KABBALAH

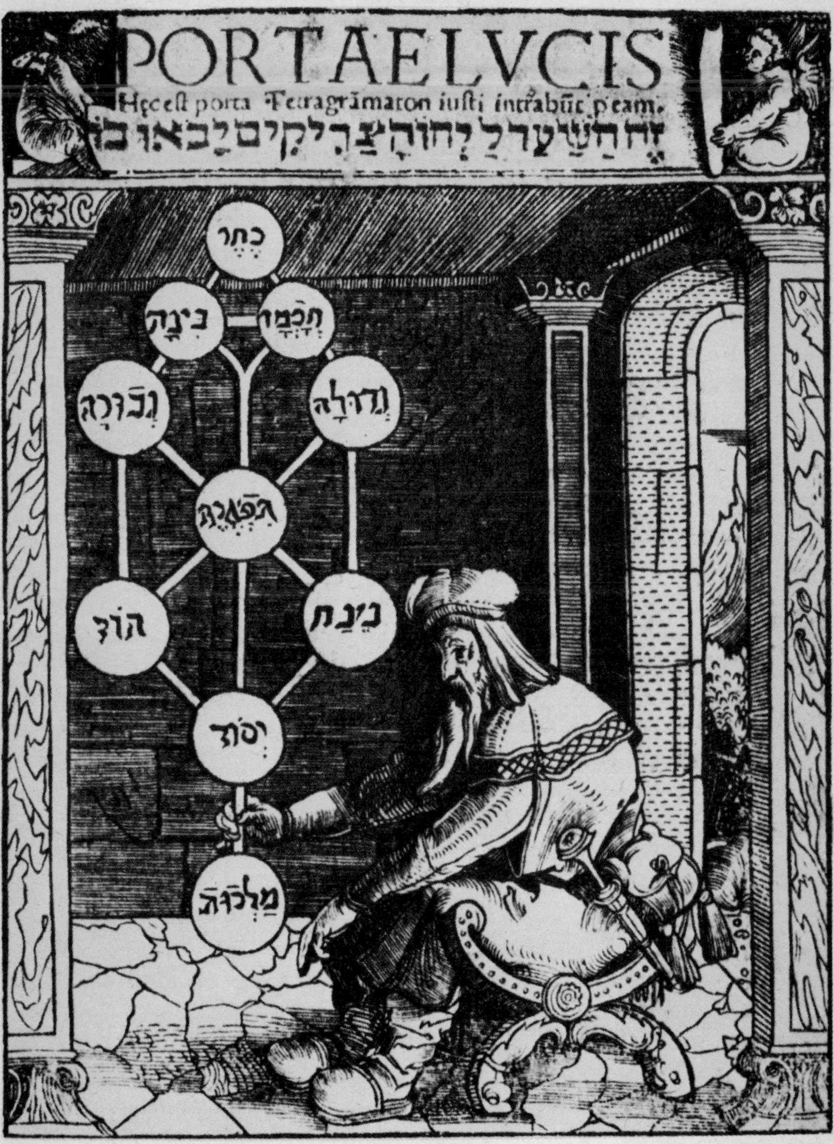

Title page of *Portae Lucis*, a Latin translation by Paulus Ricius of J. Gikatilla, *Sha'arei Orah*, Augsburg, 1516. Pictured is a man holding a tree with the ten *Sefirot*.

KABBALAH

GERSHOM SCHOLEM

A MERIDIAN BOOK
NEW AMERICAN LIBRARY
TIMES MIRROR
NEW YORK AND SCARBOROUGH, ONTARIO

This is an authorized reprint of a hardcover edition published
by Times Books.

MERIDIAN TRADEMARK REG. U.S. PAT. OFF. AND FOREIGN COUNTRIES
REGISTERED TRADEMARK—MARCA REGISTRADA
HECHO EN WESTFORD, MASS., U.S.A.

SIGNET, SIGNET CLASSICS, MENTOR, PLUME, MERIDIAN
and NAL BOOKS are published *in the United States* by
The New American Library, Inc., 1633 Broadway,
New York, New York 10019, *in Canada* by
The New American Library of Canada Limited,
81 Mack Avenue, Scarborough, Ontario M1L 1M8

First Meridian Printing, March, 1978

4 5 6 7 8 9 10 11 12

PRINTED IN THE UNITED STATES OF AMERICA

KABBALAH

CONTENTS

[Dates in parentheses appearing after titles of books in the text refer to date of first or primary edition.]

Part One
KABBALAH

1
INTRODUCTION

GENERAL NOTES

"Kabbalah" is the traditional and most commonly used term for the esoteric teachings of Judaism and for Jewish mysticism, especially the forms which it assumed in the Middle Ages from the 12th century onward. In its wider sense it signifies all the successive esoteric movements in Judaism that evolved from the end of the period of the Second Temple and became active factors in Jewish history.

Kabbalah is a unique phenomenon, and should not be considered to be identical with what is known in the history of religion as "mysticism." It is mysticism in fact; but at the same time it is both esotericism and theosophy. In what sense it may be called mysticism depends on the definition of the term, a matter of dispute among scholars. If the term is restricted to the profound yearning for direct human communion with God through annihilation of individuality (*bittul ha-yesh* in ḥasidic terminology), then only a few manifestations of Kabbalah can be designated as such, because few kabbalists sought this goal, let alone formulated it openly as their final aim. However, Kabbalah may be considered mysticism insofar as it seeks an apprehension of God and creation whose intrinsic elements are beyond the grasp of the intellect, although this is seldom explicitly belittled or rejected by the kabbalists. Essentially these elements were perceived through contemplation and illumination, which is often presented in the Kabbalah as the transmission of a primeval revelation concerning the nature of the Torah and other religious matters. In essence, however, the Kabbalah is far removed from the rational and intellectual approach to religion. This was the case even among those kabbalists who thought that basically religion was subject to rational enquiry, or that, at least, there was some accord between the path of intellectual perception and the development of the mystical approach to the subject of creation. For some kabbalists the intellect itself became a mystical phenomenon. So we find in Kabbalah a paradoxical emphasis on the congruence between intuition and tradition. It is this emphasis, together with the historical association already hinted at in the term "kabbalah" (something handed down by tradition), that points to the basic differences between the Kabbalah and other kinds of religious mysticism which are less closely identified with a people's history. Nevertheless, there are elements common to Kabbalah and both Greek and Christian mysticism, and even historical links between them.

Like other kinds of mysticism, Kabbalah too draws upon the mystic's awareness of both the transcendence of God and His immanence within the true religious life, every facet of which is a revelation of God, although God Himself is most clearly perceived through man's introspection. This dual and apparently contradictory experience of the self-concealing and self-revealing God determines the essential sphere of mysticism, while at the same time it obstructs other religious conceptions. The second element in Kabbalah is that of theosophy, which seeks to reveal the mysteries of the hidden life of God and the relationships between the divine life on the one hand and the life of man and creation on the other. Speculations of this type occupy a large and conspicuous area in kabbalistic teaching. Sometimes their connection with the mystical plane becomes rather tenuous and is superseded by an interpretative and homiletical vein which occasionally even results in a kind of kabbalistic *pilpul* (casuistry).

In its form the Kabbalah became to a large extent an esoteric doctrine. Mystical and esoteric elements coexist in Kabbalah in a highly confusing fashion. By its very nature, mysticism is knowledge that cannot be communicated directly but may be expressed only through symbol and metaphor. Esoteric knowledge, however, in theory can be transmitted, but those who possess it are either forbidden to pass it on or do not wish to do so. The kabbalists stressed this esoteric aspect by imposing all kinds of limitations on the propagation of their teachings, either with regard to the age of the initiates, the ethical qualities required of them, or the number of students before whom these teachings could be expounded. Typical of this is the account of the conditions for initiates in Kabbalah found in Moses Cordovero's *Or Ne'erav*. Often these limitations were disregarded in practice, despite the protests of many kabbalists. The printing of kabbalistic books and the influence of Kabbalah on widening circles broke down such restrictions, especially as far as the teachings on God and man were concerned. Nevertheless, there remained areas where these limitations were still more or less adhered to; for example, in the meditations on the letter-combinations (*ḥokhmat ha-ẓeruf*) and practical Kabbalah.

Many kabbalists denied the existence of any kind of historical development in the Kabbalah. They saw it as a kind of primordial revelation that was accorded to Adam or the early generations and that endured, although new revelations were made from time to time, particularly when the tradition had been either forgotten or interrupted. This notion of the nature of esoteric wisdom was expressed in apocryphal works like the Book of Enoch, was again stressed in the Zohar, and served as the basis for the dissemination of kabbalistic teaching in *Sefer ha-Emunot* by Shem Tov b. Shem Tov (c. 1400) and in *Avodat ha-Kodesh* by Meir b. Gabbai (1567). It became widely accepted that the Kabbalah was the esoteric part of the Oral Law given to Moses at Sinai. Several of the genealogies of the tradition appearing in kabbalistic literature, which were intended to support the idea of the continuity of the secret tradition, are themselves faulty and misconceived, lacking in any historical value. In actual fact, some kabbalists themselves give concrete instances of the historical development of their ideas, since they regard them either as having deteriorated to some extent from the original tradition, which found its expression in the increase of kabbalistic systems, or as part of a gradual progress toward the complete revelation of the secret wisdom. Kabbalists themselves rarely attempt to attain a historical orientation, but some examples of such an approach may be found in *Emunat Ḥakhamim* by Solomon Avi'ad Sar-Shalom Basilea (1730), and in *Divrei Soferim* by Zadok ha-Kohen of Lublin (1913).

From the beginning of its development, the Kabbalah embraced an esotericism closely akin to the spirit of Gnosticism, one which was not restricted to instruction in the mystical path but also included ideas on cosmology, angelology, and magic. Only later, and as a result of the contact with medieval Jewish philosophy, the Kabbalah became a Jewish "mystical theology," more or less systematically elaborated. This process brought about a separation of the mystical, speculative elements from the occult and especially the magical elements, a divergence that at times was quite distinct but was never total. It is expressed in the separate usage of the terms *Kabbalah iyyunit* ("speculative Kabbalah") and *Kabbalah ma'asit* ("practical Kabbalah"), evident from the beginning of the 14th century – which was simply an imitation of Maimonides' division of philosophy into "speculative" and "practical" in chapter 14 of his *Millot ha-Higgayon.* There is no doubt that some kabbalistic circles (including those in Jerusalem up to modern times) preserved both elements in their secret doctrine, which could be acquired by means of revelation or by way of initiation rites.

Once rabbinic Judaism had crystallized in the *halakhah*, the majority of the creative forces aroused by new religious stimuli, which neither tended nor had the power to change the outward form of a firmly established halakhic Judaism, found expression in the kabbalistic movement. Generally speaking, these forces worked internally, attempting to make of the traditional Torah and of the life led according to its dictates a more profound inner experience. The general tendency is apparent from a very early date, its purpose being to broaden the dimensions of the Torah and to transform it from the law of the people of Israel into the inner secret law of the universe, at the same time transforming the Jewish *ḥasid* or *ẓaddik* into a man with a vital role in the world. The kabbalists were the main symbolists of rabbinic Judaism. For Kabbalah, Judaism in all its aspects was a system of mystical symbols reflecting the mystery of God and the universe, and the kabbalists' aim was to discover and invent keys to the understanding of this symbolism. To this aim is due the enormous influence of the Kabbalah as a historical force, which determined the face of Judaism for many centuries, but it too can explain the perils, upheavals, and contradictions, both internal and external, which the realization of this aim brought in its wake.

TERMS USED FOR KABBALAH

At first the word "kabbalah" did not especially denote a mystical or esoteric tradition. In the Talmud it is used for the extra-Pentateuchal parts of the Bible, and in post-talmudic literature the Oral Law is also called "kabbalah." In the writings of Eleazar of Worms (beginning of the 13th century), esoteric traditions (concerning the names of the angels and the magical Names of God) are referred to as "kabbalah," e.g., in his *Hilkhot ha-Kisse* (in *Merkabah Shelemah*, 1921), and *Sefer ha-Shem*. In his commentary to the *Sefer Yeẓirah* (c. 1130), when he is discussing the creation of the Holy Spirit, i.e., the *Shekhinah*, Judah b. Barzillai states that the sages "used to transmit statements of this kind to their students and to sages privately, in a whisper, through kabbalah." All this demonstrates that the term "kabbalah" was not yet used for any one particular field. The new, precise usage originated in the circle of Isaac the Blind (1200) and was adopted by all his disciples.

Kabbalah is only one of the many terms used, during a period of more than 1,500 years, to designate the mystical movement, its teaching, or its adherents. The Talmud speaks of *sitrei torah* and *razei torah* ("secrets of the Torah"), and parts of the secret tradition are called *ma'aseh bereshit* (literally, "the work of creation") and *ma'aseh merkabah* ("the work of the chariot"). At least one of the mystical groups called itself *yoredei merkabah* ("those who descend to the chariot"), an extraordinary expression whose meaning eludes us (perhaps it means those who reach down into themselves in order to perceive the chariot). In the mystical literature from the close of the talmudic period and afterward, the terms *ba'alei ha-sod* ("masters of the mystery") and *anshei emunah* ("men of belief") already occur, and the latter also appears as early as the Slavonic Book of Enoch. In the period of the Provençal and Spanish kabbalists the Kabbalah is also called *ḥokhmah penimit* ("inner wisdom"), perhaps a phrase borrowed from Arabic, and the kabbalists are often called *maskilim* ("the understanding ones"), with reference to Daniel 12:10, or *doreshei reshumot* ("those who interpret texts"), a talmudic expression for allegorists. In the same way as the word Kabbalah came to be restricted in meaning to the mystical or esoteric tradition, so, at the beginning of the 13th century, the words *emet* ("truth"), *emunah* ("faith"), and *ḥokhmah* ("wisdom") were used to designate the mystical or inner truth. Hence the widespread use of *ḥokhmat ha-emet* ("the science of truth") and *derekh ha-emet* ("the way of truth"). There is also found the expression *ḥakhmei lev* ("the wise-hearted"), after Exodus 28:3. The kabbalists are also called *ba'alei ha-yedi'ah* ("the masters of knowledge" – Gnostics) or *ha-yode'im* ("those who know") beginning with Naḥmanides. Naḥmanides also coined the phrase *yode'ei ḥen* ("those who know grace"), after Ecclesiastes 9:11, where *ḥen* is used as an abbreviation for *ḥokhmah nistarah* ("secret wisdom"). The author of the Zohar uses terms such as *benei meheimnuta* ("children of faith"), *benei heikhala de-malka* ("children of the king's palace"), *yade'ei ḥokhmeta* ("those who know wisdom"), *yade'ei middin* ("those who know measures"), *meḥaẓdei ḥakla* ("those who reap the field"), and *inon de-allu u-nefaku* ("those who have entered and left, i.e., unharmed"), after *Ḥagigah* 14b. Several authors call the kabbalists *ba'alei ha-avodah* ("masters of service"), i.e., those who know the true, inner way to the service of God. In the main part of the Zohar the term Kabbalah is not mentioned, but it is used in the later strata, in the *Ra'aya Meheimna* and the *Sefer ha-Tikkunim*. From the beginning of the 14th century the name Kabbalah almost completely superseded all other designations.

2

THE HISTORICAL DEVELOPMENT OF KABBALAH

THE EARLY BEGINNINGS OF MYSTICISM AND ESOTERICISM

The development of the Kabbalah has its sources in the esoteric and theosophical currents existing among the Jews of Palestine and Egypt in the era which saw the birth of Christianity. These currents are linked with the history of Hellenistic and syncretistic religion at the close of antiquity. Scholars disagree on the measure of the influence exerted by such trends, and also by Persian religion, on the early forms of Jewish mysticism. Some stress the Iranian influence on the general development of Judaism during the period of the Second Temple, and particularly on certain movements such as the Jewish apocalyptic, a view supported by many experts on the different forms of Gnosticism, like R. Reitzenstein and G. Widengren. That there was an extensive degree of Greek influence on these currents is maintained by a number of scholars, and various theories have been adduced to explain this. Many specialists in the Gnosticism of the first three centuries of the common era see it as basically a Greek or Hellenistic phenomenon, certain aspects of which appeared in Jewish circles, particularly in those sects on the fringes of rabbinic Judaism – *ha-minim*. The position of Philo of Alexandria and his relationship with Palestinian Judaism is of especial weight in these controversies. In contrast to scholars like Harry Wolfson who see Philo as fundamentally a Greek philosopher in Jewish garb, others, like Hans Lewy and Erwin Goodenough, interpret him as a theosophist or even a mystic. Philo's work, they believe, should be seen as an attempt to explain the faith of Israel in terms of Hellenistic mysticism, whose crowning glory was ecstatic rapture. In his monumental book, *Jewish Symbols in the Greco-Roman Period* (13 vols. 1953–68), Goodenough maintains that, in contrast to Palestinian Judaism, which found expression in *halakhah* and *aggadah* and in the esoteric ideas which were indigenous developments, Diaspora Judaism showed little evidence of Palestinian influence. Instead, he avers, it had a specific spirituality based on a symbolism which is not rooted solely in the *halakhah,* but which is endowed with an imaginative content of a more or less mystical significance. He believes that the literary evidence, such as the writings of Philo and Hellenistic Judaism, provides extremely useful keys to an understanding of the archaeological and pictorial documentation which he has assembled in such abundance. Although considerable doubt has been cast on Goodenough's basic theories there is sufficient material in his great work to stimulate investigation into previously neglected aspects of Judaism and into evidence which has been insufficiently examined. His argument on the basically mystical significance of the pictorial symbols cannot be accepted, but he did succeed in establishing a link between certain literary evidence extant in Greek, Coptic, Armenian, and esoteric teachings prevalent in Palestinian Judaism. A similar link between Philonic ideas and the viewpoint of the *aggadah*, including the *aggadah* of the mystics, was also suggested by Yitzhak Baer.[1] Philo's book *De Vita Contemplativa* (*About the Contemplative Life*, 1895) mentions the existence of a sectarian community of "worshipers of God" (Therapeutes), who had already formulated a definitely mystical understanding of the Torah as a living body, and this paved the way for a mystical exegesis of Scripture.

An important element common to both Alexandrian and Palestinian Judaism is the speculation on Divine Wisdom which has its scriptural roots in Proverbs 8 and Job 28. Here wisdom is seen as an intermediary force by means of which God creates the world. This appears in the apocryphal Wisdom of Solomon (7:25) as "a breath of the power of God, and a clear effluence of the glory of the Almighty . . . For she is an effulgence from everlasting light and an unspotted mirror of the working of God, And an image of His goodness" (Charles). In the Slavonic Book of Enoch God commands His Wisdom to create man. Wisdom is here the first attribute of God to be given concrete form as an emanation from the Divine Glory. In many circles this Wisdom soon became the Torah itself, the "word of God," the form of expression of the Divine Power. Such views of the mystery of Wisdom demonstrate how parallel development could take place, on the one hand through rabbinic exegesis of the words of Scripture, and on the other through the influence of Greek philosophical speculations on the Logos. It should be noted that there is no definite proof that Philo's writings had an actual direct influence on rabbinic Judaism in the post-tannaitic period, and the attempt to prove that the *Midrash ha-Ne'lam* of the Zohar is nothing but a Hellenistic Midrash (S. Belkin, in: *Sura,* 3 (1958), 25–92) is a failure. However, the fact that the Karaite Kirkisānī (tenth century) was familiar with certain quotations drawn from Philonic writings shows that some of his ideas found their way, perhaps through Christian-Arab channels, to members of Jewish sects in the Near East.[2] But it should not be deduced from this that there was a continuous influence up to this time, let alone up to the time of the formulation of the Kabbalah in the Middle Ages. Specific parallels between Philonic and kabbalistic exegesis should be put down to the similarity of their exegetical method, which naturally produced identical results from time to time.

The theories concerning Persian and Greek influences tend to overlook the inner dynamism of the development taking place within Palestinian Judaism, which was in itself capable of producing movements of a mystical and esoteric nature. This kind of development can also be seen in those circles whose historical influence was crucial and decisive for the future of Judaism, e.g., among the Pharisees, the *tannaim* and *amoraim*, that is to say, at the very heart of established rabbinic Judaism. In addition, there were similar tendencies in other spheres outside the mainstream, in the various currents whose influence on subsequent Judaism is a matter of controversy: the Essenes, the Qumran sect (if these two are not one and the same), and the different Gnostic sects on the periphery of Judaism whose existence is attested to by the writings of the Church Fathers. Some have thought to demonstrate the existence of mystical trends even in biblical times (Hertz, Horodezky, Lindblom, Montefiore), but it is almost certain that the phenomena which they connected with mysticism, like prophecy and the piety of certain psalms, belong to other strands in the history of religion. Historically speaking, organized closed societies of mystics have been proved to exist only since the end of the Second Temple era; this is clearly attested to by the struggle taking place in this period between different religious forces, and by the tendency then current to delve more deeply into original religious speculation.

APOCALYPTIC ESOTERICISM AND MERKABAH MYSTICISM

Chronologically speaking, it is in apocalyptic literature that we find the first appearance of ideas of a specifically mystical character, reserved for the elect. Scholars do not agree on whether the origins of this literature are to be found among the Pharisees and their disciples or among the Essenes, and it is quite possible that apocalyptic tendencies appeared in both. It is known from Josephus that the Essenes possessed literature which was both magical and angelological in content. His silence concerning their apocalyptic ideas can be understood as his desire to conceal this aspect of contemporary Judaism from his gentile readers. The discovery of the literary remains of the Qumran sect shows that such ideas found a haven among them. They possessed the original Book of Enoch, both in Hebrew and Aramaic, although it is quite likely that it was composed in the period preceding the split between the Pharisees and the members of the Qumran sect. In fact, traditions resembling those embedded in the Book of Enoch found their way into rabbinic Judaism at the time of the *tannaim* and *amoraim*, and it is impossible to determine precisely the breeding ground of this type of tradition until the problems presented by the discovery of the Qumran writings have been solved. The Book of Enoch was followed by apocalyptic writing up to the time of the *tannaim*, and, in different ways, even later. Esoteric knowledge in these books touched not only upon the revelation of the end of time and its awesome terrors, but also upon the structure of the hidden world and its inhabitants: heaven, the Garden of Eden, and Gehinnom, angels and evil spirits, and the fate of the souls in this hidden world. Above this are revelations concerning the Throne of Glory and its Occupant, which should apparently be identified with "the wonderful secrets" of God mentioned by the Dead Sea Scrolls. Here a link can be established between this literature and the much later traditions concerning the *ma'aseh bereshit* and the *ma'aseh merkabah.*

It is not just the content of these ideas which is considered esoteric; their authors too hid their own individuality and their names, concealing themselves behind biblical characters like Enoch, Noah, Abraham, Moses, Baruch, Daniel, Ezra, and others. This self-concealment, which was completely successful, has made it extremely difficult for us to determine the historical and social milieu of the authors. This pseudepigraphical pattern continued within the mystical tradition in the centuries that followed. The clear tendency toward asceticism as a way of preparing for the reception of the mystical tradition, which is already attested to in the last chapter of the Book of Enoch, becomes a fundamental principle for the apocalyptics, the Essenes, and the circle of the Merkabah mystics who succeeded them. From the start, this pietist asceticism aroused active opposition entailing abuse and persecution, which later characterized practically the whole historical development of pietist tendencies (*ḥasidut*) in rabbinic Judaism.

The mysteries of the Throne constitute here a particularly exalted subject which to a large extent set the pattern for the early forms of Jewish mysticism. It did not aspire to an understanding of the true nature of God, but to a perception of the phenomenon of the Throne on its Chariot as it is described in the first chapter of Ezekiel, traditionally entitled *ma'aseh merkabah.* The mysteries of the world of the Throne, together with those of the Divine Glory which is revealed there, are the parallels in Jewish esoteric tradition to the revelations on the realm of the divine in Gnosticism. The 14th chapter of the Book of Enoch, which contains the earliest example of this kind of literary description, was the source of a long visionary tradition of describing the world of the Throne and the visionary ascent to it, which we find portrayed in the books of the Merkabah mystics. In addition to interpretations, visions, and speculations based on the *ma'aseh merkabah*, other esoteric traditions began to crystallize round the first chapter of Genesis, which was called *ma'aseh bereshit.* These two terms were subsequently used to describe those subjects dealing with these topics. Both Mishnah and Talmud (Ḥag. 2:1 and the corresponding *Gemara* in both the Babylonian and Jerusalem Talmud) show that, in the first century of the common era, esoteric traditions existed within these areas, and severe limitations were placed on public discussion of such subjects: "The story of creation should not be expounded before two persons, nor the chapter on the Chariot before one person, unless he is a sage and already has an independent understanding of the matter." Evidence concerning the involvement of Johanan b. Zakkai and his disciples in this sort of exposition proves that this esotericism could grow in the very center of a developing rabbinic Judaism, and that consequently this Judaism had a particular esoteric aspect from its very beginning. On the other hand, it is possible that the rise of Gnostic speculations, which were not accepted by the rabbis, made many of them tread very warily and adopt a polemical attitude. Such an attitude is expressed in the continuation of the Mishnah quoted above: "Whoever ponders on four things, it were better for him if he had not come into the world: what is above, what is below, what was before time, and what will be hereafter." Here we have a prohibition against the very speculations which are characteristic of Gnosticism as it is defined in the "Excerpts from the writings of [the Gnostic] Theodutus" (*Extraits de Thédote*, ed. F. Sagnard (1948), para. 78). In actual fact, this prohibition was largely ignored, as far as can be judged from the many statements of *tannaim* and *amoraim* dealing with these matters which are scattered throughout the Talmud and the Midrashim.

In an age of spiritual awakening and deep religious turmoil there arose in Judaism a number of sects with heterodox ideas resulting from a mixture of inner compulsion and outside influence. Whether Gnostic sects existed on the periphery of Judaism before the advent of Christianity is a matter of controversy (see below); but there is no doubt that *minim* ("heretics") did exist in the tannaitic period and especially in the third and fourth centuries. In this period a Jewish Gnostic sect with definite antinomian tendencies was active in Sepphoris. There were also of course intermediate groups from which members of these sects gained an extended knowledge of theological material on *ma'aseh bereshit* and *ma'aseh merkabah*, and among these should be included the Ophites (snake worshipers) who were basically Jewish rather than Christian. From this source a considerable number of esoteric traditions were transmitted to Gnostics outside Judaism, whose books, many of which have been discovered in our own time, are full of such material – found not only in Greek and Coptic texts of the second and third centuries but also in the early strata of Mandaic literature, which is written in colloquial Aramaic. Notwithstanding all the deep differences in theological approach, the growth of Merkabah mysticism among the rabbis constitutes an inner Jewish concomitant to Gnosis, and it may be termed "Jewish and rabbinic Gnosticism."

Within these circles theosophical ideas and revelations connected with them branched out in many directions, so that it is impossible to speak here of one single system. A particular mystical terminology was also established. Some of it is reflected in the sources of "normal" Midrashim, while part is confined to the literary sources of the mystics: the literature of the *heikhalot* and the *ma'aseh bereshit.* Verbs like *histakkel, ẓafah, iyyen*, and *higgi'a* have specific meanings, as do nouns like *ha-kavod, ha-kavod ha-gadol, ha-kavod ha-nistar, mara di-revuta, yoẓer bereshit, heikhalot, ḥadrei merkabah,* and others. Particularly important is the established usage of the term *Kavod* ("glory") as a name both for God when He is the object of profound mystical enquiry and also for the general area of theosophical research. This term acquires a specific meaning, distinct from its scriptural usage, as early as the Book of Tobit and the end of the Book of Enoch, and it continues to be used in this way in apocalyptic literature. In contrast, the use of the word *sod* ("mystery") in this context was relatively rare, becoming general only in the Middle Ages, whereas *raz* ("secret") is used more often in the earlier texts.

Merkabah terminology is found in a hymn-fragment in the Dead Sea Scrolls, where the angels praise "the image of the Throne of the Chariot" (Strugnell). Members of the sect combined ideas concerning the song of the angels, who stand before the Chariot, with other ideas about the names and duties of the angels, and all this is common to the sect of Qumran and to later traditions of the *ma'aseh merkabah.* From the very beginning these traditions were surrounded by an aura of particular sanctity. Talmudic *aggadah* connects exposition of the Merkabah with the descent of fire from above which surrounds the expositor. In the literature of the *heikhalot* other and more daring expressions are used to describe the emotional and ecstatic character of these experiences. Distinct from the exposition of the Merkabah which the rabbis gave while on earth below was the ecstatic contemplation of the Merkabah experienced as an ascent to the heavens, namely "descent to the Merkabah," through entering *pardes* ("paradise"). This was not a matter for exposition and interpretation but of vision and personal experience. This transition, which once again connects the revelations of the Merkabah with the apocalyptic tradition, is mentioned in the Talmud alongside the exegetic traditions (Ḥag. 14b). It concerns the four sages who "entered *pardes*." Their fate demonstrates that here we are dealing with spiritual experiences which were achieved by contemplation and ecstasy. Simeon b. Azzai "looked and died"; Ben Zoma "looked and was smitten" (mentally); Elisha b. Avuyah, called *aḥer* ("other"), forsook rabbinic Judaism and "cut the shoots," apparently becoming a dualistic Gnostic; R. Akiva alone "entered in peace and left in peace," or, in another reading, "ascended in peace and descended in peace." So R. Akiva, a central figure in the world of rabbinic Judaism, is also the legitimate representative of a mysticism within its boundaries. This is apparently why Akiva and Ishmael, who was his companion and also his adversary in halakhic matters, served as the central pillars and chief mouthpieces in the later pseudepigraphic literature devoted to the mysteries of the Merkabah. In addition, the striking halakhic character of this literature shows that its authors were well rooted in the halakhic tradition and far from holding heterodox opinions.

In mystic circles particular conditions were laid down for the entry of those fit to be initiated into the doctrines and activities bound up with these fields. The basic teachings were communicated in a whisper (Ḥag. 13b; *Bereshit Rabbah,* Theodor Albeck edition (1965), 19–20). The earliest conditions governing the choice of those suitable were of two types. In the *Gemara* (Ḥag. 13b) basically intellectual conditions were formulated, as well as age limits ("at life's half-way stage"); and in the beginning of *Heikhalot Rabbati* certain ethical qualities required of the initiate are enumerated. In addition to this, from the third and fourth centuries, according to Sherira Gaon (*Oẓar ha-Ge'onim* to *Ḥagigah* (1931), *Teshuvot*, no. 12, p. 8), they used external methods of appraisal based on physiognomy and chiromancy *(hakkarat panim ve-sidrei sirtutin). Seder Eliyahu Rabbah*, chapter 29, quotes an Aramaic *baraita* from the Merkabah mystics concerning physiognomy. A fragment of a similar *baraita*, written in Hebrew in the name of R. Ishmael, has been preserved, and there is no doubt that it was a part of Merkabah literature. Its style and content prove its early date.[3] (Another fragment from the Genizah was published by I. Gruenwald.)[4]

ESOTERIC LITERATURE: THE *HEIKHALOT*, THE *MA'ASEH BERESHIT*, AND THE LITERATURE OF MAGIC

This literature occupies an extremely important place in the development of esotericism and mysticism. It is connected at innumerable points with traditions outside its boundaries, in the Talmuds and Midrashim, and these traditions sometimes explain each other. In addition, esoteric literature contains a wealth of material that is found nowhere else. Many scholars, including Zunz, Graetz, and P. Bloch, have tried to show that a vast distance, both in time and subject matter, separates the early Merkabah ideas from those embedded in Talmud and Midrash, and they ascribed the composition of Merkabah literature to the geonic era. Even though it is quite possible that some of the texts were not edited until this period, there is no doubt that large sections originated in talmudic times, and that the central ideas, as well as many details, go back as far as the first and second centuries. Many of the texts are short, and in various manuscripts there is a considerable amount of basic material quite devoid of any literary embellishment. (For a list of the books belonging to this literature see Merkabah Mysticism p. 373.) The traditions assembled here are not all of the same kind, and they indicate different tendencies among the mystics. We find here detailed descriptions of the world of the Chariot, of the ecstatic ascent to that world, and of the technique used to accomplish this ascent. As in non-Jewish Gnostic literature, there is a magical and theurgic aspect to the technique of ascent, and there are very strong connections between Merkabah literature and Hebrew and Aramaic theurgic literature from both this and the geonic period. The earliest stratum of the *heikhalot* strongly emphasizes this magical side, which in the practical application of its teachings is linked to the attainment of the "contemplation of the Chariot." It is very similar to a number of important texts preserved among the Greek magic papyri and to Gnostic literature of the *Pistis Sophia* type which originated in the second or third century C.E.

This literature refers to historical figures, whose connection with the mysteries of the Chariot is attested by Talmud and Midrash. The ascent of its heroes to the Chariot (which in the *Heikhalot Rabbati* is deliberately called "descent") comes after a number of preparatory exercises of an extremely ascetic nature. The aspirant placed his head between his knees, a physical position which can induce altered states of consciousness and self-hypnosis. At the same time, he recited hymns of an ecstatic character, the texts of which are extant in several sources, particularly in the *Heikhalot Rabbati*. These poems, some of the earliest *piyyutim* known to us, indicate that "Chariot hymns" like these were known in Palestine as early as the third century. Some of them purport to be the songs of the holy creatures (*ḥayyot*) who bear the Throne of Glory, and whose singing is already mentioned in apocalyptic literature. The poems have their own specific style which corresponds to the spirit of "celestial liturgy," and they have a linguistic affinity with similar liturgical fragments in the writings of the Qumran sect. Almost all of them conclude with the *kedushah* ("sanctification") of Isaiah 6:3, which is used as a fixed refrain. Isaac Nappaḥa, a third-century Palestinian *amora*, puts a similar poem in the mouth of the kine who bore the ark of the covenant (I Sam. 6:12), in his interpretation of "And the kine took the straight way" (*va-yisharnah*, interpreted as "they sang"; Av. Zar. 24b), for he sees a parallel between the kine who bear the ark singing and the holy creatures who bear the Throne of Glory with a glorious festive song. These hymns clearly show their authors' concept of God. He is the holy King, surrounded by "majesty, fear, and awe" in "the palaces of silence." Sovereignty, majesty, and holiness are

His most striking attributes. He is not a God Who is near but a God Who is afar, far removed from the area of man's comprehension, even though His hidden glory may be revealed to man from the Throne. The Merkabah mystics occupy themselves with all the details of the upper world, which extends throughout the seven palaces in the firmament of *aravot* (the uppermost of the seven firmaments); with the angelic hosts which fill the palaces *(heikhalot)*; the rivers of fire which flow down in front of the Chariot, and the bridges which cross them; the *ofan* and *ḥashmal*; and with all the other details of the Chariot described by Ezekiel. But the main purpose of the ascent is the vision of the One Who sits on the Throne, "a likeness as the appearance of a man upon it above" (Ezek. 1:26). This appearance of the Glory in the form of supernal man is the content of the most recondite part of this mysticism, called *Shi'ur Komah* ("measure of the body").

The teaching on the "measure of the body" of the Creator constitutes a great enigma. Fragments of it appear in several passages in the *ma'aseh merkabah* literature, and other fragments are preserved separately. They enumerate the fantastic measurements of parts of the head as well as some of the limbs. They also transmit "the secret names" of these limbs, all of them unintelligible letter combinations. Different versions of the numbers and the letter combinations have survived and so they cannot be relied upon, and, all in all, their purpose (whether literal or symbolic) is not clear to us. However, the verse which holds the key to the enumeration is Psalms 147:5: "Great is Our Lord, and mighty in power," which is taken to mean that the extent of the body or of the measurement of "Our Lord" is alluded to in the words *ve-rav ko'aḥ* ("and mighty in power") which in *gematria* amount to 236. This number (236 × 10,000 leagues, and, moreover, not terrestrial but celestial leagues) is the basic measurement on which all the calculations are based. It is not clear whether there is a relationship between speculations on "the greatness of the Lord of the world" and the title *mara di-revuta* ("Lord of greatness") which is one of the predications of God found in the Genesis Apocryphon (p. 2, line 4). The terms *gedullah* ("greatness"; e.g., in the phrase "*ofan* [wheel] of greatness") and *gevurah* ("might") occur as names for God in several texts of the Merkabah mystics. We should not dismiss the possibility of a continuous flow of specific ideas from the Qumran sect to the Merkabah mystics and rabbinic circles in the case of the *Shi'ur Komah* as well as in other fields. The paradox is that the vision of the *Shi'ur Komah* is actually hidden "from the sight of every creature, and concealed from the ministering angels," but "it was revealed to R. Akiva in the *ma'aseh merkabah*" *(Heikhalot Zutrati)*. The mystic, therefore, grasps a secret which even the angels cannot comprehend.

In the second half of the second century a Hellenized version of this speculation is to be found in the Gnostic Markos' description of the "body of truth." There also exist a number of Gnostic gems which, like the Hebrew fragments of *Shi'ur Komah*, bear the figure of a man whose limbs are inscribed with magical combinations of letters, obviously corresponding to their secret names (cf. C. Bonner, *Hesperia*, 23 (1954), 151). A clear reference to this doctrine is found as early as the Slavonic Book of Enoch (13:8)[5] "I have seen the measure of the height of the Lord, without dimension and without shape, which has no end." The passage reflects the precise Hebrew terminology. At least two versions of this doctrine were current in later talmudic and post-talmudic times, one in the name of R. Akiva and one in the name of R. Ishmael (both published in the collection *Merkavah Shelemah* (Jerusalem (1922). fol. 32–43). Two manuscripts from the tenth or 11th centuries (Oxford Hebr. C. 65, and Sassoon 522) contain the oldest available texts, but even these are in different stages of corruption. According to the testimony of Origen (third century), it was not permitted to study Song of Songs in Jewish circles before the age of full maturity, obviously because of esoteric teachings like the *Shi'ur Komah* doctrine which were connected with it. The Midrashim on the Song of Songs reflect such esoteric understanding in many passages. The fragments of *Shi'ur Komah* were known in the sixth century, if not earlier, to the poet Eleazar ha-Kallir.

The provocative anthropomorphism of these passages perplexed many rabbis, and was the object of attacks by the Karaites – so much so that even Maimonides, who at first regarded the *Shi'ur Komah* as an authoritative work requiring interpretation (in his original Ms. of his commentary to the Mishnah, Sanh. 10), later repudiated it, believing it to be a late forgery (*Teshuvot ha-Rambam* (1934), no. 117). In fact, the *Shi'ur Komah* was an early and genuine part of mystic teaching in the days of the *tannaim.* The theory does not imply that God in Himself possesses a physical form, but only that a form of this kind may be ascribed to "the Glory," which in some passages is called *guf ha-Shekhinah* ("the body of the Divine Presence"). *Shi'ur Komah* is based on the descriptions of the beloved in Song of Songs (5:11–16), and it apparently became a part of the esoteric interpretation of this book. Perhaps the idea of the "tunic" and garment of God also belonged to the *Shi'ur Komah*. This "tunic" is of great significance in the *ma'aseh bereshit* of the *Heikhalot Rabbati*. and echoes of this idea can be found in the rabbinic *aggadot* concerning the garment of light in which the Holy One, blessed be He, wrapped himself at the moment of creation.

The ascent and passage through the first six palaces are described at length in the *Heikhalot Rabbati*, with details of all the technical and magical means which assist the ascending spirit and save it from the dangers lying in wait for it. These dangers were given much emphasis in all Merkabah traditions. Deceptive visions meet the ascending soul and angels of destruction try to confound it. At the gates of all the palaces it must show the doorkeepers "the seals," which are the secret Names of God, or pictures imbued with a magical power (some of which are extant in the Gnostic *Pistis Sophia*), which protect it from attack. The dangers especially increase in number at the entrance to the sixth palace where it appears to the Merkabah mystic as if "one hundred million waves pour down, and yet there is not one drop of water there, only the splendor of the pure marble stones which pave the palace." It is to this danger in the ecstatic ascent that the words of R. Akiva refer in the story of the four who entered *pardes:* "when you come to the place of pure marble stones, do not say 'water, water.' " The texts also mention a "fire which proceeds from his own body and consumes it." Sometimes the fire is seen as a danger (*Merkabah Shelemah* (1921), 1b) and at other times as an ecstatic experience which accompanies the entry into the first palace: "My hands were burned, and I stood without hands or feet" (Ms. Neubauer, Oxford 1531, 45b). The *pardes* which R. Akiva and his companions entered is the world of the celestial Garden of Eden or the realm of the heavenly palaces and the ascent or "rapture" is common to several Jewish apocalypses, and is mentioned by Paul (II Cor. 12:2–4) as something which needs no explanation for his readers of Jewish origin. In contrast to the dangers which attend those who, although unfit for them, indulge in these matters and in the magical science of theurgy, great emphasis is laid on the illumination which comes to the recipients of the revelations: "There was light in my heart like lightning," or "the world changed into purity around me, and my heart felt as if I had entered a new world" (*Merkabah Shelemah* 1a, 4b).

An early passage enumerating the basic subjects of the mystery of the Chariot is to be found in the Midrash to Proverbs 10, and, in a different version, in Azriel's *Perush ha-Aggadot* (ed. Tishby (1945), 62). The subjects mentioned are the *ḥashmal*, the lightning, the cherub, the Throne of Glory, the bridges in the Merkabah, and the measurement of the limbs "from my toenails to the top of my head." Other subjects which are of great importance in a number of sources are not mentioned. Among these are ideas concerning the *pargod* ("curtain" or "veil") which separates the One Who sits on the Throne from the other parts of the Chariot, and upon which are embroidered the archetypes of everything that is created. There are different, highly colored traditions concerning the *pargod*. Some take it to be a curtain which prevents the ministering angels from seeing the Glory (Targ. of Job 26:9), while others hold that "the seven angels that were created first" continue their ministry inside the *pargod* (*Massekhet Heikhalot*, end of ch. 7). In another form, this concept of the *pargod* was taken over by second century non-Jewish Gnostics.

There was no fixed angelology, and different views, and indeed complete systems, have been preserved, ranging from those found in the Ethiopic Book of

Enoch to the Hebrew Enoch found among the literature of the *heikhalot*. These ideas occupy a considerable place in the extant Merkabah literature, and, as would be expected, they reappear in various forms of a practical nature in incantations and theurgical literature. Knowledge of the names of the angels was already part of the mysticism of the Essenes, and it developed in both rabbinic and heterodox circles up to the end of the geonic period. Together with the concept of the four or seven key angels (archangels), there developed (about the end of the first or the beginning of the second century) a new doctrine concerning the angel Metatron (*sar ha-panim*, "the prince of the Presence"). (See details in the separate section on Metatron, p. 377.)

In Merkabah literature the names of the angels easily intermingle with the secret Names of God, many of which are mentioned in the fragments of this literature still extant. Since many of these names have not been completely explained it has not yet been possible to ascertain whether they are meant to convey a specific theological idea – e.g., an emphasis on a particular aspect of God's revelation or activity – or whether they have other purposes which we cannot fathom. Fragments of *heikhalot* literature mention names like Adiriron, Zoharariel, Zavodiel, Ta'zash, Akhtriel (found also in a *baraita* emanating from this circle in Ber. 7a). The formula "the Lord, God of Israel" is very often added to the particular name, but many of the chief angels also have this added to their names (e.g., in the Hebrew Enoch) so it cannot be deduced from this whether the phrase refers to the name of an angel or to the name of God. Sometimes the same name serves to designate both God and an angel. An example of this is Azbogah ("an eightfold name") in which each pair of letters adds up, through *gematria*, to the number eight. This "eightfold" name reflects the Gnostic concept of the *ogdoas*, the eighth firmament above the seven firmaments, where the Divine Wisdom dwells. In the *Heikhalot Zutrati* it is defined as "a name of power" *(gevurah)*, i.e., one of the names of the Divine Glory, while in the Hebrew Enoch chapter 18 it becomes the name of one of the angelic princes; its numerical significance is forgotten and it is subject to the customary aggadic interpretation of names. The same is true of the term *ziva rabba*, which from one angle is no more than an Aramaic translation of *ha-kavod ha-gadol* ("the great glory") found in the apocalypses and also in Samaritan sources as a description of the revealed God. But it also occurs in the lists of the mysterious names of the angel Metatron, and it is found with a similar meaning in Mandaic literature. Just as non-Jewish Gnostics sometimes used Aramaic formulae in their Greek writings, so Greek elements and Greek formulae found their way into Merkabah literature. The dialogue between the mystic and the angel Dumiel at the gate of the sixth palace in the *Heikhalot Rabbati* is conducted in Greek.[6] One of the names of God in this literature is Totrossiah, which signifies the *tetras* of the four letters of the name YHWH. The reverse parallel to this is the name Arbatiao which is found frequently in the magic papyri of this period.

The different tendencies of Merkabah mysticism established ways of contemplating ascent to the heavens – ways which were understood in their literal sense. Their basic conception did not depend on scriptural interpretation but took on its own particular literary form. The magical element was strong in the early stages of *heikhalot* literature only, becoming weaker in later redactions. From the third century onward interpretations appear which divest the subject of the Chariot of its literal significance and introduce an ethical element. Sometimes the different palaces correspond to the ladder of ascent through the virtues;[7] and sometimes the whole topic of the Chariot completely loses its literal meaning. This kind of interpretation is especially evident in the remarkable mystic utterance of the third-century *amora* Simeon b. Lakish: "the patriarchs are the Chariot" (Gen. Rabbah, 475, 793, 983, with regard to Abraham, Isaac, and Jacob). Statements like these opened the door to the type of symbolic interpretation which flourished afterward in kabbalistic literature.

The first center for this type of mysticism was in Palestine, where a large part of *heikhalot* literature was written. Mystical ideas found their way to Babylonia at least as early as the time of Rav (mid-third century), and their influence is recognizable, among other places, in the magical incantations which were inscribed on bowls to afford "protection" from evil spirits and demons, and which reflect popular Babylonian Judaism from the end of the talmudic period to the time of the *geonim*. In Babylonia, apparently, a number of magical prayers were composed, as well as treatises on magic, like the *Ḥarba de-Moshe* (ed. Gaster, 1896), *Sefer ha-Malbush* (Sassoon Ms. 290, pp. 306–11), *Sefer ha-Yashar* (British Museum, Margoliouth Ms. 752, fol. 91ff.), *Sefer ha-Ma'alot, Havdalah de-R. Akiva* (Vatican Ms. 228), *Pishra de R. Ḥanina b. Dosa* (Vatican Ms. 216, fols. 4–6), and others, some of which were written in Babylonian Aramaic. In all these the influence of Merkabah ideas was very strong. In Palestine, perhaps at the end of the talmudic period, the *Sefer ha-Razim* was composed, which contains descriptions of the firmaments greatly influenced by *heikhalot* literature, while the "practical" part, concerning incantations, has a different style, partly adopted verbatim from Greek sources. From circles such as these emanated the magical usage of the Torah and Psalms for practical purposes.[8] This practice was based on the theory that essentially these books were made up from the Sacred Names of God and His angels, an idea that first appeared in the preface to the *Shimmushei Torah*; only the midrashic introduction, with the title *Ma'yan ha-Ḥokhmah*, has been printed (Jellinek, *Beit ha-Midrash*, part 1 (1938), 58–61), but the whole work is extant in manuscript. Of the same type is the book

Shimmushei Tehillim, which has been printed many times in Hebrew and also exists in manuscript in an Aramaic version.

The poetical content of the literature of the *ma'aseh merkabah* and the *ma'aseh bereshit* is striking; we have already noted the hymns sung by the *ḥayyot* and the ministering angels in praise of their Creator. Following the pattern of several of the Psalms, the view was developed that the whole of creation, according to its nature and order, was singing hymns of praise. A hymnology was established in the various versions of the *Perek Shirah*, which without any doubt derives from mystical circles in the talmudic period. Connected with this poetical element is the influence that the Merkabah mystics had on the development of specific portions of the order of prayer, particularly on the morning *kedushah,*[9] and later on the *piyyutim* which were written for these portions *(silluk, ofan, kedushah)*.

JEWISH GNOSIS AND THE *SEFER YEZIRAH*

In these stages of Jewish mysticism, the descriptions of the Chariot and its world occupy a place which in non-Jewish Gnosticism is filled by the theory of the "aeons," the powers and emanations of God which fill the *pleroma*, the divine "fullness." The way in which certain *middot*, or qualities of God, like wisdom, understanding, knowledge, truth, faithfulness, righteousness, etc., became the "aeons" of the Gnostics is paralleled in the tradition of the *ma'aseh bereshit*, although it did not penetrate the basic stages of Merkabah mysticism. The ten sayings by which the world was created (Avot 5:1) became divine qualities according to Rav (Ḥag. 12a). There is also a tradition that *middot* such as these "serve before the Throne of Glory" (ARN 37), thus taking the place occupied by the *ḥayyot* and the presiding angels in the Merkabah system. The semi-mythological speculations of the Gnostics which regarded the qualities as "aeons" were not admitted into the rabbinic tradition of the Talmud or the Midrashim, but they did find a place in the more or less heterodox sects of the *minim* or *ḥizẓonim*. To what extent the growth of Gnostic tendencies within Judaism itself preceded their development in early Christianity is still the subject of lively scholarly controversy. Peterson, Haenchen, and Quispel, in particular, along with several experts on the Dead Sea Scrolls, have tried to prove that Jewish forms of Gnosis, which retained a belief in the unity of God and rejected any dualistic notions, came into being before the formation of Christianity and were centered particularly around the idea of primordial man (following speculation on Gen. 1:26; "Adam Kadmon"). The image of the Messiah, characteristic of the Christian Gnostics, was absent here. These scholars have interpreted several of the earliest documents of Gnostic literature as Gnostic Midrashim on cosmogony and Haenchen in particular has argued that their basic Jewish character is clearly recognizable in an analysis of the teaching of Simon Magus, apparently the leader of Samaritan Gnosis, a first-century heterodox Judaism. Even before this, M. Friedlaender had surmised that antinomian Gnostic tendencies (which belittled the value of the Commandments) had also developed within Judaism before the rise of Christianity. Although a fair number of these ideas are based on questionable hypotheses, nevertheless there is a considerable measure of truth in them. They point to the lack of Iranian elements in the early sources of Gnosis, which have been exaggerated by most scholars of the last two generations, whose arguments rest on no less hypothetical assumptions. The theory of "two principles" could have been the result of an internal development, a mythological reaction within Judaism itself, just as easily as a reflection of Iranian influence. The apostasy of the *tanna* Elisha b. Avuyah to a Gnostic dualism of this kind is connected in the Merkabah tradition with the vision of Metatron seated on the Throne like God. Mandaic literature also contains strands of a Gnostic, monotheistic, non-Christian character, which many believe originated in a Transjordanian Jewish heterodox sect whose members emigrated to Babylonia in the first or second century. The cosmogony of some of the most important Gnostic groups, even of those of an antinomian character, depends not only on biblical, but to a very large measure also on aggadic and esoteric Jewish elements. The earliest strata of the *Sefer ha-Bahir* (see p. 312), which came from the East, prove the existence of definitely Gnostic views in a circle of believing Jews in Babylonia or Syria, who connected the theory of the Merkabah with that of the "aeons." These early sources are partly linked with the book *Raza Rabba,* which was known as an early work at the end of the geonic period; fragments of it can be found in the writings of the Ḥasidei Ashkenaz (see below). Concepts which did not originate exclusively in Jewish mysticism, like the idea of the *Shekhinah* and the hypostases of stern judgment and compassion, could easily have been interpreted according to the theory of the "aeons" and incorporated with Gnostic ideas. The "exile of the *Shekhinah,*" originally an aggadic idea, was assimilated in Jewish circles at a particular stage with the Gnostic idea of the divine spark that is in exile in the terrestrial world, and also with the mystic view of the Jewish concept of the *keneset Yisrael* ("the community of Israel") as a heavenly entity that represents the historical community of Israel. In the elaboration of such motifs, Gnostic elements could be added to rabbinic theories of the Merkabah and to ideas of Jewish circles whose connection with rabbinism was weak.

THE *SEFER YEZIRAH*

Speculation on the *ma'aseh bereshit* was given a unique form in a book, small in size but enormous in influence, the *Sefer Yeẓirah* ("Book of Creation"), the earliest extant Hebrew text of systematic, speculative thought. Its brevity – less than 2,000 words altogether even in its longer version – allied to its obscure and at the same time laconic and enigmatic style, as well as its terminology, have no parallel in other works on related subjects. The result of all these factors was that for over 1,000 years the book was expounded in a great many different ways, and not even the scientific investigations conducted during the 19th and 20th centuries succeeded in arriving at unambiguous and final results.

Sefer Yeẓirah is extant in two versions: a shorter one which appears in most editions as the book itself, and a longer version which is sometimes printed as an appendix.[10] Both versions were already in existence in the tenth century and left their imprint on the different types of the numerous manuscripts, the earliest of which (from the 11th century?) was found in the Cairo *Genizah* and published by A. M. Habermann (1947). In both versions the book is divided into six chapters of *mishnayot* or *halakhot*, composed of brief statements which present the author's argument dogmatically, without any explanation or substantiation. The first chapter in particular employs a sonorous, solemn vocabulary, close to that of the Merkabah literature. Few biblical verses are quoted. Even when their wording is identical, the different arrangement of the *mishnayot* in the two versions and their resultant altered relationship one with the other color the theoretical appreciation of the ideas.

The central subject of *Sefer Yeẓirah* is a compact discourse on cosmology and cosmogony (a kind of *ma'aseh bereshit*, "act of creation," in a speculative form), outstanding for its clearly mystical character. There is no foundation for the attempts by a number of scholars to present it as a kind of primer for schoolchildren,[11] or as the first Hebrew composition on Hebrew grammar and orthography (according to P. Mordell). The book's strong link with Jewish speculations concerning divine wisdom *(ḥokhmah)* is evident from the beginning, with the declaration that God created the world by means of "32 secret paths of wisdom." These 32 paths, defined as "ten *Sefirot beli mah*" and the "22 elemental letters" of the Hebrew alphabet, are represented as the foundations of all creation. Chapter I deals with the *Sefirot* and the other five chapters with the function of the letters. Apparently the term *Sefirot* is used simply to mean "numbers," though in employing a new term (*sefirot* instead of *misparim*), the author seems to be alluding to metaphysical principles or to stages in the creation of the world.

The use of the term *Sefirot* in *Sefer Yeẓirah* was later explained – particularly in Kabbalah literature – as referring to a theory of emanation, although the book does not mention that the first *Sefirah* itself emanated from God and was not created by Him as an independent action. The author emphasizes, though ambiguously, the mystical character of the *Sefirot*, describing them in detail and discussing the order of their grading. At least the first four *Sefirot* emanate from each other. The first one is the "spirit (*ru'aḥ*) of the Living God" (the book continues to use the word *ru'aḥ* in its dual meaning of abstract spirit and air or ether). From the first *Sefirah* comes forth, by way of condensation, "one Spirit from another"; that is first the primal element of air, and from it, issuing one after the other as the third and fourth *Sefirot*, water and fire. From the primal air God created, or "engraved" upon it, the 22 letters; from the primal waters, the cosmic chaos; and from the primal fire, the Throne of Glory and the hosts of the angels. The nature of this secondary creation is not sufficiently clear because the precise terminological meaning of the verbs employed by the author – e.g., engraved, hewed, created – can be interpreted in various ways. The last six *Sefirot* are of a completely different nature, representing the six dimensions (in the language of the book the *keẓavot*, "extremities") of space, though it is not expressly said that they were created from the earlier elements. Even so it is emphasized that the ten *Sefirot* constitute a closed unit, for "their end is in their beginning and their beginning in their end" and they revolve in each other; i.e., these ten basic principles constitute a unity – although its nature is not sufficiently defined – which is not considered as identical with the divinity except insofar as the first stage of its creation expresses the ways of divine "Wisdom."

The author, no doubt intentionally, employs expressions borrowed from the description of the *ḥayyot* ("living creatures") who carry the Throne of Glory in the chariot (*merkavah*; Ezek. 1), and seems to be establishing a certain correlation between the "living beings" and the *Sefirot*, describing the latter as the king's servants who obey his commands and prostrate themselves before his throne. At the same time they are also the dimensions *(amakim)* of all existence, of good and even of evil. The fact that the theory of the significance of the 22 letters as the foundation of all creation in chapter 2 partly conflicts with chapter 1 has caused many scholars to attribute to the author a conception of a double creation: the one ideal and pure brought about by means of the *Sefirot*, which are conceived in a wholly ideal and abstract manner; and the other one real, effected by the interconnection of the elements of speech, which are the letters. According to some views, the obscure word *"belimah,"* which always accompanies the word *Sefirot*, is simply a composite, *beli mah* – without anything, without actuality, ideal. However, judging from the literal meaning, it would seem that it should be understood as signifying "closed," i.e., closed within itself. The text offers no more detailed explanation of the relationship between the *Sefirot* and the letters, and the *Sefirot* are not referred to again. Some scholars have believed that two separate cosmogonic doctrines basically differing from one another were fused in the book, and were united by a method resembling neo-Pythagorean theory current in the second and third century B.C.E.

All the real beings in the three strata of the cosmos: in the world, in time, and in man's body (in the language of the book: world, year, soul) came into existence through the interconnection of the 22 letters, and especially by way of the "231 gates"; i.e., the combinations of the letter into groups of two perhaps representing the roots of the Hebrew verb (it appears that the author held that the Hebrew verb is based on two consonants, but see N. Aloni). The logical number of 231 combinations does not appear in the earliest manuscripts, which fixed 221 gates or combinations, and which are enumerated in a number of manuscripts. Every existing thing somehow contains these linguistic elements and exists by their power, whose foundation is one name; i.e., the Tetragrammaton, or, perhaps, the alphabetical order which in its entirety is considered one mystical name. The world-process is essentially a linguistic one, based on the unlimited combinations of the letters. In chapters 3–5 the 22 basic letters are divided into three groups, according to the author's special phonetic system. The first contains the three matrices – *immot* or *ummot* (meaning elements, in the language of the Mishnah) – *alef, mem, shin* (אמש), which in turn represent the source of the three elements mentioned in a different context in chapter 1 – air, fire, water – and from these all the rest came into being. These three letters also have their parallel in the three seasons of the year (according to a system found among Greek and Hellenistic writers) and the three parts of the body: the head, torso, and stomach. The second group consists of seven "double" letters, i.e., those consonants which have a hard and soft sound when written with or without a *dagesh (bet, gimmel, dalet,* and *kaf, pe, resh, tav).* The presence of the letter *resh* in this group gave rise to various theories.[12] Through the medium of the "double" letters were created the seven planets, the seven heavens, the seven days of the week, and the seven orifices of the body (eyes, ears, nostrils, mouth), and they also allude to the basic opposites *(temurot)* in man's life. The 12 remaining "simple" letters *(ha-peshutot)* correspond to what the author considers as man's chief activities; the 12 signs of the zodiac in the heavenly sphere, the 12 months, and the 12 chief limbs of the body *(ha-manhigim).* In addition he gives also a completely different phonetic division of the letters, in accordance with the five places in the mouth where they are articulated (gutterals, labials, velars, dentals, and sibilants). This is the first instance in which this division appears in the history of Hebrew linguistics and it may not have been included in the first version of the book. The combination of these "basic letters" contains the roots of all things and also the contrast between good and evil (עֹנֶג וְנֶגַע, *oneg ve-nega*).

There is an obvious connection between this linguistic-mystical cosmogony, which has close parallels in astrological speculation, and magic which is based on the creative, magical power of the letters and words. In fact it might well be said that *Sefer Yeẓirah* speaks of "the letters in which heaven and earth were created," as according to the Talmud, Bezalel, the architect of the tabernacle, possessed the knowledge of their combinations (Berakhot 55a). From this point stem the ideas connected with the creation of the *golem* by an ordered recitation of all the possible creative letter-combinations. Whether *Sefer Yeẓirah* itself initially was aimed at magical ideas of this type is a subject on which opinions differ, but it is not impossible. According to a talmudic legend (Sanh. 65b) R. Ḥanina and R. Hoshaiah (fourth century) used to occupy themselves with *Sefer Yeẓirah,* or – as an ancient variant has it – with *Hilkhot Yeẓirah;* by means of it a "calf three years old" was created for them, which they ate. Whether these *Hilkhot Yeẓirah* are simply the book in question or its early version cannot be decided for the moment, but it must be stressed that accompanying the very earliest texts of *Sefer Yeẓirah* were introductory chapters emphasizing magical practices which are presented as some kind of festive ritual to be performed on the completion of the study of the book (Judah b. Barzillai's commentary, 103–268).

TIME OF COMPOSITION

Zunz,[13] Graetz in his later works, Bacher, Block, and others were of the opinion that *Sefer Yeẓirah* was composed in the period of the *geonim,* around the eighth century. This dating was in line with the general tendency of those scholars to assign a late date to the composition of the mystical works on the mysteries of the creation and Merkabah, a trend which modern scholarship can no longer uphold. They also talked of hypothetical Arab influence (which was not actually proved). In his early work on Gnosticism and Judaism (1846), Graetz tended to correlate the time of its composition with that of the Mishnah or the beginning of the period of the Talmud, and this view was shared by Abraham Epstein, Louis Ginzberg, and others, who dated its composition between the third and sixth centuries. Leo Baeck tried to prove that *Sefer Yeẓirah* was written under the Neoplatonic influence of Proclus, possibly in the sixth century. The Hebrew style, however, points to an earlier period. Epstein already proved its proximity to the language of the Mishnah, and additions can be made to his linguistic proofs. The book contains no linguistic form which may not be ascribed to second- or third-century Hebrew. In addition, a number of links with the doctrine of divine wisdom and with various Gnostic and syncretistic views indicate an earlier period; analogies between *Sefer Yeẓirah* and the views of Markos the Gnostic of the school of Valentinus had already been noticed by Graetz.

The doctrine of the *Sefirot* and the language system hint at neo-Pythagorean and Stoic influences. Stoic is the emphasis on the double pronunciation of *"bagad kafat."* Some of the terms employed in the book were apparently translated from Greek, in which the term *στοιχεῖα* indicates both elements and letters; this duality finds its expression in the Hebrew term *otiyyot yesod* ("elemental letters"), i.e., letters which are also elements. The material which F. Dornsieff [14] collected from the linguistic mysticism of Greek syncretism contains many parallels with *Sefer Yeẓirah.* Illuminating, in this connection, is *Sefer Yeẓirah's* view of the "sealing" of the six extremities of the world by the six different combinations of the name YHW (יהו) which (unlike in the Bible) occurs here as an independent, fundamental Name of God, playing the part of its corresponding name in Greek transcription *ἰάω*, which is extremely frequent in the documents of the Gnostics and in religious and magical syncretism. The idea that every act of creation was sealed with the name of God is one of the earliest tenets of Merkabah mysticism and is already found in *Heikhalot Rabbati* (ch. 9); in Gnostic systems and some which are close to Gnosis this name has its function in establishing the cosmos and in defining fixed boundaries for the world. Combinations of this name, which in Greek consists of vowels and not of consonants, appear frequently in Greek magical papyri. The author of *Sefer Yeẓirah* did not yet know the symbols for the Hebrew vowels and in place of the Greek vowels he employed the Hebrew consonants יהו, which are both vowel letters and components of the Tetragrammaton. There is common ground here between the speculations of *Sefer Yeẓirah* and the projections of Gnostic or semi-Gnostic speculations on the fringe of Judaism or outside it during the early centuries of the Common Era. It is difficult to decide whether the ten *Sefirot* or the rules of the 32 paths have to be explained or understood in the spirit of the Gnostic aeon doctrine or in that of the Pythagorean school, both views being possible. The function of the letters of the Hebrew alphabet in the construction of the world is mentioned in an ancient fragment from *Midrash Tanḥuma* dealing with the creation: "The Holy One, Blessed be He, said: 'I request laborers.' The Torah told Him: 'I put at Your disposal 22 laborers, namely the 22 letters which are in the Torah, and give to each one his own.' "[15] This legend is extremely close to the basic idea in *Sefer Yeẓirah*, chapter 2, and it is impossible to know which was the earlier.

To sum up, it may be postulated that the main part of *Sefer Yeẓirah*, though it contains post-talmudic additions, was written between the third and sixth centuries, apparently in Palestine by a devout Jew with leanings toward mysticism, whose aim was speculative and magical rather than ecstatic. The author, who endeavored to "Judaize" non-Jewish speculations which suited his spirit, presents a parallel path to Jewish esotericism of the *Heikhalot* type of literature, which has its roots in the same period. This "Judaizing" is also apparent at the end of the book, which presents Abraham, the first to believe in the oneness of God, as the one who first studied the ideas expressed in the book and actually practiced them – maybe an allusion to the use of magic mentioned above. From this derived the late view claiming Abraham as the author of the book, called in several manuscripts *Otiyyot de-Avraham Avinu*. The attribution of *Sefer Yeẓirah* to R. Akiva only makes its appearance in the Kabbalah literature from the 13th century onward, no doubt in the wake of the late Midrash *Otiyyot de-Rabbi Akiva.*

COMMENTARIES ON SEFER YEẒIRAH

The earliest reference to *Sefer Yeẓirah* appears in the *Baraita di-Shemu'el* and the poems by Eleazar ha-Kallir (c. sixth century). Later on the book was of great importance both to the development of Jewish philosophy before Maimonides and to the Kabbalah, and scores of commentaries were written on it. Saadiah Gaon explained the book (at the beginning of the tenth century) as an early authoritative text. On the basis of the longer version which was at his disposal he introduced changes and new divisions. The Arabic text with a French translation by M. Lambert was published in Paris in 1891 and by Josef Kafiḥ, Jerusalem 1972, with a Hebrew one. Saadiah's commentary was translated into Hebrew several times from the 11th century onwards and had a considerable circulation. In 955/6 the commentary on the short version by Abu Sahl Dunash ibn Tamim was made in Kairouan. Parts of this Arabic original were discovered in the Cairo *Genizah,* and it was preserved in various editions originating from a later revision and an abbreviated form of the original version, mainly in different Hebrew translations. One of these was published by M. Grossberg in 1902. The commentary was apparently based on the lectures of Isaac Israeli, Abu Sahl's teacher. G. Vajda made a detailed study of this commentary. A third commentary from the tenth century was written in southern Italy by Shabbetai Donnolo and published by D. Castelli in 1880, with a comprehensive introduction. The most important of all literal commentaries is the one composed at the beginning of the 12th century by Judah b. Barzillai of Barcelona, published by S. Z. H. Halberstamm (Berlin, 1885). Judah Halevi commented on many parts of the *Sefer Yeẓirah* in his *Kuzari* (4:25). Abraham ibn Ezra's commentary on the first chapter, which was known to Abraham Abulafia, was lost, as were some other commentaries from the 11th and 12th centuries, including one by the rabbis of Narbonne. In the 11th century poems were even composed on the doctrines of *Sefer Yeẓirah,* e.g., by Ibn Gabirol[16] and by Ẓahallal b. Nethanel Gaon.[17]

A great many commentaries on *Sefer Yeẓirah* were written within the circles of the Ḥasidei Ashkenaz, among them that of Eleazar b. Judah of Worms which was published in its entirety in Przemysl in 1889, and one later attributed to Saadiah Gaon (from the beginning of the 13th century), of which only a part is printed in the usual editions; also noteworthy is the commentary by Elhanan b. Yakar of London (c. 1240), edited by G. Vajda (in *Koveẓ al Yad,* 6 (1966), 145–97). The number of commentaries written in the spirit of the Kabbalah and according to the kabbalists' conception of the doctrine of the *Sefirot* comes close to fifty. The earliest of these, by Isaac the Blind, is also one of the most difficult and important documents from the beginnings of Kabbalah (see below, p.42.) The commentary of Isaac's pupil Ariel b. Menahem of Gerona appears in the printed editions as the work of Naḥmanides. The actual commentary by Naḥmanides (only on the first chapter) was published by G. Scholem.[18] Almost the entire commentary by Abraham Abulafia (Munich Ms. 58) is contained in the *Sefer ha-Peli'ah* (Korets, 1784, fols. 50–56). This kabbalist, in one of his works, enumerates 12 commentaries which he studied in Spain (Jellinek, *Beit ha-Midrash,* 3 (1855), 42). From the 14th century come the comprehensive commentary by Joseph b. Shalom Ashkenazi, written in Spain and erroneously attributed in printed editions to R. Abraham b. David;[19] the commentary by Meir b. Solomon ibn Sahula of 1331 (Rome, Angelica library, Ms. Or. 45); as well as the *Meshovev Netivot* (Ms. Oxford) by Samuel ibn Motot. Around 1405 Moses Botarel wrote a commentary citing a considerable number of false quotations from his predecessors. A number of commentaries were composed in Safed, among them one by Moses b. Jacob Cordovero (Ms. Jerusalem) and by Solomon Toriel (Ms. Jerusalem). From then on commentaries in the spirit of Isaac Luria proliferated; for example, by Samuel b. Elisha Portaleone (Ms. Jews' College, London), by David Ḥabillo (Ms. of the late Warsaw community); from among these the commentary by Elijah b. Solomon, the Gaon of Vilna (1874), and the book *Otot u-Mo'adim* by Joshua Eisenbach of Prystik (Pol. Przystyk, 1903) were printed.

PRINTED EDITIONS AND TRANSLATIONS

Sefer Yeẓirah was first printed in Mantua in 1562 with the addition of several commentaries, and has since been reprinted a great many times, with and without commentaries. In the Warsaw 1884 edition – the most popular one – the text of some commentaries is given in a considerably distorted form. *Sefer Yeẓirah* was translated into Latin by the Christian mystic G. Postel and printed even before the Hebrew edition (Paris, 1552). Another Latin edition with commentaries was published by S. Rittangel in 1652. Translations appeared, mostly with commentaries, in English, by I. Kalisch (1873), A. Edersheim (1883), P. Davidson (1896), W. Westcott (1911), K. Stenring (1923), Akiva ben Joseph (*The Book of Formation,* 1970); in German by J. F. von Meyer (1830), L. Goldschmidt (1894; which, quite unfoundedly, professes to give a critical Hebrew text), E. Bischoff (1913); in French by Papus (1888), Duchess C. de Cimara (1913), Carlo Suarès (1968); in Italian by S. Savini (1923); in Hungarian by B. Tennen (1931); and in Czech by O. Griese (1921).

MYSTICISM IN THE GEONIC PERIOD

The mishnaic and talmudic periods were times of irrepressible creativity in the field of mysticism and esoteric inquiry. In the geonic era (from the seventh to the 11th centuries) little that was essentially original emerged, and the various streams already mentioned continued to exist and to intermingle. The center of mystical activity shifted to Babylonia, although its continuing influence in Palestine is evident in several chapters of later midrashic literature and particularly in the *Pirkei de-R. Eliezer.* The poems of Eleazar Kallir, which are influenced by Merkabah literature and the *Shi'ur Komah,* belong to the end of the earlier period or were composed between the two eras. The poet made no attempt to conceal ideas which had been transmitted through old esoteric theories. As mysticism developed in this period, in both Palestine and Babylonia, it followed the pattern of the earlier period. Apocalyptic writing continued with great momentum; examples are extant from the time of the *amoraim* almost to that of the Crusades, and they were collected in Judah Even-Shemuel's great anthology, *Midrashei Ge'ullah* (1954^2), most of them from the geonic period. They display a marked connection with the Merkabah tradition and several have been preserved in manuscripts of works by mystics. Simeon b. Yoḥai appears here for the first time, side by side with R. Ishmael, as a bearer of apocalyptic tradition (in the *Nistarot de-R. Shimon b. Yoḥai*). Apocalypses were also attributed to the prophet Elijah, Zerubbabel, and Daniel.

At the other extreme there grew and flourished in these circles an angelology and a theurgy which produced a very rich literature, much of it extant from this period. Instead of, or in addition to, the contemplation of the Chariot, this presents a many-sided practical magic associated with the prince or princes of the Torah, whose names vary. Many incantations addressed to the angel Yofiel and his companions, as princes of wisdom and of Torah, are found in a large number of manuscripts of magical manuals, which continue the tradition of the earlier magical papyri. There was also a custom of conjuring up these princes particularly on the day before the Day of Atonement or even on the night of the Day of Atonement itself.[20] Formulae for more mundane purposes have also been preserved in many incantations written in Babylonian Aramaic by Jewish "Masters of the Name," and not always on behalf of Jewish customers. (See Baal Shem p. 310) This may have something to do with the origin of the medieval stereotype of the Jew as magician and sorcerer. Concepts from the Merkabah mystics' circle, as well as mythological and aggadic ideas – some unknown from other sources – filtered through to groups which were far removed indeed from mysticism and much closer to magic. A demonology, extremely rich in detail, also grew up side by side with the angelology. Many examples of these (published by Montgomery C. Gordon, and others) were found on clay bowls which were buried, according to custom, beneath the threshold of houses. They have important parallels among the incantations transmitted through literary tradition in the fragments of the *Genizah* and in the material which found its way as far as the Hasidei Ashkenaz (e.g. in the *Havdalah de-R. Akiva*). The theology and angelology of the incantations were not always explained correctly by their editors, who saw in them a heterodox theology.[21] It was in Babylonia also, apparently, that the book *Raza Rabba* ("The Great Mystery") was composed. Attacked by the Karaites as a work of sorcery, the book does indeed contain magical material but the extant fragments show that it also has some Merkabah content, in the form of a dialogue between R. Akiva and R. Ishmael. As the angelology in these fragments has no parallel in other sources, it would seem that the work is a crystallization of an early form of a theory of the "aeons" and of speculations of a Gnostic character. The style, quite different from that of the *heikhalot,* indicates a much later stage. These fragments have been published by G. Scholem in *Reshit ha-Kabbalah* (1948), 220–38.

The beginnings of new trends in this period can be discerned in three areas:

(1) The utterances employed in the creation of the world were conceived either as forces within the Chariot or as "aeons," *middot,* or hypostases. To what extent this speculation is associated with the view of the ten *Sefirot* in the *Sefer Yeẓirah* is not altogether clear. It is evident, however, that in Jewish Gnostic circles the concept of the *Shekhinah* occupied a completely new position. In the early sources "*Shekhinah*" is an expression used to denote the presence of God Himself in the world and is no more than a name for that presence; it later becomes a hypostasis distinguished from God, a distinction that first appears in the late Midrash to Proverbs (Mid. Prov. 47a: "the *Shekhinah* stood before the Holy One, blessed be He, and said to Him"). In contrast to this separation of God and His *Shekhinah,* there arose another original concept – the identification of the *Shekhinah* with *keneset Yisrael* ("the community of

Israel"). In this obviously Gnostic typology, the allegories which the Midrash uses in order to describe the relationship of the Holy One, blessed be He, to the community of Israel are transmuted into this Gnostic concept of the *Shekhinah* or "the daughter" in the eastern sources which are embedded in *Sefer ha-Bahir.*[22] Gnostic interpretations of other terms, like wisdom, and of various talmudic similies in the spirit of Gnostic symbolism, can be understood as going back to the early sources of the *Sefer ha-Bahir* (*ibid.*, 78–107). Several of the book's similes can be understood only against an oriental background, and Babylonia in particular, as, for example, the statements concerning the date palm and its symbolic significance. The ascent of repentance to reach the Throne of Glory is interpreted in a late Midrash (*Pesikta Rabbati* 185a) as an actual ascent of the repentant sinner through all the firmaments, and so the process of repentance is closely connected here with the process of ascent to the Chariot.

(2) In this period the idea of the transmigration of souls *(gilgul)* also became established in various eastern circles. Accepted by Anan b. David and his followers (up to the tenth century) – although later rejected by the Karaites – it was also adopted by those circles whose literary remains were drawn upon by the redactors of the *Sefer ha-Bahir*. For Anan (who composed a book specifically on this subject) and his followers the idea, which apparently originated among Persian sects and Islamic Mutazilites, had no mystical aspects. It is apparent, however, that the mystics' idea of transmigration drew upon other sources, for in the sources of the *Sefer ha-Bahir* it makes its appearance as a great mystery, alluded to only through allegory, and based on scriptural verses quite different from those quoted by the sect of Anan and repeated by Kirkisānī in his *Kitāb al-Anwār*, "Book of Lights" (pt. 3, chs. 27–28).

(3) A new element was added to the idea of the Sacred Names and angels which occupied such a prominent position in the theory of the Merkabah. This was an attempt to discover numerological links through *gematria*, between the different types of names and scriptural verses, prayers and other writings. The numerological "secrets," *sodot*, served two purposes. They ensured, firstly, that the names would be spelled exactly as the composers of *gematriot* received them through written or oral sources – though this system did not entirely save them from mutilation and variation, as is clearly shown by the mystical writings of the Ḥasidei Ashkenaz. Secondly, by this means they were able to give mystical meanings and "intentions" *(kavvanot)* to these names, which served as an incentive to deeper meditation, especially since many of the names lacked any significance. This process seems to be connected with a decline in the practical use of this material during preparation for the soul's ecstatic ascent to heaven. Names which originated through intense emotional excitement on the part of the contemplatives and visionaries were stripped of their meaning as technical aids to

ecstatic practice, and so required interpretations and meanings on a new level of *kavvanah.* All the names, of whatever kinds, have therefore a contemplative content; not that ascent to the Merkabah completely disappeared at this time, for the various treatises in many manuscripts on the methods of preparation for it testify to the continuity of their practical application. However, it is clear that this element gradually became less significant. Another new factor must be added to this: the interpretation of the regular prayers in the search for *kavvanot* of this numerical type.

It is impossible to determine with any certainty from the evidence that remains where the secrets of the names and the mysteries of prayer according to this system of *gematria* first made their appearance. The new interpretations of prayer link the words of phrases of the liturgy generally with names from the Merkabah tradition and angelology. Perhaps this link was first formulated in Babylonia; but it is also possible that it grew up in Italy, where the mysteries of the Merkabah and all the associated material spread not later than the ninth century. Italian Jewish tradition, particularly in the popular forms it assumed in the *Megillat Aḥima'aẓ* by Ahima'az of Oria, clearly shows that the rabbis were well versed in matters of the Merkabah. It also tells of the miraculous activity of one of the Merkabah mystics who emigrated from Baghdad, namely Abu Aharon (Aaron of Baghdad), who performed wonders through the power of the Sacred Names during the few years that he lived in Italy. The later tradition of the Ḥasidei Ashkenaz (12th century) maintained that these new mysteries were transmitted about the year 870 to R. Moses b. Kalonymus in Lucca by this same Abu Aharon, the son of R. Samuel ha-Nasi of Baghdad. Afterward, R. Moses went to Germany where he laid the foundations of the mystical tradition of the Ḥasidei Ashkenaz, which grew up around this new element. The personality of Abu Aharon remains obscure in all these traditions, and the recent attempts (in several papers by Israel Weinstock) to see him as a central figure in the whole development of the Kabbalah and as author and editor of many mystical works, including the *heikhalot* literature and the *Sefer ha-Bahir,* are founded on an extreme use of *gematriot* and on dubious hypotheses.[23] In any event, there is no doubt that at the end of the geonic period mysticism spread to Italy, in the form of Merkabah literature and perhaps also in the form of the above-mentioned theory of names, which served as an intermediate link between the orient and the later development in Germany and France.

These ideas reached Italy through various channels. The magical theurgic elements in them came to the fore, while the speculative side became weaker. This latter was represented in the main by the commentary of the physician Shabbetai Donnolo (913–c. 984) to the *Sefer Yeẓirah* which was indisputably influenced by the commentary of Saadiah b. Joseph Gaon (882–942) to the same work. It is impossible to say to what extent theosophic writings of a Gnostic character, in Hebrew or Aramaic, also passed through these channels, but this possibility should not be denied.

From the numerous remains of mystical literature extant from the talmudic and geonic periods it can be deduced that these types of ideas and attitudes were widespread in many circles, wholly or partially restricted to initiates. Only on very rare occasions is it possible to establish with certainty the personal and social identity of these circles. There is no doubt that, apart from the individual *tannaim* and *amoraim* whose attachment to mystical studies is attested by reliable evidence, there were many whose names are unknown who devoted themselves to mysticism and even made it their chief preoccupation. In addition to the rabbis that have already been mentioned, R. Meir, R. Isaac, R. Levi, R. Joshua b. Levi, R. Hoshaya, and R. Inyani b. Sasson (or Sisi) were involved with mystical ideas. The identity of those who studied theurgy (who were called, in Aramaic, "users of the Name," *ba'alei ha-Shem*) is completely unknown, and most of them, of course, did not come from rabbinic circles. Our knowledge of the exponents of mysticism and esotericism in the geonic period is even more limited. Geonic responsa reveal that such traditions did spread to the leading academies, but there is no proof that the foremost *geonim* themselves were steeped in these teachings or that they actually practiced them. The material touching on Merkabah traditions in the responsa and in the commentaries of the *geonim*[24] is notable for its extreme caution, and occasionally for its forbearance. The main attempt to link the theories of the *Sefer Yeẓirah* with contemporary philosophical and theological ideas was made by Saadiah Gaon, who wrote the first extensive commentary to the book. He refrained from dealing in detail with the subject matter of the Merkabah and the *Shi'ur Komah,* but at the same time he did not disown it despite the attacks of the Karaites. In several instances Sherira b. Ḥanina Gaon and Hai Gaon set out to discuss matters in this field, but without connecting their explanations with the philosophical ideas expressed elsewhere in their writings. Hai Gaon's opinion in his responsum concerning the Secret Names, such as the 42- and 72×3-lettered Name, led others to attribute to him more detailed commentaries on these subjects, and some of these came into the possession of the Ḥasidei Ashkenaz.[25]

The words that Hai Gaon addressed to the rabbis of Kairouan show that the esoteric teaching on names had an impact even on the more distant Diaspora, but they also demonstrate that there was no tradition and little textual distribution of the *heikhalot* tracts, of which the *gaon* says "he who sees them is terrified by them." In Italy this literature did spread, particularly among the rabbis and the poets *(paytanim)*, and an important section of the work of Amittai b. Shephatiah (ninth century) consists of Merkabah poems. As these traditions passed into Europe, some circles of rabbinic scholars became once more the principal but not the only exponents of mystical teaching.

Aggadot and Midrashim with angelogical and esoteric tendencies were also written in this period. The *Midrash Avkir,* which was still known in Germany up to the end of the Middle Ages, contained material rich in otherwise unknown mythical elements concerning angels and names. The remains of it which appear in the *Likkutim mi-Midrash Avkir* were collected by S. Buber in 1883. Various parts of the *Pesikta Rabbati* also reflect the ideas of the mystics. The *Midrash Konen* is made up of different elements;[26] the first part contains a remarkable combination of ideas concerning the Divine Wisdom and its role in creation and the theory of the *Shekhinah,* while the rest of the work includes different versions of angelology and a version of *ma'aseh bereshit.* An element of *gematria* also appears. Judging from the Greek words in the first part, the extant text was edited in Palestine or in Southern Italy. In the tradition of the Ḥasidei Ashkenaz (British Museum Ms. 752 fol. 132b) a fragment of a Midrash survives concerning the angels active during the Exodus from Egypt, which is also based to a large extent on the exegesis of *gematriot,* and it would seem that there were other Midrashim of this type whose origin is not known.

While many ideas concerning God and His manifestation are expressed or implied in the Merkabah literature, no particular concentrated attention is paid in these early stages of mysticism to the teaching about man. The emphasis of the Merkabah mystics is on the ecstatic and contemplative side, and man interested them only insofar as he received the vision and revealed it to Israel. Their speculations contain no specific ethical theory nor any new concept of the nature of man.

ḤASIDIC MOVEMENTS IN EUROPE AND EGYPT

Religious impulses which were mystical in the sense of involving man's powerful desire for a more intimate communion with God and for a religious life connected with this developed in the Judaism of the Middle Ages in different places and by various means; not all are associated exclusively with Kabbalah. Such tendencies resulted from a fusion of internal drives with the external influence of the religious movements present in the non-Jewish environment. Since their proponents did not find the answer to all their needs in the talmudic and midrashic material which purported to bind man closer to God – although they utilized it as far as they could and also at times based far-fetched interpretations on it – they drew extensively on the literature of the Sufis, the mystics of

Islam, and on the devout Christian ascetic tradition. The intermingling of these traditions with that of Judaism resulted in tendencies which were regarded as a kind of continuation of the work of the Ḥasideans (pietists) of the tannaitic period, and they stressed the value of *ḥasidut* as a way of bringing man nearer to *devekut* ("communion" with God) although this term was not yet used to designate the culmination of *ḥasidut*. Extremism in ethical and religious behavior, which in the sayings and literature of the rabbis characterized the term *"ḥasid"* ("pious") as against *"ẓaddik'* ("righteous"), became the central norm of these new tendencies. They found their classical literary expression, first and foremost, in 11th-century Spain in the *Ḥovot ha-Levavot* ("Duties of the Heart") by Baḥya ibn Paquda, originally written in Arabic. The material dealing with the life devoted to communion of the true "servant" – who is none other than the *ḥasid* yearning for the mystical life – is taken from Sufi sources and the author's intention was to produce an instructional manual of Jewish pietism which culminated in a mystical intent. A Hebrew translation of the *Ḥovot ha-Levavot* was made in 1160 on the initiative of Meshullam ben Jacob and the early circle of kabbalists in Lunel. The book's great success, especially in Hebrew, shows how much it answered the religious needs of the people even beyond the confines of the Kabbalah. The obvious connection with talmudic tradition, which served as the point of departure for explanations of a remarkable spiritual intent, was a distinguishing feature in works of this kind, which also clearly reveal neoplatonic philosophical elements. Such elements facilitated formulations of a mystical character, and this philosophy became one of the most powerful means of expression. Several of the poems of Solomon ibn Gabirol, Baḥya's older contemporary, evidence this trend toward a mystical spirituality, and it is expressed particularly in the concepts of his great philosophical work, *Mekor Ḥayyim*, which is saturated with the spirit of neoplatonism. The extent to which his poems reflect individual mystical experiences is controversial.[27] In Spain, after a century or more, these tendencies intermingled with the emerging Kabbalah, where traces of Gabirol may be seen here and there, especially in the writings of Isaac b. Latif.

Parallel with this was a growth of *ḥasidut* of a mystical bent in Egypt in the days of Maimonides and his son Abraham b. Moses b. Maimon; this, however, found no echo in the Kabbalah, remaining an independent occurrence of a Jewish Sufi type which is recorded as late as the 14th or even the 15th century. No mere figure of speech, the epithet "Ḥasid" was a description of a man who followed a particular way of life, and it was appended to the names of several rabbis from the 11th century onward, in both the literary and the personal records that survived in the *Genizah*. The Egyptian trend of *ḥasidut* turned into "an ethically oriented mysticism" (S.D. Goitein), particularly in the literary productions of Abraham b. Moses b. Maimon (d.1237). The mystical aspect of his book *Kifāyat al-'Ābidīn*[28] is entirely based on Sufi sources and bears no evidence of any similar Jewish tradition known to the author. The circle of Ḥasidim which grew up around him stressed the esoteric aspect of their teaching (S.D. Goitein), and his son Obadiah also followed this path.[29] A much later work of the same kind was discussed by F. Rosenthal.[30] What remains of this literature is all written in Arabic, which may explain why it found no place in the writings of the Spanish kabbalists, most of whom had no knowledge of the language.

An essentially similar religious movement grew up in France and Germany, beginning in the 11th century. It reached its peak in the second half of the 12th and in the 13th century, but it continued to have repercussions for a long time, particularly in the Judaism of the Ashkenazi world. This movement – known as the Ḥasidei Ashkenaz – has two aspects: the ethical and the esoteric-theosophical. On the ethical plane a new ideal developed of extreme *ḥasidut* linked to a suitable mode of life, as described particularly in the *Sefer Ḥasidim* of Judah b. Samuel he-Ḥasid, extant in two versions, one short and the other long. Along with specific pietistic customs there grew up a particular method of repentance which, remarkable for its extremism, had a marked influence on Jewish ethical teaching and behavior. The common factor in all the ḥasidic movements of Spain, Egypt, and Germany was the violent opposition that they aroused, attested by the Ḥasidim themselves. A Ḥasidism which does not arouse opposition in the community cannot, according to their own definition, be considered a true one. Equanimity of spirit, indifference to persecution and ignominy; these are the distinguishing traits of the Ḥasid, to whichever particular circle he belongs. Although the Ḥasidei Ashkenaz reflect to some extent the contemporary Christian asceticism, nevertheless they developed mainly within the framework of a clear talmudic tradition, and the basic principles were often identical with the principles of this tradition. All these movements had from the beginning a social significance intended "to revive the hearts." The Ḥasidei Ashkenaz did not, relatively speaking, lay great stress on the mystical element associated with the ḥasidic ideal. Despite the paradox inherent in the situation, they tried as far as possible to integrate the Ḥasid, ostensibly an unnatural phenomenon, into the general Jewish community, and to make him responsible in practice to the community. The Ḥasid who renounced his natural impulses and always acted "beyond the limit of strict justice" was the true embodiment of the fear and love of God in their purest essence. Many of these Ḥasidim attained the highest spiritual levels, and were considered to be masters of the holy spirit, or even prophets, a term applied to several men who are known for their activity in tosafist circles, e.g. R. Ezra ha-Navi ("the prophet") of Montcontour, and also to others who are otherwise completely unknown, e.g. R. Nehemiah ha-Navi and R. Troestlin ha-Navi from Erfurt. These men's attainment of such spiritual heights was connected not only with their behavior on the ethical plane but also with the distinction they achieved in the realm of esoteric theosophy. The latter was assigned an important position; in it all earlier trends were maintained, joined and mingled with new forces. Remaining the main object of enquiry, and even a practical guide toward the "ascent to heaven," the teaching on the Merkabah became largely interwoven with number mysticism and the speculations based on it. In addition to the ecstatic or visionary ascent to heaven, there developed a tendency toward deep meditation, toward prayer and the mysteries of prayer, which were communicated orally. Philosophy introduced a new element, mainly through Saadiah Gaon's commentary to the *Sefer Yeẓirah* (which had been translated into Hebrew as early as the 11th century), and through the early translation of his *Emunot ve-De'ot* in a style reminiscent of the *piyyutim* of the Kallir school. This was the source of the theory of the *Kavod* ("Glory"), transmitted through ḥasidic literature, which saw the Divine Glory as the first created entity, although the mystics dared speak of it only in trembling awe. Despite their distinction between God and the *Kavod* which is also called *Shekhinah*, they continued to refer to the *Shekhinah* in terms of the talmudic and midrashic conception of it as an attribute of God. An additional factor from the 12th century onward was the influence of rabbis of the neoplatonic school, especially Abraham ibn Ezra, and Abraham b. Ḥiyya. Perhaps Ibn Ezra's travels to France and his personal contacts there contributed to this influence as well as his books. In all the literature they inherited from Saadiah and the Spanish rabbis, the Ḥasidim concentrated on that part that was closest to their thought, practically turning these authors into theosophists. Arriving at no unified systemization of these disparate and contradictory elements, in formulating their ideas they contented themselves with eclectic presentations.

The ideas of the Merkabah and the *Shi'ur Komah* were already known in France at the beginning of the ninth century, as witnessed by the attacks on them by Agobard, bishop of Lyons. Here and there glimpses of these traditions appear in the writings of Rashi and the tosafists of the 12th and 13th centuries. The study of the *Sefer Yeẓirah* was looked upon as an esoteric discipline, consisting both of revelations concerning creation and the mysteries of the world, and of a profound knowledge of the mysteries of language and the Sacred Names. Traditions of this type have come down from Jacob b. Meir Tam, Isaac of Dampierre, Elhanan of Corbeil, and Ezra of Montcontour. The last, claiming divine revelation, aroused messianic excitement in France and beyond in the second decade of the 13th century.[31] These traditions were given written form in France in the *Sefer ha-Ḥayyim* (Jerusalem, 1973), written around 1200. However, following Ibn Ezra, its basic doctrine assimilated other theosophical elements concerning the divine attributes and their place in the *Kavod* and beneath the Throne whose affinity with the kabbalistic outlook is clear.

In all aspects, including the esoteric, the movement reached its peak in Germany, first within the widespread Kalonymus family from the 11th century on. In Worms, Speyer, and Mainz, and afterward in Regensburg, the main upholders of the tradition are known: Samuel b. Kalonymus, Judah b. Kalonymus of Mainz, and his son, Eleazar of Worms; his teacher, Judah b. Samuel he-Ḥasid (d.1217); Judah b. Kalonymus of Speyer (author of *Sefer Yiḥusei Tanna'im ve-Amora'im*), and the descendants of Judah he-Ḥasid who were scattered throughout the German cities of the 13th century. They and their pupils gave a far-reaching popular expression to the movement, and several of them wrote books of wide compass which embodied a major part of their traditions and ideas. In addition to the bulk of the *Sefer Ḥasidim* Judah he-Ḥasid, the movement's central figure in Germany, wrote other books known to us only through citation in other works, particularly the *Sefer ha-Kavod.* According to J. Dan he was also the author of a large work extant in Oxford manuscript 1567. His pupil, Eleazar of Worms, included in books large and small (most of which have been preserved in manuscript) the major part of the material he had received concerning the teachings of the *ma'aseh merkabah,* the *ma'aseh bereshit,* and the doctrine of Names. They are a mixture of mythology and theology, of Midrash and speculation on one side, and of theurgy on the other. All the tendencies already mentioned above find expression in his work, existing side by side, as in his *Sodei Razayya* (considerable parts of which were published in the *Sefer Razi'el,* and all of which is extant in British Museum, Margoliouth 737) or in those texts which are arranged in the form of *halakhot: Hilkhot ha-Malakhim, Hilkhot ha-Kisse, Hilkhot ha-Kavod, Hilkhot ha-Nevu'ah* (printed under the title of *Sodei Razayya,* 1936), and also in many others that remain unpublished. The scope of this literature is very wide,[32] and it contains some fragments of traditions of an unusual type, Gnostic in character, which apparently traveled from the east by way of Italy. The mysteries of prayer and the extensive interpretation of Scripture through number mysticism were further developed in Germany, partly through the chain of tradition of the Kalonymus family and partly through other developments which went so far that the emphasis on the search for associations by way of *gematriot* was considered by Jacob b. Asher (Tur OḤ 113) to be the most characteristic feature of the Ḥasidei Ashkenaz. In the 13th century a very rich literature grew up, grounded on the different aspects of ḥasidic tradition but still independent of the kabbalistic literature that developed in the same period. The names of many rabbis who trod the path of ḥasidic theosophy are recorded in these sources, most of which are in manuscript. Many of their sayings were incorporated in Eleazar Hirẓ Treves' commentary to the liturgy (in *Siddur ha-Tefillah,* 1560), and in the *Arugat ha-Bosem* of Abraham b. Azriel, an early 13th-century commentary on the *piyyutim* of the *maḥzor* of the Ashkenazi rite.[33] In this circle the *Sefer Yeẓirah* was nearly always interpreted in the manner of Saadiah and Shabbetai Donnolo, with an added tendency to see the book as a guide for both mystics and adepts of magic. The study of the book was considered successful when the mystic attained the vision of the *golem,* which was connected with a specific ritual of a remarkably ecstatic character. Only in later times did this inner experience assume more tangible forms in popular legend.[34]

The theological views of the Ḥasidim are summarized in the *Hilkhot ha-Kavod,* and in the *Sha'arei ha-Sod ve-ha-Yiḥud ve-ha-Emunah*[35] and in the various versions of the *Sod ha-Yiḥud* from Judah he-Ḥasid to Moses Azriel at the end of the 13th century.[36] In addition to the ḥasidic version of the concept of the *Kavod*, another view developed in a particular circle in the 11th or 12th century which is not mentioned in the writing of Judah he-Ḥasid and his school. This is the idea of *keruv meyuḥad* ("the special cherub") or *ha-keruv ha-kadosh* ("the holy cherub"). According to this view, it is not the *Kavod* pure and simple which sits upon the Throne but a special manifestation in the shape of an angel or a cherub, to whom the mysteries of the *Shi'ur Komah* refer. In the writings of Judah he-Ḥasid and Eleazar of Worms, and in the *Sefer ha-Ḥayyim,* there are a nnmber of variations on the theme of the *Kavod* and various ways of presenting the idea. Sometimes a distinction is made between the revealed and the hidden *Kavod* and so on. The special cherub appears as an emanation from the great fire of the *Shekhinah* or from the hidden *Kavod,* which has no form. In this circle the two basic divine attributes are contrasted with one another: God's "holiness," which denotes the presence of the *Shekhinah* in all things and the hidden *Kavod,* and God's "greatness" or "sovereignty," which has both appearance and size. Such an idea is somewhat reminiscent of the speculations of eastern sects, such as that of Benjamin b. Moses Nahawendi, who believed that the world was created through an angelic intermediary (a concept which also had precedents among early heterodox sects during the development of Gnosis). This idea becomes apparent among the Ḥasidim in the pseudepigraphical text called the *Baraita of Yosef b. Uzziel,* which appears, from its language, to have been written in Europe. Joseph b. Uzziel is taken to be the grandson of Ben Sira. The *baraita* is found in several manuscripts and was published in part by A. Epstein.[37] This idea was accepted by several rabbis, including Avigdor ha-Ẓarefati (12th century?); the author of *Pesak ha-Yir'ah ve-ha-Emunah,* which was mistakenly combined by A. Jellinek with the *Sha'arei ha-Sod ve-ha-Yiḥud;* the anonymous author of the commentary to the *Sefer Yeẓirah,* which was apparently composed in France in the 13th century and printed under the name of Saadiah Gaon in the editions of the *Sefer Yeẓirah;* and finally, Elhanan b. Yakar of London, in the first half of the 13th century.[38] In the course of time such ideas, and particularly that of the special cherub, became combined and confused with Spanish Kabbalah, and in Germany in the 14th century several texts were composed which reflect this combination; some are still extant.[39]

Ḥasidic ideology, particularly in its French manifestations and in the form given it by Elhanan of London, adopted the theory of the five worlds. Mentioned by Abraham b. Ḥiyya in his *Megillat ha-Megalleh* and originating among the Islamic neoplatonists in Spain, this theory enumerates in order the worlds of light, of the divine, of the intellect, of the soul, and of nature.[40] Occasionally the writings of this circle incorporated material which originally came from Latin Christian literature, as G. Vajda demonstrated in connection with Elhanan of London.[41] The views of the Hasidim were reflected to a large extent in their own special prayers, composed either in the style associated with Saadia's concept of the *Kavod* (e.g. in the *Shir ha-Yiḥud* a hymn which was perhaps written by Judah he-Hasid or even earlier), or frequently based on the Secret Names, alluded to in the acronym. Many of these have survived in the writings of Eleazar of Worms, particularly in manuscripts of his commentary to the *Sefer Yeẓirah.* There are also prayers and poems which their authors intended to represent the songs of heavenly beings, a king of continuation of the *heikhalot* hymns, the songs of the sacred *ḥayyot.* Generally speaking, these prayers were not accorded a fixed place in the liturgy, and they were apparently the preserve of a chosen few. At a much later time they were included in liturgical anthologies in Italy and Germany, collected by kabbalists in the Safed period, and many of them were finally published in the *Sha'arei Ẓiyyon* by Hannover (ch.3). Several of them were attributed in manuscript to Spanish kabbalists, e.g. Jacob ha-Kohen, who was in fact personally connected with the Ḥasidei Ashkenaz, of Solomon Alkabez.[42]

Eleazar of Worms clearly recognized the esoteric character of those subjects that merited special study, and he enumerates with some variations the areas involved: "The mystery of the Chariot, the mystery of Creation, and the mystery of the Unity [*Sod ha-Yiḥud,* a new concept] are not to be communicated except during a fast" (*Ḥokhmat ha-Nefesh* (1876) 3c). He defines "the science of the soul," to which he devotes one of his main works, as the means and gateway to the "mystery of the Unity," which he apparently saw as the root of mystical theology. In the *Sodei Razayya* he enumerates "three kinds of mystery," those of the Chariot, the Creation, and the Commandments. The question of whether the commandments also have an esoteric purpose is also discussed in the *Sefer Ḥasidim* (ed. Wistinetzki (1891), no. 1477). This book (no. 984) makes mention of "the profundity of piety *[hasidut]*, the profundity of the laws of the Creator, and the profundity of His Glory *[Kavod]*," and initiation in these subjects depends on the fulfillment of the conditions laid down in the Talmud in connection with the *ma'aseh merkabah.* The mystics *(ḥakhmei ha-ḥidot)* are "nourished" in this world on the savor of some of the mysteries that originate in the heavenly academy, most of which are treasured up for the righteous in the world to come (no. 1056). Associated with the ḥasidic affinity for mysticism was their desire to synthesize the early material, including the anthropomorphic elements, with the spiritual interpretation that denies these elements. Aroused by this compromise, Moses Taku (writing in the early 13th century) denied the Saadian principles and defended a corporeal point of view. His attack was included in the *Ketav Tammim,* of which two extensive fragments survive (*Oẓar Neḥmad,* 3 (1860), 54–99, and *Arugat ha-Bosem,* vol. 1, 263–8). Seeing in the new tendencies "a new religion" which smacked of heresy, he also denounced the attention that the Ḥasidim paid to the mysteries of prayer, and particularly the dissemination of these mysteries in their books. By his attack he shows how widespread the ideas and literature of the Ḥasidim were in his time.

THE ESTABLISHMENT OF THE KABBALAH IN PROVENCE

Contemporaneously with the growth of *ḥasidut* in France and Germany, the first historical stages of the Kabbalah emerged in southern France, although there is no doubt that there were earlier steps in its development which cannot now be discerned. These earlier stages were connected with the existence of a Jewish Gnostic tradition, associated in particular eastern circles with Merkabah mysticism. The main remnants were incorporated in the early parts of *Sefer ha-Bahir* (see p. 312) and also in a few records preserved in the writings of the Ḥasidei Ashkenaz. *Sefer ha-Bahir,* ostensibly an ancient Midrash, appeared in Provence some time between 1150 and 1200 but no earlier; it was apparently edited there from a number of treatises which came from Germany or directly from the East. An analysis of the work leaves no doubt that it was not originally written in Provence,[43] and to a large extent confirms the mid-13th-century kabbalistic tradition concerning the history of the book and its sources before it reached the early Provençal mystics in a mutilated form. That the book reflects opinions which were not current in Provence and Spain is quite clearly shown by the commentary to the *Sefer Yeẓirah* by Judah b. Barzillai, written in the first third of the 12th century and containing all that the author knew of the traditions of the *ma'aseh bereshit* and especially the *ma'aseh merkabah.* In his interpretations of the ten *Sefirot* of the *Sefer Yeẓirah* there is no mention of them as "aeons" or divine attributes, or as powers within the Merkabah, as they appear in the *Bahir.* His commentary is impregnated throughout with the spirit of Saadiah Gaon, quite unlike the *Bahir,* which is completely unconcerned with philosophical ideas or with any attempt to reconcile philosophy with the concepts it advances. Cast in the form of interpretations of scriptural verses, particularly passages of mythological character, the *Bahir* transforms the Merkabah tradition into a Gnostic tradition concerning the powers of God that lie within the Divine Glory *(Kavod),* whose activity at the creation is alluded to through symbolic interpretation of the Bible and the *aggadah.* Remnants of a clearly Gnostic terminology and symbolism are preserved, albeit through a Jewish redaction, which connects the symbols with motifs already well known from the *aggadah.* This is especially so with regard to anything that impinges on *keneset Yisrael,* which is identified with the *Shekhinah,* with the *Kavod,* and with the *bat* ("daughter"), who comprises all paths of wisdom. There are indications in the writings of Eleazar of Worms that he too knew this terminology, precisely in connection with the symbolism of the *Shekhinah.* The theory of the *Sefirot* was not finally formulated in the *Sefer ha-Bahir,* and many of the book's statements were not understood, even by the early kabbalists of western Europe. The teaching of the *Bahir* is introduced as *ma'aseh merkabah,* the term "Kabbalah" not yet being used. The theory of transmigration is presented as a mystery, an idea which is self-explanatory and has no need for philosophical justification, despite the opposition of Jewish philosophers from the time of Saadiah onward.

The book *Raza Rabba* may be identified as one of the sources of the *Bahir,* but there is no doubt that there were other sources, now unknown. The earliest signs of the appearance of the Gnostic tradition, and of religious symbolism constructed upon it, are to be found in the mid-12th century and later, in the leading circle of the Provençal rabbis: Abraham b. Isaac of Narbonne, the author of *Sefer ha-Eshkol*, his son-in-law Abraham b. David (Rabad), the author of the "animadversions" (glosses) to Maimonides' *Mishneh Torah,* and Jacob Nazir of Lunel. Their works did not deal specifically with the subject of mysticism, but fragments of their opinions scattered here and there prove their association with kabbalistic views and with kabbalistic symbolism.[44] In addition to this, according to the reliable testimony of the Spanish kabbalists, they were considered as men inspired from above, who attained "a revelation of Elijah," that is, a mystical experience of spiritual awakening, through which something novel was revealed. Since main points of the theory of the *Sefirot* in its theosophical formulation are already contained in the *Sefer ha-Bahir,* it cannot be regarded as the basic content of these revelations; these were apparently connected with a new idea of the mystical purpose of prayer, based not on *gematriot* and secret Names but on contemplation of the *Sefirot* as a means of concentrating on the *kavvanah* ("meditation") in prayer. Within this circle Jacob Nazir belonged to a special group – called *perushim* in rabbinic parlance and "nazirites" in biblical terminology – whose members did not engage in commerce, but were supported by the communities so that they could devote all their time to the Torah. From its very nature, this group was akin to the Ḥasidim, and there is evidence that several of them led a ḥasidic life. Within this group a contemplative life could develop in which mystic aspirations could easily be aroused. The rabbis mentioned above did not share one consistent system of thought: there are several different and conflicting tendencies in their writings. The idea of the *Kavod,* in its plain Saadian meaning, was not regarded particularly as a mystery, but interpretations in the spirit of the theory of the *Sefirot* in the *Bahir* were considered to be "the great mystery." In the school of Abraham b. David, traditions of this type were transmitted orally, and mysteries relating to the profundities of the Divine were added to the new theory concerning mystical *kavvanah* during prayer.

This circle of the early kabbalists in Provence worked in a highly charged religious and cultural environment. Rabbinic culture had reached a high stage of development there, and even Maimonides considered those proficient in the *halakhah* to be great exponents of the Torah. Their minds were open to the philosophical tendencies of their age. Judah ibn Tibbon, head of the renowned family of translators, worked in this circle, and translated for his colleagues many of the greatest philosophical books, among them works of a distinctly neoplatonic tendency. He also translated Judah Halevi's *Kuzari* from Arabic, and its profound influence derived from this circle. The early kabbalists absorbed the *Kuzari's* ideas concerning the nature of Israel, prophecy, the Tetragrammaton, the *Sefer Yeẓirah* and its meaning, in the same way as they assimilated the writings of Abraham ibn Ezra and Abraham b. Ḥiyya, with their tendency toward neoplatonism. Jewish versions of neoplatonic theories of the Logos and the Divine Will, of emanation and of the soul, acted as a powerful stimulus. But philosophical theories concerning the Active Intellect as a cosmic force, association with which could be attained by the prophets and the select few, also penetrated these circles. The close proximity of this theory to mysticism stands out clearly in the history of medieval Islamic and Christian mysticism, and not surprisingly it acts as an important link in the chain which connects many kabbalists with the ideas of Maimonides. The influence of the asceticism of *Ḥovot ha-Levavot* has already been mentioned, and it continued to play an active role in the ethics of the Kabbalah and in its theory of mystical communion. In the last thirty years of the 12th century the Kabbalah spread beyond the circle of Abraham b. David of Posquières. The encounter between the Gnostic tradition contained in the *Bahir* and neoplatonic ideas concerning God, His emanation, and man's place in the world, was extremely fruitful, leading to the deep penetration of these ideas into earlier mystical theories. The Kabbalah, in its historical significance, can be defined as the product of the interpenetration of Jewish Gnosticism and neoplatonism.

In addition, Provence in these years was the scene of a powerful religious upheaval in the Christian world, when the Catharist sect gained control of a large part of the Languedoc, where the first centers of Kabbalah were to be found. It is not yet clear to what extent if any there was a connection between the new upsurge in Judaism in the circles of the *perushim* and the Ḥasidim, and the profound upheaval in Christianity which found expression in the Catharist movement. In their ideology there is practically nothing in common between the ideas of the kabbalists and those of the Cathari, except for the theory of transmigration, which kabbalists in fact took from the eastern sources of the *Sefer ha-Bahir*. The dualistic theology of the Cathari was clearly opposed to the Jewish view; nevertheless, it remains a possibility that there were some contacts which can no longer be discerned between the different groups, united as they were by a deep and emotional religious awakening. There is some evidence that the Jews of Provence were well aware of the existence and the beliefs of the sect as early as the first decades of the 13th century.[45] Points of possible doctrinal contacts between the *Bahir* and Catharism regarding the nature of evil have been discussed by Sh. Shachar.[46]

Fragments of the kabbalist tradition that was familiar to Abraham b. David and Jacob Nazir are found in the writings of the kabbalists, and the clear contradictions between them and later ideas, whether on the teaching on God or on the question of the *kavvanah*, testifies to their authenticity. Abraham b. David's statement in his criticism of Maimonides (*Hilkhot Teshuvah* 3,7) defending those who believe in God's corporality becomes clarified when it is seen against the background of his kabbalistic views, which distinguish the "Cause of Causes" from the Creator, who is the subject of the *Shi'ur Komah* in the early *baraita*. His interpretation of the *aggadah* in *Eruvim* 18a, that Adam was at first created with two faces, also reflects kabbalistic speculation on the divine attributes – the *Sefirot*.

Abraham b. David's son, Isaac the Blind (d. c. 1235), who lived in or near Narbonne, was the first kabbalist to devote his work entirely to mysticism. He had many disciples in Provence and Catalonia, who spread kabbalistic ideas in the form they had received them from him, and he was regarded as the central figure of the Kabbalah during his lifetime. His followers in Spain have left some record of his sayings and his habits, and a few letters and treatises written at his dictation are also extant: their style is quite different from that of any of his known disciples. Generally he couched his ideas elliptically and obscurely, and he used his own peculiar terminology. Something of his opinions can be learned from the common elements in the writings of his pupils. At all events, he is the first kabbalist whose historical personality and basic ideas clearly emerge. Entrusting his writings only to a few chosen individuals, he definitely opposed the public dissemination of the Kabbalah, seeing in this a dangerous source of misunderstanding and distortion. At the close of his life he protested in a letter to Naḥmanides and Jonah Gerondi against popularization of this sort in Spain, in which several of his pupils were engaged.[47] When the Spanish kabbalists of the 13th century speak of "the Ḥasid" they refer to Isaac the Blind. He developed a contemplative mysticism leading to communion with God through meditation on the *Sefirot* and the heavenly essences *(havayot).* The earliest instructions on detailed meditations associated with basic prayers, according to the concept of the *Sefirot* as stages in the hidden life of God, came from him. There is no doubt that he inherited some of his main ideas from his father, on whom he sometimes relied, but he had also recognized the value of the *Sefer ha-Bahir* and he built on its symbolism. His commentary to the *Sefer Yeẓirah*[48] is the first work to explain the book in the light of a systematic *Sefirot* theory in the spirit of the Kabbalah. At the head of the world of divine qualities he puts the "thought" *(maḥashavah),* from which emerged the divine utterances, the "words" by means of which the world was created. Above the "thought" is the Hidden God, who is called for the first time by the name *Ein-Sof* ("the Infinite"; see below). Man's thought ascends through mystic meditation until it reaches, and is absorbed into, Divine "Thought." Along with the theory of the *Sefirot* he developed the concept of the mysticism of language. The speech of men is connected with divine speech, and all language, whether heavenly or human, derives from one source – the Divine Name. Profound speculations on the nature of the Torah are found in a long fragment from Isaac's commentary on the beginning of the *Midrash Konen.* The neoplatonic character of his ideas is striking, and distinguishes them completely from the *Bahir.*[49]

There were other circles in Provence who spread the kabbalistic tradition on the basis of material which perhaps reached them directly from anonymous eastern sources. On the one hand they continue the neoplatonic, speculative trend of Isaac the Blind, especially in his commentary to the *Sefer Yeẓirah* and on the other hand they connect his trend with new ideas concerning the world of the Merkabah and the spiritual powers from which it is composed. There is a marked tendency to particularize and name these powers, and the theory of the *Sefirot* occupies only an incidental place among other attempts to delineate the world of emanation and the forces which constitute it. While Isaac the Blind and his disciples revealed their identities and refrained from writing pseudepigraphically, these circles concealed their identities as far as possible, both in Provence and in Spain, and produced a rich kabbalistic pseudepigrapha imitating the literary forms used in Merkabah literature and the *Sefer ha-Bahir.* One portion of this pseudepigraphic literature is neoplatonic and speculative in character, while another is angelogical, demonological, and theurgic. This latter tendency in particular found a home in some Castilian communities, e.g. Burgos and Toledo. Among the early kabbalists of Toledo are mentioned the Hasid Judah ibn Ziza, Joseph ibn Maẓah, and Meir b. Todros Abulafia.[50] How, and in what circumstances, the Kabbalah arrived there around the year 1200 is not known, but there is evidence linking the Provençal kabbalists with the citizens of Toledo. The Provençal scholar Samuel ben Mordecai mentions as sources the traditions of the Provençal teachers, Abraham b. David and his father-in-law, Ḥasidim of Germany, and Judah ibn Ziza from Toledo.[51] The pseudepigraphic literature used names from the time of Moses up to the later *geonim* and the Ḥasidim of Germany. Provence was undoubtedly the place of composition of the *Sefer ha-Iyyun* ascribed to Rav Ḥamai Gaon, the *Ma'ayan ha-Ḥokhmah,* which was communicated by an angel to Moses, the *Midrash Shimon ha-Ẓaddik,* and other texts, while the home of most of the writings attributable to the circle of the *Sefer ha-Iyyun* could have been either Provence or Castile. More than 30 texts of this kind are known, most of them very short.[52] New interpretations of the ten *Sefirot* are found side by side with notes and expositions of the "32 paths of wisdom," the Tetragrammaton, and the 42-lettered Name of God, as well as various cosmogonic speculations. Platonic and Gnostic tendencies are interwoven in them. Knowledge of the "intellectual lights," which fill the place previously occupied by the Chariot, competes with theories of the ten *Sefirot* and of the mystical names. The authors of these works had their own solemn, abstract terminology, but the terms are given differing interpretations as they recur in various places. The order of emanation varies from time to time, and it is clear that these speculations had not yet reached their final state. There were considerable differences of opinion within this circle, and each individual author seems to have been trying to define the content of the world of emanation as it was disclosed to his vision or contemplation. Even where the theory of the *Sefirot* was accepted it underwent remarkable changes. One group of texts interprets the 13 attributes of divine mercy as the sum of the powers which fill the world of emanation, some authors adding three powers to the end of the list of *Sefirot,* while in other texts the three powers are added to the top, or are considered to be intellectual lights shining within the first *Sefirah.* This view, which stimulated many speculations as the development of the Kabbalah continued, occurs in the responsa attributed to Hai Gaon on the relationship of the ten *Sefirot* to the 13 attributes.

There are clear connections leading from Saadiah's theory of the *Kavod* and his concept of "the ether which cannot be grasped," stated in his commentary to the *Sefer Yeẓirah,* to his circle, which made use of his ideas through the early translation of the *Emunot ve-De'ot.* The circle seems to have had little use for the *Sefer ha-Bahir.* The stress on the mysticism of the lights of the intellect is near in spirit, although not in detail, with later neoplatonic literature, e.g., the "Book of the Five Substances of Pseudo-Empedocles" (from the school of Ibn Masarra in Spain). For example, the supernal essences which are revealed, according to the *Sefer ha-Iyyun* and several other texts, from "the highest hidden mystery" or "the primeval darkness," are: primeval wisdom, wonderful light, the *ḥashmal,* the mist *(arafel)*, the throne of light, the wheel *(ofan)* of greatness, the cherub, the wheel of the Chariot, the surrounding ether, the curtain, the throne of glory, the place of souls, and the outer place of holiness. This mixture of terms from widely different fields is characteristic of the blending of sources and of a hierarchical arrangement that does not depend on the theory of the *Sefirot,* although it too is incorporated in some of the writings of this circle. A theurgic tendency also appears along with a desire to indulge in philosophical speculations on the Sacred Names. In addition to the influence of Arab neoplatonism, there are indications of some links with the Christian Platonic tradition transmitted through the *De Divisione Naturae* of John Scotus Erigena, but this question needs further research.

THE KABBALIST CENTER OF GERONA

Under the influence of the first kabbalists, their ideas spread from Provence to Spain, where they found a particular response in the rabbinic circle of Gerona, in Catalonia, between the Pyrenees and Barcelona. Here, from the beginning of the 13th century, a center of great and far-ranging importance came into being which fulfilled an essential role in the establishment of the Kabbalah in Spain and in the development of kabbalistic literature. For the first time, books were written here which, despite their emphasis on the esoteric side of Kabbalah, sought to bring its major ideas to a wider public. Sometimes allusions to these ideas are found in works which are not basically kabbalistic – e.g., works of *halakhah,* exegesis, ethics, or homiletics – but there were a number of books which were entirely or largely devoted to the Kabbalah. Several letters from members of this group have survived which contain important evidence of their feelings and their participation in contemporary disputes and discussions. The main figures in this group were a mysterious individual by the (pseudonymous?) name Ben Belimah;[53] Judah b. Yakar, Naḥmanides's teacher and for a certain time *dayyan* in Barcelona (1215), whose commentary to the liturgy[54] contains kabbalistic statements; Ezra b. Solomon and Azriel; Moses b. Naḥman (Naḥmanides); Abraham b. Isaac Gerondi, the *ḥazzan* of the community; Jacob b. Sheshet Gerondi; and the poet Meshullam b. Solomon Da Piera[55] (his poems were collected in *Yedi'ot ha-Makhon le-Ḥeker ha-Shirah,* 4(1938)). In addition, their pupils should also be included, although many of them spread further afield to the Aragonese communities.

A personal and literary link between the kabbalists of Provence and those of Gerona may be seen in Asher b. David, a nephew of Isaac the Blind. A number of his writings were very widely scattered in manuscript.[56] In content, his writings are very similar to thoses of Ezra and Azriel, who were apparently among the first to write works entirely devoted to Kabbalah and composed mainly in the first third of the 13th century. Ezra wrote a commentary to the Song of Songs (which was published under Naḥmanides' name), interpreted the *aggadot* to several tractates of the Talmud wherever he was able to connect them with the Kabbalah, and summarized traditions, the greater part of which doubtless derived from Provençal kabbalists. His younger companion, Azriel, made an independent rendering of his interpretation of the *aggadot* (ed. Tishby, 1943), wrote a commentary to the liturgy (*Perush ha-Tefillot;* French translation by G. Séd, 1973) according to the theory of *kavvanot*, a commentary to the *Sefer Yeẓirah* published in editions of that work under the name of Naḥmanides, and two small books on the nature of God, *Be'ur Eser Sefirot* (also entitled *Sha'ar ha-Sho'el*), and *Derekh ha-Emunah ve-Derekh ha-Kefirah.* These two kabbalists also left separate "mysteries" on several subjects (e.g. "the mystery of sacrifices"), and letters on kabbalistic questions, including a long letter from Azriel to the kabbalists of Burgos.[57] Azriel stands out above other members of the group because of the systematic nature of his thought and the depth of his intellect. He is the only one of the group whose work is connected in style and content with the writings of the circle of the *Sefer ha-Iyyun* mentioned above. In his books, the interpretation of neoplatonic and Gnostic elements reached their first apex. The neoplatonic element came largely from the writings of Isaac b. Solomon Israeli, some of which were undoubtedly known in Gerona.[58] Jacob b. Sheshet, in his polemical work against Samuel ibn Tibbon, *Meshiv Devarim Nekhoḥim* (ed. Vajda, 1968), combined philosophical enquiry with kabbalistic speculation. Two of his books were devoted to the latter: *Sefer ha-Emunah ve-ha-Bitaḥon,* later attributed to Naḥmanides and published under his name, and *Sha'ar ha-Shamayim,* a rhymed summary of kabbalistic ideas (*Ozar Neḥmad,* 3 (1860), 133–65).

It is doubtful if these kabbalists, who were known only to a small circle and who composed no works outside the field of Kabbalah, would have had the great influence that they did if it had not been for the stature of their colleague Naḥmanides (c.1194–1270), the highest legal and religious authority of his time in Spain. The fact that he joined the ranks of the kabbalists as a young man prepared the way for reception of the Kabbalah in Spain, just as the personality of Abraham b. David had prepared the way for the reception of the Kabbalah in Provence. The names of these two men were a guarantee to most of their contemporaries that, despite their novelty, kabbalistic ideas did not stray from the accepted faith and the rabbinic tradition. Their undisputed conservative character protected the kabbalists from accusations of deviation from strict monotheism or even heresy. Charges of this kind were made, provoked mainly by the wider publicity given the earlier works of Kabbalah and to their oral propagation in a number of communities. Isaac the Blind refers to polemics between the kabbalists and their opponents in Spain, and evidence of similar arguments in Provence (between 1235 and 1245) is extant in the accusations of Meir b. Simeon of Narbonne, a reply to which, in defense of the Kabbalah, is included in the works of Asher b. David.[59]

From the very beginning two opposing tendencies appear among the kabbalists, the first seeking to limit the Kabbalah to closed circles as a definitely esoteric system, and the second wishing to spread its influence among the people at large. Throughout the history of the Kabbalah right down to recent times these two tendencies have been in conflict. Parallel with this, from the time of the appearance of the Kabbalah in Gerona, two attitudes developed concerning the relationships of the bearers of rabbinic culture to the Kabbalah. The kabbalists were accepted as proponents of a conservative ideology and as public defenders of tradition and custom, but at the same time they were suspected, by a substantial number of rabbis and sages, of having non-Jewish leanings and of being innovators whose activities must be curtailed wherever possible. Most of the kabbalists themselves saw their role in terms of the preservation of tradition, and in fact their first public appearance was associated with their taking the traditionalists' side in the controversy over Maimonides' writings and the study of philosophy in the 13th century.[60] In these disputes the Kabbalah of the Gerona scholars seemed to be a symbolic interpretation of the world of Judaism and its way of life, based on a theosophy which taught the inner secrets of the revealed Godhead and on a rejection of rationalist interpretations of the Torah and the Commandments. Nevertheless, it cannot be ignored that the system of thought elaborated by a man like Azriel did not invalidate the philosophic teaching of his time but rather added to it a new dimension, that of theosophy, as its crowning glory. In particular this school contributed a new spiritual dimension to the exegesis of Genesis I, one of the main topics of Jewish philosophical thought.[61]

In several of his works Naḥmanides gives room to the Kabbalah, particularly in his commentary to the Torah, where his many veiled and unexplained allusions to interpretations "according to the true way" were meant to arouse the curiosity of those readers who had never heard of that "way." He also used kabbalistic symbolism in some of his *piyyutim.* And his views on the fate of the soul after death and the nature of the world to come, expressed in *Sha'ar ha-Gemul* at the end of his halakhic work *Toledot Adam,* represent the ideas of his circle and are in contrast to Maimonides' views on this subject. His commentary to the book of Job is based on the theory of transmigration (without mentioning the term *gilgul* itself) and on the views of his companion, Ezra, concerning the *Sefirah Ḥokhmah.* Naḥmanides wrote no works specifically on the Kabbalah, apart from a commentary to the first chapter of the *Sefer Yeẓirah*[62] and, rather surprisingly, a sermon on the occasion of a wedding.[63] Since the 14th century, several books by other authors were attributed to him. In the writings of the Gerona kabbalists there is a definite, well-established symbolic framework which is related first and foremost to the theory of the *Sefirot* and to the way in which this theory interprets scriptural verses and homilies dealing with the acts of God. This symbolism served as the main basis for the development of the Kabbalah in this group, and numerous anonymous kabbalists of this and later periods made out lists and tables, mostly brief, of the order of the *Sefirot,* and of the nomenclature in Scripture and *aggadah* which fitted them. In points of detail practically every kabbalist had his own system but there was a wide measure of agreement on fundamentals.[64]

Contacts were made between the Spanish kabbalists and the Ḥasidei Ashkenaz, either through individual Ḥasidim who visited Spain or through books which were brought there, e.g., the works of Eleazar of Worms. Abraham Axelrod of Cologne, who traveled through the Spanish communities between 1260 and 1275 approximately, wrote *Keter Shem Tov* dealing with the Tetragrammaton and the theory of the *Sefirot.* It exists in various versions, one of which was published in Jellinek's *Ginzei Ḥokhmat ha-Kabbalah* (1853), while another gives the author's name as Menahem, a pupil of Eleazar of Worms. This combination of the theory of the Sacred Names and speculations using the methods of *gematria* with the theory of the *Sefirot* of the Gerona kabbalists contains, at least in a third version of the book, a powerful renewal of ecstatic tendencies, which took on the new form of "prophetic Kabbalah."[65] Other kabbalists from Castile also established contacts with one of the pupils of Eleazar of Worms who lived in Narbonne in the middle of the 13th century.

It is almost certain that an anonymous kabbalist from the Gerona circle, or one of the Provençal kabbalists, was the author of the book *Temunah* (written before 1250), which was attributed several generations later to R. Ishmael, the high priest. The style of the book is very difficult, and its contents are obscure at many points. An interpretation of the "image of God" through the shapes of the Hebrew letters, it became the basis of several other texts, composed in a similar fashion and perhaps even by the same author; e.g., interpretations of the secret 72-lettered Name of God mentioned in the mystical literature of the geonic period. The importance of the book lies in its detailed though enigmatic explanation of the theory of *shemittot* (see below), to which the Gerona kabbalists alluded without a detailed explanation. The difficult style of the *Temunah* was elucidated to some extent by an old commentary, also anonymous (published with the book itself in 1892), which was written at the end of the 13th century. *Temunah* had a distinct influence on Kabbalah up to the 16th century.

OTHER CURRENTS IN 13TH CENTURY SPANISH KABBALAH

The combination of theosophic-Gnostic and neoplatonic-philosophical elements, which found expression in Provence and Gerona, led to the relative, or sometimes exaggerated, dominance of one element over the other in other currents from 1230 onward. On one side there was an extreme mystical tendency, expressed in philosophical terms and creating its own symbolism which was not based on the theory or nomenclature of the *Sefirot* found among the Gerona kabbalists. Refuting some of the suppositions of the latter (e.g. the theory of transmigration), nevertheless it saw itself as the true "science of Kabbalah." Its first and most important exponent was Isaac ibn Latif, whose books were written (perhaps in Toledo) between 1230 and 1270. "He had one foot inside [the Kabbalah], and one foot outside [in philosophy]" as Judah Ḥayyat said of him (preface to *Minḥat Yehudah* on *Ma'arekhet ha-Elohut*). Becoming a kind of independent mystic, he drew his philosophical inspiration from the writings in both Arabic and Hebrew of the neoplatonists, and especially from Ibn Gabirol's *Mekor Ḥayyim* and the works of Abraham ibn Ezra, although at times he completely transformed their meaning. His main work, *Sha'ar ha-Shamayim* (written in 1238), was intended to be, in a speculative mystical vein, both a continuation of and a substitute for Maimonides' *Guide of the Perplexed.* Together with most of the Gerona kabbalists he accorded the highest place to the Primeval Will, seeing in it the source of all emanation. The theory of the Divine Logos, which he took from the Arabic neoplatonic tradition, became divided into the Will – which remained completely within the Divine and was identified with the Divine Word (Logos) which brought forth all things – and into the "first created thing," the Supreme Intellect that stands at the top of the hierarchy of all beings, and was presented in symbols which in other places belong to the Logos itself. But Ibn Latif is not consistent in his highly personal use of symbolism and often contradicts himself, even on important points. From the "first created thing" *(nivra rishon)* emanated all the other stages, called symbolically light, fire, ether, and water. Each of these is the province of one branch of wisdom: mysticism, metaphysics, astronomy, and physics. Ibn Latif created a complete and rich system of the universe, basing his views on a far-fetched allegorical interpretation of Scripture, although he was opposed to the extreme allegorists who regarded allegory as a substitute for the literal interpretation and not simply an addition to it. His ideas about prayer and true understanding have a distinctly mystical tinge, and in this respect exceed the theory of *kavvanah* and meditation prevalent among the kabbalists of Gerona. The influence of Ibn Gabirol is most noticeable in his *Ẓurat ha-Olam* (1860) which contains specific criticisms of kabbalistic theosophy. Nevertheless, Ibn Latif regards Kabbalah as superior to philosophy both in nature and efficacy, in particular because it takes hold of truth which is of a temporal nature, whereas philosophical truth is atemporal (*Rav Pe'alim* (1885), no. 39). Ibn Latif had personal connections with exponents of Kabbalah whose conceptions were completely opposed to his, and he dedicated *Ẓeror ha-Mor* to Todros Abulafia of Toledo, one of the leaders of the Gnostic trend of Kabbalah. His books were read by kabbalists and philosophers alike, e.g. the philosopher Isaac Albalag (Vatican Ms, 254, fol. 97b), who criticized his *Ẓurat ha-Olam.* According to Ibn Latif, the highest intellectual understanding reaches only the "back" of the Divine, whereas a picture of the "face" is disclosed only in a supra-intellectual ecstacy, which involves experience superior even to that of prophecy (*Ginzei ha-Melekh,* chs. 37 and 41). This perception he calls "the beatitude of supreme communion." True prayer brings the human intellect into communion with the Active Intellect "like a kiss," but from there it ascends even to union with the "first created thing"; beyond this union, achieved through words, is the union through pure thought intended to reach the First Cause, i.e., the Primeval Will, and at length to stand before God Himself (*Ẓeror ha-Mor,* ch. 5).

The second exponent of philosophic-mystical tendencies distinct from the theosophical Kabbalah of the Gerona school and aspiring toward an ecstatic Kabbalah was Abraham Abulafia (1240–after 1292). The striking image of this man derives from his outstanding personality. He came into contact with a group whose technique of letter combination and number mysticism stimulated his own ecstatic experiences. At least part of his inspiration was derived from the German Ḥasidei Ashkenaz and perhaps also through the influence of Sufi circles, whom he met with during his travels in the east in his early years. Abulafia's teacher was the *ḥazzan* Barukh Togarmi (in Barcelona?), who, judging by his name, came from the east. From him he learned the fundamental teachings of prophetic Kabbalah to whose dissemination he devoted his life, after he had attained illumination in Barcelona in 1271. His prophetic and perhaps also messianic claims aroused strong opposition both in Spain and in Italy, but his books were widely read from the end of the 13th century, especially those where he expounded his system of Kabbalah as a kind of guide to the upward journey from philosophical preoccupations of the Maimonidean type to prophecy and to those mystical experiences which he believed partook of the nature of prophecy. Abulafia was also a copious borrower of kabbalistic ideas whenever he found them relevant, but those aspects which were foreign to his nature he opposed even to the point of ridicule. A passionate admirer of Maimonides, he believed that his own system was merely a continuation and elaboration of the teaching of the *Guide of the Perplexed.* Unlike Maimonides, who dissociated himself from the possibility of prophecy in his time, Abulafia defended such a prospect, finding in "the way of the Names," i.e., a specific mystical technique also called "the science of combination," *ḥokhmat ha-ẓeruf,* a means realizing and embodying human aspirations toward prophecy.

So inspired, he himself wrote 26 prophetic books of which only one, *Sefer ha-Ot,* has survived.[66] *Derekh ha-Sefirot* ("the way of the *Sefirot*"), he believed, is useful for beginners, but is of little value compared with *Derekh ha-Shemot* ("the way of the Names"), opening up only after deep study of the *Sefer Yeẓirah* and the techniques to which it alludes. Abulafia saw his Kabbalah, therefore, as another layer added to the earlier Kabbalah, which did not contradict such major works as the *Bahir,* the *Temunah*, and the writings of Naḥmanides. His promise to expound a way which would lead to what he called "prophecy," and his practical application of kabbalist principles, found a distinct echo in Kabbalah from the 14th century onward, first in Italy and later in other countries. His great manuals (*Sefer he-Ẓeruf, Or ha-Sekhel* and especially *Ḥayyei ha-Olam ha-Ba,* and others), which have been copied right down to recent times, are textbooks of meditation, the objects of which are the Sacred Names and the letters of the alphabet and their combinations, both comprehensible and incomprehensible. It was precisely this kind of manual which had been lacking in the usual type of kabbalistic literature, which had confined itself to symbolic descriptions, and refrained from advancing in writing techniques for mystic experience. The work of Abulafia filled this need, and the fierce criticism of him which was heard here and there did not prevent their absorption and influence. One of Abulafia's pupils wrote (perhaps in Hebron) at the end of 1294 a small book on prophetic Kabbalah, *Sha'arei Ẓedek,* which includes an important autobiographical description of his studies with his teacher, and of his mystical experiences.[67]

On the other side of this twofold development of the Kabbalah was a school of kabbalists who were more attracted to Gnostic traditions, whether genuine or only apparently so, and who concentrated on the Gnostic and mythological element rather than on the philosophical. The exponents of this trend set out to find and assemble fragments of documents and oral traditions, and added to them just as much themselves, until their books became an astonishing mixture of pseudepigrapha with the authors' own commentaries. In contrast with the Kabbalah of Gerona, the pseudepigraphic element was very strong in this branch, although it is not absolutely certain that the authors of these books themselves invented the sources which they quoted. This school, which might properly be called "the Gnostic reaction," includes the brothers Jacob and Isaac, sons of Jacob ha-Kohen of Soria, who traveled in Spain and Provence (c. 1260–80) and met their older kabbalist predecessors: Moses b. Simeon, their pupil and successor, rabbi of Burgos; and Todros b. Joseph Abulafia of Burgos and Toledo, one of the leaders of Castilian Jewry of his day. Their main work belongs to the second half of the 13th century. In Kabbalist circles Moses of Burgos was widely considered to be endowed with particular authority, and he was also the teacher of Isaac ibn Sahula, author of *Mashal ha-Kadmoni.* It is extraordinary that such a complete rationalist and devotee of philosophical enquiry as Isaac Albalag could see three members of this school as the true exponents of Kabbalah in his time, with Moses of Burgos at their head: "His name has spread throughout the country: Moses has received *[kibbel]* the [authentic] kabbalist tradition."[68]

The speculative side is not altogether absent in this school, and some fragments of one of Isaac ha-Kohen's books[69] in particular show some relationship between him and Ibn Latif, but its true characteristics are quite different. He developed the details of the theory of the left, demonic, emanation, whose ten *Sefirot* are the exact counterparts of the Holy *Sefirot.* A similar demonic emanation is already mentioned in the writings of the *Sefer ha-Iyyun* group, and in the works of Nahmanides, and it is possible that its origins stemmed from the east. In the evidence extant, this theory appeared in pseudepigraphic texts and its roots were mainly in Provence and Castile. From these traditions came the zoharic theory of the *sitra aḥra* (the "other side"). There is also a strong tendency here to arrange long lists of beings in the world below the realm of the *Sefirot* – that are given specific names – and so establish a completely new angelology. These emanations of the second rank are presented partly as "curtains" *(pargodim)* in front of the emanations of the *Sefirot,* and as "bodies" and "garments" for the inner souls, which are the *Sefirot.* This multiplicity of personified emanations and the listing of them recall similar tendencies in the later development of several Gnostic systems, and in particular the book *Pistis Sophia.* To everything in the world below there is a corresponding force in the world above, and in this way a kind of strange mythology without precedent in other sources is created. This theme runs through all the writings of Isaac b. Jacob ha-Kohen, and through some of the work of his elder brother Jacob. The novelty of the names of these forces and their description is obvious, and some of the details of the *Sefirot* and their nomenclature occasionally assume a form different from that in the Kabbalah of Gerona. In the writings of Todros Abulafia the kabbalists who are exponents of the Gnostic trend are given the specific name of *ma'amikim* ("those who delve deeply"), in order to distinguish them from the others. The Spanish kabbalists of the 14th century made an additional distinction between the Kabbalah of the Castilian kabbalists, which belonged to the Gnostic school, and that of the Catalonian kabbalists. In this circle we can observe quite clearly the growth of the magical element and the tendency to preserve theurgic traditions of which there is no trace in the Gerona school.

This new gnostic bent did not stop the individual mystical or visionary experience. The two elements go hand in hand in the writings of Jacob ha-Kohen, who wrote the extensive *Sefer ha-Orah,* which has no link with earlier kabbalistic tradition but is based entirely on visions which "were accorded him" in heaven. The Kabbalah of these visions is completely different from the traditionalist portion of his other writings, and it is not taken up anywhere else in the history of the Kabbalah. It is based on a new form of the idea of Logos which assumes here the image of Metatron. The theory of emanation also acquires another garb, and concern with the *Sefirot* makes way for speculations on "the holy spheres" *(ha-galgalim ha-kedoshim)* through which the power of the Emanator is invisibly dispersed until it reaches the sphere of Metatron, which is the central cosmic force. This very personal theosophy, nourished and inspired by vision, has no relationship with the theosophy of the Gerona kabbalists but it has some connection with the Ḥasidei Ashkenaz. Jacob ha-Kohen was the first Spanish kabbalist to build all his mystical teachings concerning the reasons for the Commandments and other matters on *gematriot.* Metatron, to be sure, was created, but came into being simultaneously with the emanation of the inner heavenly spheres, and the verse "Let there be light" alludes to the "formation of the light of the intellect" in the shape of the Metatron. There is little doubt that Jacob ha-Kohen knew about the art of "combination" as a prerequisite for mystical perception, but had no knowledge of those mysteries derived from it through rationalist interpretation characteristic of Abraham Abulafia. *Sefer ha-Orah* has not been preserved in its entirety, but large parts of it exist in various manuscripts (Milan 62, Vatican 428, etc.). Apart from Ibn Latif's writings, it is the most striking example of how an entirely new Kabbalah could be created side by side with the earlier one, and it is as if each one of them speaks on a different plane. In his *Oẓar ha-Kavod* on the legends of the Talmud (1879), and in his *Sha'ar ha-Razim* on Psalm 19 (Munich Ms. 209) Todros Abulafia strove to combine the Kabbalah of Gerona with the Kabbalah of the Gnostics, but he never alluded to the revelations accorded to Jacob ha-Kohen.

THE ZOHAR (see also p.213).

The mingling of the two trends emanating from the Gerona school and from the school of the Gnostics is to a certain extent paralleled in the main product of Spanish Kabbalah. This is the *Sefer ha-Zohar* written mainly between 1280 and 1286 by Moses b. Shem Tov de Leon in Guadalajara, a small town northeast of Madrid. In this city there also lived two kabbalist brothers, Isaac and Meir b. Solomon ibn Sahula, and it is in Isaac's books that the first quotations are found from the earliest stratum of the Zohar, dating from 1281.[70] Many kabbalists were active at this time in the small communities around Toledo, and there is evidence of mystical experience even among the unlearned. An example of this is the appearance as a prophet in Avila in 1295 of Nissim b. Abraham, an ignorant artisan, to whom an angel revealed a kabbalistic work, *Pil'ot ha-Ḥokhmah,* and who was opposed by Solomon b. Abraham Adret (Responsa of Solomon b. Adret, no. 548). This was the community where Moses de Leon passed the last years of his life (d. 1305). The Zohar is the most important evidence for the stirring of a mythical spirit in medieval Judaism. The origin of the book, its literary and religious character, and the role that it has played in the history of Judaism, have been subjects of prolonged argument among scholars during the last 130 years, but most of it has not been based on historical and linguistic analysis. In an analysis of this kind we can establish a precise place for the Zohar in the development of Spanish Kabbalah, which has set its seal on the book. In so doing we must resist continually recurring apologetic attempts to antedate its composition by turning its late literary sources into evidence for the earlier existence of the book, or by proclaiming ancient strata in it – of whose presence there is no proof whatsoever (J.L. Zlotnik, Belkin, Finkel, Reuben Margaliot, Chavel, M. Kasher, and others).

The mingling of these two currents – the Kabbalah of Gerona and the Kabbalah of the "Gnostics" of Castile – became in the mind of Moses de Leon a creative encounter which determined the basic character of the Zohar. Instead of the brief allusions and interpretations of his predecessors he presents a broad canvas of interpretation and homiletics covering the whole world of Judaism as it appeared to him. He was far removed from systematic theology, and indeed there are fundamental problems of contemporary Jewish thought which do not arise in his work at all, such as the meaning of prophecy and the questions of predestination and providence; however, he reflects the actual religious situation, and expounds it through kabbalistic interpretation. In a pseudepigraph attributed to Simeon b. Yoḥai and his friends, Moses de Leon clothed his interpretation of Judaism in an archaic garb – in the form of long and short Midrashim of the Torah and the three books Song of Songs, Ruth, and Lamentations. The explanations in the book revolve round two poles – one consisting of the mysteries of the world of the *Sefirot* that constitute the life of the Divine, which is also reflected in many symbols in the created world; and the other of the situation of the Jew and his fate both in this world and in the world of souls. The deepening and broadening of a symbolic view of Judaism was very daring in an age when the kabbalists still preserved in some measure the esoteric character of their ideas. The appearance of what purported to be an ancient Midrash which actually reflected the basic viewpoints of the Spanish kabbalists, and successfully expressed them in an impressive literary synthesis, sparked off a number of arguments among the kabbalists of the day. However, it also served to spread knowledge of the Kabbalah and ensure its acceptance. The author's viewpoint progressed from a tendency toward philosophy and allegoric interpretation to Kabbalah and its symbolic ideas. The steps in this progress can still be recognized in the differences between the *Midrash ha-Ne'lam,* the earliest part of the Zohar, and the main body of the book. There is little doubt that the aim of the book was to attack the literal conception of Judaism and the neglect of the performance of the *miẓvot,* and this was accomplished by emphasizing the supreme value and secret meaning of every word and Commandment of the Torah. As in most great mystical texts, inner perception and the way to "communion" are connected with the preservation of the traditional framework, whose value is increased sevenfold. The mystical viewpoint served to strengthen the tradition and indeed became a conscious conservative factor. On the other hand, the author of the Zohar concentrated frequently on speculations on the profundities of the nature of Divinity, which other kabbalists did not dare dwell upon, and his boldness was an important contributory factor in the renewed development of Kabbalah several generations later. When the Zohar appeared few kabbalists turned their attention to this original aspect. Instead they used the Zohar as a distinguished aid to strengthening their conservative aims. In his Hebrew books written in the years after 1286, after he had finished his major work in the Zohar, Moses de Leon himself concealed many of his more daring speculations (which the obscure Aramaic garb had suited very well). On the other hand he stressed in them the principles of *Sefirot* symbolism, with its value for the comprehension of the Torah and of prayer, and also the homiletical and moral element of the Zohar. His Hebrew books expanded, here and there, themes which were first adumbrated with some variations in the Zohar. These works have largely been preserved, and some of them were copied many times, but only one has been published before modern times (*Sefer ha-Mishkal,* also called *Sefer ha-Nefesh ha-Ḥakhamah,* 1608). It is hard to say to what extent Moses de Leon expected his work in the Zohar actually to be accepted as an ancient and authoritative Midrash, or how far he intended to create a compendium of Kabbalah in a suitable literary form which would be perfectly clear to the discerning eye. Many kabbalists in the succeeding generation used similar forms and wrote imitations of the Zohar, something which they would not have dared to do in the case of genuine Midrashim, thus showing that they did not take the framework of the book too seriously. This does not detract from (indeed it may add to) the value of the Zohar from a historical point of view, whether for its own sake of for the sake of the influence that it exerted.

Moses de Leon was certainly very closely associated with another kabbalist, who began as a disciple of Abraham Abulafia himself. This was Joseph Gikatilla, who wrote *Ginnat Egoz* in 1274 and later a number of other works under the inspiration of his first master. However, while still young he also became associated with Gnostic circles and afterward he struck up a friendship with Moses de Leon; each came under the other's influence. Turning his attention from the mysteries of letters, vowels, and names, Gikatilla embarked on a profound study of the theosophy of the *Sefirot* system, and his books provide an independent and valuable parallel to the writings of Moses de Leon. *Sha'arei Orah,* written about 1290, already shows the influence of certain parts of the Zohar, although there is no mention of it. An important summary of, and introduction to, the interpretation of *Sefirot* symbolism, this book became one of the major works of Spanish Kabbalah. It is worth noting that three different streams, the Kabbalah of Gerona, the Kabbalah of the Zohar, and the Kabbalah of Abulafia, were able to meet and be reconciled in Gikatilla's mind, a very rare occurrence in this period. His *Ginnat Egoz* in the latest source, insofar as we know, utilized by the author of the Zohar.

Two works written in the 1290s or in the earliest years of the 14th century, the *Ra'aya Meheimna* and the *Sefer ha-Tikkunim,* compromise the latest strands in the zoharic literature. They are the work of an unknown kabbalist who was familiar with the major part of the Zohar and wrote his books as a kind of continuation of it (albeit with some change in literary style and framework). The books contain a new interpretation of the first chapters of Genesis and a tabulated explanation of the reasons for the Commandments. Elevating the importance of the Zohar as the final revelation of the mysteries, these two works connected its appearance with the beginning of the redemption: "Through the merits of the Zohar they will go forth from exile in mercy," i.e. without the dread pains of the redemption (Zohar 3: 124b). The author exaggeratedly blends the image of the biblical Moses with Moses the revealer of the Zohar on the eve of the final redemption. It is possible that he was very close to the circle of Moses de Leon, and perhaps his name was also called Moses. These books are the first of a whole line of Kabbalistic works which were written in the pseudo-Aramaic style of the Zohar and as a continuation of it. Some authors also wrote in Hebrew, adding interpretations in the name of zoharic characters but reflecting their own ideas. In this category mention should be made of *Mar'ot ha-Ẓove'ot* (Sassoon Ms. 978) by David b. Judah he-Ḥasid, known from his other writings as a grandson of Naḥmanides (*Ohel David,* 1001–06); and *Livnat ha-Sappir* (on Gen., 1914; on Lev. British Museum Ms. 767) by Joseph Angelino, written in 1325–27, and wrongly ascribed by several kabbalists to David b. Judah Ḥasid. This latter David was the first to compose a garbled Hebrew translation and elaboration of the speculations in the *Idra Rabba* of the Zohar, called *Sefer ha-Gevul* (Jerusalem Ms.).[71] He also wrote a long commentary, *Or Zaru'a,* on the liturgy, and several other books.[72]

An important pseudepigraph written at the time of the appearance of the Zohar was *Sod Darkhei ha-Shemot,* "The Mystery of the Names, Letters, and Vowels, and the Power of the [Magical] Operations, according to the Sages of Lunel," which is found in several manuscripts under different names (Vatican Ms. 441). Attributed to the circle of Abraham b. David, the book is actually based on the works of Gikatilla and Moses de Leon, and connects speculations on the letters, vowels, and Sacred Names with the theory of practical Kabbalah. Its author, who gave the words of the late 13th century kabbalists a new pseudepigraphic frame, also compiled the kabbalist anthology *Sefer ha-Ne'lam* (Paris Ms. 817), using similar source material. An obscure figure in zoharic imitation literature is Joseph "who came from the city of Shushan" (i.e. from Hamadan in Persia). Perhaps this is a completely fictitious name concealing a Spanish kabbalist who lived about 1300 or a little later and wrote a lengthy work on the Torah section of *Terumah,* the Song of Songs, and Kohelet, which is largely written in the style of the Zohar and develops the ideas of the zoharic *Idras* concerning the *Shi'ur Komah.* This extensive work is preserved (British Museum Ms. 464) and was disseminated even in comparatively late times.[73] The book is full of strange ideas not to be found in other kabbalistic texts, and the author introduces opinions which are quite foreign to the Zohar, although couched in its style. According to A. Altmann he is to be identified with the anonymous author of the *Sefer Ta'amei ha-Miẓvot,* which was used as the source of a literary plagiarism by Isaac ibn Farḥi in the 16th century.[74] This author also wrote the comprehensive work *Toledot Adam,* partly printed under the erroneous title

Sefer ha-Malkhut.[75] The third book in this category in the *Sefer ha-She'arim* or *She'elot la-Zaken* (Oxford Ms. 2396) from the first quarter of the 14th century. The old man *(zaken)* who replies to the questions of his disciples is none other than Moses himself. The bulk of the book is written in Hebrew and only a minor section in the zoharic style. Also a completely independent work, it relies a great deal on allusion without fully explaining its ideas.

THE KABBALAH IN THE 14TH CENTURY UP TO THE EXPULSION FROM SPAIN

The 14th century was a period of intellectual development which produced an extremely rich literature. The Kabbalah spread through most of the communities of Spain and beyond, in particular to Italy and the East. Once the gates were opened wide through the books that revealed mystical ideas, all the preceding trends found their continuators and their interpreters; with this expansion all the different trends mingled with one another to a certain extent, and attempts were made to find a compromise between them.

The Kabbalah of Gerona was continued through the prolific literary activity of the disciples of Naḥmanides' pupils, who were taught by Solomon b. Abraham Adret (Rashba) and Isaac b. Todros, author of a commentary to the *maḥzor* according to Kabbalah (Paris Ms. 839). Members of this school, who did not favor the prevailing pseudepigraphic style, produced many books attempting to clarify the kabbalistic passages of Naḥmanides' commentary to the Torah. An unknown author writing at the beginning of the 14th century composed *Ma'arekhet ha-Elohut* (1558), a compendium which expounded the doctrine of Kabbalah in a terse and systematic fashion. This book was very widely read, especially in Italy, and its influence was felt as late as the 16th century. Although Solomon b. Abraham Adret was very cautious in his dealings with kabbalistic matters, he often alluded to them in his commenatry to the *aggadot* (Vatican Ms. 295), and he also composed a long prayer in the kabbalistic way. His pupils, however, assigned a central place to the Kabbalah. To this school belong: Baḥya b. Asher from Saragossa, whose commentary to the Torah contributed greatly to the dissemination of the Kabbalah and was the first kabbalistic book to be printed in its entirety (1492); Joshua ibn Shu'ayb from Tudela, author of the important *Derashot* (homilies) on the Torah (1523), the first book in this genre to assign a central place to the Kabbalah, and the real author of the *Be'ur Sodot ha-Ramban* ("Explanation of [the kabbalistic] secrets of Nahmanides' Commentary"), which was printed (1875) under the name of his pupil, Meir b. Solomon Ibn Sahula; Ḥayyim b. Samuel of Lerida, author of

Ẓeror ha-Ḥayyim, which contains a kabbalistic exposition of halakhic matters (Ms. Musajoff); Shem Tov b. Abraham ibn Gaon from Soria, who began a large-scale literary activity on the Kabbalah between 1315 and 1325, emigrated to Ereẓ Israel with his friend Elhanan b. Abraham ibn Eskira, and settled in Safed. Elhanan's *Yesod Olam* (Guenzburg Ms. 607), written partly in Arabic, merges the Gerona tradition with neoplatonic philosophical Kabbalah. In the school of Solomon Adret a large amount of of raw material was assembled which has been preserved in *collectanea* of considerable value (Vatican Ms. 202, Parma Mss. 68 and 1221, and others). In the same way several anonymous texts have been preserved which interpret the hidden meanings in Naḥmanides. The main storehouse for all the traditions of this school is *Me'irat Einaim* by Isaac b. Samuel of Acre, who also dealt at length in other books with completely different aspects of the Kabbalah, under the joint influence of the Zohar and the school of Abraham Abulafia. In contrast to the attempts to seek a compromise between Kabbalah and philosophy, he insisted on the independence and supreme worth of kabbalist theosophy. Parts of the collection of revelations that were granted to him in various ways were assembled in *Oẓar ha-Ḥayyim* (Guenzburg Ms. 775), parts of which have been frequently copied. He was associated with many contemporary kabbalists, and he was the first of this circle to write an autobiography, which, however, is lost.

Another kabbalist who migrated to Spain and became acquainted with the Kabbalah there was Joseph b. Shalom Ashkenazi, author of an extensive commentary to the *Sefer Yeẓirah* (which has been printed in editions of the book under the name of Abraham b. David). He also wrote a commentary to the *bereshit* section of the *Midrash Genesis Rabbah* (KS, 4 (1928), 236–302), under the title *Parashat Bereshit* The former book was already used in the works of David b. Judah Ḥasid. These works develop the theory of the *Sefirot* to the extreme, assigning to everything a precise place in the world of the *Sefirot* Joseph b. Shalom engaged in the kabbalistic critique of philosophy, but he interpreted its principles kabbalistically in a very bold way. Like most of the kabbalists of his time he was taken much with the idea of the *shemittot* which gained much ground in this period. Among the most important versions of this theory is that lucidly presented in *Sod Ilan ha-Aẓilut* by R. Isaac.[76] Joseph b. Shalom expounded an extreme conception of the theory of transmigration of souls, turning it into a cosmic law involving a change of form which affected every part of creation from the *Sefirah* of *Ḥokhmah* down to the lowest grade of inanimate objects.

Together with the influence of the Zohar and the school of Solomon Adret the Spanish Kabbalah began to spread into Italy, particularly through the writings of Menahem Recanati who wrote, early in the 14th century, a commentary "according to the path of truth" on the Torah (1523) and a work on the mystical reasons for the commandments (complete ed. 1963). But there was little independence in Italian Kabbalah, and for a long time it consisted of no more than compilations and interpretations, following the Zohar and the *Ma'arekhet ha-Elohut,*[77] and, to an even greater extent than in Spain itself, the writings of Abraham Abulafia. One exception is the *Iggeret Purim,*[78] whose author gives an unusual symbolic interpretation of the theory of the *Sefirot.* The outstanding Italian kabbalist of the 14th century was Reuben Ẓarfati. In Germany also there was little independent creativity in the Kabbalah. German kabbalists contented themselves with mingling the Zohar and the *Ma'arekhet* with the tradition of Ḥasidei Ashkenaz. Avigdor Kara (d. 1439), who achieved fame there as a kabbalist,[79] wrote *Kodesh Hillulim* on Psalm 150 (Zurich Ms. 102). In the second half of the 14th century Menahem Ẓiyyoni of Cologne wrote *Sefer Ẓiyyoni* on the Torah, and Yom Tov Lipmann Muelhausen devoted part of his literary activity to the Kabbalah, e.g. *Sefer ha-Eshkol* (ed. Judah Even-Shemuel (Kaufmann), 1927). From the beginning of the 14th century the Kabbalah also spread to the East. In Persia, Isaiah b. Joseph of Tabriz wrote *Ḥayyei ha-Nefesh* (1324; Jerusalem Ms. 8° 544; part of it was published in 1891); and in Constantinople Nathan b. Moses Kilkis, who says that he studied in Spain, wrote the voluminous *Even Sappir* (1368–70; Paris Ms. 727–8).

These last two books belong to the strain which attempted to combine Kabbalah and philosophy in more or less radical ways. Originating mainly among the Spanish kabbalists of the period, these attempts became quite common, and their proponents attacked the opposite tendency to emphasize the two sides' basic differences of approach. The unequivocal neoplatonic line of Ibn Latif was continued (about 1300) by David b. Abraham ha-Lavan in his *Masoret ha-Berit.* Joseph b. Shalom, mentioned above, linked Kabbalah with Aristotelian metaphysics and with natural philosophy, showing how even abstract philosophical concepts could be given a mystical content. Obviously, some tended toward a more philosophical view, while others concentrated on the specifically kabbalistic side. Two of the chief exponents of these tendencies wrote in Arabic, an extremely rare occurrence in kabbalistic literature. One was Judah b. Nissim ibn Malka from Fez, who wrote in 1365; his works have been analyzed by G. Vajda (1954), who has done a great deal of research on the relationship between Kabbalah and philosophy in this period. The other, who lived a generation earlier, was Joseph b. Abraham ibn Waqar of Toledo. In his lengthy work entitled *al-Maqāla al-Jamī'a bayna al-Falsafa wa-ash-Shar'i'a* ("A Synthesis of Philosophy and Kabbalah"), he set down the views of the philosophers, the kabbalists, and the astrologers, evaluated their ideas according to their relative merits, and tried to establish a basis common to them all.[80] His book also includes a lexicon of *Sefirot* symbolism, which was translated into Hebrew and circulated widely. The author was deeply indebted to Naḥmanides and Todros Abulafia, but he warns "that many errors have crept into" the Zohar. Ibn Waqar wrote poems on the Kabbalah.[81] His personal friend was Moses Narboni, who was inclined basically toward philosophy; however, in the *Iggeret al Shi'ur Komah* and in other places in his writings, through a positive albeit somewhat reluctant approach to Kabbalah, Narboni tries to explain kabbalistic statements as if they were in agreement with philosophy.[82]

An attempt to weight the balance in favor of Kabbalah found expression in the criticism of the work of Judah ibn Malka attributed to Isaac of Acre.[83] Samuel b. Saadiah Motot in Guadalajara (c. 1370) also followed Ibn Waqar in his commentary to the *Sefer Yeẓirah* called *Meshovev Netivot,* and his commentary to the Torah, *Megalleh Amukot* (to Ex., Oxford Ms. 286, and Lev. to Deut., Jerusalem, National Library, Ms. 8° 552). But the Zohar had a very strong influence on him. In the discussions of the philosophical kabbalists a great deal of attention was paid to the question of the relationship between the theosophic theory of the *Sefirot,* the philosophers' theory of the separate intelligences, and the neoplatonic idea of the cosmic soul. Attempts were made to explain the *Guide of the Perplexed* in a kabbalistic manner, or at least to clarify certain problems in it from the standpoint of the Kabbalah, using methods different from that of Abraham Abulafia; e.g. in the critique attributed to Joseph Gikatilla,[84] or in the *Tish'ah Perakim mi-Yiḥud* attributed to Maimonides.[85] Following Abulafia, the urge to make a kabbalist of Maimonides was emphasized in the legend that he had a change of heart at the end of his life and turned to the Kabbalah,[86] a tale that was current from the year 1300 and appears in several versions. In this period the *Megillat Setarim* was also written, which was said to be a letter of Maimonides concerning the Kabbalah.[87]

Totally in contrast to these tendencies toward compromise were two important phenomena which were absolutely opposed to the world of philosophy. The first is connected with the growth of meditative movements leading to contemplation, whether of the inner world of the *Sefirot* and the innumerable hidden lights concealed therein, or of the inner world of the Sacred Names which themselves conceal mystic lights. As a rule this contemplation follows the methods of prophetic Kabbalah, but by changing it and bringing it into the realm of Gnostic theosophy. The 13th-century theory of the *Sefirot* is subordinated to the contemplation of the lights of the intellect, which originated in the writings of the *Sefer ha-Iyyun* school, and produced a voluminous literature, wavering between pure inner contemplation and magic. There is no doubt that Isaac of Acre was very much inclined to this trend. Practically the whole of this literature is still concealed in manuscript form, no doubt because of the self-censorship of the kabbalists, who regarded it as the truly esoteric part of Kabbalah. One characteristic example, however, did find its way into print, namely the *Berit Menuḥah* (1648), which dates from the second half of the 14th century and was wrongly attributed to Abraham b. Isaac of Granada. It deals at length with meditations on the inner lights sparkling from the various vocalizations of the Tetragrammaton. This literature represents a continuation of Abulafia's "science of combination" with the addition of the theory of *kavvanah* of the theosophical Kabbalah. The *Sefer ha-Malkhut,* also a treatise on letter combinations, was written about 1400 by the kabbalist David ha-Levi from Seville (printed in the collection *Ma'or va-Shemesh,* 1839). Intended as practical manuals for initiates these books are of little interest for kabbalistic theory or philosophy.

The second phenomenon is connected with the composition of two pseudepigraphic works: the *Sefer ha-Peli'ah* (1784) on the first section of the Torah and the *Sefer ha-Kanah* (1786) on the (meaning of) the Commandments. The author, who wrote between 1350 and 1390, speaks in the guise of the grandson of R. Neḥunya b. ha-Kanah, the supposed author of the *Sefer ha-Bahir.* Actually, a large part of the first book consists of an anthology of earlier kabbalistic literature. The author, a considerable talmudist, adapted these sources and added a comparable amount to them. His main object was to prove,through the use of talmudic argument, that the *halakhah* has no literal meaning but mystical significance alone, and that the true literal meaning is mystical. With sweeping enthusiasm, these works go to greater lengths than the Zohar in their insistence that Judaism has no true meaning outside the world of the Kabbalah, thus representing the peak of kabbalistic extremism.[88] Clearly, in such a case there is no room for a philosophical approach. The anti-philosophical line was continued in the works of Shem Tov b. Shem Tov, who wrote two systematic books on the Kabbalah around 1400. His *Sefer ha-Emunot* (1556) demonstrates how completely the Zohar had become accepted, a century after its appearance, as the central work of Kabbalah. A large portion of the second book, whose title is unknown, is extant (British Museum Ms. 771). In this work the anti-philosophical tendency, which was perhaps influenced by contemporary events, and by the persecution of 1391, is expressed quite clearly: there is no longer any room for compromise between mysticism and the demands of rationalistic thought. It cannot be affirmed, however, that this point of view dominated the Kabbalah in its entirety, for in the years that followed, up to the beginning of the 16th century, there were various moves toward reconciliation, especially noticeable among the Italian kabbalists.

In contrast with the clear direction followed by the pseudepigraphy of the *Sefer ha-Peli'ah,* there is no obvious goal in the voluminous pseudepigraphic activity of the Provençal kabbalist Moses b. Isaac Botarel. He wrote a large number of books around 1400, including a long commentary to the *Sefer Yeẓirah,* filling them with fabricated quotations from the works of kabbalists and others, both historical and imaginary figures. However, this method was not at all like that of the Zohar and he also cultivated a conciliatory attitude toward philosophy, in complete contrast to Shem Tov b. Shem Tov. While the author of *Sefer ha-Peli'ah* and *Sefer ha-Kanah* put forward the Kabbalah as the only interpretation which could save Judaism from deteriorating and disintegrating, in other circles, imbued with a distinct talmudic and ethical spirit, it was regarded as a complementary element, through a stress on its moral and ascetic ideas. It is clear that the Kabbalah had already attained a firm status in the mind of the public, and quite obvious kabbalistic elements had begun to appear in the ethical literature of the 14th and 15th centuries. In this connection the *Menorat ha-Ma'or* by Israel al-Nakawa of Toledo (d.1391) is very important. It is a comprehensive work on Judaism with a firm halakhic standpoint. Wherever ethical questions are discussed in this book, which was intended for a wide public, statements are quoted from the Zohar (in Hebrew, under the name of *Midrash Yehi Or*) and from the other kabbalists, including specifically the *Ḥibbur ha-Adam im Ishto,* a treatise on marriage and sexuality written by an anonymous kabbalist (perhaps Joseph of Hamadan) at the end of the 13th century and later attributed to Naḥmanides under the title *Iggeret ha-Kodesh.* [89]

The literature of the kabbalists themselves testifies to the continuous existence in various circles of a strong opposition to Kabbalah and its claims – among halakhisists, literalists, and philosophers. Beginning with the polemic of Meir b. Simeon of Narbonne (1250) this opposition continued to be expressed, either *en passant* as was the case with Isaac Polkar and Menahem Meiri, or in specific works; e.g., in the *Alilot Devarim* of Joseph b. Meshullam (?) who wrote in Italy in 1468 (*Oẓar Neḥmad,* 4 (1763), 179–214), and in several writings of Moses b. Samuel Ashkenazi of Candia, 1460 (in Vatican Ms. 254). Even with the expansion of the Kabbalah's influence to much wider circles these voices were not silenced, particularly not in Italy.

In Spain kabbalistic creativity diminished considerably in the 15th century. The original stimulus of the Kabbalah had already reached its fullest expression. There were many kabbalists still to be found in Spain, and the numerous manuscripts written there testify to the large numbers who were engaged in Kabbalah, but their work shows very little originality. In 1482 Joseph Alcastiel from Jativa wrote responsa to 18 questions on various kabbalistic subjects which had been addressed to him by Judah Ḥayyat, and in them he adopts a very independent approach. [90] Joshua b. Samuel ibn Naḥmias in his book *Migdol Yeshu'ot* (Musajoff Ms.), Shalom b. Saadiah ibn Zaytun from Saragossa, and the pupils of Isaac Canpanton, who occupied a central position in the Judaism of Castile in the middle of the 15th century, were among the chief exponents of Kabbalah. Many kabbalists had crossed into Italy even before the expulsion from Spain, e.g., Isaac Mar-Ḥayyim who wrote in 1491, en route for Ereẓ Israel, two long letters on problems concerning the beginning of emanation.[91] Joseph ibn Shraga (d. 1508/9), who was called in his time "the kabbalist from Argenta," and Judah Ḥayyat, the author of a long commentary, *Minḥat Yehudah,* on the *Ma'arekhet ha-Elohut* (1558), were also among the chief transmitters of Spanish Kabbalah to Italy. The book *Ohel Mo'ed* (Cambridge Ms.) was written by an unknown kabbalist before 1500 – in Italy or even still in Spain – in order to defend the Kabbalah against its detractors. Abraham b. Eliezer ha-Levi and Joseph Taitaẓak, too, began their kabbalistic activities while still in Spain. The latter's book of revelations, *Sefer ha-Meshiv,* in which the speaker is said to be God Himself, was perhaps composed before the expulsion.[92] The activity of the migrants strengthened the Kabbalah, which acquired many adherents in Italy in the 14th and 15th centuries. Reuben Ẓarfati interpreted the theory of the *Sefirot;* Jonathan Alemano, who united Kabbalah with philosophy, wrote a commentary to the Torah in *Einei ha-Edah* (Paris Ms.), and to the Song of Songs in *Ḥeshek Shelomo;* and he also compiled a large anthology of kabbalistic miscellanies (Ms. Oxford). He also composed an unnamed work on the Kabbalah.[93] Only the introduction of his commentary to the Song of Songs has been published (1790). Judah b. Jehiel Messer Leon of Mantua opposed the tendencies of the later kabbalists and defended the view that kabbalistic principles agreed with Platonic ideas.[94] This emphasis on kabbalistic Platonism undoubtedly suited the spiritual temperament of the humanists of the circle of Marsilio Ficino and Pico della Mirandola. The poet Moses Rieti devoted part of his long poem *Mikdash Me'at* to a rhymed discourse on kabbalistic ideas, and Elijah Ḥayyim of Gennazano wrote an introduction to the Kabbalah entitled *Iggeret Ḥamudot* (1912).

THE KABBALAH AFTER THE EXPULSION FROM SPAIN AND THE NEW CENTER IN SAFED

The expulsion from Spain in 1492 produced a crucial change in the history of the Kabbalah. The profound upheaval in the Jewish consciousness caused by this catastrophe also made the Kabbalah public property. Despite the fact that the Kabbalah had spread in preceding generations, it still remained the preserve of relatively closed circles, who only occasionally emerged from their aristocratic seclusion. The aims of certain individuals like the author of the Zohar or the *Sefer ha-Peli'ah,* who intended quite consciously to create a work of historical and social importance, were not fully achieved until the 16th century. It was not until this period also that the eschatological mood prevalent among particular individuals in Spain was combined with the more basic stimuli of the Kabbalah. With the expulsion, messianism became part of the very core of Kabbalah. The earlier generations centered their thoughts on the return of man to the wellspring of his life, through the contemplation of the upper worlds, and on instruction in the method of his return through mystic communion to his original source. An ideal which could be realized in any place and at any time, this communion was not dependent on a messianic framework. Now it became combined with messianic and apocalyptic trends which laid greater stress on man's journey toward redemption than on his contemplated future return to the source of all existence in God. This combination of mysticism with messianic apocalyptic turned Kabbalah into a historic force of great dynamism. Its teachings still remained profound, abstruse, and difficult for the masses to assimilate, but its aims lent themselves easily to popularization, and many kabbalists sought to extend its influence throughout the general community. The Kabbalah penetrated many areas of popular faith and custom, overcoming the unceasing opposition of some individuals. It should be noted that the highly original development of the Kabbalah after the expulsion did not start in Italy, although that country was a center of a flourishing Jewish culture, and fruitful kabbalistic activity could be found there. The real creative force came from the new center which was established in Ereẓ Israel about 40 years after the expulsion. The religious movement which originated in Safed, and which manifested a renewal of the Kabbalah in all its intensity, is particularly important because it was the last movement in Judaism to have such a wide scope and such a decisive and continuous influence on the Diaspora as a whole, in both Europe, Asia and North Africa. This influence was maintained even after the break-up of the Shabbatean movement, which testifies to the degree to which it had become rooted in the national consciousness.

A connection between the appearance of new aspects of the Kabbalah and its rapid dissemination, and the imminent redemption of Israel, had already been established by a few of the Spanish kabbalists, like the author of the *Ra'aya Meheimna,* and the author of the *Sefer ha-Peli'ah.* But it was only after the expulsion that this became a dynamic and all-embracing force. A clear indication of this is the statement of an unknown kabbalist: "The decree from above that one should not discuss kabbalistic teaching in public was meant to last only for a limited time – until 1490. We then entered the period called 'the last generation,' and then the decree was rescinded, and permission given . . . And from 1540 onward the most important *miẓvah* will be for all to study it in public, both old and young, since this, and nothing else, will bring about the coming of the Messiah" (quoted in Abraham Azulai's introduction to his *Or ha-Ḥammah* on the Zohar).

The exiles themselves studied the Kabbalah mostly in its earlier forms, but they sought to respond to the interest in the Kabbalah aroused in Italy, North Africa, and Turkey by means of systematic and complete presentations, which at this time, however, did not contain any new points of view. The main exponents of the Kabbalah were Judah Ḥayyat, in his extensive commentary to *Ma'arekhet ha-Elohut* which was plagiarized by several Italian kabbalists;[95] Abraham Saba and Joseph Alashkar, in their commentaries to Scripture and Mishnah; Abraham Adrutiel, in an anthology of earlier traditions entitled *Avnei Zikkaron*,[96] and particularly Meir b. Gabbai, in his exhaustive presentation in *Avodat ha-Kodesh* (1568), which was perhaps the finest account of kabbalistic speculation before the resurgence of the Kabbalah in Safed. There was intensive activity along traditional lines in Italy and Turkey in particular. Among those active in Italy were Elijah Menahem Ḥalfan of Venice, Berakhiel b. Meshullam Cafman of Mantua (*Lev Adam*, 1538, in Kaufmann Ms. 218), Jacob Israel Finzi of Recanati (commentary on the liturgy, Cambridge Ms.), Abraham b. Solomon Treves ha-Ẓarfati (b. 1470) who lived in Ferrara and had "a revelation of Elijah," and Mordecai b. Jacob Rossillo (*Sha'arei Ḥayyim*, Munich Ms. 49). A panentheistic view of the relationship between God and the world was quite clearly stated in *Iggeret ha-Ẓiyyurim* by an unknown kabbalist of the first half of the 16th century in Italy (JTS Ms.). An important center was formed in Salonika, then in Turkey. Among the leaders there were Joseph Taitaẓak; Ḥayyim b. Jacob Obadiah de Bosal (*Be'er Mayim Ḥayyim*, 1546); Isaac Shani (*Me'ah She'arim*, 1543); and Isaac b. Abraham Farḥi, who circulated in his own name the anonymous *Ta'amei ha-Miẓvot*, which had actually been written about 1300. The kabbalist philosopher David b. Judah Messer Leon left Italy to work in Salonika, but his book *Magen David* (London Jews' College Ms. 290) on the philosophical principles of the Kabbalah was apparently written in Mantua; this work influenced several later kabbalists, including Meir ibn Gabbai and Moses Cordovero.[97] Solomon Alkabeẓ also began working in this circle before he went to Safed.

We also know of considerable kabbalistic activity in Morocco. Abraham Sabba's *Ẓeror ha-Mor* (1523), written between 1498 and 1501 in Fez, became a classic of kabbalistic exegesis on the Torah. Joseph Alashkar wrote most of his books in Tlemçen (*Ẓofenat Pa'neaḥ*, 1529, Jerusalem Ms. 2° 154; and several other books in the *Katalog der Handschriften . . . E. Carmoly*, 1876), but the main center in this area was Dra (or Dar'a), whose kabbalists were renowned. There Mordecai Buzaglo wrote the *Ma'yenot ha-Ḥokhmah*, which was hidden by the kabbalists (Goldschmidt Ms. Copenhagen), and a commentary on the liturgy (*Malkhei Rabbanan*

(1931), 86–87). This was the environment where the *Ginnat Bitan* was written, an introduction to the theory of the *Sefirot* by Isaac b. Abraham Cohen (Gaster Ms. 720). This work should not be confused with the *Ginnat ha-Bitan* which has two commentaries attributed to the Spanish kabbalists Jacob b. Todros and Shem Tov ibn Gaon (Gaster Ms. 1398), and which is, from the beginning to end (as shown by E. Gottlieb), a late 16th-century forgery based on *Ma'arekhet ha-Elohut* and Judah Ḥayyat's commentary to it. The most important book produced by the Moroccan kabbalists in this period was *Ketem Paz* by Simeon ibn Labi of Fez, the only commentary on the Zohar that was not written under the influence of the new Kabbalah of Safed. Consequently, it is frequently closer to the primary meaning of the text (the part on Genesis was printed in 1795). Several kabbalists were working in Jerusalem and Damascus. Some of them were emigrants from Spain, and some from the Musta'rabim. Among the emigrants from Portugal was Judah b. Moses Albotini (d. 1520), who wrote an introduction to prophetic Kabbalah,[98] and devoted many chapters of his book *Yesod Mishneh Torah* on Maimonides to the Kabbalah.[99] In Damascus, in the middle of the century, Judah Ḥaleywa, a member of a Spanish family, wrote the *Sefer ha-Kavod* (Jerusalem Ms. 8° 3731). In the main, however, this was the center of activity of Joseph b. Abraham ibn Ẓayyaḥ, one of the rabbis of the Musta'rabim who lived for several years in Jerusalem and in 1538 wrote there *Even ha-Shoham*,[100] in 1549 *She'erit Yosef* (Ms. of the Vienna community, Schwarz catalogue 260), and also several other kabbalistic works. Noteworthy for their theoretical speculations on details of the *Sefirot* system and for their profound meditation on the mysticism of the infinite number of luminaries which shine in the *Sefirot*, his books represent the culmination of a certain approach, and at the same time reveal a strong leaning toward practical Kabbalah and matters concerning the *sitra aḥra*.

Books written by the Ashkenazim after the expulsion from Spain were mainly of the anthological type: like the *Shoshan Sodot* of Moses b. Jacob of Kiev (partially printed 1784, and extant in its entirety in Oxford Ms. 1656); *Sefer ha-Miknah* of Joseph (Josselmann) of Rosheim (1546, partly edited 1970); and the commentary to the liturgy by Naphtali Hirz Treves (1560). The writings of Eliezer b. Abraham Eilenburg on Kabbalah and philosophy show how different fields became intertwined in the mind of a German kabbalist who studied in Italy and traveled in several countries. Eilenburg edited the books of the original kabbalists together with additional material of his own, some of it autobiographical.[101] The Kabbalah was established in Germany long before it found its way into Poland, where it penetrated only in the second half of the century through the work of Mattathias Delacrut, David Darshan, and Mordecai Yaffe.

The printing of several classical works contributed a great deal to the dissemination of the Kabbalah, particularly in the middle of the 16th century. At first no opposition was roused – neither when Recanati's book was produced in Venice (1523) nor when several other books came out in Salonika and Constantinople – although these works did not receive the *haskamah* ("approval") of the rabbinic authorities. However, when the printing of the Zohar itself and the *Ma'arekhet ha-Elohut* (1558) was contemplated, the plan gave rise to bitter arguments among the Italian rabbis; a few of the leading kabbalists violently opposed it, saying that they were afraid that these things would fall into the hands of men who were both ignorant and unprepared and so be liable to lead people into error. The burning of the Talmud in Italy on the order of Pope Julius III (1553) played a part in this controversy, for there were those who feared that the widespread publication of kabbalistic works would in itself tend to stimulate missionary activity. Some kabbalists who at first were opposed to the idea later became the chief protagonists of the printing of the Zohar, e.g. Isaac de Lattes, the author of a decision in favor of the printing of the Zohar, which appears at the beginning of the Mantua edition. At length, the protagonists prevailed, and the publication of other works of Kabbalah in Italy, Germany, Poland, and Turkey met with no further opposition.[102]

In addition to the traditional Kabbalah, during the first 40 years after the expulsion from Spain there arose a remarkable apocalyptic movement, whose leading exponents among the émigrés were active in Palestine and Italy. Abraham b. Eliezer ha-Levi, who traveled through many countries and settled in Jerusalem about 1515, devoted most of his energies to the propagation of a kabbalistic apocalyptic which was then causing a great stir. A few years after the expulsion a book appeared which affords striking evidence of this movement; called *Kaf ha-Ketoret* (Paris Ms. 845), it is an interpretation of the Psalms as battle-hymns for the war at the end of time, and was apparently written in Italy. At this time messianic movements also sprang up among the Marranos in Spain,[103] and emerged in Italy around the kabbalist Asher Lemlein of Reutlingen (1502). This too was the time of the first account of the attempt of the Spanish kabbalist Joseph della Reina (c. 1470) to bring about the final redemption by means of practical Kabbalah.[104] The story subsequently went through many adaptations and was very widely publicized.[105] The commentator Isaac Abrabanel also turned his attention to the propagation of apocalyptic views, whose adherents fixed the date of redemption variously at 1503, 1512, 1540, and 1541. The most serious repercussion was the agitation marking the appearance of David Reuveni and his supporter Solomon Molcho, whose kabbalistic expositions (*Sefer ha-Mefo'ar,* 1529) were favorably received by the Salonika kabbalists. Molcho's visions and discourses were a mixture of Kabbalah and incitement to political activity for messianic purposes among the Christians. With his martyrdom (1532) he was finally established in the Jewish community as one of the "saints" of the Kabbalah.

For the apocalyptists the advent of Martin Luther was another portent, a sign of the break-up of the Church and the approach of the end of days.

After its failure as a propagandist movement, the apocalyptic awakening penetrated to deeper spiritual levels. Both Christian and Jewish apocalyptists began to perceive that on the eve of redemption light would be revealed through the disclosure of mysteries that had perviously been hidden. The most profound expression of this new movement was that Ereẓ Israel became the center of Kabbalah. First Jerusalem and from 1530 onward Safed were for decades the meeting places of many kabbalists from all corners of the Diaspora; they became the leaders of the religious awakening which elevated Safed to the position of spiritual center of the nation for two generations. Here the old and the new were combined: the ancient traditions together with an aspiration to reach new heights of speculation which almost completely superseded the older forms of Kabbalah, and which in addition had a profound influence on the conduct of the kabbalistic life and on popular custom. Even such great halakhic authorities as Jacob Berab and Joseph Caro were deeply rooted in the Kabbalah, and there is no doubt that their messianic expectations set the scene for the great controversy over the reintroduction of ordination, which Jacob Berab wanted to organize in 1538 when Safed had already been established as a center. Sephardim, Ashkenazim, and Musta'rabim all contributed something to this movement, which attracted sympathizers from far afield and was also responsible for a great upsurge in the Diaspora, where communities far and wide accepted the supreme religious authority of the sages of Safed. The spread of a pietistic way of life was a practical expression of the movement and it prepared the ground for the colorful legends which quickly grew up around the major kabbalists of Safed. As with the beginning of Kabbalah in Provence, so here too profound rational speculations were combined with revelations which welled up from other sources, and they took the form (especially after the expulsion from Spain) of the revelations of *maggidim:* angels or sacred souls who spoke through the lips of the kabbalists or made them write down their revelations. Far from merely a literary device, this was a specific ritual experience, as indicated by Josef Taitaẓak's *Sefer ha-Meshiv* (perhaps the first work of this type) and Joseph Caro's *Maggid Mesharim.*[106] Once more as in the beginning of Kabbalah in Provence and Spain, here too there were two opposing trends of a philosophic and theoretical nature on the one hand, and of a mythical and anthropomorphic kind on the other.

The earlier forms of the Kabbalah were represented by David b. Solomon ibn Zimra (known as Radbaz, d. 1573), first in Egypt and later in Safed: in *Magen David* (1713) on the shape of the letters; *Migdal David* (1883) on the Song of Songs; *Meẓudat David* (1862) on the meaning of the Commandments and also in his poem *Keter Malkhut,* which is a kabbalistic imitation of the famous poem of the same name by Solomon ibn Gabirol (in the collection *Or Kadmon,* 1703). In contrast, a new system was propounded by Solomon b. Moses Alkabez, who emigrated to Ereẓ Israel from Salonika, and by his pupil and brother-in-law Moses b. Jacob Cordovero (known as Remak, 1522–70). In Cordovero Safed produced the chief exponent of Kabbalah and its most important thinker. Combining intensive religious thought with the power to expound and explain it, he was the main systematic theologian of the Kabbalah. His theoretical philosophy was based on that of Alkabeẓ and was completely different from the earlier Kabbalah, especially with regard to the theory of the *Sefirot.* It also developed greatly between his first major work *Pardes Rimmonim,* written in 1548, and the second, *Elimah Rabbati,* composed 19 years later; this later work followed his long commentary on the Zohar, *Or Yakar,* which interprets the book in the light of his own system. Cordovero interprets the theory of the *Sefirot* from the standpoint of an immanent dialectic acting upon the process of emanation, which he sees as a causative process. According to his view there is a formative principle subject to a specific dialect, which determines all the stages in the revelation of the Divine *(Ein Sof)* through emanation. The Divine, as it reveals itself when it emerges from the depths of its own being, acts like a living organism. These and other ideas give his system quite a different appearance from that adopted in Gabbai's *Avodat ha-Kodesh,* which was written (1531) shortly before the establishment of the center at Safed, although both are based on the Zohar. It would appear that Alkabeẓ' systematic presentation was written down only after the *Pardes Rimmonim (Likkutei Hakdamot le-Ḥokhmat ha-Kabbalah,* Oxford Ms. 1663). Cordovero was followed by his disciples, Abraham ha-Levi Berukhim, Abraham Galante, Samuel Gallico, and Mordecai Dato, who introduced his master's Kabbalah to Italy, his birthplace and the scene of his prolific kabbalistic activity. Eliezer Arikri and Elijah de Vidas, both students of Cordovero, wrote in Safed the two classical works on kabbalistic ethics which were destined to have a wide public among students of Torah: *Sefer Ḥaredim* and *Reshit Ḥokhmah.* Not only did they have a great influence in their own right but these books opened the way to a whole literary genre of works on ethics and conduct in the kabbalistic manner which appeared in the 17th and 18th centuries and were widely popular. This literature did more for the mass dissemination of Kabbalah than those books dealing with Kabbalah in the narrower sense whose mystical content was comprehensible only to a few.

One book which is not dependent on Cordovero's Kabbalah, but which is saturated with the atmosphere of Safed, where the idea of transmigration held an important place, is the *Gallei Razayya* by an unknown author. Doubtfully attributed to Abraham ha-Levi Berukhim, this comprehensive book was written in 1552–53, and the most important section is devoted to the theory of the soul and its transmigrations. Especially striking is the attempt to explain the lives of the biblical heroes, in particular their more unscrupulous deeds and their relationships with foreign women, in terms of transmigration. The book is among the more original creations of the Kabbalah; only part of it has been printed (1812), although the whole work is extant (Oxford Ms. 1820). Its daring psychology became a precedent for the paradoxical approach of the Shabbateans in their interpretation of the sins of the biblical characters.[107] Curiously enough, it did not arouse any recorded opposition.

In the magnetism of his personality and the profound impression he made on all, Isaac Luria Ashkenazi, the "Ari" (1534–72), was greater than Cordovero (see page 420). The central figure of the new Kabbalah, he was the most important kabbalistic mystic after the expulsion. Although he worked in Safed during the last two or three years of his life only, he had a profound influence on the closed circle of students – some of them great scholars – who after his death propagated and interpreted various versions of his ideas and his way of life, mainly from the end of the 16th century onward. Immediately after his death a rich tapestry of legend was woven around him, in which historical fact was intermingled with fantasy.[108] Luria's powers as a thinker cannot be compared with those of Cordovero, with whom he studied for a short while in 1570; but his personal and historical influence went far deeper, and in the whole history of Kabbalah only the influence of the Zohar can measure up to his. Developed from speculations of a mythical character on the Zohar, in general his system depended more than was previously thought on Cordovero, although he effected a kind of remythicization of the latter's theoretical concepts. In particular Cordovero's interpretations of the ideas in the *Idra* of the Zohar, voiced in his *Elimah Rabbati*, had a marked influence on Luria, who based the details of his system to a large extent on the *Idrot*. With Luria these ideas are bound up with his preoccupation with letter combinations as a medium for meditation. A large area of his system does not lend itself to complete intellectual penetration, and in many instances it can only be reached through personal meditation. Even in his theory of creation (see below), which from its inception is associated with the extreme mysticism of language and the Holy Names in which the divine power is concentrated, we quickly arrive at the point – the details of the idea of the *tikkun ha-parzufim* ("the restoration of the faces [of God]") – which is beyond the scope of intellectual perception. Here we are dealing with an extreme case of Gnostic reaction in the Kabbalah which finds its expression in the placing of innumerable stages among the degrees of emanation, and the lights which sparkle in them. This Gnostic reaction, and with it the mythical tendency in the Kabbalah, reached its highest point in Luria, while at the same time its relationship with the philosophical trends of Spanish Kabbalah and of Cordovero also was at its most tenuous.

Those passages which are comprehensible, and which are related to the origin of the process of creation, are quite dissimilar from the starting-points of the neo-platonists, but they are of great importance for the history of mysticism and their historical influence was astounding. It is precisely in these sections that we find important differences in the various versions of Lurianic Kabbalah. Some concealed particular parts of these speculations, as did Moses Jonah with regard to the whole theory of *ẓimẓum* ("contraction") in his *Kanfei Yonah,* and Ḥayyim Vital (see p.443) with the problem of *berur ha-dinim,* the progressive removal of the powers of rigor and severity from the *Ein-Sof* in the process of contraction and emanation. Some added new ideas of their own, like Israel Sarug, in his theory of the *malbush* ("garment") which is formed by the inner linguistic movement of the *Ein-Sof* and is the point of origin, preceding even the *ẓimẓum.* The original aspects of Luria's work, both in general and in particular, were both profound and extreme, and despite the fact that they were rooted in earlier ideas, they gave the Kabbalah a completely new appearance. A new terminology and a new more complex symbolism are the outstanding features of the literature of this school. There was much originality in the ideas concerning the *ẓimẓum* which preceded the whole process of emanation and divine revelation; the dual nature of the evolution of the world through the *hitpashetut* ("egression") and *histallekut* ("regression") of the divine forces, which introduced a fundamental dialectical element into the theory of emanation (already apparent in Cordovero); the five *parẓufim* ("configurations") as the principal units of the inner world, which are simply configurations of the *Sefirot* in the new arrangements in the face of which the ten *Sefirot* lose their previous independence; the growth of the world out of the necessary catastrophe which overtook Adam; and the slow *tikkun* ("restoration") of the spiritual lights which have fallen under the domination of the *kelippot* ("shells, husks"; forces of evil). The Gnostic character of these ideas, which constitute a new mythology in Judaism, cannot be doubted. Parallel to the cosmogonic drama there exists a psychological drama, just as complex, concerning the nature of original sin and the restoration of the souls condemned to transmigration because of that sin. The theory of prayer and mystical *kavvanah* ("intent") once more becomes central to the Kabbalah, and the emphasis it receives far surpasses any previously accorded to the subject. This mysticism of prayer proved to be the most important factor in the new Kabbalah because of the steady stimulus it provided for contemplative activity. A fine balance existed in Lurianic Kabbalah between theoretical speculations and this practical activity. The messianic element is far more noticeable here than in other kabbalistic systems, for the theory of *tikkun* confirmed the interpretation of the whole meaning of Judaism as an acute messianic tension. Such tension finally broke in the Shabbatean messianic movement, whose particular appeal and historical power may be explained through the combination of messianism with Kabbalah. A messianic explosion like this was unavoidable at a time when apocalyptic tendencies could easily be resusciatated in large sections of the people because of the dominance of the Lurianic Kabbalah. Not that this form of Kabbalah was distinct from other streams in its tendency to practical application or its association with magic. These two elements also existed in other systems, even in that of Cordovero. The theory of *kavvanah* in prayer and in the performance of the *miẓvot* undoubtedly contained a strong magical element intended to influence the inner self. The *yiḥudim,* exercises in meditation based on mental concentration on the combinations of Sacred Names which Luria gave to his disciples, contained such an element of magic, as did other devices for attaining the holy spirit.

Luria's disciples saw him as the Messiah, son of Joseph, who was to prepare the way for later revelation of the Messiah, son of David,[109] but for a whole generation after his death they kept themselves in esoteric groups and did little to spread their belief among the people.[110] Only occasionally did written fragments and various anthologies or summaries of Luria's teachings penetrate beyond Ereẓ Israel. In the meantime, in Ereẓ Israel itself, a complete literature of "Lurianic writings" came into being, which originated in the circles of his disciples together with their own disciples. Only a minimal portion of these works come from Luria's own writings.[111] In addition to the disciples mentioned above, Joseph ibn Tabul, Judah Mishan, and others also took part in this activity, but not one of them became a propagandist or was active outside Ereẓ Israel. This work began only at the end of the 16th century with the journeys of Israel Sarug to Italy and Poland,[112] and then through a scholar who, despite his pretensions, was not one of Luria's pupils in Safed but only a disciple in the spiritual sense. Up to about 1620 the Kabbalah remained largely under the influence of the other Safed kabbalists, Cordovero in particular.

As the Kabbalah began to radiate outward from Safed to the Diaspora it was accompanied by a great wave of religious excitement, particularly in Turkey, Italy, and Poland. In Italy particular importance attaches to the work of Mordecai Dato, who also engaged in literary messianic propaganda around the year 1575, which many considered to be the actual year of redemption.[113] Equally important was his pupil Menahem Azariah Fano (d. 1623), who was regarded for many years as the most prominent kabbalist of Italy, who produced a considerable number of works, following Cordovero first of all and later Lurianic Kabbalah in the version spread by Sarug. He and his disciples, particularly Aaron Berechiah b. Moses of Modena (d. 1639) and Samuel b. Elisha Portaleone, made Italy into one of the most important centers of Kabbalah. Preachers in Italy and Poland began to speak of kabbalistic matters in public, and kabbalistic phraseology became public property.

Some attempts were also made to explain kabbalistic ideas without using technical language. This is seen particularly in the writings of Judah Loew b. Bezalel (Maharal of Prague) and in the *Bet Mo'ed* of Menahem Rava of Padua (1608). The spread of the Kabbalah also brought with it a mingling of popular belief and mystic speculation, which had widespread results. The new customs of the kabbalists in Safed found their way to the wider public, especially after the appearance of *Seder ha-Yom* by Moses ibn Makhir from Safed (1599). Penitential manuals based on the practice of the Safed kabbalists and new prayers and customs became widespread. In Italy, and later in other lands too, special groups were established for their propagation. Small wonder that the movement resulted also in the revival of religious poetry, rooted in the world of the Kabbalah. Beginning in Safed too, where its main exponents were Eliezer Azikri, Israel Najara, Abraham Maimin, and Menahem Lonzano, this poetry spread to Italy and was exemplified in the works of Mordecai Dato, Aaron Berechiah Modena, and Joseph Jedidiah Carmi; in the years that followed it was echoed extensively. Many poets owed a major stimulus of their creativity to Kabbalah, especially the great Yemenite poet Shalom (Salim) Shabbazi, Moses Zacuto, and Moses Ḥayyim Luzzatto. In their works they revealed the imaginative and poetic value of kabbalistic symbols, and many of their poems found their way into prayer books, both of the community and of individuals.[114]

As long as Ḥayyim Vital, Luria's chief disciple, refused to allow his writings to be publicized – a process which did not begin in earnest until after Vital's death (1620) – detailed knowledge of Lurianic Kabbalah came to the Diaspora at first through the versions of Moses Jonah and Israel Sarug. Nearly all the works of the Kabbalah which were devoted to the spread of these ideas through the press in the first half of the 17th century bear the imprint of Sarug. But in his book *Shefa Tal* (1612) Shabbetai Sheftel Horowitz of Prague based his attempt to reconcile the Lurianic theory of *ẓimẓum* with the Kabbalah of Cordovero on the writings of Joseph ibn Tabul. Abraham Herrera, a pupil of Sarug who connected the teaching of his master with neoplatonic philosophy, wrote *Puerto del Cielo,* the only kabbalistic work originally written in Spanish, which came to the knowledge of many European scholars through its translations into Hebrew (1655) and (partly) into Latin (1684).

At first Lurianic ideas appeared in print in an abbreviated form only, as in the *Appiryon Shelomo* of Abraham Sasson (Venice, 1608); but in 1629–31 the two volumes by Joseph Solomon Delmedigo were published, *Ta'alumot Ḥokhmah* and *Novelot Ḥokhmah,* which also included source material from the writings of Sarug and his pupils. The latter volume also contains Delmedigo's lengthy studies of these ideas and a number of attempts to explain them philosophically. During these years manuscripts of Vital's teachings were disseminated and in 1648 there appeared in Amsterdam the *Emek ha-Melekh* of Naphtali Bacharach (see p.394), which contained an extremely detailed presentation of Lurianic doctrine based on a mixture of the two traditions of Vital and Sarug. It had an enormous influence although it also aroused protest and criticism. It was followed by the publication of other sources which sought to interpret the new teaching; e.g., *Hatḥalat ha-Ḥokhmah* from the Sarug school, published by a Polish kabbalist, Abraham Kalmanks of Lublin, who assumed authorship of the book under the title *Ma'ayan ha-Ḥokhmah* (Amsterdam, 1652). However, the books published in the field of Kabbalah, which continued to increase in number during the 17th century, only partially reflect the great tidal waves of Kabbalah which were sweeping both East and West. From Ereẓ Israel and Egypt spread a great variety of different editions and redactions of all kinds of Lurianic teachings, which captivated those who were mystically inclined. A large amount of this output was the work of men at the center established in Jerusalem between 1630 and 1660 whose leaders, Jacob Ẓemaḥ, Nathan b. Reuben Spiro, and Meir Poppers, labored unstintingly both in editing Vital's writings and in composing their own works. Of these only the books of Nathan Spiro, who spent some of his later years in Italy, were actually printed (*Tuv ha-Areẓ,* 1655, *Yayin ha-Meshummar,* 1660, and *Maẓẓat Shimmurim,* all in Venice). The way in which the Kabbalah penetrated every aspect of life can be seen not only in the long list of homiletic works of a completely kabbalistic nature and of ethical works written under its influence (especially the *Shenei Luḥot ha-Berit* of Isaiah Horowitz), but also in the interpretations of legal and halakhic details based on kabbalistic principles. Ḥayyim b. Abraham ha-Kohen of Aleppo was particularly distinguished in this field and his book, *Mekor Ḥayyim,* with its various parts paved the way for a new type of kabbalistic literature.

The rise of the Kabbalah and its complete dominance in many circles was accompanied by some hostile reaction. It is true, of course, that the support given to the Kabbalah by men of renowned rabbinic authority prevented vituperative attacks and, in particular, open charges of heresy, but many intellectuals of a more conservative nature were suspicious of the Kabbalah and some even expressed their hostility openly in their books. Among these should be mentioned Elijah Delmedigo in his *Beḥinat ha-Dat,* and Mordecai Corcos in a special work now lost. A bitter attack on the Kabbalah was launched by Moses b. Samuel Ashkenazi of Candia (c. 1460) in a number of writings preserved in Vatican Ms. 254. An anonymous work, *Ohel Mo'ed* (of the Spanish expulsion period; Jerusalem Ms.), was written in answer to the rabbis who belittled and mocked the Kabbalah. As the Kabbalah spread more widely in the community Leone (Judah Aryeh) Modena of Venice (about 1625) wrote the classical polemical work against it, *Ari Nohem,* but he did not dare publish it in his lifetime (ed. N. Libowitz, 1929). However, his book, widely known in manuscript, provoked many reactions. Joseph Solomon Delmedigo also criticized the Kabbalah severely in his *Iggeret Aḥuz,* which also circulated in manuscript only (published by Abraham Geiger in *Melo Chofnajim,* Berlin, 1840).

In its continued advance, the Kabbalah reached Poland from the second half of the 16th century.[115] Public enthusiasm reached such proportions that "he who raises objections to the science of the Kabbalah" was considered "liable to excommunication" (R. Joel Sirkes in his responsa, first ser. (1834), no. 5). At first Cordovero's approach was in the forefront, but from the beginning of the 17th century Luria's Kabbalah began to dominate. Nevertheless, before 1648, the actual systematic ideas of the Kabbalah had little influence, as far as can be judged from the writings of Aryeh Loeb Priluk (commentaries to the Zohar), Abraham Kohen Rappaport of Ostrog (in his homilies at the end of the collection of responsa *Eitan ha-Ezrahi*), Nathan b. Solomon Spira of Cracow (*Megalleh Amukot,* 1637), Abraham Chajes (in *Holekh Tamim,* Cracow, 1634), and others. Here also the writings of the Sarug school were the first to be circulated; apparently the visit of Sarug himself to Poland shortly after 1600, which is convincingly documented, also left its mark. Great stress was laid here on the war against the power of the *sitra aḥra* crystallized in the *kelippot,* which was divorced from its association with the Lurianic idea of *tikkun* and treated as a basic principle in its own right. The tendency to personify these powers in various demonological forms is featured particularly in the work of Samson b. Pesaḥ Ostropoler, who after his death (in the Chmielnicki massacres of 1648) was considered one of the greatest Polish kabbalists. The attempt to create a complete demonological mythology gave this particular stream of Kabbalah a unique character. To some extent it was based on writings falsely ascribed to Isaac Luria, but really composed in Poland.[116]

THE KABBALAH IN LATER TIMES

A generation later Lurianic Kabbalah had become widely established, the messianic tension embodied within it burst out into the Shabbatean movement. Although there were, of course, various local factors involved in the extent to which people's minds were open to the announcement of the Messiah's coming, nevertheless the growing dominance of the Kabbalah in the popular consciousness of the time, and particularly among the fervently religious, must be seen as the general background which made the movement possible and determined its mode of expression. The profound upheaval which the messianic experience brought in its wake opened the way for great changes in the world of traditional Kabbalah – or in the Kabbalah that the generations preceding Shabbateanism considered to be traditional. When large groups of people continued to hold fast to their faith in the messianic claim of Shabbetai Ẓevi even after his apostasy, two factors combined to create an abnormal and audacious Shabbatean Kabbalah which was regarded as heretical by the more conservative kabbalists: (1) the idea that the beginning of redemption made it already possible to see the changes that redemption would effect in the structure of the worlds, and that the mystery of creation could be unraveled in terms of visionary revelations which had not been possible before; and (2) the need to fix the place of the Messiah in this process and to justify in this way the personal career of Shabbetai Ẓevi despite all its contradictions. Consequently it is clear that the whole Shabbatean Kabbalah was new, full of daring ideas which had considerable appeal. Whatever essential originality later Kabbalah contains is derived mainly from the Kabbalah of the Shabbateans, whose principle ideas were the creation of Nathan of Gaza (d. 1680), Shabbetai's prophet, and of Abraham Miguel Cardozo (d. 1706). Although their books were not printed, they were frequently copied, and the influence of their ideas on those who were secret adherents of Shabbateanism is easily recognizable, even in several works that did in fact reach the press. The fact that some of the greatest rabbis were to be counted among the concealed Shabbatean faithful meant that there was a twilight area in their printed writings. This new Kabbalah showed its strength mainly in the period from 1670 to 1730.

By contrast, originality in the work of the kabbalists who remained outside the Shabbatean camp was limited. Continuators rather than original thinkers, they concentrated their efforts in two directions: (1) to continue the way that had emerged through the development of the Kabbalah from the Zohar to Isaac Luria; to examine and interpret the works of the earlier authorities; and generally to act as if nothing had happened and as if the Shabbatean explosion had never taken place; and (2) to limit the spread of the Kabbalah among the populace, because of the dangerous consequences they feared Shabbateanism had had for traditional Judaism; and to restore the Kabbalah to its former position, not as a social force but as an esoteric teaching restricted to a privileged few. Hence the predominantly conservative character of the "orthodox" Kabbalah from 1700 onward. Careful not to burn themselves on the hot coals of messianism, its adherents emphasized rather the aspects of meditation, of praying with *kavvanah,* of theosophy, and of moral teaching in the spirit of Kabbalah. New revelations were suspect. Differences of approach began to crystallize particularly around the question of how exactly the teachings of Isaac Luria should be understood as they had been formulated in the different schools of his disciples or their disciples. There was here room for quite striking differences of opinion. There were even some kabbalists who, secretly influenced by Shabbateanism, drew a clear boundary between the traditional Lurianic Kabbalah and the area of new revelations and researches which remained closed to outsiders. It was as if there were no point of contact between these two areas, and they were able to remain side by side within the same domain. This was the case, for example, with Jacob Koppel Lifschuetz (one of the secret Shabbateans) in his *Sha'arei Gan Eden* (Koretz, 1803) and, in a different way, with Moses Ḥayyim Luzzatto (d. 1747), who tried to make a distinction between his systematic studies of Lurianic Kabbalah (in *Pitḥei Ḥokhmah* and *Addir ba-Marom,* etc.) and the studies based on the revelations granted to him through his *maggid.*

Most of those who were considered the foremost kabbalists devoted themselves to cultivating the Lurianic tradition, sometimes attempting to combine it with Cordovero's system. The enormous literary output, of which only a fraction has been printed, reflects this state of affairs. In addition to this, selections or anthologies were made, most outstanding of which was the *Yalkut Reuveni* by Reuben Hoeshke, arranged in two parts (Prague, 1660, and Wilmersdorf, 1681; see below, p. 193). This collection of the aggadic output of the kabbalists had a wide circulation. Anthologies of this type were composed mainly by the Sephardi rabbis up to recent times mostly with the addition of their own interpretations; e.g. the valuable *Midrash Talpiyyot* of Elijah ha-Kohen ḥa-Itamari (Smyrna, 1736).

Apart from works of Kabbalah in the precise sense of involvement in, and presentation of, its ideas, a more popular Kabbalah began to spread from the end of the 17th century. Emphasizing mainly the basic ethical foundation and teaching concerning the soul, this popular Kabbalah chose a few isolated ideas from other kabbalistic teachings and embroidered them with general aggadic homilies. The influence of these books was no less than that of the works of technical Kabbalah. Literature of this kind was initiated by great preachers like Bezalel b. Solomon of Slutsk, Aaron Samuel Kaidanover and his son Ẓevi Hirsch, author of *Kav ha-Yashar,* and Berechiah Berakh Spira of Poland. Among the Sephardim were Ḥayyim ha-Kohen of Aleppo in his *Torat Ḥakham,* Elijah ha-Kohen ha-Itamari of Smyrna, Ḥayyim ibn Attar of Morocco in *Or ha-Ḥayyim,* and Sassoon ben Mordecai (Shandookh) (*Davar be-Itto,* 1862–64) of Baghdad. Commentaries in this vein on midrashic literature also circulated; e.g., *Nezer ha-Kodesh* by Jehiel Mikhal b. Uzziel (on Gen. R., 1719) and *Zikkukin de-Nura* by Samuel b. Moses Heida (on *Tanna de-Vei Eliyahu,* Prague, 1676). Under the influence of the Kabbalah, the *Midrashei ha-Peli'ah* were composed in Poland in the 17th century. These extremely paradoxical and mystifying sayings, often couched in an early Midrashic style, can be understood only through a mixture of kabbalistic allusion and ingenuity. According to Abraham, the son of the Gaon of Vilna (in *Rav Pe'alim,* 97), a collection of this type, *Midrashei Peli'ah,* was printed in Venice in the 17th century. Other such collections are known from the 19th century.

In this period there were important kabbalistic centers in Morocco where a very rich literature was produced, although most of it remained in manuscript. The Kabbalah was dominant in other North African countries and the emphasis was mainly on Lurianic Kabbalah in all its ramifications. A mixture of all the systems is evident among the kabbalists of Yemen and Kurdistan, where the Kabbalah struck very deep roots, particularly from the 17th century onward. The most prominent Yemenite kabbalists, both from Sana, were the poet Shalom b. Joseph Shabbazi (17th century), who also authored the *Midrash Ḥemdat Yamin* on the Torah (Jerusalem, 1956) and Joseph Ẓalaḥ (d. 1806), author of the commentary *Eẓ Ḥayyim* on the liturgy according to the Yemeni rite (*Tikhlal,* Jerusalem, 1894). The Hariri family of kabbalists was active in Ruwandiz in Kurdistan in the 17th and 18th centuries, and most of their writings are extant in manuscript. Later centers were formed in Aleppo and Baghdad, whose kabbalists were renowned in their own lands. In all these parts, and also in Italy, religious poetry of a kabbalistic nature developed and spread widely. The main later poets were Moses Zacuto, Benjamin b. Eliezer ha-Kohen, and Moses Ḥayyim Luzzatto in Italy, Jacob b. Ẓur in Morocco (*Et le-Khol Ḥefeẓ,* Alexandria, 1893), Solomon Molcho (the second) in Salonika and Jerusalem (d. 1788), and Mordecai Abadi in Aleppo.

In contrast to these regional centers, a special position was occupied by the new center established in Jerusalem in the middle of the 18th century, headed by the Yemenite kabbalist Shalom Mizraḥi Sharabi (ha-Reshash; d. 1777), the most important kabbalist throughout the Orient and North Africa. He was thought to be inspired from on high and in respect equalled only by Isaac Luria himself. In his personality and in the yeshivah Bet El which continued his tradition for nearly 200 years in the Old City of Jerusalem (it was destroyed in an earthquake in 1927), a twofold approach crystallized: (1) a definite, almost exclusive, concentration on Lurianic Kabbalah based on the writings of Vital, particularly his *Shemonah She'arim,* and the adoption of the doctrine of *kavvanot* and mystical contemplation during prayer as being central to Kabbalah in both its theoretical and practical aspects; (2) a complete break with activity on the social level and a shift toward the esotericism of a spiritual elite, who embody the exclusive, pietist life. There are obvious points of similarity between this later form of Kabbalah and the type of Muslim mysticism (Sufism) prevailing in those lands from which Bet El drew its adherents. Sharabi himself wrote a prayer book (printed in Jerusalem in 1911) with detailed elaborations of the *kavvanot*, outnumbering even those transmitted in the *Sha'ar ha-Kavvanot* in the name of Luria. The training of the members of this circle, popularly known as the *Mekhavvenim,* required them to spend many years on the spiritual mastering of these *kavvanot,* which every member was duty-bound to copy in their entirety. From the first two generations after Bet El was founded a number of *shetarei hitkasherut* ("bills of association") still exist, in which the signatories pledged themselves to a life of complete spiritual partnership both in this world and in the world to come. Apart from Sharabi, the leaders of the group in the first generation were Yom Tov Algazi (1727–1802), Ḥayyim Joseph David Azulai (1724–1806) and Ḥayyim della Rosa (d. 1786). As in the case of the writings of Isaac Luria, Sharabi's books also gave rise to an abundant exegetical and textual literature.[117] The supreme authority of this circle as the true center of Kabbalah was quickly established throughout all Islamic countries and its position was very strong. Many kabbalistic legends were woven around Sharabi. The last of the chief mainstays of Bet El were Mas'ud Kohen Alḥadad (d. 1927), Ben-Zion Ḥazan (1877–1951), and Ovadiah Hadayah (1891–1969).

Only a few chosen individuals, naturally, went to the center at Bet El. Among those leaders of the Kabbalah who remained in their own countries in the East, particular mention should be made of Abraham Azulai of Marrakesh (d. 1741), Abraham Tobiana of Algiers (d. 1793), Shalom Buzaglo of Marrakesh (d. 1780), Joseph Sadboon of Tunis (18th century), and Jacob Abiḥaẓera (d. 1880). Sassoon b. Mordecai Shandookh (1747–1830) and Joseph Ḥayyim b. Elijah (d. 1909) were the main kabbalists of Baghdad. Several of the Turkish and Moroccan kabbalists of the 18th century were wavering with regard to Shabbateanism, like Gedaliah Ḥayon of Jerusalem, Meir Bikayam of Smyrna, Joseph David and Abraham Miranda of Salonika, and David di Medina of Aleppo. The classic work to emerge from the kabbalists of these circles, who clung to all the minutiae of the tradition but at the same time did not sever their links with Shabbateanism, was *Ḥemdat Yamim,* by an anonymous author (Smyrna, 1731–32), which was enormously influential in the East.

The later development of the Kabbalah in Poland did not lead to the establishment of a center like Bet El, but a center of a slightly similar type existed between 1740 and the beginning of the 19th century in the Klaus *(kloiyz)* at Brody. In this era the *Yoshevei ha-Klaus* ("the Sages of the Klaus") constituted an organized institution of kabbalists who worked together and were consulted as men of particular authority. At the head of this group were Ḥayyim b. Menahem Zanzer (d. 1783), and Moses b. Hillel Ostrer (from Ostrog; d. 1785). When the new ḥasidic movement developed in Podolia and became an additional and independent stage in the growth of Jewish mysticism and of the wider popularization of the kabbalistic message, the kabbalists of the Klaus remained outside it and indeed aloof from it. In this center, too, great emphasis was laid on profound study of the Lurianic Kabbalah. The only link between the two centers was provided by Abraham Gershon of Kuttow (Kuty), the brother-in-law of Israel b. Eliezer, the Ba'al Shem Tov, who was at first a member of the Klaus at Brody and who then went to Ereẓ Israel and in his later years joined the kabbalists of Bet El, or at least was close to them in spirit. Many of the kabbalistic works published in Poland in the 18th century received the official approval of the Klaus group, but even before the establishment of this center the study of Kabbalah flourished in many places in Poland, as well as in Germany and other Hapsburg lands.

At this time many kabbalists came in particular from Lithuania, like Judah Leib Poḥovitzer at the end of the 17th century, and Israel Jaffe, the author of *Or Yisrael* (1701). In the 18th century the foremost Lithuanian kabbalists were Aryeh Leib Epstein of Grodno (d. 1775) and R. Elijah, the Gaon of Vilna, whose approach set the pattern for most 19th-century Lithuanian kabbalists. Especially notable among the latter were Isaac Eizik (Ḥaver) Wildmann, author of *Pitḥei She'arim,* and Solomon Eliashov (1841–1924), who wrote *Leshem Shevo ve-Aḥlamah;* both works are systematic presentations of Lurianic Kabbalah. Many kabbalistic works appeared in Poland and Germany from the end of the 17th century, and just as many ethical treatises based on kabbalistic principles. Attempts at systematization occur in *Va-Yakhel Moshe* by Moses b. Menahem Graf de Prague (Dessau, 1699) and several books by Eliezer Fischel b. Isaac of Stryzów. Literature which based its religious fervor on the power of "revelation from above" was generally suspected, not without reason, of Shabbatean tendencies, but books of this genre did exist within the more conservative Kabbalah, e.g., *Sefer Berit Olam* by Isaac b. Jacob Ashkenazi (vol. 1 Vilna, 1802, vol. 2 Jerusalem, 1937). The development in Poland in the 18th century was linked to a great extent with the influence of Italian kabbalists, and particularly with the *Shomer Emunim* of Joseph Ergas and the *Mishnat Ḥasidim* and *Yosher Levav* of Immanuel Ḥai Ricchi, which presented different approaches to an understanding of Lurianic teaching. The kabbalistic revelations of David Moses Valle of Modena (d. 1777) remained a closed book, but copies of the writings of Moses Ḥayyim Luzzatto reached the Lithuanian kabbalists, and some of them were known to the early Ḥasidim, on whom they made a great impression. Ergas was followed by Baruch of Kosov (Kosover) in his various introductions to the Kabbalah, which remained unpublished until some 100 years after his death (*Ammud ha-Avodah,* 1854). An orthodox systematic presentation was made by the kabbalist Jacob Meir Spielmann of Bucharest in *Tal Orot* (Lvov, 1876–83). Attempts were made once again to link Kabbalah with philosophic studies, as in *Ma'amar Efsharit ha-Tiv'it* by Naphtali Hirsch Goslar, the early writings of Solomon Maimon,[118] which remained in manuscript, and particularly the *Sefer ha-Berit* of Phinehas Elijah Horowitz of Vilna (Bruenn, 1897) and the *Imrei Binah* by Isaac Satanow, one of the first *maskilim* in Berlin.

In contrast to these attempts at a deeper study of Kabbalah, the ḥasidic movement broadened the canvas and strove to make kabbalistic ideas more and more popular, often by means of a new and more literal interpretation of its principles. In this movement Jewish mysticism proved to be once again a living force and a social phenomenon. In the Ḥabad branch of Ḥasidim an original form of Kabbalah was created, which had a clear psychological objective and produced a variegated literature; but in the ḥasidic camp too there were currents that went back to a study of Lurianic Kabbalah. This Kabbalah flourished anew for a century, particularly in the school of Ẓevi Hirsch Eichenstein of Zhidachov (Zydaczów; d. 1831) which produced a rich literature. The heads of this school were Isaac Eizik Jehiel Safrin of Komarno (d. 1874), Isaac Eizik of Zhidachov (d. 1873), and Joseph Meir Weiss of Spinka (1838–1909).

At the beginning of the nationalist ferment of the 19th century two kabbalists were active – Elijah Guttmacher in Graetz (1796–1874) and Judah Alkalai in Belgrade (1798–1878); the latter's Zionist writings are suffused with the spirit of the Kabbalah. In Central and Western Europe the influence of the Kabbalah swiftly declined, particularly after the conflict between Jacob Emden and Jonathan Eyebeschuetz concerning the latter's association with Shabbateanism. Nathan Adler in Frankfort (d. 1800) gathered around himself a circle which had strong kabbalistic tendencies, and his pupil, Sekel Löb Wormser, "the Ba'al Shem of Michelstadt" (d.1847), was for some time removed by the government from the rabbinate of his city, "because of his superstitious kabbalistic faith" – apparently as the result of intrigue by the *maskilim*. While Phinehas Katzenelenbogen, the rabbi of Boskovice in the middle of the 18th century, was cataloging the kabbalistic dreams and experiences of his family (Oxford Ms. 2315), and in the circle of Nathan Adler, as in the circles of the later Frankists in Offenbach, claims to prophetic dreams were made, the rabbis were withdrawing further and further from any manifestation of a mystical tendency or a leaning toward the Kabbalah. When Elhanan Hillel Wechsler (d. 1894) published his dreams concerning the holocaust which was about the befall German Jewry (1881), the leading Orthodox rabbis tried to prevent him from doing so, and his kabbalistic leanings led to his being persecuted. The last book by a German kabbalist to be printed was *Torei Zahav* by Hirz Abraham Scheyer of Mainz (d. 1822) published in Mainz in 1875. However, various kinds of kabbalistic literature continued to be written in Eastern Europe and the Near East up to the time of the Holocaust, and in Israel until the present. The transformation of kabbalistic ideas into the forms of modern thought may be seen in the writings of such 20th-century thinkers as R. Abraham Isaac Kook *(Orot ha-Kodesh, Arpilei Tohar, Reish Millin)*; in the Hebrew books of Hillel Zeitlin; and in the German writings of Isaac Bernays (*Der Bibel'sche Orient,* 1821) and Oscar Goldberg (*Die Wirklichkeit de Hebraeer,* Berlin, 1925).

The fervent assault on the Kabbalah by the Haskalah movement in the 19th century limited its deep influence in Eastern Europe to a marked degree; but it succeeded hardly at all in breaking the influence of the Kabbalah in Oriental countries, where the life of the Jewish community was affected by it until recent times. An exception was the antikabbalistic movement of the Yemen known as *Dor De'ah* ("Doerde"). Headed by Yiḥya Kafaḥ (Kafiḥ) of Sana (d. 1931), it caused much strife among the Jews of Yemen. Apart from the accusatory and defamatory writings from 1914 onward, there appeared in connection with this controversy the *Milḥamot ha-Shem* of Kafaḥ and the reply of the Yemeni rabbis, authored by Joseph Jacob Zabiri, *Emunat ha-Shem* (Jerusalem, 1931 and 1938).

3

THE BASIC IDEAS OF KABBALAH

As is apparent from the preceding account, the Kabbalah is not a single system with basic principles which can be explained in a simple and straightforward fashion, but consists rather of a multiplicity of different approaches, widely separated from one another and sometimes completely contradictory. Nevertheless, from the date of the appearance of the *Sefer ha-Bahir* the Kabbalah possessed a common range of symbols and ideas which its followers accepted as a mystical tradition, although they differed from one another in their interpretation of the precise meaning of these symbols, of the philosophical implications inherent in them, and also of the speculative contexts through which it became possible to regard this common framework as a kind of mystical theology of Judaism. But even within this framework two stages must be differentiated: (1) the range of symbols of the early Kabbalah up to and including the Safed period, i.e., the theory of the *Sefirot* as it crystallized in Gerona, in the various parts of the Zohar, and in the works of kabbalists up to Cordovero; and (2) the range of symbols created by Lurianic Kabbalah, which in the main dominated kabbalistic thinking from the 17th century until recent times. The Lurianic system goes beyond the doctrine of the *Sefirot,* although it makes a wide and emphatic use of its principles, and is based on the symbolism of the *parẓufim.*

In addition to this, two basic tendencies can be discerned in kabbalistic teaching. One has a strongly mystical direction expressed in images and symbols whose inner proximity to the realm of myth is often very striking. The character of the other is speculative, an attempt to give a more or less defined ideational meaning to the symbols. To a large extent this outlook presents kabbalistic speculation as a continuation of philosophy, a kind of additional layer superimposed upon it through a combination of the powers of rational thought and meditative contemplation. The speculative expositions of kabbalistic teaching largely depended on the ideas of neoplationic and Aristotelian philosophy, as they were known in the Middle Ages, and were couched in the terminology customary to these fields. Hence the cosmology of the Kabbalah is borrowed from them and is not at all original, being expressed in the common medieval doctrine of the separate intellects and the spheres. Its real originality lies in the problems that transcend this cosmology. Like Jewish philosophy, the speculative Kabbalah moved between two great heritages, the Bible and talmudic Judaism on the one hand and Greek philosophy in its different forms on the other. The original and additional feature, however was the new religious impulse which sought to integrate itself with these traditions and to illuminate them from within.

GOD AND CREATION

All kabbalistic systems have their origin in a fundamental distinction regarding the problem of the Divine. In the abstract, it is possible to think of God either as God Himself with reference to His own nature alone or as God in His relation to His creation. However, all kabbalists agree that no religious knowledge of God, even of the most exalted kind, can be gained except through contemplation of the relationship of God to creation. God in Himself, the absolute Essence, lies beyond any speculative or even ecstatic comprehension. The attitude of the Kabbalah toward God may be defined as a mystical agnosticism, formulated in a more or less extreme way and close to the standpoint of neoplatonism. In order to express this unknowable aspect of the Divine the early kabbalists of Provence and Spain coined the term *Ein-Sof* ("Infinite"). This expression cannot be traced to a translation of a Latin or Arabic philosophical term. Rather it is a hypostatization which, in contexts dealing with the infinity of God or with His thought that "extends without end" (*le-ein sof* or *ad le-ein sof*), treats the adverbial relation as if it were a noun and uses this as a technical term. *Ein-Sof* first appears in this sense in the writings of Isaac the Blind and his disciples, particularly in the works of Azriel of Gerona, and later in the Zohar, the *Ma'arekhet ha-Elohut,* and writings of that period. While the kabbalists were still aware of the origin of the term they did not use it with the definite article, but treated it as a proper noun; it was only from 1300 onward that they began to speak of *ha-Ein-Sof* as well, and generally identify it with other common epithets for the Divine. This later usage, which spread through all the literature, indicates a distinct personal and theistic concept in contast to the vacillation between an idea of this type and a neutral impersonal concept of *Ein-Sof* found in some of the earlier sources. At first it was not clear whether the term *Ein-Sof* referred to "Him who has no end" or to "that which has no end." This latter, neutral aspect was emphasized by stressing that *Ein-Sof* should not be qualified by any of the attributes or personal epithets of God found in Scripture, nor should such eulogies as *Barukh Hu* or *Yitbarakh* (found only in the later literature) be added to it. In fact, however, there were various attitudes to the nature of *Ein-Sof* from the very beginning; Azriel, for example, tended toward an impersonal interpretation of the term, while Asher b. David employed it in a distinctly personal and theistic way.

Ein-Sof is the absolute perfection in which there are no distinctions and no differentiations, and according to some even no volition. It does not reveal itself in a way that makes knowledge of its nature possible, and it is not accessible even to the innermost thought *(hirhur ha-lev)* of the contemplative. Only through the finite nature of every existing thing, through the actual existence of creation itself, is it possible to deduce the existence of *Ein-Sof* as the first infinite cause. The author of *Ma'arekhet ha-Elohut* put forward the extreme thesis (not without arousing the opposition of more cautious kabbalists) that the whole biblical revelation, and the Oral Law as well, contained no reference to *Ein-Sof,* and that only the mystics had received some hint of it. Hence the author of this treatise, followed by several other writers, was led to the daring conclusion that only the revealed God can in reality be called "God," and not the hidden *"deus absconditus,"* who cannot be an object of religious thought. When ideas of this kind returned in a later period in Shabbatean and quasi-Shabbatean Kabbalah, between 1670 and 1740, they were considered heretical.

Other terms or images signifying the domain of the hidden God that lies beyond any impulse toward creation occur in the writings of the Gerona kabbalists and in the literature of the speculative school. Examples of these terms are *mah she-ein ha-maḥshavah masseget* ("that which thought cannot attain" – sometimes used also to describe the first emanation), *ha-or ha-mit'allem* ("the concealed light"), *seter ha-ta'alumah* ("the concealment of secrecy"), *yitron* ("superfluity" – apparently as a translation of the neoplatonic term *hyperousia*), *ha-aḥdut ha-shavah* ("indistinguishable unity," in the sense of a unity in which all opposites are equal and in which there is no differentiation), or even simply *ha-mahut* ("the essence"). The factor common to all these terms is that *Ein-Sof* and its synonyms are above or beyond thought. A certain wavering between the personal and the neutral approach to the concept of *Ein-Sof* can also be seen in the main part of the Zohar, while in the later stratum, in the *Ra'aya Meheimna* and the *Tikkunim,* a personal concept is paramount. *Ein-Sof* is often (not always) identified with the Aristotelian "cause of all causes," and, through the kabbalistic use of neoplatonic idiom, with the "root of all roots." While all the definitions above have a common negative element, occasionally in the Zohar there is a remarkable positive designation which gives the name *Ein-Sof* to the nine lights of thought that shine from the Divine Thought, thus bringing *Ein-Sof* out of its concealment and down to a more humble level of emanation (the contrast between the two concepts emerges through comparison between various passages, e.g., 1:21a and 2:239a with 2:226a). In later development of Lurianic Kabbalah, however, in distinct opposition to the view of the earlier kabbalists, several differentiations were made even within *Ein-Sof*. In Kabbalah, therefore, *Ein-Sof* is absolute reality, and there was no question as to its spiritual and transcendent nature. This was so even though the lack of clarity in some of the expressions used by the kabbalists in speaking of the relationship of the revealed God to His creation gives the impression that the very substance of God Himself is also immanent within creation (see below on Kabbalah and pantheism). In all kabbalistic systems, light-symbolism is very commonly used with regard to *Ein-Sof*, although it is emphasized that this use is merely hyperbolical, and in later Kabbalah a clear distinction was sometimes made between *Ein-Sof* and "the light of *Ein-Sof*." In the popular Kabbalah which finds expression in ethical writings and ḥasidic literature, *Ein-Sof* is merely a synonym for the traditional God of religion, a linguistic usage far removed from that of the classical Kabbalah, where there is evidence of the sharp distinction between *Ein-Sof* and the revealed Divine Creator. This can be seen not only in the formulations of the early kabbalists (e.g., Isaac of Acre in his commentary to the *Sefer Yeẓirah*, in: KS 31 (1956), 391) but also among the later ones; Baruch Kosover (c. 1770) writes: "*Ein-Sof* is not His proper name, but a word which signifies his complete concealment, and our sacred tongue has no word like these two to signify his concealment. And it is not right to say '*Ein-Sof*, blessed be He' or 'may He be blessed' because He cannot be blessed by our lips" (*Ammud ha-Avodah*, 1863, 211d).

The whole problem of creation, even in its most recondite aspects, is bound up with the revelation of the hidden God and His outward movement – even though "there is nothing outside Him" (Azriel), for in the last resort "all comes from the One, and all returns to the One," according to the neoplatonic formula adopted by the early kabbalists. In kabbalistic teaching the transition of *Ein-Sof* to "manifestation," or to what might be called "God the Creator," is connected with the question of the first emanation and its definition. Although there were widely differing views on the nature of the first step from concealment to manifestation, all stressed that no account of this process could be an objective description of a process in *Ein-Sof;* it was no more than could be conjectured from the perspective of created beings and was expressed through their ideas, which in reality cannot be applied to God at all. Therefore, descriptions of these processes have only a symbolic or, at best, an approximate value. Nevertheless, side by side with this thesis, there is detailed speculation which frequently claims objective reality for the process it describes. This is one of the paradoxes inherent in Kabbalah, as in other attempts to explain the world in a mystical fashion.

The decision to emerge from concealment into manifestation and creation is not in any sense a process which is a necessary consequence of the essence of *Ein-Sof;* it is a free decision which remains a constant and impenetrable mystery (Cordovero, at the beginning of *Elimah*). Therefore, in the view of most kabbalists, the question of the ultimate motivation of creation is not a legitimate one, and the assertion found in many books that God wished to reveal the measure of His goodness is there simply as an expedient that is never systematically developed. These first outward steps, as a result of which Divinity becomes accessible to the contemplative probings of the kabbalist, take place within God Himself and do not "leave the category of the Divine" (Cordovero). Here the Kabbalah departs from all rationalistic presentations of creation and assumes the character of a theosophic doctrine, that is, one concerned with the inner life and processes of God Himself. A distinction in the stages of such processes in the unity of the Godhead can be made only by human abstraction, but in reality they are bound together and unified in a manner beyond all human understanding. The basic differences in the various kabbalistic systems are already apparent with regard to the first step, and since such ideas were presented in obscure and figurative fashion in the classical literature, such as the *Bahir* and the Zohar, exponents of widely differing opinions were all able to look to them for authority. The first problem, which from the start elicited different answers, was whether the first step was one toward the outer world at all, or rather a step inward, a withdrawal of *Ein-Sof* into the depths of itself. Early kabbalists and Cordovero adopted the former view, which led them to a theory of emanation close to the neoplatonic although not absolutely identical with it. But Lurianic Kabbalah, which took the latter position, speaks not only of a return of created things to their source in God but also of a return *(regressus)* of God into the depths of Himself preceding creation, a process identifiable with that of emanation only by means of interpreting it as a mere figure of speech. Such an interpretation did, in fact, appear before long (see below, Lurianic Kabbalah, p. 128). The concepts which occur most frequently in the description of this first step mainly concern will, thought, *Ayin* ("absolute Nothingness"), and the inner radiation of *Ein-Sof* in the supernal lights called "splendors" *(ẓahẓaḥot),* which are higher than any other emanation.

WILL

If *Ein-Sof* is denied any attributes than it must be separated from the Divine Will, however exalted the latter is and however clearly connected with its possessor, which is *Ein-Sof.* The kabbalists of Gerona frequently speak of the hidden God working through the Primal Will, which is, as it were, encompassed by

Him and united with Him. This, the highest of emanations, which is either emanated from His essence, or concealed within His power, constitutes the ultimate level to which thought can penetrate. Mention is made of "the infinite will" *(ha-razon ad ein-sof)*, "infinite exaltation" *(ha-rom ad ein-sof)* or "that which thought can never attain," and the reference is to that unity of action between *Ein-Sof* and its first emanation, which is bound to and returns constantly to its source. In some works, e.g., Azriel's *Perush ha-Aggadot,* there is hardly any mention of *Ein-Sof* at all; instead, the Primal Will appears in expressions which are generally connected with *Ein-Sof* itself. Was this Will coeternal with *Ein-Sof* itself, or did it originate only at the time of its emanation, so that it is possible to think of a situation in which *Ein-Sof* existed without Will, i.e., volition to create or be manifested? Several of the kabbalists of Gerona and their followers tended to believe that the Primal Will was eternal, and thus they fixed the beginning of the process of emanation at the second step or *Sefirah,* which was consequently called *reshit* ("beginning"), identified with the Divine Wisdom of God (see below). Most of the statements in the main part of the Zohar follow this view. What is called "the infinite Will," in the sense of the unity of *Ein-Sof* with the Will and their joint manifestation in the first *Sefirah,* is given the figurative name *Attika Kaddisha* ("the Holy Ancient One") in the Zohar. Also, in those passages which speak of *Ein-Sof* and the beginning of emanation, this beginning *(reshit)* is always related to the second *Sefirah,* there being no mention that what preceded it also came into being in time and had not been eternally emanated. Therefore in some cases the first emanation is seen as only an external aspect of *Ein-Sof:* "It is called *Ein-Sof* internally and *Keter Elyon* externally" (*Tikkunei Zohar,* end of *Tikkun* 22). However, this ordering occurs only in those passages which discuss the process in detail; in those dealing with the process of emanation in general there is no differentiation between the status of the first *Sefirah* and that of the other *Sefirot.* As the Kabbalah developed in Spain the tendency prevailed to make a clear distinction between *Ein-Sof* and the emanation, which now began to be considered neither eternal nor pre-existent. Among the kabbalists of Safed, indeed, the contrary view was considered almost heretical, since it made possible the identification of *Ein-Sof* with the first *Sefirah.* In fact this identification is actually found in several early kabbalistic sources, and the anonymous author of *Sefer ha-Shem,* mistakenly attributed to Moses de Leon (c. 1325, printed in *Heikhal ha-Shem,* Venice, 1601, 4b), criticizes the Zohar because of it, saying it is contrary to "the view of the greatest kabbalists" and an error made possible only by the false assumption that the *Ein-Sof* and the first emanation are one.

The early kabbalists, particularly Azriel of Gerona and Asher b. David, considered the Divine Will as that aspect of the Divine Essence which alone was active in creation, and was implanted there by the power of *Ein-Sof.* Communion with the Supreme Will was the final aim of prayer, for it was "the source of all life," including emanation itself. Does this specific concept of the Will as the supreme Divine Power, which, according to the Gerona kabbalists and the Zohar, takes precedence even over Divine thought and pure intellect, contain traces of the direct influence of Solomon ibn Gabirol's central idea in his book *Mekor Ḥayyim*? A historical connection seems clearly apparent in the teachings of Isaac ibn Latif (fl. 1230–60), who apparently lived in Toledo and could have read Gabirol's book in the Arabic original. His theory is a mixture of Gabirol's ideas and those of the first generation of Spanish Kabbalah. His view of the Will can be found mainly in his *Ginzei ha-Melekh* and *Ẓurat ha-Olam.* "The primordial Will" *(ha-ḥefeẓ ha-kadmon)* is not completely identical with God, but is a garment "clinging to the substance of the wearer on all sides." It was "the first thing to be emanated from the true pre-existent Being" in a continuing process which had no real beginning. Above matter and form, this Will unites the two in their first union, thus bringing into being what Ibn Latif calls "the first created thing" *(ha-nivra ha-rishon).* His description of the details of the processes that take place below the level of the Will differs from that of the other kabbalists; it was not accepted nor did it have any influence on the theory of emanation as it was formulated in later Kabbalah. As the tendency to all but identify *Ein-Sof* with the first *Sefirah* became less and less pronounced, so the distinction between *Ein-Sof* and the Will was emphasized to a correspondingly greater degree, although the question as to whether the Will was created or eternal continued to be surrounded by controversy, or was consciously obscured.

THOUGHT

Another concept basic to the whole problem of the first manifestation of *Ein-Sof* is that of "Thought" *(maḥshavah).* In the *Sefer ha-Bahir* and the writings of Isaac the Blind no special status is accorded to the Will, whose place is taken by "the Thought which has no end or finality," and which exists as the highest state, from which all else has emanated, without being designated as an emanation itself. Accordingly, the first source of all emanation is sometimes also called "pure Thought" – a domain impenetrable to merely human thought. According to this theory, the whole creative process depends on an intellectual rather than a volitional act, and the history of Kabbalah is marked by a struggle between these two views of creation. The essential identity of Will and Thought was insisted on by Ibn Latif alone. For most kabbalists, that Thought which thinks only itself and has no other content was demoted to a level below that of Will and became identified with the Divine Wisdom, which proceeded to contemplate not only itself but the whole plan of creation and the paradigma of all the universe. Therefore, the Gerona kabbalists and the author of the Zohar speak of "the Will of Thought," i.e., the Will which activates Thought, and not vice versa. The highest aspect of *ḥokhmah* ("Wisdom"), which the Gerona kabbalists speak of a great deal, is called *haskel* (from Jer. 9:23), a term denoting divine understanding, the activity of the *sekhel* ("divine intellect"), whatever the content of this might be, and not, as with *ḥokhmah*, its crystallization into a system of thought. The concept of *haskel* took the place of Will among those who were disinclined to accept the theory or were perplexed by it, particularly in the school of Isaac the Blind. It corresponds to the role of divine *intelligere* in the teachings of Meister Eckhart 100 years later.

NOTHINGNESS

More daring is the concept of the first step in the manifestation of *Ein-Sof* as *ayin* or *afisah* ("nothing," "nothingness"). Essentially, this nothingness is the barrier confronting the human intellectual faculty when it reaches the limits of its capacity. In other words, it is a subjective statement affirming that there is a realm which no created being can intellectually comprehend, and which, therefore, can only be defined as "nothingness." This idea is associated also with its opposite concept, namely, that since in reality there is no differentiation in God's first step toward manifestation, this step cannot be defined in any qualitative manner and can thus only be described as "nothingness." *Ein-Sof* which turns toward creation manifests itself, therefore, as *ayin ha-gamur* ("complete nothingness"), or, in other words: God Who is called *Ein-Sof* in respect of Himself is called *Ayin* in respect of His first self-revelation. This daring symbolism is associated with most mystical theories concerning an understanding of the Divine, and its particular importance is seen in the radical transformation of the doctrine of *creatio ex nihilo* into a mystical theory stating the precise opposite of what appears to be the literal meaning of the phrase. From this point of view it makes no difference whether *Ein-Sof* itself is the true *ayin* or whether this *ayin* is the first emanation of *Ein-Sof*. From either angle, the monotheistic theory of *creatio ex nihilo* loses its original meaning and is completely reversed by the esoteric content of the formula. Since the early kabbalists allowed no interruption of the stream of emanation from the first *Sefirah* to its consolidation in the worlds familiar to medieval cosmology, *creatio ex nihilo* may be interpreted as creation from within God Himself. This view, however, remained a secret belief and was concealed behind the use of the orthodox formula; even an authoritative kabbalist like Naḥmanides was able to speak in his commentary to the Torah of *creatio ex nihilo* in its literal sense as the free creation of the primeval matter from which everything was made, while simultaneously implying, as shown by his use of the word *ayin* in his commentary to Job 28:12 and by kabbalistic allusions in his commentary to Genesis 1, that the true mystical meaning of the text is the emergence of all things from the absolute nothingness of God. Basing their speculations on the commentary to the *Sefer Yeẓirah* by Joseph Ashkenazi (attributed in the printed editions to Abraham b. David), kabbalists who held an undoubted theistic view tried to rescue the original significance of the formula by defining the first *Sefirah* as the first effect, which is absolutely separated from its cause, as if the transition from cause to effect involved a great leap from *Ein-Sof* to *ayin,* a view which indeed conformed with the traditional theological picture. However, in order to escape the inner logic of the early theory, a few later kabbalists, from the 16th century onward, tried to add a new act of *creatio ex nihilo* after the emanation of the *Sefirot* or at each stage of emanation and creation. Doubts of this kind did not exist in Spanish Kabbalah, nor in the works of Cordovero, although in the *Elimah Rabbati* he found it hard to decide between a symbolic and a literal interpretation of the formula. David b. Abraham ha-Lavan in *Masoret ha-Berit* (end of 13th century) defined the *ayin* ("nothingness") as "having more being than any other being in the world, but since it is simple, and all other simple things are complex when compared with its simplicity, so in comparison it is called 'nothing.' "[1] We also find the figurative use of the term *imkei ha-ayin* ("the depths of nothingness"), and it is said that "if all the powers returned to nothingness, the Primeval One who is the cause of all would remain in equal oneness (or: unity without distinctions) in the depths of nothingness."

THE THREE LIGHTS

Another idea connected with the transition from the Emanator to the emanated originated in a responsum (early 13th century) attributed to Hai Gaon, and subsequently aroused a great deal of speculation.[2] There it is stated that, above all emanated powers, there exist in "the root of all roots" three hidden lights which have no beginning, "for they are the name and essence of the root of all roots and are beyond the grasp of thought." As the "primeval inner light" spreads throughout the hidden root two other lights are kindled, called *or meẓuḥzaḥ* and *or ẓaḥ* ("sparkling light"). It is stressed that these three lights constitute one essence and one root which is "infinitely hidden" *(ne'lam ad le-ein sof),* forming a kind of kabbalistic trinity that precedes the emanation of the ten *Sefirot.* However, it is not sufficiently clear whether the reference is to three lights between the Emanator and the first emanation, or to three lights irradiating one another within the substance of the Emanator itself – both possibilities can be supported. In the terminology of the Kabbalah these three lights are called *ẓaḥẓaḥot* ("splendors"), and they are thought of as the roots of the three upper *Sefirot* which emanate from them (see Cordovero, *Pardes Rimmonim,* ch. 11). The need to posit this strange trinity is explained by the urge to make the ten *Sefirot* conform with the 13 attributes predicated of God. It is hardly suprising that Christians later found an allusion to their own doctrine of the trinity in this theory, although it contains none of the personal hypostases characteristic of the Christian trinity. In any case, the hypothesis of the *ẓaḥẓaḥot* led to further complication in the theory of emanation and to the predication of roots in the essence of *Ein-Sof* to everything that was emanated. In the generation following the publication of the Zohar, David b. Judah Ḥasid, in his *Mare'ot ha-Ẓove'ot,* mentions ten *ẓaḥẓaḥot* placed between *Ein-Sof* and the emanation of the *Sefirot.*

EMANATION AND THE CONCEPT OF THE *SEFIROT*

Scholars have long been engaged in a controversy over whether or not the Kabbalah teaches emanation as the emergence of all things from within God Himself. In this controversy there is considerable conceptual confusion. Like several scholars before him, A. Franck interpreted the Kabbalah as a pure emanist system, which he considered identical with a clearly pantheistic approach. He therefore thought of emanation as an actual going-forth of the substance of God and not simply of the power of the Emanator. He based his interpretation on the Zohar, and especially on later Lurianic teaching, although neither of these two sources contains any reference to a direct theory of substantive emanation. In contrast to Franck, D.H. Joel set out to prove that the Zohar and early Kabbalah in general contained nothing of the theory of emanation, which Joel believed first appeared in the writings of "the modern commentators" of the 16th century, where it is the result of faulty interpretation. In his opinion there is no significant difference between "the pure theology" of Jewish medieval thinkers, and "the true Kabbalah," the very foundation of which is the idea of free creation of primeval substance *ex nihilo* in the literal meaning of the term. There is no doubt that Joel and Frank were equally mistaken, and that both were at fault in interpreting the basic content of Lurianic Kabbalah in pantheistic terms. Inasmuch as early Kabbalah needed a theoretical foundation it was largely influenced by neoplatonism; and although it proposed a definite process of emanation – the theory of the emanation of the *Sefirot* – this was a kind of activity

אל תאמר אינו כי ישנו וכאשר תמנה מימינך לשמאלך
תמנה עשרה ותראה כי הכתר בית לכלן ומקור כלן

מנה שהקודם לאצילות גדול מקיף הכל והמאוחר לאצילות
קטן ומוקף מהכל וכלול מכלן וזהו כגלדי הבצלים וכמו
והארץ השפלה הזאת היא קטנה והיא באמצע כל הכבראיב

Perspective diagram of the world of the ten *Sefirot*, composed of the initial letters of the names of each *Sefirah*, starting with the first *Sefirah* and going to the last. From Moses Cordovero, *Pardes Rimmonim*, Cracow, 1592.

which took place within the Divine itself. The God who manifests Himself in His *Sefirot* is the very same God of traditional religious belief, and consequently, despite all the complexities such an idea involves, the emanation of the *Sefirot* is a process within God Himself. The hidden God in the aspect of *Ein-Sof* and the God manifested in the emanation of *Sefirot* are one and the same, viewed from two different angles. There is therefore a clear distinction between the stages of emanation in the neoplatonic systems, which are not conceived as processes within the Godhead, and the kabbalistic approach. In Kabbalah, emanation as an intermediate stage between God and creation was reassigned to the Divine, and the problem of the continuation of this process outside the Godhead gave rise to various interpretations. At first there was no need to conclude that worlds below the level of the *Sefirot*, and the corporeal world itself, were also emanated from the *Sefirot.* Perhaps intentionally, the kabbalists dealt with this point in a highly obscure fashion, frequently leaving open the way to the most diverse interpretations. God's actions outside the realm of the *Sefirot* of emanation led to the emergence of created beings separated from the *Sefirot* by an abyss, although few kabbalists maintained unambiguously that the process of emanation came to an absolute end with the final *Sefirah* and that what followed constituted a completely new beginning. The early kabbalists agreed that all creatures below the *Sefirot* had an existence of their own outside the Divine, and were distinguished from it in their independent existence since their state was that of created beings, although they had their archetypes in the *Sefirot.* Even given the belief that from the point of view of God they have their root in His being, nevertheless they are in themselves separated from His essence and possess a nature of their own. Distinctions of this kind are common to the Kabbalah and to other mystical theologies, like those of medieval Islam and Christianity, but they were generally neglected in most kabbalistic discussions of emanation, with all the consequent unclarity that this entailed. Particularly in a number of important books which do not attempt to build their own doctrines on a firm theoretical foundation, such as the *Bahir,* the Zohar, and the works of Isaac b. Jacob ha-Kohen, the authors often use highly ambiguous terms and speak of "creation" even when they mean "emanation." This ambiguity can be explained in the light of the history of the Kabbalah, which was at first concerned with the description of a religious and contemplative experience and not with questions of purely theoretical systematization. In addition, the developing Kabbalah was heir to a strong, mythically inclined Gnostic heritage of speculation on the aeons (whose nature was also subject to many theoretical interpretations). Thus, when their figurative and symbolic language was put to a logical test, sources like the above were accorded many different theological and analytical interpretations.

As the Kabbalah developed in Provence and Spain and the Gnostic tradition was confronted with neoplatonism, a host of short tracts were written in which it was attempted to give an independent description of the processes of emanation. Most of these works belong to the circle of the *Sefer ha-Iyyun* (see above). They show quite clearly that, aside from the theory of the *Sefirot,* there were other approaches to a description of the spiritual world, such as in terms of a world of powers *(koḥot),* lights, or divine intellects, which were sometimes given identical names but which were ordered each time in quite different ways. Obviously these were the first gropings toward the establishment of a definitive order in the degrees and stages of emanation. However, as they did not correspond with the symbolism that had been constructed in a more or less unified fashion from the time of Isaac the Blind up to the Zohar, they were almost completely disregarded.

Unlike these first hesitant steps, the theory of the *Sefirot* ultimately became the backbone of Spanish kabbalistic teaching and of that basic system of mystical symbolism which had such important repercussions on the kabbalists' view of the meaning of Judaism. Right from the beginning, ideas concerning emanation were closely bound up with a theory of language. On the one hand, much is written about the manifestation of the power of *Ein-Sof* through various stages of emanation which are called *Sefirot* and are no more than the various attributes of God or descriptions and epithets which can be applied to Him – that is, about a continuous process of emanation. Yet at the same time this very process was described as a kind of revelation of the various Names peculiar to God in His capacity of Creator. The God who manifests Himself is the God who expresses Himself. The God who "called" His powers to reveal themselves named them, and, it could be said, called Himself also by appropriate names. The process by which the power of emanation manifests itself from concealment into revelation is paralleled by the manifestation of divine speech from its inner essence in thought, through sound that as yet cannot be heard, into the articulation of speech. Through the influence of the *Sefer Yeẓirah,* which speaks of "the ten *Sefirot* of *belimah,*" the number of the stages of emanation was fixed at ten, although in this early work the term refers only to the ideal numbers which contain the forces of creation. In kabbalistic usage, on the other hand, it signifies the ten powers that constitute the manifestations and emanations of God. Since the *Sefirot* are intermediary states between the first Emanator and all things that exist apart from God, they also represent the roots of all existence in God the Creator.

That many themes are united, or sometimes simply commingled, in this concept is demonstrated by the profusion of terms used to describe it. The term *Sefirah* is not connected with the Greek σφαῖρα ("sphere"), but as early as the *Sefer ha-Bahir* it is related to the Hebrew *sappir* ("sapphire"), for it is the radiance of God which is like that of the sapphire. The term is not used at all in the main part of the Zohar, appearing only in the later stratum, but other kabbalists too employed a wealth of synonyms. The *Sefirot* are also called *ma'amarot* and *dibburim* ("sayings"), *shemot* ("names"), *orot* ("lights"), *koḥot* ("powers"), *ketarim* ("crowns"; since they are "the celestial crowns of the Holy King"), *middot* in the sense of qualities, *madregot* ("stages"), *levushim* ("garments"), *marot* ("mirrors"), *neti'ot* ("shoots"), *mekorot* ("sources"), *yamim elyonim* or *yemei kedem* ("supernal or primordial days"), *sitrin* (i.e., "aspects," found mainly in the Zohar), *ha-panim ha-penimiyyot* ("the inner faces of God"). (A long list of other designations for the *Sefirot* can be found in Herrera, *Sha'ar ha-Shamayim,* 7:4.) Terms like "the limbs of the King" or "the limbs of the *Shi'ur Komah,*" the mystical image of God, allude to the symbolism of the supernal man, also called *ha-adam ha-gadol,* or primordial man. Sometimes this term is used for one specific *Sefirah,* but often it denotes the whole world of emanation. The term *ha-adam ha-kadmon* ("primordial man") occurs for the first time in *Sod Yedi'at ha-Meẓi'ut,* a treatise from the *Sefer ha-Iyyun* circle. The different motifs of the *Sefirot,* which express themselves in this proliferation of names, tend to vary both with the specific context and with the overall inclinations of the kabbalist making use of them.

No agreed canonical definition exists. The conceptual connection between the *ma'amarim* or the *ketarim*, as the *Sefirot* were called in the *Sefer ha-Bahir*, and the intermediate substances between the infinite and the finite, the one and the many, of neoplatonism, originated mainly in the work of Azriel, who was determined to divest the idea of the *Sefirot* of its Gnostic character. His definitions, which appear in *Perush Eser Sefirot* and *Derekh ha-Emunah ve-Derekh ha-Kefirah,* and those of his companion Asher b. David, were largely instrumental in fixing the concept of the *Sefirot* in Spanish Kabbalah, although the tendency to portray them as Gnostic aeons did not entirely disappear. According to Azriel, things were created in a specific order, since creation was intentional, not accidental. This order, which determines all the processes of creation and of generation and decay, is known as *Sefirot,* "the active power of each existing thing numerically defineable." Since all created things come into being through the agency of the *Sefirot,* the latter contain the root of all change, although they all emanate from the one principle, *Ein-Sof,* "outside of which there is nothing." In terms of their origin in the *Ein-Sof* the *Sefirot* are not differentiated, but in respect of their activity within the finite realm of creation they are. Existing alongside these Platonic definitions is the theosophic conception of the *Sefirot* as forces of the divine essence or nature, through which absolute being reveals itself; they therefore constitute the inner foundation and the root of every created being in a way which is generally not specifically defined, but not necessarily as "intermediaries" in the philosophical sense. The contrast with the neoplatonic pattern is very definitely expressed in a doctrine, common to all kabbalists of every age (even to Azriel), concerning the dynamic of these powers. Although there is a specific hierarchy in the order of the *Sefirot,* it is not ontologically determined: all are equally close to their source in the Emanator (this is already so in the *Sefer ha-Bahir*). It is possible for them to join together in mystical unions, and some of them move up and down within the framework of the hidden life of God (both Gnostic motifs), which does not fit the Platonic point of view. In other words, within a conceptual Platonic system a theosophic understanding of God came to the fore.

The nature or essence of these *Sefirot,* that is the relationship of the manifested world of the Divine to the created world and to the hidden being of the Emanator, was a widely disputed subject. Were the *Sefirot* identical with God or not, and, if not, wherein lay the difference? At first this question did not arise, and the imagery used to describe the *Sefirot* and their activity was not aimed at a precise definition. The description of the *Sefirot* as vessels for the activity of God, the Emanator, which occurs, for example, as early as Asher b. David, does not contradict the idea that in essence they are identical with God. The term *ko'aḥ* ("force," "power," "potency"), which is common in kabbalistic literature, does not always indicate a precise distinction between "force" and "essence" in the Aristotelian sense. It is also used to refer to the independent existence of "potencies," hypostases which are emanated from their source, without any preceding indication of whether this emanation is an expansion of the latter's essence or only of its radiation that was previously concealed in potentiality and now is activated. In purely figurative descriptions of the world of the *Sefirot* these philosophical distinctions did not come to the forefront, but once questions of this sort were raised it was impossible to evade them.

Most of the early kabbalists were more inclined to accept the view that the *Sefirot* were actually identical with God's substance or essence. This is stated in many documents from the 13th century, and stressed later in the school of R. Solomon b. Adret, and particularly in the *Ma'arekhet ha-Elohut,* which was followed in the 16th century by David Messer Leon, Meir ibn Gabbai, and Joseph Caro. According to this view, the *Sefirot* do not constitute "intermediary beings" but are God Himself. "The Emanation is the Divinity," while *Ein-Sof* cannot be subject to religious investigation, which can conceive of God only in His external aspect. The main part of the Zohar also tends largely toward this opinion, expressing it emphatically in the interchangeable identity of God with His Names or His Powers: "He is They, and They are He" (Zohar, 3:11b, 70a). In the latter stratum, however, in the *Ra'aya Meheimna* and the *Tikkunim,* and subsequently in the *Ta'amei ha-Mizvot* of Menahem Recanati, the *Sefirot* are seen not as the essence of God but only as vessels or tools: although they are indeed neither separated from Him nor situated outside Him like the tools of a human artisan, nevertheless they are no more than means and instruments which He uses in His work. Recanati states that most of the kabbalists of his time disagreed with this view. In the writings of Joseph Ashkenazi (Pseudo-Rabad) this theory is developed to the extreme where the *Sefirot,* being intermediaries, pray to God Himself and are actually unable to perceive the nature of their Emanator, a view which was first presented in the writings of Moses of Burgos and subsequently appeared in many kabbalistic works. Cordovero tried to reconcile these two opposing views and to accord a certain measure of truth to each one. Just as in all organic life the soul (the essence) cannot be distinguished from the body (the vessels) except *in abstracto* and in fact they cannot be separated at all when they are working together, so it may be said of God that He works, so to speak, as a living organism, and thus the *Sefirot* have two aspects, one as "essence," and the other as "vessels." Dominating this theosophic organism is a metabiological principle of measure and form called *kav ha-middah* (according to specific statements in the Zohar which use this term to express the nature of the activity of the first *Sefirah*). From this point of view the *Sefirot* are both identical with the essence of God and also separated from Him (see *Pardes Rimmonim,* ch. 4). In later Kabbalah this view became paramount.

The *Sefirot* emanate from *Ein-Sof* in succession – "as if one candle were lit from another without the Emanator being diminished in any way" – and in a specific order. Nevertheless, in contrast to the neoplatonic concept in which the intermediaries stand completely outside the domain of the "One," they do not thereby leave the divine domain. This influx is given the name *hamshakhah* ("drawing out"), that is to say, the entity which is emanated is drawn out from its source, like light from the sun or water from a well. According to Naḥmanides (in his commentary to Num. 11:17) and his school, the second term, *aẓilut,* expresses the particular position of this emanation. The term is understood as deriving from *eẓel* ("near by," or "with"), for even the things that are emanated remain "by Him," and act as potencies manifesting the unity of the Emanator. Naḥmanides' anti-emanist interpretation of the term *aẓilut* was apparently intended only for the unitiated, for in his esoteric writings he also uses the term *hamshakhah* (in his commentary to the *Sefer Yeẓirah*). Generally speaking, stress is laid on the fact that the God who expresses Himself in the emanation of the *Sefirot* is greater than the totality of the *Sefirot* through which He works and by means of which He passes from unity to plurality. The personality of God finds expression precisely through His manifestation of the *Sefirot.* It is therefore surprising that, in those circles close to Naḥmanides, the nature of the Emanator which remained concealed beyond all emanation was thought to be a closely guarded tradition. Naḥmanides himself refers to it as "the hidden matter at the top of the *Keter*," at the head of the first *Sefirah*, a designation which deprives it of any personal quality (commentary to the *Sefer Yeẓirah*). As noted above, however, some of his contemporary kabbalists, like Abraham of Cologne (1260–70) in *Keter Shem Tov*, completely rejected the idea by denying an impersonal aspect to God and by identifying *Ein-Sof* with the first *Sefirah*.

Deriving *aẓilut* from *eẓel* does not necessarily imply that the process of emanation is eternal: it simply signifies the contrast between two domains – the *olam ha-yiḥud* ("the world of unification") and the *olam ha-perud* ("the world of separation"). Emanation is the world of unification, not of the static unity of *Ein-Sof* but of the process which occurs in God, who is Himself unified in the dynamic unity of His powers ("like the flame linked to a burning coal"). In contrast to this, "the world of separation" refers to the domain which results from the act of creation, whose theosophic inner nature is expressed in the emanation of the *Sefirot*. But this process of emanation of the *Sefirot* is not a temporal one, nor does it necessitate any change in God Himself; it is simply the emergence from potentiality into actuality of that which was concealed within the power of the Creator.

However, the opinion differed on the question of the emanation and time. Azriel taught that the first *Sefirah* was always within the potentiality of *Ein-Sof*, but that other *Sefirot* were emanated only in the intellectual sense and had a beginning in time; there were also *Sefirot* that were emanated only "now, near to the creation of the world." Others maintained that the concept of time had no application to the process of emanation, while Cordovero held that this process occurred within "non-temporal time," a dimension of time which involved as yet no differentiation into past, present, and future. A dimension of this type was also important in the thinking of the later neoplatonists, who spoke of *sempiternitas*. This supermundane concept of time was defined "as the twinkling of an eye, without any interval" between the various acts which were part of emanation (so in *Emek ha-Melekh* and *Va-Yakhel Moshe* by Moses Graf). Joseph Solomon Delmedigo in *Navelot Ḥokhmah*, and Jonathan Eybeschuetz in *Shem Olam*, also posited the coeternity of the *Sefirot*, but generally speaking this idea aroused a great deal of opposition. As early as the 13th century the counter-doctrine was formulated that "the essences existed but emanation came into being.[3] If the essences preceded emanation then they must of necessity have existed in the will or thought of *Ein-Sof*, but they were made manifest by an act which had something of the nature of new creativity although not in the usual sense of creativity in time.

In the literature of the Kabbalah the unity of God in His *Sefirot* and the appearance of plurality within the One are expressed through a great number of images which continually recur. They are compared to a candle flickering in the midst of ten mirrors set one within the other, each a different color. The light is reflected differently in each, although it is the same single light. The daring image of the *Sefirot* as garments is extremely common. According to the Midrash *(Pesikta de-Rav Kahana),* at the creation of the world God clothed Himself in ten garments, and these are identified in the Kabbalah with the *Sefirot,* although in the latter no distinction is made between the garment and the body – "it is like the garment of the grasshopper whose clothing is part of itself," an image taken from the Midrash *Genesis Rabbah.* The garments enable man to look at the light, which without them would be blinding. By first growing used to looking at one garment man can look progressively further to the next and the next, and in this way the *Sefirot* serve as rungs of the ladder of ascent toward the perception of God (Asher b. David, *Perush Shem ha-Meforash*).

The doctrine of the *Sefirot* was the main tenet clearly dividing the Kabbalah from Jewish philosophy. The subject matter of philosophy – the doctrine of divine attributes and in particular "the attributes of action" as distinct from "the essential attributes" – was transformed in Kabbalah into the theosophic conception of a Godhead that was divided into realms or "planes" which, in the eyes of the beholder at least, existed as lights, potencies, and intelligences, each of unlimited richness and profundity, whose content man could study and seek to penetrate. Each one was like "a world unto itself," although it was also reflected in the totality of all the others. As early as the beginning of the 13th century, after the appearance of the *Sefer ha-Bahir,* the view was propounded that there were dynamic processes not only between the *Sefirot* but also within each separate *Sefirah.* This tendency toward an increasingly more complex doctrine of the *Sefirot* was the most distinctive characteristic of the development of kabbalistic theory. The number ten provided the framework for the growth of a seemingly endless multiplicity of lights and processes. In the circle of the *Sefer ha-Iyyun*, where this development began, we find an enumeration of the names of the intellectual lights and powers, which only partially fit the traditional symbolism of the *Sefirot* (see below) and sometimes diverge widely from it. The writings of "the Gnostic circle" in Castile expanded the framework of emanation and added potencies bearing personal names which gave a unique coloring to the world of the *Sefirot* and to all that existed outside it. This tendency was continued by the author of the Zohar, whose descriptions of the first acts of creation, and particularly those in the *Idra Rabba* and the *Idra Zuta* concerning the configurations of the forces of emanation (called *Attika Kaddisha, Arikh Anpin* and *Ze'eir Anpin*), are very different from the original simple concept of the *Sefirot.* Here is the beginning of the anatomical and physiological symbolism of the *Shi'ur Komah* – a description of the image of God based on analogy with human structure – which shook the very foundations of the *Sefirot* doctrine and introduced into it new differentiations and combinations. An additional complexity resulted when the theory of the *Sefirot* was combined with prophetic Kabbalah and "the science of combination" of the school of Abraham Abulafia. Every different combination of letters and vowels could be seen in the radiance of that intellectual light which appears under certain circumstances in the meditations of the mystic. Whole books like the *Berit Menuḥah* (second half of the 14th century), *Toledot Adam* (printed in part in Casablanca in 1930 in *Sefer ha-Malkhut*), and *Avnei Shoham* by Joseph ibn Sayyaḥ[4] reflect this view. These complexities in the doctrine of the *Sefirot* reached their most extreme expression in Cordovero's *Elimah Rabbati* and, finally, in the Lurianic theory of the *parẓufim* (see below).

The *Sefirot*, both individually and collectively, subsume the archetype of every created thing outside the world of emanation. Just as they are contained within the Godhead, so they impregnate every being outside it. Thus, the limitation of their number to ten necessarily involves the supposition that each one is composed of a large number of such archetypes.

DETAILS OF THE DOCTRINE OF THE *SEFIROT* AND THEIR SYMBOLISM

Both theosophical and theological approaches are equally evident in kabbalistic speculation about the *Sefirot* in general and their relationship to the Emanator in particular. When it comes to the sequential development of the *Sefirot*, on the other hand, and to the individual function of each, especially from the second *Sefirah* onward, a strong Gnostic and mythic element begins to predominate. The kabbalists continuously stressed the subjective nature of their descriptions: "everything is from the perspective of those who receive" *(Ma'arekhet ha-Elohut);* "all this is said only from our view, and it is all relative to our knowledge" (Zohar 2: 176a). However, this did not prevent them from indulging in the most detailed descriptions, as if they were speaking after all of an actual reality and objective occurrences. The progressive movement of the hidden life of God, which is expressed in a particular structural form, established the rhythm for the development of the created worlds outside the world of emanation, so that these first innermost structures recur in all secondary domains. Hence there is basic justification for a single comprehensive symbolic system. An inner reality that defies characterization or description because it is beyond our perception can only be expressed symbolically. The words of both the Written and the Oral Law do not describe mundane matters and events alone, situated in history and concerned with the relations between Israel and its God, but also, when interpreted mystically, they speak of the interaction between the Emanator and the emanated, between the different *Sefirot* themselves, and between the *Sefirot* and the activities of men through Torah and prayer. What in the literal sense is called the account of creation is really a mystical allusion to the process which occurs within the world of emanation itself and therefore can be expressed only symbolically. General speaking, such symbolism interested the kabbalists far more than all the theoretical speculation on the nature of the *Sefirot,* and the greater part of kabbalistic literature deals with this aspect and its detailed application. Most of the commentaries to the Torah, to Psalms, and to the *aggadot,* as well as the voluminous literature on the reasons for the Commandments *(ta'amei ha-mizvot),* are based on this approach. As noted above, however, none of this symbolism has any bearing on *Ein-Sof,* although there were nevertheless kabbalists who did attribute to the latter specific expressions in Scripture or in the *Sefer Yezirah.*

The common order of the *Sefirot* and the names most generally used for them are: (1) *Keter Elyon* ("supreme crown") or simply *Keter;* (2) *Ḥokhmah* ("wisdom"); (3) *Binah* ("intelligence"); (4) *Gedullah* ("greatness") or *Ḥesed* ("love"); (5) *Gevurah* ("power") or *Din* ("Judgment," also "rigor"), (6) *Tiferet* ("beauty") or *Raḥamim* ("compassion"); (7) *Neẓaḥ* ("lasting endurance"); (8) *Hod* ("majesty"); (9) *Ẓaddik* ("righteous one") or *Yesod Olam* ("foundation of the world"); (10) *Malkhut* ("kingdom") or *Atarah* ("diadem"). This terminology was greatly influenced by the verse in I Chronicles 29:11, which was interpreted as applying to the order of the *Sefirot.* Although the *Sefirot* are emanated successively from above to below, each one revealing an additional stage in the divine process, they also have a formalized structure. Three such groupings are most commonly found. In their totality the *Sefirot* make up "the tree of emanation" or "the tree of the *Sefirot,*" which from the 14th century onward is depicted by a detailed diagram which lists the basic symbols appropriate to each *Sefirah.* The cosmic tree grows downward from its root, the first *Sefirah,* and spreads out through those *Sefirot* which constitute its trunk to those which make up its main branches or crown. This image is first found in the *Sefer ha-Bahir:* "All the divine powers of the Holy One, blessed be He, rest one upon the other, and are like a tree." However, in the *Bahir* the tree starts to grow by being watered with the waters of Wisdom, and apparently it includes only those *Sefirot* from *Binah* downward. Alongside this picture we have the more common image of the *Sefirot* in the form of a man. While the tree grows with its top down, this human form has its head properly on top, and is occasionally referred to as the "reversed tree." The first *Sefirot* represent the head, and, in the Zohar, the three cavities of the brain; the fourth and the fifth, the arms; the sixth, the torso; the seventh and eighth, the legs; the ninth, the sexual organ; and the tenth refers either to the all-embracing totality of the image, or (as in the *Bahir*) to the female as companion to the male, since both together are needed to constitute a perfect man. In kabbalistic literature this symbolism of primeval Man in all its details is called *Shi'ur Komah.* The most common pattern is:

	Keter	
Binah		*Ḥokhmah*
Gevurah		*Gedullah*
	Tiferet	
Hod		*Neẓaḥ*
	Yesod	
	Malkhut	

Sometimes the three *Sefirot, Keter, Ḥokhmah,* and *Binah,* are not depicted in a triangle, but in a straight line, one below the other. On the whole, however, the overall structure is built out of triangles.

From the end of the 13th century onward a complementary *Sefirah,* called *Da'at* ("knowledge"), appears between *Ḥokhmah* and *Binah,* a kind of harmonizing of the two that was not considered a separate *Sefirah* but rather "the external aspect of *Keter.*" This addition arose from the desire to see each group of three *Sefirot* as a unit comprising opposing attributes and as a synthesis which finally resolved them. This was not, however, the original motivation of the pattern. In the *Sefer ha-Bahir,* and in several early texts of the 13th century, the *Sefirah Yesod* was thought of as the seventh, preceding *Neẓaḥ* and *Hod,* and only in Gerona was it finally assigned to the ninth place. On the model of the neoplatonic hierarchy, according to which the transition from the one to the many was accomplished through the stages of intellect, universal soul, and nature, many kabbalists, Azriel in particular, thought of the *Sefirot* as also comprising these stages (although they still remained within the domain of deity). *Keter, Ḥokhmah,* and *Binah* were "the intellectual" *(ha-muskal); Gedullah, Gevurah,* and *Tiferet* were "the psychic" *(ha-murgash); Neẓaḥ, Hod,* and *Yesod* were "the natural" *(ha-mutba).* Apparently it was intended that these three stages should be understood as the sources of the independent realms of intellect, soul, and nature, which were fully activated and developed only at a lower level. It is obvious that this was an artificial compromise with neoplatonic ontology.

Since the *Sefirot* were conceived of as the progressive manifestation of the Names of God, a set of equivalences between the latter and the names of the *Sefirot* was established:

	Ehyeh	
YHWH (vocalized as *Elohim*)		*Yah*
Elohim		*El*
	YHWH	
Elohim Ẓeva'ot		YHWH *Ẓeva'ot*
	El Ḥai or *Shaddai*	
	Adonai	

According to the Kabbalah these are "the ten names which must not be erased," seven of which are mentioned in the Talmud (*Shevu'ot,* 35a), and compared with them all other names are mere epithets. The Zohar designates *Shaddai* as the name particularly related to the *Sefirah Yesod,* while Joseph Gikatilla associates this *Sefirah* with *El Ḥai.*

The division of the *Sefirot* was also determined by other criteria. Sometimes they were divided into five and five, i.e., the five upper *Sefirot* corresponding to the five lower, an equal balance between the hidden and the revealed being maintained. On the basis of the statement in the *Pirkei de-R. Eliezer* "with ten sayings was the world created, and they were summarized in three," they were also divided into seven and three. In this case there was a differentiation between three hidden *Sefirot* and "the seven *Sefirot* of the building," which are also the seven primordial days of creation. Six of these were also equated with the six sides of space in the *Sefer Yeẓirah.* How these six were complemented by a seventh was never decisively established. Some thought that the seventh was the sacred palace which stood in the center, as in the *Sefer Yeẓirah.* Others considered it to be represented by Divine Thought, while for others it was a symbolic Sabbath. The correlation of the "*Sefirot* of the building" with the days of creation became extremely complex. Many kabbalists, including the author of the bulk of the Zohar, could not agree on the automatic association of each *Sefirah* with one particular day, and they regarded creation, which from the mystical viewpoint was the completion of "the building" of emanation, as having been already completed by the fourth day. They were particularly perplexed by the problem of the Sabbath, which many interpreted as a symbol of *Yesod,* since it paralleled the original seventh place of this *Sefirah,* while many others saw in it an allusion to the last *Sefirah,* especially since the powers came to an end there. Just as each day performed an act specific to it, apart from the seventh, so each *Sefirah* performed it own specific activities by which it was characterized, except for the last *Sefirah,* which had no such active force, but comprised the totality of all the *Sefirot* or the specific principle that received and united the active forces without adding anything particular of its own. On the contrary it is the absence of activity and the tenth *Sefirah's* function as an all-inclusive entity which constitutes its uniqueness. The division of the *Sefirot* into three lines or columns was especially important: the right hand column includes *Ḥokhmah, Gedullah,* and *Neẓaḥ;* the left hand column includes *Binah, Gevurah,* and *Hod;* and the central column *(kav emẓa'i)* passes from *Keter* through *Tiferet* and *Yesod* to *Malkhut.*

All of these groupings testify to the kabbalists' belief that there was a definite structure to the *Sefirot,* no matter how great the possibilities of variation may have been. In contrast to them all is yet another arrangement which presents the *Sefirot* either as adjoining arcs of a single circle surrounding the central Emanator, or as ten concentric spheres (called "circles") with the power of emanation diminishing as it moves further away from the center. This latter concept is related to the medieval cosmological picture of a universe of ten spheres, which could be imagined in terms of the outward gyration of these spiritual circles. The circular concept appears especially from the 14th century onward (Pseudo-Rabad to the *Sefer Yeẓirah,* 1, 2). In Lurianic Kabbalah every one of these diagrammatic arrangements, circular or linear, is accorded a specific place in the plan of emanation.

When we come to deal with the symbolism of the *Sefirot* we must distinguish between the general symbolic systems appertaining to the processes of emanation as a whole and the symbolism related to each individual *Sefirah* or to a particular combination of *Sefirot.* The overall symbolic systems are based on both mathematical and organic imagery. In the system depending on mathematical concepts, which is sometimes linked with images of light and rivers, the first *Sefirah* is nothingness, zero, and the second is the manifestation of the primordial point, which at this stage has no size but contains within it the possibility of measurement and expansion. Since it is intermediate between nothingness and being, it is called *hatḥalat ha-yeshut* ("the beginning of being"). And since it is a central point it expands into a circle in the third *Sefirah,* or it builds around itself a "palace" which is the third *Sefirah.* When this point is represented as a source welling up from the depths of nothingness, the third *Sefirah* becomes the river that flows out from the source and divides into different streams following the structure of emanation until all its tributaries flow into "the great sea" of the last *Sefirah.* The first point is established by an act of Divine Will, taking its first step toward creation. In the Zohar the appearance of the supernal point (which is called *reshit,* "beginning," part of the first word of the Bible) is preceded by a number of acts that take place between *Ein-Sof* and the first *Sefirah* or within the first *Sefirah.* As well as being nothingness *(ayin)* and the will of God, this *Sefirah* is also the primordial ether *(avir kadmon)* which surrounds *Ein-Sof* like an eternal aura. From the mystery of *Ein-Sof* a flame is kindled and inside the flame a hidden well comes into being. The primordial point shines forth in being when the well breaks through the ether (1:15a). It is as if all the possible images were assembled together within this description.

The organic symbolism equates the primordial point with the seed sown in the womb of "the supernal mother," who is *Binah*. "The palace" is the womb which is brought to fruition through the fertilization of the semen and gives birth to the children, who are the emanations. In another organic image *Binah* is compared to the roots of a tree which is watered by *Ḥokhmah* and branches out into seven *Sefirot*. In another symbolic pattern – very common in the 13th century and particularly in the Zohar – the first three *Sefirot* represent the progress from will to thought and thence to intellect, where the general content of wisdom or thought is more precisely individuated. The identification of the following *Sefirot* as love, justice, and mercy links this doctrine with the aggadic concept of the divine attributes. References to male and female appear not only in the symbolism of father and mother, son and daughter *Ḥokhmah*, and *Binah*, *Tiferet* and *Malkhut*) but also in the striking use of sexual imagery which is a particular characteristic of the Zohar and Lurianic Kabbalah. The use of such phallic and vaginal images is especially prominent in the description of the relationships between *Tiferet* and *Yesod* on the one hand and *Malkhut* on the other. Many kabbalists did their utmost to minimize the impact of this symbolism, which afforded much scope for mythical images and daring interpretations.

A general symbolism of a different type is related to the stages in the manifestation of the personal, individual identity of God. The first *Sefirah* contains only "He"; sometimes this "He" is hidden and no mention is made of Him because of His extreme self-concealment, as, for example, within the verb *bara* ("He created") at the beginning of the Bible. Thus *bereshit bara Elohim* (usually "in the beginning God created") is interpreted mystically to refer to the first three *Sefirot:* through the medium (the prefix *be*) of *Ḥokhmah* (called *reshit*), the first *Sefirah* – the force hidden within the third person singular of the word *bara* – produced by an act of emanation the third *Sefirah (Binah)*, which is also called *Elohim*. *Elohim* ("God") is thus not the subject but the object of the sentence. This daring interpretation is common to almost all 13th century kabbalists. But as His manifestation continues, God becomes "Thou," whom man is now able to address directly, and this "Thou" is related to *Tiferet* or to the totality of the *Sefirot* in *Malkhut*. However, God reaches His complete individuation through His manifestation in *Malkhut*, where He is called "I." This conception is summed up in the common statement that through the process of emanation "Nothingness changes into I" *(Ayin le-Ani)*. The three letters or elements which make up *Ayin* ("Nothingness") – *alef, yod, nun* – are also contained in *Ani*, that is in both the beginning and the end of the process, but like the forces which they denote they are combined in a different way. In a similar fashion the name YHWH denotes just one *Sefirah (Tiferet)* but also contains within it all the fundamental stages of emanation: the spike at the top of the *yod* represents the source of all in *Ayin,* the *yod* itself is *Ḥokhmah,* the first *he* is *Binah,* the *vav* is *Tiferet* or, because of the numerical value of the letter *vav,* the totality of the six *Sefirot* and the final *he* is *Malkhut.* Since the latter comprises the other *Sefirot* and has no independent power, it cannot be assigned a letter of its own but only that *he,* which has already appeared at the beginning of the emanation of the structure of the *Sefirot* and whose manifestation has reached its final development at the end of the process. The other names of God in the Bible are also interpreted in a similar fashion, their letters alluding to an inner progress in the process of emanation.

Emanation in its totality is the "Celestial Chariot" and individual components are "parts of the Chariot" which are interpreted in particular in the commentaries on the Chariot by Jacob Kohen of Soria, his brother Isaac Kohen, Moses de Leon, and Joseph Gikatilla. Biblical figures are also connected with this. "The patriarchs are the Chariot" *(Genesis Rabbah),* for Abraham represents the attribute of abundant love *(Ḥesed),* Isaac the attribute of strict justice *(Din)* and Jacob the attribute of mercy *(Raḥamim),* which is a combination of the other two. These three, together with King David, the founder of the kingship *(Malkhut)* of Israel, constitute the "four legs of the Throne" in the Chariot. And when Moses and Aaron are added, as representing the sources of prophecy in *Neẓaḥ* and *Hod,* and then Joseph – according to the talmudic picture of him as "Joseph the righteous," keeper of the covenant, who resists the temptations of the sexual instinct – we have the seven *Sefirot* portraying the heroes of the Bible, who are called the "seven shepherds" or guests *(ushpizin).* This kind of symbolism conveys the moral content of the *Sefirot* as specific ethical attributes. The righteous, each of whom is inspired by a characteristic moral quality, embody the rule of the divine attributes in the world.

In addition to this ethical symbolism we find several cosmological systems. The four elements, the four winds, and even the four metals (gold, silver, copper, and lead) are indications of *Gedullah, Gevurah, Tiferet,* and *Malkhut;* the sun and the moon of *Tiferet* or *Yesod* and *Malkhut.* The moon, which receives its light from the sun and has no light of its own, and which waxes and wanes according to a fixed cycle, occupies an important place in the very rich symbolism of the last *Sefirah.* However, the most important of these symbols are the *Keneset Yisrael* ("the community of Israel") and the *Shekhinah* ("the Divine Presence"). The Kingdom of Heaven, which is realized in time in the historical *Keneset Yisrael,* represents therefore the latter's meta-historical aspect as well. The supernal *Keneset Yisrael* is the mother *(matrona),* the bride, and also the daughter of the "king," and they appear in countless midrashic parables on the ralationship between God and the Jewish people. In her capacity as bride *(kallah)* she is also, by a mystical etymology, "the consummation of all" *(kelulah mi-ha-kol).* She is the receptive aspect of "the holy nuptial" of the symbols of "king" and "queen." Other of her features are to be seen in the symbols of her as freedom, the Torah, and the trees in the Garden of Eden. The *Sefirah Binah* is the "supernal Jubilee," in which everything emerges into freedom and returns to its source, and therefore *Binah* is also called *Teshuvah* ("return"). But the last *Sefirah* is the *shemittah,* the seventh year when the earth rests and is renewed. The Written Law is woven from the name YHWH, and alludes to an emanation which already has some manifestation but has yet to be fully articulated. The Oral Law, which gives a detailed interpretation of the ways of the Written Law and of its application to life, is embodied in *Keneset Yisrael,* both in heaven and on earth. And similarly with regard to the trees: the Tree of Life is the *Sefirah Yesod* (though later on it is mainly *Tiferet*), while the Tree of Knowledge is a symbol of *Malkhut,* or of the Oral Law. In the early *aggadah* the *Shekhinah* is a synonym for God, indicating His presence, His "dwelling" in the world, or in any specified place. In the Kabbalah, on the other hand, from the *Sefer ha-Bahir* onward, it becomes the last attribute through which the Creator acts in the lower world. It is "the end of thought," whose progressive unfolding demonstrates God's hidden life. From its source at "the beginning of thought" in *Ḥokhmah* ("wisdom"), the thought of creation pursues its task through all the worlds, following the laws of the process of the *Sefirot* themselves. The emphasis placed on the female principle in the symbolism of the last *Sefirah* heightens the mythical language of these descriptions. Appearing from above as "the end of thought," the last *Sefirah* is for man the door or gate through which he can begin the ascent up the ladder of perception of the Divine Mystery.

The symbols mentioned so far form only part of a rich symbolism which drew on material from every sphere. Often there are differences in the details of its presentation, and there was a certain amount of freedom in the way given symbols were connected to a given *Sefirah,* but as far as basic motifs were concerned there was a great degree of agreement. Yet works explaining the attributes of the *Sefirot* were written from the time of the Gerona kabbalists onward, and the differences between them should not be minimized. Even in the Zohar itself there are many variations within a more or less firmly established framework. Such differences can also be seen between the symbolism of Moses de Leon and that of Joseph Gikatilla. The best sources for an understanding of this symbolism are: *Sha'arei Orah* (1560; best ed. Jerusalem, 1970) and *Sha'arei Ẓedek* by Gikatilla; *Shekel ha-Kodesh* (1911) by Moses de Leon; *Sefer ha-Shem* written by another unidentified Moses; *Sod Ilan ha-Aẓilut* by R. Isaac (*Kovez al-Yad,* 68, 5 (1951), 65–102); *Ma'arekhet ha-Elohut,* chs. 3–7; *Sefer ha-Shorashim* by Joseph ibn Wakkar (translation of the section on symbolism from his Arabic work, found separately in many Mss.); *Sha'ar Arkhei ha-Kinuyim* in *Pardes Rimmonim* by Cordovero, ch. 23; *Sefat Emet* by Menahem Azariah Fano (Lobatschov, 1898); *Arkhei ha-Kinuyim* by Jehiel Heilprin (Dyhrenfurth, 1806); *Kehillat Ya'akov* by Jacob Ẓevi Jolles (Lemberg, 1870) and its second part entitled *Yashresh Ya'akov* (Brooklyn, about 1961). The attributes of the *Sefirot* according to Lurianic Kabbalah are described in detail in *Me'orot Natan* by Meir Poppers (text) and Nathan Nata Mannheim (notes) (Frankfort, 1709); *Regal Yesharah* by Ẓevi Elimelech Schapira (Lemberg, 1858), *Emet le-Ya'akov* by Jacob Shealtiel Niño (Leghorn, 1843); and *Or Einayim* by Eliezer Ẓevi Safrin (Part 1, Premysl, 1882, Part 2, Lemberg, 1886).

From the 13th century onward we find the idea that each *Sefirah* comprises all others successively in an infinite reflection of the *Sefirot* within themselves. This formal method of describing the rich dynamic that exists within each *Sefirah* was also expressed in other ways. So, for example, we read of the 620 "pillars of light" in *Keter,* of the 32 "ways" in *Ḥokhmah,* of the 50 "gates" of *Binah,* of the 72 "bridges" in *Ḥesed,* and so on (in the *Tefillat ha-Yiḥud* ascribed to R. Neḥunya b. ha-Kanah), and of forces which are called by magical names whose meaning cannot be communicated but which denote the various concentrations of power that can be differentiated in emanation. As early as Moses of Burgos and Joseph Gikatilla it is stressed that from each *Sefirah* are suspended worlds of its own that do not form part of the hierarchical order of the worlds that follow the world of emanation. In other words, the total power of each *Sefirah* cannot be expressed simply with reference to the known creation. There are aspects that have other purposes: hidden worlds of love, of justice, and so on. Gikatilla speaks of millions of worlds.[5] In the Zohar descriptions of this type occur only in relation to the world of *Keter (Arikh Anpin,* lit. "the long face," properly "the long-suffering God") and the world of *Tiferet* (*Ze'eir Anpin,* lit. "the short face," properly "the impatient One") and take the form of a description of the anatomy of "the white head," written with an extreme tendency to anthropomorphism. Parts of the "head" symbolize the ways in which God acts: the brow refers to His acts of grace, the eye to His providence, the ear to His acceptance of prayer, the beard to the 13 facets of mercy, and so on. An allegorization of the theological concepts in the doctrine of the attributes, a symbolism which views its own imagery as an accurate allusion to that which is beyond all images, and an attempt to reconcile the apparently incompatible doctrines of the *Sefirot* and the earlier *Shi'ur Komah* – all meet in these symbols of the *Idrot* of the Zohar. The author never states openly that his descriptions entail a positing of "*Sefirot* within *Sefirot*" (which are mentioned in the bulk of the Zohar and also in the Hebrew writings of Moses de Leon, but only incidentally and without any detail). Apparently he saw no need to offer any speculative theory to justify his use of corporeal images, so difficult to probe rationally in any detail. His world was symbolic rather than conceptual. However, the kabbalists from the beginning of the 14th century did give such "revelations" a theoretical interpretation, starting with the *Sefer ha-Gevul* (based on the *Idra Rabba* in the Zohar) by David b. Judah he-Ḥasid and ending with Cordovero's *Elimah Rabbati* and his commentary to the Zohar. A similar doctrine is also evident in the writings of Joseph b. Shalom Ashkenazi. In their meditations on these internal reflections of the *Sefirot* within one another some kabbalists, such as Joseph ibn Sayyaḥ went as far as to describe in detail the play of lights inside the *Sefirot* to the fourth "degree," as, for example, the "*Tiferet* which is in *Gedullah* which is in *Binah* which is in *Keter.*" Cordovero too went further along this path than most kabbalists.

In Cordovero's teachings this theory of *Sefirot* within *Sefirot* is connected with another – that of the *beḥinot,* the infinite number of aspects which can be differentiated within each *Sefirah* and whose main purpose is to explain how each *Sefirah* is connected with both the preceding and the following ones. According to Cordovero, there are, in the main, six of these aspects in each *Sefirah*: (1) its concealed aspect before its manifestation in the *Sefirah* which emanates it; (2) the aspect in which it is manifested and apparent in the emanating *Sefirah*; (3) the aspect in which it mat rializes in its correct spiritual location, that is to say, as an independent *Sefirah* in it own right; (4) the aspect which enables the *Sefirah* above it to instill within it the power to emanate further *Sefirot;* (5) the aspect by which it gains the power to emanate the *Sefirot* hidden within it to their manifested existence within its own essence; and (6) the aspect by which the following *Sefirah* is emanated to its own place, at which point the cycle begins again. This complete array of *beḥinot* is seen as causal relationship, each *beḥinah* causing the awakening and the manifestation of the following *beḥinah* (*Pardes Rimmonim* ch. 5, 5). But there are many other "aspects" in the *Sefirot* as well and their discovery depends on the perspective of their investigator. Each *Sefirah* "descends into itself," and the process of this descent is infinite in its internal reflections. At the same time, however, it is also finite, in that it begets or brings into being from within itself another *Sefirah.* This concept necessitates the premise that the roots of emanation have a concealed "aspect" in *Ein-Sof* itself, and Cordovero interprets the three *ẓaḥẓaḥot* mentioned above as the three hidden *beḥinot* of *Keter* in *Ein-Sof.* He is thus forced to demolish the natural boundary between *Ein-Sof* and the first *Sefirah,* despite his clear desire to establish such a natural division. He therefore postulates that the *beḥinot* of *Keter* within *Keter* within *Keter* and so on, although they potentially continue *ad infinitum,* do not in fact reach an identity with the essence of the Emanator, so that the propinquity of *Ein-Sof* and *Keter* remains asymptotic. All this, of course, is stated from the point of view of created beings for even the supernal awakening of "aspects" of the Will within the Will within the Will and so on does not reveal *Ein-Sof,* and it is this differential which comprises the leap from the essence of the Emanator to that of the emanated. On the other hand, the differential gap closes when it is regarded from the point of view of the Emanator Himself. Cordovero's doctrine of the *beḥinot* shows how closely he approached a clearly dialectic mode of thought within the framework of kabbalistic ideas. With Cordovero the *Sefirot* are more than emanations which manifest the attributes of the Emanator, though they are this too. They actually become the structural elements of all beings, even of the self-manifesting God Himself. The implied contradiction between the processes of emanation and structuralism was never fully resolved by Cordovero himself, and it appears even in the systematic presentation of his ideas in *Shefa Tal* by Shabbetai Sheftel Horowitz. In such works as *Elimah Rabbati* and *Shefa Tal* zoharic Kabbalah undergoes an extremely profound speculative transformation in which as far as possible theosophy dispenses with its mythical foundations. Nevertheless, it is evident that this speculative trend does not turn Kabbalah into philosophy, and that the acknowledgement of a hidden life within the deity – the process of the emanation of the *Sefirot* – depends finally on mystical intuition, for by it alone can this domain be understood. In the Zohar this intuition is called "fleeting vision [of the eternal]" (*istakluta le-fum sha'ata;* 2:74b; ZḤ 38c), and this is the element that the prophet and the kabbalist have in common (1:97a and b).

In addition to the process of emanation which takes place between the *Sefirot*, there are two symbolistic modes of expressing the way in which each *Sefirah* radiates upon the others:

(1) Reflected light. This is based on the premise that, in addition to the direct light which spreads from one *Sefirah* to the next, there is a light which is reflected back from the lower *Sefirot* to the upper. The *Sefirot* can be seen as both a medium for the transference of the light from above to below, and as a mirror serving to reflect the light back to its source. This reflected light can re-ascend from any *Sefirah,* particularly from the last one, back up to the first, and it acts on its return path as an additional stimulus that causes the differentiation of still further *beḥinot* in each *Sefirah.* Reflected light, according to Cordovero (*Pardes* 15), fulfills a great task in the consolidation of the potencies and *beḥinot* of judgment *(din)* in each *Sefirah*, for it functions through a process of restrictive contraction rather than free expansion. Only marginally based on early Kabbalah – e.g., the statements in the Zohar on the relationships among the first three *Sefirot* – this doctrine was developed by Solomon Alkabez

and Cordovero alone and it formed an important factor in their dialectical reasoning.

(2) Channels. This is based on the premise that specific *Sefirot* stand in particular relationships of radiation with other *Sefirot* (though not necessarily with all of them). The face of one *Sefirah* turns toward another and consequently there develops between them a "channel" *(ẓinnor)* of influence which is not identical with actual emanation. Such channels are paths of reciprocal influence between different *Sefirot.* This process is not a one-way influx from cause to effect; it also operates from effect to cause, dialectically turning the effect into a cause.

It is not clear to what extent there is any identity between the symbols of reflected light and channels nor, if there is none at all, what their relationship is. Any interruption in the return influx from below to above is called a "breaking of the channels" (*shevirat ha-ẓinnorot;* Gikatilla, *Sha'arei Orah*), an idea which serves to explain the relations between the lower and upper worlds on the occasion of sin and divine disapproval. These channels are alluded to by the Gerona kabbalists, Gikatilla, Joseph of Hamadan *(Shushan ha-Birah),* if this is the real name of the author of a commentary to Song of Songs and to the *parashah Terumah* in British Museum Ms. Margoliouth 464, mentioned above, as well as other kabbalists of the 14th and 15th centuries, and the doctrine is presented in detail in chapter 7 of *Pardes Rimmonim.*

EARLIER WORLDS, LOWER WORLDS, AND COSMIC CYCLES (THE DOCTRINE OF THE *SHEMITTOT*)

The emergence of God from the depths of Himself into creation, which constitutes the foundation of the doctrine of the *Sefirot,* was not always understood as a single, uninterrupted, straightforward process. In other views of the process of emanation and creation, a vital role was played by the midrashic legend concerning the worlds which were created and destroyed before the creation of our present world. An important variation of this idea lies at the root of a doctrine of the *Idrot* in the Zohar, in which the *Midrash* and other similar *aggadot* are connected with a description of how God entered into the form of the *Adam Kadmon* or Primordial Man, or into the different configurations of this form. Here we have a motif whose origin is in no way consistent with the classical formulation of the *Sefirot* doctrine, as can be easily seen from its reversed treatment of the male-female principle. Unlike in classical tradition, the male principle is considered here to be the principle of *din* or strict judgment which needs softening and "sweetening" by the female principle. A creation dominated solely by the forces of judgment could not survive. The exact nature of such earlier, unsuccessful creations, however – called in the Zohar "the Kings of Edom" or "the Primeval Kings" (*malkhei Edom* or *malkin Kadma'in*) – is not made plain. It was only when the form of Primordial Man was fashioned perfectly, with a harmonious balance between the male and the female forces, that creation was able to sustain itself. This balance is called in the Zohar *matkela* ("the scales"), and only through its power did our world come into being. The biblical list of the kings of Edom (Gen. 35:31 ff.) was interpreted in the light of this doctrine, for Edom was understood to represent the principle of judgment.

The author of the Zohar also expressed this doctrine in other ways. The worlds which preceded ours and were destroyed were like the sparks that scatter and die away when the forger strikes the iron with his hammer. This doctrine, in a completely new version, acquired a central place in Lurianic Kabbalah, while still other kabbalists tried to divest it of its literal meaning because of its theological difficulties. Cordovero's interpretation related it to the emanation of the *Sefirot* themselves, and to the dialectical process within each *Sefirah* – an interpretation quite out of keeping with the original idea. Other kabbalists of the Zohar period, such as Isaac ha-Kohen of Soria, expressed similar ideas, which they connected with the development of a "left-sided" emanation, that is, of an emanation of the forces of evil. The common element in all these doctrines is the supposition that during the first steps toward emanation certain abortive developments took place that had no direct effect on the actual creation of the present worlds, although remnants of these destroyed worlds did not entirely disappear and something of them still hovers disruptively among us.

Spanish Kabbalah concentrated its thinking on the emanation and structure of the *Sefirot*, a subject which is not dealt with at all in the writings of the philosophers. As regards the continuity of this process below the level of the last *Sefirah*, the kabbalists were in the main deeply influenced by medieval philosophical cosmology. Most kabbalists agreed that there was no essential break in the continuity of the influx of emanation which led to the development of additional areas of creation as well, such as the world of the intellect, the world of the spheres, and the lower world. But they maintained that whatever preceded these secondary stages was part of the divine domain, which they symbolically portrayed as a series of events in the world of emanation, whereas from this point on, the outward movement departed from the realm of the Godhead and was thought of as a creation distinct from the divine unity. This fundamental distinction between "the world of unity" of the *Sefirot* and "the world of separate intelligences" that was below them was made as early as the beginning of the 13th century. When the philosophers spoke of "separate intelligences," however, which they identify with the angels, they thought of them as immaterial beings representing pure form, whereas in kabbalistic language the term refers rather to a separation from the sefirotic unity of the divine domain.

As the Kabbalah developed, the world of the Merkabah (see above p.10) described in the *heikhalot* literature became quite clearly distinguished from the world of the divine above it. The former was now often called "the domain of the Throne," and a rich angelology developed around it which was only partly identical with the earlier angelology of the Merkabah literature. In the bulk of the Zohar there are detailed descriptions of the inhabitants of the seven "palaces" which spread out below the *Sefirah Malkhut* and are the products of its emanative influx, and which have little in common with the *heikhalot* of earlier literature. No fixed hierarchical order had been established in earlier Kabbalah for the world of the angels, and the writings of various 13th- and 14th-century kabbalists contain quite different angelogical systems. Such systems occupy an important place in the works of Isaac ha-Kohen, his brother Jacob, and their pupil Moses of Burgos, all of whom spoke in detail of secondary emanations which served as garments for the *Sefirot* and were situated even higher than the most prominent angels in the traditional angelology, such as Michael, Raphael, Gabriel, and so on. Other systems occur in the *Tikkunei Zohar,* in the *Sod Darkhei ha-Nekuddot ve-ha-Otiyyot* attributed to the school of Abraham b. David of Posquières, in the books of David b. Judah ha-Ḥasid and Joseph of Hamadan. Sometimes a distinction was made between the Merkabah as a symbol of the world of the *Sefirot* themselves, and the *mirkevet ha-mishneh,* or "second chariot," which represented the domain that came after the *Sefirah Malkhut,* and was itself divided into ten *Sefirot* of its own. Everything below the last *Sefirah* is subject to time and is called *beri'ah* ("creation") since it is outside *(le-var)* the Godhead.

The general scheme of a world of the Godhead and the *Sefirot,* and of the intelligences and the spheres, did not prevent many kabbalists, such as the author of the Zohar and Gikatilla, from supposing the existence of a very large number of secondary worlds within each one of these primary worlds. This expansion of an originally narrower cosmological framework is analogous to similar motifs in Indian thought, although there is no need to try to establish a direct historical link between the two. Every stage in the process of creation is crystallized in a specific world where the creative power of the Creator achieves the perfect expression of one of its many aspects. At the same time, we can trace the development of a unified doctrine of a series of worlds from above to below forming one basic vector along which creation passes from its primeval point to its finalization in the material world.[6] The outcome of this development, in which Jewish, Aristotelian, and neoplatonic principles were all mingled together, was a new doctrine of four basic worlds, called *olam ha-aẓilut* (the world of emanation – the ten *Sefirot*), *olam ha-beriah* (the world of creation – the Throne and the Chariot), *olam ha-yeẓirah* (the world of formation – sometimes the world of the angels centered around Metatron), and *olam ha-asiyyah* (the world of making – which sometimes includes both the whole system of the spheres and the terrestrial world, and sometimes the terrestrial world only). This arrangement, although mostly without the nomenclature of "worlds," is already mentioned by Moses de Leon and some parts of the Zohar, particularly in the *Tikkunei Zohar.* It appears in the form of four actual worlds in the *Massekhet Aẓilut,* a pseudepigraphic treatise from the beginning of the 14th century (ed. in Jellinek, *Answahl Kabbalistischer Mystik,* 1853). Isaac of Acre also made frequent use of this arrangement and gave it, for the first time, the abbreviated name *abiya (aẓilut, beri'ah, yeẓirah, asiyyah).* However, the doctrine was not fully developed until the 16th century when the kabbalists of Safed went into the details even of the worlds of *beri'ah* and *yeẓirah,* particularly Cordovero and the school of Isaac Luria. In the *Tikkunei Zohar* the world of *asiyyah* was understood as the domain of the material world and of evil spirits, while according to the *Massekhet Aẓilut* it included the whole range of creation from the angels (known as *ofannim*) through the ten spheres to the world of matter. According to Lurianic Kabbalah, all the worlds, including the world of *asiyyah,* were originally spiritual, but through the "breaking of the vessels" the world of *asiyyah,* after its descent from its earlier position, was commingled with the *kelippot* or impure "husks", which in principle should have remained completely separate and produced a world of matter that contained nothing spiritual. The ten *Sefirot* are active in all four worlds according to their adaptation to each one, so that it is possible to speak of the *Sefirot* of the world of *beri'ah,* the *Sefirot* of the world of *yeẓirah,* and so on. Some concomitant of the *Sefirot* may be seen in the lower world also. Even the image of *Adam Kadmon* is reflected in each of these worlds (*adam di-veriyah, adam de-aẓilut,* etc., as in the writings of Moses de Leon, in the *Ra'aya Meheimna* and the *Tikkunim*). Even the terrestrial world of nature may be called *adam ha-gadol* ("the great man"; macroanthropos). In another kabbalistic view dating to the period of the expulsion from Spain, nature is defined as *ẓel Shaddai,* that is the shadow of the Divine Name.

Beginning in the 13th century, and especially from the 15th and 16th centuries, the kabbalists tried to make pictorial representations of the structure of creation as it progressed from *Ein-Sof* downward. Such diagrams were generally called *ilanot* ("trees"), and the obvious differences between them reflect divergences among the various doctrines and schemes of symbolism. Drawings of this kind are found in a large number of manuscripts. A detailed pictorial representation of the Lurianic system, called *ilan ha-gadol* ("the great tree"), which was made by Meir Poppers, has been published, first in the form of a long scroll (Warsaw, 1864) and later as a book (Warsaw, 1893). Another detailed Lurianic "tree" *(tabula)* was included in Knorr Von Rosenroth, *Kabbalah Denudata* I, part 5, 193–255 (in 16 plates).

These speculations were accorded a unique form in the doctrine of the *shemittot* or cosmic cycles which was based on a fixed periodicity in creation. Although dependent on aggadic motifs, this doctrine displays some relationship with similar non-Jewish systems, whose influence on Jewish authors can be traced in Muslim countries and in Spain, particularly in the writings of Abraham bar Ḥiyya. In his *Megillat ha-Megalleh,* he speaks of unnamed "philosophers" who believed in a long, even infinite series of cyclical creations. Some of them, he said, maintained that the world would last for 49,000 years, that each of the seven planets would rule for 7,000 years, and that God would then destroy the world and restore it to chaos in the 50th millennium, only to subsequently recreate it once again. These were astrological ideas drawn from Arabic and Greek sources, which could easily be assimilated to certain views expressed in the *aggadah,* such as the statement of Rav Katina (Sanh. 97a) that the world would last for 6,000 years and be destroyed in the seventh millennium, in which a parallel is drawn between the days of creation and those of the world, seen as a great cosmic week, at the end of which it "rests" and is destroyed. The earlier kabbalists related these ideas to their own doctrine of emanation. Their new teaching concerning the cycles of creation, which was widely referred to and even summarized in the Kabbalah of Gerona, was fully articulated, although in a highly cryptic style, in the *Sefer ha-Temunah,* which was written about 1250. The main point of this doctrine is that it is the *Sefirot* and not the stars that determine the progress and span of the world. The first three *Sefirot* remain concealed and do not activate "worlds" outside themselves – or at least not worlds that we can recognize as such. From the *Sefirah Binah,* also called "the mother of the world," the seven apprehendable and outgoing *Sefirot* are emanated. Each one of these *Sefirot* has a special role in one creation-cycle, which comes under its dominion and is influenced by its specific nature. Each such cosmic cycle, bound to one of the *Sefirot,* is called a *shemittah* or sabbatical year – a term taken from Deuteronomy 15 – and has an active life of 6,000 years. In the seventh millennium, which is the *shemittah* period, the Sabbath-day of the cycle, the sefirotic forces cease to function and the world returns to chaos. Subsequently, the world is renewed through the power of the following *Sefirah,* and is active for a new cycle. At the end of all the *shemittot* there is the "great jubilee," when not only all the lower worlds but the seven supporting *Sefirot* themselves are reabsorbed into *Binah.* The basic unit of world history is therefore the 50,000 year jubilee, which is subdivided as described above. The details of this doctrine in the *Sefer Temunah* are complicated by the fact that, according to the author, the *Sefirah Yesod,* which is also called *Shabbat,* does not activate a manifest *shemittah* of its own. Rather, its *shemittah* remains concealed and works through the power of the other cosmic cycles. Nor is there explicit mention here of any new cycle of creation after the jubilee. According to the kabbalists of Gerona, the laws in the Torah concerning the sabbatical and jubilee years refer to this mystery of recurrent creation.

An even more radical doctrine came into being in the 13th century, according to which the world-process lasts for no less than 18,000 jubilees (Baḥya b. Asher, on the Torah portion *Be-Ha'alotekha*). Moreover, the actual chronology of these calculations is not to be taken literally, because the *Sefer ha-Temunah* teaches that in the seventh millennium there sets in a gradual and progressive retardation in the movement of the stars and the spheres, so that the measurements of time change and become longer in geometrical progression. Fifty thousand "years" therefore becomes a much longer period. Hence, other kabbalists, and Isaac of Acre in particular, arrived at truly astronomical figures for the total duration of the world. Some kabbalists thought that after each "great jubilee" a new creation would begin *ex nihilo,* a view which passed from Baḥya b. Asher to Isaac Abrabanel, and from him to his son Judah, who mentioned it in his famous Italian work, *Dialoghi di Amore.* These views were also accepted much later by the author of *Gallei Razaya* (1552), and even by Manasseh Ben Israel. No kabbalist posited an infinite number of jubilees. In contrast to such enormous vistas, others maintained that we do not know what will follow the jubilee and that investigation of the subject is forbidden.

There were also divergent views on the question of which *shemittah* in the jubilee period we are living in now. Generally speaking, the accepted position was that of the *Sefer ha-Temunah,* namely, that we are now in the *shemittah* of judgment, dominated by the *Sefirah Gevurah,* and the principle of strict justice. Consequently, this must have been preceded by the *shemittah* of *Ḥesed* or lovingkindness, which is described as a kind of "golden age," akin to that of Greek mythology. According to another view (for example that of the *Livnat ha-Sappir* by Joseph Angelino), we are in the last *shemittah* of the present jubilee period. Each *shemittah* experiences a revelation of the Torah, which is simply the complete articulation of the Divine Name or Tetragrammaton, but comprehension of it, that is, the combination of its letters, differs in every *shemittah*. Therefore, in the previous *shemittah* the Torah was read completely differently and did not contain the prohibitions which are the product of the power of judgment; similarly, it will be read differently in the *shemittot* to come. The *Sefer ha-Temunah* and other sources contain descriptions of the final *shemittah* which are of a distinctly utopian character. In their view, some souls from the previous *shemittah* still exist in our own, which is governed by a universal law of transmigration that includes the animal kingdom as well. As the power of judgment is mitigated in subsequent *shemittot*, so laws and customs will be relaxed also. This doctrine allowed tremendous play to the power of the imagination, which was particularly exploited by Isaac of Acre. It should be noted that in itself the premise that one and the same Torah could be revealed in a different form in each *shemittah* did not at the time arouse any open opposition, and was even extended by some who maintained that the Torah was read differently in each of the millions of worlds involved in the complex of creation – a view first expressed in Gikatilla's *Sha'arei Ẓedek.*[7] One of the most extreme manifestations of this belief was the theory that in the present *shemittah* one of the letters of the alphabet is missing and will be revealed only in the future. Thus the reading of the Torah will obviously be absolutely transformed.

The influence of the *Sefer ha-Temunah* and the doctrine of the *shemittot* was extremely strong and still had its champions as late as the 17th century. However, the author of the Zohar ignored it completely, apparently out of some fundamental disagreement, although he too held that there was a great jubilee lasting 50,000 years in the world. As the Zohar became increasingly recognized as the authoritative and chief source for later Kabbalah, this silence on the subject strengthened opposition to the doctrine. Joseph ibn Zayyaḥ, Cordovero, and Isaac Luria rejected it as a mistaken or unnecessary hypothesis, at least in the version found in the *Sefer ha-Temunah,* and as a result of their influence it more or less disappeared from later kabbalistic literature. However, Mordecai Yaffe, a contemporary of Isaac Luria, was still teaching at the end of the 16th century that sequences of *shemittot* existed, even within the limits of historical time. The *shemittah* of *Din* ("judgment") began precisely at the time of the giving of the Torah, while everything that preceded it still belonged to the end of the *shemittah* of *Ḥesed* ("lovingkindness"). Its visionary utopianism and its mystical theory concerning the changing manifestations of the essence of the Torah were without doubt among the main reasons why the doctrine of *shemittot* was accepted so widely in kabbalistic circles. The disciples of Shabbetai Ẓevi made much of it, stressing its inherently antinomian implications.

THE PROBLEM OF EVIL

The question of the origin and nature of evil was one of the principal motivating forces behind kabbalistic speculation. In the importance attached to it lies one of the basic differences between kabbalistic doctrine and Jewish philosophy, which gave little original thought to the problem of evil. Various kabbalistic solutions were proffered. The *Ma'arekhet ha-Elohut* reveals the influence of the conventional neoplatonist position that evil has no objective reality and is merely relative. Man is unable to receive all the influx from the *Sefirot,* and it is this inadequacy which is the origin of evil, which has therefore only a negative reality. The determining factor is the estrangement of created things from their source of emanation, a separation which leads to manifestations of what appears to us to be the power of evil. But the latter has no metaphysical reality, and it is doubtful whether the author of the *Ma'arekhet ha-Elohut* and his disciples believed in the existence of a separate domain of evil outside the structure of the *Sefirot.* On the other hand we already find in the *Sefer ha-Bahir* a definition of the *Sefirah Gevurah,* as "the left hand of the Holy One blessed be He," and as "a quality whose name is evil" and which has many offshoots in the forces of judgment, the constricting and limiting powers in the universe. As early as Isaac the Blind this led to the conclusion that there must of necessity be a positive root of evil and death, which was balanced within the unity of the Godhead by the root of goodness and life. During the process of differentiation of these forces below the *Sefirot,* however, evil became substantified as a separate manifestation. Hence the doctrine gradually developed which saw the source of evil in the superabundant growth of the power of judgment which was made possible by the substantification and separation of the quality of judgment from its customary union with the quality of lovingkindness. Pure judgment, untempered by any mitigating admixture, produced from within itself the *sitra aḥra* ("the other side"), just as a vessel which is filled to overflowing spills its superfluous liquid on the ground. This *sitra aḥra,* the domain of dark emanations and demonic powers, is henceforth no longer an organic part of the World of Holiness and the *Sefirot.* Though it emerged from one of the attributes of God, it cannot be an essential part of Him. This view became dominant in the Kabbalah through the writings of the Gerona kabbalists and the Zohar.

According to the "Gnostics" of Castile and, in a different version, the Zohar also, there exists a complete hierarchy of the "emanation of the left," which is the power of uncleanliness that is active in creation. However, this objective reality lasts only as long as it continues to receive fresh strength from the *Sefirah Gevurah,* which is in the holy order of the *Sefirot,* and in particular, only as long as man revives and fortifies it through his own sinful deeds. According to the Zohar, this *sitra aḥra* has ten *Sefirot* ("crowns") of its own, and a similar view, albeit with several variations and the addition of certain mythical elements, is expressed in the writings of Isaac ha-Kohen and in *Ammud ha-Semali* by his pupil, Moses of Burgos. Isaac ha-Kohen taught that the first worlds that were destroyed were three dark emanations, which perished because of the overly concentrated power of strict judgment that they contained. The force of evil in this world, he argues, does not come from the *Sefirah Gevurah* but is a continuation of the *Sefirah Binah* that was substantified in the destructive potencies corresponding to the seven constructive *Sefirot* of creation. These two forces battle with one another from the beginning of creation itself.

In the Zohar too it is implied that the evil in the universe originated from the leftovers of worlds that were destroyed. The power of evil is compared to the bark *(kelippah)* of the tree of emanation, a symbol which originated with Azriel of Gerona[8] and became quite common from the Zohar onward. Some kabbalists called the totality of the emanation of the left "the outer tree" *(ha-ilan ha-ḥiẓon)*. Another association, found in the Gerona kabbalists, and following them in the Zohar as well, is with "the mystery of the Tree of Knowledge." The Tree of Life and the Tree of Knowledge were bound together in perfect harmony until Adam came and separated them, thereby giving substance to evil, which had been contained within the Tree of Knowledge of Good and Evil and was now materialized in the evil instinct *(yeẓer ha-ra)*. It was Adam therefore who activated the potential evil concealed within the Tree of Knowledge by separating the two trees and also by separating the Tree of Knowledge from its fruit, which was now detached from its source. This event is called metaphorically "the cutting of the shoots" *(kiẓẓuẓ ha-neti'ot)* and is the archetype of all the great sins mentioned in the Bible, whose common denominator was the introduction of division into the divine unity. The essence of Adam's sin was that it introduced "separation above and below" into what should have been united, a separation of which every sin is fundamentally a repetition – apart, that is, from sins involving magic and sorcery, which according to the kabbalists join together what should have remained separate. In actual fact, this view too tends to stress the separation of the power of judgment contained within the Tree of Knowledge from the power of lovingkindness contained within the Tree of Life. The latter pours out its influx unstintingly, while the former is a restrictive force with a tendency to become autonomous. This it can do either as the result of man's actions or of a metaphysical process in the upper worlds.

Both these views appear concurrently in kabbalistic literature without any clear distinction being drawn between them. The cosmic evil stemming from the inner dialectic of the process of emanation is not differentiated here from the moral evil produced by human action. The Zohar tries to bridge these two realms by positing that the disposition toward moral corruption, toward evil in the guise of human temptation, derives from the cosmic evil which is the domain of the *sitra aḥra* (3: 163a). The basic difference between the Zohar and the writings of the Gnostics in Castile was that the latter indulged in exaggerated personifications of the powers in this domain, resorting on occasion to earlier demonological belief, and calling the potencies of "the emanation of the left" by proper names, whereas the author of the Zohar generally kept to more impersonal categories, with the exception of the figures of Samael – the kabbalistic equivalent of Satan – and his mate Lilith (see p.356 and p.385), to whom he assigned a central role in the realm of evil. Another departure from this rule is his detailed description of the "palaces of impurity" with their guardians in his commentary on Exodus 38–40 (2:262–9), which follows a parallel description of the "palaces of holiness."

In the symbolism of the Zohar concerning the *sitra aḥra,* a number of different themes confront and occasionally even conflict with one another. The *kelippot* ("shells" or "husks" of evil) are sometimes understood neoplatonically as the last links of the chain of emanation where all turns to darkness, as "the end of days" in the metaphor of the Zohar. At other times they are defined simply as intermediaries between the upper and lower worlds, and as such they are not necessarily seen as evil. Indeed, every mediating principle is a "shell" from the perspective of that which is above it but a "kernel" from the point of view of that which is below (Zohar, 1:19b). In other descriptions the domain of evil is delineated as the natural waste product of an organic process and is compared to bad blood, a bitter branch on the tree of emanation, foul waters (2:167b), the dross which remains after the gold has been refined *(hittukhei ha-zahav),* or the dregs from good wine. Such descriptions of the *sitra aḥra* in the Zohar are particularly rich in mythical images. The identification of evil with physical matter, though it occurs occasionally in the Zohar and in other kabbalistic books, never became an accepted doctrine of either. The equivocation of medieval philosophy between the Aristotelian and the Platonic-emanatist concepts of matter is equally strongly felt in the Kabbalah, although the problem of how matter is emanated is referred to only infrequently. Generally speaking, the question of the nature of matter is not central in the Kabbalah, where the major interest was rather the question of how the Divine was reflected in matter. Occasional discussions of the nature of matter from a neoplatonic viewpoint can already be found in the literature of the *Sefer ha-Iyyun* circle. Cordovero, in his *Rabbati Elimah,* explains the emanation of matter from spirit by means of a dialectic treatment of the concept of form that was common in medieval philosophy.

According to the Zohar there is a spark of holiness even in the domain of "the other side," whether from an emanation of the last *Sefirah* or as an indirect result of man's sin, for just as the fulfillment of a commandment strengthens the side of holiness, so a sinful act revitalizes the *sitra aḥra.* The realms of good and evil are to an extent commingled, and man's mission is to separate them. In contrast to this view which acknowledges the metaphysical existence of evil, an alternative approach has found its basic expression in Gikatilla, who defined evil as an entity which was not in its rightful place: "every act of God, when it is in the place accorded to it at creation, is good; but if it turns and leaves its place, it is evil." These two views – that of the Zohar, which accords evil actual existence as the fire of God's anger and justice, and that of Gikatilla, which attributes to it only a potential existence that nothing can activate save the deeds of men – occur throughout kabbalistic literature without any victory of one over the other. Even in the different versions of Lurianic doctrine the two are perpetually in conflict. (On the problem of evil in the Lurianic Kabbalah see below.) A subsequent and final development in regard to the problem of evil occurred in the doctrine of the Shabbateans, as formulated particularly in the writings of Nathan of Gaza. According to him, there were from the very beginning two lights in *Ein-Sof*: "the light which contained thought" and "the light which did not contain thought." The first had in it from the very beginning the thought of creating worlds, while in the latter there was no such thought, its whole essence striving toward remaining concealed and resting within itself without emerging from the mystery of *Ein-Sof*. The first light was entirely active and the second light entirely passive and immersed in the depths of itself. When the thought of creation arose in the first light, it contracted to make room for this creation, but the thought-less light which had no share in creation remained in its place. Since it had no other purpose but to rest in itself, it passively resisted the structure of emanation which the light containing thought had built in the vacuum created by its own contraction. This resistance turned the light without thought into the ultimate source of evil in the work of creation. The idea of a dualism between matter and form as being the root of good and evil here assumes a most original pattern: the root of evil is a principle within *Ein-Sof* itself, which holds itself aloof from creation and seeks to prevent the forms of the light which contains thought from being actualized, not because it is evil by nature but only because its whole desire is that nothing should exist apart from *Ein-Sof*. It refuses to receive within itself the light that contains thought, and consequently it strives to frustrate and destroy whatever is constructed by that light. Evil is therefore the outcome of a dialectic between two aspects of the light of *Ein-Sof* itself. Its activity arises from its opposition to change. The affinity of this idea to the neoplatonic view of matter as the principle of evil is obvious. The struggle between the two lights is renewed at every stage of creation, nor will it come to an end until the time of final redemption, when the light that contains thought will penetrate through and through the light without thought and delineate therein its holy forms. The *sitra aḥra* of the Zohar is no more than the totality of the structure which the light without thought is forced to produce as a result of this struggle. As the process of creation goes on, the struggle becomes sharper, because the light of thought wants by its very nature to penetrate all the space that has been vacated by its contraction and to leave nothing untouched in that formless, primordial realm that Nathan calls *golem* (the formless *hyle*). The premise that the principles of both good and evil exist together in the supreme mind of God and that there is no other possible logical solution to the problem of evil in a monotheistic system was shared by Leibnitz, who approached the problem similarly some 40 years later in his *Théodicée.*

Although there is no doubt that most kabbalists held that evil did have a real existence at various levels, even though it functioned through negation, they were divided in their views concerning the eschatological problem of how it would finally be terminated both in the world and in man. Would the power of evil be totally destroyed in the time to come? Would it perhaps survive, but without any possibility of influencing the redeemed world once good and evil, which had become intermingled, had now been finally separated? Or would evil perhaps be transformed into good once more? The view that in the future world, whenever that would be, all things would return to their original holy state, had eminent advocates from the days of the Gerona kabbalists onward. Naḥmanides spoke of "the return of all things to their true essence" – a concept drawn perhaps from Christian eschatology and the doctrine of *apokatasis* (reintegration) – and he meant by this the reascent of every created being to its source in emanation which would no longer leave room for the continued existence of the realm of evil in creation or of the power of the evil instinct in man. It would appear, indeed, that this return was connected in his view with the great jubilee, according to the doctrine of the *shemittot.* Such a position accepted the reality of evil within the different *shemittot,* in each *shemittah* according to its specific nature.

Generally speaking, kabbalistic arguments about the ultimate fate of evil limited themselves to the time of the redemption and the final day of judgment. The dominant view was that the power of evil would be destroyed and disappear, since there would be no longer any justification for its continued existence. However, others held that the evil domain would survive as the place of eternal punishment for the wicked. A certain vacillation between these two beliefs is found in both the Zohar and Lurianic Kabbalah. On the whole, the Zohar emphasizes that the power of the *kelippot* will be terminated and "broken" in the time to come, and in a number of places it states quite plainly that the *sitra aḥra* "will pass from the world" and the light of holiness will shine "without hindrance." Gikatilla states, on the other hand, that in the time to come "God will take the attribute of [punishing] misfortune [i.e., the power of evil] to a place where it will not be able to be malignant" (*Sha'arei Orah,* ch. 4).

Those who upheld the doctrine that evil would once more become good claimed that Samael himself would repent and be transformed into an angel of holiness, which would automatically cause the disappearance of the realm of the *sitra aḥra.* This view is expressed in the book *Kaf ha-Ketoret* (1500), and particularly in the *Asarah Ma'amarot* of Menahem Azariah Fano, but is opposed in the writings of Vital, who took a less liberal position. A powerful symbolic statement of Samael's future return to sanctity, and one particularly common from the 17th century onward, was the view that his name would be changed, the letter *mem* signifying death *(mavet)* dropping out to leave Sa'el, one of the 72 holy Names of God.

THE DOCTRINE OF CREATION IN LURIANIC KABBALAH

The one factor common to all kabbalistic doctrines of emanation and creation before Isaac Luria was their belief in an inner uni-directional development that led from the first stirring of *Ein-Sof* toward creation by means of more or less continuous stages. This process was prone to assume more complex forms and to go beyond the general doctrine of the ten *Sefirot,* to delve into the inner dynamic of the *Sefirot* themselves, or to describe the world of emanation through other symbolic systems, such as that of the mutually evolving, mutually conjoining Names of God. But the basic theme always remained the same: the progressive manifestation of *Ein-Sof* as articulated through the processes of emanation and creation. Even the classic formulation of this doctrine in the books of Cordovero, with all its dialectic complexity, does not diverge from this basic line. In contrast to this, we find a crucial turning-point in Lurianic cosmogony, whose very dramatic conception introduced far-reaching changes in the structure of kabbalistic thought. The details of this system are extremely complex even where they are clearly expounded, as for example, with regard to the principal acts of the creation drama, to say nothing of its many obscurities that mystical meditation alone can perhaps comprehend. Lurianic doctrine created an enormous chasm between *Ein-Sof* and the world of emanation, which in previous kabbalistic teachings had been closely bound together, and then proceeded to fill it with divine acts of which the earlier Kabbalah had known nothing, although they can often be better understood against the background of older motifs. The principal accounts of the stages of creation found in the different versions of Lurianic doctrine given in the writings of his disciples and their pupils (on these sources, see the section on Luria p. 420) are basically similar, but they vary in emphasis and in the speculative interpretations they give to the significance of the main acts of creation. It may indeed be said that with Isaac Luria a new period of kabbalistic speculation was inaugurated which must be distinguished from earlier Kabbalah in almost all respects.

This new Kabbalah was based on three main doctrines, which determined its character: *ẓimẓum;* "the breaking of the vessels" *(shevirah);* and *tikkun.*

ẒIMẒUM ("CONTRACTION")

The basic source of this doctrine is found in an early fragment from the circle of the *Sefer ha-Iyyun* (a preface to a commentary on "the 32 paths of wisdom" in a Florence Ms.) which speaks of an act of divine contraction that preceded emanations: "How did He produce and create this world? Like a man who gathers in and contracts *(meẓamẓem)* his breath [Shem Tov b. Shem Tov has, "and contracts Himself"], so that the smaller might contain the larger, so He contracted His light into a hand's breadth, according to His own measure, and the world was left in darkness, and in that darkness He cut boulders and hewed rocks." Here the reference is to the creation of *Keṭer*, which was thought to evolve from an act of contraction that left room for that darkness which alone was *Keter.* This was also in fact Naḥmanides view in his commentary to the *Sefer Yeẓirah,* but not until Luria was the idea elevated to a basic cosmological principle.

The main originality of this Lurianic doctrine lay in the notion that the first act of *Ein-Sof* was not one of revelation and emanation, but, on the contrary, was one of concealment and limitation. The symbols employed here indicate an extremely naturalistic point of departure for understanding the beginning of creation and their audacity made them problematic. Not surprisingly, therefore, important points of Luria's doctrine, which was preserved in its original wording in Luria's own literary remains and in Joseph ibn Tabul's version, were either obfuscated (as in Vital's *Eẓ Ḥayyim*) or completely suppressed (as in *Kanfei Yonah* by Moses Jonah). The starting point of this theory is the idea that the very essence of *Ein-Sof* leaves no space whatsoever for creation, for it is impossible to imagine an area which is not already God, since this would constitute a limitation of His Infinity. (This problem was not a source of concern to either the Zohar or Cordovero.) Consequently, an act of creation is possible only through "the entry of God into Himself," that is, through an act of *ẓimẓum,* whereby He contracts Himself and so makes it possible for something which is not *Ein-Sof* to exist. Some part of the Godhead therefore withdraws and leaves room, so to speak, for the creative processes to come into play. Such a retreat must precede any emanation.

Unlike the midrashic use of the word *(meẓamẓem),* which speaks of God contracting Himself into the Holy of Holies in the abode of the cherubs, kabbalistic contraction has quite the reverse significance: it is not the concentration of God's power *in* a place, but its withdrawal *from* a place. The place from which He retreats is merely "a point" in comparison with His infinity, but it comprises from our point of view all levels of existence, both spiritual and corporeal. This place is primordial space, and it is called *tehiru*, a term taken from the Zohar (1:15a). Luria also answers the question of how this *ẓimẓum* actually took place. Before *ẓimẓum* all the forces of God were stored within His infinite Self and equitably balanced without any separation between them. Hence, even the forces of *Din* ("judgment") were stored there but were not distinguishable as such. When the primal intention to create came into being, *Ein-Sof* gathered together the roots of *Din*, which had been previously concealed within Him, to one place, from which the power of mercy had departed. In this way the power of *Din* became concentrated. *Ẓimẓum* therefore was an act of judgment and self-limitation, and the process thus initiated was intended to continue by means of a progressive extraction and catharsis of the power of *Din* that was left in primordial space, where it was intermingled in a confused fashion with the remnants of the light of *Ein-Sof* that had remained behind even after *ẓimẓum*, like the drops of oil that remain in a vessel after it has been emptied. This residue was called *reshimu*. Into this inchoate mixture, which is the hylic aspect of the future universe, there descends from the primordial, space-encompassing *Ein-Sof* a *yod*, the first letter of the Tetragrammaton, which contains a "cosmic measure" or *kav ha-middah*, that is, the power of formation and organization. This power may be seen as belonging to the attribute of overflowing mercy *(Raḥamim)*.

Creation, therefore, is conceived of as a double activity of the emanating *Ein-Sof* following on *ẓimẓum:* the Emanator acts both as a receptive substratum through the light of the *reshimu*, and as a form-giving force which descends from the essence of *Ein-Sof* to bring order and structure to the original confusion. Thus, both the subject and the object of the process of creation have their origin in God but were differentiated from each other in the *ẓimẓum*. This process is expressed in the creation of "vessels" *(kelim)* in which the divine essence that remained in primordial space is precipitated out: at first this takes place still hylically, in the vessel called "primordial air" *(avir kadmon)*, but subsequently it assumes a clearer form in the vessel called "primordial man" *(Adam Kadmon)* that is created by a raising and lowering of the "cosmic measure," which serves as a permanent connection between *Ein-Sof* and the primordial space of *ẓimẓum*.

This version of the doctrine of *ẓimẓum* was obscured to a great extent by Vital, although occasional allusions to it remain scattered here and there in his works. At the beginning of his *Ez Ḥayyim,* however, there is a much simpler account. Without mentioning either the gathering out of the roots of *Din* or *reshimu*, he describes a process whereby as a result of the act of divine contraction an empty vacuum was formed in the midst of *Ein-Sof* into which emanated a ray of light that filled this space with ten *Sefirot.* Since the *ẓimẓum* took place equally on all sides, the resulting vacuum was circular or spherical in shape. The light which entered it in a straight line after the *ẓimẓum* has, therefore, two aspects from the start: it arranges itself both in concentric circles and in a unilinear structure, which is the form of *Adam Kadmon le-khol ha-kedumim,* "the primordial man that preceded all other primordials." The form of a circle and of a man are henceforth the two directions in which every created thing develops. Just as the first movement in creation was in reality composed of two movements – the ascent of *Ein-Sof* into the depths of itself and its partial descent into the space of *ẓimẓum* – so this double rhythm is a necessarily recurring feature of every stage in the universal process. This process works through the double beat of the alternately expanding movement of *Ein-Sof* and its desire to return to itself, *hitpashtut* ("egression") and *histalkut* ("regression"), as the kabbalists call it. Every movement of regression toward the source has something of a new *ẓimẓum* about it. This double-facedness in the process of emanation is typical of the dialectical tendency of Lurianic Kabbalah. Every stage in the development of the emanating light has not only a circular and linear aspect but also the modes of both an "inner light" within the vessels that are produced and a "surrounding light," as well as the modes of *aẓmut ve-kelim* ("substance and vessels"), and "direct light and reflected light," that are taken from the teachings of Cordovero. Luria's special interest in the structure of the spiritual worlds and their emergence through dialectical processes is also expressed in the distinction he makes between the structural "totality" *(kelalut)* of the forces of emanation and the structural "individuality" *(peratut)* of each such power that is active in a given overall structure.

Our earliest sources for the doctrine of *ẓimẓum* clearly show that Luria did not differentiate between the substance of *Ein-Sof* and its light, in both of which *ẓimẓum* occurred. Such a distinction was made only when probiems arose concerning the harmonization of this doctrine with the idea of God's immutability. This desire for consistency had two consequences: (1) a differentiation between the substance of *Ein-Sof* and its light (i.e., its will), which made it possible to argue that the *ẓimẓum* occurred only in the latter and not in its "possessor"; and (2) the insistence that the concept of *ẓimẓum* was not to be taken literally, being only figurative and based on a human perspective. These two beliefs were particularly stressed in the school of Israel Sarug, whose teachings on the subject were based on a combination of Ibn Tabul's redaction of Lurianic doctrine with that of Moses Jonah in his *Kanfei Yonah,* which makes no mention of *ẓimẓum* but speaks only of an emanation of one primal point comprising all the *Sefirot* without going into the details of how the latter came into being. To this Sarug added original ideas of his own which had a great influence on later Kabbalah; a summary of them can be found in his book *Limmudei Aẓilut* later attributed to Vital. According to him, the *ẓimẓum* was preceded by processes of an even more inward nature within *Ein-Sof* itself. In the beginning *Ein-Sof* took pleasure in its own autarkic self-sufficiency, and this "pleasure" produced a kind of "shaking" *(ni'anu'a)* which was the movement of *Ein-Sof* within itself. Next, this movement "from itself to itself" aroused the root of *Din,* which was still indistinguishably combined with *Raḥamim.* As a result of this "shaking," "primordial points" were "engraved" in the power of *Din,* thus becoming the first forms to leave their markings in the essence of *Ein-Sof.* The contours of this "engraving" were those of the primordial space, that was to come into being as the end-product of this process. As the light of *Ein-Sof* outside this "engraving" acted upon the points within it, the latter were activated from their potential state and the primordial Torah, the ideal world woven in the substance of *Ein-Sof* itself, came into being. This Torah, the linguistic movement of *Ein-Sof* within itself, is called a *malbush* ("garment"), though in fact it is inseparable from the divine substance and is woven within it "like the grasshopper whose clothing is part of itself," to use the language of the Midrash. Sarug described the structure of this "garment" in great detail. Its length was made up of the alphabets of the *Sefer Yeẓirah* and had 231 "gates" (i.e., possible combinations of the 22 letters of the Hebrew alphabet in the progression אב. אג. אד etc.) which form the archistructure of divine thought. Its breadth was composed of an elaboration of the Tetragrammaton according to the numerical value of the four possible spellings of the fully written names of its letters, viz., the "name" 45 (יוד. הא. ואו. הא), the "name" 52 (יוד, הה, וו, הה), the "name" 72 (יוד. הי. ויו. הי), and the "name" 63 (יוד. הי. ואו. הי), which were the "threads" and the "weave" that were originally situated in the hem of the garment. This primordial Torah contained potentially all that could possibly be revealed through the Torah to be given on earth. In effect, it was a kabbalistic version of the Platonic world of ideas. The size of this garment was twice the area necessary for the creation of all the worlds. After it had been woven, it was folded in two: half of it ascended and its letters stood behind the letters of the other half. The "names" 45 and 52 were arranged behind the "names" 72 and 63, and consequently the last *yod* of the "name" 63 was left without a partner in the folded garment. This folding constituted a contraction *(ẓimẓum)* of the garment to half its area, and with the removal of half of it from its previous place, something was created in *Ein-Sof* that no longer partook of its substance. All that remained in this primordial square was the unmatched *yod*, which now assumed the dynamic task of transferring the light of *Ein-Sof*, which spread in circles, to the area produced by the act of *ẓimẓum*, as in the version of Ibn Tabul. The empty area created by the folding of the garment is not an actual vacuum but is merely deprived of the garment or of the light of its substance. Yet the hidden law of the whole of creation that is inscribed within the "engraving" of *Ein-Sof* is henceforward active and expresses itself throughout all subsequent processes through the power invested in this one intruding *yod*. Made manifest in the vacated space are both the residue *(reshimu)* of the remaining light of its essence and some of the light of *Ein-Sof* itself, which acts as the soul that sustains all and without which all would return to *Ein-Sof* as before. This soul too contracts to a point, which is none other than the *anima mundi* of the philosophers. Moreover, the various movements of the *ẓimẓum*, and the ascents and descents of *yod*, produce still other points in space that constitute the primordial "world of points" *(olam ha-nekudot)*, which at this stage still has no definite structure and in which the divine lights exist in an atomized, punctiform state. According to Sarug, not one but many contractions occur in the place of the *reshimu*, and even more so thereafter. Elsewhere he states that there are two kinds of *reshimu*, one of the divine substance and one of the folded garment, and that only the second is articulated in the world of the points. Only upon the return of the *yod*, which ascends to *Ein-Sof* and re-descends from it, is that supernal light created in the primordial space which is known as the *tehiru* or primal matter of every being.

The dialectical complication apparent in Sarug's presentations bears witness to the uncertainty and excitement caused by the new idea of *ẓimẓum*. The importance of the power of *Din* in those acts which led to its embodiment in primal matter is obliterated to a much greated extent in Sarug's presentation than in that of Ibn Tabul, though it does not disappear altogether. The contradiction inherent in the opposing conceptions of the vacated primordial space, now as a square and now a sphere created by the activity of the emanating *yod*, posed an additional problem in Sarug's work that was not found elsewhere and that had no consistent solution. In any case, extreme naturalistic descriptions in these accounts were qualified by the stress laid on their symbolic character.

One of the most interesting of the further speculative attempts to explain the theories of *ẓimẓum*, which continued to be made for more than 200 years, is the daring interpretation of Shabbetai Sheftel Horowitz in his *Shefa Tal*. Horowitz tried to revise the doctrine of *ẓimẓum* once again and to regard it as merely a symbolic account of the emanation of the *Sefirah Keter*. Following Tabul's and Sarug's presentation, although without mentioning the *malbush* ("garment"), he attempted to equate the different stages in *ẓimẓum* with what he considered to be the parallel stages in the emanation of *Keter* in Cordovero's teachings. The emergence of the *tehiru* was no longer produced by the *ẓimẓum* itself but by the emanation of the light of *Ein-Sof* from within the essence of *Ein-Sof* itself. Only within this emanated *tehiru* did a contraction take place of the light of *Ein-Sof,* a residue of which mingled with some of the emanated substance to form the *reshimu.* Thus, the soul came into being as a supernal point in the *Sefirah Keter.* This transformation of the *ẓimẓum* into a second divine act following an original act of emanation made the doctrine once more compatible with Cordovero, who had also acknowledged the existence of a *ẓimẓum* within the chain of emanations, in which the power of the Creator became inevitably restricted in a progressive manner. Thus, Horowitz' interpretation removed the paradoxical thrust which was inherent in the doctrine of *ẓimẓum* from its very conception and indeed its most original feature.

From the 17th century onward kabbalistic opinion was divided on the doctrine of *ẓimẓum.* Was it to be taken literally? Or was it to be understood symbolically as an occurrence in the depths of the Divine, which the human mind could only describe in figurative language? The question was a bone of contention in the many arguments that took place between the kabbalists and the more philosophically inclined who found kabbalistic speculation distasteful, for all that the concept of *ẓimẓum* was in fact very close to the ideas that later developed in modern idealist philosophies, such as those of Schelling and Whitehead. As a result of the exposition of the doctrine given by the author of *Emek ha-Melekh,* many kabbalists were inclined to take the *ẓimẓum* literally, a view that became especially popular among the Shabbateans, whose entire creed made a non-literal interpretation impossible. This position was clearly expressed in the writings of Nathan of Gaza and Nehemiah Ḥayon. It was Ḥayon's determined defense of the literalist interpretation, in fact, that prompted Joseph Ergas to stress even more keenly Abraham Herrera's view that the *ẓimẓum* doctrine was symbolic. This dispute, which was also bound up with the anthropomorphistic doctrine of the Shabbateans in general, broke out in 1714 and was summed up by Ergas in his *Shomer Emunim* (1736), which is our main source for that fundamental reinterpretation that restored Lurianic doctrine to its Cordoveroan starting point. By then the Shabbatean side of the argument was no longer a factor, so that the literalist position was defended again, even in the camp of the orthodox kabbalists, whose chief spokesman was Immanuel Ḥai Ricchi in his *Yosher Levav* (1737). Ergas' system, on the other hand, was expanded in the *Amud ha-Avodah* by Baruch Kosover (written about 1763, but not printed until 1854). Ergas greatly influenced ḥasidic literature, especially the Ḥabad teachings of Shneur Zalman of Lyady and his pupil Aaron ha-Levi of Staroselye, who devoted a profound dialectical discussion to the subject in his *Avodat ha-Levi* (1862). In his *Tanya* Shneur Zalman maintained that the Gaon of Vilna mistakenly took *ẓimẓum* literally, but it is an open question if he was justified in interpreting the Gaon's teachings in this way. Aaron ha-Levi's system is based on the premise of a double *ẓimẓum.* The first *ẓimẓum,* also called *beki'ah* ("piercing"), is a contraction in the substance of *Ein-Sof* which renders possible the appearance of the Infinite in general and which is completely beyond our understanding. It leads to a revelation of the light of *Ein-Sof,* but is so unfathomable that there is not the slightest mention of it in Ḥayyim Vital's *Ez Ḥayyim.* It is only after this *beki'ah,* which is conceived of as a "leap" from absolute *Ein-Sof* to relative *Ein-Sof,* that the second contraction occurs, whereby the Infinite light of *Ein-Sof* is made to appear finite. In fact, however, the finite has no existence at all and is made possible only through the emission of a line or a ray from the Infinite. The cathartic concept of *ẓimẓum* mentioned above was developed independently in the writings of Moses Ḥayyim Luzzatto, who believed the crux of *ẓimẓum* to lie in the fact that the Creator "overcomes, as it were, His innate law of goodness in creation, so that His creatures should not be made perfect, even seen from their own point of view, let alone seen from that of God." The metaphysical root of evil is inherent in the very privation that the act of *ẓimẓum* involves, and the whole development of created beings depends on their being given an opportunity to perfect themselves according to their merits and to separate the power of evil from the power of good.

In sum, we can say that those kabbalists who wrote with one eye on the philosophers tended to stress the non-literal nature of *ẓimẓum,* whereas those kabbalists who had little use for Aristotelian philosophy to begin with presented the doctrine literally and unadorned. Nor should we overlook the close connection in the view of many kabbalists between *ẓimẓum* and the existence of the hylic matter which served as the basis for creation as a whole. Even Ḥayyim Vital himself defined the Infinite as the Nothing, which only through *ẓimẓum* became manifest in *Keter* which is the hylic matter in the whole of creation (*Ez Ḥayyim,* ch. 42, para. 1). Others connected the existence of the *hyle* with the *reshimu,* the primordial space, or the primordial air which was made manifest through *ẓimẓum.* A special discussion of the subject occurs in Eliakim b. Abraham Hart's *Ẓuf Novelot* (London, 1799), summarizing the far longer elaboration in *Novelot Ḥokhmah* by Joseph Solomon Delmedigo (1631).

THE BREAKING OF THE VESSELS

The point in *Ein-Sof* that was vacated in the act of *ẓimẓum* was subsequently filled with a proliferation of words and ontological events, each one of which tends in Lurianic Kabbalah to become the subject of a description whose complexity verges on the extreme. Moreover, these descriptions themselves vary widely in the different redactions of Ibn Tabul, Moses Jonah, and Ḥayyim Vital, and highly contradictory versions of them can even be found in several of Vital's own works. Israel Sarug's attempts to make a unified whole out of this confusion only added still further to it. Nevertheless, in each of these many presentations the same broad outlines appear. Isaac Luria's main preoccupation, it would appear, was to trace the further development of the vessels that received the light of emanation which shone into the primordial space after the act of *ẓimẓum* In the actual emergence of these vessels a part was played both by the lights that were located in the *tehiru* after the *ẓimẓum* and by the new lights that entered with the ray. The purpose of this process was the elimination *(berur)* of the forces of *Din* that had collected, a catharsis that could have been attained either by eliminating these forces from the system entirely or else by integrating them within it by first "softening" and purifying them – two conflicting approaches which we frequently encounter side by side. In either case, however, in order to further those processes that were a necessary prelude to the complex hierarchy of creation, a progressive differentiation was called for in the vessels themselves, without which the emanating streams would have been unable to regulate themselves and function properly. To this end, the various conjunctions of the first emanated lights as they collided with each other resulted in the creation of vessels, which "crystallized out," as it were, from certain modes that these lights contained.

All the Lurianic redactions agree that the ray of light that comes from *Ein-Sof* in order to organize the *reshimu* and the forces of *Din* that have filled the primordial space functions in two opposing fashions which inform all the developments in this space from beginning to end. These are the two aspects of "circle and line" *(iggul ve-yosher)*. Practically speaking, a point can expand evenly in one of two ways, circularly or linearly, and herein is expressed a basic duality that runs through the process of creation. The more harmonious of the two forms, which partakes of the perfection of *Ein-Sof,* is the circle; the latter conforms naturally to the spherical space of the *ẓimẓum* while the straight ray of light goes back and forth to seek its ultimate structure in the form of man, who represents the ideal aspect of *yosher* ("lineaform" structure). Thus, while the circle is the natural form, the line is the willed form that is directed toward the figure of a man. Moreover, because the line of light comes directly from *Ein-Sof,* it is of a higher degree than the circle, whose shape is a reflection of the *ẓimẓum.* The former, according to Isaac Luria, comprehends the principle of the *ru'aḥ,* the latter the principle of the *nefesh* or natural perfection. Essentially, this doctrine is a restatement of the Pythagorean geometrical symbolism that dominated natural philosophy until the 17th century. Every act of emanation, therefore, contains these two aspects, and should one be missing various disruptions or unexpected developments will take place. All purposeful, teleological movements are basically dominated by natural, immanent necessity.

The first form that emanation assumes after the *ẓimẓum* is that of *Adam Kadmon* ("primordial man"), which in the Lurianic system stands for a realm above the four worlds of *aẓilut, beri'ah, yeẓirah,* and *asiyyah* with which pre-Lurianic Kabbalah began. Isaac Luria did, it is true, seek to support this belief with a number of citations from the Zohar and the *Tikkunim,* but in fact it represented a completely new departure. Though he and his disciples maintained that many of the processes that take place in the *Adam Kadmon* are mysteries beyond human knowledge, they nevertheless discussed in great detail the manner in which the forces of emanation were organized after the *ẓimẓum* in this form. Throughout their treatment of this figure and of the supernal lights that radiated from it, the double dialectical movement mentioned above remains dominant. Thus, the ten *Sefirot* first took shape in the *Adam Kadmon* in the form of concentric circles, of which the outermost, the circle of *Keter,* remained in close contact with the surrounding *Ein-Sof.* This was the *nefesh* of the *Adam Kadmon.* Next the ten *Sefirot* rearranged themselves as a line, in the form of a man and his limbs, though of course this must be understood in the purely spiritual sense of the incorporeal supernal lights. This was the *ru'aḥ* of the *Adam Kadmon.* The higher aspects of the *nefesh,* known as *neshamah, ḥayah,* and *yeḥidah,* are also rooted in the upper *Sefirot* in their linear configurations. All of these lights possess vessels which are still so subtle and "pure" that they can hardly be considered vessels at all. The promotion of the *Adam Kadmon* to the rank of the first being to emerge after the *ẓimẓum* accounts for the strong anthropomorphic coloring that accompanies all descriptions of the process of emanation in the Lurianic system. The *Adam Kadmon* serves as a kind of intermediary link between *Ein-Sof,* the light of whose substance continues to be active in him, and the hierarchy of worlds still to come. In comparison with the latter, indeed, the *Adam Kadmon* himself could well be, and sometimes was, called *Ein-Sof.*

From the head of the *Adam Kadmon* tremendous lights shone forth and aligned themselves in rich and complex patterns. Some assumed the form of letters while others took on still other aspects of the Torah or the Holy Tongue, such as cantillations *(te'amim),* the vowel points, or the scribal affixes *(tagim),* which too are components of Holy Writ. Thus, two essentially different symbolisms – that of light, and that of language and writing – are here joined. Every constellation of light has its particular linguistic expression, though the latter is not directed toward the lower worlds but rather inward toward its own hidden being. These lights combine to form "names" whose concealed potencies become active and are made manifest through concealed "configurations" *(millu'im)* where each letter is fully written out by its name in the alphabet. This primordial world described by linguistic symbols was precipitated from the lights of *Adam Kadmon's* forehead, which issued from the spot where the phylactery-of-the-head is laid. The lights issuing from the *Adam Kadmon's* ears, nose, and mouth, however, expanded linearly only, nor did their *Sefirot* have special vessels, since they were at first joined together in a common vessel in accord with the "collectivity" that was their structural nature. Vital called this sphere *olam ha-akudim,* meaning a world where the *Sefirot* were not yet differentiated (lit. were bound together). The function assigned to these lights in the drama of creation was never clearly defined. The lights of the eyes, on the other hand, were differentiated into single *Sefirot.* In theory these lights should have issued from the navel, but the place of their appearance was deflected by a medium acting within the *Adam Kadmon* and referred to as *parsa* (apparently a reference to the diaphragm). This displacement is described as the result of another *ẓimẓum* within the lights themselves. Having changed their path, these lights issued from their eyes both linearly and circularly, and each of their *Sefirot* commanded a vessel of its own. Vital calls these separated lights "the world of dots" *(olam ha-nikkudim),* but in other Lurianic writings they are grouped together with the light of the *tehiru* and referred to as "the world of points" *(olam ha-nekudot)* or "the world of chaos" *(olam ha-tohu)* – the latter because at this stage the punctiform lights of the *Sefirot* had not yet attained a stable structural arrangement. All the lights of these *Sefirot* were given vessels, themselves made of thicker light, in which to arrange themselves and function.

At this point, however, there occurred what is known in Lurianic Kabbalah as "the breaking of the vessels" or "the death of the kings." The vessels assigned to the upper three *Sefirot* managed to contain the light that flowed into them, but the light struck the six *Sefirot* from *Ḥesed* to *Yesod* all at once and so was too strong to be held by the individual vessels; one after another they broke, the pieces scattering and falling. The vessel of the last *Sefirah, Malkhut,* also cracked but not to the same degree. Some of the light that had been in the vessels retraced its path to its source, but the rest was hurled down with the vessels themselves, and from their shards the *kelippot,* the dark forces of the *sitra aḥra,* took on substance. These shards are also the source of gross matter. The irresistible pressure of the light in the vessels also caused every rank of worlds to descend from the place that had been assigned to it. The entire world process as we now know it, therefore, is at variance with its originally intended order and position. Nothing, neither the lights nor the vessels, remained in its proper place, and this development – called after a phrase borrowed from the *Idrot* of the

Zohar, "the death of the primeval kings" – was nothing less than a cosmic catastrophe. At the same time, the breaking of the vessels, which corresponds to the destruction of the first, unsuccessful worlds in earlier Kabbalah, was not understood in Lurianic writings to be an anarchic or chaotic process; rather it took place in accord with certain clear internal laws that were elaborated extensively. Similarly, the emergence of the *kelippot* as the root of evil was described as a process followed by fixed rules and involving only the shards of those vessels that had been struck by the first sparks of light. These lights remained "captured" among the *kelippot,* which are nourished by them; they, in fact, provide the life-force for the entire world of *kelippot,* which in one degree or another interpenetrated the whole hierarchy of worlds once the vessels had been broken. The broken vessels too, of course, were subjected to the process of *tikkun* or restoration which began immediately after the disaster, but their "dross" was unaffected, and from this waste matter, which can be compared to the necessary by-products of any organic process, the *kelippot*, in their strict sense as the powers of evil, emerged. The catastrophic aspects of the breaking of the vessels were especially stressed in the simplified versions of the story that appeared in more popular kabbalistic literature which described the entire process in highly mythical imagery.

Widely differing explanations for the breaking of the vessels were offered in Lurianic writings. Some commentators were content to attribute it to the weak and atomized inner structure of "the world of points," whose isolated, unorganized parts were too unstable to prevent the occurrence. Another explanation was that since the first emanations of the points were all circular rather than partly linear, an inevitable imbalance was created. In some texts it is stated that only the "branches" of the points went forth from *Adam Kadmon* while the "roots" remained within him, and that the former lacked the power by themselves to withstand the pressure of the light. All of these explanations are based on the premise that the unsound structure of the world of points was at fault, and view the breaking of the vessels as a mishap in the existence of the life-process of the Godhead. (See Tishby, *Torat ha-ra ve-ha-kelippah be-kabbalat ha-Ari,* 39–45). Other explanations which seem to derive from Isaac Luria himself actually seek to justify this unsound structure by viewing it as a reaction to the roots of *Din* and the *kelippot* that were from the start present in the emanation. According to this view, the main design of the emanative process was to bring about a catharsis of these harsh elements and of the waste matter in the divine system. The presence of the roots of the *kelippot* in the emanation was the true inner reason for the breaking of the vessels. This cathartic explanation is frequently associated with the teleological view that the vessels were broken in order to pave the way for reward and punishment in the lower worlds that were due to emerge as the last phase of the creation. Differently stressed versions of such explications can be found in Moses Jonah, Vital, and Ibn Tabul. The cathartic and teleological explanations represent basically different approaches and well illustrate the tension in Lurianic Kabbalah between mythic and theological modes of thought. Later kabbalists ruled that the teleological explanation was indeed the literally correct one but that the cathartic explanation represented the mystical truth (Meir Bikayam, *Me'orei Or,* 1752, 15c). In the Lurianic school of Israel Sarug an additional, organic analogy was offered: the world of points was like a sown field whose seeds could not bear fruit until they had first split open and rotted.

TIKKUN

The breaking of the vessels marks a dramatic turning-point in the relations between the *Adam Kadmon* and all that develops beneath him. All the subsequent processes of creation come about to restore this primal fault. In its imaginative boldness, the belief that such an event could take place within a realm that, according to all opinions, was still part of the self-manifesting Godhead can be compared only to the doctrine of the *ẓimẓum* itself. Indeed, it was even suggested that the *ẓimẓum* too represented a kind of primordial "breakage" within *Ein-Sof.* The laws by which the process of cosmic restoration and reintegration *(tikkun)* works itself out constitute the largest part of Lurianic Kabbalah, for they touch on all the realms of creation, including the "anthropological" and "psychological" ones. The details of the doctrine of *tikkun* are extremely complex and seem to have been intentionally designed as a challenge to mystical contemplation. The most crucial element in this doctrine is the concept that the chief medium of *tikkun,* that is, of the restoration of the universe to its original design in the mind of its Creator, is the light that issued from *Adam Kadmon's* forehead to reorganize the disorderly confusion that resulted from the breaking of the vessels. The main support of these lights comes from the linear *Sefirot* of "the world of points," which did not undergo any breakage and henceforth have the task of encouraging the formation of balanced and stable structures in the future realms of creation. These new structures are called *parẓufim,* that is, configurations or *gestalten,* and each comprises an organic pattern of hierarchies of *Sefirot* with its own dynamic laws.

These *parẓufim* (literally, "faces" or "physiognomies") now take the place of the *Sefirot* as the principal manifestations of *Adam Kadmon.* In each of them newly emanated forces are bonded together with others that were damaged in the breaking of the vessels; thus, each *parẓuf* represents a specific stage in the process of catharsis and reconstruction. The *Sefirah Keter* is now re-formed as the *parzuf* of *Arikh Anpin* (literally, "the long-faced one," i.e., "the indulgent one" or "forbearing one," a phrase borrowed from the Zohar, where it appears as an Aramaic translation of the biblical *erekh-appayin,* "long-suffering"), or *Attika* ("the ancient one"), which are sometimes treated as two separate aspects of the same *parzuf.* The *Sefirot Ḥokhmah* and *Binah* now become the *parzufim,* of *Abba* and *Imma* ("father and mother"), which function in a dual capacity: they exist as a medium for the reindividuation and redifferentiation of all the emanated beings into transmitters and receivers of influx, and they also serve as the supreme archetype for that procreative "coupling" *(zivvug)* which, in its metaphorical aspect of "looking face-to-face" *(histakkelut panim-be-fanim),* is the common root of all intellectual and erotic unions. This "coupling" is aroused by the reascent of the 288 sparks that had been in the broken vessels and returned to the bowels of *Binah* where they play the role of animating and quickening forces within a structure whose function is primarily receptive. Without such assisting forces, which are referred to as "female waters" *(mayim nukbin)* there can be neither "coupling" nor unification even in the world of *azilut.* From the union of *Abba* and *Imma* a new *parzuf* is born, known as *Ze'eir Anpin* (literally, "the short-faced one," i.e., "the impatient" or "unindulgent one"), which is comprised of the six lower *Sefirot,* from *Gedullah* to *Yesod.* Here we have the center for the cathartic processes that take place in all the *parzufim* in order to mitigate the harsh powers of *Din;* their ultimate success depends on a long, almost endless series of developments. The self-manifestation of *Ein-Sof* in the created worlds takes place largely through this *parzuf,* which undergoes an embryonic development *(ibbur)* in the depths of *Imma* followed by "birth," "suckling," and the progressive emergence of the formative powers known as "immaturity" *(katnut)* and "maturity" *(gadlut).* The latter in turn are re-invigorated through a second "conception" by means of new powers that join them from other *parzufim.* The structural unity of *Ze'eir Anpin* is assured by the workings of a principle called *zelem* ("image," after the verse in Gen. 1:27), which involves the activity of certain lights that help serve as a constituent element in all the *parzufim* but are especially centered in *Ze'eir Anpin.* The last and tenth *Sefirah, Malkhut,* in also converted into a *parzuf,* which is named *Nukba de-Ze'eir,* "the female of *Ze'eir,*" and represents the latter's complementary feminine aspect. The main source of this boldly anthropomorphic symbolism is in the *Idrot* of the Zohar, but in its development in the Lurianic Kabbalah it took a radical turn. Isaac Luria himself undoubtedly viewed the *parzufim* as power centers through which the creative dynamism of the Godhead was able to function and assume form. The various names, configurations, and sub-configurations that accompany these symbolic descriptions were probably intended to mute this almost provocatively conspicuous anthropomorphism to some extent. Over and above the five *parẓufim* just mentioned, whose inner dialectic is extensively explained in Ḥayyim Vital's *Eẓ Ḥayyim,* there are still other, secondary *parẓufim* that constitute the articulation of certain powers in the *Ze'eir Anpin* and its feminine *Nukba,* such as *Yisrael Sava, Tevunah, Raḥel,* and *Leah.* Indeed, in Isaac Luria's richly associative thought, practically every biblical personage was immediately transformed into a metaphysical figure from which sprang new hypostases and *parẓufim.* An outstanding example of this tendency can be found in chapter 32 of the *Eẓ Ḥayyim,* where all that happened to the "generation of the desert" is construed as representing processes of the *parẓufim* of the three upper *Sefirot* of the *Ze'eir Anpin* and its female counterpart.

The five principal *parẓufim* of *Arikh Anpin, Abba, Imma, Ze'eir Anpin,* and *Nukba de-Ze'eir* constitute the final figure of the *Adam Kadmon* as it evolves in the first stages of *tikkun,* which is quite different from the figure of *Adam Kadmon* that existed before the breaking of the vessels. These *parẓufim* also comprise "the world of balance" *(olam ha-matkela),* which is identical with the world of *aẓilut* of earlier Kabbalah. From this world, though not its substance, an influx of spiritual light descends downward to the lower worlds of *beri'ah, yeẓirah,* and *asiyyah.* At the bottom of each world is a "curtain" which serves to filter out the sefirotic substance that properly corresponds to the nature of that world and to let all else pass on through a secondary reflex which in turn becomes the substance of a subsequent stage. The basic structure of the world of *aẓilut* repeats itself with certain modifications in the three lower worlds. The *tikkun,* however, has not yet been completed. As a result of the breaking of the vessels, none of the worlds is located in its proper place. Each one of them stands a rank lower than it should be, the original place of the world beneath it. In consequence, the world of *asiyyah,* which in essence is also a spiritual world (like the Ideal Nature of the neoplatonist), has descended and commingled with the lowest part of the realm of the *kelippot* and with the physical matter that is dominant there.

The main concern of Lurianic Kabbalah, as has been mentioned, is with the details of the process of *tikkun* and the developments that take place in the *parẓufim* of the different worlds, in the *"adam* of *aẓilut,"* the *"adam* of *beri'ah,"* etc. (Over three-quarters of the *Eẓ Ḥayyim* is devoted to this subject.) The crucial point in the various Lurianic discussions of these developments is that although the *tikkun* of the broken vessels has almost been completed by the supernal lights and the processes stemming from their activity, certain concluding actions have been reserved for man. These are the ultimate aim of creation, and the completion of *tikkun,* which is synonymous with the redemption, depends on man's performing them. Herein lies the close connection between the doctrine of *tikkun* and the religious and contemplative activity of man, which must struggle with and overcome not only the historic exile of the Jewish people but also the mystic exile of the *Shekhinah,* which was caused by the breaking of the vessels.

The object of this human activity, which is designed to complete the world of *tikkun,* is the restoration of the world of *asiyyah* to its spiritual place, its complete separation from the world of the *kelippot,* and the achievement of a permanent, blissful state of communion between every creature and God which the *kelippot* will be unable to disrupt or prevent. Of crucial importance here is the Lurianic distinction between the inward and outward aspects of the supernal lights and the worlds of creation themselves: the *tikkun* of the outward aspects of the worlds is not up to man at all, whose mission is solely concerned with certain aspects of inwardness. In the Lurianic system the hierarchical rank of the inward is always lower than that of the outward, but precisely because of this it is within reach of the truly spiritual, inward individual, to some extent at least. Should the latter perform his task properly, the "female waters" that enable the supernal couplings to take place will be aroused, and the work of the outward *tikkun* will be completed by the supernal lights that have remained concealed in the *parẓuf* of *Attika* and are due to reveal themselves only in the messianic future. At the very least, human activity in accordance with the Torah can prepare the way for the *tikkun* of the lower worlds.

The Gnostic character of this cosmogony cannot be denied, though the detailed manner in which it is worked out is drawn entirely from internal Jewish sources. Typically Gnostic, for example, are the depiction of the creation as a cosmic drama centered around a profoundly fateful crisis within the inner workings of the Godhead itself, and the search for a path of cosmic restoration, of a purging of the evil from the good, wherein man is assigned a central role. The fact that such an unrecognized Gnostic theology was able to dominate the mainstream of Jewish religious thought for a period of at least two centuries must surely be considered one of the greatest paradoxes in the entire history of Judaism. At the same time, side by side with this Gnostic outlook, we find a most astonishing tendency to a mode of contemplative thought that can be called "dialectic" in the strictest sense of the term as used by Hegel. This tendency is especially prominent in attempts to present formal explanations of such doctrines as that of the *ẓimẓum,* the breaking of the vessels, or the formation of the *parẓufim.*

In addition to the redaction of Luria's teachings mentioned above, the basic tenets of Lurianic Kabbalah are systematically and originally presented in the following works: *Ma'amar Adam de-Aẓilut,* included by Moses Pareger in his *Va-Yakhel Moshe* (Dessau, 1699); Joseph Solomon Delmedigo's *Novelot*

Ḥokhmah (Basle, actually Hanau, 1631); *Keleḥ* [138] *Pitḥei Ḥokhmah* by Moses Ḥayyim Luzzatto (Koretz, 1785); Jacob Meir Spielmann's *Tal Orot* (Lvov, 1876–83); Isaac Eisik Ḥaver's *Pitḥei She'arim* (1888); Solomon Eliashov's *Leshem Shevo ve-Aḥlamah* (1912–48); and Judah Leib Ashlag's *Talmud Eser ha-Sefirot* (1955–67). Well-known expositions of Lurianic Kabbalah by Abraham Herrera and Joseph Ergas were greatly influenced by their tendency to reconcile or at least to correlate the Lurianic system with the teachings of Cordovero, as can be seen in Ergas' allegorization of the Lurianic doctrine of *ẓimẓum*.

THE KABBALAH AND PANTHEISM

The question of whether, and to what degree, the Kabbalah leads to pantheistic conclusions has occupied many of its investigators from the appearance in 1699 of J.G. Wachter's study *Der Spinozimus im Jüdenthumb* attempting to show that the pantheistic system of Spinoza derived from kabbalistic sources, particularly from the writings of Abraham Herrera. Much depends here, of course, on the definition of a concept which has been employed in widely different meanings. A teaching can be considered pantheistic when it insists that "God is everything" and that "everything is God," yet we must distinguish between occasional formulas which have this kind of pantheistic coloring and the exact place assigned them within the framework of a systematic theology. Such formulas are found extensively in Christian and Muslim mysticism as well, yet their actual content does not always conform to their outward pantheistic appearance. This is equally true of many similar utterances in kabbalistic literature, especially those which occur in expositions of kabbalistic thought deliberately intended for popular consumption, as in a great deal of hasidic writing. On the other hand, the opposite phenomenon may occur as well, and here and there we find explicitly theistic formulas that belie their inner pantheistic or near-pantheistic content. All depends on the internal context of a given system of thought. Apparent theistic tendencies can serve to conceal actually pantheistic views, while general formulas can more often than not be variously interpreted and do not therefore prove a great deal. Examples of this are Azriel's pronouncement that "nothing is outside" *Ein-Sof*, Meir ibn Gabbai's declaration that "everything is in Him and He is in everything," or the recurring insistence in the Zohar that God "is everything" and that everything is unified in Him, "as is known to the mystics" (2:85b). Such statements can also be found in orthodox theistic systems of thought where they serve to underline the belief that nothing could exist without a first, divine cause and that the latter, since it is the cause of all, includes and comprehends within itself whatever it has caused. In this respect God can be said to be present and immanent in all that He has caused, and were He to discontinue His presence all caused existence would thereby be annihilated. The neoplatonic principle that every effect is included in its cause greatly influenced such formulations in the Kabbalah without casting them in a necessarily pantheistic mold.

Strictly speaking, however, the problem of pantheism does occur in connection with a number of specific questions that greatly preoccupied kabbalistic speculation and to which pantheistic doctrines were at least able to offer unambiguous answers. Such questions were: (1) Is there a unity of substance between the Emanator and the emanated? Does the actual substance of God go forth into all or only the radiated potency of that substance? (2) If there is a unity of substance between *Ein-Sof* and the *Sefirot,* is there also such a unity between *Ein-Sof* and created beings? (3) Is God the soul of the world or identical with the world? (4) Does God exist in created beings (or, in the language of the philosophers, is He immanent in them), or even in them alone? Wherever we find positive answers to these questions there is good reason to assume that we are dealing with pantheism, and wherever we do not, we can assume the converse.

The majority of kabbalists from Isaac the Blind on rejected the notion that God's substance manifests itself in the world of emanation and insisted, as did most medieval neoplatonists, that God's power alone, as opposed to his substance, goes forth in the emanative process. Some of the earliest kabbalists, however, in particular the author of the *Ma'arekhet ha-Elohut,* did believe the emanated *Sefirot* to be of one substance with the emanating *Ein-Sof.* Only in the realms below the *Sefirot,* they held, was the divine potency alone active as the cause of beings that were separate from the Godhead. On the whole, we find that this school of thought had clearly theistic tendencies. Isaac b. Samuel Mar Ḥayyim (1491) distinguished between an "emanation of essence," which is the beaming forth of the *Sefirot* within the substance of *Ein-Sof,* and an "emanation of influx," which is the potency of the Emanator as it manifests itself in accordance with the receptive capacity of the given medium. Those kabbalists who identified *Ein-Sof* with the *Sefirah Keter* were obliged to consider the *Sefirot* as consubstantial with *Ein-Sof.* Yet those who held this view also explicitly denied that there could be any oneness of substance between God and the separate intellects, much less between God and other created beings. Such, for instance, was the opinion of Joseph Gikatilla in his glosses on the *Guide of the Perplexed.* Even he, however, did not restrain himself from declaring that "He fills all and He is all." Many other kabbalists, on the other hand, denied the consubstantiality of God with the emanated world, in which they professed to see only His emanating potency. In carrying on the thought of Cordovero (see

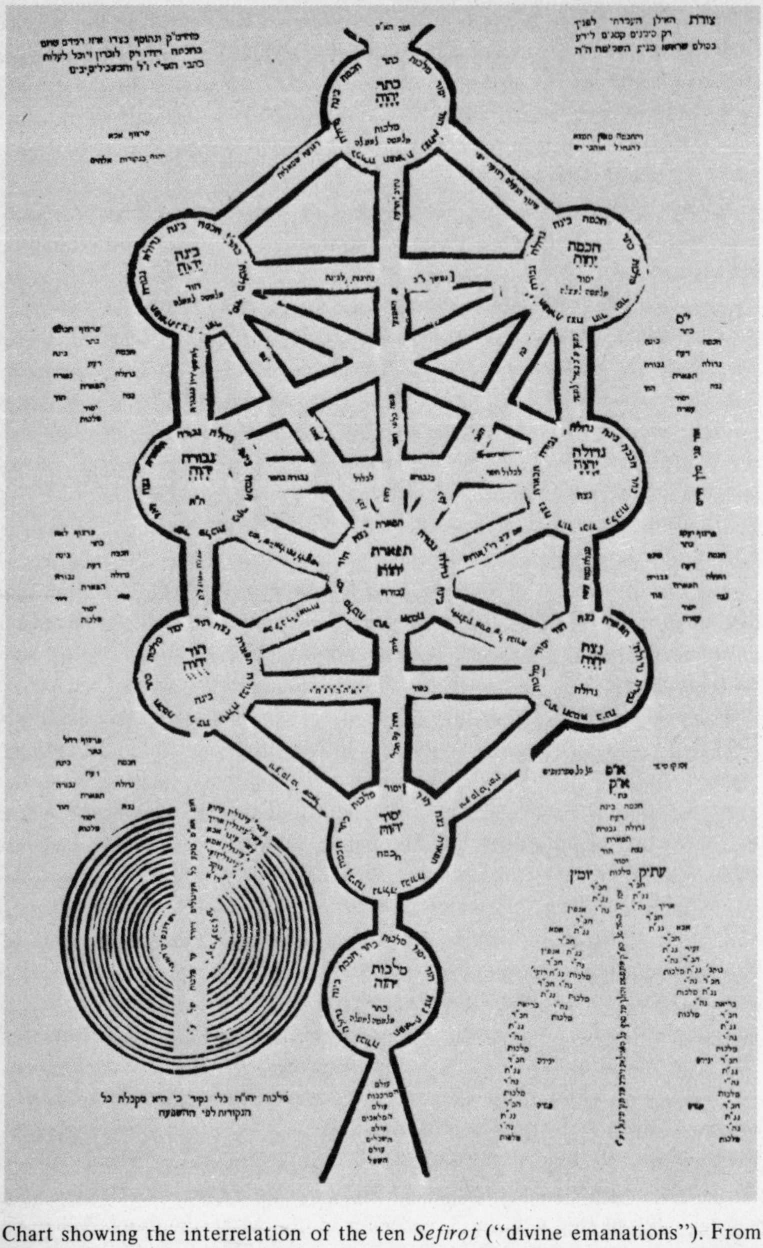

Chart showing the interrelation of the ten *Sefirot* ("divine emanations"). From *Pa'amon ve-Rimmon*, Amsterdam, 1708.

below), the disciples of his school emphasized the separate substance of the emanated as opposed to the substance of the Emanator whose "garment" the former was.

The author of the Zohar was not especially concerned with this problem and was content to dispose of it with conceptually vague formulations which were open to conflicting interpretations, but in Moses de Leon's Hebrew works there is a more discernible tendency to stress the unity of all beings in a continuous chain of being. There are no qualitative jumps in the links of this chain, and God's true essence is "above and below, in heaven and on earth, and there is no existence besided Him" *(Sefer ha-Rimmon).* In the theophany at Mount Sinai God revealed all the worlds to the children of Israel, who saw that there was nothing in them that was not His manifest glory and essence. Implied here is the suggestion that every being has a secondary existence of its own apart from the Godhead but that this disappears before the penetrating gaze of the mystic which uncovers the unity of essence behind it. The pantheistic tendencies in this line of thought are cloaked in theistic figures of speech, a device characteristic of a number of kabbalists. On the one hand such writers describe *Ein-Sof* in personalistic terms and stress its absolute transcendence over everything, even the *Sefirot,* which have no apprehension of it, while on the other hand they make much of its "clothing itself" in the latter, and through them in the lower worlds as well. There is also a certain ambiguity in their double interpretation of the *creatio ex nihilo,* sometimes insisting that it be taken literally, which would of course rule out any pantheistic approach, and sometimes explaining it symbolically, rejecting a simple literalism in order to leave the door open to the possibility that all being has its place, at least partially, in the divine reality. The true nothingness from which all was created manifests itself in the transition from *Ein-Sof* to the first *Sefirah,* nor is there in reality any jump or discontinuity in the structure of being. The creation from nothingness is a manifestation of the divine wisdom where human thought reaches its limit, or of that nothingness which is the first emanation, *Keter.* In those systems where *Ein-Sof* was identified with the *Keter,* it was *Ein-Sof* itself that became the Divine Nothingness in which all has its source. Such views left room for the belief that God, who is one with *Ein-Sof,* comprehends much more than what proceeds from Him in the emanative and creative processes but that He encompasses the latter within Himself as well. All is comprehended within the Godhead but not everything is identical with it. In the early 19th century the term "panentheism" was coined to distinguish such a view from pure pantheism. There is no doubt that the term could apply to a number of well-known kabbalists, who were able to argue – with some measure of justice – that a similar position was already implied in the statement in the Midrash (Gen. R. 68) that "The Holy One blessed be He is the place of the world but the world is not His place." The panentheist view offered a clear compromise between pure theism and pure pantheism and left room for a personalistic depiction of the Godhead.

It is evident, therefore, that while not a single kabbalist school of thought ever claimed that God has no existence apart from created beings, the position most commonly held was that He was nevertheless to be found within them in various definable ways. Hence, too, the neoplatonic assertion frequently encountered in kabbalistic literature that God is "the soul of souls," a claim which is not entirely free of pantheistic nuances although it lends itself to other interpretations as well. This phrase was already favored by the Zohar, but it must be observed that "soul" *(neshamah)* in its precise sense often does not imply in such writings an actual inherence in or existence contingent on the body but rather a higher mode of being. The *neshamah* proper does not descend to the lower worlds at all but radiates downward to the mode that we call man's "soul." Such, for instance, was the opinion of Isaac Luria. Other kabbalists, on the other hand, especially Moses de Leon, considered the human soul "a part of God above" (Job 31:2), not just in a figurative sense, as it was generally understood to be, but quite literally. Thus, their thought was based on the assumption that there is something in the soul consubstantial with God. It was this same assumption that led Moses de Leon in his *Mishkan ha-Edut*[9] to challenge the view that the punishment of the souls of the damned in hell is eternal, for how is it possible that God should inflict such suffering on Himself? This opinion is also indirectly hinted at in the Zohar, where it is stated that that highest part of the soul *(nefesh)* that is called *neshamah* is incapable of sinning and departs from the sinner at the moment that a sin is committed. Shabbetai Sheftel Horowitz was in agreement with this view and conceded only a quantitative distinction between the soul and the substance of God, a position that, because of its pantheistic implications, was challenged, especially by Manasseh Ben Israel in his *Nishmat Ḥayyim* (1652).

In contrast to the bulk of the Zohar, its later strata (the *Ra'aya Meheimna* and the *Tikkunim*) have a markedly theistic flavor. Here too, however, it is especially stressed that if God stands apart from the world He is also within it ("He is outside as much as He is inside"), and that He "fills all and causes all" without this immanence precluding a personalistic and theistic view of Him. Such formulations in the Zohar became expremely popular among later kabbalists and in the writings of Ḥasidism, where they were used to bridge theistic and pantheistic opinions abounding in these texts. Kabbalistic works written between 1300 and 1500 tended on the whole to obscure the problem, as can be seen in the writings of the disciples of Solomon b. Adret and in the *Sefer ha-Peliah.* Similarly, popular kabbalistic texts written at the time of the expulsion from Spain show a marked preference for decidedly theistic formulations (Abraham b. Eliezer ha-Levi, Judah Ḥayyat, Abraham b. Solomon Adrutiel), which in rare cases only conceal a different content between the lines.

A detailed discussion of the problematics of pantheism can be found in the writings of Cordovero, whose own panentheistic outlook was more carefully worked out than that of any other kabbalist, especially in his *Sefer Elimah* and *Shi'ur Komah.* His presentation of the question is extremely subtle and has nothing in common with that "Spinozist" approach which, in its more vulgar sense, a number of authors have sought to attribute to him. Cordovero understood full well that the salient point of the whole theory of emanation was the transition from *Ein-Sof* to the *Sefirah Keter* and he devoted great effort to its solution. The *Sefirot,* he argues, owe the source of their existence to *Ein-Sof,* but this existence is "hidden" in the same sense that the spark of fire is hidden in the rock until it is struck with metal. Moreover, this aspect of their existence is incomparably more rarified than their existence once they have been emanated to their respective places, for in their emanated existence they assume a totally new guise. Even in their ultimate, "hidden" mode of existence, however, when they are comprehended in the substance of *Ein-Sof* and united with it perfectly, they are nevertheless not truly identical with this substance, which apprehends them while remaining unapprehended by them. This being the case, should it be said that the first change in their ontological status takes place in their hidden existence or not until their manifest one? Cordovero avoided giving an unequivocal answer to this question, while at the same time developing the theory that even the highest aspects of the *Keter* which he called "the *Keter* of the *Keter,*" "the *Keter* of the *Keter* of the *Keter,*" and so forth, approach the substance of *Ein-Sof* asymptotically until the human intellect can no longer distinguish them. Nevertheless they retain an identity distinct from it, so that there is a kind of leap between *Ein-Sof* and their hidden existence within it that continually approaches to infinity. The existence of these inward stages is considered by Cordovero to represent an entirely new departure within the Godhead, and the coming into being of this hidden existence, or "Will of Wills" as he calls it, is what constitutes the act of creation from nothingness in its literal sense. The initial awakening of the Divine Will in this chain of wills *(re'utin)* is, he argues, the one occasion on which true creation from nothingness takes place, a view whose paradoxical nature testifies to the manner in which he felt torn between the theistic and the pantheistic approach. From the divine point of view God comprehends all, inasmuch as He encompasses the "wills" both by virtue of being their cause and of embracing them in His essence, but from the human point of view all of these subsequent stages comprise a secondary reality existing separately from *Ein-Sof* and contingent on it, so that they cannot possibly share a true identity with the substance of the Emanator. Even at the highest levels this substance clothes itself in "vessels" which are by their very nature secondary and preceded by a state of privation *(he'eder).*

In all of these processes, therefore, it is necessary to distinguish between the substance of the Emanator, which clothes itself in vessels, and the substance of the emanated. Though this distinction is somewhat obscured in the *Pardes Rimmonim,* it is emphasized in the *Sefer Elimah,* where Cordovero asserts that while in the act of emanation the divine substance goes forth into vessels, these vessels *(kelim)* or garments *(levushim)* assume an increasingly less refined existence as the process continues downward. And yet behind these infinite garments there is not a single link in the chain where the substance of *Ein-Sof* does not remain present and immanent. Even from the viewpoint of the human condition it is potentially possible to contemplatively "undress" these garments and reveal "the processions of the substance" *(tahalukhei ha-ezem)* which clothe themselves in them. Such a moment of revelation is the supreme happiness to which the mystic can attain in his lifetime. Yet again, this immanence of *Ein-Sof* in everything is not identical with the specific existence of the vessels: "The products of causation as they descend do not share one substance with their cause but rather . . . are diminished from their cause as they descend until the lowest [level of] existence." Only as they reascend toward their cause are they reunified with it, until they reach the Supreme Cause of all, which is the *Keter,* where there is no longer any distinction between the agent and the products of its action, for they adhere to it as far as is in any way possible and are truly united to *Ein-Sof,* "where there is no cause or caused but everything is cause" (*Elimah,* 18c). The single most definitive statement in Cordovero's treatment of the problem can be classed as panentheistic: "God is all that exists, but not all that exists is God" (*Elimah,* 24d). To be sure, this reascent toward first causes must be taken as applying to the culminating process of all creation in its return to the bosom of the emanator rather than to the mystical experience of the individual. Moreover, in many passages Cordovero further dilutes the concept by warning against misunderstanding: the caused beings themselves will not be reabsorbed into the substance of *Ein-Sof* but only their "spirituality" once their separate garments have been cast off. What has been forever sundered from the Godhead cannot be redeified.

Lurianic Kabbalah tended on the whole to avoid even the panentheistic formulations of Cordovero and to adopt an openly theistic position. The doctrine of the *zimzum,* by stressing the discontinuity between *Ein-Sof* and the world of emanation, heightened this proclivity even more. Granting even that something of the divine substance goes forth into the *Adam Kadmon* and even into the *parzufim* that emanate from him, clothing itself in them, this process comes to a definite end with the emanated *Sefirot* in the first world of *aẓilut*. Beneath them stretches a "curtain" which prevents the divine substance from finding garments for itself in the worlds of *beri'ah*, *yeẓirah*, and *asiyyah* as well. Of course it is possible to speak of a radiation of *Ein-Sof* into all the worlds, *asiyyah* included, but not of its substance being immanent in them. On the other hand, though such theistic arguments dominate most of the writings of Ḥayyim Vital and Ibn Tabul, even here there are occasional statements that are closer to Cordovero's position. Indeed, the doctrine that every higher principle "clothes itself" in a lower one, which in the final analysis is a doctrine of divine immanence, was sometimes carried to extremes. Above all the kabbalist was expected to understand "how all the worlds share a single mode of being as garments of *Ein-Sof*, so that *Ein-Sof* clothes itself in them and surrounds *[sovev]* them and nothing goes beyond it. Everything can be seen under one aspect and all the worlds are bound to the Emanator," although caution decrees that "it would be inadvisable to reveal more of this matter" (*Sha'ar ha-Hakdamot*, Hakdamah 4). Others such as Ibn Tabul emphasized that only God's "inner light" *(ha-or ha-penimi)* was filtered out by the "curtains," whereas His "comprehensive light" *(ha-or ha-mekif)* was not curtained off at all. Inasmuch as the latter comprises the main part of the divine substance that goes forth into the world of emanation, a door was here opened once again for a return to the panentheistic views of Cordovero.

Whether the light of *Ein-Sof* that goes forth into the vacuum of the *ẓimẓum* and clothes itself in vessels can be considered part of the Godhead even though it does not partake of the latter's substance remained an open question which most Lurianic kabbalists emphatically answered in the affirmative. The Lurianists held that without question the world of *aẓilut* with its inner dynamic processes belonged to the Godhead. Nevertheless, many of them denied that there was a unity of substance between the manifestations of the Godhead in *aẓilut* and the substantive properties of *Ein-Sof*. Even the highest circle of the *Sefirot* of the *Adam Kadmon*, they argued, was closer to the lowliest worm than to *Ein-Sof*. Such analogies bear witness to a continual equivocation between two inherently conflicting points of view. One radical solution to this ambivalence was the strict theistic doctrine of Moses Ḥayyim Luzzatto, who insisted that *aẓilut* could be called a "world" *(olam)* in the figurative sense only, because in it the Godhead manifested itself directly, whereas all the other worlds were created by a free act of God from literal nothingness. No statement to the effect that these lower worlds had evolved or developed out of the world of *aẓilut* was to be taken literally, for at most it could mean that they had been patterned after *aẓilut*. "We must not think that there can be any bond *[hitkashrut]* between what is created and the Creator." It would appear that Luzzatto had an especially firm grasp of the built-in contradiction between the doctrine of emanation and that of a paradigmatic creation in the clash between which lay the crux of the problem of pantheism in the Kabbalah. Generally speaking, most kabbalistic texts that were written for the benefit of a wider audience, such as Ḥayyim Vital's *Sha'arei Kedushah*, were theistic on the surface, sometimes concealing beneath it the germs of a different, essentially panentheistic interpretation. These germs, such as the Lurianic doctrines of the creative ray, the residue or *reshimu*, the primordial space of the *ẓimẓum*, the unity of the chain of being, and so forth, nourished panentheistic tendencies which subsequently came to the fore once more in a number of the classic texts of Ḥasidism.

MAN AND HIS SOUL (PSYCHOLOGY AND ANTHROPOLOGY OF THE KABBALAH)

Over and above disagreements on specific details that tend to reflect different stages in the Kabbalah's historical development, there exists a basic consensus among kabbalists on man's essential nature. The fundamental doctrine of a hidden life of the Godhead which through a dynamism of its own determines the life of creation as a whole had inevitable implications as regards the human condition, in which the same theosophic process, though with certain significant differences, was thought to repeat itself. At opposite poles, both man and God encompass within their being the entire cosmos. However, whereas God contains all by virtue of being its Creator and Initiator in whom everything is rooted and all potency is hidden, man's role is to complete this process by being the agent through whom all the powers of creation are fully activated and made manifest. What exists seminally in God unfolds and develops in man. The key formulations of this outlook can already be found in the Kabbalah of Gerona and in the Zohar. Man is the perfecting agent in the structure of the cosmos; like all the other created beings, only even more so, he is composed of all ten *Sefirot* and "of all spiritual things," that is, of the supernal principles that constitute the attributes of the Godhead. If the forces of the *Sefirot* are reflected in him, he is also the "transformer" who through his own life and deeds amplifies these forces to their highest level of manifestation and redirects them to their original source. To use the neoplatonic formula, the process of creation involves the departure of all from the One and its return to the One, and the crucial turning-point in this cycle takes place within man, at the moment he begins to develop an awareness of his own true essence and yearns to retrace the path from the multiplicity of his nature to the Oneness from which he originated. The essential correspondence or parallelism between the inward aspects of man, God, and creation introduces a mutual interplay among them that was frequently dramatized in the Kabbalah by means of anthropomorphic symbols, though the latter are nearly always accompanied by warnings that they are only to be understood "as if." If the *Sefirot* in which God reveals Himself assume the form of man, making him a microcosm in himself – a doctrine which found universal acceptance among the kabbalists – then man on earth is obviously capable of exerting an influence upon the macrocosm and upon primordial man above. Indeed it is this which bestows on him the enormous importance and the dignity that the kabbalists went to great lengths to describe. Because he and he alone has been granted the gift of free will, it lies in his power to either advance or disrupt through his actions the unity of what takes place in the upper and lower worlds. His essence is unfathomably profound; he is "a face within a face, an essence within an essence, and a form within a form" (Ezra of Gerona). Even man's physical structure corresponds to that of the *Sefirot,* so that we find Ezra of Gerona's description of the last *Sefirah* as "the form *[temunah]* that includes all forms" applied in the Zohar to man himself, who is called "the likeness *[deyokna]* that includes all likenesses." Such speculations about man's essence were most pithily expressed in various statements about Adam before his fall. Though his original harmony was disrupted by his sin, his principal mission remained to bring about a *tikkun* or restoration of this world and to connect the lower with the upper, thereby "crowning" creation by setting the Creator upon His throne and perfecting His reign over all His handiwork.

Man's essence has a spiritual nature for which his body serves only as an outer cloak. One widespread belief was that prior to Adam's sin his body too was spiritual, a kind of ethereal garment which became corporealized only after his fall. (In support of this view, the statement in Gen. 3:21 that God made "garments of skin," *kotnot ʿor,* for Adam and Eve after their expulsion from Eden, was taken as meaning that previously they had worn "garments of light," *kotnot ʾor.*) Had it not been for Adam's sin, the supreme divine will would have continued to work unbroken in Adam and Eve and all their descendants, and all of creation would have functioned in perfect harmony, transmitting the divine influx downward from above and upward from below, so that there would have been no separation between the Creator and His creation that adhered to Him. This uninterrupted communion, which is the goal of creation, was broken off at the time of Adam's sin when his lower will was parted from the divine will by his own free volition. It was then that his individuality, whose origin lay in his separation from God with its attendant proliferation of multiplicity, was born. What had been intended to be nothing more than a series of periodic fluctuations within a single harmonic system now turned into an opposition of extremes that found their expression in the fierce polarization of good and evil.

It is the concrete destiny of the human race, and of the Jew as the principal bearer of this mission and the recipient of God's revelation through the Torah, to overcome this polarization from within the human condition created by the first sin.

It is at this point that the problem of man in the world and the problem of evil in the world are interlaced. The sin which gave evil an active existence lies in man's failure to achieve his primal purpose, a failure which occurred again and again in history. It is the function of good in the world, whose tools are the Torah and its commandments, to bridge the abyss of separation that was formed by man's sin and to restore all existence to its original harmony and unity. The final goal, in other words, is the reunification of the divine and the human wills. It is likely that this kabbalistic doctrine of the corruption of the world through man's first sin originated as a result of direct contact with Christian beliefs, although it is also possible that these Christian ideas were derived from the same sources from which homologous *aggadot* in the Midrash took their inspiration. There can be no doubt that the kabbalists accepted the doctrine that the entire creation was fundamentally flawed by man's sin, after which the *sitra aḥra* or "other side" achieved a dominion over man which will not be finally abolished until the ultimate redemption in which all things will revert to their original state. The crucial Christian element, however, is lacking here, for unlike Christian dogma of original sin, the Kabbalah does not reject the idea that every man has the power to overcome this state of corruption, to the extent that he too is affected by it, by means of his own innate powers and with the help of divine aid prior to and independently of the final redemption. Speculations of this sort concerning the essence of sin as a disruption of the primordial order of things, the effects of which as it were reach up to and include the world of the *Sefirot* themselves, and concerning the means to achieve a *tikkun* whereby creation will be restored to its former grandeur, assumed a central place in the kabbalistic doctrine of man. This teaching developed out of purely religious motifs that only incidentally became motivated in the course of time with certain psychological motifs as well. Judah Halevi's metaphor in the *Kuzari* of Israel constituting the heart of the nations was taken over by the author of the Zohar and the kabbalists of Gerona, who spoke of the Jewish people as being "the heart of the cosmic tree" *(lev ha-ilan)*, a symbol borrowed from the *Sefer ha-Bahir.* Within this basic context, a fuller understanding of Israel's mission depends on the kabbalistic teachings on the structure of man's soul.

The kabbalists adopted the psychological doctrines of neoplatonism and tried to adapt them to the language of Jewish tradition. The Zohar occasionally mentions the three faculties or dispositions of a unified human soul as they are spoken of in the philosophy of Aristotle, but generally the Zohar refers to three essentially different parts of tne soul that form a sequence from lower to higher and are designated by the Hebrew terms *nefesh, ru'aḥ,* and *neshamah.* True, here too a unity was posited among these parts, but for the most part it remained problematic. The *nefesh* or first element is to be found in every man, for it enters him at the moment of birth and is the source of his animal vitality *(ḥiyyut)* and of the totality of his psychophysical functions. Whatever is necessary for the well-being of these functions is already contained in it and it is equally the property of all human beings. The two other parts of the soul, on the other hand, are postnatal increments that are found only in the man who has awakened spiritually and made a special effort to develop his intellectual powers and religious sensibilities. The *ru'aḥ* or *anima* is aroused at an unspecified time when a man succeeds in rising above his purely vitalistic side. But it is the highest of the three parts of the soul, the *neshamah* or *spiritus,* which is the most important of all. It is aroused in a man when he occupies himself with the Torah and its commandments, and it opens his higher powers of apprehension, especially his ability to mystically apprehend the Godhead and the secrets of the universe. Thus, it is the intuitive power that connects mankind with its Creator. It is only in the most general terms, however, that this tripartite division was adopted by all the various kabbalistic schools of thought. The terminology indeed remains the same, but the meanings and interpretations assigned to it differ widely in detail.

The fundamental division of the soul into three parts and the use of the terms *nefesh, ru'aḥ,* and *neshamah* (*naran* in the kabbalistic acronym) to describe them came from such Jewish neoplatonists as Abraham ibn Ezra and Abraham bar Ḥiyya, but in the course of the Kabbalah's development in the 13th century the philosophical content of these categories became considerably blurred and yielded to occultist associations under whose influence the strictly defined concepts of neoplatonic psychology took on fantastic and mythic dimensions. This process can be clearly traced in the classic texts of early Kabbalah. Already for the kabbalists of Gerona, though they still retained the original identification of the *neshamah* with the rational soul of the philosophers, the rational faculty of the soul was merged with the intuitive and mystic. Only the *neshamah,* they held, which was like a divine spark in man, was emanated directly from the Godhead itself rather than evolved from the separate intellects like the *ru'aḥ* or from the four elements like the *nefesh.* There is still an echo here of the philosophical division of the soul into its animal or vital, vegetative, and rational faculties and of the association of the soul's origin with the world of intellects, and particularly of the active intellect, as in the philosophy of Isaac Israeli. Within this system man's *nefesh* is still a common denominator between him and the animal world, while only the rational *neshamah,* whose origin is in the world of the *Sefirot,* and more precisely in the *Sefirah Binah,* truly deserves to be called the human soul, for it is a divine spark, one that was created from nothingness, to be sure, but from a nothingness that belongs nonetheless to the realm of the Godhead itself. Some of the kabbalists of Gerona even held that the source of the *neshamah* was in the *Sefirah* of Divine Wisdom or *Ḥokhmah,* a difference of opinion which bore on the question of the heights to which man's mystical cognition could attain.

The different strata of the Zohar reflect the varying psychological doctrines toward which its author leaned at different times. In the *Midrash ha-Ne'elam* there is still a clear debt to the psychology of the school of Maimonides with its doctrine of the "acquired intellect" which is activated in man through his pursuit of the Torah and its commandments and which alone has the power to bestow on him immortality of the soul. Together with this, however, we find the characteristic Aristotelian division of the soul, though minus the identification with the *nefesh, ru'aḥ,* and *neshamah,* and in connection with a number of functions that are peculiar to Moses de Leon alone. Thus, for instance, we find a distinction between the "speaking soul" *(ha-nefesh ha-medabberet)* and the "rational soul" *(ha-nefesh ha-sikhlit),* the latter alone possessing the supernal power which can bring man to perfection and which is identical with the true soul or *neshamah.* In effect the faculty called *nefesh* embraces all three forces, the animal, the vegetative, and the cognitive *(medabber),* which comprise the psycho-physical totality of man. The *neshamah,* in contrast, is a power concerned exclusively with mystical cognition, while the *ru'aḥ* represents an intermediate stage that involves the ethical power to distinguish between good and evil. The *neshamah* itself, on the other hand, by virtue of being "a part of God above," is capable of performing good only. It is impossible to speak here of a consistent approach: purely religious motifs alternate freely with philosophical ones, a confusion that extends to the relationship between intellectual awareness and the *neshamah* itself. In some instances the author, who expresses his views through the mouths of various rabbinic sages, even abandons the tripartite division of the soul entirely in favor of a twofold distinction between the vital soul *(ha-nefesh ha-ḥayyah)* and the *neshamah.* In the main corpus of the Zohar these divergent opinions are consolidated into a unified position of sorts in which religious motifs predominate over traditional philosophical and psychological ones. Here a fundamental contradiction emerges between the belief that the soul is universally the same for all mankind and another, double standard according to which the soul of the Jew and the soul of the gentile are dissimilar. The kabbalists of Gerona knew only of the former doctrine, that is, of the soul that is universally shared by all the descendants of Adam, and it is in the bulk of the Zohar that we read for the first time of a twofold though corresponding division of souls into non-Jewish and Jewish. The first group has its source in the "other side" or *sitra aḥra,* the second in the "holy side" or *sitra di-kedusha.* Interest in the Zohar is almost entirely confined to the psychic structure of the Jew. In the later Kabbalah, particularly in the works of Ḥayyim Vital, this duality between the "divine soul" *(ha-nefesh ha-elohit)* and the "natural soul" *(ha-nefesh ha-tiv'it)* is given enormous emphasis.

An important problem for the Kabbalah was the different sources of the different parts of the soul in the different worlds of emanation. According to the *Midrash ha-Ne'elam* even the highest *neshamah* emanates only from the Throne of Glory, that is, from the realm beneath that of the *Sefirot* though above that of the intellects. It is thus considered to be something created, though a creation of the highest order. In the main corpus of the Zohar this view is abandoned and each part of the soul is assigned a root in the world of the *Sefirot:* the *nefesh* originates in the *Sefirah Malkhut,* the *ru'aḥ* in the *Sefirah Tiferet,* and the *neshamah* in the *Sefirah Binah.* The descent of the supernal *neshamah* is brought about by the "holy union" of the "king" *(melekh)* and the "queen" *(matronita),* who are synonymous with the *Sefirot Tiferet* (or *Yesod*) and *Malkhut.* In its root every soul is a composite of male and female, and only in the course of their descent do the souls separate into masculine souls and feminine souls. The symbolism used to describe the descent of the souls from the world of emanation has a strongly mythical flavor. Especially prominent are the images of the tree of souls on which each soul blooms, and of the river which carries the souls downward from their supernal source. In both symbolisms the *Sefirah Yesod* is considered to be a halfway station through which all the souls must pass before entering the "treasure-house of souls" *(oẓar ha-neshamot),* which is located in the celestial paradise *(gan eden shel ma'alah),* where they live in bliss until they are called to descend still further and assume a human form. Many differences in detail exist among the various accounts of this process, but all the kabbalists agree as to the preexistence of the soul, especially in the latter's more strictly defined sense. Undisputed too is the belief that the soul originates on a plane higher than that of the angels, a doctrine that is referred to repeatedly in discussions of the human condition, for if man is capable of plunging to indescribable depths of depravity, he also has the capacity, when he fulfills his true density, of rising even above the angelic realm. No angel has that potential power to restore the worlds to a state of *tikkun* which has been granted to man.

In addition to the three parts of the soul that were collectively referred to by the acronym *naran,* kabbalists after the Zohar came to speak of two more additional, higher parts of the soul which they called *ḥayyah* and *yeḥidah* and which were considered to represent the sublimest levels of intuitive cognition and to be within the grasp only of a few chosen individuals. In Lurianic Kabbalah these five parts of the soul (*naran-ḥai* in acronym) became associated with the five *parẓufim* of *Adam Kadmon* in each of the worlds of *aẓilut, beri'ah, yeẓirah,* and *asiyyah,* so that a tremendous multiplicity of potential soul-ranks was created in accordance with the particular world of emanation and *parẓuf* from which a given soul stemmed. The highest soul having its source in the *yeḥidah* of the *Sefirah Keter* of the world of *aẓilut* was believed to be that of the Messiah. Unlike the masses of souls which are subject to the general laws of transmigration, such high-ranking souls were thought to remain concealed among the supernal lights until their time arrived and not enter the cycle of reincarnation at all.

From the Zohar and through the works of the disciples of Isaac Luria mention is made of an aspect of man that is referred to in the Kabbalah as the *ẓelem* (the "image," on the basis of Gen. 1:26, "Let us make man in our image, after our likeness") and which is not identical with any of the parts of the soul referred to above. The *ẓelem* is the principle of individuality with which every single human being is endowed, the spiritual configuration or essence that is unique to him and to him alone. Two notions are combined in this concept, one relating to the idea of human individuation and the other to man's ethereal garment or ethereal (subtle) body which serves as an intermediary between his material body and his soul. Because of their spiritual nature, the *neshamah* and *nefesh* are unable to form a direct bond with the body, and it is the *ẓelem* which serves as the "catalyst" between them. It is also the garment with which the souls clothe themselves in the celestial paradise before descending to the lower world and which they don once again after their reascent following physical death; during their sojourn on earth it is hidden within man's psycho-physical system and is discernible only to the intellectual eye of the kabbalist. The source of this belief is undoubtedly the similar doctrine held by the later neoplatonists concerning the ethereal or subtle body that exists in every man and that reveals itself to the mystical experience of those endowed with the gift of vision. Unlike the soul, the *ẓelem* grows and develops in accordance with the biological processes of its possessor. The kabbalists made use of a play on words to draw a parallel between man's *ẓelem* and his shadow *(ẓel).* The Zohar apparently considers the shadow to be a projection of the inner *ẓelem,* a belief that brought with it various popular magical superstitions that were widespread in Europe during the Middle Ages. Supposedly the *ẓelem* was the repository of the years a man lived and it departed with the approach of his death. According to another view, the *ẓelem* was woven as a garment for the soul from a man's good deeds and served as a kind of supernal appearance that protected and clothed him after his death. An ancient belief concerning such an ethereal body, whose source lies in Persian religion and which reached the author of the Zohar through later legends to become associated in his mind with various occultist ideas, was that the *ẓelem* was actually a man's true self. In Lurianic Kabbalah the *nefesh, ru'aḥ,* and *neshamah* were each assigned a *ẓelem* of their own which made it possible for them to function in the human body. Without the *ẓelem* the soul would burn the body up with its fierce radiance.

Moses de Leon, in his Hebrew writings, connects Maimonides' teachings that man's mission in this world is the full realization of his intellectual power with the doctrines of the Kabbalah. In his *Ha-Nefesh ha-Ḥakhamah* (1290), De Leon writes: "The purpose of the soul in entering the body is to exhibit its powers and abilities in the world . . . And when it descends to this world it receives power and influx to guide this vile world and to undergo a *tikkun* above and below, for it is of high rank, [being] composed of all things, and were it not composed in a mystic manner of what is above and below, it would not be complete . . . And when it is in this world, it perfects itself and completes itself from this lower world . . . And then it is in a state of perfection, which was not the case in the beginning before its descent."

According to an even earlier belief, which is already present in the *heikhalot* literature, all the souls are initially woven into a curtain *(pargod)* that hangs before the Throne of Glory, and this symbol of "the curtain of souls" was both adopted and adapted by a number of classic kabbalistic texts. The entire past history and future destiny of each single soul is recorded in this curtain. The *pargod* is not just a mystical fabric composed of spiritual ether which contains or is capable of receiving a record of each man's life and works; it is in addition the abode of all those souls that have returned from below to their native land. The souls of the wicked will find no place in it.

The kabbalistic doctrine of man and his soul dealt at great length with such eschatological problems as the fate of the soul after death, and its ascent crossing a river of fire, which resembles a kind of purgatory, to the terrestrial paradise and from there to the still sublimer pleasures of the celestial paradise and the realm referred to by the early kabbalists as "eternal life" (*ẓeror ha-ḥayyim,* literally: the bundle of life), which is sometimes synonymous with the celestial paradise and sometimes taken to refer to one of the *Sefirot* themselves, to which the soul returns to partake of the life of the Godhead. Human life on earth, therefore, must be seen in the broad context of the soul's life before birth and after death; hence the great interest of the Kabbalah in descriptions of heaven and hell such as those that we find in extensive and imaginative detail in the works of the kabbalists of Gerona or the Zohar, which inaugurated a long and influential tradition that flourished especially in the more popularly oriented literature of the Kabbalah until recent generations. Much was made here of the beliefs that were already to be found in the *aggadah,* particularly in a number of small, late

Midrashim, and which were reinterpreted in the light of kabbalistic symbolism and embellished with further details. Many obvious parallels exist between such material and similar eschatological motifs in Christianity and Islam. None of these teachings was ever given a definitive or authoritative form, thus enabling them to preserve a great deal of imaginative freedom in which folkloristic and mystic elements came together. The kabbalists of the 13th century in particular, among them the author of the Zohar, were attracted to such speculations and devoted considerable attention to such questions as the garments of the souls in paradise, the nature of their perceptions, the expansion of their consciousness in the apprehension of the divine, and the unification of the highest level of the *neshamah* with God.

Generally speaking, however, the kabbalists were wary about speaking of an actual mystic union of the soul with God and preferred to talk in terms of a spiritual communion *(devekut)* and no more. In his commentary on the letters of the Hebrew alphabet, Jacob b. Jacob Kohen (1270) speaks of mystic union without defining its nature. Moses de Leon mentions a supreme but temporary condition in which the soul finds itself standing before God in a state of contemplation and ultimate bliss without any garment between it and Him, though as a rule it must don a garment of ether or light even in the celestial paradise. Descriptions of the soul's union with God in terms of a divine nuptial are rare in the Kabbalah, though there are occasional examples, such as commentaries on the Song of Songs interpreting it as a conjugal dialogue between God and the soul. Even here, however, the love that is described is that between a father and daughter rather than of an erotic nature nor is anything said about the dissolution of the soul in the substance of God but merely about its temporary rapture in His presence. Only in the writings and poetry of the Kabbalists of Safed is there an obviously strong erotic overtone. Whether later schools of kabbalistic thought tended to the extreme mystical position, such as that found in Ḥabad Ḥasidism, some of whose speakers held that the soul loses its selfhood entirely in God, remains open to question. The author of the Zohar (2:253a) writes of the souls passing before God in the "room of love" from which the new souls depart to descend, but not in terms of conjugal imagery. On the contrary, the outcome of this divine "reception" is that God makes the soul swear to fulfill its earthly mission and attain to the "knowledge of the mysteries of the faith" which will purify it for its return to its homeland. By means of its awakening through the Torah and its commandments it gains new strength and helps complete the mystical figure of the *Keneset Yisrael* or Community of Israel, which is one with the *Shekhinah.* Only a few rare souls, such as those of Enoch and Elijah, ever achieve a permanent communion *(devekut)* with God; among the other biblical heroes of righteousness there are infinite degrees and differences of rank. Nor does a single fate await the different parts of the soul after death. The *nefesh* remains for a while in the grave, brooding over the body; the *ru'aḥ* ascends to the terrestrial paradise in accordance with its merits; and the *neshamah* goes directly back to its native home. Punishment and retribution are the lot of the *nefesh* and *ru'aḥ* alone. According to Moses de Leon, once in a cosmic jubilee the soul ascends from its communion with the *Shekhinah* to the hidden, celestial paradise in the world of the divine mind, that is, to the *Sefirah Ḥokhmah.*

The teachings of the Kabbalah concerning the soul are inextricably connected with the doctrine of transmigration, a basic kabbalistic principle that frequently came into conflict with other beliefs, such as that in the reward and punishment that are meted out to man in heaven and hell. (For further details, see the section *Gilgul* p.344). In the course of the development of the Kabbalah the idea of transmigration was radically expanded from that of a punishment restricted to certain sins to that of a general law encompassing all the souls of Israel, and, in a later stage, the souls of all human beings and even, in its most radical form, of all creation from the angels to insentient things. Thus, transmigration ceased to be considered merely a punishment and came also to be viewed as an opportunity for the soul to fulfill its mission and make up for its failures in previous transmigrations.

In comparison with the Zohar, the teachings of the Lurianic Kabbalah in regard to man's psychic structure are far more complex, concerning both the source of soul and man's inner make-up. In the works of Ḥayyim Vital there is also a discrepancy between his presentation of the subject in books meant for popular consumption, such as his *Sha'arei Kedushah,* and his more esoteric writings. In the former work Vital distinguishes clearly between three "quarries" *(maḥẓevim):* the quarry of the *Sefirot,* which is all divinity, the quarry of the souls, and the quarry of the angels, who are not themselves divine. His explanation of the coming-into-being of the souls through the emanative process in his *Eẓ Ḥayyim,* on the other hand, is far more complex and largely parallels his outline of the development of the lights that manifest the divine existence in the worlds of *aẓilut* and *beri'ah.* Just as the supernal lights in the *parẓufim* of *aẓilut* develop through conjunctions and "couplings" *(zivvugim)* of the *parẓufim,* so are the souls born through corresponding processes. Within the *Sefirah Malkhut* of each *parẓuf* are concealed souls in a potential state that ascend to the highest modes of that *parẓuf* and are actualized as a result of the "unions" of the *Sefirot.* At the outset these souls exist only in the state of "female waters" *(mayyim nukbin);* that is, they are passive potencies that possess the power of active arousal but still lack harmony and form, for their supernal source lies in those 288 sparks of light that fell into the *kelippot* at the time of the breaking of the vessels. Only through additional "couplings" of the *parẓuf* of *Ze'eir Anpin* with its female counterpart or *nukba* do they receive the actual structure of souls. With each new arousal of the "female waters" in these *parẓufim,* new opportunities arise for the creation of souls. Such a process occurs in all four worlds of emanation, the possible variations in modes of souls being practically infinite. Each of these souls recapitulates in miniature the structure of the worlds through which it passed in the process of being created, so that when it descends to enter a body in this world it will be able to work toward the latter's *tikkun* and uplifting and, to some extent, toward the uplifting of the higher worlds as well. On the other hand, a number of Lurianic texts stress the view that in substance the souls as such remain above and do not enter into bodies at all but rather radiate sparks of themselves that can be called souls *(neshamot)* by analogy only. The true soul hovers over a man, whether from near or afar, and maintains an immediate magic tie with its spark below. Popular expositions of these doctrines were always much simpler than their original elucidations, which tended to have a strong Gnostic flavor.

The soul of Adam was composed of all the worlds and was destined to uplift and reintegrate all the sparks of holiness that were left in the *kelippot.* Its garment was of spiritual ether and it contained within it all of the souls of the human race in perfect condition. It had 613 limbs, one for each of the commandments in the Torah, the spiritual aspect of which it was Adam's mission to uplift. Each of these limbs formed a complete *parẓuf* in itself known as a "great root" *(shoresh gadol),* which in turn contained 613, or according to other versions, up to 600,000 "small roots." Each "small root," which was also referred to as a "great soul" *(neshamah gedolah),* concealed within it 600,000 sparks or individual souls. These sparks too were apt to fission still further, but there remained a special affinity and power of attraction between all the sparks that descended from a common root. Each of these sparks formed a complete structure or *komah* in itself. Had Adam fulfilled his mission through the spiritual works of which he was capable, which called for contemplative action and deep meditation, the living chain between God and creation would have been closed and the power of evil, the *kelippah,* would have undergone that complete separation from holiness that, according to Luria, was the aim of the entire creative process. Thus, Adam had within him the fully developed powers of the *Adam Kadmon* in all his *parẓufim* and the depth of his fall when he sinned was equal to the great height of his cosmic rank beforehand (see below). Instead of uplifting everything, however, he caused it to fall even further. The world of *asiyyah,* which had previously stood firmly on its own base, was now immersed in the realm of the *kelippot* and subjected to their domination. Where the *Adam Kadmon* had stood a satanic creature now rose up, the *Adam Beliyya'al* who gained power over man. As a result of the admixture of the world of *asiyyah* with the *kelippah,* Adam assumed a material body and all his psycho-physical functions were corporealized. Moreover, his soul shattered and its unity was smashed to pieces. In it were elements of high rank known as "upper light" *(zihara ila'ah)* which refused to participate in Adam's sin and departed for above; these will not return to this world again until the time of the redemption. Other souls remained in Adam even after his spiritual stature was diminished from cosmic to mundane dimensions; these were the holy souls that did not fall into the clutches of the *kelippot,* and among them were the souls of Cain and Abel, which entered their bodies through direct hereditary transmission rather than through the process of transmigration. The bulk of the souls that were in Adam, however, fell from him and were subjugated by the *kelippot;* it is these souls that must achieve their *tikkun* through the cycle of transmigration, stage after stage. In a manner of speaking, Adam's fall when he sinned was a repetition of the catastrophe of the breaking of the vessels. The Lurianic Kabbalah went to great lengths to play up the dramatic elements in Adam's sin and its consequences. The inner history of the Jewish people and the entire world was identified with the recurrent reincarnations through which the heroes of the Bible struggled to achieve *tikkun.* Among these heroes were both "original souls" *(neshamot mekoriyyot),* which embraced a great and powerful psychic collectivity and were capable of great powers of *tikkun* whereby the whole world stood to benefit, and other, private, individual souls which could achieve a *tikkun* only for themselves. Souls descending from a single "root" comprised "families" who had special relations of affinity and were especially able to help each other. Now and then, though only very rarely, some of the upper souls that had not even been contained in the soul of Adam might descend to earth in order to take part in some great mission of *tikkun.* A complete innovation in Lurianic Kabbalah was the stress laid on the high rank of the souls of Cain and Abel, and particularly of the former. These two sons of Adam were taken to symbolize the forces of *gevurot* and *ḥasadim,* that is, the restrictive and outgoing powers of creation. Though the outgoing power of *ḥesed* is at present greater than the restrictive power of *gevurah* and *din,* this order will be reversed in the state of *tikkun.* Paradoxically, therefore, many of the great figures of Jewish history are represented as stemming from the root of Cain, and as the messianic time approaches, according to Isaac Luria, the number of such souls will increase. Ḥayyim Vital himself believed that he was of the root of Cain.

The nature of Adam's sin itself was never authoritatively defined in kabbalistic literature and highly differing views of it can be found. The problem of the first sin is closely connected with the problem of evil discussed above. According to the Spanish Kabbalah, the crux of the sin lay in "the cutting of the shoots" *(kizzuz ha-netiyyot),* that is, in the separation of one of the *Sefirot* from the others and the making of it an object of a special cult. The *Sefirah* that Adam set apart was *Malkhut,* which he "isolated from the rest." In the *Ma'arekhet Elohut,* nearly all the major sins mentioned in the Bible are defined as different phases of "the cutting of the shoots," or as repetitions of Adam's sin which prevented the realization of the unity between the Creator and His creation. Such were the drunkenness of Noah, the building of the Tower of Babel, Moses' sin in the desert, and above all the sin of the golden calf, which destroyed everything that had been accomplished in the great *tikkun* that took place during the theophany at Mount Sinai. In the final analysis, even the destruction of the Temple and the exile of the Jewish people were the results of misinformed meditations that brought division into the emanated worlds. Such sins wreaked havoc above and below, or, in the symbolism of the Zohar, caused division between the "king" *(melekh)* and the "queen" *(matronita)* or *Shekhinah.* The exile of the *Shekhinah* from her husband was the main metaphysical outcome of these sins. The good deeds of the biblical heroes, on the other hand, especially those of the patriarchs Abraham, Isaac, and Jacob, came to set this fundamental fault in creation aright and to serve as a paradigm for those who came after. It is noteworthy that the author of the Zohar himself was reticent in his remarks on the nature of Adam's sin. The author of the *Tikkunei ha-Zohar* was less circumspect. Adam's sin, he held, took place above all in the divine mind itself, that is, in the first or second *Sefirah,* from which it caused God's departure, indeed, it was Adam's sin alone that caused God to become transcendent (*Tikkun* 69). As far as the effect of the first sin is concerned, we find two conflicting lines of thought: (1) Whereas previously good and evil had been mixed together, the sin separated evil out as a distinct reality in its own right (as in Meir ibn Gabbai's *Avodat ha-Kodesh*); (2) Good and evil were originally separate, but the sin caused them to become mixed together (such was Gikatilla's position, and in general, that of the Lurianic Kabbalah). In the tradition of earlier teachings, such as those in the *Ma'arekhet ha-Elohut* and the *Sefer ha-Peli'ah,* Lurianic Kabbalah also occasionally explained the first sin as a "technical" mishap, though one with grave consequences, in the procedure of *tikkun.* This occurred because Adam was in a hurry to complete the *tikkun* before its appointed time, which was to have been on the first Sabbath of creation, starting late in the afternoon of the sixth day. The tendency in such explanations is to emphasize that essentially the greatest biblical sinners meant to do good but erred in their choice of means.

The principal instrument for repairing the primal fault in the metaphysical aspect of completing the *tikkun* of the broken vessels and in relation to Adam's sin which disrupted the channels of communication between the lower and upper worlds, is human engagement in holiness through Torah and prayer. This activity consists of deeds, which restore the world in its outward aspects, and of prayer and meditations, which effect it inwardly. Both have profound mystical dimensions. In the act of revelation God spoke and continues to speak to man, while in the act of prayer it is man who speaks to God. This dialogue is based on the inner structure of the worlds, on which each human action has an effect of which man is not always aware. The actions of the man who is conscious of their significance, however, have the greatest effect and help speed the ultimate *tikkun.* Because the world became material as a result of the first sin, the great majority of the commandments in the Torah acquired a material meaning, because every instrument must be adjusted to the end it is meant to serve. Yet this does not detract from the inward spiritual dimension that each commandment possesses, whose collective purpose is the restoration and perfection of the true stature of man in all 613 of the limbs of his soul. The same Torah which prescribes a practical way of life for human beings in the light of revelation simultaneously provides an esoteric guide for the mystic in his struggle to commune with God. Evident in such an approach is the conservative character of the Kabbalah as a factor working to defend and deepen Jewish values. Observance of the Torah was sanctified as the way to abolish division in the world, and every man was called upon to play his part in this task in accordance with the rank of his soul and the role that was allotted him. The spiritual light that shines in every commandment connects the individual with the root of his soul and with the supernal lights in general. Thus, a mission was entrusted to the collective body of the souls of Israel which could not easily be carried out and involved many descents and reascents before all obstacles could be overcome, but which in the final analysis had a clear and urgent purpose: the *tikkun* and final redemption of the world.

EXILE AND REDEMPTION

It therefore follows that the historical exile of the Jewish people also has its spiritual causation in various disturbances and faults in the cosmic harmony for which it serves as a concrete and concentrated symbol. The situation of the spiritual worlds at the time of the exile was completely different from that ideal state in which they were supposed to exist according to the divine plan and in which they will find themselves at the time of redemption. In one form or another this belief recurs throughout the development of the Kabbalah. The kabbalists of Gerona held that for as long as the exile continues the *Sefirot* do not function normally; as they are withdrawn toward the source of their original emanation, Israel lacks the power to adhere to them truly by means of the Divine Spirit, which has also departed for above. Only through individual effort can the mystic, and he alone, still attain to a state of *devekut.* In some texts we are told that only the five lower *Sefirot* continue to lead an emanated existence below, whereas the upper *Sefirot* remain above. When the Jewish people still lived in its own land, on the other hand, the divine influx descended from above to below and reascended from below to above all the way to the highest *Keter.* The letters of the Tetragrammaton, which contain all the emanated worlds, are never united for the duration of the exile, especially the final *vav* and *he,* which are the *Sefirot Tiferet* and *Malkhut,* and which were already parted at the time of Adam's first sin, when the exile in its cosmic sense began. Since then there has been no constant unity between the "king" and "queen," and this will be restored only in the future when the queen, who is the *Shekhinah* and the *Sefirah Malkhut,* reascends to be rejoined with the *Sefirah Tiferet.* Similarly, only in messianic times will man return to that paradisical state in which "he did of his own nature that which it was right to do, nor was his will divided against itself" (Naḥmanides on Deut. 30:6). It was in these same Spanish circles that there first arose the belief in the mystical nature of the Messiah which supposedly consisted in a harmony of all the levels of creation from the most rarified to the most gross, so that he possessed "a divine power, and an angelic power, and a human power, and a vegetative power, and an animal power" (Azriel in his Epistle to Burgos). The Messiah will be created through the special activity of the *Malkhut,* and this origin will serve to elevate his powers of cognition above those of the angels. The Zohar too takes the position that the crux of the redemption works itself out in the uninterrupted conjunction of *Tiferet* and *Malkhut,* and that redemption of Israel is one with the redemption of God Himself from His mystic exile. The source of this belief is talmudic and can be found in both the Palestinian Talmud, *Sukkah* 4, 3 and in the Midrash Lev. R. 9, 3: "The salvation of the Holy One blessed be He is the salvation of Israel." At the time of the redemption "all the worlds will be in a single conjunction *[be-zivvug eḥad],*" and in the year of the grand jubilee *Malkhut* will be joined not only with *Tiferet* but with *Binah* as well. In the *Ra'aya Meheimna* and the *Tikkunei Zohar* we find the idea that whereas during the period of the exile the world is in thrall to the Tree of Knowledge of Good and Evil, in which the realms of good and evil struggle between themselves so that there are both holiness and impurity, permitted acts and forbidden acts, sacred and profane, in the time of the redemption dominion will pass to the Tree of Life and all will be as before Adam's sin. The utopian motifs in the messianic idea are given their ultimate expression in these works and in those composed under their influence. The future abolition of the commandments mentioned in the Talmud (Nid. 61b) was taken by the kabbalists to refer to the complete spiritualization of the commandments that would take place under the dominion of the Tree of Life. The details of this vision tended to vary greatly according to the homiletic powers of the particular kabbalist who embraced it.

In Lurianic Kabbalah too the exile of Israel is connected with Adam's sin, the outcome of which was the scattering of the holy sparks, both of the *Shekhinah* and of Adam's soul. When the sparks became diffused even further in Adam's descendants, the mission of gathering them and raising them up, that is, of preparing the way for redemption, was awarded to Israel. The exile is not, therefore, merely a punishment and a trial but is a mission as well. The Messiah will not come until the good in the universe has been completely winnowed out from the evil, for in Vital's words "the ingathering of the exiles itself means the gathering of all the sparks that were in exile." The exile may be compared to a garden that has been abandoned by its gardener so that weeds have sprung all over it (*Ez Ḥayyim,* ch. 42, para.4). The *tikkun* progresses in predetermined stages from one generation to the next and all the transmigrations of souls serve this purpose. As the exile draws to an end, the *tikkun* of the human structure of the *Sefirot* reaches the "feet" *(akevayyim);* thus, the souls that go forth in "the footsteps of the Messiah" are unusually obdurate and resistant to *tikkun,* from whence stem the special ordeals that will occur on the eve of the redemption.

Opinions varied as to whether the Messiah's soul too entered the cycle of transmigration: some kabbalists held that his soul had also been incarnated in Adam and in David (according to other views, in Moses as well), while others contended (a view first found in the *Sefer ha-Bahir*) that it was not subject to the law of transmigration. According to the Lurianic Kabbalah, each of the *parẓufim* of the *Adam Kadmon* had a female counterpart *(nukba)* except for the *parẓuf* of *Arikh Anpin,* which was instrumental in creating the world through a process of autogeny *(zivvug minnei u-vei),* that is, of "coupling" with itself. At the time of the redemption, however, it will be able to "couple" through the pairing of its *Yesod* with its *nukba* (the waxing *Sefirah Malkhut*), and the offspring of this act will be the most hidden root of the soul of the Messiah Son of David, which is its *yeḥidah.* The descent of this soul depends on the state of *tikkun* prevailing in the different worlds, for in every generation there is one righteous man who has the disposition to receive it if only the age is worthy. The soul of the Messiah Son of Joseph, on the other hand, who is the harbinger of the Messiah Son of David, is subject to the regular cycle of transmigration. The redemption will not come all at once but will rather manifest itself in stages, some of which will be inwardly hidden in the spiritual worlds and others of which will be more apparent. The final redemption will come only when not a single spark of holiness is left among the *kelippot.* In the writings of Luria's school different views can be found on whether the Messiah himself has an active role to play in the process of redemption through his unique ability to raise up certain last sparks that are beyond the power of anyone else. This question assumed particular importance in the development of the Shabbatean movement. In the course of the redemption certain hitherto concealed lights from the *parẓuf* of *Attika* will manifest themselves and alter the structure of creation. In the final analysis, national and even nationalistic motifs blend with the cosmic ones in the Lurianic Kabbalah to form a single great myth of exile and redemption.

THE TORAH AND ITS SIGNIFICANCE

The role of the Torah in the Kabbalah as an instrument and a way of life in the service of a universal *tikkun* has already been discussed. The central position of the Torah in the Kabbalah, however, goes far beyond such definitions. The kabbalistic attitude to the Pentateuch, and in a somewhat lesser degree to the Bible as a whole, was a natural corollary of the overall kabbalistic belief in the symbolic character of all earthly phenomena. There was literally nothing, the kabbalists held, which in addition to its exterior aspect did not also possess an interior aspect in which there existed a hidden, inner reality on various levels. The kabbalists applied this view of the "transparency" of all things to the Torah as well, but inasmuch as the latter was the unique product of divine revelation, they also considered it the one object which could be apprehended by man in its absolute state in a world where all other things were relative. Regarded from this point of view in its quality as the direct word of God and thus unparalleled by any other book in the world, the Torah became for the kabbalists the object of an original mystical way of meditation. This is not to say that they sought to deny the concrete, historical events on which it was based, but simply that what interested them most was something quite different, namely, the conducting of a profound inquiry into its absolute nature and character. Only rarely did they discuss the relationship among the three parts of the Bible, the Pentateuch, the Prophets, and the Hagiographa, and for the most part their attention was concentrated almost exclusively on the Torah in its strict sense of the Five Books of Moses. The Zohar (3:35a) actually attempts in one place to assert the absolute superiority of these books and their students over the Prophets and the Hagiographa and their students, yet only in the context of commenting on the talmudic statement that "the sage is preferable to the prophet." In his *Ginnat Egoz* (1612, 34dff.), Joseph Gikatilla also sought to attach a kabbalistic interpretation to the tripartite division of the Bible. On the whole, however, where kabbalistic commentaries do exist on the Prophets and the later writings (and especially on the Book of Psalms), their approach to these texts is essentially no different from that of the commentaries on the Torah.

The classic formulations of this approach appear as early as the 13th century, nor do later and bolder restatements of them, even in the Lurianic school, add anything fundamentally new. A large part of the literature of the Kabbalah consists of commentaries on the Pentateuch, the Five Scrolls, and the Book of Psalms, and the Zohar itself was largely written as a commentary on the Pentateuch, Ruth, and the Song of Songs. Books such as the commentaries on the Pentateuch by Menahem Recanati, Baḥya b. Asher, Menahem Ẓiyyoni, and Abraham Sabba became classic kabbalistic texts. Noteworthy too is the fact that there are practically no kabbalistic commentaries to speak of on entire books of the Prophets or on the Book of Job and the Book of Daniel. Only a few, isolated exegeses of fragments of these texts tend to recur regularly in connection with certain mystical interpretations. The only known kabbalistic commentary ever to have been composed on the entire Bible is the 16th-century *Minḥat Yehudah*, written in Morocco by an unknown author, large sections of which have been preserved in various manuscripts. Outside the Pentateuch, the Song of Songs alone was made the subject of a large number of kabbalistic commentaries, beginning with Ezra of Gerona's and continuing down to several written in recent generations.

The main basis of the kabbalistic attitude toward the Torah is, as was mentioned above, the fundamental kabbalistic belief in the correspondence between creation and revelation. The divine emanation can be described both in terms of symbols drawn from the doctrine of *Sefirot* and of the emanated, supernal lights, and of symbols drawn from the sphere of language and composed of letters and names. In the latter case, the process of creation can be symbolized as the word of God, the development of the fundamentals of divine speech, and as such it is not essentially different from the divine processes articulated in the Torah, the inwardness of which reveals the same supreme laws that determine the hierarchy of creation. In essence, the Torah contains in a concentrated form all that was allowed to develop more expansively in the creation itself. Strictly speaking, the Torah does not so much mean anything specific, though it in fact means many different things on many different levels, as it articulates a universe of being. God reveals Himself in it as Himself rather than as a medium of communication in the limited human sense. This limited, human meaning of the Torah is only its most eternal aspect. The true essence of the Torah, on the other hand, is defined in the Kabbalah according to three basic principles: the Torah is the complete mystical name of God; the Torah is a living organism; and the divine speech is infinitely significant, and no finite human speech can ever exhaust it.

THE TORAH AS THE MYSTICAL NAME OF GOD

Underlying this principle is an originally magic belief which was transformed into a mystical one. Such a magical belief in the structure of the Torah can already be found in the *Midrash Tehillim* (on Ps.3): "Had the chapters of the Torah been given in their correct order, anyone who read them would have been enabled to raise the dead and work miracles; therefore, the Torah's [true] order has been hidden and is known [only] to God." The magical uses of the Torah are discussed in the book *Shimmushei Torah,* which dates at the very latest from the geonic period, and in which it is related that together with the accepted reading of the Torah, Moses received yet another reading composed of Holy Names possessing magical significance. To read the Torah "according to the names" (Naḥmanides introduction to his commentary on the Pentateuch) does not, therefore, have any concrete human meaning but rather one that is completely esoteric: far from having to do with historical narrations and commandments, the Torah thus read is solely concerned with concentrations of the divine power in various combinations of the letters of God's Holy Names. From the magical belief that the Torah was composed of God's Holy Names, it was but a short step to the mystical belief that the entire Torah was in fact nothing else than the Great Name of God Himself. In it God expressed His own being insofar as this being pertained to creation and insofar as it was able to manifest itself through creation. Thus, the divine energy chose to articulate itself in the form of the letters of the Torah as they express themselves in God's Name. On the one hand this Name comprises the divine potency; on the other hand it comprehends within it the totality of the concealed laws of creation. Obviously, such an assumption about the Torah did not refer to the physical text written on parchment but rather to the Torah in its pre-existential state in which it served as an instrument of the creation. In this sense, the creation of the Torah itself was simply a recapitulation of the process by which the *Sefirot* and the individual aspects of the Divine Names were emanated from the substance of *Ein-Sof.* Nor is the Torah separate from this substance, for it represents the inner life of God. In its earliest and most hidden existence it is called "the primordial Torah," *Torah Kedumah,* which is occasionally identified with the *Sefirah Hokhmah.* Thereafter it develops in two manifestations, that of the Written Torah and that of the Oral Torah, which exist mystically in the *Sefirot Tiferet* and *Malkhut,* while on earth they exist concretely and are geared to the needs of man.

The relationship between the Torah as the all-comprehensive Name of God and the Ineffable Name or Tetragrammaton was defined by Joseph Gikatilla in his *Sha'arei Orah:* "The entire Torah is like an explication of, and a commentary on, the [Ineffable] Name of God." In what way is it essentially an explication of the Ineffable Name? In that it is a single "fabric" woven out of the epithets of God in which the Ineffable Name unfolds. Thus, the Torah is a structure the whole of which is built on one fundamental principle, namely, the Ineffable Name. It can be compared to the mystic body of the Godhead, and God Himself is the soul of its letters. This view evolved among the kabbalists of Gerona, and can be found in the Zohar and in contemporaneous works.

THE TORAH AS A LIVING ORGANISM

The weaving of the Torah from the Ineffable Name suggests the analogy that the Torah is a living texture, a live body in the formulation of both Azriel of Gerona and the Zohar. The Torah "is like an entire building; just as one man has many organs with different functions, so among the different chapters of the Torah some seem important in their outward appearance and some unimportant," yet in actual fact all are bound together in a single organic pattern. Just as man's unified nature is divided up among the various organs of his body, so the living cell of God's Name, which is *the* subject of revelation, grows into the earthly Torah that men possess. Down to the last, seemingly insignificant detail of the masoretic text, the Torah has been passed on with the understanding that it is a living structure from which not even one letter can be excised without seriously harming the entire body. The Torah is like a human body that has a head, torso, heart, mouth, and so forth, or else it can be compared to the Tree of Life, which has a root, trunk, branches, leaves, bark, and pith, though none is distinct from another in essence and all form a single great unity. (According to Philo of Alexandria, a similar conception of the Torah as a living organism inspired the sect of Therapeutes, as it did to a certain extent his own biblical commentaries, without there of course being any demonstrable historical filiation between such sources and the Kabbalah.) This organic approach was well able to explain the apparent stylistic discrepancies in the Bible, which was part narrative (and sometimes even seemingly superfluous narrative), part law and commandment, part poetry, and part even raw statistic. Behind all these different styles stood the mystic unity of the great Name of God. Such outward appearances were simply the garments of the hidden inwardness that clothed itself in them, and "Woe is he who looks only at the garments!" Connected with this is the view that the Torah is revealed in a different form in each of the worlds of creation, starting with its primordial manifestation as a garment for *Ein-Sof* and ending with the

Torah as it is read on earth – a view that was especially promulgated by the school of Israel Sarug (see above p.131). There is a "Torah of *azilut,*" a "Torah of *beri'ah,*" and so forth, each one reflecting the particular function of the mystical structure of a given phase of creation. In each of these phases there is a relativization of the Torah's absolute essence, which is in itself unaffected by these changes, great though they may be. Similarly, as was explained above, the single Torah appears in different forms in the different *shemmitot* or cosmic cycles of creation.

THE INFINITE SIGNIFICANCE OF THE DIVINE SPEECH

A direct consequence of this belief was the principle that the content of the Torah possessed infinite meaning, which revealed itself differently at different levels and according to the capacity of its contemplator. The unfathomable profundity of the divine speech could not possibly be exhausted at any one level alone, an axiom that applied as well to the concrete, historical Torah revealed by God in the theophany at Mount Sinai. From the outset this Torah possessed the two aspects mentioned above, a literal reading formed by its letters that combined to make words of the Hebrew language, and a mystical reading composed of the divine Names of God. But this was not all. "Many lights shine forth from each word and each letter," a view that was summed up in the well-known statement (itself an epigrammatic rendering of a passage in the *Otiyyot de-Rabbi Akiva*) that "the Torah has 70 faces." The conventional four categories by which the Torah was said to be interpretable, the literal *(peshat),* the allegorical *(remez),* the hermeneutical or homiletical *(derash),* and the mystical *(sod),* served only as a general framework for a multiplicity of individual readings, a thesis which from the 16th century on was expressed in the widespread belief that the number of possible readings of the Torah was equal to the number of the 600,000 children of Israel who were present at Mount Sinai – in other words, that each single Jew approached the Torah by a path that he alone could follow. These four categories were first collectively given the acronym *pardes* (literally, "garden") by Moses de Leon. Basically, this "garden of the Torah" was understood as follows. The *peshat* or literal meaning did not embrace only the historical and factual content of the Torah but also the authoritative Oral Law of rabbinic tradition. The *derash* or hermeneutical meaning was the path of ethical and aggadic commentary. The *remez* or allegorical meaning comprised the body of philosophical truths that the Torah contained. The *sod* or mystical meaning was the totality of possible kabbalistic commentaries which interpreted the words of the Torah as references to events in the world of the *Sefirot* or to the relationship to this world of the biblical heroes. The *peshat,* therefore, which was taken to include the corpus of talmudic law as well, was only the Torah's outermost aspect, the "husk" that first met the eye of the reader. The other layers revealed themselves only to that more penetrating and latitudinous power of insight which was able to discover in the Torah general truths that were in no way dependent on their immediate literal context. Only on the level of *sod* did the Torah become a body of mystical symbols which unveiled the hidden life-processes of the Godhead and their connections with human life. This fourfold exegetical division was apparently influenced by the earlier yet similar categories of Christian tradition (literal, moral, allegorical, mystical). Literal, aggadic, and philosophical-allegorical commentaries had previously been known to Jewish tradition as well, and Joseph ibn Aknin's long commentary on the Song of Songs, for example, which was composed early in the 13th century, combined all three of these approaches. Baḥya b. Asher was the first biblical commentator (1291) to introduce all the four aspects into his textual explications, though he did not use the acronym *pardes* and referred to the philosophical reading of the Torah as "the way of the intellect." Explication on the level of *sod,* of course, had limitless possibilities, a classic illustration of which is Nathan Spira's *Megalleh Amukkot* (1637), in which Moses' prayer to God in Deuteronomy 3:23ff. is explained in 252 different ways. In the main corpus of the Zohar, where use of the term "Kabbalah" is studiously avoided, such mystical interpretations are referred to as "mysteries of the faith" *(raza de-meheimnuta),* that is, exegesis based on esoteric beliefs. The author of the Zohar, whose belief in the primacy of kabbalistic interpretation was extreme, actually expressed the opinion (3:152a) that had the Torah simply been intended as a series of literal narratives, he and his contemporaries would have been able to compose a better book! Occasionally kabbalistic interpretations would deliberately choose to stress certain words or verses that seemed insignificant on the surface and to attribute to them profound symbolic importance, as can be seen in the Zohar's commentary on the list of the kings of Edom in Genesis 36 or on the deeds of Benaiah the son of Jehoiada related in II Samuel 23.

Since the Torah was considered to be essentially composed of letters that were nothing less than configurations of the divine light, and since it was agreed that it assumed different forms in the celestial and terrestrial worlds, the question arose of how it would appear in paradise or in a future age. Certainly its present reading had been affected by the corporealization of its letters that took place at the time of Adam's sin. The answer given to this conundrum by the kabbalists of Safed was that the Torah contained the same letters prior to Adam's sin but that in a different sequence that corresponded to the condition of the worlds at that time. Thus, it did not include the same prohibitions or laws that we read in it now, for it was adjusted in its entirety to Adam's state before his fall. Similarly, in future ages the Torah will cast off its garments and will again appear in a purely spiritual form whose letters will assume new spiritual meanings. In its primordial existence, the Torah already contained all the combinational possibilities that might manifest themselves in it in accordance with men's deeds and the needs of the world. Had it not been for Adam's sin, its letters would have combined to form a completely different narrative. In messianic times to come, therefore, God will reveal new combinations of letters that will yield an entirely new content. Indeed, this is the "new Torah" alluded to in the Midrash in its commentary on Isaiah 51:4, "For Torah shall go forth from Me." Such beliefs continued to be widespread even in ḥasidic literature.

The most radical form that this view took was associated with the talmudic *aggadah* according to which prior to the creation of the world the whole of the Torah was written in black fire on white fire. As early as the beginning of the 13th century the daring notion was expressed that in reality the white fire comprised the true text of the Torah, whereas the text that appeared in black fire was merely the mystical Oral Law. Hence it follows that the true Written Law has become entirely invisible to human perception and is presently concealed in the white parchment of the Torah scroll, the black letters of which are nothing more than a commentary on this vanished text. In the time of the Messiah the letters of this "white Torah" will be revealed. This belief is referred to in a number of the classic texts of Ḥasidism as well.

THE MYSTIC WAY

DEVEKUT

Life in the framework of Judaism, through the study of Torah and prayer, offered the kabbalist a way of both active and passive integration in the great divine hierarchy of creation. Within this hierarchy, the task of the Kabbalah is to help guide the soul back to its native home in the Godhead. For each single *Sefirah* there is a corresponding ethical attribute in human behavior, and he who achieves this on earth is integrated into the mystic life and the harmonic world of the *Sefirot.* Cordovero's *Tomer Devorah* is dedicated to this subject. The kabbalists unanimously agreed on the supreme rank attainable by the soul at the end of its mystical path, namely, that of *devekut,* mystical cleaving to God. In turn, there might be different ranks of *devekut* itself, such as "equanimity" (*hishtavvut,* the indifference of the soul to praise or blame), "solitude" (*hitbodedut,* being alone with God), "the holy spirit," and "prophecy." Such is the ladder of *devekut* according to Isaac of Acre. In contrast, a running debate surrounded the question of what was the highest quality preparatory to such *devekut,* the love of God or the fear of God. This argument recurs throughout the literature of the Kabbalah with inconclusive results, and continued into the later *musar* (moralist) literature that was composed under kabbalist influence. Many kabbalists considered the worship of God in "pure, sublime fear," which was quite another thing from the fear of punishment, to be an even higher attainment than the worship of Him in love. In the Zohar this "fear" is employed as one of the epithets of the highest *Sefirah,* thus giving it supreme status. Elijah de Vidas, on the other hand, in his *Reshit Ḥokhmah,* defended the primacy of love. In effect, both of these virtues lead to *devekut.*

The early Kabbalah of Provence already sought to define *devekut* both as a process by which man cleaves to his Creator and as an ultimate goal of the mystic way. According to Isaac the Blind: "The principal task of the mystics *[ha-maskilim]* and of those who contemplate on His Name is [expressed in the commandment] 'And ye shall cleave unto Him' [Deut. 13:5]. And this is a central principle of the Torah, and of prayer, and of [reciting] the blessings, to harmonize one's thought with one's faith as though it cleaved to [the worlds] above, to conjoin God in His letters, and to link *[likhlol]* the ten *Sefirot* in Him as a flame is joined to a coal, articulating his epithets aloud and conjoining Him mentally in His true structure." In a more general sense, Naḥmanides, in his commentary on Deuteronomy 11:22, defines *devekut* as the state of mind in which "You constantly remember God and His love, nor do you remove your thought from Him . . . to the point that when [such a person] speaks with someone else, his heart is not with them at all but is still before God. And indeed it may be true of those who attain this rank, that their soul is granted immortal life *[ẓerurah bi-ẓeror ha-ḥayyim]* even in their lifetime, for they are themselves a dwelling place for the *Shekhinah.*" Whoever cleaves in this way to his Creator becomes eligible to receive the holy spirit (Naḥmanides, *Sha'ar ha-Gemul*). Inasmuch as human thought derives from the rational soul in the world of *aẓilut* it has the ability to return to its source there, "And when it reaches its source, it cleaves to the celestial light from which it derives and the two become one" (Meir ibn Gabbai). In his commentary on Job 36:7, Naḥmanides refers to *devekut* as the spiritual level that characterizes the true *ḥasid,* and in fact Baḥya ibn Pakuda's definition of *ḥasidut* in his *Ḥovot ha-Levavot* (8, 10) is very similar to Azriel of Gerona's definition of *devekut* in his *Sha'ar ha-Kavvanah,* for both speak in almost identical terms of the effacement of the human will in the divine will or of the encounter and conformity of the two wills together. On the other hand, kabbalistic descriptions of *devekut* also tend to resemble the common definitions of prophecy and its various levels. In his Epistle to Burgos, Azriel of Gerona speaks of the way to prophecy as being also the way to *devekut,* while in his *Perush ha-Aggadot* (ed. Tishby, 40), he virtually equates the two.

Devekut results in a sense of beatitude and intimate union, yet it does not entirely eliminate the distance between the creature and its Creator, a distinction that most kabbalists, like most Ḥasidim, were careful not to obscure by claiming that there could be a complete unification of the soul and God. In the thought of Isaac of Acre, the concept of *devekut* takes on a semi-contemplative, semi-ecstatic character.[10] Here and there ecstatic nuances can be found in the conceptions of *devekut* of the other kabbalists.[11]

PRAYER, *KAVVANAH,* AND MEDITATION

The main path traveled by the mystic was of course associated in the kabbalistic mind with the practical observance of the commandments, yet the two were not intrinsically connected, for essentially the mystic way involved the ascent of the soul to a state of ecstatic rapture through a process of concentrated thought and meditation. Above all, in the Kabbalah it is prayer that serves as the principal realm for this ascent. Prayer is unlike the practical commandments, each of which demands a certain well-defined action, the performance of which does not leave much room for meditation and mystical immersion. True, every commandment has its mystical aspect whose observance creates a bond between the world of man and the world of the *Sefirot,* but the full force of spirituality can express itself far better in prayer. The mystical intention or *kavvanah* that accompanies every commandment is in effect a concentration of thought upon the kabbalistic significance of the action at the time that it is performed; prayer, on the other hand, stands independent of any outward action and can easily be transformed into a comprehensive exercise in inward meditation. The tradition of mystical prayer accompanied by a system of meditative *kavvanot* that focused on each prayer's kabbalistic content developed as a central feature of the Kabbalah from its first appearance among the Ḥasidei Ashkenaz and the kabbalists of Provence and on through the Lurianic Kabbalah and the latter's last vestiges in modern times. The greatest kabbalists were all great masters of prayer, nor would it be easy to imagine the Kabbalah's speculative development without such permanent roots in the experience of mystical prayer. In its kabbalistic guise, the concept of *kavvanah* was given new content far beyond that bestowed on it in earlier rabbinic and halakhic literature.[12]

Kabbalistic doctrine sought a way out of the dilemma, which the kabbalists themselves were aware of, that was posed by the theologically unacceptable notion that prayer could somehow change or influence the will of God. The

Kabbalah regarded prayer as the ascent of man to the upper worlds, a spiritual peregrination among the supernal realms that sought to integrate itself into their hierarchical structure and to contribute its share toward restoring what had been flawed there. Its field of activity in kabbalistic thought is entirely in the inward worlds and in the connections between them. Using the traditional liturgical text in a symbolic way, prayer repeats the hidden processes of the universe which, as was explained above, can themselves be regarded as essentially linguistic in nature. The ontological hierarchy of the spiritual worlds reveals itself to the kabbalist in the time of prayer as one of the many Names of God. This unveiling of a divine "Name" through the power of the "word" is what constitutes the mystical activity of the individual in prayer, who meditates or focuses his *kavvanah* upon the particular name that belongs to the spiritual realm through which his prayer is passing. In early Kabbalah, it is the name of the appropriate *Sefirah* on which the mystic concentrates when reciting the prayers and into which he is, as it were, absorbed, but in later Kabbalah, and especially in the Lurianic school, this is replaced by one of the mystical Names of God. Thus, while prayer has an aspect of "inward magic" by which it is empowered to help order and restore the upper worlds, it has no outwardly magical efficacy. Such "inward magic" is distinguished from sorcery in that its meditations or *kavvanot* are not meant to be pronounced. The Divine Names are not called upon, as they are in ordinary operational magic, but are aroused through meditative activity directed toward them. The individual in prayer pauses over each word and fully gauges the *kavvanah* that belongs to it. The actual text of the prayer, therefore, serves as a kind of banister onto which the kabbalist holds as he makes his not unhazardous ascent, groping his way by the words. The *kavvanot,* in other words, transform the words of the prayer into holy names that serve as landmarks on the upward climb.

The practical application of mystical meditation in the Kabbalah, therefore, is connected mainly, if not exclusively, with the moment of prayer. In terms of Jewish tradition, the principal innovation in this approach lay in the fact that it shifted the emphasis from group prayer to individual mystical prayer without in any way destroying the basic liturgical framework itself. Indeed, in their effort to preserve this framework, the first generations of kabbalists largely refrained from composing original prayers of their own that would reflect their beliefs directly. Only from the 16th century onward and especially under the influence of the Lurianic school, were large numbers of kabbalistic prayers added to the old. The short meditations of the early kabbalists were now replaced by increasingly lengthy and involved *kavvanot* whose execution led to a considerable lengthening of the service. The system of *kavvanot* reached its maximum development in the school of the Yemenite kabbalist Shalom Sharabi, where prayer required an entire congregation of mystical meditators who were capable of great psychical exertion. Several such groups are actually known to have existed. According to Azriel of Gerona, he who meditates mystically in his prayer "drives away all obstacles and impediments and reduces every word to its 'nothingness.' " To achieve this goal is in a sense to open a reservoir whose waters, which are the divine influx, pour down on the praying individual. Because he has properly prepared himself for these supernal forces, however, he is not overwhelmed and drowned by them. Having completed his upward ascent, he now descends once again with the aid of fixed *kavvanot,* and in this manner unites the upper and the lower worlds. An excellent example of this circle of ascent and descent can be found in the *kavvanot* to the *Shema.*

In contrast to the contemplative character of prayer in the Kabbalah of Gerona and the Zohar, Lurianic Kabbalah emphasized its more active side. Every prayer was now directed not only toward the symbolic ascent of him who prays, but also toward the upraising of the sparks of light that belonged to his soul. "From the day the world was created until the end of time, no one prayer resembles another." Despite the fact that there is a common collectivity to all the *kavvanot,* each one has its completely individual nature, and every moment of prayer is different and demands its own *kavvanah.* In this way, the personal element in prayer came to be highly stressed. Not even all the *kavvanot* listed in the writings devoted to them exhausted the totality of possibilities, just as a musical score cannot possibly contain the personal interpretation that the musician brings to it in the act of performance. In answer to the question in the Talmud, "From where can it be known that God Himself prays?" the Kabbalah replied that through the mystical prayer man was drawn upward or absorbed into the hidden, dynamic life of the Godhead, so that in the act of his praying God prayed too. On the other hand, the theory can also be found in kabbalistic literature that prayer is like an arrow shot upward by its reciter with the bow of *kavvanah.* In yet another analogy from the Lurianic school, which had a great impact on ḥasidic literature, the process of *kavvanah* is defined in terms of the drawing downward of the spiritual divine light into the letters and words of the prayer book, so that this light can then reascend to the highest rank (A. Azulai, *Ḥesed le-Avraham,* 2 par. 44). In the opinion of the Zohar (2:215b), the individual passes through four phases in his prayer: he accomplishes the *tikkun* of himself, the *tikkun* of this lower world, the *tikkun* of the upper world, and, finally, the *tikkun* of the Divine Name. Similarly, the morning service as a whole was interpreted as representing a symbolic progression, at the end of which the reciter was ready to risk all for God, whether by yielding to a near-ecstatic rapture or by wrestling with the *sitra aḥra* in order to rescue the imprisoned holiness from its grasp. In Lurianic prayer a special place was reserved for *yiḥudim* ("acts of unification"), which were meditations on one of the letter combinations of the Tetragrammaton, or on configurations of such names with different vocalizations, such as Isaac Luria was in the habit of giving to his disciples, to each "in accordance with the root of his soul." As employed in such individual *yiḥudim,* the *kavvanot* were detached from the regular liturgy and became independent instruments for uplifting the soul (a practice paralleled in many other mystical systems of meditation). They also were sometimes used as a method of communing with other souls, particularly with the souls of the departed *ẓaddikim.*

A wide kabbalistic literature was devoted to the path of prayer and to mystical interpretations of the traditional liturgy. Such interpretations were less commentaries in the ordinary sense than systematic manuals for mystical meditation in prayer. Among the best known of these are Azriel of Gerona's *Perush ha-Tefillot* (extant in many Mss., French translation by G. Séd, 1973); Menahem Recanati's *Perush ha-Tefillot* (1544); David b. Judah he-Ḥasid's *Or Zaru'a,*[13] and a commentary by an anonymous author (c. 1300), the long introduction to which has been published (*Koveẓ Madda'i le-Zekher Moshe Shor,* 1945, 113–26). Among such books written in the 16th century were Meir ibn Gabbai's *Tola'at Ya'akov* (1560); Jacob Israel Finzi's *Perush ha-Tefillot* (in Cambridge Ms.); and Moses Cordovero's *Tefillah le-Moshe* (1892). The rise of Lurianic Kabbalah led to an enormous outpouring of books of *kavvanot* and mystical prayers. The most detailed among the are Ḥayyim Vital's *Sha'ar ha-Kavvanot* and *Peri Eẓ Ḥayyim,* and Emmanuel Ḥai Ricchi's summary *Mishnat Ḥasidim* (1727). As early as Vital's circle the practice developed of compiling special prayer books with the corresponding *kavvanot* and many redactions of these circulated in manuscript under the title *Siddur ha-Ari* ("The Prayer Book of Isaac Luria"). A number of such prayer books were published, among them *Sha'arei Raḥamim* (Salonika, 1741); *Ḥesed le-Avraham* (Smyrna, 1764); Aryeh Loeb Epstein's *Mishnat Gur Aryeh* (Koenigsberg, 1756); and the *Siddur ha-Ari* of the kabbalists of the Brody *klaus* (Zolkiew, 1781); and the kabbalistic prayer books of Asher Margoliot (Lvov, 1788), Shabbetai Rashkover (1794), and Jacob Kopel Lifschuetz, whose *Kol Ya'akov* (1804) is full of Shabbatean influence. The acme of such books was the prayer book of Shalom Sharabi, the bulk of which was published in Jerusalem in a long series of volumes beginning in 1910. To this day there are groups in Jerusalem who pray according to Sharabi's *kavvanot*, although the spiritual practice of this can take many years to master. Other guides to prayer from this period are Isaiah Horowitz's *Siddur ha-Shelah* (Amsterdam, 1717); Solomon Rocca's *Kavvanot Shelomo* (Venice, 1670); Moses Albaz's *Heikhal ha-Kodesh* (Amsterdam, 1653); and Ḥayyim Vital's son Samuel's *Ḥemdat Yisrael* (1901). In his *Sha'ar Ru'aḥ ha-Kodesh* (with commentary by

Joseph Sadboon of Tunis, 1874), Ḥayyim Vital discusses the *yiḥudim.* Numerous kabbalist prayer books were compiled for various specific occasions, a genre that began with Nathan Hannover's *Sha'arei Ẓiyyon* (1662).

ECSTASY

Beside the mystical meditation of prayer a number of other mystical "disciplines" developed in Kabbalah. (On the ecstatic ascents of the Merkabah mystic see above p.10.) From the beginning of the geonic period there is a text called *Sefer ha-Malbush* describing a half-magical, half-mystical practice of "putting on the Name" *(levishat ha-Shem),* whose history apparently goes back even further. Of central importance in this context is the "prophetic Kabbalah" of Abraham Abulafia, in which an earlier tradition of systematic instruction based on "the science of combination," *ḥokhmat ha-ẓeruf* (a play on the double meaning of the word in *ẓeruf ha-otiot,* "the combination of letters," and *ẓeruf ha-levavot,* "the purification of hearts"), was refashioned. This mystical discipline made use of the letters of the alphabet, and especially of the Tetragrammaton and the other Names of God, for the purpose of training in meditation. By immersing himself in various combinations of letters and names, the kabbalist emptied his mind of all natural forms that might prevent his concentrating on divine matters. In this way he freed his soul of its natural restraints and opened it to the divine influx, with whose aid he might even attain to prophecy. The disciplines of *kavvanah* and letter combination became linked together toward the end of the 13th century and from then on mutually influenced each other. The Lurianic *kavvanot* were especially heavily influenced by *ḥokhmat ha-ẓeruf.* The doctrine of the *Sefirot* was also absorbed by these disciplines, though Abulafia himself regarded it as a less advanced and less valuable system than "the science of combination" as the latter was expounded in his books.

In the further course of the development of the Kabbalah, many kabbalists continued to regard such disciplines as the most esoteric side of Kabbalah and were reluctant to discuss them in their books. Abulafia himself described quite explicitly, and in a seemingly objective manner, just what were the obstacles and dangers, as well as the rewards, that such mystical experience could bring. He drew a clear parallel between "the science of combination" and music, which too could conduct the soul to a state of the highest rapture by the combination of sounds. The techniques of "prophetic Kabbalah" that were used to aid the ascent of the soul, such as breathing exercises, the repetition of the Divine Names, and meditations on colors, bear a marked resemblance to those of both Indian Yoga and Muslim Sufism. The subject see flashes of light and feels as though he were divinely "anointed." In certain stages he lives through a personal identification with an inner spiritual mentor or *guru* who is revealed to him and who is really Metatron, the prince of God's countenance, or in some cases, the subject's own true self. The climactic stage of this spiritual education is the power of prophecy. At this point Abulafia's Kabbalah coincides with the discipline of *kavvanot* developed by the kabbalists of Gerona, which was also intended to train its practitioner so that "whoever has mastered it ascends to the level of prophecy."

Here and there mention is made in the Kabbalah of various other occult phenomena, but on the whole there is a clear-cut tendency to avoid discussing such things, just as most kabbalists refrained from recording their personal experiences in the autobiographical form that was extremely common in the mystical literature of both Christianity and Islam. Descriptions exist of the mystical sensation of the subtle ether or "aura," called also "the ether of the *ẓelem,*" by which man is surrounded, of mystical visions of the primordial letters in the heavens (Zohar, 2:130b), and of invisible holy books that could be read only with the inward senses.[14] In a number of places prophecy is defined as the experience wherein a man "sees the form of his own self standing before him and relating the future to him."[15] One anonymous disciple of Abulafia actually composed a memoir about his experiences with *ḥokhmat ha-ẓeruf.*[16] Generally speaking, however, the autobiographical confession was strictly disapproved of by most kabbalists. In the Zohar, a description of mystical ecstasy occurs only once, and that in a highly circumspect account of the experience of the high priest in the Holy of Holies on the Day of Atonement (3:67a, and in the *Zohar Ḥadash,* 19a). Even in those writings that essentially continue the tradition of Abulafia, there is little of the latter's ecstatic extravagance, and ecstasy itself is moderated into *devekut.* Not until the golden period of the ḥasidic movement in the late 18th century, particularly in the circle of the Maggid of Mezhirech, are descriptions of ecstatic abandon once again encountered in the literature of Judaism. Several books or sections of books that dealt openly and at length with the procedure to be followed for the attainment of ecstasy and the holy spirit, such as Judah Albotoni's *Sulam ha-Aliyah* (c. 1500) and the last part of Ḥayyim Vital's *Sha'arei Kedushah,* called *Ma'amar Hitbodedut,* "On Solitary Meditation" (Ginzburg Ms. 691, British Museum 749), were suppressed in their day and preserved only in manuscript. The only such book to have been actually published was the *Berit Menuḥah* (Amsterdam, 1648), the work of an anonymous 14th-century author that has been mistakenly attributed to Abraham of Granada. This book, which contains lengthy descriptions of visions of the supernal lights attained by meditating on various vocalizations of the Tetragrammaton with the aid of a symbolic system unparalleled elsewhere in the Kabbalah, borders on the frontier between "speculative Kabbalah" *(kabbalah iyyunit),* whose primary interest was in the inner spiritual guidance of the individual, and "practical Kabbalah" *(kabbalah ma'asit),* which was concerned above all with magical activity.

PRACTICAL KABBALAH

The disciplines discussed in the preceding section, though they deal with practical instructions for the spiritual life, do not belong to the realm of "practical Kabbalah" in the kabbalistic sense of the term, which refers rather to a different set of preoccupations. For the most part, the realm of practical Kabbalah is that of purely motivated or "white" magic, especially as practiced through the medium of the sacred, esoteric Names of God and the angels, the manipulation of which may affect the physical no less than the spiritual world. Such magical operations are not considered impossible in the Kabbalah, or even categorically forbidden, though numerous kabbalistic writings do stress the prohibitions against them. In any case, only the most perfectly virtuous individuals are permitted to perform them, and even then never for their private advantage, but only in times of emergency and public need. Whoever else seeks to perform such acts does so at his own grave physical and spiritual peril. Such warnings were generally observed in the breach, however, as is demonstrated by the extensive literature of practical Kabbalah that has survived. In actual practice, moreover, the boundary between physical magic and the purely inward "magic" of letter combination and *kavvanot* was not always clear-cut and could easily be crossed in either direction. Many early scholarly investigators of the Kabbalah did not distinguish clearly between the two concepts and frequently used the term "practical Kabbalah" to refer to the Lurianic school as opposed to Cordovero and the Zohar. This confusion can be traced as far back as Pico della Mirandola, whose usage of the term is highly ambiguous and contradictory. He considered the Kabbalah of Abulafia to belong to the "practical" variety. Abulafia himself, however, was well aware of the distinction and in many of his books he fiercely attacked the "masters of names" *(ba'alei shemot)* who defiled themselves with magical practices. The anonymous author of a text once attributed to Maimonides (*Megillat Setarim,* published in *Ḥemdah Genuzah* 1 (1856), 45–52), who himself belonged to the Abulafian school, differentiates between three kinds of Kabbalah, "rabbinic Kabbalah," "prophetic Kabbalah," and "practical Kabbalah." The latter is identified with theurgy, the magical use of Sacred Names, which is not at all the same thing as the meditation on such names. Before the term "practical Kabbalah" came into use, the concept was expressed in Hebrew by the phrase *hokhmat ha-shimmush,* which was a translation of the technical Greek term *(praxis)* used to denote magical activity. The Spanish kabbalists made a clear distinction between traditions that had come down to them from "masters of the doctrine of the *Sefirot*" *(ba'alei ha-sefirot)* and those that derived from magicians or "masters of the names." Also known to them were certain magical practices that were referred to as "great theurgy" *(shimmusha rabba)* and "little theurgy" (*Shimmusha zutta;* see *Tarbiz,* 16 (1945), 196–209). Unlike Abulafia, however, Gikatilla, Isaac ha-Kohen, and Moses de Leon all mention such "masters of the name" and their expositions without holding them up to reproach. From the 15th century on the semantic division into "speculative" and "practical" Kabbalah became prevalent, though it was not necessarily meant to be prejudicial to the latter. On the whole, however, general summaries of kabbalistic doctrine rarely referred to its "practical" side except incidentally, such as in Cordovero's angelology *Derishot be-Inyanei ha-Mal'akhim* (at the end of R. Margaliot's *Malakhei Elyon,* 1945).

Historically speaking, a large part of the contents of practical Kabbalah considerably predate those of speculative Kabbalah and are not dependent on them. In effect, what came to be considered practical Kabbalah constituted an agglomeration of all the magical practices that developed in Judaism from the talmudic period down through the Middle Ages. The doctrine of the *Sefirot* hardly ever played a decisive role in these practices, despite occasional attempts from the late 13th century on to integrate the two. The bulk of such magic material to have been preserved is found in the writings of the Ḥasidei Ashkenaz, which for the most part were removed from the theological influences of Kabbalism, both in texts that were especially written on the subject, such as Eleazer of Worms' *Sefer ha-Shem,* and in collected anthologies. Most earlier theurgical and magical works, such as the *Ḥarba de-Moshe* or the *Sefer ha-Razim,* were eventually assimilated into practical Kabbalah. Various ideas and practices connected with the concept of the *golem* also took their place in practical Kabbalah through a combination of features drawn from the *Sefer Yeẓirah* and a number of magical traditions. The ostensible lines drawn by the kabbalists to set the boundaries of permissible magic were frequently overstepped and obscured, with the consequent appearance in practical Kabbalah of a good deal of "black" magic – that is, magic that was meant to harm others or that employed "the unholy names" (*shemot ha-tum'ah,* Sanhedrin 91a) of various dark, demonic powers, and magic used for personal gain. The open disavowal of practical Kabbalah by most kabbalists, to the extent that it was not simply an empty formality, was for the most part in reaction to practices like these. Such black magic embraced a wide realm of demonology and various forms of sorcery that were designed to disrupt the natural order of things and to create illicit connections between things that were meant to be kept separate. Activity of this sort was considered a rebellion of man against God and a hubristic attempt to set himself up in God's place. According to the Zohar (1:36b), the source of such practices was "the leaves of the Tree of Knowledge," and they had existed among men since the expulsion from the Garden of Eden. Alongside this view, there continued the ancient tradition, first found in the Book of Enoch, that the rebellious angels who had fallen from heaven were the original instructors of the magic arts to mankind. To this day, the Zohar relates (3:208a, 212a–b), the sorcerers journey to "the mountains of darkness," which are the abode of the rebel angels Aza and Azael, to study under their auspices (a Jewish version of the late-medieval idea of the "Sabbat" of the witches and sorcerers). The biblical archetype of the sorcerer is Balaam. Such black magic is called in the Kabbalah "apocryphal science" *(ḥokhmah ḥiẓonah)* or "the science of the Orientals" (*ḥokhmat benei kedem,* on the basis of I Kings 5:10), and though a theoretical knowledge of it is permitted – several kabbalistic books in fact treat of it at length – its practice is strictly forbidden. The sorcerer draws forth the spirit of impurity from the *kelippot* and mixes the clean and the unclean together. In the *Tikkunei Zohar* the manipulation of such forces is considered justifiable under certain circumstances, inasmuch as the *sitra aḥra* must be fought with its own weapons.

The opposition of the speculative kabbalists to black magic was unable to prevent a conglomeration of all kinds of magical prescriptions in the literature of practical Kabbalah. Often the white-magical practices of amulets and protective charms can be found side by side with the invocation of demons, incantations, and formulas for private gain (e.g., magical shortcuts, the discovery of hidden treasure, impregnability in the face of one's enemies, etc.), and even sexual magic and necromancy. The international character of magical tradition is evident in such collections, into which many originally non-Jewish elements entered, such as Arab demonology and German and Slavic witchcraft. It was this indiscriminate mixture that was responsible for the rather gross image of practical Kabbalah that existed in the Jewish popular mind and eventually reached the Christian world too, where the theoretical kabbalistic distinction between forbidden and permitted magical practices was of course overlooked completely. The widespread medieval conception of the Jew as a powerful sorcerer was further nourished to no small extent by the practical kabbalistic sources that fostered this confusion. As early as the geonic period the title *ba'al shem* or "master of the name" signified a master of practical Kabbalah who was an expert at issuing amulets for various purposes, invoking angels or devils, and exorcising evil spirits who had taken possession of a human body. On the whole such figures were clearly identified with white magic in the popular mind, as opposed to sorcerers, witches, and wizards.

Among earlier kabbalistic works that are especially rich in material taken from practical Kabbalah are the Zohar, the writings of Joseph b. Shalom Ashkenazi and Menahem Ẓiyyoni, and the *Berit Menuḥah,* while in the post-Lurianic period the *Emek ha-Melekh* is outstanding in this respect. Magical prayers attributed to some of the leading *tannaim* and *amoraim* were already composed long before the development of speculative Kabbalah, and indeed magical material that has been preserved in sources like the *Sefer ha-Razim* and later ones from the geonic age contains many similarities to magical Greek papyri that have been discovered in Egypt. Contemporaneous with such sources are various magical reworkings of the *shemoneh esreh* prayer, such as the *Tefillat Eliyahu* (Cambridge Ms. 505), which was already known to Isaac the Blind, or the maledictory version of the same prayer, quoted from the archives of Menahem Recanati in the complete manuscript of *Shoshan Sodot.* Almost all such compositions have been preserved in manuscript only, except for occasional borrowings from them in more popular anthologies. Among the most important known manuscripts of practical Kabbalah with its characteristic mixture of elements are Sassoon Ms. 290;[17] British Museum Ms. 752; Cincinnati Ms. 35; and Schocken Ms. 102. Literature of this sort was extremely widespread, however, and hundreds of additional manuscripts also exist. Noteworthy also are the anonymous *Sefer ha-Ḥeshek*[18] and *Shulḥan ha-Sekhel* (in Sassoon Ms.), and Joseph ibn Ẓayyaḥ's *She'erit Yosef* (1549, formerly in the Jewish Library of Vienna). In none of these books, however, is there any serious attempt at a systematic exposition of the subject. In many popular anthologies, which were widely circulated, both practical Kabbalah and folk medicine were combined together.

Other prominent works of practical Kabbalah include Joel Ba'al Shem's *Toledot Adam* (1720) and *Mif'alot Elohim* (1727); *Derekh ha-Yashar* (Cracow, 1646); Ẓevi Chotsh's *Derekh Yasharah* (Fuerth, 1697); *Ta'alumot Ḥokhmah* (Venice, 1667); Zechariah Plongian's *Sefer ha-Zekhirah* (Hamburg, 1709); Abraham Ḥammawi's anthologies *He'aḥ Nafshenu* (1870), *Davek me-Aḥ* (1874), *Abi'ah Ḥidot* (1877), *Lidrosh Elohim* (1879), and *Nifla'im Ma'asekha* (1881); and Ḥayyim Palache's *Refu'ah ve-Ḥayyim* (1874). A great deal of valuable material from the realm of practical Kabbalah can be found in *Mitteilungen der Gesellschaft fuer juedische Volkskunde* (1898–1929), and *Jahrbuecher fuer juedische Volkskunde,* 1–2 (1923–24). Ḥayyim Vital too compiled an anthology of practical Kabbalah mixed with alchemical material (Ms. in the Musayof Collection, Jerusalem). His son Samuel composed an alphabetical lexicon of practical Kabbalah called *Ta'alumot Ḥokhmah* which has been lost. Moses

Zacuto's comprehensive lexicon *Shorshei ha-Shemot,* on the other hand, has been preserved in many manuscript copies (selections from it were published in French by M. Schwab, 1899). Clear proof exists of several books on the subject of practical Kabbalah written by some outstanding kabbalists, but these have not been preserved. Among the great masters of practical Kabbalah in the eyes of kabbalistic tradition itself were figures like Judah he-Ḥasid, Joseph Gikatilla, Isaac of Acre, Joseph della Reina, Samson of Ostropol, and Joel Ba'al Shem Tov.

To the realm of practical Kabbalah also belong the many traditions concerning the existence of a special archangelic alphabet, the earliest of which was "the alphabet of Metatron." Other such alphabets of *kolmosin* ("[angelic] pens") were attributed to Michael, Gabriel, Raphael, etc. Several of these alphabets that have come down to us resemble cuneiform writing, while some clearly derive from early Hebrew or Samaritan script. In kabbalistic literature they are known as "eye writing" *(ketav einayim)* because their letters are always composed of lines and small circles that resemble eyes. Under exceptional circumstances, as when writing the Tetragrammaton or the Divine Names Shaddai and Elohim, these alphabets were occasionally used even in a text otherwise written in ordinary Hebrew characters. Such magical letters, which were mainly used in amulets, are the descendants of the magical characters that are found in theurgic Greek and Aramaic from the first centuries C.E. In all likelihood their originators imitated cuneiform writing that could still be seen in their surroundings, but which had become indecipherable and had therefore assumed magical properties in their eyes.

The well-known medieval book, *Clavicula Salomonis* ("Solomon's Key"), was not originally Jewish at all, and it was only in the 17th century that a Hebrew edition was brought out, a mélange of Jewish, Christian, and Arab elements in which the kabbalistic component was practically nil. By the same token, *The Book of the Sacred Magic of Abra-Melin* (London, 1898), which purported to be an English translation of a Hebrew work written in the 15th century by a certain "Abraham the Jew of Worms" and was widely regarded in modern European occultist circles as being a classical text of practical Kabbalah, was not in fact written by a Jew, although its anonymous 16th century author had an uncommon command of Hebrew. The book was originally written in German and the Hebrew manuscript of it found in Oxford (Neubauer 2051) is simply a bad translation. Indeed, the book circulated in various editions in several languages. It shows the partial influence of Jewish ideas but does not have any strict parallel in kabbalistic literature.

The relationship of the Kabbalah to other "occult sciences" such as astrology, alchemy, physiognomy, and chiromancy was slight. Astrology and alchemy play at most a marginal role in kabbalistic thought. At the same time, practical Kabbalah did manifest an interest in the magical induction of the pneumatic powers of the stars through the agency of specific charms. This use of astrological talismans, which clearly derived from Arabic and Latin sources, is first encountered in the *Sefer ha-Levanah* (London, 1912), cited by Naḥmanides. Another text of astrological magic is the Hebrew translation of the *Picatrix, Takhlit he-Ḥakham* (Arabic original and German translation, 1933 and 1962). This genre of magical book is also referred to in the Zohar (1: 99b), and several tracts on the subject have been preserved in manuscripts of practical Kabbalah. A number of kabbalistic works dealing with the preparation of magical rings combine astrological motifs with others taken from "the science of combination." A book in this vein that claims to have been divinely revealed has been preserved in Sassoon Ms. 290. The *Sefer ha-Tamar,* which has been attributed to Abu Aflaḥ Syracuse (ed. G. Scholem, 1927), was preserved in practical kabbalistic circles but did not derive from them, having its source rather in Arabic astrological magic. Interestingly, kabbalistic attitudes toward astrological magic were highly ambivalent, and some leading kabbalists, such as Cordovero, actually approved of it.

Alchemy too had relatively little influence on the Kabbalah. Indeed, there was a basic symbolic divergence between the two from the start, for while the alchemist considered gold to be the symbol of perfection, for the kabbalist gold, which symbolized *Din,* had a lower rank than silver, which symbolized *Ḥesed.* Nevertheless, efforts were made to harmonize the two systems and allusions to this can already be found in the Zohar. Joseph Taitaẓak, who lived at the time of the Spanish expulsion, declared the identity of alchemy with the divine wisdom of the Kabbalah.[19] In 17th-century Italy a kabbalistic alchemical text called *Esh Meẓaref* was composed in Hebrew, but the original has been lost; large parts have been preserved in Latin translation in Knorr von Rosenroth's *Kabbala Denudata* vol. I (assembled in English by Robert Kelum, A Short Enquiry Concerning the Hermetick Art, London, 1714, and in a new edition, 1894). Ḥayyim Vital spent two years of his youth studying alchemy exclusively and composed a book on alchemical practices which he publicly repented of in old age. No kabbalistic reworkings of physiognomy are known, but there are several treatments of chiromancy (see p.317), especially in the Zohar and in traditions of the Lurianic school. Some kabbalists believed that the lines of the hand and the forehead contained clues to a man's previous reincarnations.

The practice of practical Kabbalah raised certain problems concerning occult phenomena (see also preceding section). A number of these come under the category of *giluy einayim,* whereby a man might be granted a vision of something that, generally speaking, only the rare mystic was permitted to see. Such visions included a glimpse of the "sapphiric ether" *(ha-avir ha-sappiri)* that surrounds all men and in which their movements are recorded, "the book in which all one's deeds are expressly written down" (especially in the works of Menahem Azariah Fano). The concept of the *ẓelem* was often associated with this ether, according to Lurianic sources, as was that of the angelic "eye-writing" (mentioned above), and invisible letters that spelled out the secret nature of each man's thoughts and deeds which hovered over every head and might be perceived by initiates. Sometimes, especially during the performance of certain commandments such as circumcision, the initiate might also be granted a vision of the Tetragrammaton in the form of fiery letters that "appear and disappear in the twinkling of an eye." A *mohel* who was also a kabbalist could tell by the hue of this fire what the fortune of the newborn child would be (*Emek ha-Melekh,* 175b). The *aggadah* about the rays of light that shone from Moses' forehead (Midrash Ex. R. 47) fathered the kabbalistic notion of a special halo that circled above the head of every righteous man (*Sefer Ḥasidim,* par. 370). This belief became widespread, although the halo was sometimes considered to appear only shortly before the *ẓaddik's* death. Visions of angels were explained in a similar fashion: the angel's form was imprinted in an invisible ether that was not the same as ordinary air, and could be seen by a select few, not because they were prophets but because God had opened their eyes as a reward for having purified their corporeal bodies (Cordovero in his *Derushei Mal'akhim*). Sorcerers who saw demons constituted an analogous phenomenon. Automatic writing is mentioned in a number of sources. Thus, Joseph b. Todros Abulafia, for example, composed a kabbalistic tract under the influence of "the writing name" (*Kerem Ḥemed,* 8, 105). Such "names" that facilitated the process of writing are referred to in a number of practical kabbalistic manuscripts. In describing a "revelation" that was granted to him, Joseph Taitaẓak speaks of "the mystic secret of writing with no hand." The anthology *Shoshan Sodot* (Oxford Ms., par. 147) mentions the practice of automatic writing, "making marks *[ḥakikah]* by the pen," as a method of answering vexing or difficult questions. A number of other spiritualistic phenomena, both spontaneous and deliberately induced, are also mentioned in various sources, among them the "levitating table," which was particularly widespread in Germany from the 16th century on. According to one eyewitness report, the ceremony was accompanied by a recital of Divine Names taken from practical Kabbalah and the singing of psalms and hymns (Wagenseil, *Sota,* 1674, 530). An acquaintance of Wagenseil's told him (*ibid.,*1196) of how he had seen some yeshivah students from Wuerzburg who had studied in Fuerth lift such a table with the aid of Divine Names. Specific instructions for table levitation have been preserved in a number of kabbalistic manuscripts (e.g.,

Jerusalem 1070 8°, p. 220). The use of divining rods is also known in such literature, from the 15th century on at the latest.[20]

Certain magical names or *shemot* were prescribed for certain special activities. The *shem ha-garsi* was invoked in the study of Talmud or any rabbinic text *(girsa)*; the *shem ha-doresh* was invoked by the preacher *(darshan)*. There was a "name of the sword" *(shem ha-ḥerev)*, a "name of the Ogdoad" *(shem ha-sheminiyut)*, and a "name of the wing" *(shem ha-kanaf)*. Some of these invocations were borrowed from non-Jewish sources, as for example the name "Parakletos Jesus b. Pandera" that was recommended by a preacher for use in synagogue (*Hebr. Bibl.*, 6 (1863), 121; G. Scholem, *Kitvei Yad be-Kabbalah* (1930), 63).

4

THE WIDER INFLUENCES OF AND RESEARCH ON KABBALAH

THE INFLUENCE OF THE KABBALAH ON JUDAISM

Though it has been evaluated differently by different observers, the influence of the Kabbalah has been great, for it has been one of the most powerful forces ever to affect the inner development of Judaism, both horizontally and in depth. Jewish historians of the 19th century, while conceding the Kabbalah's significant role, considered it to have been overwhelmingly baleful and even catastrophic, but the appraisal of 20th-century Jewish historiography has been far more positive, no doubt due in part to profound changes in the course of Jewish history itself since the beginnings of the Zionist revival. There has been a new readiness in recent decades to acknowledge the wealth of rich symbolism and imagery that the kabbalistic imagination added to Jewish life as well as to recognize the contributing role of the Kabbalah in strengthening the inner life of collective Jewry and the individual Jew. The reappraisal has made itself felt especially in the last two generations, both in literature and historical studies. Indeed, at times it has assumed panegyric proportions, as in the works of S.A. Horodezky, which have done little to further a fruitful discussion of the religious motives that found their expression in the Kabbalah with results that, if all is said and done, were sometimes problematic.

As was pointed out at the beginning of this exposition, the Kabbalah represented a theological attempt, open to only a relative few, whose object was to find room for an essentially mystical world-outlook within the framework of traditional Judaism and without altering the latter's fundamental principles and behavioral norms. To what extent if at all this attempt was successful remains open to debate, but there can be no doubt that it achieved one very important result, namely, that for the three-hundred-year period roughly from 1500 to 1800 (at the most conservative estimate) the Kabbalah was widely considered to be *the* true Jewish theology, compared with which all other approaches were able at best to lead an isolated and attenuated existence. In the course of this period an open polemical attack on the Kabbalah was practically unheard of, and characteristically, when such an attack appeared, it was almost always in the guise of a rebuke addressed to the later kabbalists for having misrepresented and corporealized the pure philosophy of their predecessors, rather than an open criticism of the Kabbalah itself. Examples of this tactic, which was dictated by necessity, can be found in the anonymous polemic written in Posen in the middle of the 16th century[21] and in Jacob Francis of Mantua's anti-kabbalistic poems from the middle of the 17th century. When Mordecai Corcos, on the other hand, wished to publish a book openly opposed to the Kabbalah itself in Venice in 1672, he was prevented from doing so by the Italian rabbinical authorities.

In the area of *halakhah,* which determined the framework of Jewish life in accordance with the laws of the Torah, the influence of the Kabbalah was limited though by no means unimportant. As early as the 13th century there began a tendency to interpret the *halakhah* in kabbalistic terms without actually seeking to effect halakhic rulings or discussions by this means. In the main such kabbalistic interpretations touched on the mystical reasons for the commandments. At times there was an undeniable tension between the kabbalists and the strict halakhists, which in some cases expressed itself partly in kabbalistic outbursts rooted both in the natural feeling of superiority, which, whether justified or not, is frequently found in mystics and spiritualists (as in the case of Abraham Abulafia), and partly in the lack of a certain religious intensity, that kabbalists believed characterized the outlook of some leading halakhists. The attacks on cut-and-dried legalism that can be found in Baḥya ibn Paquda's *Ḥovot ha-Levavot* and in the *Sefer Ḥasidim* clearly reflect an attitude that did not exist only in the imagination of the mystics and was responsible for the fierce polemical assaults of the authors of the *Ra'aya Meheimna* and the *Sefer ha-Peli'ah* against the "talmudists," that is, the halakhists. Popular witticisms directed against such scholars, such as the ironic reading of the word *ḥamor* ("ass") as an acronym for the phrase *ḥakham mufla ve-rav rabanan* ("a great scholar and rabbi of rabbis"; see Judah b. Barzilai's *Perush Sefer Yeẓirah,* 161), have their echoes in the *Ra'aya Meheimna* (3: 275b), whose author does not shrink from the pejorative expression *ḥamor de-matnitin* ("mishnaic ass"), and in the mystical homily 1:27b, in a passage belonging to the *Tikkunei Zohar* that refers to the Mishnah in a double-entendre as "the burial place of Moses." Other similar discourses, such as the exegesis *(ibid.)* relating the verse in Exodus 1:4, "And they made their lives bitter with hard service," to talmudic studies, or the angry descriptions of rabbinic scholars in the *Sefer ha-Peli'ah,* reveal a good deal of resentment. On the other hand, there is no historical basis for the picture drawn by Graetz of an openly anti-talmudic campaign waged by the kabbalists, who in reality insisted in their own writings on a scrupulous observance of halakhic law, albeit of course from a mystical perspective. At the same time, however, true antinomian tendencies could easily spring from the Kabbalah when it joined forces with messianism, as happened in the case of the Shabbatean movement.

A trend toward actually ruling on moot halakhic question by treating them according to kabbalistic principles first appears in the mid-14th century, in the *Sefer ha-Peli'ah* and especially in discussions of the commandments in the *Sefer ha-Kanah.* Dating from the same period or shortly after are a number of similarly minded rabbinic responsa that have been attributed to Joseph Gikatilla (first published in the *Festschrift* for Jacob Freimann (1937) 163–70). Yet this school of thought remained in the minority, and most kabbalists, to the extent that they were also leading authorities on the *halakhah,* such as David b. Zimra, Joseph Caro, Solomon Luria, Mordecai Yaffe, and Hayyim Joseph David Azulai, deliberately refrained from adopting halakhic positions that conflicted with talmudic law. The accepted rule among them was that decisions were only to be made on the basis of the Zohar when no clear talmudic guideline could be found (*Beit Yosef le-Oraḥ Ḥayyim* par. 141). The entire question of whether halakhic rulings could ever be made on the basis of the Zohar or other kabbalistic texts led to considerable controversy. No less accomplished a kabbalist than David b. Zimra declared that, apart from the Zohar itself, it was forbidden to cite a kabbalistic work in opposition to even an isolated halakhic authority. A differing view was expressed by Benjamin Aaron Selnik, a disciple of Moses Isserles, in his volume of responsa, *Mas'at Binyamin* (1633): "If all the [halakhic] writers since the closing of the Talmud were placed in one pan of the scales, and the author of the Zohar in the other, the latter would outweigh them all." The laws and regulations that could be gleaned from the Zohar were collected by Issachar Baer b. Pethahiah of Kremnitz in his *Yesh Sakhar* (Prague, 1609). Joseph Solomon Delmedigo (1629) assembled a large amount of material dealing with the attitudes of the halakhic authorities to various kabbalistic innovations (*Maẓref le-Ḥokhmah* (1865), 66–82). The tremendous growth of new customs influenced by Lurianic Kabbalah led a number of kabbalists to seek to elevate Isaac Luria himself to a halakhically authoritative status. Even Ḥayyim Joseph David Azulai who generally accepted as authoritative the halakhic opinions of Joseph Caro, wrote that Isaac Luria's interpretations of *halakhah* took precedence over Caro's Shulḥan Arukh *(Shiyurei Berakhah* on *Oraḥ Ḥayyim).* The tendency to refer to kabbalistic sources in the course of halakhic discussions was much more prominent in the post-Lurianic period among the Sephardim than among the Ashkenazim. The influence of the Kabbalah was particularly felt in connection with observances involving prayer, the Sabbath, and holidays, and was much less pronounced in more purely legal matters. It was common practice to comment on halakhic fine points from a kabbalistic perspective without actually claiming for the latter any halakhic authority. Outstanding examples of this are the *Mekor Ḥayyim* (1878–79) of Ḥayyim ha-Kohen of Aleppo, a disciple of Ḥayyim Vital, and Jacob Ḥayyim b. Isaac Baruch of Baghdad's *Kaf ha-Ḥayyim* (1912–29), a voluminous compilation of all the kabbalistic matter connected with the *Oraḥ Ḥayyim* of the Shulḥan Arukh.

In the realm of the *aggadah,* the Kabbalah was unrestricted, and many kabbalists made use of this opportunity not only to compose far-reaching interpretations of the early *aggadot* of the Midrash, in which they saw the key to many of their mystic doctrines, but also to create a rich new body of aggadic legend bearing a strongly mythic character. In general, they were more at home in aggadic expression than in systematic exposition, and it is to this "kabbalization" of the *aggadah* that much of the enormous attraction of the Zohar must be credited. As for the fresh aggadic material created by the kabbalists themselves, it largely consisted of a mystical dramatization of the epos of creation and of the interaction of upper and lower worlds in the lives of the biblical heroes. The latter are portrayed as acting against a broad cosmic background, drawing sustenance from supernal powers and affecting them in turn by their deeds. The classic anthology of nearly 500 years of this kabbalistic *aggadah* is Reuben Hoeshke of Prague's *Yalkut Re'uveni,* a first edition of which (Prague, 1660) was organized topically, while its second, enlarged version (Wilmersdorf, 1681), which was modeled after the early midrashic anthology, *Yalkut Shimoni,* was arranged as a commentary on the Torah. Another comprehensive collection of both exoteric and esoteric *aggadot* on the period from the first week of creation to Adam's sin is Nahum Breiner's *Yalkut Naḥmani* (1937).

The main influence of Kabbalah on Jewish life must be sought in the three areas of prayer, custom, and ethics. Here the Kabbalah had practically unlimited freedom to exert its influence, which expressed itself in the creation of a broad body of literature that was directed at every Jewish home. From the middle of the 17th century onward, kabbalistic motifs entered the everyday prayer book and inspired special liturgies intended for a variety of specific occasions and rituals, many of which were in essence kabbalistic creations. This development began in Italy with books by Aaron Berechiah Modena and Moses Zacuto, and above all, with the appearance of Nathan Hannover's *Sha'arei Ẓiyyon* (Prague, 1662), one of the most influential and widely circulated of all kabbalistic works. In this volume the Lurianic doctrines of man's mission on earth, his connections with the powers of the upper worlds, the transmigrations of his soul, and his striving to achieve *tikkun* were woven into prayers that could be appreciated and understood by everyone, or that at least could arouse everyone's imagination and emotions. Such liturgies reached the farthest corners of the Diaspora and continued to be popular among Jews in Muslim countries long after they were excised from the prayer book by the Jewish communities of Central Europe as a consequence of the decline of the Kabbalah there in the 19th century. Sizeable anthologies of highly emotional prayers composed under kabbalistic inspiration were published mainly in Leghorn, Venice, Constantinople, and Salonika. Especially important in this realm were the activities of Judah Samuel Ashkenazi, Abraham Anakawa, and above all, Abraham Hammawi, who published a series of such books in Leghorn for the Jews of North Africa *(Bet Oved, Bet El, Bet ha-Kaporet, Bet ha-Beḥirot, Bet Av, Bet Din, Bet ha-Sho'evah, Bet Menuḥah).* The liturgical anthology *Oẓar ha-Tefillot* (1914) reflects the last lingering kabbalistic influences on the prayers of Eastern European Jewry.

Popular customs and popular faith were also highly affected by the spread of the Kabbalah. Many kabbalistic concepts were absorbed at the level of folk beliefs, such as the doctrine of man's first sin as the cause of a disruption in the upper worlds, the belief in transmigration of souls, the kabbalistic teachings about the Messiah, or the demonology of the later Kabbalah. Throughout the Diaspora, the number of folk customs whose origins were kabbalistic was enormous; many were taken directly from the Zohar, and many others from Lurianic tradition, the observances of which were codified in the middle of the 17th century by Jacob Ẓemaḥ in his *Shulḥan Arukh ha-Ari* (ca. 1660; best edition Jerusalem, 1961) and *Naggid u-Meẓavveh* (1712). A more recent guide to Lurianic customs was the compilation *Ta'amei ha-Minhagim* (1911–12). Such customs came on the whole to fulfill four mystical functions: the establishment of a harmony between the restrictive forces of *Din* and the outgoing forces of *Raḥamim;* to bring about or to symbolize the mystical "sacred marriage" *(ha-zivvug ha-kadosh)* between God and His *Shekhinah;* the redemption of the *Shekhinah* from its exile amid the forces of the *sitra aḥra,* the protection of oneself against the forces of the *sitra aḥra* and the battle to overcome them. Human action on earth assists or arouses events in the upper worlds, an interplay that has both its symbolic and its magical side. Indeed, in this conception of religious ceremony as a vehicle for the workings of divine forces, a very real danger existed that an essentially mystical perspective might be transformed in practice into an essentially magical one. Undeniably, the social effects of the Kabbalah on popular Jewish custom and ceremony were characterized by this ambivalence. Alongside the tendency to greater religious inwardness and insight was the tendency to a complete demonization of all life. The conspicuous growth of this latter trend at the expense of the former was undoubtedly one of the factors which, by reducing Kabbalah to the level of popular superstition, ultimately helped eliminate it as a serious historical force. (See G. Scholem, *The Kabbalah and its Symbolism* (1965), 118–57.)

Among kabbalistic customs that became particularly widespread were the holding of midnight vigils for the exile of the *Shekhinah*, the treating of the eve of the new moon as "a little Day of Atonement," and the holding of dusk-to-dawn vigils, which were dedicated to both ordinary and mystical study, on the nights of Pentecost, Hoshanah Rabba, and the seventh day of Passover. All such ceremonies and their accompanying liturgies and texts were referred to as *tikkunim* (e.g., "the *tikkun* of midnight" for the exile of the *Shekhinah* etc.). A special atmosphere of solemn celebration surrounded the Sabbath, which was thoroughly pervaded with kabbalistic ideas about man's role in the unification of the upper worlds. Under the symbolic aspect of "the marriage of King and Queen," the Sabbath was enriched by a wealth of new customs that originated in Safed, such as the singing of the mystical hymn *Lekhah Dodi* and the recital of the Song of Songs and Chapter 31 of Proverbs ("A woman of valor who can find?"), all of which were intended as meditations on the *Shekhinah* in her aspect as God's mystical bride. Mystical and demonic motifs became particularly interwined in the area of sexual life and practices to which an entire literature was devoted, starting with the *Iggeret ha-Kodesh*, later mistakenly ascribed to Naḥmanides (see G. Scholem, in: KS 21 (1944), 179–86; and Monford Harris, in: HUCA 33 (1962), 197–220) and continuing up to Naḥman of Bratslav's *Tikkun ha-Kelali.* Connected with these motifs were also a number of common burial customs, such as the circling of corpses and the forbidding of sons to attend their fathers' funerals. Similar ideas were behind the fast days in the months of Tevet and Shevat for "the *tikkun* of the *shovevim,*" that is, of the demonic offspring of nocturnal emission.

This penetration of kabbalistic customs and beliefs, which left no corner of Jewish life untouched, is especially well documented in two highly influential books: Isaiah Horowitz's *Shenei Luḥot ha-Berit* (Amsterdam, 1648), which was accorded a particularly prominent place among Askenazi Jewry, and the anonymous *Ḥemdat Yamim* (Izmir, 1731), which was written by a moderate Shabbatean in the early 18th century. The latter book was circulated first in Poland as well, but once its Shabbatean character came under attack its influence became largely restricted to the Sephardi world, where it fostered an entire literature of breviaries and study texts for special occasions. Despite the bulkiness of both works, their expressive power and rich contents made them classics of their kind. Noteworthy among more recent examples of this literature is Sassoon ben Mordecai of Baghdad's *Davar be-Itto* (1862–64). A custom that became particularly widespread among the Sephardim was that of reciting the Zohar aloud, paying no attention to its contents, simply as "salutary for the soul."

Most of the popular ethical works of *musar* literature, especially the more prominent of them, bear the stamp of kabbalistic influences from the 1570s until the beginning of the 19th century, and even until the latter's end in the Sephardi world. The pioneer works in this respect were Eliezer Azikri's *Sefer Ḥaredim* (Venice, 1601), and Elijah de Vidas' *Reshit Ḥokhmah* (Venice, 1579), a comprehensive and exhaustive volume on all ethical aspects of Jewish life which served as a link between the motifs of medieval aggadic and *musar* literature and the new world of popular Kabbalah. Contemporaneous homiletic literature, much of which was also devoted to ethical instruction, also contains strong kabbalistic elements, which were further reinforced by the spread of Lurianic beliefs. The Lurianic doctrines of *tikkun,* the transmigration of souls, and the struggle with the *sitra aḥra* were subjected to especially intensive popular treatment. Such exhortative works as Ḥayyim Vital's *Sha'arei Kedushah* (Constantinople, 1734), Ẓevi Hirsch Kaidanover's *Kav ha-Yashar* (Frankfort, 1705), Elijah ha-Kohen's *Shevet Musar* (Constantinople, 1712), and many others down to the *Nefesh ha-Ḥayyim* of Ḥayyim of Volozhin, a disciple of the Gaon of Vilna, manifest indebtedness to kabbalistic sources on every page. Even the crowning masterpiece of this type of ethical literature, Moses Ḥayyim Luzzatto's *Mesillat Yesharim* (Amsterdam, 1740), was basically inspired by a conception of the ethical education of the Jew as a stage on the way to mystical communion with God, despite its restricted use of kabbalistic citations and symbols. Similar works of ethical exhortation composed in Poland in the middle of the 18th century are highly charged with attitudes and ideas that clearly served as a prelude to the beginnings of Ḥasidism. Examples of such books are Moses b. Jacob of Satanov's *Mishmeret ha-Kodesh* (Zolkiew, 1746), the *Bet Pereẓ* (Zolkiew, 1759), of Pereẓ b. Moses who was a kabbalist of the Brody *Klaus,* and Simḥah of Zalosicz's *Lev Simḥah* and *Neti'ah shel Simḥah* (Zolkiew, 1757 and 1763). In the 20th century the deep influence of kabbalistic *musar* literature can still be felt in the works of R. Abraham Kook. Similarly, in the middle of the 19th century, we find R. Judah Alkalai of Belgrade, one of the earliest heralds of Zionism, still totally immersed in the ethical world of the Kabbalah (see his collected writings in Hebrew, Jerusalem 1944).

THE CHRISTIAN KABBALAH

From the late 15th century onward, in certain Christian circles of a mystical and theosophical persuasion a movement began to evolve with the object of harmonizing kabbalistic doctrines with Christianity, and above all, of demonstrating that the true hidden meaning of the teachings of the Kabbalah points in a Christian direction. Naturally, such views did not meet with a friendly reception from the kabbalists themselves, who expressed nothing but derision for the misunderstandings and distortions of kabbalistic doctrine of which Christian Kabbalah was full; but the latter undeniably succeeded in arousing lively interest and debate among spiritualistic circles in the West until at least the middle of the 18th century. Historically, Christian Kabbalah sprang from two sources. The first was the christological speculations of a number of Jewish converts who are known to us from the end of the 13th century until the period of the Spanish expulsion (G. Scholem, in *Essays Presented to Leo Baeck* (1954), 158–93), such as Abner of Burgos (Yiẓhak Baer, *Tarbiz* 27 (1958), 152–63), and Paul de Heredia, who pseudepigraphically composed several texts of Christian Kabbalah entitled *Iggeret ha-Sodot* and *Galei Rezaya* in the name of Judah ha-Nasi and other *tannaim.* Another such tract put out by Jewish converts in Spain toward the end of the 15th century, and written in imitation of the styles of the *aggadah* and the Zohar, circulated in Italy. Such compositions had little effect on serious Christian spiritualists, nor was their clearly tendentious missionary purpose calculated to win readers. Another matter entirely, however, was the Christian speculation about the Kabbalah that first developed around the Platonic Academy endowed by the Medicis in Florence and was pursued in close connection with the new horizons opened up by the Renaissance in general. These Florentine circles believed that they had discovered in the Kabbalah an original divine revelation to mankind that had been lost and would now be restored, and with the aid of which it was possible not only to understand the teachings of Pythagoras, Plato, and the Orphics, all of whom they greatly admired, but also the secrets of the Catholic faith. The founder of this Christian school of Kabbalah was the renowned Florentine prodigy Giovanni Pico della Mirandola (1463–94), who had a considerable portion of kabbalistic literature translated for him into Latin by the very learned convert Samuel ben Nissim Abulfaraj, later Raymond Moncada, also known as Flavius Mithridates. Pico began his kabbalistic studies in 1486, and when he displayed his 900 famous theses for public debate in Rome he included among them 47 propositions taken directly from kabbalistic sources, the majority from Recanati's commentary on the Torah, and 72 more propositions that represented his own conclusions from his kabbalistic research.

The theses, especially the daring claim that "no science can better convince us of the divinity of Jesus Christ than magic and the Kabbalah," first brought the Kabbalah to the attention of many Christians. The ecclesiastical authorities fiercely rejected this and other of Pico's propositions, and there ensued the first real debate on the subject of the Kabbalah ever to take place in humanistic and clerical circles. Pico himself believed that he could prove the dogmas of the Trinity and the Incarnation on the basis of kabbalistic axioms. The sudden discovery of an esoteric Jewish tradition that had hitherto been completely unknown caused a sensation in the Christian intellectual world, and Pico's subsequent writings on the Kabbalah helped to further increase the interest of Christian Platonists in the newly uncovered sources, particularly in Italy, Germany, and France. Under Pico's influence the great Christian Hebraist Johannes Reuchlin (1455–1522) also took up the study of Kabbalah and published two Latin books on the subject, the first ever to be written by a non-Jew, *De Verbo Mirifico* ("On the Miracle-working Name," 1494) and *De Arte Cabalistica* ("On the Science of the Kabbalah," 1517). The years between these two dates also witnessed the appearance of a number of works by the learned convert Paul Ricius, the private physician of Emperor Maximilian, who took Pico's and Reuchlin's conclusions and added to them through an original synthesis of kabbalistic and Christian sources. Reuchlin's own main contribution was his association of the dogma of the Incarnation with a series of bold speculations on the kabbalistic doctrine of the Divine Names of God. Human history, Reuchlin argued, could be divided into three periods. In the first or natural period, God revealed Himself to the patriarchs through the three-lettered name of Shaddai (שדי). . In the period of the Torah He revealed Himself to Moses through the four-lettered name of the Tetragrammaton. But in the period of grace and redemption He revealed Himself through five letters, namely, the Tetragrammaton with the addition of the letter *shin,* signifying the Logos, thus spelling Yehoshua יהושה or Jesus. In the name of Jesus, which is the true Miraculous Name, the formerly forbidden name of God now became pronounceable. In Reuchlin's schematic arrangement, which was able to draw for support on the common abbreviation for Jesus in medieval manuscripts, JHS, Jewish beliefs in three world ages (Chaos, Torah, and Messiah) blended with the tripartite Christian division of the millennialist school of Joachim of Fiore into a reign of the Father, a reign of the Son, and a reign of the Holy Ghost.

Pico's and Reuchlin's writings, which placed the Kabbalah in the context of some of the leading intellectual developments of the time, attracted wide attention. They led on the one hand to considerable interest in the doctrine of Divine Names and in practical Kabbalah, and on the other hand to further speculative attempts to achieve a synthesis between kabbalistic motifs and Christian theology. The place of honor accorded to practical Kabbalah in Cornelius Agrippa of Nettesheim's great compendium *De Occulta Philosophia* (1531), which was a widely read summary of all the occult sciences of the day, was largely responsible for the mistaken association of the Kabbalah in the Christian world with numerology and witchcraft. Several Christian kabbalists of the 16th century made a considerable effort to master the sources of the Kabbalah more deeply, both in Hebrew and in Latin translations prepared for them, thus widening the basis for their attempts to discover common ground between the Kabbalah and

Christianity. Among the most prominent of these figures were Cardinal Egidio da Viterbo (1465–1532). whose *Scechina* (ed. F. Secret, 1959) and "On the Hebrew Letters" were influenced by ideas in the Zohar and the *Sefer ha-Temunah,* and the Franciscan Francesco Giorgio of Venice (1460–1541), the author of two large and at the time widely read books, *De Harmonia Mundi* (1525) and *Problemata* (1536), in which the Kabbalah assumed a central place and manuscript material from the Zohar was used extensively for the first time in a Christian work. He also gave to his disciples an elaborate commentary on Pico's kabbalistic theses (Ms. Jerusalem), later plagiarized by his pupil Archangelo de Burgonovo (two parts; 1564 and 1569). The admiration of these Christian authors for the Kabbalah aroused an angry reaction in some quarters, which accused them of disseminating the view that any Jewish kabbalist could boast of being a better Christian than an orthodox Catholic. A more original mystical thinker who was also better acquainted with the Jewish sources was the renowned Frenchman Guillaume Postel (1510–1581), one of the outstanding personalities of the Renaissance. Postel translated the Zohar and the *Sefer Yeẓirah* into Latin even before they had been printed in the original, and accompanied his translations with a lengthy theosophic exposition of his own views. In 1548 he published a kabbalistic commentary in Latin translation on the mystical significance of the *menorah,* and later a Hebrew edition as well. These authors had many connections in Jewish circles.

During this period, Christian Kabbalah was primarily concerned with the development of certain religious and philosophical ideas for their own sake rather than with the desire to evangelize among the Jews, though this latter activity was often stressed to justify a pursuit that was otherwise suspect in many eyes. On of the most dedicated of such Christian kabbalists was Johann Albrecht Widmanstetter (Widmanstadius; 1560–1557), whose enthusiasm for the Kabbalah led him to collect many kabbalistic manuscripts that are extant in Munich. Many of his contemporaries, however, remained content to speculate in the realm of Christian Kabbalah without any firsthand knowledge of the sources. Indeed, in the course of time the knowledge of Jewish sources diminished among the Christian kabbalists, and consequently the Jewish element in their books became progressively slighter, its place being taken by esoteric Christian speculations whose connections with Jewish motifs were remote. The Lurianic revival in Safed had no effect on these circles. Their commitment to missionary work increased, yet the number of Jewish converts to Christianity from kabbalistic motives, or of those who claimed such motives retrospectively, remained disproportionately small among the numbers of converts in general. There is no clear evidence in the writings of such Christian theosophists to indicate whether or not they believed the Jewish kabbalists to be hidden or unconscious

Christians at heart. In any event, Christian Kabbalah occupied an honored place both in the 16th century, primarily in Italy and France, and in the 17th century, when its center moved to Germany and England.

In the 17th century Christian Kabbalah received two great impetuses, one being the theosophical writings of Jacob Boehme, and the other Christian Knorr von Rosenroth's vast kabbalistic compendium *Kabbala Denudata* (1677–84), which for the first time made available to interested Christian readers, most of whom were undoubtedly mystically inclined themselves, not only important sections of the Zohar but sizeable excerpts from Lurianic Kabbalah as well. In this work and in the writings of the Jesuit scholar Athanasius Kircher the parallel is drawn for the first time between the kabbalistic doctrine of *Adam Kadmon* and the concept of Jesus as primordial man in Christian theology. This analogy is pressed particularly in the essay entitled *Adumbratio Kabbalae Christinae* which appears at the end of the *Kabbala Denudata* (Fr. trans., Paris, 1899). Its anonymous author was in fact the well-known Dutch theosophist, Franciscus Mercurius van Helmont, all of whose works are shot through with kabbalistic ideas. It was Van Helmont who served as the link between the Kabbalah and the Cambridge Platonists led by Henry More and Ralph Cudworth, who made use of kabbalistic motifs for their own original speculative purposes, More especially. Somewhat earlier, students (as well as opponents) of Jacob Boehme had discovered the strong affinity between his own theosophical system and that of the Kabbalah, though there would seem to be no historical connection between them. In certain circles, particularly in Germany, Holland, and England, Christian Kabbalah henceforward assumed a Boehmian guise. In 1673 a large chart was erected in a Protestant church in Teinach (southern Germany), which had as its purpose the presentation of a kind of visual summary of this school of Christian Kabbalah. Several different interpretations were given to it.

As early as the late 16th century a pronounced trend had emerged toward the permeation of Christian Kabbalah with alchemical symbolism, thus giving it an oddly original character in its final stages of development in the 17th and 18th centuries. This mélange of elements typifies the works of Heinrich Khunrat, *Amphitheatrum Sapientiae Aeternae* (1609), Blaise de Vigenère, *Traité du Feu* (1617), Abraham von Frankenberg (1593–1652), Robert Fludd (1574–1637), and Thomas Vaughan (1622–1666), and reaches its apogee in Georg von Welling's *Opus Mago-Cabbalisticum* (1735) and the many books of F.C. Oetinger (1702–1782), whose influence is discernible in the works of such great figures of German idealist philosophy as Hegel and Schelling. In yet another form this mixture reappears in the theosophical systems of the Freemasons in the second half of the 18th century. A late phase of Christian Kabbalah is represented by Martines de Pasqually (1727–1774) in his *Traité de la réintégration des êtres,* which greatly influenced theosophical currents in France. The author's disciple was the well-known mystic Louis Claude de St. Martin. Pasqually himself was suspected during his lifetime of being a secret Jew, and modern scholarship has in fact established that he was of Marrano ancestry. The sources of his intellectual indebtedness, however, have still to be clarified. The crowning and final achievement of Christian Kabbalah was Franz Josef Molitor's (1779–1861) comprehensive *Philosophie der Geschichte oder Ueber die Tradition*, which combined profound speculation in a Christian kabbalistic vein with highly suggestive research into the ideas of the Kabbalah itself. Molitor too still clung to a fundamentally christological view of the Kabbalah, whose historical evolution he completely failed to understand, yet at the same time he revealed an essential grasp of kabbalistic doctrine and an insight into the world of the Kabbalah far superior to that of most Jewish scholars of his time.

SCHOLARSHIP AND THE KABBALAH

As implied above, the beginnings of scholarly investigation of the Kabbalah were bound up with the interests of Christian Kabbalah and its missionary zeal. A number of Christian kabbalists were led to study the literature of the Kabbalah first hand, one of the first being Reuchlin, who resorted primarily to the works of Gikatilla and to a large collection of early kabbalistic writings that has been preserved in Halberstamm Ms. 444 (in the Jewish Theological Seminary in New York). Though a significant number of kabbalistic works had been translated by the middle of the 16th century, only a few of these translations, such as one of Gikatilla's *Sha'arei Orah* (1516), had been published, while the majority remained in manuscript where they did little to stimulate further research. In addition, the theological presuppositions of the Christian kabbalists ruled out any historical, to say nothing of critical, perspective on their part. A crucial turning-point was the publication of Knorr von Rosenroth's *Kabbala Denudata* despite its many erroneous translations which were further compounded in the retranslation of some of its parts into English and French (see MGWJ 75 (1932), 444–8). The appearance of this book aroused the interest of several scholars who had not previously had any attachment to Christian Kabbalah, such as Leibniz. Completely at variance with its premises was Johann Georg Wachter's study of Spinozistic tendencies in Judaism, *Der Spinozismus im Juedenthumb* [sic!] (Amsterdam, 1699), which was the first work to interpret the theology of the Kabbalah pantheistically and to argue that the kabbalists were not disguised Christians but rather disguised atheists. Wachter's book greatly influenced discussions on the subject throughout the 18th century. Early in the 18th century J.P. Buddeus proposed the theory of a close connection between the early Gnostics and the Kabbalah in his "Introduction to the History of the Philosophy of the Jews" (in Latin, Halle, 1720), which was largely devoted to the Kabbalah. J.K. Schramm too, in his "Introduction to the Dialectics of the Kabbalists" (Braunschweig, 1703) sought to discuss the subject in scientific and philosophical terms, while G. Sommer's *Specimen Theologiae Soharicae* (Gotha, 1734) presented an anthology of all the passages from the Zohar that were in the author's opinion close to Christian doctrine. A particularly valuable though now totally forgotten book was Hermann von der Hardt's *Aenigmata Judaeorum Religiosissima* (Helmstadt, 1705), which dealt with practical Kabbalah. J.P. Kleuker published a study in 1786 in which he argued the case for a decisive Persian influence on the kabbalistic doctrine of emanation. Common to all these early scholars was the belief that the Kabbalah was in essence not Jewish at all, but rather Christian, Greek, or Persian.

Scholarly investigation of the Kabbalah by Jews also first served a tendentious purpose, namely, to polemicize against what was felt to be the Kabbalah's baleful influence on Jewish life. The first critical work to be written in this vein was Jacob Emden's highly influential *Mitpaḥat Sefarim* (Altona, 1768), which grew out of the author's lifelong battle against Shabbateanism and was intended to weaken the authority of the Zohar by proving that many of its passages were late interpolations. In the 19th century also most Jewish scholarship on the Kabbalah bore a polemical character primarily aimed against kabbalistic influences as they appeared in Ḥasidism. For the most part such scholars too considered the Kabbalah to have been an essentially foreign presence in Jewish life. At the time, indeed, Kabbalah was still a kind of stepdaughter in the field of Jewish scholarship whose actual literary sources were studied by only a few. Even from this limited perspective, however, important contributions to the investigation of the Kabbalah were made by Samuel David Luzzatto, Adolphe Franck, H.D. Joel, Senior Sachs, Aaron Jellinek, Isaac Meises, Graetz, Ignatz Stern, and M. Steinschneider. The works of the single Jewish scholar of this period to devote in-depth studies to the Zohar and other important kabbalistic texts, Eliakim Milsahagi (Samiler), remained almost completely unpublished and were eventually forgotten and largely lost. All that has been preserved of them is his analysis of the Zohar (Jerusalem Ms. 4° 121), and the *Sefer Raziel.* Works on the Kabbalah during the Haskalah period are almost all practically worthless, such as the many tracts and books of Solomon Rubin. The only two scholars of the age to approach the Kabbalah out of a fundamental sympathy and even affinity for its teachings were the Christian F.J. Molitor in Frankfurt and the Jew Elijah Benamozegh in Leghorn. The many books written on the subject in the 19th and 20th centuries by various theosophists and mystics lacked any basic knowledge of the sources and very rarely contributed to the field, while at times they even hindered the development of a historical approach. Similarly, the activities of French and English occultists contributed nothing and only served to create considerable confusion between the teachings of the Kabbalah and their own totally unrelated inventions, such as the alleged kabbalistic origin of the Tarot-cards. To this category of supreme charlatanism belong the many and widely read books of Eliphas Levi (actually Alphonse Louis Constant; 1810–1875), Papus (Gérard Encausse; 1868–1916), and Frater Perdurabo (Aleister Crowley; 1875–1946), all of whom had an infinitesimal knowledge of Kabbalah that did not prevent them from drawing freely on their imaginations instead. The comprehensive works of A.E. Waite (*The Holy Kabbalah,* 1929), S. Karppe, and P. Vulliaud, on the other hand, were essentially rather confused compilations made from secondhand sources.

The profoundly altered approach to Jewish history that followed in the wake of the Zionist revival and the movement for national rebirth led, particularly after World War I, to a renewal of interest in the Kabbalah as a vital expression of Jewish existence. A new attempt was made to understand, independently of all polemic or apolegetic positions, the genesis, development, historical role, and social and intellectual influence of the Kabbalah within the total context of the internal and external forces that have determined the shape of Jewish history. The pioneers of this new approach were S.A. Horodezky, Ernst Müller, and G. Scholem. In the years following 1925 an international center for kabbalistic research came to reside in the Hebrew University of Jerusalem. Among the foremost representatives of the school of historical criticism that developed there were G. Scholem, I. Tishby, E. Gottleib, J. Dan, Rivka Schatz, and J. Ben-Shlomo. Elsewhere important contributions to kabbalistic scholarship were made too, particularly by G. Vajda, A. Altmann, and François Secret. With the development of new perspectives in recent years, scholarly investigation of the Kabbalah is only now emerging from its infancy. Ahead of it lies a great deal of room for fruitful expansion that will yet take in kabbalistic literature in the whole of its richness and its many implications with regard to the history, thought, and life of the Jewish people.

BIBLIOGRAPHY

For editions of English translations of individual works, see the respective sections. **Bibliography and Sources**: J.C. Wolf, *Bibliotheca Hebraea,* 2 (1721), 1191–1247; 4 (1733), 734ff.; Steinschneider, Cat. Bod; idem, *Die hebraeischen*

Handschriften der k. Hof-undStaatsbibliothek in Muenchen (1897); Neubauer, Cat, 537ff.: Margoliouth, Cat. 3 (1909), 1–155; G. Scholem, *Bibliographia Kabbalistica* (1927); idem, *Kitvei Yad be-Kabbalah ha-Nimẓa'im be-Bet ha-Sefarim ha-Leummi ve-ha-Universita'i be-Yrushalayim* (1930); Shunami, Bibl, 739–48; C. Knorr von Rosenroth, *Kabbalah Denudata*, 2 vols. (1677–84; Eng. tr. by S.L. MacGregor Mathers, 1887, repr. 1962).

General: Scholem, Mysticism; idem, *Perakim le-Toledot Sifrut ha-Kabbalah* (1931); idem, *Von der mystischen Gestalt der Gottheit* (1962); idem, *Ursprung und Anfaenge der Kabbala* (1962; *Les Origines de la Kabbale*, 1966); idem, *On the Kabbalah and its Symbolism* (1965); idem, *Ueber einige Grundbegriffe des Judentums* (1970); idem. *Judaica III, Studien zur juedischen Mystik* (1973); D. Kahana, *Toledot ha-Mekubbalim, ha-Shabbeta'im ve-ha-Ḥasidim*, 2 vols. (1913); M.D.G. Langer. *Die Erotik der Kabbala* (1923); P. Vulliaud, *La Kabbale juive*, 2 vols. (1923); S.A. Horodezky, *Ha-Mistorin be-Yisrael*, 3 vols. (1931–52); idem, *Yahadut ha-Sekhel ve-Yahadut ha-Regesh*, 2 vols. (1947); idem, *Kivshono shel Olam* (1950); Hayyim ben Shelomo Araki (ed.), *Emunat ha-Shem* (1937); H. Sérouya, *La Kabbale: ses origines, sa psychologie mystique, sa metaphysique* (1947): L. Schaya, *The Universal Meaning of the Kabbalah* (1970); H. Zeitlin, *Be-Fardes ha-Ḥasidut ve-ha-Kabbalah* (1960); A. Safran, *La'Cabale* (1960); G. Vajda. *Recherches sur la philosophie et la Kabbale dans la pensée juive du moyen-âge* (1962); B. Dinur, *Yisrael ba-Golah*, 2. pt. 4 (1969), 275–435; pt. 6 (1972), 258–77; I. Weinstock, *Be-Ma'aglei ha-Nigleh ve-ha-Nistar* (1969); I. Tishby, *Netivei Emunah u-Minut* (1964); I. Baeck, *Jewish Mysticism*, in: JJS, 2 (1950), 3–16.

Early Beginnings: N.I. Weinstein, *Zur Genesis der Agada*, 2 (1901); M. Friedlaender, *Die religioesen Bewegungen innerhalb des Judentums im Zeitalter Jesu* (1905); E. Bischoff, *Babylonisch-astrales in Weltbilde des Thalmud und Midrasch* (1907); J. Abelson, *Immanence of God in Rabbinical Literature* (1912); W. Schencke, *Die Chokma (Sophia) in der juedischen Hypostasenspekulation* (1913); B.J. Bamberger, *Fallen Angels* (1952); H.J. Franken, *Mystical Communion with JHWH in the Book of Psalms* (1954); C.L. Montefiore, *Mystic Passages in the Psalms*, in: JQR, 1 (1889). 143–61; D. Castelli, *Gli antecedenti della Cabbala nella Bibbia e nella letteratura talmudica*, in: *Actes du Xllme Congres des Orientalistes*, 3 (1899), 57–109; G.F. Moore, *Intermediaries in Jewish Theology*, in: HTR, 15 (1922), 41–85; J. Hertz, *Mystic Currents in Ancient Israel*, in: *Jews at the Close of the Bible Age* (1926), 126–56; J. Lindblom, *Die Religion der Propheten und die Mystik*, in: ZAW, 57 (1939), 65–74; R. Marcus, *On Biblical Hypostases of Wisdom*, in: HUCA, 23 (1950–51), 157–71; I. Efros, *Holiness and Glory in the Bible*, in: JQR, 41 (1950/51), 363–77; I.F. Baer, *Le-Berurah shel Torat Aḥarit ha-Yamim bi-Yemei ha-Bayit ha-Sheni*, in: *Zion*, 23–24 (1958/59), 3–34, 141–65.

Apocalyptic Esotericism and Merkabah Mysticism: M.D. Hoffman, *Toledot Elisha ben Avuya* (1880); H. Kraus, *Begriff und Form der Haeresie nach Talmud und Midrasch* (1896); A. Jellinek, *Elischa ben Abuja–Acher* (1891); M. Buttenwieser, *Outline of the Neo-Hebraic Apocalyptic Literature* (1901); H. Bietenhard, *Die himmlische Welt im Urchristentum und Spaetjudentum* (1951); J. Maier, *Vom Kultus zur Gnosis* (1964); M.J. Bin-Gorion, *Erekh "Aḥer,"* in:

Ha-Goren, 8 (1912), 76–83; V. Aptowitzer, *Bet ha-Mikdash shel Ma'alah al Pi ha-Aggadah*, in: *Tarbiz*, 2 (1931), 137–85; A. Buechler, *Die Erloesung Elisa b. Abujahs aus dem Hoellenfeuer*, in: MGWJ, 76 (1932), 412–56; H. Hirschberg, *Once Again – the Minim*, in: JBL, 67 (1948), 305–18; A. Neher, *Le voyage mystique des quatre*, in: RHR, 140 (1951), 59–82; J. Strugnell, *The Angelic Liturgy at Qumran 4Q, Serek Širot 'Olat Hassabbat*, in: suppl. to VT, 7 (1960), 318–45; W.C. van Unnik, *Die juedische Komponente in der Entstehung der Gnosis*, in: *Vigilaie Christianae*, 15 (1961), 65–82; E. Haenchen, *Gab es eine vorchristliche Gnosis?* in: *Gott und Mensch* (1965), 265ff.; E.E. Urbach, *Ha-Masorot al Torat ha-Sod bi-Tekufat ha-Tanna'im*, in: *Mehkarim . . . G. Scholem* (1967), 1–28.

Esoteric Literature: B. Jacob, *Im Namen Gottes* (1903); J.A. Montgomery, *Aramaic Incantation Texts from Nippur* (1913); A. Ravenna, *I sette santuari (Hekhalot)* (1964); G. Scholem, *Jewish Gnosticism, Merkabah Mysticism and Talmudic Tradition* (1965[2]); C. Gordon, *Five Papers on Magical Bowls and Incantations (Jewish and Mandaean)*, in: *Archiv Orientálni*, 6 (1934), 319–34, 466–74; 9 (1937), 84–106; 18 (1949), 336–41; 20 (1951), 306–15; A. Altmann, *Gnostic Themes in Rabbinic Cosmology*; in: *Essays . . . J.H. Hertz* (1943), 19–32: idem. *A Note on the Rabbinic Doctrine of Creation* in: JJS, 7 (1956), 195–206; E.R. Goodenough, *A Jewish-Gnostic Amulet of the Roman Period*, in: *Greek and Byzantine Studies* (1958), 71–81; B.Z. Bokser, *The Thread of Blue*, in: PAAJR, 31 (1963), 1–32; J. Maier, in: *Kairos*, 5 (1963), 18–40 (Ger.): N. Séd, *Une Cosmologie juive du haut Moyen-Age, la Berayta du Ma'aseh Beresit*, in: REJ, 123 (1964), 259–305; 124 (1965), 23–123; idem, *Les hymnes sur le Paradis de Saint Ephrem et les traditions juives* in: *Le Muséon*, 81 (1968), 455–501; R. Loewe, *The Divine Garment and Shi'ur Qomah*, in: HTR, 58 (1965), 153–60; I. Gruenwald, *Piyyutei Yannai ve-Sifrut ha-Merkavah*, in: *Tarbiz*, 36 (1967), 257–77.

Jewish Gnosis and the Sefer Yeẓirah: H. Graetz, *Gnosticismus und Judenthum* (1846); M. Friedlaender, *Ben Dosa und seine Zeit* (1872); idem, *Der vorchristliche juedische Gnosticismus* (1898); U. Bianchi (ed.), *Le origini dello gnosticismo (Colloquio de Messina)* (1967); A. Epstein, *Recherches sur le Séfer Yecira*, in: REJ, 28 (1894) 94–108; 29 (1894), 61–78; P. Mordell, *The Origin of Letters and Numerals According to the Sefer Yetzirah*, in: JQR, 2 (1911/12); 3 (1912/13); A.M. Habermann, *Avanim le-Ḥeker Sefer Yeẓirah*, in: *Sinai*, 20 (1946), 241–65; G. Vajda, *Le commentaire kairouanis sur le 'Livre de la Création,'* in: REJ, 107 (1947), 5–62; 110 (1949/50), 67–92; 112 (1953), 5–33; idem. *Nouveaux fragments arabes du commentaire de Dunash b. Tamim sur le 'Livre de la Création,' ibid.*, 113 (1954); *ibid.*, idem, *Notes et Mélanges* 122 (1963), 149–66; idem, *Sa'adya Commentateur du 'Livre de la Création'* in: *Ecole Pratique des Hautes Etudes*, Section des Sciences Religieuses, *Extrait de l'Annuaire 1959–60* (1960), 1–35; idem, *Les lettres et les sons de la langue arabe d'après Abu Hatim Al-Razi*, in: *Arabica*, 18 (1961), 113–30; K. Schubert, *Der gegenwaertige Stand der Erforschung der in Palaestina neu gefundenen hebraeischen Handschriften, 25: Der Sektenkanon von En Fescha und die Anfaenge der juedischen Gnosis*, in: *Theologische Literaturzeitung*, 8/9 (1953), 496–506; G. Quispel, *Christliche Gnosis und* *juedische Heterodoxie*, in: *Evangelische Theologie* (1954), 1–11; S. Loewenstamm, *Mah le-Ma'alah u-Mah le-Matah, Mah le-Fanim u-Mah le-Aḥor*, in: *Sefer ha-Yovel le-Yeḥezkel Kaufmann* (1960), 112–22; S. Morag, *Sheva Kefulot Begad Kafrat*, in: *Sefer Tur-Sinai* (1960), 207–42; J. Neusner, *Masa al Ma'aseh Merkavah*, in: *Ha-Eshnav* (1961); M. Smith, *Observations on Hekhalot Rabbati*, in: Brandeis University, *Studies and Texts*, 1 (1963), 142–60; P. Merlan, *Zur Zahlenlehre in Platonismus (Neuplatonismus) und in Sefer Yeẓira*, in: *Journal of the History of Philosophy*, 3 (1965), 167–81; N. Séd, *Le Memar samaritain, Le Séfer Yesira et les trente-deux sentiers de la Sagesse*, in: RHR, 170 (1966),159–84; E. Rosh-Pinnah (Ettisch), in: JQR, 57 (1967), 217–26; I. Gruenwald, *A Preliminary Critical Edition of S. Yeẓira*, in: *Israel Oriental Studies I*, (1971), 132–77; I. Weinstock, in: *Temirin*, 1 (1972), 9–61; N. Aloni, *ibid.*, 63–99.

Geonic Period: E.E. Hildesheimer, *Mystik und Agada im Urteile der Gaonen R. Scherira und R. Hai* (1931); I. Weinstock, *Oẓar Razim Kadmon ve-Gilgula*, in: *Shanah be-Shanah 5723* (1962), 345–58; idem, *Demut Aharon ha-Bavli bi-Megillat Aḥima'aẓ*, *ibid.*, *5724* (1963); 242–65; idem, *Gilluy Izavon ha-Sodot shel Abu Aharon ha-Bavli*, in: *Tarbiz*, 32 (1962/63), 153–9; idem, *Oẓar ha-Sodot shel Abu Aharon – Dimyon o Meẓi'ut*, in: *Sinai*, 54 (1963), 226–59; G. Scholem, *Ha-Im nitgalleh Izavon ha-Sodot shel Abu Aharon ha-Bavli?*, in: *Tarbiz*, 32 (1963), 252–65.

Ḥasidic Movements in Europe and Egypt: J. Freimann, *Mavo le-Sefer Ḥasidim* (1924); J. Dan, *Torat ha-Sod shel Ḥasidut Ashkenaz* (1968); idem, *Sefer ha-Ḥokhmah le-R. Eleazar mi-Worms u-Mashma'uto le-Toledot Toratah ve-Sifrutah shel Ḥasidut Ashkenaz*, in: *Zion*, 29 (1964), 167–81; idem, *Sefer ha-Navon*, in: *Koveẓ al Yad*, 16 (1966). 201–23; idem, *Beginnings of Jewish Mysticism in Europe*, in: C. Roth (ed.), *World History of the Jewish People*, vol. 2, *Dark Ages* (1966), 282–90, 455–6; idem, *Ḥug ha-Kruv ha-Meyuḥad bi-Tenu'at Ḥasidut Ashkenaz*, in: *Tarbiz*, 35 (1966), 349–72; idem, *Ḥokhmath Ha-Egoz, Its Origin and Development*, in: JJS, 17 (1966), 73–82; A. Epstein, *Le-Korot ha-Kabbalah ha-Ashkenazit*, in: *Ha-Ḥoker*, 2 (1894), 37–48; idem, *R. Shemu'el he-Ḥasid ben R. Kalonimus ha-Zaken*, in: *Ha-Goren*, 4 (1903), 81–101; G. Vajda, *The Mystical Doctrine of Rabbi Obadyah, Grandson of Moses Maimonides*, in: JJS, 6 (1955), 213–25; idem, *Perusho ha-Rishon shel Rabbi Elḥanan Yiẓḥak ben Yakar mi-London le-Sefer Yeẓirah*, in: *Koveẓ al Yad*, 16 (1966), 147–97; A. Altmann, *Eleazar of Worms' Ḥokhmath ha-Egoz*, in: JJS, 11(1960), 101–13; A. Rubin, *Concept of Repentance Among the Ḥasidey Ashkenaz*, in: JJS, 16(1965), 161–76; R. Edelmann, *Das 'Buch der Frommen' als Ausdruck des volkstuemlichen Geisteslebens der deutschen Juden im Mittelalter*, in: *Miscellanea Mediaevalia* (1966), 55–71; S.D. Goitein, *A Treatise in Defence of the Pietists by Abraham Maimonides*, in: JJS, 17 (1966), 105–14; idem, *Abraham Maimonides and his Pietist Circle*, in: *Jewish Medieval and Renaissance Studies* (1967), 145–64; I.F. Baer, *Shenei Perakim shel Torat ha-Hashgaḥah be-Sefer Ḥasidim*, in: *Meḥkarim . . . G. Scholem* (1967), 47–62.

Kabbalah in Provence: G. Scholem, *Te'udah Ḥadashah le-Toledot Reshit ha-Kabbalah*, in: *Sefer Bialik* (1934), 141–62; Ch. Wirszubski, *Akdamot le-Bikoret ha-Nusaḥ shel Perush Sefer Yeẓirah le-R. Yiẓḥak Sagi-Nahor*, in: *Tarbiz*, 27

(1958), 257–64; E. Werner, *Die Entstehung der Kabbala und die . . . Katharer,* in: *Forschungen und Fortschritte,* 37 (1963), 86–89.

In Gerona: G. Scholem, *Ursprung und Anfaenge der Kabbala* (1962), 324-419; G. Vajda, *Le commentaire d'Ezra de Gérone sur le cantique des cantiques* (1969); I. Tishby, *Kitvei ha-Mekubbalim R. Ezra ve-R. Azriel mi-Gerona,* in: *Sinai,* 16 (1945), 159–78; idem, *Ha-Mekubbalim R. Ezra ve-R. Azriel u-Mekomam be-Ḥug Gerona,*in: *Zion,* 9 (1944), 178–85; A. Altmann, *The Motif of of the 'Shells, in Azriel of Gerona,* in: JJS, 9 (1958), 73–80; G. Séd-Rajna, *De quelques commentaires kabbalistiques sur le rituel dans les manuscrits de la Bibliothèque nationale de Paris,* in: REJ, 124 (1965), 307–51; E. Gottlieb, *Mashma'utam u-megammatam shel Perushei Ma'aseh Bereshit be-Reshit ha-Kabbalah,* in: *Tarbiz,* 37 (1968), 294–317; N. Séd, *Le Sefer ha-Temunah et la doctrine des cycles cosmiques,* in: REJ, 126 (1967), 399–415.

Other Currents: S.O. Heller-Wilensky, *Sha'ar ha-Shamayim,* in: *Tarbiz* 32 (1963), 277–95; idem, *Isaac Ibn Latif – Philosopher or Kabbalist?* in: *Jewish Medieval and Renaissance Studies,* ed. A. Altmann (1967), 185–223; idem, in: *Fourth World Congress of Jewish Studies* (1968), 317–26. M.H. Landauer, *Vorlaeufiger Bericht. . . .,* in: *Literaturblatt des Orients,* 6 (1845), 322ff; A. Jellinek, *Philosophie und Kabbala* (1854); Scholem, Mysticism, ch. 4; A. Berger, in: *Essays in Honor of S.W. Baron* (1959), 55–61; Ch. Wirszubski, *Liber Redemptionis,* in: *Israel Academy of Sciences and Humanities, Proceedings* (Hebrew Series), 3 (1969), 135–49; G. Scholem, *Kabbalot R. Ya'akov ve-R. Yiẓḥak Kohen* (1927); idem, *Ha-Kabbalah shel Sefer ha-Temunah ve-shel Abraham Abulafia* (1965); idem, *Le-Ḥeker Kabbalat R. Yiẓḥak ben Ya'akov ha-Kohen,* in: *Tarbiz,* 2 (1931), 188–217, 415–42; 3 (1932), 33–66, 258–86; 4 (1933), 54–77, 207–25; 5 (1934), 50–60, 180–98, 305–28; I. Tishby, *Mishnat ha-Zohar,* 1 (1949, 1957[2], with F. Lachower); 2 (1961); Baer, Spain, 1 (1961), ch. 6; E. Gottlieb, *Ha-Kabbalah be-Kitvei Rabbenu Baḥya ben Asher* (1970); G. Vajda, *Le traite Pseudo-Maimonidien – Neuf chapitres sur l'unité du Dieu,* in: *Archives d'Histoire Doctrinale et Litteraire du Moyen Age* (1953), 83–98; J. Finkel, *The Alexandrian Tradition and the Midrash ha-Ne'elam,* in: *Leo Jung Jubilee Volume,* (1962), 77–103; S. O. Heller-Wilensky, *Le-she'elat Meḥabro shel Sefer Sha'ar ha-Shamayim ha-Meyuḥas le-Avraham ibn Ezra,* in: *Tarbiz,* 32 (1963), 277–95; A. Altmann, *Li-She'elat Ba'aluto shel Sefer Ta'amei ha-Miẓvot ha-Meyuḥas le-R. Yiẓḥak ibn Farḥi,* in KS, 40(1965), 256–412; idem. *Midrash al Pi Derekh ha-Kabbalah ha-Penimit al Bereshit 24,* in: *Sefer ha-Yovel Tiferet Yisrael. . . Brodie* (1966), 57–65; M. H. Weiler, *Iyyunim ba-Terminologiyah ha-Kabbalit shel R. Yosef Gikatilla ve-Yaḥaso la-Rambam,* in: HUCA, 37 (1966), Hebr. part, 13–44; idem, in: *Temirin,* 1 (1972), 157–86; I. Gruenwald, *Shenei Shirim shel ha-Mekubbal Yosef Gikatilla,* in: *Tarbiz,* 36 (1967), 73–89; E. Gottlieb, *Berurim be-Kitvei R. Yosef Gikatilla,* in: *Tarbiz,* 39 (1969–70), 62–89.

14th Century: G. Scholem, *Seridei Sifro shel R. Shem Tov ibn Gaon al Yesodot Torah ha-Sefirot,* in: KS, 8 (1931/32), 397–408, 534–42; 9 (1932/33), 126–33; idem, *Perusho shel R. Yiẓḥak de-min Akko le-Ferek Rishon shel Sefer Yeẓirah,* in: KS, 31 (1955/56), 379–96; idem, *Li-Yedi'at ha-Kabbalah bi-Sefarad Erev he-Gerush,* in: *Tarbiz,* 24 (1954/55), 167–206; G. Vajda, *Les observations* *critiques d'Isaac d'Acco sur les ouvrages de Juda ben Nissim ibn Malka,* in: REJ, 115 (1956), 25–71; idem, *Un chapitre de l'histoire du conflit, entre la-Kabbale et la Philosophie. La polemique anti-intellectualiste de Joseph ben Shalom Ashkenazi de Catalogne,* in: *Archives d'Histoire Doctrinale et Litteraire du Moyen Age* (1956), 45–144; idem, *Deux chapitres du 'Guide des Egares' repenses par un Kabbaliste,* in: *Mélanges . . . Etienne Gilson* (1959), 651–9; idem, *Recherches sur la synthèse philosophico-kabbalistique de Samuel ibn Motot,* in: *Archives d'Histoire Doctrinale et Litteraire du Moyen Age* (1960), 29–63; D.S. Lewinger, *R. Shemtov b. Abraham b. Gaon,* in: *Sefunot,* 7 (1963), 9–29.

After the Expulsion from Spain – The New Center in Safed: P. Bloch, *Die Kabbalah auf ihren Hoehepunkt und ihre Meister* (1905); A. Ben-Israel, *Alumot* (1952); Moses Cordovero, *Palm Tree of Deborah,* tr. by L. Jacobs (1960); R.J.Z. Werblowsky, *Joseph Karo, Lawyer and Mystic* (1962); M. Benayahu, *Toledot ha-Ari* (1967); idem, *R. Yehudah b. R. Mosheh Botini ve-Sifro 'Yesod Mishneh Torah,'* in: *Sinai* (1955), 240–74; idem, *Hanhagot Mekubbalei Ẓefat be-Meron,* in: *Sefunot,* 6 (1962), 11–40; D. Tamar, *Meḥkarim be-Toledot ha-Yehudim be-Ereẓ Yisrael u-ve-Italyah* (1970); S. Assaf, *La-Pulmus al Hadpasat Sifrei ha-Kabbalah,* in: *Sinai,* 5 (1939/40), 360–5; G. Scholem, *Shtar ha-Hitkashrut shel Talmidei ha-Ari,* in: *Zion,* 5 (1940), 133–60; idem, *Yisrael Sarug – Talmid ha-Ari? ; ibid.,* 214–41; J. Dan, *"R. Yosef Karo – Ba'al Halakhah u-Mistikan" le-R.J.Z. Werblowsky,* in: *Tarbiz,* 33 (1964), 86–96; G. *Séd-Rajna, Le rôle de la Kabbale . . . selon Ḥ. Vital,* in: RHR, 167 (1965), 177–96.

Later Times: M. Wiener, *Die Lyrik der Kabbalah: eine Anthologie* (1920); A. Bension, *Sar Shalom Sharabi* (1930); Y. Kafah, *Sefer Milḥamot ha-Shem* (1931); F. Lachower, *Al Gevul ha-Yashan ve-ha-Ḥadash* (1951); S. Ratner, *Le-Or ha-Kabbalah* (1962); H. Weiner, *Nine and One Half Mystics; the Kabbalah Today* (1969); E. Tcherikower, *Di Komune fun Yerushaylayimer Mekubolim 'Ahavas Shalom' in Mitn dem 18ten Yorhundert,* in: *Historishe Shriftn fun YIVO,* 2 (1937), 115–39; I. Gruenwald, *Le-Toledot ha-Mekubbalim be-Ungaryah,* in: *Sinai,* 24 (1949), 2–22; G. Scholem, *Die letzten Kabbalisten in Deutschland,* in: *Judaica III* (1973), 218-46.

Lurianic Kabbalah: I. Tishby, *Torat ha-Ra ve-ha-Klippah be-Kabbalat ha-Ari* (1942); S.A. Horodezky, *Torat ha-Kabbalah shel Rabbi Yiẓḥak Ashkenazi ve-Rabbi Ḥayyim Vital* (1947); L.I. Karkovsky, *Kabbalah: The Light of Redemption* (1950); J. von Kempski, *Zimzum: Die Schoepfung aus dem Nichts,* in: *Merkur,* 14 (1960), 1107–26; Moses Ḥayyim Luzzatto, *General Principles of the Kabbalah* (New York, 1970).

Kabbalah and Pantheism: M.S. Freystadt, *Philosophia cabbalistica et Pantheismus* (1832); J. Ben-Shlomo, *Torat ha-Elohut shel R. Moshe Cordovero* (1965).

Man and His Soul: M.D.G. Langer, *Die Erotik der Kabbala* (1923).

Exile and Redemption: G. Scholem, *The Messianic Idea in Judaism and Other Essays* (1971); I. Klausner, *'Kol Mevasser' le-Rabbi Yehudah Alkalay,* in: *Shivat Ẓiyyon,* 2 (1953), 42–62; H.H. Ben-Sasson, in: *Sefer Yovel le-Yiẓḥak Baer* (1960), 216–27.

The Torah and its Significance: G. Scholem, *The Meaning of the Torah in*

Jewish Mysticism, in: *On the Kabbalah and its Symbolism* (1965), 32–86; E. Lipiner, *Idiyalogiya fun Yidishn Alef-Beis* (1967).

The Mystic Way: Dov Baer of Lubavitch, *Tract on Ecstasy*, tr. by L. Jacobs (1963); A.J. Heschel, *Al Ru'aḥ ha-Kodesh bi-Yemei ha-Beinayim*, in: *Sefer ha-Yovel . . . A. Marx* (1950), 175–208; G. Vajda, *Continence, mariage et vie mystique selon doctrine du Judaisme*, in: *Mystique et Continence, Etudes Carmélitaines* (1952), 82–92; R.J.Z. Werblowsky, *Tikkun Tefillot le-Rabbi Shelomoh ha-Levi ibn Alkabets*, in: *Sefunot*, 6 (1962), 137–82.

Practical Kabbalah: G. Brecher, *Das Transcendentale, Magie und magische Heilarten im Talmud* (1850); D. Joel, *Der Aberglaube und die Stellung des Judenthums zu demselben*, 2 vols. (1881–83); L. Blau, *Das altuedische Zauberwesen* (1898); J. Guenzig, *Die Wundermaenner im juedischen Volke* (1921); G. Scholem, *Alchemie und Kabbalah*, in: MGWJ, 69 (1925), 13–30, 95–110, 371–74; 70 (1926), 202–9; J. Trachtenberg, *Jewish Magic and Superstition* (1939); T. Schrire, *Hebrew Amulets: Their Decipherment and Interpretation* (1966); J. Dan, *Sippurim Dimonologiyim mi-Kitvei R. Yehuda he-Ḥasid*, in: *Tarbiz*, 30 (1961), 273–89; idem, *Sarei Kos ve-Sarei Bohen, ibid.*, 32 (1963), 359–69; I. Shahar, *The Feuchtwanger Collection of Jewish Tradition and Art* (Heb., 1971), 227–305 (amulets).

Influence of Kabbalah on Judaism: G. Scholem, *On the Kabbalah and its Symbolism* (1965), 118–57; I. Weinstock, *Be-Ma'aglei ha-Nigleh ve-ha-Nistar* (1969), 249–69; I.D. Wilhelm, *Sidrei Tikkunim*, in: *Alei Ayin* (1948-52), 125–46; J.L. Avida, *Ha-Malakhim ha-Memunim al ha-Shofar ha-Ma'alim et ha-Teki'ot*, in: *Sinai*, 33 (1953), 3–23; M. Benayahu, *Hanhagot Mekubbalei Ẓefat be-Meron*, in: *Sefunot*, 6 (1962), 11–40; Y. Yaari, *Toledot ha-Hillula be-Meron*, in: *Tarbiz*,31 (1962), 71–101.

Christian Kabbalah: Johannes Pistorius, *Artis Cabalisticae Scriptores*, 1 (Basel, 1587); Johann Steudner, *Juedische ABC Schul vom Geheimnuss dess dreyeiningen wahren Gottes . . .* (Augsburg, 1665); F.C. Oetinger, *Offentliches Denckmal der Lehrtafel der Prinzessin Antonia* (Tuebingen, 1763); D. Saurat, *Literature and Occult Tradition: Studies in Philosophical Poetry* (1930); E. Anagnine, *G. Pico della Mirandola: sincretismo religioso-filosofico 1463–1494* (1937); J.L. Blau, *The Christian Interpretation of the Cabala in the Renaissance* (1944); F. Secret, *Le Zôhar chez les Kabbalistes chrétiens de la Renaissance* (1958); idem, in: *Bibliothèque d'Humanisme et Renaissance*, 17 (1955), 292–5; 20 (1958), 547–55; idem, *Les debuts du kabbalisme chrétien en Espagne et son histoire à la Renaissance*, in: *Sefarad*, 17 (1957), 36–48; idem, *Le symbolisme de la kabbale chrétienne dans la 'Scechina' de Egidio da Viterbo*, in: *Archivo di Filosofia* (1958), 131–54; idem, *Pedro Ciruelo: Critique de la Kabbale et de son usage par les chrétiens*, in: *Sefarad*, 19 (1959), 48–77; idem, in: *Rinascimento*, 11 (1960), 169–92; 14 (1963), 251–68; idem, *L'hermeneutique de G. Postel*, in: *Archivo di Filosofia* (1963), 91–117; idem, *Le soleil chez les Kabbalistes chrétiens*, in: *Le Soleil à la Renaissance* (1965), 213–40; idem, *Nouvelles précisions sur Flavius Mithridates maître de Pic de la Mirandole et traducteur de commentaires de Kabbale*, in: *L'opera e il pensiero di G. Pico della Mirandola*, 2 (1965), 169–87; idem, *"L'ensis Pauli" de Paulus de Heredia*, in: *Sefarad*, 26

(1966), 79–102, 253–71, idem, *La Revelacion de Sant Pablo, ibid.*, 28 (1968), 45–67; E. Benz, *Die christliche Kabbala: Ein Stiefkind der Theologie* (1958); Ch. Wirszubski, *Sermo de passione Domini* (1963); idem, *Giovanni Pico's Companion to Kabbalistic Symbolism,* in: *Studies . . . G. Scholem,* (1967), 353–62; idem, in: *Journal of the Warburg and Courtauld Institutes,* 32 (1969), 177–99; idem, *Mors Osculi. Poetic Theology and Kabbala in Renaissance Thought,* in: *Proceedings of the Israel Academy of Sciences and Humanities* (1971); M. Brod, *Johannes Reuchlin und sein Kampf* (1965); G. Scholem, *Zur Geschichte der Anfaenge des christlichen Kabbala,* in: *Essays . . . Leo Baeck* (1954), 158–93; R.J.Z. Werblowsky, *Milton and the Conjectura Cabbalistica,* in: *Journal of the Warburg and Courtauld Institutes,* 18 (1955), 90–113; W.A. Schulze, *Schelling und die Kabbala,* in: *Judaica,* 13 (1957), 65–98, 143–70, 210–232; idem, *Der Einfluss der Kabbala auf die Cambridger Platoniker Cudworth und More, ibid.*, 23 (1967), 75–126, 136–60, 193–240; I. Sonne, *Mekomah shel ha-Kabbalah bi-Fe'ulat ha-Hassatah shel ha-Kenesiyah ba-Me'ah ha-Sheva-Esreh,* in: *Bitzaron,* 36 (1957), 7–12, 57–66; I.F. Baer, *Torat ha-Kabbalah be-Mishnato ha-Kristologit shel Avner mi-Burgos,* in: *Tarbiz,* 27 (1958), 278–89; R.T. Lewellyn, *Jacob Boehmes Kosmogonie in ihrer Beziehung zur Kabbala,* in: *Antaios,* 5 (1963), 237–50; F. Haeussermann, in: *Blaetter fuer Wuertembergische Kirchengeschichte,* 66–67 (1966/67), 65–153; 68–69 (1968/69), 207–346.

Research on the Kabbalah: G. Scholem, *Die Erforschung der Kabbala von Reuchlin bis zur Gegenwart* (1969); G. Kressel, *Kitvei Elyakim ha-Milzahagi,* in: KS, 17 (1940), 87–94; G. Vajda, *Les origines et le dévelopement de la Kabbale juive d'après quelques travaux récents.*, in: RHR, 134 (1948), 120–67; idem, *Recherches recentes sur l'ésotérisme juif (1947–1953; 1954–1062),* in: RHR, 147 (1955), 62–92; 164 (1963), 191–212.

Part Two
TOPICS

1

The Zohar

The Zohar (Heb. זֹהַר : "[The Book of] Splendor") is the central work in the literature of the Kabbalah. In some parts of the book the name "Zohar" is mentioned as the title of the work. It is also cited by the Spanish kabbalists under other names, such as the *Mekhilta de-R. Simeon b. Yoḥai,* in imitation of the title of one of the halakhic Midrashim, in *Sefer ha-Gevul* of David b. Judah he-Ḥasid; the *Midrash de-R. Simeon b. Yoḥai,* in several books dating from the period of the pupils of Solomon b. Abraham Adret, in the *Livnat ha-Sappir* of Joseph Angelino, the homilies of Joshua ibn Shu'ayb, and the books of Meir ibn Gabbai; *Midrash ha-Zohar,* according to Isaac b. Joseph ibn Munir [1]; *Midrash Yehi Or* in the *Menorat ha-Ma'or* of Israel al-Nakawa, apparently because he had a manuscript of the Zohar which began with a commentary on the verse "Let there be light" (Gen. 1:3). Manuscripts of this type are extant. Several statements from the Zohar were quoted in the first generation after its appearance, under the general title of *Yerushalmi,* in the writings of, for example, Isaac b. Sahula, Moses de Leon, and David b. Judah he-Ḥasid, and in the (fictitious) responsa of Rav Hai in the collection *Sha'arei Teshuvah.*

The Literary Form of The Zohar. In its literary form the Zohar is a collection of several books or sections which include short midrashic statements, longer homilies, and discussions on many topics. The greater part of them purport to be the utterances of the *tanna* Simeon b. Yoḥai and his close companions *(ḥavrayya),* but there are also long anonymous sections. It is not one book in the accepted sense of the term, but a complete body of literature which has been united under an inclusive title. In the printed editions the Zohar is composed of five volumes. According to the division in most editions, three of them appear under the name *Sefer ha-Zohar al ha-Torah;* one volume bears the title *Tikkunei ha-Zohar;* the fifth, entitled *Zohar Ḥadash,* is a collection of sayings and texts found in the manuscripts of the Safed Kabbalists after the printing of the bulk of the Zohar and assembled by Abraham b. Eliezer ha-Levi Berukhim. Page references in the most common editions of the Zohar and the editions of the *Tikkunim* are generally uniform.

References here to the *Zohar Ḥadash* (ZḤ) are to the Jerusalem edition of 1953. Some of the editions of the book exist separately in manuscript. The sections which make up the Zohar in its wider sense are essentially:

(1) The main part of the Zohar, arranged according to the weekly portions of the Torah, up to and including the portion *Pinḥas.* From Deuteronomy there are only *Va-Ethannan,* a little on *Va-Yelekh,* and *Ha'azinu.* Basically it is a Kabbalistic Midrash on the Torah, mixed with short statements, long expositions, and narratives concerning Simeon b. Yoḥai and his companions. Some of it consists also of common legends. The number of verses interpreted in each portion is relatively small. Often the exposition digresses to other subjects quite divorced from the actual text of the portion, and some of the pieces are quite skillfully constructed. The expositions are preceded by *petiḥot* ("introductions") which are usually based on verses from the Prophets and the Hagiographa, especially Psalms, and which end with a transition to the subject matter of the portion. Many stories act as a framework for the homilies of the companions, e.g., conversations while they are on a journey or when they rest for the night. The language is Aramaic, as it is for most of the other sections of the work (unless otherwise stated). Before the portion of *Bereshit* there is a *hakdamah* ("preface"), which would appear to be a typical collection of writings and not a preface as such, unless perhaps it was intended to introduce the reader to the spiritual climate of the book. Many expositions are found in various manuscripts in different places and sometimes there is some doubt as to which particular portion they really belong. There are also discourses which recur in different contexts in two or three places. Aaron Zelig b. Moses in *Ammudei Sheva* (Cracow, 1635) listed about 40 such passages which are found in parallel editions of the Zohar. A few expositions in the printed editions break off in the middle, and their continuation is printed solely in the *Zohar Ḥadash.* In the later editions, beginning with that of Amsterdam, 1715, these completions are printed as *hashmatot* ("omissions") at the end of each volume.

(2) Zohar to the Song of Songs (printed in ZḤ fols. 61d–75b); it extends only to the greater part of the first chapter and, like (1), consists of kabbalistic expositions.

(3) *Sifra de-Ẓeni'uta* ("Book of Concealment"), a kind of fragmented commentary on the portion *Bereshit,* in short obscure sentences, like an anonymous Mishnah, in five chapters, printed at the end of portion *Terumah* (2:176b–179a). In several manuscripts and in the Cremona edition (1559–60) it is found in the portion *Bereshit.*

(4) *Idra Rabba* ("The Greater Assembly"), a description of the gathering of Simeon b. Yoḥai and his companions, in which the most profound mysteries are expounded concerning the revelation of the Divine in the form of *Adam Kad-*

mon ("Primordial Man"). It is of a superior literary construction and the most systematic discourse found in the Zohar. Each of the companions says his piece and Simeon b. Yoḥai completes their pronouncements. At the end of this solemn assembly three of the ten participants meet with an ecstatic death. Among the early kabbalists it was called *Idra de-Naso* and it is printed in the portion *Naso* (3:127b–145a). It is, in a way, a kind of Gemara to the Mishnah of the *Sifra de-Ẓeni'uta.*

(5) *Idra Zuta* ("The Lesser Assembly"), a description of the death of Simeon b. Yoḥai and his closing words to his followers before his death, a kind of kabbalistic parallel to the death of Moses. In contains a companion discourse to that in the *Idra Rabba,* with many additions. Among the early kabbalists it was called *Idra de-Ha'azinu.* This portion concludes the Zohar (3:287b–96b).

(6) *Idra de-Vei Mashkena,* a study session conducted by Simeon b. Yoḥai with some of his students concerning the exposition of certain verses in the section dealing with the tabernacle. Most of it deals with the mysteries of the prayers. It is found at the beginning of the *Terumah* (2: 127a–146b). The note in later editions that the section 2:122b–3b is the *Idra de-Vei Mashkena* is a mistake. This part is mentioned at the beginning of the *Idra Rabba.*

(7) *Heikhalot,* two descriptions of the seven palaces in the celestial garden of Eden in which the souls take their delight when prayer ascends and also after their departure from the world. One version is short and is inserted in the portion *Bereshit* (1:38a–48b). The other version is very long, because it expands on the mysteries of prayer and angelology. It is found at the end of the portion *Pekudei* (2:244b–62b). At the end of the longer version there is an additional section on the "seven palaces of uncleanness," which is a description of the abodes of hell (2:262b–8b). In kabbalistic literature it is called the *Heikhalot de-R. Simeon b. Yoḥai.*

(8) *Raza de-Razin* ("The Secret of Secrets"), an anonymous piece of physiognomy and chiromancy, based on Exodus 18:21, in the portion *Yitro* (2:70a–75a). Its continuation is to be found in the omissions and in *Zohar Ḥadash* (56c–60a). A second section on the same subject, cast in a different form, was inserted in a parallel column in the bulk of the Zohar (2:70a–78a).

(9) *Sava de-Mishpatim* ("Discourse of the Old Man"), an account of the companions' encounter with R. Yeiva, an old man and a great kabbalist, who disguises himself in the beggarly appearance of a donkey driver, and who delivers himself of an extensive and beautifully constructed discourse on the doctrine of the soul, based on a mystical interpretation of the laws of slavery in the Torah. It is inserted in the bulk of the Zohar on the portion *Mishpatim* (2:94b–114a).

(10) *Yanuka* ("The Child"), the story of a wonder child, the son of the old man, Rav Hamnuna, who teaches the companions profound interpretations of

the Grace after Meals and other matters, when they happen to be lodging in his mother's house. Stories concerning other children like this are found in other parts of the Zohar. In some manuscripts this story constitutes the section of the Zohar on the portion *Devarim.* In the printed edition it is found in the portion *Balak* (3:186a–92a).

(11) *Rav Metivta* ("Head of the Academy"), an account of a visionary journey undertaken by Simeon b. Yoḥai and his pupils to the Garden of Eden, and a long exposition by one of the heads of the celestial academy on the world to come and the mysteries of the soul. It is printed as part of the portion *Shelaḥ Lekha* (3:161b–174a). The beginning is missing, as are certain parts from the middle and the end.

(12) *Kav ha-Middah* ("The Standard of Measure"), an explanation of the details of the mysteries of emanation in an interpretation of the *Shema,* in the form of a discourse by Simeon b. Yoḥai to his son, printed in *Zohar Ḥadash* (56d-58d).

(13) *Sitrei Otiyyot* ("Secrets of the Letters"), a discourse by Simeon b. Yoḥai on the letters of the Divine Names and the mysteries of emanation, printed in *Zohar Ḥadash* (1b–10d).

(14) An interpretation of the vision of the chariot in Ezekiel, chapter 1, printed without a title in *Zohar Ḥadash* (37c–41b).

(15) *Matnitin* and *Tosefta,* numerous short pieces, written in a high-flown and obscure style, serving as a kind of Mishnah to the Talmud of the Zohar itself. The connection between these pieces and the expositions in the portions of the Zohar is clear at times and at others tenuous. Most of the pieces appear as utterances of a heavenly voice which is heard by the companions, and which urges them to open their hearts to an understanding of the mysteries. Many of them contain a summary of the idea of emanation and other major principles of Zohar teaching, couched in an enigmatic style. These pieces are scattered all over the Zohar. According to Abraham Galante in his *Zoharei Ḥammah* (Venice, 1650), 33b, "when the editor of the Zohar saw an exposition which belonged to an argument in a particular exposition from the *mishnayot* and *tosafot* he put it between those pieces in order to give the exposition added force from the Tosefta and the Mishnah."

(16) *Sitrei Torah* ("Secrets of the Torah"), certain pieces on verses from the Book of Genesis, which were printed in separate columns, parallel to the main text of the Zohar, in the portions *No'aḥ, Lekh Lekha, Va-Yera,* and *Va-Yeẓe,* and in *Zohar Ḥadash* on the portions *Toledot* and *Va-Yeshev.* There are several pieces entitled *Sitrei Torah* in the printed editions – e.g., *Sitrei Torah* to the portion *Aḥahrei Mot* in *Zohar Ḥadash* – but it is doubtful whether they really do belong to the *Sitrei Torah.* Similarly, there are manuscripts which designate the

systematic interpretation of creation in 1:15a–22a as the *Sitrei Torah* to this section. However, its character is different from the other examples of *Sitrei Torah,* which contain mainly allegorical explanations of verses on the mysteries of the soul, whereas this piece explains the theory of emanation (in an anonymous discourse) in the style of the main part of the Zohar and the *Matnitin.*

(17) *Midrash ha-Ne'lam* ("Esoteric Midrash") on the Torah. This exists for the sections *Bereshit, No'aḥ, Lekh Lekha* in *Zohar Ḥadash;* for *Va-Yera, Ḥayyei Sarah,* and *Toledot* in the main body of the Zohar, in parallel columns; and for *Va-Yeẓe* in *Zohar Ḥadash.* The beginning of the section *Va-Yeḥi* in the printed editions, 1:211–6, is marked in some sources as the *Midrash ha-Ne'lam* to this portion, but there is some reason to believe, with several kabbalists, that these pages are a later addition. From their literary character and the evidence of several manuscripts, the pages 2:4a–5b, and particularly 14a–22a, belong to the *Midrash ha-Ne'lam* to the portion *Shemot,* and 2:35b–40b to the *Midrash ha-Ne'lam* to the portion *Bo.* From this point onward only a few separate short pieces occur in *Zohar Ḥadash*, on the portions *Be-Shallaḥ* and *Ki Teẓe.* Several pieces, very close in spirit to the *Midrash ha-Ne'lam,* are found here and there in the main part of the Zohar, e.g. in the exposition of Ray Huna before the rabbis, in the portion *Terumah,* 2:174b–175a. It is also possible that the pages in the portion *Bo* are of this kind. The language of this part is a mixture of Hebrew and Aramaic. Many rabbis are mentioned in it, and in contrast to the long expositions of the earlier parts we find here mostly short pieces similar to the original aggadic Midrashim. Here and there we can recognize the transition to a more lengthy expository method, but there are no artistically constructed and extensive expositions. As to content, the material is centered mainly around discussions on creation, the soul, and the world to come, with a few discussions on the nature of God and emanation. Most of the sections, after the portion *Bereshit,* expound biblical narratives, notably the deeds of the patriarchs, as allegories of the fate of the soul.

(18) *Midrash ha-Ne'lam* to the book of Ruth, similar in style and content to the preceding. It is printed in *Zohar Ḥadash,* and was originally printed as a separate work called *Tappuḥei Zahav* or *Yesod Shirim* in Thiengen in 1559. It exists in many manuscripts as an independent book.

(19) The beginning of the *Midrash ha-Ne'lam* to the Song of Songs. It is printed in *Zohar Ḥadash* and is merely a prefatory exposition to the book, without any continuation.

(20) *Ta Ḥazei* ("Come and See"), another interpretation of the portion *Bereshit* in short anonymous comments, most of them beginning with the words, *ta ḥazei,* and written in an obviously kabbalistic vein. The first part is found in *Zohar Ḥadash,* 7a, after the *Sitrei Otiyyot,* and the rest was first printed in the

Cremona edition, 55–75, continuing in the *hashmatot* of the Zohar, at the end of volume I. In some manuscripts (like Vatican 206, fols. 274–86), the two sections are found together, but in most they are missing altogether.

(21) *Ra'aya Meheimna* ("The Faithful Shepherd") – the reference is to Moses – a separate book on the kabbalistic significance of the commandments. It is found in some manuscripts as an independent work, and in the printed editions it is scattered piecemeal among the sections in which the particular commandments are mentioned and printed in separate columns. The greater part occurs in portions from Numbers and Deuteronomy, and particularly in *Pinḥas, Ekev,* and *Ki Teẓe.* The setting of the book is different from that of the main part of the Zohar. In it Simeon b. Yoḥai and his companions, apparently through a visionary revelation, meet Moses, "the faithful shepherd," along with *tannaim* and *amoraim* and other figures from the celestial world, who appear to them and talk with them about the mysteries of the commandments, as if the academy on high had descended to the earth below. This work is quite clearly dependent on the Zohar itself, since it is quoted several times under the name of "the former [or first] book," particularly in the portion *Pinḥas.* The enumeration of the commandments, which is extant in several places and which points to an original order, has become confused (see also below, The Unity of the Work, Order of Composition).

(22) *Tikkunei Zohar,* also an independent book whose setting is similar to that of the *Ra'aya Meheimna.* It comprises a commentary to the portion *Bereshit,* each section *(tikkun)* beginning with a new interpretation of the word *bereshit* ("in the beginning"). The book was designed to contain 70 *tikkunim* conforming to "the 70 aspects of the Torah," but in actual fact there are more, and some of them are printed as additions at the end of the book. Two completely different arrangements are found in the manuscripts, and these are reflected in the different editions of Mantua (1558), and of Orta Koj (1719). The later editions follow Orta Koj. The expositions in the book digress widely from the subject matter of the portion and deal with quite different topics which are not discussed in the main body of the Zohar, like the mysteries of the vowel points and accents, mysteries concerning halakhic matters, prayer, and so on. The pages in the Zohar, 1:22a–29a, belong to this book and occur in manuscripts as parts of *tikkun* no. 70. Here and there, there is a change in the narrative framework, when it imitates that of the main body of the Zohar and, sometimes apparently continuing the discussion, appears as if it were being held in the celestial academy. The book also has a preface *(hakdamah)* on the model of the preface in the Zohar. Long additional expositions, parallel with the book's opening sections and mixed with other interpretations on the same pattern, are printed at the end of *Zohar Ḥadash* (93–123), and they are usually introduced

as *tikkunim* of *Zohar Ḥadash.* Many of these were meant to serve as a preface to the book of *Tikkunim.*

(23) An untitled work on the portion *Yitro,* a redaction, in the spirit of the *tikkunim,* of the physiognomy found in the *Raza de-Razin,* printed in *Zohar Ḥadash* (31a–35b).

(24) A few tracts printed in *Zohar Ḥadash,* like the "Zohar to the portion *Tissa*" (43d–46b), and the anonymous piece printed as the portion *Ḥukkat* in *Zohar Ḥadash* (50a–53b). These pieces must be regarded as imitations of the Zohar, but they were written without doubt very soon after the appearance of the book, and the first is already quoted in the *Livnat ha-Sappir,* which was written in 1328 (Jerusalem, 1914, 86d).

In addition to these sections there were others known to various kabbalists which were not included in the printed editions, and some of them are completely lost. A continuation of the *Sefer ha-Tikkunim* on other portions known to the author of *Livnat ha-Sappir* (95b–100a) was a long piece on the calculation of the time of redemption. The pieces, which were printed in the *Tikkunei Zohar Ḥadash* (117b–121b), and interpret various verses concerning Abraham and Jacob, seem to belong to this continuation. The "sayings of *Ze'ira*" ("the little one"), which are mentioned in *Shem ha-Gedolim* as being "quasimidrashic homilies," are extant in Paris Ms. 782 and were included by Ḥayyim Vital in an anthology which still exists. The Zohar to the portion *Ve-Zot ha-Berakhah* is preserved in the same Paris manuscript (fols. 239-42), and is a mixture of fragments from the Midrash on Ruth and unknown pieces. It would appear that Moses Cordovero saw a *Midrash Megillat Esther* from the Zohar, according to *Or Ne'erav* (Venice, 1587, 21b). His pupil Abraham Galante, in his commentary to *Sava de-Mishpatim,* quotes a text called *Pesikta,* from a manuscript Zohar, but its content is not known. There is no direct connection between the literature of the Zohar and the later literary imitations of it that are not included in the manuscripts, such as the Zohar on Ruth, which was printed under the title *Har Adonai* (Amsterdam, 1712). This piece was composed in Poland in the 17th century.

The opinion of the kabbalists themselves concerning the composition and editing of the Zohar was formed after the circulation of the book. At first the view was widely held that this was the book written by Simeon b. Yoḥai while he was in hiding in the cave, or at least during his lifetime, or at the latest in the generation that followed. Among the kabbalists of Safed, who generally believed in the antiquity of the whole of the Zohar, Abraham Galante, in his commentary to the portion *Va-Yishlaḥ* in the Zohar, thought that the whole work was put together in geonic times from the writings of R. Abba, who was Simeon b. Yoḥai's scribe, and that the book did not receive its present form until that time.

This view, which tries to explain a number of obvious difficulties in the chronology of the rabbis who are mentioned in the Zohar, also occurs in *Netiv Miẓvotekha* by Isaac Eisik Safrin of Komarno. In the 16th century the legend grew up that the present Zohar, which contains about 2,000 closely printed pages, was only a tiny remnant of the original work, which was some 40 camel loads in weight (in *Ketem Paz,* 102a). These ideas are not substantiated by a critical examination of the Zohar.

The Unity of the Work. The literature contained in the Zohar can be divided basically into three strata, which must be distinguished from one another: (a) the main body of the Zohar, comprising items (1)–(15) in the list above; (b) the stratum of the *Midrash ha-Ne'lam* and *Sitrei Torah,* i.e., items (16)–(19); and (c) the stratum of the *Ra'aya Meheimna* and the *Tikkunim,* i.e., (21)–(23). Items (20) and (24) are doubtful as regards their literary relationship, and perhaps they belong to material that was added after the appearance of the Zohar in the 14th century. There are, to be sure, definite links between the different strata which establish a chronological order, but a detailed investigation shows quite clearly that each stratum has a definite unity of its own. The question of the unity of the main body of the Zohar is particularly important. The apparent differences are merely external and literary, e.g., the choice of a laconic and enigmatic style at times, and at others, the use of a more expansive and occasionally verbose style.

Style. This unity is evident in three areas; those of literary style, language, and ideas. Ever since the historical critique of the Zohar first began, there have been views that regard the Zohar as a combination of ancient and later texts, which were put together only at the time of the Zohar's appearance. At the very least it contains a homiletic prototype, a creation by many generations which cannot be attributed essentially to one single author. This view has been held, for example, by Eliakim Milsahagi, Hillel Zeitlin, Ernst Mueller, and Paul Vulliaud, but they have contented themselves with a general conclusion, or with a claim that the *Sifra di-Ẓeni'uta,* the *Matnitin,* or the *Idrot,* are ancient sources of this type. The only scholar who attempted to investigate the early strata in the expositions of the other parts of the Zohar was I. Stern. A detailed examination of his arguments, and also of the general arguments, shows that they are extremely weak. In particular there is no evidence that the *Sifra di-Ẓeni'uta* differs from the other parts of the body of the Zohar except in the allusive style in which it was intentionally written. In actual fact, the literary connections between the different parts of the Zohar are extremely close. Many of the sections are constructed with great literary skill and the different parts are related to one another. There is no real distinction, either in language or thought, between the short pieces in the true midrashic style and the longer expositions which follow the methods of the medieval preachers, who used to weave together different ideas into a single fabric, which begins with a particular verse, ranges far and wide, and then finally returns to its starting point. Practically all the sections are built on an identical method of composition, stemming from variations of different literary forms. From the point of view of construction there is no difference also between the various narrative frameworks, such as the transmission of expositions which originated during the companions' journeys between one city and another in Palestine, especially in Galilee, or the type of dramatic composition that is to be found in the *Idrot,* the *Sava,* and the *Yanuka.* The breaking-up of the material into a conversation among the companions, or into an expository monologue, does not basically alter the subject matter of the composition itself. Even in the monologues several opinions are concerning a particular verse are mentioned side by side while in other parts the different opinions are divided up and assigned to different speakers. Quotations of, or references to, expositions in other parts of the Zohar occur throughout the main body of the book. Some matters, which are discussed extremely briefly in one place, are treated more fully in another exposition. The Zohar, unlike the Midrash, loves to allude either to a previous discussion or to a subject which is to be dealt with later, and this is typical of medieval homilists. An examination of these cross-references, whether of exact verbal citations or of subject matter without precise quotation, shows that the main part of the Zohar is a literary construction all of one piece, despite superficial variations. Statements or ideas which are not reflected in more than one place do exist but they are very few and far between. Even those sections which have a particularly characteristic subject matter, like that dealing with physiognomy in the portion *Yitro,* are connected in many ways with other sections of the Zohar, which deal more fully with topics only briefly mentioned in the former. On the relationship of the *Midrash ha-Ne'lam* to the main body of the Zohar, see below.

One element in the constructional unity of the Zohar is that of the scene and the dramatis personae. The Zohar presupposes the existence of an organized group of "companions" *(ḥavrayya),* who, without doubt, were originally meant to be ten in number, but most of them are no more than shadowy figures. These ten companions are Simeon b. Yoḥai, his son Eleazar, Abba, Judah, Yose, Isaac, Hezekiah, Ḥiyya, Yeisa, and Aḥa. Several of them are *amoraim* who have been transferred by the author to the age of the *tannaim,* like Abba, Hezekiah, Ḥiyya, and Aḥa. What is narrated of them here and there shows that the author utilized stories in talmudic sources which concerned *amoraim* with these names, and these are not therefore unknown historical figures. These basic characters are joined by certain other rabbis, who usually appear indirectly, or as figures from the generation that preceded Simeon b. Yoḥai. In this connection, one particular error of the Zohar is very important. In several stories it consistently turns Phineḥas b. Jair, Simeon b. Yoḥai's son-in-law (according to Shab. 33b), into his father-in-law. Similarly, the father-in-law of Eleazar, Simeon's son, is called Yose b. Simeon b. Lekonya, instead of Simeon b. Yose b. Lekonya. In addition to the regular companions there occasionally appear other characters whom the designation *sava* ("old man") places in the preceding generation, e.g., Nehorai Sava, Yeisa Sava, Hamnuna Sava, and Judah Sava. There is a recognizable tendency to create a fictional framework in which the problems of anachronism and chronological confusion do not arise. On the other hand, neither Akiva nor Ishmael b. Elisha is mentioned as a master of mystical tradition, whereas both appear in the *heikhalot* and the Merkabah literature. Akiva is introduced only in stories and quotations which come from the Talmud.

The Palestinian setting of the book is also fictional, and, in the main, has no basis in fact. The Zohar relies on geographical and topographical ideas about Palestine taken from older literature. Sometimes the author did not understand his sources, and created places which never existed, e.g., Kapotkeya, as the name of a village near Sepphoris, on the basis of a statement in the Palestinian Talmud (Shev. 9:5), which he combined with another statement in the Tosefta, *Yevamot* 4. He produces a village in Galilee by the name of Kefar Tarsha which he identified with Mata Meḥasya, and tells in this connection of the rite of circumcision which is based on material quoted in geonic literature with regard to Mata Meḥasya in Babylonia. Occasionally a place-name is based on a corrupt text in a medieval manuscript of the Talmud, e.g., Migdal Ẓor at the beginning of *Sava de-Mishpatim.* In the matter of scene and characters there are very close links between the main body of the Zohar and the stratum of the *Midrash ha-Ne'lam,* which follows the same path of mentioning places which do not actually exist. In this section Simeon b. Yoḥai and his companions already constitute a most important community of mystics, but other groups are mentioned as well, and particularly later *amoraim* or scholars with fictitious names who do not reappear in the Zohar. In recent times, several attempts have been made to explain the geographical difficulties, and to give a nonliteral interpretation of statements in the Talmud and the Midrashim in order to make them fit the Zohar, but they have not been convincing. Several times the Zohar uses the expression *selik le-hatam* ("he went up thither"), a Babylonian idiom for those who went up from Babylonia to Palestine, thereby changing the scene from Palestine to the Diaspora – "thither" is an impossible expression if the book was actually written in Palestine.

Sources. As to the question of the sources of the Zohar, we must distinguish between those that are mentioned explicitly and the true sources that are alluded to in only a general way("they have established it," "the companions have discussed it"), or are not mentioned at all. The sources of the first type are fictitious works which are mentioned throughout the Zohar and the *Midrash ha-Ne'lam,* e.g., the *Sifra de-Adam* the *Sifra de-Ḥanokh,* the *Sifra de-Shelomo Malka,* the *Sifra de-Rav Hamnuna Sava,* the *Sifra de-Rav Yeiva Sava* and in a more enigmatic form, *Sifrei Kadma'ei* ("ancient books"), the *Sifra de-Aggadeta,* the *Raza de-Razin, Matnita de-Lan* (i.e., the mystical Mishnah in contradistinction to the usual Mishnah). With regard to the mystery of the letters of the alphabet, the *Atvan Gelifin* ("Engraved Letters") is quoted, or the "Engraved Letters of R. Eleazar." Works of magic are also quoted, e.g., the *Sifra de-Ashmedai,* the *Zeini Ḥarshin de-Kasdi'el Kadma'ah* ("Various Kinds of Sorcery of the Ancient Kasdiel"), the *Sifra de-Ḥokhmeta di-Venei Kedem* ("Book of Wisdom of the Sons of the East"). Some names are based on earlier sources, like the *Sifra de-Adam,* and the *Sifra de-Ḥanokh,* but matters are referred to by these names which really belong entirely to the Zohar and to its world of ideas. In contrast to this fictitious library, which is clearly emphasized, the actual literary sources of the Zohar are concealed. These sources comprise a great many books, from the Talmud and Midrashim to the kabbalistic works which were composed in the 13th century. A single approach in the use of these sources can be detected, both in the sections of the Zohar itself and in the *Midrash ha-Ne'lam.* The writer had expert knowledge of the early material and he often used it as a foundation for his expositions, putting into it variations of his own. His main sources were the Babylonian Talmud, the complete *Midrash Rabbah,* the *Midrash Tanḥuma,* and the two *Pesiktot,* the Midrash on Psalms, the *Pirkei de-Rabbi Eliezer,* and the Targum Onkelos. Generally speaking they are not quoted exactly, but translated into the peculiar style of the Zohar and summarized. If a particular subject exists in a number of parallel versions in the earlier literature, it is not often possible to establish the precise source. But, on the other hand, there are many statements which are quoted in a form which exists in only one of the different sources. Less use is made of the halakhic Midrashim, the Palestinian Talmud, and the other Targums, and of the Midrashim like the *Aggadat Shir ha-Shirim,* the Midrash on Proverbs, and the *Alfabet de-R. Akiva.* It is not clear whether the author used the *Yalkut Shimoni,* or whether he knew the sources of its *aggadah* separately. Of the smaller Midrashim he used the *Heikhalot Rabbati,* the *Alfabet de-Ben Sira,* the *Sefer Zerubabel,* the *Baraita de-Ma'aseh Bereshit,* the *Perek Shirah* in his aggadic descriptions of *Gan Eden,* and the tractate *Ḥibbut ha-Kever,* and also, occasionally, the *Sefer ha-Yashar.* Sometimes the author makes use of *aggadot* which no longer remain, or which are extant only in the *Midrash ha-Gadol;* this is not to be wondered at because aggadic Midrashim like this were known to many medieval writers, e.g., in the homilies of Joshua ibn Shu'ayb, who wrote in the generation following the appearance of the Zohar. The Zohar continues the thought patterns of the *aggadah* and transfers them to the world of the Kabbalah. The references to parallels in rabbinic literature which Reuben Margulies quotes in his *Niẓoẓei Zohar* in the Jerusalem edition of the Zohar (1940-48) often reveal the sources of the expositions.

From medieval literature the author makes use, as W. Bacher has shown, of Bible commentators like Rashi, Abraham ibn Ezra, David Kimḥi, and the *Lekaḥ Tov* of Tobiah b. Eliezer. Apparently he also knew the commentaries of the tosafists. He was noticeably influenced by the allegorical commentators of the Maimonides' school, particularly in the *Midrash ha-Ne'lam* but also in some of the expositions in the main body of the Zohar. The last commentator whom he used as a source was Naḥmanides in his commentaries both to the Torah and to Job. Certain verbal usages in the Zohar can be explained only by reference to the definitions in the *Sefer he-Arukh,* and in the *Sefer ha-Shorashim* of David Kimḥi. An important exposition in the section *Balak* is based on a combination of three pieces from the *Kuzari* of Judah Halevi. In connection with certain customs he bases himself on the *Sefer ha-Manhig* of Abraham b. Nathan ha-Yarḥi. Rashi's commentary to the Talmud serves as the foundation of several statements in the Zohar, and not only in connection with the Talmud. Of the works of Maimonides, he makes slight use of the commentary to the Mishnah and the *Moreh Nevukhim,* and uses the *Mishneh Torah* more extensively. Several attempts to prove that Maimonides knew the Zohar and made use of it in several of his *halakhot* (more recently that of R. Margulies, *Ha-Rambam ve-ha-Zohar,* 1954) only serve to show the dependence of the Zohar on Maimonides.

The sources of the Zohar among the kabbalistic works which preceded it are also unclear. The *Sefer Yeẓirah* is clearly mentioned only in the later stratum. The *Sefer ha-Bahir, Ma'yan ha-Ḥokhmah* attributed to Moses, the writings of the Ḥasidei Ashkenaz and particularly of Eleazar of Worms, R. Ezra's commentary to the Song of Songs, and the commentary to the liturgy by Azriel of Gerona, were all known to the author of the Zohar, and he develops tendencies which appeared first in the writings of the circle of the Gnostics in Castile in the middle of the 13th century. Similarly, the kabbalistic terminology of the Zohar reflects the development of the Kabbalah from the *Sefer ha-Bahir* up to Joseph Gikatilla, and the term *nekuddah ḥada* ("one point") in the sense of "center" is taken from Gikatilla's *Ginnat Egoz,* which was written in 1274. Terms scattered in several places, like *Ein-Sof, avir kadmon, ayin* (in the mystical sense), *mekora de-ḥayei, re'uta de maḥshavah, alma de-peiruda,* have their source in the development of the Kabbalah after 1200. The term *ḥaluk* or *ḥaluka de-rabbanan*, for the soul's garment in Eden, and ideas relating to the formation of this garment, are taken from the *Ḥibbur Yafeh min ha-Yeshu'ah* of Nissim b. Jacob (1050). Often the author of the Zohar draws on the Midrashim indirectly by means of the commentaries on them written by the kabbalists who preceded him.

The medieval environment can be recognized in many details of the Zohar apart from those already mentioned. Historical references to the Crusades and to Arab rule in Palestine after the wars are put together with material based on the laws and customs found in the Spanish environment of the author. In the same way his ethical diatribe directed against certain particular immoralities in the life of the community belongs to a specific period of time, as Yiẓhak Baer has shown. The common customs are characteristic of Christian lands in medieval times. The author's ideas on medicine fit this particular period, which was dominated by the views of Galen. The Zohar does not have any clear ideas concerning the nature of idolatry, and it is dependent on the views of Maimonides which, for their part, were based on the fictitious "literature" of the sect of the Sabeans in Ḥarran. The cultural and religious background to which most of the book, including its polemical parts, is related, is Christian and monogamous. But occasionally we come across allusions to Islam and to contacts with Muslims, and this fits the identification of Castile as the place where the book was written.

Where the ideas of the Zohar concerning Satan and the ranks of the powers of uncleanness, devils, and evil spirits, and also necromancy and sorcerers, are not taken from talmudic sources, they bear the clear impress of the Middle Ages, e.g., the compact between the sorcerer and Satan, and the worship of Satan by the sorcerers. References to these matters are scattered throughout the Zohar, but they are of one and the same type. The liturgy, which is expounded at length in the sections *Terumah* and *Va-Yakhel*, is not the original liturgy of Palestine, but the Spanish and French version in use in the Middle Ages. The literary form given to all these expositions as though they were spoken in the tannaitic period is only superficial. The author of the third stratum, in the *Ra'aya Meheimna* and the *Tikkunim*, reveals his environment through some additional material, and it is almost as if he did not wish to conceal it at all. This is particularly noticeable in his lengthy treatment of the social and religious situation of the Jewish communities of his time, a favorite subject which receives a different treatment from that in the main body of the Zohar. The social conditions described here are in no way those of the earlier communities of Babylonia and Palestine but fit, in every detail, what we know of the conditions in Spain in the 13th century. His writing has a distinctly harsh polemical note directed against various groups in Jewish society, a note which is absent from other parts of the Zohar. Typical of this part is the use of the phrase *erev rav* ("mixed multitude") to designate the social stratum in the Jewish communities in which were combined all the blemishes which he noted in his own contemporaries. The author was also aware of the lively controversy between the kabbalists, called in these parts only *marei kabbalah* ("masters of kabbalah"), and their opponents, who denied both their claim that mysteries existed in the Torah and their knowledge of them.

Language. If all hopes of discovering primitive layers in the Zohar through an historical and literary analysis of its various parts are vain, they will be equally frustrated when we turn to a linguistic critique. The language of the Zohar may be divided into three types: (1) the Hebrew of the *Midrash ha-Ne'lam;* (2) the Aramaic there and in the main body of the Zohar; and (3) the imitation of (2) in the *Ra'aya Meheimna* and the *Tikkunim.* The Hebrew is, in fact, an imitation of the aggadic style, but whenever it diverges from its literary sources it is seen to be a medieval Hebrew belonging to a time when philosophical terminology was widely used. The writer uses later philosophical terms quite openly, particularly in the earlier sections and in the Midrash on Ruth. At the same time the transition from this Hebrew to the Aramaic of the *Midrash ha-Ne'lam* itself and of the main part of the Zohar, which linguistically speaking are one and the same, can be clearly distinguished. The natural Hebrew of the author is here translated into an artificial Aramaic. While his Hebrew has counterparts in medieval literature, the Aramaic of the Zohar has no linguistic parallel, since it is compounded of all the Aramaic idioms that the author knew and which he used as the foundation for his artificial construction. The very use of the word *targum* (I:89a) for the Aramaic language, instead of *leshon Arami,* which was used in the Talmud and Midrash, was a medieval practice. The Aramaic idioms are in the main the language of the Babylonian Talmud and the Targum Onkelos, together with the Galilean Aramaic of the other Targums, but they include only very little from the Palestinian Talmud. Types of different idioms are used side by side indiscriminately, even in the same passage. Similar differences may be seen in the pronouns, both subjective and possessive, demonstrative and interrogative, and also in the conjugation of the verb. The Zohar uses these interchangeably, quite freely. Sometimes the Zohar adopts the Babylonian usage of a particular form, e.g., those forms of the perfect tense preceded by *ka (ka'amar)* or the form of conjugation of the third person imperfect *(leima).* At other times the corresponding targumic forms are preferred. With the noun there is no longer any distinction between those forms which have the definitive *alef* suffix, and those which do not have it, and there is complete confusion. Even a form like *tikla ḥada* ("a pair of scales") is possible here. The constructive case is almost non-existent and is mostly replaced by the use of *di.* In addition to the usual vocabulary new words are coined by analogy with formations that already exist in other words. So words like *nehiru, neẓiẓu, ketatu* come into being (for new words in the vocabulary, see below). As for adverbs, it uses indiscriminately words from both biblical and Babylonian Aramaic, and translations of medieval terms, like *lefum sha'ata* or *kedein,* in imitation of the use of *az* to join different parts of a sentence as in medieval Hebrew. With all the confusion of these forms there is, nevertheless, some sort of system and consistency. A kind of unified language is created which is common throughout all the parts mentioned above. In addition to the basic forms drawn from the Aramaic idiom there are many characteristics which are peculiar to the language of the Zohar. The Zohar mixes up the conjunctions of the verb, using the *pe'al* instead of the *pa'el* and the *af'el (lemizkei* for *lezakka'ah, lemei'al* for *le'a'ala'ah, lemeḥdei* for *leḥadda'ah)* and also the *af'el* instead of the *pe'al,* e.g., *olifna* for *yalfinan* (among the most common words in the Zohar). It uses incorrect forms of the *itpa'al* or *etpe'el* (the two forms of the verb are indistinguishable), e.g., *itsaddar* or *itsedar, itẓayyar* or *itẓeyar, itzakkei* or *tzekei, itẓerif,* etc. In several instances, although only with certain verbs, it uses the *itpa'al* (or the *etpe'el*) as a transitive verb, e.g., *it'arna milei, le-istammara* or *le-istemara orḥoi, le-itdabbaka* or *le-itdebaka* in the sense of "to attain." it gives new meanings to words, following their medieval usage: e.g., *istallak* with regard to the death of the righteous; *it'ar,* through the influence of *hitorer,* which in the Middle Ages was used in the sense of "to discuss a certain matter"; *adbakuta* in the sense of "intellectual perception"; *ashgaḥuta* in the sense of "providence"; *shorsha* in the sense of "basic principle." The conjunctive phrase *im kol da* used throughout in the sense of "nevertheless" *(be-khol zot)* is influenced by the translators from Arabic, as is the use of the word *remez* as a term for allegory.

A large number of errors and of borrowed translations constantly recur in the Zohar. The word *pelatarin* is considered a plural form, and *galgallei yamma* a plural form from *gallei ha-yam* ("waves of the sea"). The author writes *bar-anan* instead of *bar-minan* and gives the artificial translation "limb" for *shaifa* through a mistaken guess in the interpretation of a passage in *Makkot* 11b. From the verb *gamar,* meaning "to learn," he coins the same meaning for the verb *ḥatam (le-meḥtam oraita),* and there are many examples of this kind. There are several words, whose meaning in the original sources the author of the Zohar did not know, and they are given new and incorrect meanings: e.g., the verb *ta'an* is given the meaning of "to guide a donkey from behind" (an Arabism taken from the *Sefer ha-Shorashim* of David Kimḥi) or *taya'a,* "the Jew who guides the donkey." *Tukpa* in the sense of "lap" is based on a misunderstanding of a passage in Targum Onkelos (Num. 11:12); *bozina de-kardinuta* as "a very powerful light" is based on a misunderstanding of a passage in *Pesaḥim* 7a. There are a number of words, especially nouns, which have no known source and whose meaning is often unclear. It is possible that they derive from corrupt readings in manuscripts of rabbinic literature, or the author's new coinage in imitation of foreign words which occur in that literature. Most of them begin with the letter *kof* and the letters *zayin, samekh, pe,* and *resh* are predominant: e.g., *sospita, kaftira, kospita, kirta, kozpira.* Arabic influence appears in only a very few words, but Spanish influence is noticeable in the vocabulary, idioms, and use of particular prepositions. The word *gardinim* in the sense of "guardians," derived from the Spanish *guardianes,* occurs in every part of the Zohar; the verb *besam* in the sense of "to soften" is a literal translation of the Spanish verb *endulzar;* hence also the common expression *hamtakat ha-din,* which comes from the Zohar. The borrowed translations of *ḥakal* in the sense of "battlefield," and of *kos* in the sense of the "cup of a flower," show the influence of Romance usage. Idioms like *lakeḥin derekh aḥeret, kayyama bi-she'elta, istekem al yedoi* (instead of *askem*), *osim simḥah, yateva be-reikanya* (in the sense of "being empty") are all translations borrowed from Spanish. In the *Tikkunei Zohar* there is, in addition, the use of *esh nogah* for "synagogue" (Sp. *esnoga=sinagoga).* The phrase *egoz ha-keshet* as a military term has its source in the medieval Romance languages *(nuez de ballesta).* There are many examples of the use of the preposition *min* ("from") instead of *shel* ("of"); *be* ("in") for *im* ("with"); *legabbei* ("in reference to") for *el* ("to") – all resulting from the influence of Spanish constructions.

The linguistic unity of the Zohar is apparent also in particular stylistic peculiarities which are not found at all in rabbinic literature, or which have a completely different meaning there. They occur in all parts of the Zohar, particularly in the *Midrash ha-Ne'lam,* and in the main body of the Zohar. Examples of this are the use of forms on the pattern of "active and not active" – not in the rabbinic sense of "half-active," but with the significance of spiritual activity whose profundity cannot be fathomed; the combination of words with the termination *de-kholla,* e.g., *amika de-kholla, nishmeta de-kholla, mafteḥa de-kholla;* hyperbolic forms of the type *raza de-razin, temira de-temirin, ḥedvah de-khol ḥedvan, tushbaḥta de-khol tushbeḥin;* the description of an action, whose details are not to be revealed, through the use of the form "he did what he did"; the division of a particular matter into certain categories by the use of *it . . . ve-it,* e.g., *it yayin ve-it yayin, it kayiẓ ve-it kayiẓ;* the use of hendiadys (two terms for the same object), e.g., *ḥotama de-gushpanka* ("seal of a seal"), *boẓina di-sheraga* ("light of a light"). As for syntax we notice the use of the infinitive at the beginning of a clause, even when the subject of the clause is different from that of the main sentence; e.g., *ẓaddikim re'uyyim le-hityashev ha-olam mehem; ihu heikhala di-reḥimu le-iddebaka dakhora be-nukba.* This is particularly so in the case of relative and final clauses. Another syntactical characteristic is the use of *az* or *kedein* at the beginning of subclauses. All these characteristics are typical of medieval usage, and particularly of the Hebrew of Spanish Jewry, under the influence of the philosophical style, and the author of the Zohar uses them without any concern about their being a late development. The dialectical language in the arguments of the rabbis is taken almost exclusively from the Babylonian Talmud, with the addition of a few terms from the medieval homiletical style, e.g., *it le-istakkala, it le'it'ara.* Within the context of this linguistic unity, the Zohar uses different stylistic media with great freedom. Sometimes it deals with an exposition or follows an argument at great length; and at others it is laconic and enigmatic, or adopts a solemn almost rhythmical style.

In contrast to the language used in other parts of the Zohar, the language of the *Ra'aya Meheimna* and the *Tikkunim* is poor from the point of view of both vocabulary and syntax. The writer is already imitating the Zohar itself, but he does not have the literary skill of its author. The number of Hebrew words transmuted into Aramaic is much greater here than in the Zohar. The literary goal of the author of the main part of the Zohar is quite different from that of this author, who writes an almost undisguised medieval Hebrew: it is quite clear that he never intended his work to be thought of as a tannaitic creation. The terms Kabbalah and *Sefirot,* which are not used at all in the main body of the Zohar or in the *Midrash ha-Ne'lam,* and which indeed are circumvented by the use of all kinds of paraphrastic idioms, are here mentioned unrestrainedly.

Order of Composition. An examination of the Zohar following the criteria above shows the order of composition of the main strata. The oldest parts, relatively speaking, are sections of the *Midrash ha-Ne'lam,* from *Bereshit* to *Lekh Lekha,* and the *Midrash ha-Ne'lam* to Ruth. They had already been written according to a different literary pattern, which did not yet assign everything to the circle of Simeon b. Yoḥai alone but which established Eliezer b. Hyrcanus also, following the *Heikhalot* and the *Pirkei de-Rabbi Eliezer,* as one of the main heroes of mystical thought. This section contains the basis of many passages in the main body of the Zohar, which quotes statements to be found only there, and develops its themes, stories, and ideas more expansively. The reverse cannot be maintained. In these early sections, there are no matters whose comprehension depends on a reference to the Zohar itself, whereas every part of the body of the Zohar, including the *Idra Rabba* and the *Idra Zuta,* is full of quotations from, and allusions to, matters found only in the *Midrash ha-Ne'lam.* The contradictions that occur here and there between the two strata on certain points, particularly on matters concerning the soul, may be explained, in the light of the unity that exists between them, as indications of a development in the ideas of the author whose written work emerged from a deep spiritual stirring. Some gleanings into the creative imagination of the author and its development were made possible by the discovery of a new section on the verse "Let there be lights in the firmament of heaven," which parallels one in the printed editions and in most of the manuscripts, but differs from it in the extraordinary imaginative conception of the author, and appears to be the first draft of the printed version which is toned down considerably. This new section is extant only in the oldest manuscript of the Zohar so far known[2] but it provides the first quotation from Zoharic writings to be found in Hebrew literature. In the last two sections of the *Midrash ha-Ne'lam* there are two references to matters that are to be found only in the main body of the Zohar, the writing of which seems therefore to have been started at that time. In the composition of the main body of the Zohar changes occur in literary technique, and in the transition to the exclusive use of Aramaic, and particularly in the decision to treat more expansively the writer's kabbalistic ideas, and those of his circle. The order of composition of the various sections which make up the second basic stratum cannot be precisely determined. There are so many cross-references, and we do not know whether these references were inserted in the final redaction or were there from the very beginning, either referring to something already written or to what the author intended to write later on. In any event, most of the material was written as the result of a profound creative enthusiasm and over a relatively short period of time, so that the question of the order of composition of this section is not vitally important. Even after the author had stopped working on the *Midrash ha-Ne'lam,* which was never completed, he occasionally continued to write passages in the same vein and fitted them into the structure of the main part of the Zohar. This interlocking of one layer with another, despite the obvious differences between them, occurs also between the main body of the Zohar and the later stratum, whose composition begins with the *Ra'aya Meheimna.* The differences here are so great that it is impossible to suppose that the same author wrote both the two earlier strata and the later one. But there is a link between them. The author of the main part of the Zohar began, apparently, to compose a literary work which was anonymous and not associated with any particular literary or narrative fromework and which was meant to be an interpretation of the reasons for the commandments according to his views. He did not finish this work, and the remnants of it are not extant in any one particular manuscript copy. However, the author of the *Ra'aya Meheimna,* who was probably a pupil of the former writer, knew it and used it as the starting point of his comments on several of the commandments, adding his own individual insights and the new scenery. The differences in outlook and style between these fragments – which, when they do occur, are always at the beginning of the discussion on the commandments – and the main parts of the *Ra'aya Meheimna* are very great. It is almost always possible to determine precisely the point of transition between the fragments of the original text, which may be assigned to the Zohar itself, and the *Ra'aya Meheimna,* which was added to it.

The kabbalists themselves seem to have recognized this distinction. For example, the printers of the Cremona edition of the Zohar made a division of the title page between two sections, called *Pekuda* and *Ra'aya Meheimna.* The pages of the *Pekuda* belong from every point of view to the main body of the Zohar. The author of the later stratum had very different ideas from those of the author of the first. He does not express his ideas at length like the homilists, but links things together by association, without explaining his basic principle. He progresses by means of associations, especially in the *Sefer ha-Tikkunim.*

The author of the *Midrash ha-Ne'lam* and the main body of the Zohar intended from the very beginning to create a varied literature in the guise of early rabbinic material. He did not content himself with putting together the various sections which now form part of the Zohar, but he extended his canvas. He edited a version of a collection of geonic responsa, particularly those of Hai Gaon, and he added kabbalistic material in the style of the Zohar, using particular idioms of zoharic Aramaic, and also in the style of the *Midrash ha-Ne'lam,* all of which he entitled *Yerushalmi* or the "*Yerushalmi* version." This edited version began to circulate at about the same time as the Zohar itself, in order to serve as a kind of indication that the new work was in fact known to the earlier rabbis. It was subsequently printed under the title of responsa, *Sha'arei Teshuvah* and it misled not only kabbalists of the 15th and 16th centuries but also scholars of the 19th century, who used it as a proof of the antiquity of the Zohar. One of the first of these was David Luria in his *Ma'amar Kadmut Sefer ha-Zohar.*

Similarly, the author of the *Midrash ha-Ne'lam* wrote a small book entitled *Orḥot Ḥayyim* or *Ẓavva'at R. Eliezer ha-Gadol,* which is connected throughout very closely to the Zohar. It is written in Hebrew but it has all the linguistic ingredients and stylistic peculiarities of the Zohar. In this work Eliezer b. Hyrcanus before his death, which is described at length following the late Midrash *Pirkei de-R. Eliezer,* reveals the paths of virtue and good conduct in an epigrammatic style, and in the second part, adds a description of the delights of the soul in the garden of Eden after death. These descriptions are very close indeed to particular parts of the Midrash on Ruth, and of the portions *Va-*

Yakhel, Shelaḥ Lekha, Balak, and other parts of the Zohar. The book was known at first only in kabbalistic circles. It was printed in Constantinople in 1521, and usually each of the two parts was printed separately – the description of the death and the ethical prescriptions in one part, and the description of the garden of Eden in the other. The second part is included in A. Jellinek's *Beit ha-Midrash* (3 (1938), 131–40). The first part was interpreted at length in the editions of *Orḥot Ḥayyim* by two Polish rabbis, Abraham Mordecai Vernikovsky (*Perush Dammesek Eliezer,* Warsaw, 1888), and Gershon Enoch Leiner (Lublin, 1903), who tried to prove the antiquity of the book because it was based entirely on the Zohar, and in fact they did prove that the two works were composed by the same author. There are also some grounds for thinking that the author of the Zohar intended to write a *Sefer Ḥanokh* on the garden of Eden and other kabbalistic topics, and a long description from it is quoted in the *Mishkan ha-Edut* of Moses de Leon.

Date of Composition. Calculations of the time of redemption, which are to be found in several sections of the Zohar, confirm the conclusions concerning the time of its composition. These calculations give an assurance, in various forms, and by means of different interpretations and conjectures, that the redemption will commence in the year 1300, and they expound the different stages of redemption leading to the resurrection. There are variations in the details of the precise dates, depending on the type of theme expounded. According to the Zohar 1,200 years had passed since the destruction of the Temple – a century for each of the tribes of Israel. Israel now stood at the period of transition which preceded the beginning of redemption. According to these dates (1:116–9, 139b; 2:9b; see A.H. Silver, *A History of Messianic Speculation in Israel* (1927), 90–92) it must be assumed the the main part of the Zohar and the *Midrash ha-Ne'lam* were written between 1270 and 1300. Similar calculations are to be found in the *Ra'aya Meheimna* and the *Tikkunim.* The basic date is always 1268. After this the "pangs of the Messiah" will begin, and Moses will appear and will reveal the Zohar as the end of time approaches. The period of transition will come to a halt in the year 1312, and then the various stages of the redemption itself will begin. Moses, in his final appearance, is not the Messiah but the harbinger of the Messiah – the son of Joseph, and the son of David. He will be a poor man, but rich in kabbalistic Torah. The period of transition is a period of trouble and torment for the sacred group of the people of Israel, represented by the kabbalists, who will join in fierce conflict with their opponents and detractors. The Zohar itself is a symbol of Noah's ark, through which they were saved from the destruction of the flood. God revealed Himself to the original Moses through the fire of prophecy; but to the later Moses of the final generation He will be revealed in the flames of the Torah, that is to say, through the revelation of the mysteries of Kabbalah. Something of Moses shines upon every sage or righteous man who occupies himself in whatever generation with the Torah, but at the end of time he will appear in concrete form as the revealer of the Zohar. Allusions of this type exist in every section of the latest stratum.

The Author. According to the clear testimony of Isaac b. Samuel of Acre, who assembled the contradictory information concerning the appearance and nature of the Zohar in the early years of the 14th century, the book was published, part by part, not all at once, by the Spanish kabbalist Moses b. Shem Tov de Leon, who died in 1305, after he met Isaac of Acre. This kabbalist wrote many books in Hebrew bearing his name, from 1286 until after 1293. He was connected with several kabbalists of his time, including Todros Abulafia and his son Joseph in Toledo, one of the leaders of Castilian Jewry, who supported Moses de Leon. From all that has already been said, the Zohar with its various strata was without doubt composed in the years that immediately preceded its publication, since it is impossible to uncover any section that was written before 1270. In actual fact, Moses de Leon was considered by some of Isaac of Acre's colleagues to have been the actual author of the Zohar. When he made some investigations in Avila, the last city in which Moses de Leon lived, Isaac was told that a wealthy man had proposed to marry his son to the daughter of Moses' widow provided that she would give him the original ancient manuscript from which, according to him, her deceased husband had copied the texts which he had published. However, both mother and daughter maintained that there was no such ancient manuscript, and that Moses de Leon had written the whole work on his own initiative. Opinions have been divided ever since as to the worth of this important evidence, and even the attitude of Isaac of Acre himself, whose story, preserved in Abraham Zacuto's *Sefer ha-Yuḥasin,* breaks off in the middle, is not altogether clear, for he quotes from the Zohar in a few places in his books without relying on it at length or in main points. An analysis of the Zohar gives no support to the view that Moses de Leon edited texts and fragments of ancient works that came to him from the East. The question, therefore, is whether Moses de Leon himself was author, editor, and publisher, or whether a Spanish kabbalist, associated with him, wrote the book and gave it to him to edit. A decision can be made only on the basis of a comparison of the parts of the Zohar with the Hebrew writings of Moses de Leon, and on the basis of such information as the earliest extant quotations from the Zohar. Research into these questions leads to definite conclusions. In the extant works of Moses de Leon, and also in the earliest citations from the Zohar by Spanish kabbalists between 1280 and 1310, there are no quotations from the *Ra'aya Meheimna* and the

Tikkunim. It may be supposed therefore that these latter were neither composed nor published by Moses de Leon. Of particular weight in this connection is the fact that Moses de Leon wrote a long work on the reasons for the commandments, but there is no similarity whatsoever between his *Sefer ha-Rimmon* and the *Ra'aya Meheimna.* In complete contrast to this, all his writings are extraordinarily replete with expositions, ideas, linguistic usages, and other matters to be found in the Zohar, from the stratum of the *Midrash ha-Ne'lam* and the main body of the Zohar, including those particular fragments designated above, which constitute the *Pekuda* at the beginning of some sections of the *Ra'aya Meheimna.* Often long sections like these, written here in Hebrew, contain no mention of the fact that they are derived from one source, and the author often prides himself on being the originator of ideas, which all exist nevertheless in the Zohar. Short pieces in the middle of a longer section are introduced in various ways which show that his real reference is to the Zohar: "it is expounded in the inner Midrashim"; "they say in the secrets of the Torah"; "the pillars of the world have discussed the secrets of their words"; "I have seen a profound matter in the writings of the ancients"; "I saw in the *Yerushalmi*"; "I have seen in the secrets of the depth of wisdom"; and so on. Quotations like these abound in his writings, and some of them are already presented in the Aramaic version of the Zohar. There are also a few passages which do not occur in the existing Zohar, either because these particular texts did not survive or because they were not finally published. I. Tishby's opinion is that several of them were introduced only as pointers to what the author intended to write, but he did not in fact manage to write out these matters at length. But it is more likely that the greater part of the Zohar was available to him when he wrote his Hebrew books.

Moses de Leon's Hebrew style reveals in many particulars the idiosyncrasies of the Aramaic of the Zohar indicated above, and we find especially those mistakes and errors of usage which are characteristic of the Zohar and are not found in the works of any other writer. He writes in this style even when his writing does not reflect the actual expositions of the Zohar, but expresses his own personal ideas or adds a new dimension to ideas in the Zohar. He has a completely unfettered control of the material in the Zohar and uses it like a man using his own spiritual property. He ties together expositions from different parts of the Zohar, adding to them combinations of themes and new expositions, which are in perfect accord with the zoharic spirit and show that his thinking is identical with that of the Zohar. In many cases his writings constitute an interpretation of difficult passages of the Zohar which later kabbalists did not interpret literally. Whenever in his writings he diverges freely from the subjects treated in the Zohar, his variations do not constitute any proof that he did not understand his "source." Sometimes he openly mentions the true literary sources which are concealed in the Zohar. The long passage from the Book of Enoch which is quoted in his *Mishkan ha-Edut* is written entirely in his own particular Hebrew style. Features which are peculiar to the Zohar, and which distinguish it from other contemporary kabbalistic works, recur in the works of Moses de Leon. These are in particular the exaggerated use of mythical imagery, the sexual symbolism developed with regard to the relationships between the *Sefirot,* and the striking interest shown in demonology and sorcery. Consequently, there is no reason to assume that an unknown author wrote the Zohar in the lifetime of Moses de Leon, and then passed it on to him. The authorship of Moses de Leon solves the problems raised by an analysis of the Zohar together with his Hebrew works. These books were largely written in order to prepare the ground for the publication of the parts of the Zohar which went hand in hand with this work. In particular, the *Mishkan ha-Edut* (1293) is full of recommendations and praise for the secret sources upon which it is based.

The solution of the fundamental question of the identity of the Zohar's author leaves questions which are still open on several counts; e.g., the order of composition of the sections of the main stratum of the Zohar; and the final editing of the Zohar before its texts were publicly disseminated, if indeed there was an editing at all, for there is evidence here for both possibilities. The main question still needing clarification is the relationship between Moses de Leon and Joseph Gikatilla, which apparently was very close and reciprocal. Similarly we still have to solve the problem of the author of the *Ra'aya Meheimna,* who, unlike Moses de Leon, left no other books which can identify him. Whether other kabbalists knew of Moses de Leon's plan and helped him in some way to achieve his aim is not clear. What is clear is that many kabbalists, after the appearance of the book, considered themselves free to write works in the style of the Zohar and to imitate it – a liberty which they would not have taken with Midrashim whose genuineness and antiquity were beyond question. This fact shows that they did not take seriously the claim of the Zohar to be accepted as an ancient source, even though they saw in it a fine expression of their own spiritual world.

Manuscripts and Editions. The circumstances surrounding the appearance of the Zohar are not known in detail. The first texts which circulated among a few kabbalists were of the *Midrash ha-Ne'lam* and the earliest quotations are to be found in two books by Isaac b. Solomon Abi Sahula, the *Meshal ha-Kadmoni* (Venice, c. 1546–50) and his commentary to Song of Songs, which were written in 1281 and 1283 in Guadalajara, where Moses de Leon lived at that time. He is the only author who knew and quoted the *Midrash ha-Ne'lam* before Moses de Leon himself began to write his Hebrew works. Todros Abulafia also possessed such texts and quoted from them in his books. Parts of the main body of the Zohar circulated from the late 1280s. An examination of the quotations from the Zohar found in contemporary writing shows that (1) the authors possessed only isolated parts, depending on what each of them could obtain; (2) they knew a few expositions or parts which do not appear in the Zohar we have; (3) they made use of it without regarding it as a supreme authority in Kabbalah. In about 1290 some portions of the Zohar on the Torah were known to Baḥya b. Asher, who translated several passages word for word in his commentary to the Torah without mentioning his source, and generally used the Zohar widely. Twice, however, he refers to very short passages in the name of the *Midrash R. Simeon b. Yoḥai.* Other sections, including the *Idrot,* were in the possession of Gikatilla when he wrote *Sha'arei Orah,* before 1293. From the anonymous *Ta'amei ha-Miẓvot,* which was probably written in the 1290s, it appears that some passages were known to the author. From 1300 onward there is an increase in the number of quotations actually cited under the specific name Zohar or *Midrash ha-Ne'lam,* which sometimes served as the title for the whole Zohar. Solomon b. Abraham Adret's pupils, who wrote many kabbalistic works, quote the Zohar only rarely, and they clearly exercised some restraint in the use of it. Menahem Recanati of Italy also possessed some isolated parts in this time, and he used them widely, mentioning his source in his commentary to the Torah and in his *Ta'amei ha-Miẓvot.* In the latter book he makes a distinction between the *Zohar Gadol,* which consisted mainly of the *Idra Rabba,* and the *Zohar Mufla.* The origin of this distinction is not clear. Recanati possessed only about one-tenth of the Zohar now extant, but he had access to an exposition of the mystery of sacrifices which is no longer extant. Among the authors at this time (1310–30) who used the Zohar extensively were Joseph Angelino, the author of *Livnat ha-Sappir,* and David b. Judah he-Ḥasid, who wrote *Marot ha-Ẓove'ot, Sefer ha-Gevul,* and *Or Zaru'a.*

The position with regard to the earliest quotations is matched by our knowledge of the earliest Zohar manuscripts. Complete, well-ordered manuscripts did not circulate, and it is doubtful whether they ever existed. Mystics who took an interest in the Zohar made up collections for themselves from the texts they were able to procure; hence the great differences in the contents of the early manuscripts. An example of a collection like this is the Cambridge Ms. Add. 1023, the oldest manuscript yet known. It contains material which served to complete another anthology which is now lost, and includes those parts of the Zohar which the compiler was able to obtain. This manuscript is from the last third of the 14th century, and contains a complete portion, otherwise unknown, of the *Midrash ha-Ne'lam,* which Isaac ibn Sahula also knew (see above). The Vatican Ms. 202, which is a little earlier, contains only isolated fragments from the Zohar. In the 15th century, manuscripts containing most of the portions of the Zohar were already compiled, but sometimes they still omit whole sections, e.g., the *Idrot,* the *Sava,* etc.[3]

The differences between manuscripts of the Zohar and the printed editions are mainly in the field of spelling (words are mostly written *plene* in the manuscripts and in early quotations), and in the relatively large number of romanisms, which were later obliterated; in the wider use of the preposition *bedil* instead of *begin;* and in the alteration of the grammatical forms of the Targum and the Babylonian Talmud. There are many differences in the basic text but they are relatively unimportant, and usually different readings of this kind are given in brackets in the later printed editions. There are manuscripts from the 15th century of the *Sefer Tikkunim* as well, such as Paris Ms. 778. The *Ra'aya Meheimna* also exists in separate manuscripts, but rather late ones. From 1400 onward the authority of the Zohar became more widely acknowledged in kabbalistic circles, and the criticisms of it which were heard here and there in the 14th century (e.g., by Joseph ibn Waqar who wrote: "the Zohar contains many errors of which one must be wary, to avoid being misled by them") died down. At this time the spread and influence of the Zohar were confined mainly to Spain and Italy, and it was very slow to reach the Ashkenazi lands and the East. The great elevation of the Zohar to a position of sanctity and supreme authority came during and after the period of the expulsion from Spain, and it reached its peak in the 16th and 17th centuries.

The Zohar was printed amid a fierce controversy between those who opposed its publication, among whom were some important kabbalists, and its supporters (see major essay, Kabbalah). The first two editions of the Zohar were published by competing printers in the neighboring cities Mantua (1558–60) and Cremona (1559–60). The *Tikkunei ha-Zohar* was also published separately in Mantua (1558). The editors of these two editions used different manuscripts – hence the differences in the order and in specific readings. Immanuel of Benevento who established the Mantua text used ten manuscripts, from which he arranged his edition, and chose the text which he considered to be the best. Among the correctors at Cremona was the apostate grandson of the grammarian Elijah Levita (Baḥur), Vittorio Eliano. They used six manuscripts. The Mantua Zohar was printed in three volumes in Rashi script, while the Cremona Zohar was in one large volume in square script. Both of them contain a large number of printing errors. Both include the *Ra'aya Meheimna,* but they differ as to the placing of the different *miẓvot.* According to size, the kabbalists called these two editions *Zohar Gadol* ("Large Zohar") and *Zohar Katan* ("Small Zohar"). The *Zohar Gadol* was printed on two more occasions in this form, in Lublin in 1623, and in Sulzbach in 1684. The Polish and German kabbalists up to about 1715 generally used the *Zohar Gadol.* All other editions follow the Mantua prototype. Altogether the Zohar has been printed more than 65 times and the *Tikkunei Zohar* nearly 80 times. Most of the editions come from Poland and Russia, but there are also printings from Constantinople, Salonika, Smyrna, Leghorn, Jerusalem, and Djerba. In later editions they added the variant readings of the Cremona text and corrected many printing errors. They also added variants and readings from the manuscript of the Safed kabbalists, indications of biblical sources, and introductions. The Zohar was printed twice in Leghorn with an (incorrectly) vocalized text. Those sections in the Safed manuscripts which were not found in the Mantua edition were, except for the *Midrash ha-Ne'lam* to Ruth, printed together in a separate volume in Salonika in 1597, which in the later editions was called *Zohar Ḥadash.* The best of these are Venice, 1658, and Munkacs, 1911. All the sections of the Zohar were included in the complete edition of Yehudah Ashlag, Jerusalem, 1945–58, in 22 volumes, with a Hebrew translation and textual variants from the earlier editions. The *Tikkunei ha-Zohar* began to appear in 1960, and is still not completed. A critical edition based on early manuscripts does not yet exist.

Commentaries. The crucial importance of the Zohar in the development of Kabbalah and in the life of the Jewish community can be seen in the vast exegetical literature and the large number of manuals that were composed for it. Most of these commentaries have not been printed, notably the commentary of Moses Cordovero *Or ha-Yakar,* of which seven volumes have so far appeared (Jerusalem, 1962–73) – a complete version of this exists in the library at Modena in 16 large volumes; and the commentaries of Elijah Loans of Worms, *Adderet Eliyahu,* and *Ẓafenat Pa'ne'aḥ,* which exist at Oxford in four large volumes in the author's own hand. The early commentaries to the Zohar have not survived. Although Menahem Recanati mentions his own commentary in his *Ta'amei ha-Miẓvot,* most commentaries are based on Lurianic Kabbalah and do not add much to our understanding of the Zohar itself, e.g., *Zohar Ḥai* of Isaac Eizik Safrin of Komarno, which was printed in 1875–81 in five volumes, and *Dammesek Eliezer* by his son Jacob Moses Safrin, which was printed in seven volumes in 1902–28. The most important commentary for a more literal understanding of the Zohar is *Ketem Paz* by Simeon Labi of Tripoli (written about 1570), of which only the Genesis section has been printed (Leghorn, 1795), but this also diverges quite often from the literal meaning and offers fanciful interpretations. Second in importance is the *Or ha-Ḥammah,* a compilation by Abraham b. Mordecai Azulai, which includes an abridgment of Cordovero's commentary, the commentary of Ḥayyim Vital which was written in the main before he studied with Luria, and the *Yare'aḥ Yakar,* a commentary by Abraham Galante, one of Cordovero's pupils. Azulai arranged these commentaries together corresponding to each page of the text of the original Zohar. The whole work was printed with the title *Or ha-Ḥammah* in four volumes in Przemysl in 1896–98. It reflects the Cordovero school of Zohar exposition. A very widely known commentary, half literal and half Lurianic, is the *Mikdash Melekh* of Shalom Buzaglo, a Moroccan rabbi of the 18th century, which was printed in Amsterdam in five volumes in 1750, and several times subsequently. It was printed together with the Zohar itself in Leghorn in 1858. The commentary, *Ha-Sullam,* in Yehudah Ashlag's edition of the Zohar, is part translation and part exposition. These commentaries do not consider the Zohar in comparison with earlier material in rabbinic literature or in other kabbalistic works. The commentaries of the Gaon Elijah of Vilna are important, namely *Yahel Or,* and his commentary to the *Sifra de-Ẓeni'uta,* which is characterized by his comparative approach. Both of them were printed toghether in Vilna in 1882. Among the many commentaries to the *Tikkunei Zohar,* the *Kisse Melekh* of Shalom Buzaglo must be singled out, and also the *Be'er la-Ḥai Ro'i* of Ẓevi Schapira (printed in Munkacs, 1903–21), three of whose volumes cover only about half the book.

Of the aids to the study of the Zohar the most useful are *Yesh Sakhar,* a collection of the laws in the Zohar, by Issachar Baer of Kremnitz (Prague, 1609); *Sha'arei Zohar,* a clarification of zoharic statements through their relationship to Talmud and Midrash, set out in the order of tractates and Midrashim, by Reuben Margulies (Jerusalem, 1956); a collection of zoharic statements on the Psalms by Moses Gelernter (Warsaw, 1926); and *Midrashei ha-Zohar Leket Shemu'el* by S. Kipnis, three volumes (Jerusalem, 1957–60), a collection of zoharic statements on the Bible with explanation. Indices to the subject matter of the Zohar are to be found in *Maftehot ha-Zohar,* arranged by Israel Berekhiah Fontanella (Venice, 1744), and in *Yalkut ha-Zohar* by Isaiah Menahem Mendel (Piotrikov, 1912).

Translations. The question of translating the Zohar into Hebrew had already arisen among the kabbalists of the 14th century. David b. Judah he-Ḥasid translated into Hebrew most of the quotations from the Zohar which he cited in his books. According to Abraham Azulai, Isaac Luria had "a book of the Zohar translated into the holy tongue by Israel al-Nakawa," the author of *Menorat ha-Ma'or* in which all the quotations from the Zohar, under the name of *Midrash Yehi Or,* are in Hebrew. In the Vatican manuscripts of the Zohar (nos. 62 and 186), several sections have been translated into Hebrew in the 14th or 15th century. According to Joseph Sambari, Judah Mas'ud translated the Zohar into Hebrew in the 16th century. A translation of the Zohar from the Cremona edition, dating from the year 1602, is extant in Oxford Ms. 1561, but the more esoteric passages are omitted; the translator was Barkiel Cafman Ashkenazi. The Genesis part of this work was printed by Obadiah Hadaya (Jerusalem, 1946). In the 17th century Samuel Romner of Lublin translated a large part of the Zohar under the title *Devarim Attikim* (Dembitzer, *Kelilat Yofi,* 2 (1960), 25a); this is extant in Oxford Ms. 1563, with rabbinic authorizations dated 1747, showing that they had intended to have it printed. According to Eliakim Milsahagi of Brody, about 1830, in his *Zohorei Ravyah* (Jerusalem Ms.), he translated the whole of the Zohar into Hebrew, and to judge from his excellent style this must have been the finest translation made, but it is now lost together with most of his separate studies on the Zohar. In the 20th century large sections on the Torah were translated by Judah Rosenberg in *Zohar Torah* in five volumes; and similarly, on the Zohar to Psalms and the *Megillot* in two volumes (New York, 1924–25; Bilgoraj, 1929–30). This translation is devoid of any literary qualities. The Hebrew writer Hillel Zeitlin began to translate the Zohar, but he did not continue. The preface to the Zohar in his translation was printed in *Metsudah* (London, 1 (1943), 36–82). A complete and extremely literal translation (but not without many textual misunderstandings) is contained in the edition of the Zohar by Yehudah Ashlag. Many selected pieces were translated in a meticulous and fine style by F. Lachover and I. Tishby, *Mishnat ha-Zohar* (2 vol., 1957–61).

Even before the Zohar was printed, the French mystic G. Postel had prepared a Latin translation of Gensis and of the Midrash on Ruth, which is extant in manuscript in the British Museum and in Munich. The preface to it was published by F. Secret. The Christian mystic Chr. Knorr von Rosenroth also made a Latin translation of important parts, particularly the *Idrot* and the *Sifra de-Ẓeniuta,* in his large work *Kabbala Denudata* (Sulzbach, 1677; Frankfort, 1684), and most of the quotations from the Zohar or translations of those pieces which appeared in other European languages were taken from here, together with all the mistakes of the original translator, e.g., the works of S. L. Mathers, *The Kabbalah Unveiled* (1887); Paul Vulliaud, *Traduction intégrale du Siphra de-Tzeniutha* (1930). A French translation of the three volumes of the standard editions of the Zohar was prepared by Jean de Pauly (the later name of a baptized Jew from Galicia) but it is full of distortions and adulterations and accompanied by a great many false textual references, often to books which do not contain them at all or to books which have never existed. The translation was corrected by a Jewish scholar who knew Talmud and Midrash but did not correct the mistakes in the field of Kabbalah, which he did not understand. This translation, *Sepher ha-Zohar (Le Livre de la Splendeur) Doctrine ésotérique de Israélites traduit . . . par Jean de Pauly,* was magnificently printed in six volumes in Paris (1906–11). An English translation of the main part of the Zohar, with the omission of those sections which seemed to the translators to be separate works or additions, was *The Zohar* by Harry Sperling and Maurice Simon, published in five volumes in London (1931–34). The translation is in good style but suffers from incomplete or erroneous understanding of many parts of the kabbalistic exposition. A German anthology of many characteristic quotations from the Zohar was made by Ernst Mueller, who was obviously influenced by the teaching of Rudolf Steiner (*Der Sohar, das heilige Buch der Kabbala,* 1932).

Scholarship. Scholarly research into the Zohar did not begin with the kabbalists, however deeply interested they were in its teaching: they accepted uncritically the literary romantic background of the book as historical fact. The Jewish opponents of the Kabbalah expressed doubts about the veracity of this background from the end of the 15th century onward, but they did not delve deeply into a scholarly investigation of the Zohar. Christian interest in the Zohar was not at first scholarly but theological. Many thought they would find support for Christian ideas and developed a "Christian Kabbalah," and most of the writings up to the middle of the 18th century reflect this spirit. No scholarly value can be attached to these efforts. The first critical work was the *Ari Nohem* of Leone Modena (1639) who questioned the authenticity and antiquity of the Zohar, from the point of view of language and other matters, but he did not undertake a detailed study. The book was printed as late as 1840 (Leipzig), but its circulation in manuscript aroused the wrath of the kabbalists who saw every attempt at critique as an assault upon the sacred, and they replied to it, and to later books which were written in the same vein, with a considerable number of works defending the Zohar, but these are of little historical worth. Leone Modena's critique was also stimulated by a polemic against certain claims of Christian Kabbalah, while that of Jacob Emden was connected with the struggle against the Shabbateans, who went to extreme lengths of heresy in their interpretations of the Zohar. In *Mitpaḥat Sefarim* (Altona, 1768), Emden concluded on the basis of a large number of specific errors in the Zohar that many sections, and particularly the *Midrash ha-Ne'lam,* were late, although he still assumed that there was an ancient foundation for the main body of the book. The *maskilim* followed him, especially Samuel David Luzzatto in his *Vikku'aḥ al Ḥokhmat ha-Kabbalah ve-al Kadmut Sefer ha-Zohar* ("An Argument Concerning the Wisdom of the Kabbalah and the Antiquity of the Zohar" (1827), printed in Gorizia, 1852). These two books, Emden's and Luzzatto's, elicited several replies seeking to answer the questions they raised, particularly *Ben Yoḥai* by Moses Kunitz (Vienna, 1815), and *Ta'am le-Shad* by Elia

Benamozegh (Leghorn, 1863). The profound inquiries by Eliakim Milsahagi in several books devoted to the Zohar would have much furthered historical inquiry had they been printed and not simply remained in manuscript. He towered head and shoulders above many of the writers who succeeded him. There remain only a few pages of his in the *Sefer Ravyah* (Ofen, 1837) and his introduction *Zohorei Ravyah* (Ms. in National Library, Jerusalem). The great 19th-century scholars of Judaism, Zunz, Steinschneider, and Graetz, went further than Jacob Emden and saw the Zohar as a product of the 13th century. M. H. Landauer tried to prove that the Zohar was produced by Abraham Abulafia, and A. Jellinek directed attention once more to Moses de Leon. A. Frank and D.H. Joel argued as to whether the teaching of the Zohar was of Jewish or foreign, origin, and an echo of this kind of controversy reverberated throughout most of the literature of the *maskilim,* whose very general conclusions were not based on close attention to detail and are marred by many weak arguments. Because of the lack of precise critical inquiry, scholars chose to solve the problem of the Zohar in accordance with their own subjective views, and the very widespread belief was that the Zohar was the creation of many generations and was only edited in the 13th century. There were also those who admitted that Moses de Leon had a greater or lesser share in the editing. The results of the many studies by G. Scholem and I. Tishby, which were based on detailed research, do not support these theories and lead to the view summarized above. There is no doubt that scholarly research into the Zohar has only just begun and will develop in detail in connection with research into the history of 13th-century Kabbalah in general. In the bibliography works are listed which reflect various points of view.

Bibliography: G. Scholem, *Bibliographia Kabbalistica* (1933), 166–210; M. Kunitz, *Ben Yoḥai* (1815); S. J. Rapoport, *Naḥalat Yehudah* (1873); S. Z. Anushinski, *Maẓẓav ha-Yashar* (1881–87); D. Luria, *Kadmut Sefer ha-Zohar* (1887); H. Zeitlin, *Be-Fardes ha-Ḥasidut ve-ha-Kabbalah* (1960), 55–279; D. Neumark, *Toledot ha-Filosofyah be-Yisrael,* 1 (1921), 204–45, 326–54; H. S. Neuhausen, *Zohorei Zohar* (1929); idem, in: *Oẓar ha-Ḥayyim,* 13 (1937), 51–59: J. A. Z. Margaliot, *Middot Rashbi* (1937); idem, *Kokho de-Rashbi* (1948); J. L. Zlotnik, *Midrash ha Meliẓah ha-Ivrit (1938);* Y. Baer in: *Zion,* 5 (1940), 1–44; I. Tishby, *Mishnat ha-Zohar* (1957–61); idem, in: *Perakim* (1967–68), 131–82; Scholem, Mysticism, 156–243, 385–407; idem, in: *Zion (Me'assef),* 1 (1926), 40–56; idem, in: MGWJ, 75 (1931), 347–62, 444–48; idem, in: *Tarbiz,* 19 (1948), 160–75; 24 (1955), 290–306; idem, in *Sefer Assaf* (1953), 459–95; idem, in: *Le-Agnon Shai* (1959), 289–305; idem, *On the Kabbalah and its Symbolism* (1965), 32–86; F Gottlieb, *Ha-Kabbalah be-Khitvei Rabbenu Baḥya ben Asher* (1970), 167–93; R. Margulies, *Malakhei Elyon* (1962); idem, *Sha'arei Zohar* (1956); S.A. Horodezky, *Ha-Mistorin be-*

Yisrael, 2 (1952), 266–339; P. Sandler, in: *Sefer Urbach* (1955), 222–35; M.Z. Kadari, *Dikduk ha-Lashon ha-Aramit shel ha-Zohar* (1970); idem in: *Tarbiz*, 27 (1958), 265–77; M. Kasher, in: *Sinai Jubilee Volume* (1958), 40–56; S. Belkin, in: *Sura*,25-92; 3 (1958), 25–92; A. Franck, *The Kabbalah: the Religious Philosophy of the Hebrews* (1967); A.E. Waite, *The Secret Doctrine in Israel* (1913); A. Bension, *The Zohar in Moslemand Christian Spain* (1932); R. J. Z. Werblowsky, in: JJS, 10 (1959), 25–44, 113–35; D. H. Joel, *Midrash ha-Zohar: Die Religionsphilosophie des Sohar und ihr Verhaeltnis zur allgemeinen juedischen Theologie* (1923); A. Jellinek, *Moses B. Schem-Tob de Leon und sein Verhaeltnis zum Sohar* (1851); Graetz, *Geschichte der Juden*, (1874–1908), 7, 430–48; I. Stern, in: *Ben Chananja*, 1–5 (1858–62); W. Bacher, in: REJ, 22 (1891), 33–46, 219–9; S. Karppe, *Etude sur les origines et la nature du Zohar* (1901); E. Mueller, *Der Sohar und seine Lehre* (1955); K. Preis, in: MGWJ, 72 (1928), 167–84; *Etudes et Correspondance de Jean de Pauly relatives au Sepher ha-Zohar* (1933); H. Sérouya, *La Kabbale* (1952), 198–395: V.G. Sed-Rajna *Manuscripts du Tiqquney Zohar*, in REJ 129 (1970), 161–78.

2

Shabbetai Zevi and the Shabbatean Movement

Background of the Movement. Shabbateanism was the largest and most momentous messianic movement in Jewish history subsequent to the destruction of the Temple and the Bar Kokhba Revolt. The factors giving rise to its extraordinarily widespread and deep-seated appeal are twofold. On the one hand there was the general condition of the Jewish people in exile, and the hopes for political and spiritual redemption fostered by Jewish religious tradition and given great emphasis in Jewish thought, which at all times could provide fertile soil for the blossoming of messianic movements aimed at ushering in redemption. On the other hand there were the specific conditions contributing to the impetus of the movement that began in 1665. Politically and socially, the position of the Jews in the various countries of the Diaspora was still basically the same and, with few exceptions, they pursued their specific way of life apart from the surrounding Christian or Muslim society, facing humiliation and persecution at every turn of political events and in constant awareness of their insecurity.

The great wave of anti-Jewish persecution in Poland and Russia which set in with the Chmielnicki massacres in 1648 deeply affected Ashkenazi Jewry and had wide repercussions, especially through the large number of captives in many countries whose ransom led to lively agitation. Soon after this disaster came the Russian-Swedish War (1655) which also struck those areas of Polish Jewish settlement which had not been shattered by Chmielnicki's attacks. Important as these factors undoubtedly were to the upsurge of messianic hopes in Polish Jewry, they are not sufficient to explain what actually happened, and no doubt local conditions prevailing in various parts of the Diaspora contributed their share. However the political milieu and the social events are only one part of the story.

The central and unifying factor behind the Shabbatean movement was of a religious nature, connected with the profound metamorphosis in the religious world of Judaism caused by the spiritual renewal centered in Safed in the 16th century. Its decisive feature was the rise of the Kabbalah to a dominant position in Jewish life and particularly in those circles which were receptive to new religious impulses and formed the most active sector of the Jewish communities. The new Kabbalah which went out from Safed, especially in its Lurianic forms, wedded striking concepts to messianic ideas. It could be characterized as messianism pervading mysticism, thus introducing a new element of tension into the older Kabbalah, which was of a much more contemplative nature. Lurianic Kabbalah proclaimed an intimate bond between the religious activity of the Jew as he performs the commandments of the law and meditations for prayer and the messianic message. All being has been in exile since the very beginning of creation and the task of restoring everything to its proper place has been given to the Jewish people, whose historic fate and destiny symbolize the state of the universe at large. The sparks of Divinity are dispersed everywhere, as are the sparks of the original soul of Adam; but they are held captive by the *kelippah,* the power of evil, and must be redeemed. This final redemption, however, cannot be achieved by one single messianic act, but will be effected through a long chain of activities that prepare the way. What the kabbalists called "restoration" *(tikkun)* implied both the process by which the shattered elements of the world would be restored to harmony – which is the essential task of the Jewish people – and the final result, the state of redemption announced by the appearance of the Messiah, who marks the last stage. Political liberation, and all that the national myth connected with it, were seen as no more than external symbols of a cosmic process which in fact takes place in the secret recesses of the universe. No conflict was foreseen between the traditional national and political content of the messianic idea and the new spiritual and mystical note which it acquired in Lurianic Kabbalah. Those susceptible to the kabbalistic theology of Judaism – and there were many – focused their activity on hastening the arrival of the "world of *tikkun*" by an ascetic life which, though in strict accordance with the demands of the law, was permeated with virtual messianism.

This messianism, however, was not an abstract hope for a distant future: what made Lurianism a dynamic factor in Jewish history was its proclamation that almost the whole process of restoration had been completed and that the final redemption was just around the corner. Only the last stages had to be passed through and redemption would be at hand.

As they gained ascendancy and dominated religious life, ideas like these became a common catalyst for an acute precipitation of messianic fervor. In fact, Lurianic Kabbalah became a dominant factor only about 1630–40 and the ideology of the Shabbatean movement is closely connected with this development. That the movement had an overwhelming appeal to such different centers of the Diaspora as Yemen and Persia, Turkey and North Africa, the Balkans, Italy and the Ashkenazi communities can be explained only by the fact that the intense propaganda of Lurianism had created a climate favorable to the release of the messianic energies aroused by the victory of the new Kabbalah. This is the reason why places like Amsterdam, Leghorn, and Salonika, where the Jews lived relatively free from oppression, nevertheless became crucibles of the movement and centers of Shabbatean activities.

Shabbetai Ẓevi's Early Years and Personality. The figure of the man who occupied the center of the movement is a most unexpected and surprising one. By now, his biography is one of the most completely documented of any Jew who played an important role in Jewish history. Shabbetai Ẓevi was born in Smyrna (Ismir) on the Ninth of Av, 1626 (unless the date was manipulated to conform with the tradition that the Messiah would be born on the anniversary of the destruction of the Temple). His father, Mordecai Ẓevi, came from the Peloponnesus (Patras?), probably from a family of Ashkenazi origin, and as a young man settled in Smyrna, where he first was a modest poultry merchant and later became an agent for Dutch and English traders. The great economic rise of Smyrna in those years made him wealthy and Shabbetai Ẓevi's brothers, Elijah and Joseph, were actually wealthy merchants. Shabbetai Ẓevi received a traditional education. His gifts being early recognized, he was destined by his family to become a *ḥakham,* a member of the rabbinic elite. He studied under Isaac de Alba and later under the most illustrious rabbi of Smyrna at that time, Joseph Escapa, and seems to have been ordained as a *ḥakham* when he was about 18. He had a thorough talmudic training and even his bitterest detractors never accused him of being an ignoramus. According to one source, he left the yeshivah at the age of 15, beginning a life of abstinence and solitude and studying without the help of teachers. He was emotionally closely attached to his mother and at an early period developed an intense inner life. Starting out on the path of asceticism he was beset by sexual temptations, references to which have survived. In his adolescent years he also embarked on the study of Kabbalah, concentrating mainly on the Zohar, *Sefer ha-Kanah,* and *Sefer ha-Peli'ah.* Having acquired considerable proficiency in kabbalistic learning, he attracted other young contemporaries who studied with him.

Between 1642 and 1648 he lived in semi-seclusion. During this period he began to display a character that conforms largely to what handbooks of psychiatry describe as an extreme case of cyclothymia or manic-depressive psychosis. Periods of profound depression and melancholy alternated with spasms of maniacal exaltation and euphoria, separated by intervals of normality. These states, which are richly documented throughout his life, persisted until his death. Later they were described by his followers not in psychopathological but in theological terms as "illumination" and "fall" or "hiding of the face" (the state where God hides his face from him). His mental affliction brought to the fore an essential trait of his character: during his periods of illumination he felt impelled to commit acts which ran counter to religious law, later called *ma'asim zarim* ("strange or paradoxical actions"). Their content changed from time to time but a predilection for strange and bizarre rituals and sudden innovations pervaded them all. One thing was constant to these exalted states – his inclination to pronounce the Ineffable Name of God, the Tetragrammaton prohibited by rabbinic law. In the periods of melancholy, which were of uneven length, he retired from human contact into solitude to wrestle with the demonic powers by which he felt attacked and partly overwhelmed. The exact moment that this illness broke out is not known, but at the very latest it took place in 1648 when the news of the Chmielnicki massacres reached Smyrna. Starting to utter the Name of God in public, he possibly also proclaimed himself the Messiah for the first time. Since by then he was known to be mentally afflicted nobody took this seriously and his behavior caused no more than a temporary commotion. It seems that his extravagances aroused more compassion than antagonism. Between 1646 and 1650 he contracted two marriages in Smyrna which, since they were not consummated, ended in divorce. In his home town he was considered partly a lunatic and partly a fool, but since he had a very pleasant appearance and was highly musical, endowed with a particularly fine voice, he made friends, though not adherents of his kabbalistic speculations. It is generally agreed that he exercised a strong personal magnetism. In these years he began to speak of a particular "mystery of the Godhead" which had been revealed to him through his spiritual struggles. He used to speak of the "God of his faith" with whom he felt a particularly imtimate and close relation. It is not clear whether by this he meant only the *Sefirah Tiferet* (see Kabbalah), which he saw as the essential manifestation of God, or some supernal power which clothed itself in the *Sefirah.* At any rate, the term *Elohei Yisrael* ("the God of Israel") took on a special mystical meaning in his parlance. His compulsion to violate the law in his illuminated states, which were sometimes accompanied by imagining experiences of levitation, and his repeated claims to be the Messiah, finally led the rabbis, including his teacher Joseph Escapa, to intervene: around 1651–54 they banished him from Smyrna.

For several years Shabbetai Ẓevi wandered through Greece and Thrace, staying for a long time in Salonika, where he made many friends. But this stay also ended in disaster when, during one of his exalted states, he celebrated a ceremonial nuptial service under the canopy with the Torah, and committed other acts which were considered intolerable. Expelled by the rabbis, in 1658 he went to Constantinople, where he spent nine months. There he befriended the famous kabbalist David Ḥabillo (d. 1661), an emissary of the Jerusalem

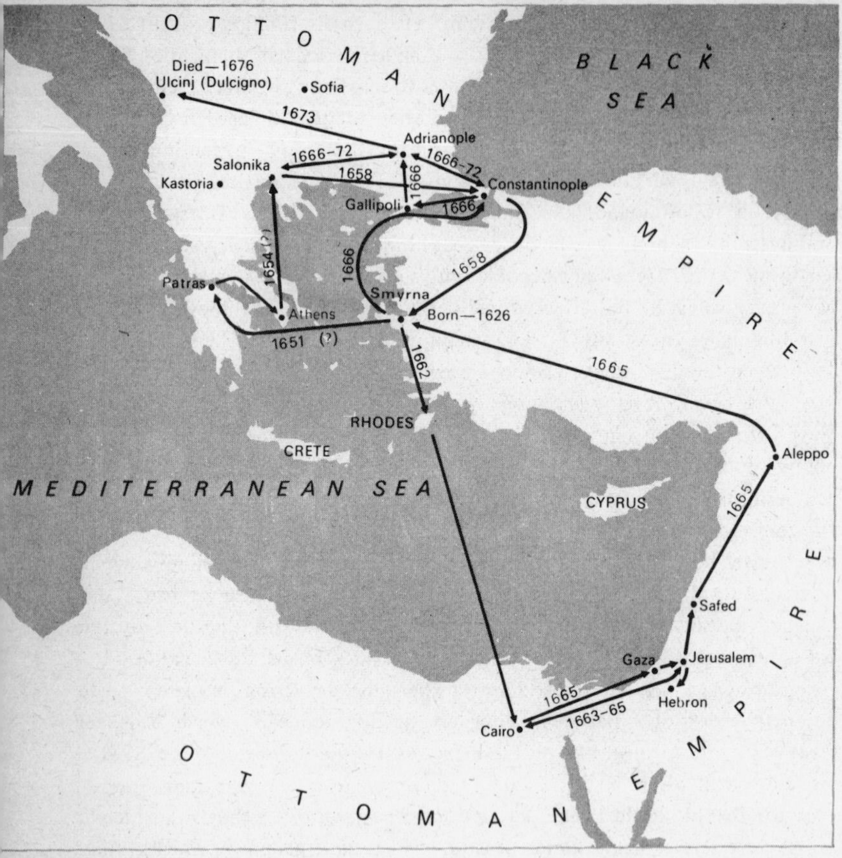

Journeys of Shabbetai Ẓevi.

community. During this period he made a first attempt to rid himself of his demonic obsessions by means of practical Kabbalah. On the other hand, during one of his ecstatic periods he not only celebrated the three festivals of Passover, Shavuot, and Sukkot all in one week, behavior which was bound to arouse hostility, but went so far as to declare the abolition of the commandments and to pronounce a blasphemous benediction to "Him who allows the forbidden." Expelled once more he returned to Smyrna, where he stayed until 1662, keeping mostly to himself and going through a prolonged period of profound melancholy. In 1662 he decided to settle in Jerusalem and traveled there via Rhodes and Cairo, where he made many contacts. Throughout this period there is no trace of any messianic agitation around him, and his genial and dignified behavior during his normal state of mind and his rabbinic and kabbalistic scholarship made him a respected figure. By the end of 1662 he reached Jerusalem, staying there for about a year, wandering around the holy places and tombs of the saints of old. His parents died about this time (his mother perhaps even earlier). There seems to have been a great deal of talk about his strange character and attacks of offensive behavior, but this was counterbalanced by his ascetic tenor of life. In a sudden emergency, in the fall of 1663, he was sent to Egypt as an emissary for Jerusalem and performed his mission with some success. He stayed in Cairo until the spring of 1665, becoming closely connected with the circle around Raphael Joseph Chelebi, the head of Egyptian Jewry, who was in deep sympathy with ascetic and kabbalistic tendencies.

From time to time Shabbetai Ẓevi's messianic fancies returned and it is probable that in one of these fits of illumination he decided to marry Sarah, an Ashkenazi girl of doubtful reputation who either had arrived by herself from Italy or was brought over on his initiative when he heard rumors about her from Italian visitors. She was an orphan of the 1648 massacres in Podolia and used to tell curious stories about herself and her upbringing by a Polish nobleman. After some years in Amsterdam she had gone to Italy, where she served with families and Jewish institutions in Mantua. Rumors that she was a woman of easy virtue preceded her and were current even later in the intimate circle of Shabbetai Ẓevi's admirers. Possibly influenced by the example of the prophet Hosea who married a whore, Shabbetai Ẓevi married Sarah in Cairo on March 31, 1664. In the winter of 1664–65, however, being troubled about his violations of the law, he tried to exorcise his demons; thus (according to his own testimony in a reliable source) he asked God to take away from him all his abnormal states, and entered an extended period of stability.

The Beginning of the Shabbatean Movement. The peripeteia in Shabbetai Ẓevi's life came with the news that a man of God had appeared in Gaza who disclosed to everyone the secret root of his soul and could give each person the particular formula for the *tikkun* that his soul needed. When the story of Nathan of Gaza's (see page 435) powers spread, Shabbetai Ẓevi "abandoned his mission and went to Gaza in order to find a *tikkun* and peace for his soul," in the words of the first report that has been preserved about the beginnings of the movement. Around mid-April 1665 he arrived in Gaza to visit the physician of the soul; by then the latter had had (in February 1665) an ecstatic vision of Shabbetai Ẓevi as the Messiah, springing no doubt from the tales about him he had heard in Jerusalem, where Nathan had studied in 1663 under Jacob Ḥagiz. These tales and the figure of the man whom the 20-year-old Nathan had often seen in the

Jewish quarter of Jerusalem had impressed themselves on his mind and crystallized in his new vision when he took up the study of Kabbalah in Gaza. Instead of curing Shabbetai Ẓevi of his malady, Nathan tried to convince him that he was indeed the true Messiah. At first refusing to pay any heed to his importunities, Shabbetai Ẓevi nevertheless accompanied Nathan on a pilgrimage to some of the holy places in Jerusalem and Hebron, during which they discussed their visions and their validity. Nathan, an outstanding young rabbi, was the first man to confirm independently Shabbetai Ẓevi's own messianic dreams and moreover, to explain the peculiar rank and nature of the Messiah's soul in the kabbalistic scheme of creation. They returned to Gaza in the beginning of Sivan (mid-May). According to one story, they were celebrating the night of Shavuot in Nathan's house along with a group of rabbis, when Nathan fell into a trance and announced Shabbetai Ẓevi's high rank before the assembly; according to another version, this happened in the absence of Shabbetai Ẓevi, who had one of his attacks of melancholy and stayed away. About this time, Nathan produced an apocryphal text attributed to one Abraham he-Ḥasid, a contemporary of the famous Judah he-Ḥasid, who as it were prophesied the appearance of Shabbetai Ẓevi and foretold his early life in apocalyptic terms, proclaiming him the redeemer of Israel. When, some days after Shavuot, Shabbetai Ẓevi entered another period of illumination, he had absorbed all these new events and, now sure of himself and of Nathan's prophetic gifts, returned to his former messianic claims with renewed strength. On the 17th of Sivan (May 31, 1665), in Gaza, he proclaimed himself as the Messiah and swept with him the whole community, including its rabbi, Jacob Najara, grandson of the celebrated poet, Israel Najara. Some weeks of frenzied excitement followed. Riding around on horseback in majestic state Shabbetai Ẓevi summoned a group of his followers, appointing them as apostles or representatives of the Twelve Tribes of Israel.

The messianic news spread like wildfire to other communities in Palestine, but encountered strong opposition from some outstanding rabbis of Jerusalem, including Abraham Amigo, Jacob Hagiz (Nathan's teacher), Samuel Garmison (Garmizan), and Jacob Ẓemaḥ, the famous kabbalist, who spoke out against Shabbetai Ẓevi. Having been denounced to the qadi of Jerusalem, he traveled to the city in a large company and succeeded in setting the mind of the qadi at rest. What exactly happened in Jerusalem in June 1665 is not clear. In kingly fashion Shabbetai Ẓevi circled Jerusalem seven times on horseback, winning over some of the rabbis like Samuel Primo, Mattathias Bloch, Israel Benjamin, and Moses Galante (the fact of Galante's adherence to Shabbetai Ẓevi was later suppressed). His conflict with the majority of the rabbis came to a head and they banished him from the town, but, after informing the rabbis of Constantinople of what happened, they apparently took no other active steps against the messianic propaganda, refraining from answering the many letters that were addressed to them about the events and maintaining an enigmatic silence throughout the following year.

Nathan, on the other hand, who now appeared as the prophet and standard-bearer of Shabbetai Ẓevi, and the group around him were very active. He proclaimed the need for a mass movement of repentance to facilitate the transition to the coming redemption, a step which was sure to win many hearts and could scarcely be opposed by the rabbinic authorities. People from the surrounding countries flocked to him to receive individual penance or wrote to him asking to reveal to them the root of their soul and tell them how to "restore it." Excessive fasts and other ascetic exercises became the order of the day, but Nathan proclaimed the abolition of the fast of the 17th of Tammuz which instead was celebrated as a day of joy in Gaza and Hebron. Letters went out, first to Egypt and the circle of Raphael Joseph, telling of the wondrous deeds of the prophet and the Messiah. One of the striking new features in these letters was the announcement that neither the prophet nor the Messiah was obliged to give proof of his mission by performing miracles, but that Israel should believe in Shabbetai Ẓevi's mission without any external proof. The actual history of the subsequent mass movement is characterized by the intrinsic contradiciton between this demand for pure faith as a redeeming value and the overwhelming wave of legends and reports of miracles which swept the Diaspora. The first reports that reached Europe were, curiously enough, not about Shabbetai Ẓevi, but about the appearance of the lost Ten Tribes of Israel, who were said to be marching under the command of a prophetic and saintly man of God about whom all sorts of miraculous stories were told. According to some versions they were conquering Mecca, according to others assembling in the Sahara Desert, and in a third version marching into Persia. Rumors of this kind, coming from Morocco, reached Holland, England, and Germany in the summer of 1665, without giving any indication of what actually had happened in Gaza or naming Shabbetai Ẓevi or making any mention of the appearance of a Messiah. By contrast, there was a great deal of commotion in the oriental Jewish communities, which had more direct communication with Palestine.

In September 1665, fortified by a new revelation, Nathan addressed a long letter to Raphael Joseph, announcing in the first part the changes which had taken place in the hidden worlds with the arrival of redemption and explaining what these changes entailed for the practice of kabbalistic devotions. The *kavvanot* ("meditations") of Isaac Luria (see p. 420) were no longer valid because the inner structure of the universe had changed and no holy sparks were left under the domination of the powers of evil, the *kelippot.* The time of redemption had come, and even though some might oppose it they could not prevent it and would do harm only to themselves. Shabbetai Ẓevi had the power to justify the greatest sinner, even Jesus, and "whoever entertains any doubts about him, though he may be the most righteous man in the world, he [Shabbetai Ẓevi] may punish him with great afflictions." In the second part of the letter Nathan predicts or rather outlines the course of events from the present moment until complete redemption is achieved. Shabbetai Ẓevi would take the crown from the Turkish king, without war, and make the sultan his servant. After four or five years he would proceed to the River Sambatyon to bring back the lost tribes and to marry Rebecca, the 13-year-old daughter of the resuscitated Moses. During this period he would put the Turkish sultan in charge, but the latter would rebel against him in his absence. This would be the period of the "birth pangs of redemption," a time of great tribulation from which only those dwelling in Gaza would be exempt. The whole tenor of this part of the letter is legendary and mythical. Between the present time and the start of the actual messianic events there would be an interval of one year and several months which should be used for doing penance all over the Jewish world. For this purpose Nathan composed liturgies, one set for the general public and another set for the initiate, comprising *kavvanot* and mystical prayers for the extended fasts prescribed by him. These were sent out to Europe and other places along with the first long announcements regarding the advent of the Messiah in the fall of 1665.

Shabbetai Ẓevi in Smyrna and Constantinople. The first reports about Shabbetai Ẓevi reached Europe early in October 1665, and in the following two months detailed accounts, deeply imbued with legendary material, arrived in Italy, Holland, Germany, and Poland. Why all the correspondents from Gaza, Jerusalem, and Egypt who became so eloquent from September 1665 onward kept silent during the three months after the events in Gaza is still unexplained. There is also a considerable gap between the events in Europe after the news finally came through and what happened in those months to Shabbetai Ẓevi himself. When he left Jerusalem under a cloud, probably before the fast of the 17th of Tammuz, he proceeded through Safed to Aleppo, where he arrived on the 8th of Av (July 20, 1665) and left on August 12. Although his fame had preceded him, he refused to appear publicly as the Messiah, but talked to several people in private, including Solomon Laniado and other members of the rabbinic court who became his enthusiastic supporters. Similarly, when he arrived in Smyrna a short time before Rosh Ha-Shanah (beginning of September 1665) he kept to himself for a long time, staying with his brother Elijah. In the meantime, a great commotion flared up in Aleppo where, in October and November, the first phenomena of Shabbatean prophesying appeared. Not only unlettered people, men and women, were swept up in the excitement, but also rabbis and scholars, such as Moses Galante from Jerusalem who had come as an emissary and was caught up in the general turmoil, also following Shabbetai Ẓevi to Smyrna and Constantinople. From Aleppo there is the first testimony, outside Palestine, about a general revivalist atmosphere in which there were reports of appearances of the prophet Elijah and a common fund was set up to maintain the poor and those who would be affected by the widespread halt in commercial activities.

Although Shabbetai Ẓevi's arrival in Smyrna was preceded by all kinds of letters and rumors which were bound to have precipitated much tension and many expectations, nothing spectacular happened for almost three months. The rabbis of Smyrna had received a letter from the rabbinate of Constantinople about Shabbetai Ẓevi's excommunication in Jerusalem, yet no action was taken against him. It was only when his state of ecstasy returned, in early December, and he became feverishly active in his own way, starting a wild commotion and performing many of his "strange acts," that the rabbis made an attempt to stop him; but by then it was too late. The enthusiasm and excitement he engendered swept Smyrna Jewry off its feet. Within a period of three weeks, the community was thrown into an uproar and the intensity and public character of the proceedings assured them the widest possible echo. There were not only several thousands of Jews but also a considerable merchant colony of English, Dutch, and Italian traders whose reports to their European friends supplemented the news that now began to stream out of Smyrna from Jewish sources. Although Shabbetai Ẓevi was in continuous correspondence with Nathan, he now acted on his own. The stormy events that followed are fully documented in many sources.

Shabbetai Ẓevi used to recite the morning prayers in one of the synagogues "with a very agreeable voice that greatly pleased those who heard him"; he gave alms very liberally; rose at midnight to perform ritual immersions in the sea; and there was nothing bizzare about his ascetic behavior. But on one of the first days of Ḥanukkah he appeared "in royal apparel" in the synagogue and created a great sensation by his ecstatic singing. About the same time a delegation arrived from Aleppo – Moses Galante and Daniel Pinto and two laymen – who had first made a visit to the prophet in Gaza and now wished to greet him officially as the Messiah of Israel. During Ḥannukkah week, Shabbetai Zevi "began to do things that seemed strange: he pronounced the Ineffable Name, ate [forbidden] fats, and did other things against the Lord and His Law, even pressing others to do likewise," behavior characteristic of his states of illumination. The infectious presence of believers spurred him on to more radical manifestations. A deep cleft became evident between the majority of "believers" and a minority of "infidels," and *ma'aminim* and *koferim* became the fixed terms for those who adhered to faith in Shabbetai Ẓevi and those who opposed him. Nathan's epistle to Raphael Joseph was widely distributed and contributed to the growing dissention. To a large extent the common people joined the camp of the believers without inhibitions or theological misgivings; the glad tidings conquered their hearts, and the fascination of Shabbetai Ẓevi's personality, with its strange mixture of solemn dignity and unrestrained license, contributed its share. Hundreds of people, largely drawn from the poorer elements of the community, accompanied him wherever he went. But from the beginning many burghers, wealthy merchants, and brokers joined the movement, as well as rabbinic scholars, including some of his former students.

The three members of the rabbinic court who were still opposed to Shabbetai Ẓevi deliberated the wisdom of opening proceedings against him. Proclaiming public prayers in reaction, Shabbetai Ẓevi once more indulged his taste for majestic pomp and behaved with great audacity. On Friday, December 11, the crowd tried to storm the house of Ḥayyim Peña, one of the leading "infidels," and on the following day matters came to a head. After beginning to recite the morning prayers in one of the synagogues, Shabbetai Ẓevi broke off and, accompanied by a large crowd, proceeded to the locked doors of the Portuguese congregation, the headquarters of his opponents. Taking up an ax, he started to smash the doors, whereupon his opponents opened them and let him in. An astonishing scene followed. Shabbetai Ẓevi read the portion of the Torah not from the customary scroll but from a printed copy; ignoring the priests and levites present, he called up to the reading of the Law his brothers and many other men and women, distributing kingdoms to them and demanding that all of them pronounce the Ineffable Name in their blessings. In a furious speech against the unbelieving rabbis, he compared them to the unclean animals mentioned in the Bible. He proclaimed that the Messiah son of Joseph, who according to aggadic tradition must precede the advent of the son of David, was a certain Abraham Zalman, who had died a martyr's death in 1648, and recited the prayer for the dead in his honor. Then he went up to the ark, took a holy scroll in his arms, and sang an ancient Castilian love song about "Meliselda, the emperor's daughter"; into this song, known as his favorite throughout his life, he read many kabbalistic mysteries. After explaining them to the congregation, he ceremonially proclaimed himself the "anointed of the God of Jacob," the redeemer of Israel, fixing the date of redemption for the 15th of Sivan 5426 (June 18, 1666). This was in conformity with a date announced by Nathan in one of his more optimistic moods, when he considered the possibility of an earlier advent than originally predicted. Shabbetai Ẓevi announced that in a short time he would seize the crown of "the great Turk." When Ḥayyim Benveniste, one of the dissenting rabbis present, asked him for proof of his mission, he flew into a rage and excommunicated him, at the same time calling on some of those present to testify to their faith by uttering the Ineffable Name. The dramatic scene amounted to a public messianic announcement and the substitution of a messianic Judaism for the traditional and imperfect one. There is reliable testimony that, besides other innovations in the law, he promised the women that he would set them free from the curse of Eve. Immediately after this Sabbath he dispatched one of his rabbinical followers to Constantinople to make preparations for his arrival.

In the wave of excitement Benveniste's doubts were carried away and on the following day he joined the camp of the believers. A smoldering conflict between him and one of the other members of the court, Aaron Lapapa, may have played some part in his conversion. At any rate, on the 5th of Tevet (December 23) Shabbetai Ẓevi engineered the expulsion of Lapapa from his office and the appointment of Benveniste as the sole chief rabbi of Smyrna. Summoned before the qadi once more to explain his behavior, Shabbetai Ẓevi again succeeded in reassuring him. In the next few days all the believers were asked to come and kiss the hand of the messianic king; most of the community did so, including some "infidels" who were afraid of the mounting terrorism of the believers. Immediately after this regal ceremony, Shabbetai Ẓevi decreed the abolition of the fast of the Tenth of Tevet. When this act aroused the opposition of some of the rabbis, the angry crowd wanted to attack them. Solomon Algazi, a great scholar and famous kabbalist who persisted in his opposition, was forced to flee to Magnesia and his house was plundered. Lapapa hid in the house of one of his colleagues. On the following Sabbath the name of the Turkish sultan was struck out from the prayer for the ruler and a formal prayer for Shabbetai Ẓevi as the messianic king of Israel was instituted, a custom later followed by many communities throughout the Diaspora. Instead of his actual name, the practice began at this time of calling him by the appellation *amirah,* an abbreviation of *Adoneinu Malkenu yarum hodo* ("our Lord and King, may his majesty be exalted") and an allusion to the term emir. The new term was widely used in Shabbatean literature up to the beginning of the 19th century.

A festive atmosphere of joy and enthusiasm marked the succeeding days. Many people from other Turkish communities arrived and joined the movement, among them Abraham Yakhini, a famous preacher and kabbalist in Constantinople, who had known Shabbetai Ẓevi since 1658 and now became one of his most active propagandists. In a fit of mass hysteria, people from all classes of society started to prophesy about Shabbetai Ẓevi. Men, women, and children fell into a trance, declaiming acknowledgments of Shabbetai Ẓevi as Messiah and biblical passages of a messianic nature. When their senses returned, they remembered nothing. About 150 "prophets" arose in Smyrna, among them Shabbetai Ẓevi's wife and the daughter of some of the "infidels." Some had

Engraving of Shabbetai Ẓevi, believed to be the only portrait done from life. From Thomas Coenen, *Ydele Verwachtinge der Joden getoont in der Persoon van Sabethai Zevi*, Amsterdam, 1669.

visions of Shabbetai Ẓevi's crown or saw him sitting on the throne, but most of them produced a mere jumble of phrases and quotations from the Bible and the prayer book, repeated over and over again. Trade and commerce came to a standstill; dancing and festive processions alternated with the penitential exercises prescribed by Nathan. Psalm 21, which had been given a Shabbatean interpretation in Gaza, was recited at each of the three daily services, a custom which spread to many other communities. As well as distributing the kingdoms of the earth among the faithful, Shabbetai Ẓevi appointed counterparts of the ancient Israelite kings from David to Zerubbabel and several of these obtained handwritten patents from the Messiah. The appointees were his main supporters in Smyrna but included some of his devotees from Palestine, Egypt, Aleppo, Constantinople, and Bursa (Brussa). Many other messianic dignitiaries were appointed. After this, his last activity in Smyrna, Shabbetai Ẓevi sailed to Constantinople on Dec. 30, 1665, accompanied by some of his "kings." His behavior during this period was as consistent as his unstable mind would allow: he was sure of his calling and believed that some supernatural intervention would bring his messianic mission to fruition. In the meantime the Turkish authorities in the capital had been aroused by the alarming reports. The news from Gaza and Smyrna had already divided the community and the waves of excitement rose high. Letters from places through which Shabbetai Ẓevi had passed combined factual reports with increasingly fanciful stories and raised the messianic fever to an even higher pitch. Even before his arrival a prophet arose in Constantinople, Moses Serviel or Suriel, a young rabbi from Burṣa who, unlike the other "prophets," revealed Shabbatean mysteries in the language of the Zohar and was credited with a particular charisma. The Messiah's arrival was considerably delayed by extremely stormy weather and in the meantime the atmosphere in the capital became critical. Some of the heads of the community seem to have warned the government, which had already taken steps to arrest Shabbetai Ẓevi in Smyrna, where the order arrived too late, or on his arrival in Constantinople. The non-Jewish population was caught up in the excitement and satirical songs about the Messiah were sung in the streets, while the Jewish masses, certain that many miracles would take place immediately after his arrival, showed a marked pride before the Gentiles.

The policy pursued by the grand vizier, Ahmed Köprülü (Kuprili), one of Turkey's ablest statesmen, is remarkable for its restraint. Revolts were frequent in Turkey and the rebels were generally speedily put to death. That this was not the immediate consequence of Shabbetai Ẓevi's arrest after interception by boat in the Sea of Marmara on Feb. 6, 1666, did much to strengthen the belief of the faithful. Amid great commotion, he was brought ashore in chains on Monday, February 8. By this time the disruption of normal life and commerce had reached a peak. One or two days after his arrest, Shabbetai Ẓevi was brought before the divan, presided over by Köprülü. Since the Turkish archives from this period were destroyed by fire, no official Turkish documents about the movement and the proceedings in this case have survived, and reports from Jewish and Christian sources in Constantinople are conflicting. It is true, however, that the vizier showed suprising leniency and patience, to which Shabbetai Ẓevi's undoubted charm and the fascination of his personality may have contributed. He may have wanted to avoid making a martyr of a Messiah who, after all, had not taken up arms against the sultan and had simply proclaimed an unrealistic mystical take-over of the crown. Shabbetai Ẓevi was put in prison, at first in a "dark dungeon" but later in fairly comfortable quarters, and the high official responsible for the police and the prison, possibly after accepting substantial bribes, permitted him to receive visits from his followers. It was said that he could have obtained his release by a very large bribe which his followers were prepared to pay, but that he refused, thereby greatly enhancing his reputation. He was still self-confident. During this period, he had returned to a normal state, led an ascetic life, preached repentance and claimed no special privileges. The rabbis of the capital who visited him in prison found a dignified scholar who bore his sufferings with an air of nobility, rather than a sinner who set himself above the Law and tradition. The rabbis were divided among themselves, some of the outstanding ones, among them Abraham Al-Nakawa, taking his side. A new set of miracles was reported in the letters written during those months from Constantinople, proving that the enthusiasm continued unabated. When the sultan and the vizier left for the war on Crete, the order was given to transfer Shabbetai Ẓevi to the fortress of Gallipoli, where important political prisoners were detained, on the European side of the Dardanelles. The transfer was made on April 19, the day before Passover. Once more in the grip of a state of illumination, Shabbetai Ẓevi sacrificed a Passover lamb and roasted it with its fat, inducing his companions to eat this forbidden food and blessing it with the now customary blessing of "He who permits the forbidden." By means of bribes, the believers soon converted his detention into honorable confinement, and the fortress became known as *Migdal Oz* ("tower of strength"), with reference to Proverbs 18:10.

The Movement in the Diaspora. The letters arriving in all parts of the Diaspora from Palestine, Egypt, and Aleppo in October and November 1665, and later from Smyrna and Constantinople, produced a tremendous excitement, and the similarity of the reactions everywhere indicates that the causes of the response went far beyond local factors. Messianic fevor took hold of communities that had no immediate experience of persecution and bloodshed as well as those which had. Social and religious factors were no doubt inextricably combined in the outbreak. Poverty and persecution bred Utopian hopes, but the situation of the Jewish people as a whole provided the relevant background. Although the Lurianic doctrine of *tikkun* and redemption expressed a social situation too, its real content was essentially religious. It is this interlocking of the various elements in the historical makeup of the Shabbatean movement which accounts for its dynamics and explosive content. Later the movement was presented in a different light in a strenuous attempt to minimize the part played by the upper strata of Jewish society and the spiritual leaders, and to ascribe the vehemence of the outbreak to the blind enthusiasm of the rabble and the poor, but this is not borne out by contemporary evidence. The response showed none of the uniformity based on class conditions. Many of the rich took a leading part in spreading the messianic propaganda, although there was no lack of those who, as the saying went at the time, "were more interested in great profits than in great prophets."

Five factors contributed to the overwhelming success of the messianic awakening: (1) The messianic call came from the Holy Land, from the center that stood for pure spirituality at its most intense. A message from there would be received in Persia, Kurdistan, or Yemen with a respect which it could scarely command had it arrived from Poland or Italy. The tremendous prestige of the new Kabbalah which emanated from Safed also played a part. (2) The renewal of prophecy with the conspicuous figure of Nathan, the brilliant scholar and severe ascetic turned prophet, helped to obsure the more dubious facets of Shabbetai Ẓevi's personality which, indeed, played little or no role in the consciousness of the mass of the believers. (3) The efficacy of traditional and popular apocalyptic beliefs, whose elements were not relinquished but reinterpreted, played its part. The old eschatological visions were retained but many new elements were absorbed. The conception of the future was, throughout 1666, thoroughly conservative. At the same time, however, the propaganda was also addressed to a widespread group of kabbalists, to whom it presented a system of ambiguous symbols. Nathan's symbolism satisfied his readers by its traditional terminology, and the apparent continuity enabled the new elements to exist, undetected, under the cover of the older kabbalism. (4) The prophet's call to repentance played a decisive role, appealing to the noblest longings in every Jewish heart. Who, even among the movement's opponents, could condemn the one demand which the prophet and the Messiah made in public? (5) There was, as yet, no differentiation between the various elements taking part in the movement. Conservative minds, responding to their sense of unbroken continuity, saw in it the promise of fulfillment of traditional expectations. At the same time the message of redemption appealed to the utopianists who longed for a new age and would shed no tears for the passing of the old order. The national character of the movement obscured these contrasts in the emotional makeup of its participants.

Since the main mass outbreaks of the movement occurred in places far removed from the scene of Shabbetai Ẓevi's own activities, and Nathan the prophet never actually left Palestine during the heyday of the events, people were dependent on letters and other means of communication which presented a wild mixture of fact and fancy, the latter no less appealing to emotion and the imagination than the former. To a large measure the movement developed out of its own momentum, adapting new features to older traditions and conceptions. There is nothing surprising in the similarity of the phenomena in places far distant; they correspond both to the basic similarity of the Jewish situation and the traditional response to it, and to the uniformity of the propaganda that came from the believers in Turkey. Of some importance in Europe were many reports from Christian sources, which of course depended mostly on Jewish informants but added exaggerations and distortions of their own. The many broadsheets and pamphlets that appeared during 1666 in English, Dutch, German, and Italian were avidly read by the Jews and often taken as independent sources confirming their own news. A secondary factor was the sympathy shown to the movement by millenarian circles in England, Holland and Germany, since it seemed to confirm the belief widespread in these groups that Christ's second coming would occur in 1666. Peter Serrarius in Amsterdam, one of the leading millenarians, did much to spread Shabbatean propaganda to his many Christian correspondents. There are, however, no grounds for the assumption that the outbreak of the movement itself was due to the influence of Christian millenarian merchants on Shabbetai Ẓevi during his years in Smyrna.

While the majority of the people in those communities of which we have firsthand knowledge, and in those influenced by them, joined in the general enthusiasm, led everywhere by a group of devoted and determined believers, there were also many instances of bitter quarrels and differences with the "infidels." A mounting wave of messianic terrorism threatened those who spoke derisively of Shabbetai Ẓevi and refused to take part in the general excitement. A number of influential rabbis, who in their hearts were skeptical about the whole upheaval (like Samuel Aboab in Venice), were careful not to antagonize their communities, and cases of open rabbinical opposition were somewhat rare. Such stubborn adversaries were Joseph ha-Levi, the preacher of the community at Leghorn, and Jacob Sasportas, who had no official position at the time, and was staying in Hamburg as a refugee from the plague in London. A highly articulate and learned letter writer, he maintained a vivid correspondence with friends and acquaintances, and even with people unknown to him, to inquire about the truth of the events and to voice carefully worded opposition to the believers, though using words of strong condemnation to those who shared his opinion. Later (in 1669) he assembled (and heavily edited) large parts of this correspondence in *Ẓiẓat Novel Ẓevi.*

Repentance alternating with public manifestations of joy and enthusiasm was the order of the day, and detailed reports from many parts of the Diaspora describe the excessive lengths to which the penitents went. Fasts and repeated ritual baths, mortifications which were frequently of an extreme character, and lavish almsgiving were practiced everywhere. Many people fasted for the whole week: those who could not manage this fasted for two or three consecutive days every week and women and children at least every Monday and Thursday. "The ritual bath was so crowded that it was almost impossible to enter there." The daily devotions for day and night arranged by Nathan were recited, and many editions of them were published in Amsterdam, Frankfort, Prague, Mantua, and Constantinople. At night people would lie down naked in the snow for half an hour and scourge themselves with thorns and nettles. Commerce came to a standstill everywhere. Many sold their houses and property to provide themselves with money for the journey to the Holy Land, while others made no such preparations, being convinced that they would be transported on clouds. More realistic wealthy believers made arrangements for renting ships to transport the poor to Palestine. Reports from small towns and hamlets in Germany prove that the messianic revival was not limited to the larger centers. From many places delegations left to visit Shabbetai Ẓevi, bearing parchments signed by the leaders of the community which acknowledged him as the Messiah and king of Israel. A new era was inaugurated: letters and even some published books were dated from "the first year of the renewal of the prophecy and the kingdom." Preachers exhorted the people to restore all ill-gotten gains, but no cases where this was actually done are on record. People waited avidly for letters from the Holy Land, Smyrna, and Constantinople which were often read in public, giving rise to great excitement and frequently to violent discussions. There were hardly any differences in the reactions of Ashkenazi, Sephardi, Italian, and Oriental Jewry. In congregations composed largely of former Marranos – such as the "Portuguese" communities of Amsterdam, Hamburg, and Salonika – the messianic fervor was particularly strong. In North Africa, where the movement struck deep roots, a former Marrano, the physician Abraham Miguel Cardozo in Tripoli, became one of the most active protagonists. Other active supporters were the rabbis of Morocco, many of whom were well acquainted with Elisha Ḥayyim b. Jacob Ashkenazi, the father of Nathan the prophet, through his visits to their country as an emissary of Jerusalem. Poems in honor of Shabbetai Ẓevi and Nathan were composed in Yemen, Kurdistan, Constantinople, Salonika, Venice,

Ancona, Amsterdam, and many other places, but at the same time one of the outstanding opponents of the movement in Italy, the poet Jacob Frances in Mantua, with the help of his brother Immanuel, composed a passionate set of verses denouncing the movement, its heroes, and followers *(Ẓevi Muddaḥ)*. But these were lone voices in the wilderness; that the Italian communities were generally enraptured is vividly revealed in the notebook of a Jew from Casale who traveled throughout northern Italy at the end of 1665 and the early months of 1666, reflecting in his spontaneous descriptions the atmosphere prevailing there (*Zion*, 10 (1945), 55–56). Moses Zacuto, the most esteemed kabbalist of Italy, gave somewhat reluctant support to the movement. Some Jews who had settled in the Holy Land sent glowing reports about the awakening to their contemporaries in the Diaspora, but it can be said in general that everyone wrote to everyone else. Even the wife of a poor wretch from Hamburg who lay in prison in Oslo faithfully reported to him in Yiddish on the latest news received in Hamburg. At the other end of the scale Abraham Pereira, said to be the richest Jew in Amsterdam and certainly a deeply devout man, lent his enormous prestige to the cause and, after publishing a comprehensive book of morals for repentant sinners *(La Certeza del Camino*, 1666), left with his entourage for the Levant, although he was held up in Leghorn. In Poland and Russia boundless enthusiasm prevailed. Preachers encouraged the repentance movement, which acquired yet more extravagant modes of expression. No opposition from the rabbinical side is recorded. In public processions of joy the Jews carried portraits of Shabbetai Ẓevi taken from Christian broadsheets, provoking riots in many places such as Pinsk, Vilna, and Lublin, until in early May 1666 the Polish king forbade such demonstrations of Jewish pride. The living memory of the massacres from 1648 to 1655 gave the movement overwhelming popular appeal.

The news of Shabbetai Ẓevi's arrest in Gallipoli in no way diminished the enthusiasm; on the contrary, the fact that he was not executed and seemingly held in an honorable state only tended to confirm his mission. Samuel Primo, whom Shabbetai Ẓevi employed as his secretary (scribe), was a past master of the majestic and bombastic phrase and his letters conveyed an aura of imperial grandeur. Shabbetai Ẓevi signed these pronouncements as the "firstborn son of God," "your father Israel," "the bridegroom of the Torah," and other high-flown titles; even when he started signing some of his letters "I am the Lord your God Shabbetai Ẓevi" only a few of the believers seem to have been shocked. Moses Galante later claimed to have left him because of this. No reliable account of Shabbetai Ẓevi's conduct during the first period of his arrest in Gallipoli has been preserved, but there are indications that he had frequent periods of melancholy. When he entered an elevated state of illumination once more, people flocked to him in great numbers and the prison, with the help of bribes, was converted into a kind of royal court. The "king," who made no bones about his messianic claims, impressed his visitors deeply. An official letter from the rabbis of Constantinople to the rabbinate of Jerusalem, asking them to set up a commission of inquiry consisting of four representatives from Jerusalem, Safed, and Hebron, remained unanswered. When in March 1666 the rabbis of Venice asked for an opinion of the Constantinople rabbinate, they were given a positive answer disguised as a commercial communication about the quality of the goat skins "which Rabbi Israel of Jerusalem has bought." They wrote: "We looked into the matter and examined the merchandise of Rabbi Israel, for his goods are displayed here under our very eyes. We have come to the conclusion that they are very valuable . . . but we must wait until the day of the great fair comes." Hundreds of prophets arose in the capital and the excitement reached fever pitch. As the fasts of the 17th of Tammuz and the Ninth of Av approached, Shabbetai Ẓevi's euphoria mounted; he not only proclaimed the abolition of the fasts but instituted new festivals in their stead. The 17th of Tammuz became the "day of the revival of Shabbetai Ẓevi's spirit" and, indulging in prescribing in minute detail the liturgy to be recited on this occasion, he turned the Ninth of Av into the festival of his birthday. In Turkey, where the news was quickly spread, almost everybody followed his instructions and the day was celebrated as a high holiday. A delegation from Poland, among whose members were the son and son-in-law of R. David ha-Levi of Lvov, the greatest rabbinic authority of his country, visited him during the week following the 17th of Tammuz and found him in an ecstatic frame of mind. His dignity and majestic deportment conquered their hearts.

Many pilgrims believed the Messiah's imprisonment to be no more than a symbolic, outward show, a belief supported by a kabbalistic tract by Nathan, "A disquisition about the dragons," written during the summer of 1666. In it Shabbetai Ẓevi's particular psychology was explained in terms of a metaphysical biography of the Messiah's soul and its struggles with the demonic powers from the time of creation until his earthly incarnation. These struggles left their mark on him and were said to explain the alternations between the times when he is held a prisoner by the *kelippot* and his periods of illumination, when the supernal light shines upon him. Even in faraway Yemen, where the excitement ran high, the details of Shabbetai Ẓevi's biography (based on a mixture of fact and legend) were expounded in a kabbalistic fashion by the anonymous author of an apocalypse, "The valley of vision" *(Gei Ḥizzayon),* written late in 1666. As early as July the delegates from Poland were handed, under Shabbetai Ẓevi's signature, a kabbalistic tract explaining the events of his life as founded on deep mysteries. Even in Palestine and Egypt, where the letters abolishing the fast of the Ninth of Av could not have been received in time, the initiative for the abolition was taken by Nathan of Gaza and his followers, among whom Mattathias Bloch was very active in Egypt. Nathan himself planned more than once to meet Shabbetai Ẓevi but actually never left Gaza. There was a minority of "infidels" in Egypt too, including some outstanding Palestinian rabbis who had settled there, but in the face of the general enthusiasm they behaved very cautiously. In Algiers and Morocco the movement encountered no serious opposition on the part of the rabbis and leaders of the community.

Shabbetai Ẓevi's Apostasy. The movement reached its climax in July and August 1666 when everyone waited expectantly for great events to unfold. The turning point came in an unforeseen way. A Polish kabbalist, Nehemiah ha-Kohen from Lvov or its vicinity, came to see Shabbetai Ẓevi, apparently on behalf of some Polish communities. Arriving on September 3 or 4, he spent two or three days with him. The reports about their meeting are conflicting and in part clearly legendary. According to one source, Nehemiah argued less on kabbalistic grounds than as a spokesman of popular apocalyptic tradition, which he interpreted in strictly literal fashion. He failed to see any correspondence between Shabbetai Ẓevi's activities and the predictions of older aggadic writings on the Messiah. Dissatisfied by kabbalistic reinterpretations, he stressed the absence of a visible Messiah ben Joseph who should have preceded Shabbetai Ẓevi. Other sources maintain that the argument was about Nehemiah's own role since he himself claimed to be the Messiah b. Joseph, an assertion rejected by his host. Whatever the fact, the acrimonious debate ended in disaster. Nehemiah suddenly declared, in the presence of the Turkish guards, his willingness to adopt Islam. He was taken to Adrianople, where he denounced Shabbetai Ẓevi for fomenting sedition. No doubt the Jewish masses blamed Nehemiah for subsequent events, and even after his later return to Judaism in Poland he was persecuted for the rest of his life for having surrendered the Messiah to the Turks. However, it is quite possible that Nehemiah's action was simply a pretext and that the Turkish authorities had by then become alarmed by the events taking place in their country. There are indications of several complaints about Shabbetai Ẓevi, including charges of immoral behavior. The bustle and exuberance at Gallipoli came to an end when, on September 12 or 13, messengers arrived from Adrianople, and took the prisoner there on September 15.

On the following day he was brought before the divan, in the presence of the sultan, who watched the proceedings from a latticed alcove. Once more, the accounts of what happened at the court are contradictory. The believers reported that he was in one of his low melancholic states, and, behaving with utter passivity, allowed events to take their course. They depicted his apostasy as an act imposed on him, in which he took no part at all. The facts were certainly different although he may well have been in one of his low states at the time. He was examined by the court or privy council and denied – as he had done before under similar circumstances – ever having made messianic claims. According to some he even made a long speech about this. Finally he was given the choice between being put to death immediately or converting to Islam. According to one source, Kasim Pasha, one of the highest officials and a little later the brother-in-law of the sultan, conducted the decisive talk, "so handling him that he was glad to turn Turk." But all other sources agree that this role was played by the sultan's physician, Mustapha Hayatizadé, an apostate Jew. He convinced Shabbetai Ẓevi to accept the court's offer, which apparently had been decided upon before he himself was brought in. The physician acted mainly as an interpreter, Shabbetai Ẓevi's Turkish being rather poor at the time. Sultan Mehmed IV, a deeply religious man, was likely to sympathize with the possibility that such an outstanding Jewish personality might induce many of his followers to take the same step, and the council's action was certainly also influenced by tactical considerations. Agreeing to apostatize and put on the turban, Shabbetai Ẓevi assumed the name Aziz Mehmed Effendi. Being considered an important convert, he was granted the honorary title of *Kapici Bashi* ("keeper of the palace gates"). A royal pension of 150 piasters per day was added to the appointment. Several of the believers who had accompanied him followed him into apostasy, as did his wife when she was brought from Gallipoli some time later. The date of the conversion, Sept. 15, 1666, is confirmed by many sources. Shabbetai Ẓevi's state of mind after his apostasy was one of deep dejection, as evidenced by a letter written one week later to his brother Elijah.

After the Apostasy Until Shabbetai Ẓevi's Death. The apostasy produced a profound shock, paralyzing leaders and followers alike. In wide circles it was simply not believed and it took some time until the truth was accepted. The waves of excitement had been high, but deeper feelings were involved: for many believers the experience of the messianic revival had taken on the dimensions of a new spiritual reality. The tremendous upheaval of a whole year had led them to equate their emotional experience with an outward reality which seemed to confirm it. Now they were faced with a cruel dilemma: to admit that their belief had been wholly in vain and that their redeemer was an impostor, or to cling to their belief and inner experience in the face of outward hostile reality and look for an explanation and justification of what had happened. That many accepted the second alternative and refused to give in proves the depth of the movement. Because of this, the movement did not come to an abrupt end with the apostasy, an act which in all other circumstances would have terminated it automatically. Who could have dreamed of a Messiah who would forswear his allegiance to Judaism? On the other hand, the rabbis and communal leaders, particularly in Turkey, acted with great circumspection. Their policy was to hush up the whole affair, to calm the excitement by pretending that little had actually happened, and to restore Jewish life to the "normal" state of exile, for which the best method was to ignore the whole course of events and to let time and oblivion heal the wound. This policy was widely followed in other countries. If it were asked how a whole nation could have been allowed to nourish such high hopes only to be deceived at the end, no discussion of God's inscrutable counsels could be allowed. There was also apprehension, particularly in Turkey, that the authorities might proceed against the Jewish leaders who had permitted the preparations for a messianic revolt, and it appears that the Turkish authorities desisted from taking such a step only after considerable vacillation. In Italy, the pages in the Jewish community records which bore witness to the events were removed and destroyed on the order of the rabbis. Official silence also descended on the literature published in Hebrew for many years. Only dim echoes of law suits connected with it and other hints at the movement of repentance appeared here and there.

The facts, however, were different. Again, Nathan of Gaza played a decisive role although it remains an open question whether the initiative for a "theological" explanation of the apostasy was taken by him or by Shabbetai Ẓevi after he had recovered from his stupor. When Nathan received the news from Shabbetai Ẓevi's circle in early November 1666 he immediately announced that it was all a deep mystery which would resolve itself in due time. He left Gaza with a large entourage in order to arrange a meeting with Shabbetai Ẓevi, who by then had received instruction in the religion of Islam. The rabbis of Constantinople, most of whom had given up their belief, took steps to prevent this. Traveling first to Smyrna, where a considerable group of believers persisted in their faith, Nathan stayed there during March and April; although very reserved in all his relations with outsiders, he began to defend the apostasy and Shabbetai Ẓevi's continued messianic mission to the believers. The central point of his argument was that the apostasy was in reality the fulfillment of a mission to lift up the holy sparks which were dispersed even among the gentiles and concentrated now in Islam. Whereas the task of the Jewish people had been to restore the sparks of their own souls in the process of *tikkun* according to the demands of the Torah, there were sparks which only the Messiah himself could redeem, and for this he had to go down into the realm of the *kelippah,* outwardly to submit to its domination but actually to perform the last and most difficult part of his mission by conquering the *kelippah* from within. In doing this he was acting like a spy sent into the enemy camp. Nathan linked this exposition with his earlier metaphysical explanation of the biography of

Shabbetai Ẓevi as a struggle with the realm of evil, to which his "strange actions" bore witness even in his earthly life. The apostasy was nothing but the most extreme case of such strange action. He had to take upon himself the shame of being called a traitor to his own people as the last step before revealing himself in all his glory on the historical scene. By placing the paradox of an apostate Messiah, a tragic but still legitimate redeemer, at the center of the new, developing Shabbatean theology, Nathan laid the foundation for the ideology of the believers for the next 100 years. He, and many others after him, searched the Bible, Talmud, Midrash, and kabbalistic literature for references to this basic paradox and came up with a rich harvest of daring, audacious, and often outright heretical reinterpretations of the older sacred texts. Once the basic paradox was admitted, everything seemed to fall in line. All the objectionable acts of the biblical heroes, strange tales of the *aggadah (aggadot shel dofi),* and enigmatic passages of the Zohar – everything seemed to point, in typological exegesis, to the scandalous behavior of the Messiah. With Shabbetai Zevi's acquiescence, these ideas were taken up by the heads of the believers and given wide circulation. The rabbis forbade discussion of these heretical ideas, which would be refuted by their very paradoxicality. In the meantime they simply ignored them.

During 1667–68 the excitement slowly ebbed. When Nathan tried to see Shabbetai Ẓevi in Adrianople, he was met in Ipsola by a delegation of rabbis who forced him to sign a promise that he would give up his design (May 31, 1667). In spite of this he visited Shabbetai Ẓevi and continued to visit him from time to time and to proclaim him as the true Messiah, announcing several dates for the expected final revelation. On Shabbetai Ẓevi's orders he went to Rome for the performance of a secret magic ritual destined to hasten the fall of the representative of Christendom. His appearance in Venice on Passover 1668 created a great sensation. The rabbis published a pamphlet summing up the interrogations in Ipsola and Venice, and claiming that Nathan had denounced his errors. Nathan repudiated all these declarations and was obviously supported by a considerable number of believers. He completed his mission in Rome and returned to the Balkans, where he spent the rest of his life, alternating between Adrianople, Sofia, Kastoria, and Salonika, all places with a strong Shabbatean following.

Shabbetai Ẓevi himself lived in Adrianople and sometimes in Constantinople until 1672, succeeding in being allowed to lead a double life, performing the duties of a Muslim but also observing large parts of Jewish ritual. The Turks expected him to act as a missionary, but the 200 heads of families whom he drew to Islam were all secret believers whom he admonished to remain together as a group of secret fighters against the *kelippah.* Periods of illumination and depression continued to alternate, and during the sometimes lengthy periods of illumination he acted in the same manner as before: he instituted new festivals, confirmed his mystical mission, and persuaded people to follow him into Islam, which by then was called "the Torah of grace," in contradistinction to Judaism, "The Torah of truth." Several reports about his libertinism during "illumination" seem well founded. In one of these periods, in April 1671, he divorced his wife, but took her back when the illumination left him although he had already made arrangements for another marriage. A Hebrew chronicle by one of his visitors, Jacob Najara, describes in detail his extraordinary behavior. Revelations by celestial agents, of which some accounts have been preserved, were frequent in his circle. Primo, Yakhini, and Nathan frequently visited him but were never asked to embrace Islam, and they were accepted by the believers in Turkey as his legitimate spokesmen. Although they were still very strong in the Balkans and Asiatic Turkey, the Shabbateans were gradually driven underground but were not actually excommunicated. The borderline between the apostates and those who remained Jews sometimes became blurred although the latter were generally noted for their extremely pious and ascetic way of life. Shabbetai Ẓevi himself, who enjoyed the sultan's favor, formed connections with some Muslim mystics among the Dervish orders. Letters between his group and the believers in North Africa, Italy, and other places spread the new theology and helped to create an increasingly sectarian spirit. After a denunciation of his double-faced behavior and sexual license by some Jews and Muslims, supported by a large bribe, Shabbetai Ẓevi was arrested in Constantinople in August 1672. The grand vizier wavered between executing or deporting him, but finally decided to exile him, in January 1673, to Dulcigo (Turkish: Ulkün) in Albania, which the Shabbateans called Alkum after Proverbs 30:31. Although allowed relative freedom, he disappeared from public view, but some of his main supporters continued their pilgrimages, apparently disguised as Muslims. In 1674 his wife, Sarah, died and he married Esther (in other sources called Jochebed), the daughter of Joseph Filosof, a respected rabbi of Salonika and one of his chief supporters. From time to time during "illuminations," he still envisioned his return to his former state and considered that the final redemption was near.

During the last ten years of his life, especially in Adrianople, he used to reveal to the elect – frequently before he demanded their submission to "mystical apostasy" – his special version of the "mystery of the Godhead." According to this the "God of Israel" was not the first cause of *Ein-Sof,* but "a second cause, dwelling within the *Sefirah Tiferet,*" that is to say manifesting itself through this *Sefirah* without being identical with it. The two main points of this doctrine, which was of crucial importance in the later development of Shabbateanism, were: (1) The distinction between the first cause and the God of Israel, implying – and this thesis was upheld in different versions by the radicals in the movement – that the first cause has no providence over creation, which is exercised only by the God of Israel who came into being only after the act of *ẓimẓum:* this doctrine aroused particular revulsion in the Orthodox camp and was considered highly dangerous and heretical. (2) The distinctly Gnostic character of the division, though with the difference that the religious evaluation of the two elements in this dualism is reversed: the second-century Gnostics thought of the hidden God as the true God, considering the "God of the Jews" as an inferior and even detestable being. Shabbetai Ẓevi, Nathan, and Cardozo, however, turned the order of values upside down: the God of Israel, although emanated from the first cause, was the true God of religion, whereas the first cause was essentially irrelevant from the religious point of view. Some time before his death Shabbetai Ẓevi dictated a longer version of this doctrine to one of his scholarly visitors, or at least induced him to write it down. This text, later known as *Raza di-Meheimanuta* ("The Mystery of the True Faith"), instituted a kind of kabbalistic trinity, called in zoharic terms the "three bonds of the faith." It consisted of The Ancient Holy One *(Attika kaddisha),* The Holy King *(Malka kaddisha),* also called The God of Israel, and his *Shekhinah.* No reference was made to the Messiah and his rank, or to his relation to these hypostases. This doctrine differed considerably from the system developed earlier by Nathan of Gaza in his *Sefer Beri'ah* ("Book of Creation"). Both texts had a profound influence on subsequent Shabbatean doctrine and their echoes are audible in the hymns sung by the later sectarians in Salonika which are extant.

A number of letters from Shabbetai Ẓevi's last years testify to his continuing belief in himself, at least during his periods of illumination. His last letter, written about six weeks before his death, asks his friends in the nearest Jewish community of Berat in Albania to send him a prayer book for the New Year and the Day of Atonement. He died quite suddenly two months after his 50th birthday, on the Day of Atonement, Sept. 17, 1676. Nathan propagated the idea that Shabbetai Ẓevi's death was merely an "occultation" and he had actually ascended to and been absorbed into the "supernal lights." Such a theory of apotheosis was in line with Nathan's earlier speculations on the gradual deification of the Messiah, but left open the question of who would then represent the Messiah on earth. Nathan himself died shortly after, on Jan. 11, 1680, in Skoplje in Macedonia. During the preceding year one of his disiples, Israel Ḥazzan of Kastoria, wrote long homilies on some psalms reflecting the state of mind of the circle closest to Shabbetai Ẓevi and the gradual construction of a heretical and sectarian doctrine.

The Shabbatean Kabbalah. As Shabbetai Ẓevi himself was not a systematic thinker and spoke mainly in hints and metaphors, Nathan of Gaza must be considered the main creator of a rather elaborate system which combined a new version of Lurianic Kabbalah with original ideas about the position of the Messiah in this new order. His ideas gained wide currency and their influence can be detected in many seemingly orthodox kabbalistic tracts in the next two generations.

Nathan accepts the Lurianic doctrine of *ẓimẓum* (see p. 129) but adds a new, even deeper layer to his conception of the Godhead. From the beginning there are in *Ein-Sof* two kinds of light or aspects – which could even be called "attributes" in Spinoza's sense – the "thoughtful light" and "the thoughtless light." The first comprises all that is focused on the purpose of creation. But in the infinite wealth of *Ein-Sof* there are forces or principles which are not aimed at creation and whose sole purpose is to remain what they are and stay where they are. They are "thoughtless" in the sense that they are devoid of any idea directed to creation. The act of *ẓimẓum,* which occurred in order to bring about a cosmos, took place only within the "thoughtful light." By this act the possibility was created for the thoughtful light to realize its thought, to project it into the primordial space, the *tehiru,* and there to erect the structures of creation. But when this light withdrew, there remained in the *tehiru* the thoughtless light, which had taken no part in creation and, by its very nature, resisted all creative change. In the dialectics of creation, it therefore became a posititively hostile and destructive power. What is called the power of evil, the *kelippah,* is in the last resort rooted in this noncreative light in God himself. The duality of form and matter takes on a new aspect: both are grounded in *Ein-Sof.* The thoughtless light is not evil in itself but takes on this aspect because it is opposed to the existence of anything but *Ein-Sof* and therefore is set on destroying the structures produced by the thoughtful light. The *tehiru* which is filled with the thoughtless light, mingled with some residue of the thoughtful light which remained even after *ẓimẓum* is called *golem,* the formless primordial matter. The whole process of creation proceeds therefore through a dialectic between the two lights; in other words, through a dialectic rooted in the very being of *Ein-Sof.*

When, after *ẓimẓum,* the thoughtful light was streaming back in a straight line *(kav ha-yosher)* into the *tehiru,* starting there processes which are very similar, but not identical, to those described in Lurianic Kabbalah, it penetrated only the upper half of the primordial space, as it were overwhelming the thoughtless light and transforming it, thereby building the world of its original thought. But it did not reach the lower half of the *tehiru,* described as "the deep of the great abyss." All the statements of Lurianic ontology and the doctrine of cosmic restoration or *tikkun* which Israel must achieve through the strength of the Torah relate to the upper part of the *tehiru* only. The lower part persists in its unreconstructed and formless condition until the advent of the Messiah, who alone can perfect it, bringing about its penetration and transformation by the thoughtful light. In fact, the thoughtless lights, too, build structures of their own – the demonic worlds of the *kelippot* whose sole intent is to destroy what the thoughtful light has wrought. These forces are called the "serpents dwelling in the great abyss." The satanic powers, called in the Zohar *sitra aḥra* ("the other side"), are none other than the other side of *Ein-Sof* itself insofar as, by its very resistance, it became involved in the process of creation itself. Nathan developed a novel theory about processes which took place in the *tehiru* even before the ray from *Ein-Sof* penetrated there, being brought about by the interaction between the residue of the thoughtful light and the forces of the *golem.* They produced modes of being connected with the first configurations of the letters which were to form the Torah and the cosmic script. Only at a later stage, after the straight line shone forth and penetrated the *tehiru,* were these first structures, called the work of primeval creation *(ma'aseh bereshit),* transformed into the more substantial structures *(ma'aseh merkavah).* All the Lurianic processes connected with the breaking of the vessels and the *tikkun* were now adapted to the dialectics of the two lights.

In this conception of creation the figure of the Messiah plays a central role from the outset. Since *ẓimẓum* the soul of the Messiah had been submerged in the lower half of the *tehiru;* that is, since the beginning of time it stayed in the realm of the *kelippot,* being one of those sparks of the thoughtful light that had remained in the *tehiru* or perhaps having been snatched in some way by the *kelippot.* This soul, invaded by the influx of the thoughtless light and the bondage to its domination, has been struggling since the beginning of the world amid indescribable suffering to free itself and set out on its great task: to open up the lower part of the *tehiru* to the penetration of the thoughtful light and to bring redemption and *tikkun* to the *kelippot.* With their final transformation a utopian equilibrium and unity would be produced between the two aspects of *Ein-Sof.* The "straight line" cannot go forth into the abyss before the Messiah has succeeded in escaping from the domination of the *kelippot.* He is essentially different from all those souls which play their part in the processes of *tikkun.* In fact, he was never under the authority of the Torah, which is the mystical instrument used by the power of the thoughtful light and the souls connected with it. He represents something utterly new, an authority which is not subject to the laws binding in the state of cosmic and historic exile. He cannot be measured by common concepts of good and evil and must act according to his own law, which may become the utopian law of a world redeemed. Both his prehistory and his special task explain his behavior after he had freed himself from the prison of the *kelippah.*

This doctrine enabled Nathan to defend each and every "strange act" of the Messiah, including his apostasy and his antinomian outbreaks. He is the mystical counterpart of the red heifer (Num. 19): he purifies the unclean but in the process becomes as it were impure himself. He is the "holy serpent" which subdues the serpents of the abyss, the numerical value of the Hebrew word *mashi'aḥ* being equal to that of *naḥash.* In a way, every soul is composed of the two lights and by its nature bound predominantly to the thoughtless light which aims at destruction, and the struggle between the two lights is repeated over and over again in every soul. But the holy souls are helped by the law of the Torah, whereas the Messiah is left completely to his own devices. These ideas were developed in the new heretic Kabbalah in great detail and in different versions, disclosing an uncanny sense for formulating paradoxical tenets of belief. They responded precisely to the particular situation of those who believed in the mission of an apostate Messiah, and the considerable dialectical force with which they were presented did not fail to impress susceptible minds. The combination of mythological images and dialectical argument added to the attraction exercised by Nathan's writings.

The Shabbatean Movement, 1680–1700. Outside the circles of the believers Shabbetai Ẓevi's death went unnoticed by the Jewish world. Among the believers it produced much soul-searching; some of his followers seem to have left the camp immediately after his death. Even his brother Elijah, who had joined him in Adrianople and had converted to Islam, returned to Smyrna and Judaism. The activities of the Shabbatean groups were mainly centered in three countries, Turkey, Italy, and Poland (particularly Lithuania), where vigorous leaders and various prophets and claimants to the succession to Shabbetai Ẓevi appeared. Though there were many believers in other parts of the Diaspora, such as Kurdistan and Morocco, these three centers were the most important. The largest groups in Turkey were in Salonika, Smyrna, and Constantinople but in most of the Balkan communities Shabbeteanism survived and not infrequently members of the rabbinical courts were secret adherents. In Constantinople, their head was Abraham Yakhini, who died in 1682. A group of rabbis and kabbalists encouraged the more unlettered believers in Smyrna, although the Orthodox regained control there too. From 1675 to 1680 Cardozo (see p. 396) occupied the leading place among the Shabbateans in Smyrna after he had been forced to leave Tripoli around 1673, and later also Tunis and Leghorn. In Smyrna he found many followers, the most important of whom were the young Rabbi Elijah b. Solomon Abraham ha-Kohen Ittamari (d. 1727), who became one of the most prolific writers and moral preachers of the next two generations and never seems to have abandoned his basic convictions, and the cantor Daniel b. Israel

Bonafoux, who claimed the powers of a medium, especially in his later years.

During these years Cardozo began a prolific literary output, composing numerous lesser and larger books and tracts in which he expounded his own brand of Shabbatean theology. Beginning with *Boker Avraham* (1672), he propagated the theory that there is a difference of principle between the first cause, which is the God of the philosophers and the pagans, and the God of Israel who revealed himself to the Patriarchs and to the people of Israel. The confusion between the two is Israel's main failure in the era of exile. The people were particularly misled by the philosophers of Judaism, Saadiah Gaon, Maimonides, and all the others. Only the teachers of the Talmud and the kabbalists had kept the flame of the true religion secretly burning. With the approach of redemption, a few elect souls would grasp the true meaning of Israel's belief, that is to say, revelation as against philosophy, and the Messiah (as prophesied by a midrashic saying) would reach the knowledge of the true God, Shabbetai Ẓevi's "mystery of the Godhead," by his own rational efforts. In the meantime, this paradoxical view could be supported by a true interpretation of traditional texts even though the blind rabbis thought it heresy. Cardozo made no use of the novel ideas of Nathan's Kabbalah but constructed a system of his own which had considerable dialectical power. In most of his writings he avoided the question of Shabbetai Ẓevi's mission, though he defended it in several epistles written at different periods of his life. For a considerable number of years, at least, he saw himself as the Messiah b. Joseph who, as revealer of the true faith and sufferer of persecution by the rabbis, must precede the fnal advent of Shabbetai Ẓevi, after which all the paradoxes of Shabbatean belief would be resolved. Between 1680 and 1697 Cardozo lived in Constantinople, Rodosto, and Adrianople, not only arousing much controversy by his teachings but also causing great unrest through his prophecies about the imminent messianic end, especially in 1682. He was finally forced to leave these parts and spent the last years of his life mainly in Candia (Crete), Chios, and, after vainly trying to settle in Jerusalem, in Egypt. The outstanding supporter of strict adherence to rabbinic tradition in practice as long as Shabbetai Ẓevi had not yet returned, he consistently battled against antinomian tendencies, although he too foresaw a complete change in the manifestation of the Torah and its practice in the time of redemption. Cardozo's influence was second only to Nathan's; his writings were copied in many countries and he maintained close relations with Shabbatean leaders everywhere. Many of his polemics were directed against Samuel Primo on the one hand, and the radical Shabbateans of Salonika on the other. Primo (d. 1708), who later became chief rabbi of Adrianople, opposed any outward Shabbatean activity and disclosed his steadfast belief and heretical ideas only in secret conclaves.

In Salonika the situation was different. The number of believers was still quite large and the family of Shabbetai Ẓevi's last wife, led by her father, Joseph Filosof, and her brother Jacob Querido, displayed their convictions quite openly. Nathan had important followers among the rabbis, including some highly respected preachers and even halakhic authorities. The continuing state of turmoil, especially after Nathan's death, produced a fresh wave of excitement and new revelations. Visions of Shabbetai Ẓevi were very common in many circles of the believers but here, in 1683, they led to the mass apostasy of about 300 families who considered it their duty to follow in the Messiah's footsteps, in contradistinction to those Shabbateans who maintained, like Cardozo, that it was of the essence of the Messiah that his acts could not be imitated or followed by anyone else. Along with the first apostates among Shabbetai Ẓevi's contemporaries, the new group, led by Filosof and Solomon Florentin, formed the sect of the Doenmeh, voluntary Marranos, who professed and practiced Islam in public but adhered to a mixture of traditional and heretical Judaism in secret. Marrying only among themselves, they were soon identified as a separate group by both Turks and Jews and developed along their own lines, forming three subsects (see p. 327). A certain amount of antinomianism was common to all their groups, but this tendency was given preeminence by the subsect under the leadership of Baruchiah Russo (Osman Baba) who, in the first years of the 18th century, created another schism by teaching that the new spiritual or messianic Torah *(Torah de-Aẓilut)* entailed a complete reversal of values, symbolized by the change of the 36 prohibitions of the Torah called *keritot* (meaning punishable by uprooting the soul and annihilating it) into positive commands. This included all the prohibited sexual unions and incest. It seems that this group also developed the doctrine of the divinity of Shabbetai Ẓevi and later of Baruchiah himself, who died in 1721. This doctrine of incarnation was later wrongly ascribed to all Shabbateans and created much confusion in the reports about them. Baruchiah's group became the most radical wing of the Shabbatean underground. Most of the believers, however, did not follow the example of the Doenmeh and stayed within the Jewish fold, even in Salonika, where they disappeared only after a considerable time. Several well-known rabbis of Salonika and Smyrna in the 18th century such as Joseph b. David, Meir Bikayam, and Abraham Miranda, were still in secret sympathy with Shabbatean teachings and beliefs. Scholars who studied with Nathan or his pupils in Salonika, like Solomon Ayllon and Elijah Mojajon, who later became rabbis of important communities such as Amsterdam, London, and Ancona, spread the teachings of the moderate wing of Shabbateanism which adhered to Judaism and even tended to excessive pietism. Between 1680 and 1740 a considerable number of the emissaries from Palestine, especially from Hebron and Safed, were "tainted" with Shabbateanism and apparently also served as links between the various groups of believers in the Diaspora.

The second center existed in Italy, first in Leghorn, where Moses Pinheiro, Meir Rofe, Samuel de Paz, and Judah Sharaf (at the end of his life) were active, and later in Modena. Abraham Rovigo in Modena was passionately devoted to Shabbateanism of a distinctly pietistic character and, being a widely reputed scholar and kabbalist as well as a member of a very rich family, became the man to whom all "believers" turned, particularly visitors passing through Italy from the Land of Israel, Poland, and the Balkans. His convictions were shared by his intimate friend Benjamin b. Eliezer ha-Kohen, the rabbi of Reggio, Hayyim Segré of Vercelli, and others. They watched for every sign of a new impulse and reported to each other the news they received from their visitors and correspondents. Revelations of heavenly *maggidim,* who confirmed Shabbetai Zevi's supernal rank and the legitimacy of his mission and also added new interpretations of the Zohar and other kabbalistic matters, were then common. Rovigo's papers, many of which have survived, show the wide distribution of Shabbatean propaganda between 1680 and 1700. Benjamin Kohen – a rabbi who displayed a portrait of Shabbetai Ẓevi in his house! – even dared to publish a commentary on Lamentations which took up in detail Nathan's aphorism that in the messianic era this biblical book would be read as a collection of hymns of joy *(Allon Bakhut,* Venice, 1712). Baruch of Arezzo, one of Rovigo's group, composed in 1682–85, probably in Midena, a hagiography of Shabbetai Ẓevi, *Zikhron le-Veit Yisrael,* the oldest biography of this kind that has survived. Nathan's writings were copied and ardently studied in these circles, and illuminates who claimed heavenly inspiration such as Issachar Baer Perlhefter and Mordecai (Mokhi'aḥ) Eisenstadt from Prague (between 1677 and 1681), and later (1696–1701) Mordecai Ashkenazi from Zholkva (Zolkiev), were received with open arms and supported by Rovigo. When Rovigo realized his plan for settling in Jerusalem in 1701, the majority of the members of the yeshivah he founded there consisted of Shabbateans. Before leaving Europe, Rovigo went with his disciple Mordecai Ashkenazi to Fuerth, where he saw through press a voluminous folio, *Eshel Avraham,* written by the latter and based on the new interpretation of the Zohar he had received from heaven. Being devoted followers of rabbinic tradition, people of Rovigo's brand of Shabbateanism deviated from halakhic practice only by secretly celebrating the Ninth of Av as a festival. Even this practice was sometimes abandoned. In general, outside the rather small circle of the Doenmeh, the followers of Shabbetai Ẓevi did not differ from other Jews in their positive attitude to halakhic practice, and the differences between them and "orthodoxy" remained in the realm of theological speculation. The latter, of course, no doubt had far-reaching implications for the

Jewish consciousness of the believers which cannot be underrated. The question of the position of the Torah in the messianic age, which was already the object of serious discussion in Shabbetai Ẓevi's own circle and in Cardozo's writings, especially in his *Magen Avraham* (1668), could not remain an abstract one. But there is no indication that before 1700 heretic practices, as opposed to ideas, were characteristic of Shabbateanism.

This also holds true of the movement in Ashkenazi Jewry. Almost immediately after Shabbetai Ẓevi's death it was speculated whether he may have been the suffering Messiah b. Joseph rather than the final redeemer. Taking this position in Prague in 1677 was Mordecai Eisenstadt, an ascetic preacher who attracted a large following during the next five years. Together with his brother, who was probably the later famous rabbi Meir Eisenstadt, he traveled through Bohemia, southern Germany, and northern Italy, exhorting the people not to lose faith in the forthcoming redemption. Learned rabbis like Baer Perlhefter from Prague who spent several years in Modena supported his claims although Baer later left his camp and perhaps Shabbateanism altogether. Even where Shabbetai Ẓevi was revered as the true Messiah as was the case in most groups, there was no lack of claimants for the role of the Messiah b. Joseph who would fill the interregnum between the "first manifestation" of Shabbetai Ẓevi and his second. Even during the latter's exile in Albania, such a claimant had already appeared in the person of Joseph ibn Zur in Meknès (Morocco), an ignoramus turned prophet who threw many communities into great agitation by proclaiming the final redemption for Passover 1675. His sudden death put an end to the upheaval, but not to the deep-rooted belief in Shabbetai Ẓevi in Morocco. More lasting was the impression created by another prophet of this type in Vilna, the former silversmith Joshua Heshel b. Joseph, generally called Heshel Ẓoref (see p. 452). Originally an unlettered craftsman, he became "reborn" during the great upheaval of 1666 and for many years was considered the outstanding prophet of the Shabbatean movement in Poland. Over a period of more than 30 years he composed the *Sefer ha-Ẓoref,* divided into five parts and said to represent something like the future Torah of the Messiah. In fact, its thousands of pages, based on mystical and numerological explanations of *Shema Yisrael,* proclaimed him as Messiah b. Joseph and Shabbetai Ẓevi as Messiah b. David. Its attitude toward rabbinical tradition remains completely conservative. Several parts of these revelations are preserved; some of them, curiously enough, came into the hands of Israel b. Eliezer Ba'al Shem Tov, the founder of later Ḥasidism, and were held in high esteem by him and his circle. In his last years Heshel Ẓoref moved to Cracow and encouraged the new movement of the Shabbatean Ḥasidim.

Another prophet of this type, a former brandy distiller called Ẓadok, appeared in 1694–96 in Grodno. The stir such men created reverbrated as far as Italy, and Rovigo and his friends carefully collected testimonies about these events from Polish visitors. One of these was the Polish Shabbatean, Ḥayyim b. Solomon, known as Ḥayyim Malakh (see p. 429), a very learned man and apparently a powerful personality. In 1691 he studied in Italy those of Nathan's writings which had not yet become available in Poland, and after his return propagated their teachings among the rabbis of Poland. Later he went to Adrianople and, under the influence of Primo, left the moderates and became a spokesman for a more radical branch of the movement. He joined forces with Judah Ḥasid from Shidlov, a famous preacher of repentance and apparently a leader of the moderates. Between 1696 and 1700 they became the moving spirits of the "holy society of Rabbi Judah Ḥasid," a group composed of many hundreds of people, most of them probably Shabbateans, who indulged in extreme ascetism and prepared to emigrate to Palestine, there to await Shabbetai Ẓevi's second manifistation. Groups of them passed through many communities in Poland and Germany, arousing great enthusiasm. Although they never declared themselves openly as Shabbateans, little doubt remains on this score. Several rabbis in large communities who were aware of the true character of these Ḥasidim unsuccessfully tried to stop the propaganda. At the end of 1698, a council of the Shabbatean leaders of the Hasidim was held in Mikulov (Nikolsburg; Moravia) and was also attended by Heshel Ẓoref.

Shabbateanism in the 18th Century and its Disintegration. The *aliyah* of the Ḥasidim to Jerusalem in 1700 represented a peak of Shabbatean activity and expectations, and in the great disappointment of its failure as after the earlier failure of Shabbetai Ẓevi, several of his followers embraced Christianity or Islam. Judah Ḥasid died almost immediately after his arrival in Jerusalem in October 1700, and conditions in Jerusalem shattered the movement. Dissension broke out between the moderates, some of whom seem to have buried their Shabbatean convictions altogether, and the more radical elements led by Malakh. He and his faction were expelled but even the moderates could not maintain their foothold in the Holy Land and most of them returned to Germany, Austria, or Poland. One influential Shabbatean who remained was Jacob Wilna, a kabbalist of great renown. Many believers had proclaimed 1706 as the year of Shabbetai Ẓevi's return and the disappointment weakened a movement that had lost its active drive. It was driven completely underground, a process hastened by the spreading rumors of the extremist antinomian and nihilist teachings of Baruchiah. Increasingly, although wrongly, Shabbateans were identified with this extreme wing whose followers were not satisfied with mystical theories and visionary experience, but drew consequences in their personal adherence to the

Law. Malakh went to Salonika, then spread the gospel of secret antinomianism in Podolia, where he found fertile ground especially in the smaller communities. There is insufficient information regarding other parts of Europe to allow a clear differentiation between the various factions in the underground movement. It is obvious, however, that the antinomian slogan propagated by the radical wing that "the nullification of the Torah was its true fulfillment," and that, like the grain that dies in the earth, the deeds of man must become in some way "rotten" in order to bring forth the fruit of redemption, had a strong emotional appeal even to some talmudists and kabbalists, though, essentially, it represented an antirabbinic revolt in Judaism. That it alarmed the rabbinic authorities, who considered the children of these sectarians as bastards and therefore no longer admissible to the fold, was only logical. On the other hand, there is evidence that not a few of the most influential moral preachers and authors of moral literature of a radical ascetic bent were secret Shabbateans of the moderate and ḥasidic wing. Many of the most influential "*musar-books*" of this period belong to this category, such as *Shevet Musar* by Elijah Kohen Ittamari (1712), *Tohorat ha-Kodesh* by an anonymous author writing in the first decade of the century (1717), and *Shem Ya'akov* by Jacob Segal of Zlatova (1716). Some kabbalists who also wrote moral tracts in Yiddish belonged to this camp, such as Ẓevi Hirsch b. Jerahmeel Chotsh, and Jehiel Michael Epstein.

Shabbatean propaganda thus polarized around two different centers. The moderates who conformed to traditional practice and even overdid it could produce a literature which, avoiding an open declaration of their messianic faith, reached a wide public unaware of the convictions of the authors. Not a few homiletical, moral, kabbalistic, and liturgical books were published whose authors hinted in devious ways at their secret belief. The radicals, who became particularly active between 1715 and 1725 after Baruchiah had been proclaimed as "Señor Santo" and an incarnation of the Shabbatean version of the "God of Israel," had to be more careful. They worked through emissaries from Salonika and Podolia and circulated manuscripts and letters expounding their "new Kabbalah." The circles in Poland known as Ḥasidim before the advent of Ba'al Shem Tov, which practiced extreme forms of ascetic piety, contained a strong element of Shabbateanism, especially in Podolia. In Moravia Judah b. Jacob, commonly called Loebele Prossnitz (see p. 441), caused upheaval after his "awakening" as a Shabbatean prophet, traveling through the communities of Moravia and Silesia and finding many followers, some of whom persisted even after his fraudulent "magical" practices were unmasked and he was put under a ban (1703–06). Meir Eisenstadt who, like a number of other outstanding rabbis, had been in sympathy with the movement and was then officiating at Prossnitz left him and turned against him; but Prossnitz remained the seat of a sizable

Shabbatean group throughout the 18th century. A little later, 1708–25, another center of Shabbateanism crystallized in Mannheim, where some members of Judah Ḥasid's society, including his son-in-law Isaiah Ḥasid from Zbarazh, found refuge in the newly established *bet ha-midrash.* About the same time Elijah Taragon, one of Cardozo's pupils, made an unsuccessful attempt to publish his master's *Boker Avraham* in Amsterdam (1712).

While all these developments took place mainly in a twilight atmosphere or underground and received little general attention, a great public scandal broke out when another Shabbatean illuminate, this time a very learned one, succeeded in publishing the only large text of Shabbatean theology printed in the 18th century. Nehemiah Ḥiyya Ḥayon (see p. 412) had been educated in Jerusalem, served as a rabbi in his home town, and was in contact with the sectarians in Salonika and with Cardozo's circle before he returned to Ereẓ Israel. There he composed an elaborate double commentary on *Raza di-Meheimanuta,* Shabbetai Ẓevi's last exposition of the mystery of the Godhead, which Ḥayon now claimed to have received from an angel or, on other occasions, to have found in a copy of the Zohar. Forced to leave Ereẓ Israel because of his Shabbatean activities, he stayed for several years in Turkey, where he made enemies and friends alike and, about 1710, arrived in Venice, either on his own initiative or as an emissary. With the support of some secret sympathizers, but in general posing as an orthodox kabbalist, he succeeded in obtaining the approbation of rabbinical authorities to publish his three books: *Raza di-Yihuda* (Venice, 1711), *Oz le-Elohim* (Berlin, 1713) and *Divrei Neḥemyah (ibid.,* 1713). Of these *Oz le-Elohim* was the main work, containing his aforementioned commentaries on Shabbetai Ẓevi's text, whose title he changed to *Meheimanuta de-Kholla.* Amid polemics against Cardozo, he expounded his own version of the doctrine regarding the "three bonds of faith," the Shabbatean trinity of *Ein-Sof,* the God of Israel, and the *Shekhinah.* He carefully avoided linking this in any way with Shabbetai Ẓevi, whose name is never mentioned in any of these books, although *Divrei Neḥemyah* contains an extremely ambiguous homily attacking and at the same time defending those who apostatized for the sake of the God of Israel, that is the Doenmeh. It was only when he came to Amsterdam at the end of 1713, where he enjoyed the protection of Solomon Ayllon, himself a former secret adherent of Shabbateanism, that the heretical character of his books and especially of *Oz le-Elohim* was recognized by Ẓevi Hirsch Ashkenazi, the rabbi of the Ashkenazi community in Amsterdam. In the ensuing violent quarrel between the Amsterdam Sephardi and Ashkenazi rabbis, which produced a lively polemical literature, Shabbatean theology was for the first time discussed in public, being attacked by rabbis like David Nieto, Joseph Ergas, and Moses Ḥagiz, and a host of other participants in the fight against the heresy. Ḥayon vigorously defended his "kabbalistic" doctrine, stoutly but vainly denying its Shabbatean character. About 120 letters concerning this controversy were published in various sources. Several rabbis who were suspected of secret Shabbateanism refused to join in the bans pronounced against Ḥayon who, by the end of 1715, was forced to leave Europe. In his attempt at vindication by the rabbis of Turkey he received only halfhearted support.

When he returned to Europe in 1725, his arrival coincided with another Shabbatean scandal and brought his efforts to naught. This latter upheaval was connected with the increasing propaganda of the extremist followers of Baruchiah who had gained a strong foothold in Podolia, Moravia, and especially in the yeshivah of Prague, where the young and already famous Jonathan Eybeschuetz (see p. 405) was widely considered their major supporter. From 1724 onward several manuscripts were circulated from Prague which contained kabbalistic explanations couched in ambiguous and obscure language but whose gist was a defense of the doctrine of the "God of Israel," his indwelling in *Tiferet,* and his intimate connection with the Messiah, without explicitly mentioning, however, his character as a divine incarnation. The testimony pointing to Eybeschuetz as the author, particularly of the kabbalistic but doubtless heretical manuscript *Va-Avo ha-Yom el ha-Ayin,* is overwelming. When this and many other Shabbatean writings from Baruchiah's sect were discovered, in Frankfort in 1725, among the luggage of Moses Meir of Kamenka (Kamionka), a Shabbatean emissary to Mannheim from Podolia, a great scandal ensued. A whole network of propaganda and connections between the several groups was uncovered, but Eybescheutz' considerable reputation as a genius in rabbinic learning prevented action against him, particularly as he placed himself at the head of those who publicly condemned Shabbetai Ẓevi and its sectarians in a proclamation of excommunication dated Sept. 16, 1725. In many other Polish, German, and Austrian communities similar proclamations were published in print, also demanding that all who heard them should denounce secret Shabbateans to the rabbinical authorities. The atmosphere of persecution which then prevailed led the remaining Shabbateans to go completely underground for the next 30 years, especially in Poland.

After these events the figure of Jonathan Eybescheutz remained in twilight, and indeed he poses a difficult psychological problem if (as may be evidenced through a study of the pertinent texts and documents) he must in fact be considered the author of the aforementioned manuscript. When, after his glorious career as a great teacher, preacher, and rabbinic authority in Prague, Metz, and Hamburg, it was discovered in 1751 that a considerable number of amulets he had given in Metz and Hamburg/Altona were in fact of a Shabbatean character, another great uproar followed, engulfing many people in Germany,

Austria, and Poland in a heated controversy. His main opponent was Jacob Emden, the son of Ḥayon's foe in Amsterdam and an indefatigable fighter against all surviving Shabbatean groups and personalities. His many polemical writings published between 1752 and 1769 often widely overshot their mark, as in the case of Moses Ḥayyim Luzzatto, but they contain much valuable information about Shabbateanism in the 18th century. Eybeschuetz' defense of the amulets was particularly weak and largely self-defeating. He argued that the text of the amulets consisted only of mystical Holy Names which had their root in kabbalistic books and could not be deciphered as a continuous text. Comparison of the amulets, however, proves the contrary. The cryptograms used differed from one item to the other, but they always contained an assertion of the messianic mission of Shabbetai Ẓevi and a reference to Shabbatean views on the "God of Israel."

The secret Shabbateans in central Europe saw Eybeschuetz as their most prominent figure, whereas the orthodox were deeply shocked by the possibility that an outstanding representative of rabbinic and kabbalistic spirituality might have leanings toward heretical ideas. Many of them refused to entertain such a possibility and stood by him. The confusion even in the camp of orthodox kabbalists was considerable and they, too, were divided. The issue under discussion was greatly complicated by personal and irrelevant factors, but the conflict demonstrated how deeply rooted were apprehensions regarding the entrenchment of the Shabbateans in many communities. This is also borne out by numerous testimonies from many sources recorded between 1708 and 1750, even before the controversy between Eybeschuetz and Emden took place. Nathan of Gaza's writings were still studied not only in Turkey, but in Morocco, Italy, and among the Ashkenazim. Several authors describe the method of Shabbatean propaganda among those who had only a modest talmudic learning or none at all but were drawn to the study of *aggadah* which the sectarians knew how to use and explain along their own lines. This method of attracting people and then slowly initiating them into the tenets of the sectarians was persistently used for more than 80 years in Poland, Moravia, Bohemia, and Germany. Much ambiguity was permitted by the widespread heretical principle that the true believer must not appear to be what he really was and that dissimulation was legitimate in a period where redemption had taken place in the secret heart of the world but not yet in the realm of nature and history. People were allowed to deny their true belief in public in order to conceal their conservation of the "holy faith." This went so far that a work presenting a summary of Shabbatean theology, like Jacob Koppel Lifschuetz' *Sha'arei Gan Eden* written in the early years of the 18th century in Volhynia, was preceded by a preface vehemently denouncing the Shabbatean heresy! This double-faced behavior came to be seen as a characteristic trait of the sectarians who, from the beginning of the 18th century, became known in Yiddish as *Shebsel* or *Shabsazviniks,* with the connotation of "hypocrites." There is full proof that a fair number of men of great talmudic learning, and even officiating rabbis, joined these groups and found it possible to live in a state of high tension between outward orthodoxy and inward antinomianism that perforce destroyed the unity of their Jewish identity. In places like Prague a number of highly respected families formed a nucleus of secret believers, and there is evidence that in some places influential Court Jews protected the sectarians or belonged to them. Many of the Moravian Shabbateans held positions of economic power. There is also evidence about the secret rituals performed in these groups, especially in Podolia, where the followers of Baruchiah were concentrated in places such as Buchach (Buczacz), Busk, Glinyany, Gorodenka, Zolkiew, Nadvornaya, Podgaitsy (Podhajce), Rogatin (Rohatyn), and Satanov. The eating of forbidden fat *(ḥelev)* or severe transgressions of sexual prohibitions were considered as initiation rites. Kabbalists and *Ba'alei Shem* (see page 310) from Podhajce who became known in Germany and England between 1748 and 1780, such as Hayyim Samuel Jacob Falk, the "Ba'al Shem of London," and Moses David Podheitser, a close associate of Eybeschuetz in Hamburg, came from these circles.

The heated controversy about the revelations of Moses Ḥayyim Luzzatto in Padua, which began in 1727, and the messianic tendencies of his group engaged much attention in the following ten years. Although even in their secret writings Luzzatto, Moses David Valle, and their companions repudiated the claims of Shabbetai Ẓevi and his followers, they were without doubt deeply influenced by some of the paradoxical teachings of Shabbatean Kabbalah, especially those concerning the metaphysical prehistory of the Messiah's soul in the realm of the *kelippot.* Luzzatto formulated these ideas in a manner which removed the obviously heretical elements but still reflected, even in his polemics against the Shabbateans, much of their spiritual universe. He even tried to find a place for Shabbetai Ẓevi, though not a messianic one, in his scheme of things. The idea of an apostate Messiah was utterly unacceptable to him as were the antinomian consequences drawn by the Doenmeh and their sympathizers, but his claims to heavenly inspiration and novel kabbalistic revelations, coming as they did immediately after the excommunication of the sectarians in 1725 and 1726, aroused grave apprehensions in Italy and some places in Germany that had special experiences with Shabbateanism. Similiarly, a generation later the first antagonists of latter-day Polish Ḥasidism suspected it to be nothing but a new branch of Shabbateanism. In both cases the suspicions were wrong but they had some foundation in the teaching and behavior of the newcomers. More complicated is the case of the voluminous work *Ḥemdat Yamim,* first published in Smyrna in 1731 and later several times in Zolkiew and twice in Italy. This anonymous work described in detail Jewish life and ritual from the point of view of Lurianic Kabbalah but was permeated with the spirit of strictly ascetic Shabbateanism as it was promoted in Jerusalem and Smyrna by kabbalists like Jacob Wilna and Meir Bikayam. Adopting several Shabbatean innovations, it included even hymns written by Nathan of Gaza and a whole ritual for the eve of the new moon whose Shabbatean character is obvious. Though feigning an earlier origin, it was probably composed between 1710 and 1730, allegedly in Jerusalem but probably somewhere else. Its very attractive style and rich content secured it a wide public, and in Turkey it was accepted as a classic, a position it maintained. However, not long after its publication in Podolia in 1742, the work was denounced by Jacob Emden as composed by Nathan of Gaza (wrongly) and propagating Shabbatean views (rightly). This opposition notwithstanding, it was still frequently quoted but withdrawn from public circulation in Poland and Germany.

Independently of the Eybeschuetz affair, a momentous explosion of Shabbateanism in its last stage occurred in 1756 in Podolia with the appearance of Jacob Frank (1726–91) as the new leader of the extremist wing. Imbued with the main ideas of Baruchiah's sectarians in Salonika, he returned to his native milieu after spending many years mainly during his childhood and adolescence in Turkey. He was already then reputed as a new leader, prophet, and reincarnation of Shabbetai Ẓevi. (For details of the movement he instigated see Jacob Frank and the Frankists, p. 287) In the stormy years between 1756 and 1760 a large part of Frank's followers converted to Catholicism, constituting a kind of Doenmeh in Poland, only in Catholic disguise. These events and especially the willingness of the Frankists to serve the interests of the Catholic clergy by publicly defending the blood libel in the disputation at Lvov (1759) deeply stirred and aroused the Jewish community in Poland and had wide repercussions even outside Poland. The majority of the Shabbateans, even of Frank's own sectarians, did not follow him into the Church and groups of Frankists remained within the Jewish fold in Poland, Hungary, Moravia, Bohemia, and Germany. Frank's main contribution was threefold. (1) He divested Shabbateanism of its kabbalistic theology and the abstruse metaphysical speculations and terms in which it was clothed, substituting instead a much more popular and colorful version, couched in mythological images. The unknown and as yet inaccessible "Good God," the "Big Brother" (also called "He Who stands before God"), and the matron or virgin or plain "she" – an amalgam of the *Shekhinah* and the Virgin Mary – constitute the Frankist trinity. Frank saw Shabbetai Ẓevi, Baruchiah, and finally himself as emissaries and somehow incarnations of the "Big Brother," whose mission would be completed by the appearance of an incarnation of the feminine element of this trinity. Frank's tendency to throw away the "old books" constrasted sharply with the continuous predilection of his followers to study them, especially those who remained Jews. (2) His version of Shabbateanism took on an unabashedly nihilistic character. Under the "burden of silence" the true believer, who has God in his secret heart, should go through all religions, rites, and established orders without accepting any and indeed annihilating all from within and thereby establishing true freedom. Organized religion is only a cloak to be put on and be thrown away on the way to the "sacred knowledge," the gnosis of the place where all traditional values are destroyed in the stream of "life." (3) He propagated this nihilistic religion as the "way to Esau" or "Edom," encouraging assimilation without really believing in it, hoping for a miraculous revival of a messianic and nihilistic Judaism through the birth pangs of a universal upheaval. This conception opened the way to an amalgamation between this last stage of Shabbatean messianism and mysticism on the one hand and contemporary enlightenment and secular and anticlerical tendencies on the other. Freemasonry, liberalism, and even Jacobinism could be seen as equally valuable means to such final ends. It is small wonder that wherever such groups existed the Jewish communities fought them vehemently even though only rather vague rumors of Frank's secret teachings reached them.

Frankists in central Europe joined forces with the older Shabbatean groups, including the admirers of Eybeschuetz, and some of Eybeschuetz' own sons and grandchildren joined the Frankist camp. In the 1760s there was still active Shabbatean propaganda in the yeshivot of Altona and Pressburg. An emissary, Aaron b. Moses Teomim from Gorodenka, propagated Shabbateanism in northern and southern Germany and, in 1767, tried to enlist the help of Christian sympathizers, claiming to have set out on his mission on behalf of the Polish prince Radziwill, a well-known protector of the Frankists. The Jewish and apostate Frankists remained in close touch, particularly through their meetings at Frank's "court" in Brno and later in Offenbach. Although they were deeply impressed by Frank's sayings and epistles, their own activities never equaled the ferocity of his subversive and nihilist visions. During the first decades of the 19th century Shabbateanism disintegrated even as a loosely organized sect and, apart from those who reverted to traditional Judaism, disappeared into the camp of Jewish liberalism and, in many cases, indifference. The sectarian groups of the Doenmeh in Turkey and the Catholic Frankists in Poland, especially in Warsaw, survived much longer, the former breaking up only in the mid-20th century and the latter probably after 1860.

Bibliography: SOURCES: J. Sasportas, *Ẓiẓat Novel Ẓevi,* ed. by I. Tishby (1954); J. Emden, *Torat ha-Kena'ot* (1752); idem, *Sefer Hitabbekut ISH* (1762); J. Eybeschuetz, *Luḥot Edut* (Altona, 1775); N. Bruell (ed.), *Toledot Shabbetai Ẓevi* (1879); A. Freimann, *Inyenei Shabbetai Ẓevi* (1912); A. M. Habermann, *"Le-Toledot ha-Pulmus Neged ha-Shabbeta'ut"* in: *Koveẓ al Yad,* n.s. 3 pt. 2 (1940), 185–215; G. Scholem, *"Gei Ḥizzayon, Apokalipsah Shabbeta'it mi-Teiman." ibid.,* n.s. 4 (1946), 103–42; idem, *Be-Ikvot Mashi'aḥ* (1944; collected writings of Nathan); M. Attias and G. Scholem (ed.), *Shirot ve-Tishbahot shel ha-Shabbeta'im* (1958); *Sefunot,* 3-4 (1959-60; *Mehkarim u-Mekorot le-Toledot ha-Tenu'ah ha-Shabbeta'it Mukdashim le-Shneur Zalman Shazar);* J. Frances, *Kol Shirei . . .,* Ed. by P. Naveh (1969). STUDIES: (Works By G. Scholem) *Sabbatai Ṣevi; the Mystical Messiah* (Princeton, 1973) includes extensive bibliography, updated version of the Hebrew *Shabbetai Ẓevi . . .*(1957); *Messianic Idea in Judaism and Other Essays* (1971); *Ḥalamotav shel ha-Shabbeta'i R. Mordekhai Ashkenazi* (1938); KS, 166 (1939–40), 320–38 (on the Emden-Eybeschuetz controversy); *"Te'udah Ḥadashah me-Reshit ha-Tenu'ah ha-Shabbeta'it," ibid.,* 33 (1958), 532–40; *Zion,* 9 (1944), 27–38, 84–88 (on Shabbateanism in missionary literature); *Sefer Dinaburg* (1948), 235–62 (on Mordecai Eisenstadt); *Alexander Marx Jubilee Volume* (Heb., 1950), 451–70 (on Elijah Kohen Ittamari and Shabbateanism); *"Le mouvement sabbataïste en Pologne,"* in: RHR, 143–4 (1953–55); *Beḥinot,* 8 (1955), 79–95; 9 (1956), 80–84 (on the book *Ḥemdat Yamim); "Perush Mizmorei Tehillim me-Ḥugo Shel Shabbetai Ẓevi be-Adrianopol,"* in: *Alei Ayin; Minḥat Devarim li-Shelomo Zalman Schocken* (1952), 157–211; *Ereẓ Israel,* 4 (1956), 188–94 (on two Mss. regarding Shabbateanism in the Adler collection); *"Iggeret Nathan ha-Azzati al Shabbetai Ẓevi ve-Hamarato,"* in: *Koveẓ al Yad,* n.s. 6 (1966), 419–56; Graetz, *Geschichte der Juden,* 7 (1896), 428–524; C. Anton, *Kurze Nachricht von dem falschen Messias Sabbathai Ẓebbi* (1752); *Nachlese zu seiner letztern Nachricht* (1753); A. Danon, *Etudes Sabbatiennes* (1910); A. Galanté, *Nouveaux Documents Sur Sabbetaï Sevi* (Istanbul, 1935); D. Kahana, *Toledot ha-Mekubbalim, ha-Shabbeta'im ve-ha-Ḥasidim,* 2 vols. (1913–14); D. Kaufman, in MGWJ, 41 (1897), 700–8 (a letter of Benjamin Cohen, dated 1691); M. Freudenthal, *"R. Michel Chasid und die Sabbatianer," ibid.,* 76 (1932), 370–85; A. Epstein, *Une lettre d'Abraham Ha-Yakhini à Nathan Gazati,"* in: REJ, 26 (1893), 209–19; A. Amarillo, *"Te'udot Shabbeta'iyyot,"* in: *Sefunot,* 5 (1961), 235–74; I. Sonne, *"Le-Toledot ha-Shabbeta'ut be-Italyah,"* in: D. Frankel (ed.). *Sefer Yovel le-Alexander Marx* (1943), 89–103; *"Overim ve-Shavim be-Veito shel Avraham Rovigo,"ibid.,* 5 (1961), 275–96; M. Friedman, *"Iggerot be-Farashat Pulmus Neḥemyah Ḥiyya Ḥayon," ibid.,* 10 (1966), 483–619; S.Z. Shazar, *Sofero shel Mashi'ah* (1970; repr. from *Ha-Shilo'ah,* 29 (1913)); idem, *"Ma'aseh Yosef Dela Reina ba-Masoret ha-Shabbeta'it,"* in: *Eder ha-Yakar, Sefer Yovel . . . S.A. Horodezky* (1947) 97–118; idem, *Ha-Tikvah li-Shenat HaTak* (1970; on I.V. Cantarini); M. Benayahu, *"Yedi'ot me-Italyah u-me-Holland al Reshitah shel ha-Shabbeta'ut,"* in: *Eretz Israel,* 4 (1956), 194–205; idem, in: *Sinai,* 46 (1960), 33–52 (on responsa regarding Shabbatean movement); idem, *"Mafte'aḥ le-Havanat ha-Te'udot al ha-Tenu'ah ha-Shabbeta'it bi-Yrushalayim,"* in: *Studies in honor* *of G. Scholem* (1968), 35–45; *"Shemu'ot Shabbeta'iyyot* (from the Italian group), in: *Michael* 1 (1973), 9–77; H. Wirshubski, *"Ha-Te'ologyah ha-Shabbeta'it shel Natan ha-Azzati,"* in: *Kenesset,* 8 (1944), 210–46; M. Perlmuter, *R. Yonatan Eybeschuetz ve-Yaḥaso el ha-Shabbeta'ut* (1947; incl. Eng. summary); A. Z. Aescoly, *Itton Flandri al Odot Tenuat Shabbatai Ẓevi,"* in: *Sefer Dinaburg* (1950), 215–36; M. Wilensky, *"Arba'ah Kunteresim Angliyyim al ha-Teun'ah ha-Shabbeta'it,"* in: *Zion,* 17 (1952), 157–72; A. Yaari, *Ta'alumat Sefer* (1954; on *Ḥemdat Yamim);* idem, *"Mi Hayah ha-Navi ha-Shabbeta'i R. Mattityahu Bloch? "* in: KS, 36 (1961) 525–34; S. Hurwitz, *"Shabbatai Zwi,"* in: *Studien zur Analytischen Psychologie C. G. Jung,* 2 (1955), 239–63; R. Schatz, in: *Beḥinot,* 10 (1956), 50–66 (on Sasportas' *Ẓiẓat Novel Zevi):* S. Simonsohn, "A Christian Report from Constantinople Regarding Shabbetai Zebi," in: JJS, 12 (1961), 33–85; Y. Tishby, *Netivei Emmunah u-Minut* (1964); A. Rubinstein, *"Bein Hasidut le-Shabbeta'ut"* in: *Bar-Ilan,* 4–5 (1965), 324–39; H. P. Salomon, "Midrash, Messianism and Heresy in Spanish-Jewish Hymns," in: *Studia Rosenthaliana,* 4, no. 2(1970), 169–80. D. Tamar, *"Maḥloket R. Ḥayyim Benveniste we-R. Aharon Lapapa",* in: *Tarbiz* 41 (1972), 411–23.

3
Jacob Frank and the Frankists

Jacob Frank (1726–1791) was the founder and central figure of a Jewish sect named after him, the Frankists, which comprised the last stage in the development of the Shabbatean movement. He was born Jacob b. Judah Leib in Korolowka (Korolevo), a small town in Podolia. His family was middle class, and his father was a contractor and merchant, apparently well respected, His grandfather lived for a time in Kalisz, and his mother came from Rzesow. Although Frank's claim before the Inquisition that his father used to serve as a rabbi appears to have no foundation there is reason to believe that he did conduct services in Czernowitz, where he moved in the early 1730s. His father is depicted as a scrupulously observant Jew. At the same time, it is very likely that he already had certain connections with the Shabbatean sect, which had taken root in many communities in Podolia, Bukovina, and Walachia. Frank was educated in Czernowitz and Sniatyn, and lived for several years in Bucharest. Although he went to *heder,* he gained no knowledge of Talmud, and in later years boasted of this ignorance and of the qualities he possessed as a *prostak* ("simple man"). His self-characterization as an ignoramus *(am ha-areẓ)* must be seen in the context of the contemporary usage of the word to mean a man who knows Bible and the *aggadah,* but who is not skilled in *Gemara.* In his memoirs he makes much of the pranks and bold adventures of his childhood and adolescence. In Bucharest he began to earn his living as a dealer in cloth, precious stones, and whatever came to hand. Between 1745 and 1755 his trade took him through the Balkans and as far as Smyrna.

Early Associations with the Shabbateans. Frank's accounts of his earliest associations with the Shabbateans are full of contradictions, but there is no doubt that these contacts go back to his youth. Apparently his teacher in Czernowitz belonged to the sect and had promised that Frank would be initiated into their faith after marriage, as was often customary among Shabbateans. He began to study the Zohar, making a name in Shabbatean circles as a man possessed of special powers and inspiration. When in 1752 he married Hannah, the daughter of a respected Ashkenazi merchant in Nikopol (Bulgaria), two

Shabbatean emissaries from Podolia were at the wedding. Shabbatean scholars like these, some of whom Frank mentions in his stories, accompanied him on his travels, and initiated him into the mysteries of "the faith." There is no doubt that these men were representatives of the extremist wing formed by the disciples of Baruchiah Russo (d. 1720), one of the leaders of the Doenmeh in Salonika. It was in the company of these teachers, themselves Ashkenazim, that Frank visited Salonika for the first time in 1753, and became involved with the Baruchiah group of the Doenmeh, but he followed the practice of the Polish disciples and did not convert to Islam. After his marriage it seems that trading became secondary to his role as a Shabbatean "prophet," and as part of his mission he journeyed to the grave of Nathan of Gaza in Skoplje, Adrianople, and Smyrna, and again spent a good deal of time in Salonika in 1755. Through their letters, his Shabbatean teachers and companions from Poland spread the news of the emergence of a new leader in Podolia, and finally persuaded him to return to his early home. Frank, who was a man of unbridled ambition, domineering to the point of despotism, had a low opinion of the contemporary Baruchiah sect in Salonika, calling it "an empty house"; whereas, as the leader of the Shabbateans in Poland, he envisaged a great future for himself. Although in the circle of his close friends he was given the Sephardi appellation *Ḥakham Ya'akov,* at the same time he was considered to be a new transmigration or a reincarnation of the divine soul which had previously resided in Shabbetai Ẓevi and Baruchiah, to whom Frank used to refer as the "First" and the "Second." At the end of the 18th century, the story that Frank had gone to Poland on an explicit mission from the Baruchiah sect was still circulating in Doenmeh groups in Salonika. In the first years of his activity he did in fact follow the basic principles of this sect, both its teaching and its customs.

Frank in Podolia. On Dec. 3, 1755, Frank, accompanied by R. Mordecai and R. Naḥman, crossed the Dniester River and spent some time with his relatives in Korolewka. After this he passed in solemn state through the communities in Podolia which contained Shabbatean cells. He was enthusiastically received by "the believers," and in the general Jewish community the news spread of the appearance of a suspected *frenk,* which was the usual Yiddish term for a Sephardi. Frank, who had spent about 25 years in the Balkans and was thought to be a Turkish subject, actually conducted himself like a Sephardi and spoke Ladino when he appeared in public. Subsequently he assumed the appellation "Frank" as his family name. His appearance in Lanskroun (Landskron) at the end of January 1756 led to a great scandal, when he was discovered conducting a Shabbatean ritual with his followers in a locked house. The opponents of the Shabbateans claimed that they surprised the sectarians in the midst of a heretical religious orgy, similar to rites which were actually practiced by members of the Baruchiah sect, especially in Podolia. Later Frank claimed that he had deliberately opened the windows of the house in order to compel the "believers" to show themselves publicly instead of concealing their actions as they had done for decades. Frank's followers were imprisoned but he himself went scot-free because the local authorities believed him to be a Turkish citizen. At the request of the rabbis an inquiry was instituted at the rabbinical court in Satanow, the seat of the Podolia district rabbinate, which examined the practices and principles of the Shabbateans. Frank crossed the Turkish frontier; returning once more to his followers, he was arrested in March 1756 in Kopyczynce (Kopichintsy) but was again allowed to go free. After this he remained for almost three years in Turkey, first in Khotin on the Dniester, and afterward mainly in Giorgievo on the Danube. There, early in 1757, he became officially a convert to Islam, and was greatly honored for this by the Turkish authorities. In June and August 1757 he made secret visits to Rohatyn, in Podolia, in order to confer with his followers. During this period, he went to Salonika a number of times, and also paid one visit to Constantinople.

When Frank appeared in Poland he became the central figure for the vast majority of the Shabbateans, particularly those in Galicia, the Ukraine, and Hungary. It would appear that most of the Moravian Shabbateans also acknowledged his leadership. The inquiry of the rabbinical court in Satanow had to a large extent uncovered the Shabbatean network of Baruchiah's followers, which had existed underground in Podolia. A considerable portion of the Satanow findings was published by Jacob Emden. From this it is clear that the suspicions concerning the antinomian character of the sect were justified, and that "the believers," who conformed outwardly to Jewish legal precepts, did in fact transgress them, including the sexual prohibitions of the Torah, with the stated intention of upholding the higher form of the Torah, which they called *Torah de-aẓilut* ("the Torah of emanation"), meaning the spiritual Torah in contradistinction to the actual Torah of the *halakhah,* which was called the *Torah de-beri'ah* ("the Torah of creation"). The results of the inquiry were laid before a rabbinical assembly at Brody in June 1756, and confirmed at a session of the Council of the Four Lands held in Konstantynow in September. In Brody a *ḥerem* ("excommunication") was proclaimed against the members of the sect, which laid them open to persecution and also sought to restrict study of the Zohar and Kabbalah before a certain age (40 years in the case of Isaac Luria's writings).

When printed and dispatched throughout the communities, the *ḥerem* provoked a wave of persecution against the members of the sect, particularly in Podolia. The Polish rabbis turned to Jacob Emden, well-known as a fierce antagonist of the Shabbateans, who advised them to seek help from the Catholic ecclesiastical authorities, his argument being that the Shabbatean faith, as a mixture of the principles of all the other religions, constituted a new religion, and as such was forbidden by canon law. However, the results of his advice were the opposite of what had been intended, as Frank's followers, who had been severely harassed, adopted the strategy of putting themselves under the protection of Bishop Dembowski of Kamieniec-Podolski, in whose diocese many of the Shabbatean communities were concentrated. If before they had acted in a two-faced manner with regard to Judaism, appearing to be outwardly Orthodox while being secretly heretical, they now decided, apparently on Frank's advice, to emphasize and even exaggerate what beliefs they held in common with the basic principles of Christianity, in order to curry favor with the Catholic priesthood, although in fact their secret Shabbatean faith had not changed at all. Proclaiming themselves "contra-talmudists," they sought the protection of the Church from their persecutors, who, they claimed, had been angered precisely because of the sympathy shown by "the believers" toward some of the important tenets of Christianity. This extremely successful maneuver enabled them to find refuge with the ecclesiastical authorities, who saw in them potential candidates for mass conversion from Judaism to Christianity. In the meantime, however, members of the sect were constantly being impelled against their will by their protectors to assist in the preparation of anti-Jewish propaganda, and to formulate declarations which were intended to wreak destruction upon Polish Jewry. These developments strengthened mutual hostility and had dire consequences. Throughout these events Frank took great care not to draw attention to himself, except to appear as a spiritual guide showing his followers the way, as it were, to draw nearer to Christianity. It should be noted that the name "Frankists" was not used at this time, becoming current only in the early 19th century. As far as the mass of Jews and rabbis were concerned there was no difference at all between the earlier Shabbateans and the Shabbateans in this new guise, and they continued to call them "the sect of Shabbetai Ẓevi." Even Frank's followers, when talking to one another, continued to refer to themselves by the usual term *ma'aminim* ("believers").

Disputations. In the events that followed, it is difficult to differentiate precisely between the steps taken by Frank's adherents and those that were initiated by the Church and resulted from ecclesiastical coercion, although there is no doubt that M. Balaban (see bibliography) is right in laying greater stress on the latter. Shortly after the *ḥerem* at Brody the Frankists asked Bishop Dembowski to hold a new inquiry into the Lanskroun affair, and they petitioned for a public disputation between themselves and the rabbis. On Aug. 2, 1756 they presented nine principles of their faith for debate. Formulated in a most ambiguous fashion, their declaration of faith asserted in brief: (1) belief in the Torah of Moses; (2) that the Torah and the Prophets were obscure books, which had to be interpreted with the aid of God's light from above, and not simply by the light of human intelligence; (3) that the interpretation of the Torah to be found in the Talmud contained nonsense and falsehood, hostile to the Torah of the Lord; (4) belief that God is one and that all the worlds were created by Him; (5) belief in the trinity of the three equal "faces" within the one God, without there being any division within Him; (6) that God manifested Himself in corporeal form, like other human beings, but without sin; (7) that Jerusalem would not be rebuilt until the end of time; (8) that Jews waited in vain for the Messiah to come and raise them above the whole world; and (9) that, instead, God would Himself be clothed in human form and atone for all the sins for which the world had been cursed, and that at His coming the world would be pardoned and cleansed of all iniquity. These principles reflect the belief of the antinomian followers of Baruchiah, but they were formulated in such a way that they seemed to refer to Jesus of Nazareth instead of to Shabbetai Ẓevi and Baruchiah. They constitute a blatant plan to deceive the Church which the priests did not understand, and which, quite naturally, they were not interested in understanding.

The rabbis managed to avoid accepting the invitation to the disputation for nearly a year. However, after great pressure from the bishop, the disputation finally took place at Kamieniec, from June 20 to 28, 1757. Nineteen opponents of the Talmud (then called Zoharites) took part, together with a handful of rabbis from communities in the area. The spokesmen for the Shabbateans were also learned men, some of them being officiating rabbis who had secret Shabbatean tendencies. The arguments in the accusations and the defense of the rabbis were presented in writing, and were later published in a Latin protocol in Lvov in 1758. On Oct. 17, 1517, Bishop Dembowski issued his decision in favor of the Frankists, imposing a number of penalties upon the rabbis, chief of which was a condemnation of the Talmud as worthless and corrupt, with an order that it be burned in the city square. All Jewish homes were to be searched for copies of the Talmud. According to some contemporary accounts many cartloads of editions of the Talmud were in fact burned in Kamieniec, Lvov, Brody, Zolkiew, and other places. The "burning of the Torah" had a crushing effect on the Jewish community and the rabbis declared a fast in memory of the event. Jews who had influence with the authorities tried to stop the burnings, which took place mainly in November 1757.

A sudden reversal of fortune, in favor of the "talmudists" and to the detriment of the sectarians, resulted from the sudden death of Bishop Dembowski on November 9, at the very time of the burnings. News of the event,

Jacob Frank, pseudo-messiah and founder of the Frankist sect.

in which Jews saw the finger of God, spread like wildfire. Persecutions of the sect were renewed with even greater vehemence, and many of them fled across the Dniester to Turkey. There several converted to Islam, and one group even joined the Doenmeh in Salonika, where they were known as "the Poles." Meanwhile the spokesmen for the "contra-talmudists" turned to the political and ecclesiastical authorities and sought the implementation of the privilege which had been promised them by Dembowski, who allowed them to follow their own faith. They also sought the return of their looted property and permission for the refugees to come back to their homes. After some internal disagreements among the Polish authorities, King Augustus III issued a privilege on June 16, 1758, which accorded the sectarians royal protection as men "who were near to the [Christian] acknowledgment of God." Most of the refugees returned to Podolia at the end of September, and gathered mainly in and around the small town of Iwanie (near Khotin). In December, or the beginning of January 1759, Frank himself also left Turkey and arrived in Iwanie. Many of "the believers" scattered throughout eastern Galicia were summoned there.

Iwanie. In fact, the Frankists constituted themselves as a special sect with a distinctive character only during those months when "the believers" lived in Iwanie, an episode which became engraved on their memory as a quasi-revelatory event. Here it was that Frank finally revealed himself as the living embodiment of God's power who had come to complete the mission of Shabbetai Ẓevi and Baruchiah, and as "the true Jacob," comparing himself to the patriarch Jacob who had completed the work of his predecessors Abraham and Isaac. It was here that he unfolded his teaching before his followers in short statements and parables, and introduced a specific order into the ritual of the sect. There is no doubt that it was here that he prepared them to face the necessity of adopting Christianity outwardly, in order to keep their true faith in secret, just as the Doenmeh had done with regard to Islam. He declared that all religions were only stages through which "the believers" had to pass – like a man putting on different suits of clothes – and then to discard as of no worth compared with the true hidden faith. Frank's originality at this time consisted in his brazen rejection of the Shabbatean theology which was well-known to "the believers" from the writings of Nathan of Gaza and from the writings which were based on the extreme Shabbatean Kabbalah in Baruchiah's version. He asked them to forget all this, proposing in its place a kind of mythology freed from all traces of kabbalistic terminology, although in fact it was no more than a popular and homiletical reworking of kabbalistic teaching. In place of the customary Shabbatean trinity of the "three knots of faith," i.e., *Attika Kaddisha, Malka Kaddisha,* and the *Shekhinah,* which are all united in the Divinity, Frank went so far as to say that the true and good God was hidden and divested of any link with creation, and particularly with this insignificant world. It is He who conceals Himself behind "the King of Kings," whom Frank also calls "the Big Brother" or "He who stands before God." He is the God of true faith whom one must strive to approach and, in doing so, break the domination of the three "leaders of the world," who rule the earth at this moment, imposing upon it an unfitting system of law. The position of "the Great Brother" is connected in some way with the *Shekhinah,* which becomes in Frank's terminology the "maiden" *(almah)* or "virgin" *(betulah).* It is obvious that he tried consciously to make this concept conform as closely as possible to the Christian concept of the virgin. Just as the extreme Shabbateans from the sect of Baruchiah saw in Shabbetai Ẓevi and Baruchiah an incarnation of *Malka Kaddisha,* who is the "God of Israel," so Frank referred to himself as the messenger of "the Great Brother." According to him, all the great religious leaders, from the patriarchs to Shabbetai Ẓevi and Baruchiah, had endeavored to find the way to his God, but had not succeeded.

In order that God and the virgin be revealed, it would be necessary to embark upon a completely new road, untrodden as yet by the people of Israel: this road Frank called "the way to Esau." In this context, Esau or Edom symbolizes the unbridled flow of life which liberates man because its force and power are not subject to any law. The patriarch Jacob promised (Gen. 33:14) to visit his brother Esau in Seir, but Scripture does not mention that he fulfilled his promise, because the way was too difficult for him. Now the time had come to set out on this way, which leads to the "true life," a central idea which in Frank's system carries with it the specific connotation of freedom and licentiouness. This path was the road to consistent religious anarchy: "The place to which we are going is not subject to any law, because all that is on the side of death; but we are going to life." In order to achieve this goal it was necessary to abolish and destroy the laws, teachings, and practices which constrict the power of life, but this must be done in secret; in order to accomplish it, it was essential outwardly to assume the garb of the corporeal Edom, i.e., Christianity. The "believers," or at least their vanguard, had already passed through Judaism and Islam, and they now had to complete their journey by assuming the Christian faith, using it and its ideas in order to conceal the real core of their belief in Frank as the true Messiah and the living God for whom their Christian protestations were really intended.

The motto which Frank adopted here was *massa dumah* (from Isa. 21:11), taken to mean "the burden of silence"; that is, it was necessary to bear the heavy burden of the hidden faith in the abolition of all law in utter silence, and it was forbidden to reveal anything to those outside the fold. Jesus of Nazareth was no more than the husk preceding and concealing the fruit, who was Frank himself. Although it was necessary to ensure an outward demonstration of Christian allegiance, it was forbidden to mix with Christians or to intermarry with them, for in the final analysis Frank's vision was of a Jewish future, albeit in a rebellious and revolutionary form, presented here as a messianic dream.

The concepts employed by Frank were popular and anecdotal, and the rejection of the traditional kabbalistic symbolic terminology, which was beyond the comprehension of simple people, called into play the imaginative faculty. Frank therefore prepared his followers in Iwanie to accept baptism as the final step which would open before them, in a real physical sense, the way to Esau, to the world of the gentiles. Even in the organization of his sect Frank imitated the evangelical tradition: he appointed in Iwanie twelve emissaries (apostles) or "brothers," who were considered his chief disciples. But at the same time he appointed twelve "sisters," whose main distinction was to serve as Frank's concubines. Continuing the tradition of Baruchiah's sect, Frank also instituted licentious sexual practices among the "believers," at least among his more intimate "brothers" and "sisters." His followers who had been used to acting in this way did not see anything blameworthy in it, but they did not take kindly to his request that they eradicate from their midst all kabbalistic books, which had been superseded by Frank's teaching, and many of them continued to use ideas from Shabbatean Kabbalah, mixing them up in their writings with Frank's new symbols.

The group remained in Iwanie for several months until the spring of 1759. Frank established there a common fund, apparently in emulation of the New Testament account of the early Christian community. During this time, when they came into close contact with Frank, people were overcome and dominated by his powerful personality, which was compounded of limitless ambition and cunning, together with a facility of expression and marked imaginative faculty which even had a tinge of poetry. Perhaps it can be said of Frank that he was a mixture of despotic ruler, popular prophet, and cunning impostor.

The Disputation in Lvov. As events unfolded, an intermingling of two tendencies became manifest. On the one hand, it became clear to Frank and his disciples that they could not remain halfway between Judaism and Christianity. If they wished to restore their position after the severe persecutions they had suffered, baptism was the only course left open to them. They were even prepared to make a public demonstration of their conversion to Christianity, as the priests required as the price for their protection. On the other hand, there were quite different but parallel interests among important sections of the Church in Poland who originally did not associate themselves with the Frankist cause.

At this time there were several instances of the blood libel in Poland, which were supported by some influential bishops and leading clergy. The Council of the Four Lands, Polish Jewry's supreme organized authority, was trying to act indirectly through different mediators with the ecclesiastical authorities in Rome, laying grave charges of deceit and insolence against those responsible for the promulgation of the blood libel. Their words did not go unheeded in Rome. It would appear that some priests in the bishoprics of Kamieniec and Lvov saw a good chance of strengthening their positon with regard to the question of the blood libel, if Jews who represented a whole group could be found to come forward and verify this unfounded accusation. At the end of February 1759, when their position at Iwanie was at its peak, Frank's disciples requested Archbishop Lubieński in Lvov to receive them into the Church, claiming to speak in the name of "the Jews of Poland, Hungary, Turkey, Moldavia, Italy, etc." They asked to be given a second opportunity to dispute publicly with the rabbinic Jews, devotees of the Talmud, and promised to demonstrate the truth not only of the tenets of Christianity but also of the blood libel. Without doubt, the text of this request was composed after consultation with priestly circles and was formulated by the Polish nobleman Moliwda (Ignacy Kossakowski, who had once been head of the Philippovian sect), who was Frank's adviser in all these negotiations, right up to the actual baptism. Lubieński himself was not able to deal with the affair, since he was appointed archbishop of Gniezno and primate of the Polish Church. He handed over the conduct of the case to his administrator in Lvov, Mikulski, a priest who became extremely active in the preparation of the great disputation in Lvov, which was planned to end in mass baptism and verification of the blood libel.

In the months that followed, the Frankists continued to send various petitions to the king of Poland and to the ecclesiastical authorities in order to clarify their intentions, and to ask for specific favors even after their conversion. They claimed that 5,000 of their adherents were prepared to accept baptism, but at the same time requested that they be allowed to lead a separate existence as Christians of Jewish identity: they should not be compelled to shave their "sideburns" *(pe'ot);* they should be allowed to wear traditional Jewish garb even after conversion, and to call themselves by Jewish names in addition to their new Christian names; they should not be forced to eat pork; they should be allowed to rest on Saturday as well as on Sunday; and they should be permitted to retain the books of the Zohar and other kabbalistic writings. In addition to all this, they should be allowed to marry only among themselves and not with anyone else. In return for being allowed to constitute this quasi-Jewish unit, they expressed their willingness to submit to the other demands of the Church. In other petitions they added the request that they should be assigned a special area of settlement in Eastern Galicia, including the cities of Busk and Glinyany, most of whose Jewish inhabitants, they claimed, were members of the sect. In this territory they promised to maintain the life of their own community, and to establish their own communal life, setting up a "productivization" into the economic structure of the usual Jewish community. Some of these petitions, printed by the priests in Lvov in 1795, circulated very widely and were translated from Polish into French, Spanish, Latin, and Portuguese; they were also reprinted in Spain and Mexico and went through several editions there. The very presentation of these requests proves that Frank's followers had no thought of assimilating or of mixing with true Christians, but sought to gain for themselves a special recognized position, like that of the Doenmeh in Salonika, under the protection of both Church and State. It is obvious that they looked upon themselves as a new type of Jew and had no intention of renouncing their national Jewish identity. These petitions also show that the more extreme pronouncements of Frank within the closed circle of his followers had not wholly taken root in their hearts and they were not prepared to follow him in every detail. The prohibition against intermarriage with gentiles reiterates Frank's own words in Iwanie, yet on other matters there was apparently lively dispute between Frank and his followers. However, these isolated requests constituted only a transitional stage in the struggle which preceded the disputation in Lvov; and the spokesmen of the sect received a negative reply. The requirement of the Church was baptism without any precondition, although at this time the priests were convinced that the Frankists' intention was sincere, since they paid no heed to Jewish representatives who warned them continually about the secret Shabbatean beliefs of those who were offering themselves for baptism. The enormous publicity given to these events after the disputation at Kamieniec stimulated missionary activity on the part of some Protestant groups. Count Zinzendorf, head of "the Fellowship of the Brethren" (later the Moravian Church) in Germany, sent the convert David Kirchhof in 1758 on a special mission to "the believers" in Podolia in order to preach to them his version of "pure Christianity" (*Judaica,* 19 (1963), 140). Among the mass of Jews, the idea spread that Frank was in reality a great sorcerer with far-reaching demonic powers, prompting the growth of various legends, which had wide repercussions, concerning his magic deeds and his success.

The Frankists tried to postpone the disputation until January 1760, when many of the nobility and merchants would gather for religious ceremonies and for the great fair at Lvov. Apparently they hoped for considerable financial help because their economic situation had suffered as a result of persecution. The authorities in Rome and Warsaw did not regard the proposed disputation favorably and, for reasons of their own, sided with the Jewish arguments against a disputation, especially one which was likely to provoke disturbances and unrest as a result of the section on the blood libel. The raising of this subject, with all the inherent risk of organized and unbridled incitement against rabbinic Judaism, was equally sure to plunge the Polish Jewish authorites into profound anxiety. In this conflict of interests between the higher authorities, who wanted the straightforward conversion of Frank's followers without any disputation, and those groups who were concerned mainly with the success of the blood libel, Mikulski acted according to his own views and sided with the latter. He therefore fixed an early date for the disputation, July 16, 1759, to be held in Lvov Cathedral, and he obliged the rabbis of his diocese to attend.

The disputation opened on July 17, attended by crowds of Poles, and was conducted intermittently at several sessions until September 10. The arguments of both sides, the theses of the "contra-talmudists" and the answers of the rabbis, were presented in writing, but in addition vehement oral disputes took place. About 30 men appeared for the rabbis, and 10–20 for the sectarians. However, the number of the actual participants was smaller. The chief spokesman, and the man who bore the main responsibility on the Jewish side, was R. Ḥayyim Kohen Rapoport, the leading rabbi of Lvov, a highly respected man of great spiritual stature. Supporting him were the rabbis of Bohorodczany and

Stanislawow. The tradition which sprang up in popular accounts circulating years later that Israel b. Eliezer Ba'al Shem Tov, the founder of Ḥasidism, was also a participant, has no historical foundation. Frank himself took part only in the last session of the disputation when the blood libel question was debated. The sect's spokesmen were three scholars who had previously been active in Podolia among the followers of Baruchiah: Leib b. Nathan Krisa from Madvornaya, R. Naḥman from Krzywcze, and Solomon b. Elisha Shor from Rohatyn. After each session, consultations took place between the rabbis and the *parnasim,* who drafted written replies. They were joined by a wine merchant from Lvov, Baer Birkenthal of Bolechov, who, unlike the rabbis, spoke fluent Polish, and he prepared the Polish text of their replies. His memoirs of this disputation in *Sefer Divrei Binah* fill in the background of the official protocol which was drawn up in Polish by the priest Gaudenty Pilulski, and printed in Lvov in 1760 with the title *Ztość Zydowska* ("The Jewish Wrath"). In Lvov the Frankists' arguments were presented in a form accommodated as far as possible to the tenets of Christianity, to an even greater extent than at the earlier disputation. However, even then, they avoided any explicit reference to Jesus of Nazareth, and there is no doubt that this silence served the express purpose of harmonizing their secret faith in Frank as God and Messiah in a corporeal form with their official support of Christianity. Indeed, according to Frank himself, Christianity was no more than a screen *(pargod)* behind which lay hidden the true faith, which he proclaimed to be "the sacred religion of Edom."

Seven main propositions were disputed: (1) all the biblical prophecies concerning the coming of the Messiah have already been fulfilled; (2) the Messiah is the true God who became incarnate in human form in order to suffer for the sake of our redemption; (3) since the advent of the true Messiah, the sacrifices and the ceremonial laws of the Torah have been abolished; (4) everyone must follow the religion of the Messiah and his teaching, for within it lies the salvation of the soul: (5) the cross is the sign of the divine trinity and the seal of the Messiah; (6) only through baptism can a man arrive a true faith in the Messiah; and (7) the Talmud teaches that the Jews need Christian blood, and whoever believes in the Talmud is bound to use it.

The rabbis refused to reply to some of these theses for fear of being offensive to the Christian faith in their answers. The disputation began at the behest of the Frankists with a statement by their protector Moliwda Kossadowski. The rabbis replied only to the first and second of the theological arguments. It was obvious from the outset that the main attention would be centered on the seventh proposition, whose effects were potentially highly dangerous for the whole of Jewry. This particular argument came up for discussion on August 27. In the preceding weeks Frank had left Iwanie and passed through the cities of Galicia, visiting his followers. He then waited a long time in Busk, near Lvov, where he was joined by his wife and children. The Frankist arguments in support of the blood libel are a mixture of quotations from books by earlier Polish apostates, and absurd arguments and nonsensical discussions based on statements in rabbinic literature containing only the slightest mention of "blood" or "red." According to Baer Birkenthal the rabbis too did not refrain from using literary stratagems in order to strengthen the impression that their replies would have on the Catholic priests, and in the oral debates they rejected all Polish translations from talmudic and rabbinic literature without exception, which resulted in some violent verbal exchanges. Behind the scenes of the disputation, contacts continued between the rabbinic representatives and Mikulski, who began to waver, both because of the opposition of the higher church authorities to the blood libel and also as a result of rabbinic arguments concerning Frankist duplicity. The debate on this point was continued in the last session on September 10, when Rabbi Rapoport made a stringent attack on the blood libel. As the disputation came to an end, one of the Frankists approached the rabbi and said: "You have declared our blood permitted – this is your 'blood for blood.' " The confused ratiocinations of the Frankists did not achieve the desired effect, and, in the end, Mikulski resolved to ask the rabbis for a detailed written answer in Polish to the Frankists' charges. However, the time for their reply was postponed until after the end of the disputation. In the meantime nothing concrete emerged from all the upheaval about the blood libel.

On the other hand, the conversion of many of the Frankists did actually take place. Frank himself was received with extraordinary honor in Lvov, and he dispatched his flock to the baptismal font. He himself was the first to be baptized on Sept. 17, 1759. There is some disagreement about the number of sectarians who were converted. In Lvov alone more than 500 Frankists (including women and children) had been baptized by the end of 1760, nearly all of them from Podolia but some from Hungary and the European provinces of Turkey. The exact numbers of converts in other places are not known, but there are details of a considerable number of baptisms in Warsaw, where Frank and his wife were baptized a second time, under the patronage of the king of Poland, in a royal ceremony, on Nov. 18, 1759; from then on he is named Josef Frank in documents. According to oral tradition in Frankists families in Poland, the number of converts was far greater than that attested by known documents, and it speaks of several thousands. On the other hand, it is known that most of the sectarians in Podolia, and in other countries, did not follow Frank all the way, but remained in the Jewish fold, although they still recognized his leadership. It would appear that all his followers in Bohemia and Moravia, and most of those in Hungary and Rumania, remained Jews and continued to lead a double life, outwardly Jews and secretly "believers". Even in Galicia there remained many cells of "believers" in an appreciable number of communities, from Podhajce (Podgaytsy) in the east to Cracow in the west.

The Social Structure of the Sect. Contradictory evidence exists concerning the social and spiritual makeup of the sectarians, both of the apostates and of those who remained within the Jewish fold, but perhaps the two types of evidence are really complementary. Many sources, particularly from the Jewish side, show that a sizeable proportion of them were knowledgeable and literate, and even rabbis of small communities. Frank's closest associates among the apostates were doubtless in this category. As far as their social status was concerned, some were wealthy and owners of property, merchants and craftsmen such as silver- and goldsmiths; some were the children of community leaders. On the other hand, a considerable number of them were distillers and innkeepers, simple people and members of the poorer classes. In Moravia and Bohemia they included a number of wealthy and aristocratic families, important merchants and state monopoly leaseholders, while in the responsa of contemporary rabbis (and also in the ḥasidic *Shivḥei ha-Besht*) incidents are related concerning scribes and *shoḥatim* who were also members of the sect. In Sziget, Hungary, a "judge of the Jews" *(Judenrichter)* is numbered among them, as well as several important members of the community.

The uncovering of the sect, which had hitherto operated in secret, and the mass apostasy which had taken place in several of the Polish communities, received wide publicity and had various repercussions. The attitude of the Jewish spiritual leaders was not uniform, many rabbis taking the view that their separation from the Jewish community and their defection to Christianity were in fact desirable for the good of the Jewish people as a whole (A. Yaari in *Sinai*, 35 (1954), 170–82). They hoped that all the members of the sect would leave the Jewish fold, but their hopes were not realized. A different view was expressed by Israel Ba'al Shem Tov after the disputation at Lvov, namely, that "the *Shekhinah* bewails the sect of the apostates, for while the limb is joined to the body there is hope of a cure, but once the limb is amputated, there can be no possible remedy, for every Jew is a limb of the *Shekhinah.*" Naḥman of Bratslav, a great-grandson of the Ba'al Shem Tov, said that his great-grandfather died of the grief inflicted by the sect and their apostasy. In many Polish communities traditions were preserved concerning Frankist families who had not apostasized, while those who were particular about family honor took care not to marry into these families because of the suspicion of illegitimacy which attached to them through their transgression of the sexual prohibitions.

Frank's Arrest. Frank's journey to Warsaw in great pomp in October 1759 provoked a number of scandalous incidents, particularly in Lublin. Even after their apostasy Frank's followers were continually watched by the priests who had doubts about their reliability and the sincerity of their conversion. Records vary of the evidence given to the ecclesiastical authorities of their real faith, and it is possible that these did in fact emanate from different sources. It was G. Pikulski in particular who in December 1759 obtained separate confessions from six of the "brethren" who had remained in Lvov, and it became apparent from these that the real object of their devotion was Frank, as the living incarnation of God. When this information reached Warsaw, Frank was arrested, on Feb. 6, 1760, and for three weeks he was subjected to a detailed investigation by the ecclesiastical court, which also confronted him with many of the "believers" who had accompanied him to Warsaw. Frank's testimony before the inquiry was a mixture of lies and half-truths. The court's decision was to exile him for an unlimited period to the fortress of Czestochowa which was under the jurisdiction of the Church, "in order to prevent him having any possible influence on the views of his followers." These latter were set free and ordered to adopt Christianity in true faith, and to forsake their leader – a result which was not achieved. Nevertheless, the "treachery" of his followers in revealing their true beliefs rankled bitterly with Frank until the end of his days. The court also issued a printed proclamation on the results of the inquiry. At the end of February, Frank was exiled and remained in "honorable" captivity for 13 years. At first he was utterly deserted, but he quickly found ways of reestablishing contact between himself and his "camp". At this time the apostates were scattered in several small towns and on estates owned by the nobility. They suffered a good deal until they finally settled down, mainly in Warsaw, with the remainder in other Polish towns like Cracow and Krasnystaw, and organized themselves into a secret sectarian society, whose members were careful to observe outwardly all the tenets of the Catholic faith. They also took advantage of the unstable political situation in Poland at the end of its independence, and several of the more important families demanded noble status for themselves, with some degree of success, on the basis of old statutes which accorded such privileges to Jewish converts.

Frank in Czestochowa. From the end of 1760 emissaries from the "believers" began to visit Frank and transmit his instructions. Following these, they became once more involved in a blood libel case in the town of Wojslawiec in 1761, as the result of which many Jews were slaughtered. Their reappearance as accusers of the Jewish people aroused great bitterness among the Jews of Poland, who saw in it a new act of vengeance. The conditions of Frank's imprisonment were gradually relaxed and from 1762 his wife was allowed to join him, while a whole group of his chief followers, both men and women, were allowed to settle near the fortress, and even to practice secret religious rites of a typical sexual orgiastic nature inside the fortress. When talking of this circle Frank added a specifically Christian interpretation to his view of the virgin as the *Shekhinah,* under the influence of the worship of the virgin which, in Poland, was actually centered in Czestochowa.

In 1765, when it was apparent that the country was about to break up, Frank planned to forge links with the Russian Orthodox Church and with the Russian government through the Russian ambassador in Poland, Prince Repnin. A Frankist delegation went to Smolensk and Moscow at the end of the year and promised to instigate some pro-Russian activity among the Jews, but the details are not known. It is possible that clandestine links between the Frankist camp and the Russian authorities date from this time. These plans became known to the Jews of Warsaw, and in 1767 a counterdelegation was sent to St. Petersburg in order to inform the Russians of the Frankists' true character. From then on, Frankist propaganda spread once more through the communities of Galicia, Hungary, Moravia, and Bohemia by means of letters and emissaries from among the learned members of the sect. Links were also formed with secret Shabbateans in Germany. One of these emissaries, Aaron Isaac Te'omim from Horodenka, appeared in Altona in 1764. In 1768–69 there were two Frankist agents in Prague and Prossnitz, the Shabbatean center in Moravia, and there they were even allowed to preach in the synagogue. At the beginning of 1770 Frank's wife died, and thenceforth the worship of "the lady" *(gevirah),* which was accorded her during her lifetime, was transferred to Frank's daughter Eva (previously Rachel), who stayed with him even when practically all of his "believers" had left the fortress and gone to Warsaw. When Czestochowa was captured by the Russians in August 1772, after the first partition of Poland, Frank was freed by the commander in chief and left the town early in 1773, going with his daughter to Warsaw. From there, in March 1773, he journeyed with 18 of his associates disguised as the servants of a wealthy merchant to Bruenn (Brno) in Moravia, to the home of his cousin Schoendel Dobruschka, the wife of a rich and influential Jew.

Frank in Bruenn and Offenbach. Frank remained in Bruenn until 1786, obtaining the protection of the authorities, both as a respected man of means with many connections and also as a man pledged to work for the propagation of Christianity among his numerous associates in the communities of Moravia.

He established a semi-military regime in his retinue, where the men wore military uniform and went through a set training. Frank's court attracted many Shabbateans in Moravia, whose families preserved for generations the swords that they wore while serving at his court. Frank went with his daughter to Vienna in March 1775 and was received in audience by the empress and her son, later Joseph II. Some maintain that Frank promised the empress the assistance of his followers in a campaign to conquer parts of Turkey, and in fact over a period of time several Frankist emissaries were sent to Turkey, working hand in glove with the Doenmeh, and perhaps as political agents or spies in the service of the Austrian government. During this period Frank spoke a great deal about a general revolution which would overthrow kingdoms, and the Catholic Church in particular, and he also dreamed of the conquest of some territory in the wars at the end of time which would be the Frankist dominion. For this, military training would be a deliberate preparation. Where Frank obtained the money for the upkeep of his court was a constant source of wonder and speculation and the matter was never resolved; doubtless some system of taxation was organized among the members of the sect. Stories circulated about the arrival of barrels of gold sent, some say, by his followers, but according to others, by his foreign political "employers". At one particular period there were in Bruenn several hundred sectarians who followed no profession or trade, and whose sole and absolute master was Frank, who ruled with a rod of iron. In 1784 his financial resources failed temporarily and he found himself in great straits, but his situation subsequently improved. During his stay in Bruenn the greater part of his teachings, his recollections, and his tales were taken down by his chief associates. In 1786 or 1787 he left Bruenn, and, after bargaining with the Prince of Ysenburg, established himself in Offenbach, near Frankfort.

In Bruenn and Offenbach, Frank and his three children played a part, which was unusually successful for a long time, in order to throw dust in the eyes of both the inhabitants and the authorities. While pretending to follow the practices of the Catholic Church, at the same time they put on a show of strange practices, deliberately "Eastern" in nature, in order to emphasize their exotic character. In his last years Frank began to spread even among his close associates the notion that his daughter Eva was in reality the illegitimate daughter of the empress Catherine of the house of Romanov, and that he was no more than her guardian. Outwardly, the Frankists shrank from social contact with Jews, so much so that many of those who had business or other dealings with the latter refused absolutely to believe Jewish charges concerning the true nature of the community as a secret Jewish sect. Even in the printed proclamations issued in Offenbach, Frank's children based their authority on their strong ties with the

Russian royal house. There is some reliable evidence to show that even the Prince of Ysenburg's administration believed that Eva should be regarded as Romanov princess.

The last center of the sect was set up in Offenbach, where members sent their sons and daughters to serve at the court, following the pattern that had been established in Bruenn. Frank had several apoplectic fits, dying on Dec. 10, 1791. His funeral was organized as a glorious demonstration by hundreds of his "believers". Frank had preserved to the end his double way of life and sustained the legendary Oriental atmosphere with which his life was imbued in the sight of both Jews and Christians.

In the period between Frank's apostasy and his death the converts strengthened their economic position, particularly in Warsaw where many of them built factories and were also active in masonic organizations. A group of about 50 Frankist families, led by Anton Czerniewski, one of Frank's chief disciples, settled in Bukovina after his death and were known there as the sect of Abrahamites; their descendants were still living a separate life there about 125 years later. Several families in Moravia and Bohemia, who had remained within the Jewish fold, also improved their social status, had close connections with the Haskalah movement, and began to combine revolutionary mystical kabbalistic ideas with the rationalistic view of the Enlightenment. Some of those who had converted in these countries under Frank's influence were accepted in the higher administration and the Austrian aristocracy, but they preserved a few Frankist traditions and customs, so that a stratum was created in which the boundaries between Judaism and Christianity became blurred, irrespective of whether the members had converted or retained their links with Judaism.

Only rarely did whole groups of Frankists convert to Christianity, as in Prossnitz in 1773, but a considerable proportion of the younger members who were sent to Offenbach were baptized there. Enlightening examples of family histories from the intermediate stratum mentioned above are those of the Hoenig and Dobruschka families in Austria. Some of the Hoenig family remained Frankist Jews even after their elevation to the nobility, and some of them were connected with the upper bourgeoisie and higher Austrian administration (the families of Von Hoenigsberg, Von Hoenigstein, Von Bienefeld), while members of the Dobruschka family converted practically en bloc and several of them served as officers in the army. Moses, the son of Schoendel Dobruschka, Frank's cousin, who was known in many circles as his nephew, was the outstanding figure in the last generation of the Frankists, being known also as Franz Thomas von Schoenfeld (a German writer and organizer of a mystical order of a Jewish Christian kabbalistic character, the "Asiatic Brethren"), and later as Junius Frey (a Jacobin revolutionary in France). Apparently he was offered the leadership of the sect after Frank's death, and, when he refused, Eva, together with her two younger brothers, Josef and Rochus, assumed responsibility for the direction of the court. Many people continued to go up to Offenbach, to *"Gottes Haus"* as the "believers" called it. However, Frank's daughter and her brothers had neither the stature nor the strength of personality required, and their fortunes quickly declined. The only independent activity that emerged from Offenbach was the dispatch of the "Red Letters" to hundreds of Jewish communities in Europe in 1799 relating to the beginning of the 19th century. In these letters the Jews were requested for the last time to enter "The holy religion of Edom." By 1803 Offenbach was almost completely deserted by the camp of the "believers," hundreds of whom had returned to Poland, while Frank's children were reduced to poverty. Josef and Rochus died in 1807 and 1813 respectively, without heirs, and Eva Frank died in 1816, leaving enormous debts. In Eva's last years a few members of the most respected families in the sect, who were supported from Warsaw, remained with her. In the last 15 years of her life she acted as if she were a royal princess of the house of Romanov, and several circles tended to believe the stories circulating in support of this.

The sect's exclusive organization continued to survive in this period through agents who went from place to place, through secret gatherings and separate religious rites, and through the dissemination of a specifically Frankist literature. The "believers" endeavored to marry only among themselves, and a wide network of inter-family relationships was created among the Frankists, even among those who had remained within the Jewish fold. Later Frankism was to a large extent the religion of families who had given their children the appropriate education. The Frankists of Germany, Bohemia, and Moravia usually held secret gatherings in Carlsbad in summer round about the Ninth of Av.

Frankist Literature. The literary activity of the sect began at the end of Frank's life, and was centered at first at Offenbach in the hands of three learned "elders", who were among his chief disciples: the two brother Franciszek and Michael Wolowski (from the well-known rabbinic family Shor) and Andreas Dembowski (Yeruham Lippmann from Czernowitz). At the end of the 18th century they compiled a collection of Frank's teachings and reminiscences, containing nearly 2,300 sayings and stories, gathered together in the book *Slowa Pańskie* ("The words of the Master"; Heb. *Divrei ha-Adon*), which was sent to circles of believers. The book was apparently composed originally in Hebrew since it was quoted in this language by the Frankists of Prague. In order to meet the needs of the converts in Poland, whose children no longer learned Hebrew, it was translated, apparently in Offenbach, into very poor Polish which needed later revisions to give it a more polished style. This comprehensive book illuminates Frank's true spiritual world, as well as his relationship with Judaism, Christianity, and the members of his sect. A few complete manuscripts were preserved in a number of families in Poland, and some were acquired by public libraries and consulted by the historians Kraushar and Balaban. These manuscripts were destroyed or lost during the Holocaust, and now only two imperfect manuscripts in Cracow University Library are known, comprising about two-thirds of the complete text. Also in Offenbach, a detailed chronicle was compiled of events in the life of Frank, which gave far more reliable information than all other documents, in which Frank did not refrain from telling lies. It also contained a detailed and undisguised description of the sexual rites practiced by Frank. This manuscript was lent to Kraushar by a Frankist family, but since then it has vanished without a trace. The work of an anonymous Frankist, written in Polish about 1800 and called "The Prophecy of Isaiah", which puts the metaphors of the biblical book to Frankist use, gives a reliable record of the revolutionary and utopian expectations of the members of the sect. This manuscript, parts of which were published in Kraushar's book, was in the library of the Warsaw Jewish community until the Holocaust. A book was recorded in Offenbach which listed the dreams and revelations of which Eva Frank and her brothers boasted, but when two younger members of the Porges family in Prague, who had been sent to the court and been disillusioned with what they saw, fled from Offenbach, they took the book with them and handed it over to the rabbinical court in Fuerth, who apparently destroyed it.

The Frankists in Prague. Another center of intensive literary activity emerged in Prague, where an important Frankist group had established itself. At its head were several members of the distinguished Wehle and Bondi families, whose forebears had belonged to the secret Shabbatean movement for some generations. They had strong connections with "the believers" in other communities in Bohemia and Moravia. Their spiritual leader, Jonas Wehle (1752–1823), was aided by his brothers, who were fervent Frankists, and his son-in-law Loew von Hoenigsberg (d. 1811), who committed to writing many of the teachings of the circle. This group acted with great prudence for a long time, particularly during the lifetime of R. Ezekiel Landau, and its members denied in his presence that they belonged to the sect. However, after his death they became more conspicuous. In 1799 R. Eleazar Fleckeles, Landau's successor, preached some fiercely polemical sermons against them, causing riotous disturbances in the Prague synagogue, and leading to the publication of libelous attacks on the group, as well as to both denunciations and defense of its members before the civil authorities. A great deal of evidence, extracted from "penitent" members of the sect in Kolin and other places, remains from this period. The important file on the Frankists in the Prague community archives was removed by the president of the community at the end of the 19th century, out of respect for the families implicated in it. The disturbances connected with the appearance of the "Red Letters" (written in red ink, as a symbol of the religion of Edom) helped to maintain a small, distinct Frankist group in Prague for years, and some of its members, or their children, were later among the founders of the first Reform temple in Prague (c. 1832). A similar distinct group existed for a long time in Prossnitz. Some of the literature of the Prague circle survived, namely, a commentary on the *aggadot* collected in the work *Ein Ya'akov* and a large collection of letters on details of the faith, as well as commentaries on various biblical passages written in German mixed with Yiddish and Hebrew by Loew Hoenigsberg in the early 19th century. Aaron Jellinek possessed various Frankist writings in German, but they disappeared after his death.

On Eva Frank's death the organization weakened, although in 1823 Elias Kaplinski, a member of Frank's wife's family, still tried to summon a conference of the sectarians, which took place in Carlsbad. After this the sect broke up, and messengers were sent to collect together the various writings from the scattered families. This deliberate concealment of Frankist literature is one of the main reasons for the ignorance concerning its internal history, allied to the decided reluctance of most of the sectarians' descendants to promote any investigation into their affairs. The only one of "the believers" who left any memoirs of his early days was Moses Porges (later Von Portheim). These he had recorded in his old age. A whole group of Frankist families from Bohemia and Moravia migrated to the United States in 1848–49. In his last will and testament, Gottlieb Wehle of New York, 1867, a nephew of Jonas Wehle, expresses a deep feeling of identity with his Frankist forebears, who appeared to him to be the first fighters for progress in the ghetto, a view held by many of the descendants of "the believers". The connection between the Frankists' heretical Kabbalah and the ideas of the new Enlightenment is evident both in surviving manuscripts from Prague, and in the traditions of some of these families in Bohemia and Moravia (where there were adherents of the sect, outside Prague, in places like Kolin, Horschitz (Horice), Holleschau (Holesov), and Kojetin).

There continued to be strong ties between the neophyte families in Poland, who had risen considerably in the social scale in the 19th century, and there may have been some kind of organization among them. In the first three generations after the apostasy of 1759/60 most of them married only among themselves, preserving their Jewish character in several ways, and only a very few intermarried with true Catholics. Copies of the "Words of the Master" were still being produced in the 1820s, and apparently it had its readers. The Frankists were active as fervent Polish patriots and took part in the rebellions of 1793, 1830, and 1863. Nevertheless the whole time they were under suspicion of Jewish sectarian separatism. In Warsaw in the 1830s most of the lawyers were descendants of the Frankists, many of whom were also businessmen, writers, and musicians. It was only in the middle of the 19th century that mixed marriages increased between them and the Poles, and later most of them moved from the liberal wing of Polish society to the nationalist conservative wing. However, there still remained a number of families who continued to marry only among themselves. For a long time this circle maintained secret contacts with the Doenmeh in Salonika. An unresolved controversy still exists concerning the Frankist affiliation of Adam Mickiewicz, the greatest Polish poet. There is clear evidence of this from the poet himself (on his mother's side), but in Poland this evidence is resolutely misinterpreted. Mickiewicz's Frankist origins were well-known to the Warsaw Jewish community as early as 1838 (according to evidence in the AZDJ of that year, p. 362). The parents of the poet's wife also came from Frankist families.

The crystallization of the Frankist sect is one of the most marked indications of the crisis which struck the Jewish society in the mid-18th century. Frank's personality reveals clear signs of the adventurer motivated by a blend of religious impulses and a lust for power. By contrast, his "believers" were on the whole men of deep faith and moral integrity as far as this did not conflict with the vicious demands made on them by Frank. In all that remains of their original literature whether in German, Polish or Hebrew, there is absolutely no reference to those matters, like the blood libel, which so aroused the Jewish community against them. They were fascinated by the words of their leader and his vision of a unique fusion between Judaism and Christianity, but they easily combined this with more modest hopes which led them to become protagonists of liberal-bourgeois ideals. Their nihilist Shabbatean faith served as a transition to a new world beyond the ghetto. They quickly forgot their licentious practices and acquired a reputation of being men of the highest moral conduct. Many Frankist families kept a miniature of Eva Frank which used to be sent to the most prominent households, and to this day some families honor her as a saintly woman who was falsely reviled.

Bibliography: J. Emden, *Sefer Shimmush* (Altona, 1762); idem, *Megillat Sefer* (1896); E. Fleckeles, *Ahavat David* (Prague, 1800); M. Balaban, *Le-Toledot ha-Tenu'ah ha-Frankit* (1934); idem, in: *Livre d'hommage à . . .S. Poznański* (1927), 25–75; N.M. Gelber, in: *Yivo Historishe Shriftn*, 1 (1929); idem, in: *Zion*, 2 (1937), 326–32; G. Scholem, *ibid.*, 35 (1920/21); idem, in: *Keneset*, 2 (1937), 347–92; idem, in: *Sefer Yovel le-Yitzhak Baer* (1960), 409–30; idem, in: RHR, 144 (1953–54), 42–77: idem, *The Messianic Idea in Judaism, and Other Essays* (1971); idem, in: *Zeugnisse T. W. Adorno zum Geburtstag* (1963),

20–32; idem, in: *Max Brod Gedenkbuch* (1969), 77–92; idem, in *Zion* 35 (1970), 127–81 (on Moses Dobruschka); idem, in: *Commentary,* 51 (Jan. 1971), 41–70; A. Yaari, in: *Sinai,* 35 (1954), 120–82; 42(1958), 294–306; A. J. Brawer, *Galizyah vi-Yhudeha* (1966), 197–275; P. Beer, *Geschichte der religioesen Sekten der Juden,* 2 (1923); H. Graetz, *Frank und die Frankisten* (1868); idem, in: MGWJ, 22, (1873); S. Back, *ibid.*, 26 (1877); A. G. Schenk-Rink, *Die Polen in Offenbach* (1866–69); A. Kraushar, *Frank i frankiści polscy* (1895); T. Jeske-Choinski, *Neofici polscy* (1904), 46–107; M. Wischnitzer, in: *Mémoires de l'Académie. . .de St. Pétersbourg,* series 8, Hist.-Phil. Section, 12 no. 3 (1914); F. Mauthner, *Lebenserinnerungen* (1918), 295–307; C. Seligman, in: *Frankfurter Israelitisches Gemeinde Blatt*, 10 (1932), 121–3, 150–2; M. Mieses, *Polacy-chrze Scijanie Pochdozenia zydowskiego. JQR 75th Anniversary Volume* (1967), 429–45; P. Arnsberg, *Von Podolien nach Offenbach* (1965); R. Kestenberg-Gladstein, *Neuere Geschichte der Juden in den boehmischen Laendern,* 1 (1969), 123–91; A. G. Duker, in: JSOS, 25 (1963), 287–333; idem, in: *Joshua Starr Memorial Volume* (1963), 191–201.

4

Ba'al Shem

Ba'al Shem (Heb. בַּעַל שֵׁם : "Master of the Divine Name"; lit. "Possessor of the Name"), was the title given in popular usage and in Jewish literature, especially kabbalistic and ḥasidic works, from the Middle Ages onward, to one who possessed the secret knowledge of the Tetragrammaton and the other "Holy Names," and who knew how to work miracles by the power of these names. The designation *ba'al shem* did not originate with the kabbalists, for it was already known to the last Babylonian *geonim.* In a responsum, Hai Gaon stated: "They testified that they saw a certain man, one of the well-known *ba'alei shem,* on the eve of the Sabbath in one place, and that at the same time he was seen in another place, several days' journey distant". It was in this sense that Judah Halevi criticized the activities of the *ba'alei shem* (*Kuzari,* 3:53). In medieval German ḥasidic tradition this title was accorded to several liturgical poets, e.g., Shephatiah and his son Amittai of southern Italy (in Abraham b. Azriel, *Arugat ha-Bosem,* 2 (1947), 181). The Spanish kabbalists used the expression *ba'alei sefirot,* the theoretical kabbalists, and the *ba'alei shemot,* the magicians, in their kabbalistic teachings. Isaac b. Jacob ha-Kohen, Todros ha-Levi Abulafia, and Moses de Leon all mentioned this tendency among kabbalists without disapproval, whereas Abraham Abulafia wrote disparingly of the *ba'alei shem.* From the end of the 13th century, the term *ba'al shem* was also used for writers of amulets based on Holy Names (*Ozar Neḥmad,* vol. 2, p. 133). There were large numbers of *Ba'alei shem,* particularly in Germany and Poland, from the 16th century onward. Some were important rabbis and talmudic scholars, such as Elijah Loans of Frankfort and Worms, Elijah Ba'al Shem of Chelm, and Sekel Isaac Loeb Wormser (the *ba'al shem* of Michelstadt). Others were scholars who devoted themselves entirely to the study of Kabbalah, such as Joel Ba'al Shem of Zamosc and Elhanan "Ba'al ha-Kabbalah" of Vienna (both 17th century), Benjamin Beinisch ha-Kohen of Krotoszyn (beginning of the 18th century), and Samuel Essingen. In the 17th and 18th centuries the number of *ba'alei shem* who were not at all talmudic scholars increased. But they attracted a following by their real or imaginary powers of healing the sick. Such a *ba'al shem* was often a combination of practical kabbalist, who performed his cures by means of prayers, amulets, and incantations, and a popular healer familiar with *segullot* ("remedies") concocted from animal, vegetable, and mineral matter. The literature of that period teems with stories and testimonies about *ba'alei shem* of this kind, some of which, however, were written in criticism of their characters and deeds. It was generally thought that the *ba'alei shem* were at their most efficacious in the treatment of mental disorders and in the exorcism of evil spirits. There is a variation to the title *ba'al shem,* known as *"ba'al shem tov".* The founder of modern Ḥasidism, Israel b. Eliezer Ba'al Shem Tov, usually referred to by the initials "BeShT", is the most famous and practically unique bearer of this title. The title *"ba'al shem tov"* existed before, but it did not designate a special quality or a distinction between bearers of this title and *ba'alei shem.* Examples are Elhanan Ba'al Shem Tov, who died in 1651; Benjamin Krotoschin, who so styled himself in his book *Shem Tov Katan* (Sulzbach, 1706); and Joel Ba'al Shem I, who actually signed himself *"BeShT"*, in common with the founder of Ḥasidism. In the 18th century, Samuel Jacob Ḥayyim Falk, the *"ba'al shem* of London," achieved considerable prominence. He was called "Doctor Falk" by Christians. The theory propounded by several scholars that these wandering *ba'alei shem* were responsible for spreading Shabbateanism has not been proved, although some of them were indeed members of the sect. Several books by these *ba'alei shem* have been published concerning practical Kabbalah, *segullot* ("remedies"), and *refu'ot* ("healing"). These include: *Toledot Adam* (1720) and *Mifalot Elohim* (1727), edited by Joel Ba'al Shem and based on the works of his grandfather Joel Ba'al Shem I, *Shem Tov Katan* (1706) and *Amtaḥat Binyamin* (1716). The deeds of the *ba'alei shem* became legendary. Fictitious characters of the same type were sometimes invented, such as Adam Ba'al Shem of Bingen, the hero of a series of miraculous stories in Yiddish which were printed as early as the 17th century. Ḥasidic legend subsequently created an imaginary connection between this character and Israel Ba'al Shem Tov. The leaders of the Haskalah generally regarded the *ba'alei shem* as charlatans and adventurers.

Bibliography: N. Prilutski, *Zamelbikher far Yidischen Folklor,* 2 (1917), 40–42; J. Guenzig, *Die "Wundermaenner" im juedischen Volke* (1921); B. Segel, in: *Globus,* 62(1892); H. Adler, in: JHSET, 5 (1908), 148–73; G. Scholem, in: *Zion,* 20(1955), 80; C. Roth, *Essays and Portraits in Anglo-Jewish History* (1962), 139–64.

5

Sefer Ha-Bahir

Sefer ha-Bahir (Heb. סֵפֶר הַבָּהִיר: "Book Bahir") is the earliest work of kabbalistic literature, i.e., the first book that adopts the specific approach and the symbolic structure characteristic of kabbalistic teaching.

Titles. Among the medieval Spanish kabbalists *Sefer ha-Bahir* was known by two names, each based on the opening sentences of the book: (1) *Midrash R. Neḥunya ben ha-Kanah* ("R. Neḥunya b. ha-Kanah said", which is the opening phrase of the first section); and (2) *Sefer ha-Bahir* based on the statement: "One verse says: 'And now men see not the light which is bright (*bahir*) in the skies'" (Job 37:21). Although the second title is the older, the first beame popular because of its use by Naḥmanides in his commentary on the Pentateuch. There is no internal evidence to support the kabbalists' attribution of the work to R. Neḥunya. The book is a Midrash in the strict literary connotation of the word: an anthology of various statements, most of them brief, attributed to different *tannaim* and *amoraim*. The main characters in the book are called "R. Amora" (or "Amorai"), and "R. Raḥmai" (or "Reḥumai"). The first name is fictitious, while the second appears to have been coined in imitation of the *amora*, Reḥumi. There are also statements attributed to R. Berechiah, R. Johanan, R. Bun, and others who are known from midrashic literature. However, only very few of these statements actually come from these sources, and all of them were attributed to rabbis mentioned in the later Midrashim, who were themselves accustomed to ascribe aggadic sayings to earlier rabbis (e.g., *Pirkei de-R. Eliezer, Otiyyot de-R. Akiva,* and similar works). There are also in *Sefer ha-Bahir* many paragraphs in which no names are mentioned at all.

Contents. Ideas and traditions on many subjects are transmitted in the form of explanations of biblical verses, short discussions between different speakers, or statements devoid of any scriptural support. In addition to familiar aggadic sayings (which are few in number), there are commentaries on the mystical significance of particular verses; on the shapes of several letters of the alphabet; on the vocalization and cantillation signs; on statements in the *Sefer Yeẓirah* (see

p. 23), and on sacred names and their use in magic. The interpretation of some verses contains explanations of the esoteric meanings of some of the commandments (e.g., *tefillin, ẓiẓit, terumot,* "sending forth of the dam" (see Deut. 22:6, 7) *lulav, etrog* and others). There is apparently no definite order in the book. Sometimes one can detect a certain train of thought in the arrangement of the various passages, but the thread is soon broken, and the sense often leaps inexplicably from one subject to another. Alternatively, statements are strung together because of some extraneous association, without any definite sequence of thought. All this gives *Sefer ha-Bahir* the appearance of a Midrash, or a collection of sayings taken from various sources. Nevertheless, it is possible to distinguish certain section which seem to have a literary unity. These are chiefly: (1) the string of statements which are based on the *Sefer Yeẓirah,* and which develop the contents of that book in a new vein; and (2) the orderly list which is given, although with frequent interruptions, of the ten *Sefirot* ("Divine Emanations"), called here the ten *ma'amarot* ("sayings"), by which the world was created.

Ideas. The book, as it has survived, confirms the tradition of the 13th-century kabbalists that *Sefer ha-Bahir* was handed down to them in extremely mutilated form, as remnants of scrolls, booklets, and traditions. It contains sections which break off in the middle of a sentence and are not connected at all with what follows. There are discussions which are begun and not completed. Additional material interrupting the sequence of the argument is found in greater proportion in those very sections which seem to have an inner consistency. In its present form the book is very short, containing about 12,000 words. The structure is extremely loose, the book being simply a collection of material brought together within a certain framework without any literary or editorial skill. The language of the book is a mixture of Hebrew and Aramaic. The style is frequently very difficult, and, even apart from the numerous errors in the printed editions, the book is hard to understand, and linguistically unclear. Nevertheless, it has in some parts a certain spiritual exaltation and even a beauty of description. There are numerous parables, sometimes embodying the very essence of an idea which cannot be expressed in any other form, or serving as replies to questions posed by speakers. Some of these sayings are mere adaptations of earlier talmudic and midrashic statements, but most have no parallel in these.

The prime importance of the *Bahir* lies in its use of symbolic language. It is the earliest source that deals with the realm of the divine attributes (*Sefirot; "logoi",* "beautiful vessels", "kings", "voices", and "crowns"), and that interprets Scripture as if it was concerned not with what happened in the created world, but also with events in the divine realm, and with the action of God's attributes. These attributes are for the first time given symbolic names, derived from the vocabulary of the interpreted verses. The principles on which the symbolism of the book is based are nowhere explained systematically, and the speakers use it as if it could be taken for granted. Only in the aforesaid list of the ten *ma'amarot* have I presented a few symbolic names, given to each *ma'amar* (logos).

The *Sefirot,* first mentioned in the *Sefer Yeẓirah* as corresponding to the ten basic numbers, became in *Sefer ha-Bahir* divine attributes, lights, and powers, each one of which fulfills a particular function in the work of creation. This divine realm, which can be described only in highly symbolic language, is the fundamental core of the book. Even the *ta'amei ha-miẓvot* (reasons for the *miẓvot*) are related to this supernal realm: the fulfillment of a certain commandment signifying the activity of a *Sefirah* or of a divine attribute (or the combined activity of several of them).

The *Bahir* adopts the view of the *Sefer Yeẓirah* that there are ten *Sefirot,* and it goes on to the general conclusion that each attribute of *Sefirah* is alluded to either in Scripture or in rabbinic writings by a very large number of names and symbols which give some idea of its nature. The descriptions of the domain of these attributes are sometimes couched only in allusive terms, which are often described in the pictorial style that gives to the book a striking mythological character. The divine powers constitute "the secret tree" from which the souls blossom forth. But these powers are also the sum of the "holy forms" which are joined together in the likeness of supernal man. Everything in the lower world, particularly everything that has sanctity, contains a reference to something in the world of the divine attributes. God is Master of all the powers, and His glorious, unique nature can be discerned in several places. Nevertheless, there is some doubt as to whether those who drew up the list of the ten *ma'amarot* distinguished Him from the first *Sefirah* (*Keter Elyon,* "the supreme crown"), or whether they considered the *Keter Elyon* itself to be God. The book emphasizes the concept of the "thought" of God in place of the "will" of God. The technical term *Ein-Sof* ("The Infinite") as an epithet for God does not yet appear in the book.

Place in Kabbalah. Generally speaking, *Sefer ha-Bahir* represents a stage in the development of the Kabbalah, displaying great variations in detail from the material usually found in later works. This also makes comprehension of the work more difficult. A great distance separates *Sefer ha-Bahir* from the Kabbalah of Isaac the Blind, to whom the book was attributed by some modern scholars. *Sefer ha-Bahir* is of the utmost importance as the only extant source for the state of the Kabbalah as it was when it came to the notice of a wider public, and for the early stages of its development prior to its dissemination beyond limited circles. There is a striking affinity between the symbolism of *Sefer ha-Behir*, on the one hand, and the speculations of the Gnostics and their theory of the "aeons", on the other. The fundamental problem in the study of the book is: is the affinity based on an as yet unknown historical link between the gnosticism of the mishnaic and talmudic era and the sources from which the material in *Sefer ha-Bahir* is derived? Or should it possibly be seen as a purely psychological phenomenon, i.e., as a spontaneous upsurge from the depths of the soul's imagination, without any historical continuity?

Sefer ha-Bahir appeared at the end of the 12th century in southern France, but the circumstances of its appearance are unknown. There are several reasons to support the theory that the book was actually compiled about this time. Some of the statements in the book show quite clearly the influence of the writings of Abraham b. Ḥiyya. Did the compilers have before them older manuscripts containing fragments, written in Hebrew, of a gnostic character, which inspired them to elaborate the new symbolic arrangement that appears in *Sefer ha-Bahir?* Was the whole book, in its present form, or in a fuller form, composed only just before its appearance, and actually in southern France? These questions had remained largely unanswered until in recent times it was proved that at least part of *Sefer ha-Bahir* was merely a literary adaptation of a much earlier book, the *Sefer Raza Rabba,* which is mentioned in the responsa of the *geonim* but which is lost, although important fragments appear in one of the books of the Ḥasidei Ashkenaz. A comparison of the parallel texts in the *Raza Rabba* and *Sefer ha-Bahir* demonstrates the link between them. But the elaboration in *Sefer ha-Bahir* adds fundamental elements of a gnostic character, which are not found in the original source. Consequently, one must presume that if there is an historical link between the symbolism of *Sefer ha-Bahir* and gnosticism, then this link was established through additional sources which are not known today. The widespread tradition among the kabbalists that parts of *Sefer ha-Bahir* came to them from Germany was strengthened considerably by the discovery of fragments of the *Raza Rabbah.* But the problem as to whether this is a collective work, the creation of a circle of 12th century mystics, or whether it is a new compilation of much earlier material, has not yet been sufficiently clarified. The complete absence of any attempt to justify opinions which contradict the accepted Jewish traditions can be explained more easily by adopting the second theory. There is no indication at all in the book that the idea of transmigration of souls which it supports had been rejected by every Jewish philosopher up to the appearance of *Sefer ha-Bahir*. All the mystical interpretations and the elucidation of the reasons for the commandments appear without any note of apology. Several paragraphs point to an Oriental environment and to a knowledge of Arabic. It is difficult to suppose that the book was compiled or composed in completely nonscholarly circles, who were unconcerned with the ideas current in contemporary literature and wrote absolutely independently. An analysis of the book's sources does not support this theory, and so the literary enigma of the earliest work of kabbalistic writing remains largely unsolved.

Influence. In Spanish kabbalist circles *Sefer ha-Bahir* was accepted as an ancient and authoritative source, "composed by the mystic sages of the Talmud" (Jacob b. Jacob ha-Kohen). It had great influence on the development of their teaching. The absence of any clear ideological formulation in the book meant that men of completely opposing views could find support in it. From this point of view it had no equal until the appearance of the Zohar. On the other hand, the book was not accepted without protest from those who were opposed to Kabbalah. Meir b. Simeon of Narbonne wrote very harshly about it and regarded it as an heretical book attributed to Neḥunya b. ha-Kanah. However, the latter was "a righteous man who did not stumble therein, and is not to be numbered with the sinners" (c. 1240).

Editions and Commentaries. Among the many manuscripts of the book there is one version which is superior to the printed edition in a large number of details, but it does not contain any new material, Ms. Munich 209. In 1331 Meir b. Solomon Ibn-Sahula, a pupil of Solomon b. Abraham Adret, wrote a commentary on *Sefer ha-Bahir* which was published anonymously in the Vilna and Jerusalem editions under the title *Or ha-Ganuz* ("The Hidden Light"). Fragments of a philosophical commentary by Elijah b. Eliezer of Candia are extant in manuscript (Vatican Ms. 431). David Habillo (d. 1661; Gaster Ms. 966) and Meir Poppers (in Jerusalem) both of whom were followers of the Lurianic Kabbalah, wrote commentaries on *Sefer ha-Bahir* which have been preserved. It is noteworthy that the various editions of the book differ in the way the book is divided into sections.

The first edition of *Sefer ha-Bahir* was printed in Amsterdam in 1651 (by an anonymous Christian scholar). The latest edition, prepared by R. Margaliot with the addition of notes and parallel material, was published in Jerusalem in 1951. The book has been translated into German by G. Scholem (1970^2).

Bibliography: G. Scholem, *Ursprung und Anfaenge der Kabbalah* (1962), 33–174; L. Baeck, *Aus drei Jahrtausenden* (1939), 398–415; Israel Weinstock, in: *Sinai* 49 (1962), 370–78; 50 (1962), 28–35, 441–52; in *Sefer Yovel . . . Ch. Albeck* (1963), 188–210; Sh. Shahar, in: *Tarbiz* 10 (1971), 483–507 (Elements common to the Cathartic scriptures and the *Bahir*).

6
Chiromancy

Chiromancy is the art of determining a man's character and frequently his fate and future from lines and other marks on the palm and fingers and was one of the mantic arts which developed in the Near East, apparently during the Hellenistic period. No early chiromantic sources from this period have been preserved, either in Greek or Latin, although they did exist. Chiromancy spread, in a much fuller form, in medieval Arabic and Byzantine Greek literature, from which it found its way to the Latin culture. It would seem that from the very beginning there were two traditions. The first linked chiromancy closely with astrology and so produced a quasi-systematic framework for its references and predictions. The second was not connected with astrology at all, but with intuition, whose methodological principles are not clear. In the Middle Ages the Christian chiromantics found a scriptural basis for chiromancy in Job 37:7: "He sealeth up the hand of every man, that all men may know his work" which could be interpreted to mean that the hand imprints are made by God for the purpose of chiromancy. This verse is adduced in Jewish tradition only from the 16th century onward.

Chiromancy appears first in Judaism in the circle of Merkabah mysticism. The fragments of their literature include a chapter entitled *Hakkarat Panim le-Rabbi Yishma'el* written in mishnaic and early midrashic Hebrew. This chapter is the earliest literary source of chiromancy which has thus far been found. It is only partly comprehensible because it is based on symbols and allusions which are still obscure, but it has no connection with astrological method. It uses the term *sirtutim* for the lines of the hand. A German translation of the chapter was published by G. Scholem.[1] Another fragment from the same period, discovered in the Genizah, presents already a mixture of astrology with chiromancy and physiognomy.[2] From a responsum of Hai Gaon (*Ozar ha-Ge'onim* on tractate *Ḥagigah*, responsa section, pg. 12), it is clear that the Merkabah mystics used chiromancy and Hellenistic physiognomy in order to ascertain whether a man was fit to receive esoteric teaching. They quoted as scriptural support for these sciences Genesis 5:1–2: "This is the book of the generations of man" (the Hebrew *Toledot* interpreted to mean "the book of man's character and fate") and "male and female created He them," which implies that chiromantic prediction varies according to the sex, the right hand being the determining factor for the male, and the left hand for the female.

Apart from the chapter mentioned above, there circulated for a long period a number of translations of an as yet unidentified Arabic chiromantic source, *Re'iyyat ha-Yadayim le-Eḥad me-Ḥakhmei Hodu* ("Reading the Hands by an Indian Sage") The sage is named in Hebrew manuscripts as Nidarnar. Of this source two translations and various adaptations have been preserved and the work became known in Hebrew not later than the 13th century. One of the adaptations was printed under the title *Sefer ha-Atidot* in the collection *Urim ve-Tummim* (1700). At the end of the 13th century the kabbalist Menahem Recanati had a copy of this text, which is based entirely on the principles of the astrological method of chiromancy relating the main lines of the palm and the various parts of the hand to the seven planets and their influences. The author was already familiar with the basic chiromantic terminology common in non-Jewish literature. His work deals not only with the meaning of the lines, or *ḥariẓim*, but also with *otiyyot*, i.e., the various marks on the hand.

Evidence of the chiromantic tradition among the early kabbalists is given by Asher b. Saul, brother of Jacob Nazir, in *Sefer ha-Minhagot* (c. 1215):[3] "[at the conclusion of the Sabbath] they used to examine the lines of the palms of the hands, because through the lines on the hands the sages would know a man's fate and the good things in store for him." In the Munich manuscript 288 (fol. 116ff.), there is a long treatise on chiromancy allegedly based on a revelation that was received by a Ḥasid in England in the 13th century. It does not differ in content from the astrological chiromancy current among contemporary Christians and the terminology is identical. A hand with chiromantical indications is found in a Hebrew manuscript of c. 1280 from France (Brit. Mus. Add. 11639, fol. 115b).

In various parts of the Zohar there are passages, some of them lengthy, which deal with the lines of both the hand and the forehead. A discipline was devoted to the latter, which corresponded to chiromancy and in the Middle Ages was called metoposcopy. Two different versions of this subject are included in the portion of Jethro and are based on Exodus 18:21, the first in the main part of the Zohar (2:70a–77a) and the second an independent treatise called *Raza de-Razin* which is printed in columns parallel to the former, and continued in the addenda to the second part of the Zohar (fol. 272a–275a). Here the lines of the forehead are discussed in detail. A third account devoted to the lines of the hand is found in Zohar, 2:77a–78a, and consists of three chapters. Although the Zohar brings out the parallel between the movement of the heavenly bodies and the direction of the lines on the hand, the influence of astrological chiromancy is not apparent in the details of the exposition, which depends in an obscure way on five letters of the Hebrew alphabet (זהספר *zayin, he, samekh, pe,* and *resh*). These are used as mystical symbols apparently referring to particular types of character. In a further elaboration of chiromancy in *tikkun* no. 70 (toward the end) of the *Tikkunei Zohar,* a relationship is established between the lines on a man's hand and forehead and the transmigrations of his soul. An interpretation of these pages in the portion of Jethro is found in *Or ha-Ḥammah* by Abraham Azulai, and was printed separately under the title *Maḥazeh Avraham* (1800). As the knowledge of the Zohar spread, several kabbalists tried to relate chiromancy back to the mysteries of the Kabbalah; especially Joseph ibn Ṣayyaḥ, at the beginning of *Even ha-Shoham,* written in Jerusalem in 1538 (Jerusalem, JNUL Ms 8°, 416); and Israel Sarug in *Limmudei Aẓilut* (1897, p. 17). Gedaliah ibn Yaḥya says in *Shalshelet ha-Kabbalah* (Amsterdam, 1697), 53a, that he himself wrote a book (1570) on the subject of chiromancy under the title *Sefer Ḥanokh* (or *Ḥinnukh*).

From the beginning of the 16th century several Hebrew books were printed summarizing chiromancy according to Arabic, Latin, and German sources; however, kabbalistic chiromancy received only incidental attention. Of these should be mentioned *Toledot Adam* (Constantinople, 1515) by Elijah b. Moses Gallena, and *Shoshannat Ya'akov* (Amsterdam, 1706) by Jacob b. Mordecai of Fulda, both of which were printed several times. Yiddish translations of the books also appeared. Abraham Hammawi included a treatise *Sefer ha-Atidot* on chiromancy in his book *Davek me-Aḥ* (1874, fols. 74ff.). Among the pupils of Isaac Luria the tradition spread that their master was an expert in chiromancy, and many traditions point to the fact that several kabbalists were knowledgeable in it. In the 19th century R. Ḥayyim Palache mentions (in *Zekhirah le-Ḥayyim,* 1880, p. 20) that the contemporary Moroccan rabbis were skilled in chiromancy.

In Hebrew books on astrological chiromancy the main lines of the hand are given the following names: (1) *Kav ha-Ḥayyim* ("the life-line"; Lat. *Linea Saturnia*); (2) *Kav ha-Ḥokhmah* ("the line of wisdom"; *Linea Sapientiae*); (3) *Kav ha-Shulḥan* ("the table line"; *Linea Martialis*); (4) *Kav ha-Mazzal* ("the line of fate") or *Kav ha-Beri'ut* ("the line of health"; *Linea Mercurii*). The idiomatic expression found in later literature, *einenni be-kav ha-beri'ut* ("I am not in the line of health"), meaning "I am not in good health", is derived from chiromantic terminology.

Bibliography: Steinschneider, Cat Bod, 939f., 1239, J. Praetorius, *Thesaurus Chiromantiae* (Jena, 1661); F. Boll, *Catalogus Codicum Astrologicorum,* 7 (1908), 236; F. Boehm, *Handwoerterbuch des deutschen Aberglaubenns,* 2 (1930), 37–53, s.v. *Chiromantie;* G. Scholem, in: *Sefer Assaf* (1953), 459–95.

7

Demonology in Kabbalah

The kabbalists made use of all of motifs current in the Talmud and Midrash in developing their system of demonology.[1] New elements were developed or added, mainly in two directions: (1) the kabbalists attempted to systematize demonology so that it would fit into their understanding of the world and thus to explain demonology in terms derived from their understanding of reality; (2) new and varied elements were added from external sources, mainly from medieval Arabic demonology, from Christian demonology, and from the popular beliefs of the Germans and Slavs. At times these elements were linked, more or less logically, to Jewish demonology and were thus "judaized" to some extent. However, frequently the link was only external; material was incorporated into Jewish demonology with almost no explicit Jewish adaptation. This is particularly true with regard to the sources of practical Kabbalah. There, real kabbalistic beliefs mingled with folk beliefs which in fact originally had no connection with the beliefs of the kabbalists. This combination gives the late Jewish demonology its markedly syncretistic character. The material pertaining to this kind of demonology can be found in innumerable sources, many still in manuscript. Extensive research in this field and its development is one of the important desiderata of Jewish studies.

The works of the kabbalists also contain contradictory conceptions of the demons. Traditions of the past as well as the cultural environment and the intellectual outlook of each individual kabbalist contributed toward the diversification of their beliefs. The ideas of the early Spanish kabbalists on this subject were formulated clearly in Naḥmanides' commentary on Leviticus 17:7 and their influence is visible in all subsequent literature. In Naḥmanides' opinion the demons *(shedim)* are to be found in waste *(shedudim),* ruined, and cold places such as in the North. They were not created out of the four elements but only out of fire and air. They have subtle bodies, imperceptible by the human senses, and these subtle bodies allow them to fly through fire and air. Because they are composed of different elements, they come under the laws of creation and decay and they die like human beings. Their sustenance is derived from water and fire, from odors and saps; hence necromancers burned incense to

Detail from a parchment amulet showing the female demon Lilith. Above her are depicted Sanoi, Sansanoi and Samnaglof.

demons. Despite the element of subtle fire which they contain, they are surrounded by a coldness that frightens off the exorcists (this detail is singled out only in later sources). By means of their flight through air they are able to approach the "princes" of the zodiac who dwell in the atmosphere and thus hear predictions of the near but not the distant future.

Naḥmanides also hints (Comm. to Lev. 16:8) that the demons belong to the patrimony of Samael, who is "the soul of the planet Mars and Esau is his subject among the nations" (the angel of Edom or Christianity). The Castilian kabbalists, Isaac b. Jacob ha-Kohen, Moses of Burgos, and Moses de Leon (in his Hebrew works and in the Zohar) linked the existence of demons with the last grades of the powers of the "left-side" emanation (the *sitra aḥra,* "other side", of the Zohar) which corresponds in its ten *Sefirot* of evil to the ten holy *Sefirot.* Their writings contain detailed descriptions of the way in which these powers emanated and explain the names of the rulers of their hosts. Their ideas are mainly based on internal development in kabbalistic circles. In the various sources entirely different names are given to the upper grades of these demonic or Satanic powers. However, they all agree in linking the hosts of demons in the sublunar world, i.e., on earth, under the dominion of Samael and Lilith who appear for the first time in these sources as a couple. Numerous details about these "dark emanations" are found in *Ammud ha-Semali* by Moses of Burgos.[2]

In contrast, the Zohar, following a talmudic legend, stresses the origin of certain classes of demons in sexual intercourse between humans and demonic powers. Some demons, such as Lilith, were created during the six days of Creation, and in particular on the Sabbath eve at twilight, as disembodied spirits. They sought to take on the form of a body through association with humans, at first with Adam when he separated from Eve and then with all his descendants. However, the demons who were created out of such unions also long for this kind of intercourse. The sexual element in the relationship of man and demons holds a prominent place in the demonology of the Zohar, as well as that of several later kabbalistic works. Every pollution of semen gives birth to demons. The details of these relationships are remarkably similar to the beliefs current in Christian medieval demonology about succubi and incubi. They are based on the assumption (contrary to the talmudic opinion) that these demons have no procreating ability of their own and need human semen in order to multiply. In the later Kabbalah it is pointed out that the demons born to man out of such unions are considered his illegitimate sons; they were called *banim shovavim* ("mischievous sons"). At death and burial they come to accompany the dead man, to lament him, and to claim their share of the inheritance; they may also injure the legitimate sons. Hence the custom of circling the dead at the cemetery to repulse these demons and also the custom (dating from the 17th century) in a number of communities of not allowing the sons to accompany their father's corpse to the cemetery in order to prevent their being harmed by their illegitimate step-brothers.

The terms *shedim* and *mazzikim* (harmful demons, *Poltergeister*) were often used as synonyms, but in some sources there is a certain differentiation between them. In the Zohar it is thought that the spirits of evil men become *mazzikim* after their death. However, there are also good-natured devils who are prepared to help and do favors to men. This is supposed to be particularly true of those demons ruled by Ashmedai (Asmodeus) who accept the Torah and are considered "Jewish demons." Their existence is mentioned by the Ḥasidei Ashkenaz as well as in the Zohar. According to legend, Cain and Abel, who contain some of the impurity of the serpent which had sexual relations with Eve, possess a certain demonic element and various demons came from them. But, in fact, the mating of female devils with human males and of male devils with female humans continued throughout history. These devils are mortal, but their kings and queens live longer than human beings and some of them, particularly Lilith and Naamah, will exist until the day of the Last Judgment (Zohar 1:55a). Various speculations were made on the death of the kings of the demons, in particular of Ashmedai.[3] There is a tradition that he died a martyr's death with the Jews of Mainz in 1096. Another kabbalistic view is that Ashmedai is merely the title of the office of the king of the demons, just as Pharaoh is the title of the office of the king of Egypt, and "every king of the demons is called Ashmedai", as the word Ashmedai in *gematria* is numerically equivalent to Pharaoh. Long genealogies of the demons and their families are found in Judeo-Arabic demonology.

Apparently, the author of the Zohar distinguishes between spirits that have emanated from the "left-side" and were assigned definite functions in the "palaces of impurity" and devils in the exact sense who hover in the air. According to later sources, the latter fill with their hosts the space of the sky between the earth and sphere of the moon. Their activity takes place mainly at night, before midnight. Devils born out of nightly pollutions are called "the stripes of the children of men" (II Sam. 7:14; see Zohar 1:54b). Sometimes the demons poke fun at men. They tell them lies about the future and mingle truth and lies in dreams. The feet of the demons are crooked (Zohar 3:229b). In numerous sources four mothers of demons are mentioned: Lilith, Naamah, Agrath, and Mahalath (who is sometimes replaced by Raḥab). The demons under their rule go out in their hosts at appointed times and constitute a danger to the world. At times, they gather on a particular mountain "near the mountains of darkness where they have sexual intercourse with Samael". This is reminiscent of the Witches' Sabbath in Christian demonology. Male and female witches also gather at this place, devote themselves to similar deeds, and learn the art of witchcraft from the arch-devils, who are here identical with the rebellious angels who have fallen from heaven (Zohar 3:194b, 212a). The author of the *Ra'aya Meheimna* in the Zohar (3:253a) distinguishes between three types of demons: (1) similar to angels; (2) resembling humans and called *shedim Yehuda'im* ("Jewish devils") who submit to the Torah; (3) who have no fear of God and are like animals. The distinction of demons according to the three main religions is found also in Arabic demonology as well as in sources of practical Kabbalah; it is mentioned in the full, uncensored text of a section of *Midrash Rut ha-Ne'lam* in the Zohar. Another division distinguishes between demons according to the various strata of the air in which they rule – an opinion common to the Zohar and to Isaac ha-Kohen who mentions details about this. On the other hand, the Zohar mentions *nukba di-tehoma rabba,* "the maw of the great abyss," as the place to which the demons return on the Sabbath when they have no power over the world. According to Baḥya b. Asher, the demons also found refuge in Noah's ark, otherwise they would not have been saved from the Flood.

The kings of the demons were given names, but not the members of their hosts, who are known by the kings' names: "Samael and his host", "Ashmedai and his host," etc. Ashmedai is generally considered as the son of Na'amah the sister of Tubal-Cain, but sometimes also as the son of King David and Agrath, the queen of the demons. Numerous names of demons have come from Arabic tradition. Among them should be mentioned Bilar (also Bilad or Bilid), the third king who succeeded Ashmedai. Bilar is merely a misspelling of Satan's name "Beliar" in several Apocalypses and in early Christian literature, which thus returned to Jewish tradition via foreign sources. He plays an important role in "practical kabbalistic" literature and from it, disguised as Bileth, he came into German magic literature associated with the story of Doctor Faust. The seal of this king is described in detail in the book *Berit Menuḥah* (Amsterdam 1648, 39b). The other demons too have seals, and those who know them can make them appear against their will. Their drawings are preserved in manuscripts of practical Kabbalah. The names of the seven kings of the demons in charge of the seven days of the week, very popular in later Jewish demonology, were derived from Arabic tradition. Prominent among them are Maimon the Black and Shemhurish, judge of the demons. Other systems originating in the Spanish Kabbalah put the three kings Ḥalama, Samael, and Kafkafuni at the head of the demons (*Sefer ha-Ḥeshek*, Ms. in Brit. Mus.).[4]

Other systems of demonology are connected with lists of the angels and the demons in charge of the night hours of the seven days of the week, or with the demonological interpretation of diseases such as epilepsy. Such sources are *Seder Goral ha-Ḥoleh* and *Sefer ha-Ne'elavim.*[5] These systems are not necessarily connected with kabbalistic ideas and some obviously preceded them. A complete system of kabbalistic demonology was presented, after the period of the Zohar, in *Sibbat Ma'aseh ha-Egel ve-Inyan ha-Shedim* (Ms. Sassoon 56), which develops internal Jewish motifs. A combination of the Zohar and Arab sources characterizes the book *Ẓefunei Ẓiyyoni* by Menahem Ẓiyyoni of Cologne (late 14th century; partly in Ms. Oxford); it enumerates a long list of important demons and their functions while preserving their Arabic names. This book was one of the channels through which Arab elements reached the practical kabbalists among the Jews of Germany and Poland, and they recur often, albeit with errors, in Ashkenazi collections of demonology in Hebrew and Yiddish. One of the most important among these is Schocken manuscript 102, dating from the end of the 18th century. Among North African and Near Eastern Jews, elements of kabbalistic and Arabic demonology were combined even without literary intermediaries; of particular interest is the collection *Shushan Yesod Olam,* in Ms. Sassoon 290. The collections of remedies and amulets composed by Sephardi scholars abound in this kind of material. An outstanding example of a complete mixture of Jewish, Arab, and Christian elements is found in the incantations of the book *Mafte'aḥ Shelomo* or *Clavicula Salomonis,* a collection from the 17th century published in facsimile by H. Gollancz in 1914. King Zauba'a and Queen Zumzumit also belong to the Arab heritage. A rich German heritage in the field of demonology is preserved in the writings of Judah he-Ḥasid and his disciples and in Menahem Ziyyoni's commentary on the Torah. According to the testimony of Naḥmanides, it was the custom of the Ashkenazi Jews to "dabble in matters concerning the demons, to weave spells and send them away, and they use them in several matters"(Responsa of Ibn Adret, attributed to Naḥmanides, no 283). The *Ma'aseh Bukh* (in Yiddish; English translation by M. Gaster, 1934) lists numerous details about this Jewish-Ashkenazi demonology of the later Middle Ages. In addition to current popular beliefs, elements originating in scholarly magic literature as well as the names of demons whose origins were in Christian magic were introduced from Christian demonology. These spread, not later than the 15th century, among the Jews of Germany. Demons such as Astarot, Beelzebub (in many forms), and their like became fixtures in incantations and lists of demons. A detailed kabbalistic system of demonology is found at the time of the expulsion from Spain in Joseph Taitaẓak's *Malakh ha-Meshiv*. In this system, the hierarchy of the demons is headed by Samael the patron of Edom and Ammon of No (Alexandria), patron of Egypt, who also represents Islam. Ammon of No recurs in numerous sources in this period.

Ḥayyim Vital tells about devils who are composed from only one of the four elements, in contrast to the opinion of Naḥmanides mentioned above. This view probably has its origin in the European demonology of the Renaissance. Isaac Luria's Kabbalah often mentions various *kelippot* ("shells") which have to be subdued via observance of the Torah and *miẓvot*, but it does not generally give them proper names or make them into devils as such. This process reached its peak in *Sefer Karnayim* (Zolkiew, 1709) by Samson of Ostropol, who gives to many *kelippot* names which were not found in any ancient source. This book is the last original text in kabbalistic demonology.

Some details: According to Isaac of Acre the devils have only four fingers and lack the thumb. The book *Emek ha-Melekh* (Amsterdam, 1648) mentions demons called *kesilim* ("fooling" spirits) who misguide man on his way and poke fun at him. Hence presumably the appellation *lezim* ("jesters") occurring in later literature and in popular usage for the lower type of demons, those who throw about household goods and the like (poltergeists). From the beginning of the 17th century the demon called *Sh. D.* (ש״ד) is mentioned, i.e., *Shomer Dappim* ("guard of the pages"); he injures a man who leaves a holy book open. According to a popular belief of German Jews, the four queens of the demons rule over the four seasons of the year. Once every three months at the turn of the season, their menstrual blood falls into the waters and poisons them, and this is said to be the reason for the older (geonic) custom which forbade the drinking of water at the change of the seasons. A special place in demonology is allotted to the Queen of Sheba, who was considered one of the queens of the demons and is sometimes identified with Lilith – for the first time in the Targum (Job, ch. 1), and later in the Zohar and the subsequent literature.[6] The motif of the battle between the prince and a dragon or a demonic reptile, representing the power of the *kelippah* who imprisoned the princess, is widespread in various forms in the demonology of the Zohar. Dragon is the name of the king of the demons who is also mentioned in *Sefer Hasidim.* According to Hayyim Vital, four queens of the demons rule over Rome (Lilith), Salamanca (Agrath), Egypt (Rahab), and Damascus (Na'amah). According to Abraham Galante, until the confusion of the languages there existed only two: the holy language (i.e., Hebrew) and the language of the demons. Belief in demons remained a folk superstition among some Jews in certain countries down to the present. The rich demonology in I. Bashevis Singer stories reflects the syncretism of Slavic and Jewish elements in Polish Jewish folklore.

Bibliography: J. Trachtenberg, *Jewish Magic and Superstition* (1934); R. Margaliot, *Malakhei Elyon* (1945), 201–94;G. Scholem, in: *Madde'ei ha-Yahadut,* 1(1926), 112–27; idem, in: KS, 10(1933/34), 68–73; idem, in: *Tarbiẓ,* vols. 3–5 (1932–34); idem, in: JJS, 16 (1965), 1–13; I. Tishby, *Mishnat ha-Zohar,* 1 (1957), 361–77: J.A. Eisenmenger, *Das entdeckte Judenthum,* 2(1700), 408–68 (a mixture of talmudic and kabbalistic ideas), P.W. Hirsch, *Megalleh Tekufot . . . oder das schaedliche Blut, welches ueber die Juden viermal des Jahrs kommt* (1717); *Mitteilugen fuer juedische Volkskunde* (1898–1926) especially M. Grunwald, in vols. for 1900, 1906, 1907: *Jahrbuch fuer Juedische Volkskunde* (1923 and 1925); M. Weinreich, in: *Landau-Bukh* (1926), 217–38.

8

The Doenmeh

The Doenmeh (Dönme) were the sect of adherents of Shabbetai Ẓevi who embraced Islam as a consequence of the failure of the Shabbatean messianic upheaval in Turkey. After Shabbetai Ẓevi converted to Islam in September 1666, large numbers of his disciples interpreted his apostasy as a secret mission, deliberately undertaken with a particular mystical purpose in mind. The overwhelming majority of his adherents, who called themselves *ma'aminim* ("believers"), remained within the Jewish fold. However, even while Shabbetai Ẓevi was alive several leaders of the *ma'aminim* thought it essential to follow in the footsteps of their messiah and to become Muslims, without, as they saw it, renouncing their Judaism, which they interpreted according to new principles. Until Shabbetai Ẓevi's death in 1676 the group which at first was centered largely in Adrianople (Edirne), numbered some 200 families. They came mainly from the Balkans, but there were also adherents from Constantinople, Izmir, Brusa, and other places. There were a few outstanding scholars and kabbalists among them, whose families afterward were accorded a special place among the Doenmeh as descendants of the original community of the sect. Even among the Shabbateans who did not convert to Islam, such as Nathan of Gaza, this group enjoyed an honorable reputation and an important mission was ascribed to it. Clear evidence of this is preserved in the commentary of Psalms (written c. 1679) of Israel Ḥazzan of Castoria.

Most of the community became converts as a direct result of Shabbetai Ẓevi's preaching and persuasion. They were outwardly fervent Muslims and privately Shabbatean *ma'aminim* who practiced a type of messianic Judaism, based as early as the 1670s or 1680s on "the 18 precepts" which were attributed to Shabbetai Ẓevi and accepted by the Doenmeh communities. (The full text was published in English by G. Scholem, in: *Essays . . . Abba Hillel Silver* (1963), 368–86.) These precepts contain a parallel version of the Ten Commandments. However, they are distinguished by an extraordinarily ambiguous formulation of the commandment "Thou shalt not commit adultery", which approximates more to a recommendation to take care rather than a prohibition. The additional commandments determine the relationship of the *ma'aminim* toward the Jews and the Turks. Intermarriage with true Muslims is strictly and emphatically forbidden.

After the death of Shabbetai Ẓevi the community's center of activities moved to Salonika and remained there until 1924. Shabbetai's last wife, Jochebed (in Islam, Ayisha), was the daughter of Joseph Filosof, one of the rabbis of Salonika, and she returned there from Albania after a brief sojourn in Adrianople. Later, she proclaimed her younger brother Jacob Filosof, known traditionally as Jacob Querido (i.e., "the beloved"), as the reincarnation of the soul of Shabbetai Ẓevi. So many different and contradictory traditions exist concerning the profound upheaval which affected the *ma'aminim* of Salonika around 1680 and afterward that, for the time being, it is impossible to say which is the most reliable. They all agree that there was considerable tension between the original Doenmeh community and the followers of Jacob Querido, among whom were several of the rabbis of Salonika. As a result of their propaganda, two to three hundred families, under the leadership of two rabbis, Solomon Florentin and Joseph Filosoph, and his son, underwent mass conversion to Islam. There are two contradictory accounts of this conversion. One dates it in the year 1683, and the other at the end of 1686. It is possible that there were two mass conversions, one after the other. Many mystical "revelations" were then experienced in Salonika, and several tracts were written reflecting the spiritual tendencies of the various groups. As time went on, most of the apostate families from other cities in Turkey migrated to Salonika and the sect was organized on a more institutional basis. During the 18th century the sect was joined by other Shabbatean groups, particularly from Poland. Jacob Querido demonstrated his outward allegiance to Islam by making the pilgrimage to Mecca with several of his followers – a course of action which the original Doenmeh community opposed. He died on his return from this journey in 1690 or 1695, probably in Alexandria.

Internal conflicts caused a split in the organization and resulted in the formation of two sub-sects: one, according to Doenmeh tradition, was called *Izmirlis (Izmirim)* and consisted of members of the original community, and the other was known as the *Jacobites,* or in Turkish *Jakoblar.* A few years after Querido's death another split occurred among the *Izmirlis,* when around 1700 a new young leader, Baruchiah Russo, appeared among them and was proclaimed by his disciples to be the reincarnation of Shabbetai Ẓevi. In 1716 his disciples proclaimed him as the Divine Incarnation. Russo was apparently of Jewish birth and the son of one of the early followers of Shabbetai Ẓevi. After his conversion he was called "Osman Baba". A third sub-sect was organized around him. Its members were called *Konyosos* (in Ladino) or *Karakashlar* (in Turkish). This was considered to be the most extreme group of the Doenmeh community. It had the reputation of having founded a new faith with a leaning toward religious nihilism. Its adherents embarked on a new missionary campaign to the chief cities of the Diaspora. Representatives were sent to Poland, Germany, and Austria, where they were a source of considerable excitement between 1720 and 1726. Branches of this sect, from which the Frankists later emerged, were established in several places. Baruchiah Russo died in 1720 while still young and his grave was an object of pilgrimage for members of the sect until recent times. His son, who became the leader of this sect, died in 1781. During the period of the French Revolution a powerful leader of one of the sects (either the *Izmirim* or the Baruchiah sect), known as "Dervish Effendi", became prominent. He is perhaps to be identified with the Doenmeh preacher and poet, Judah Levi Tovah, several of those poems and kabbalistical homilies in Ladino were preserved in manuscripts belonging to the Doenmeh and are now in a number of public collections.

It soon became clear to the Turkish authorities that these apostates, who had been expected to encourage the Jews to convert to Islam, had no intention of assimilating, but were determined to continue to lead a closed sectarian existence, although outwardly they strictly observed the practices of Islam, and were politically loyal citizens. From the beginning of the 18th century, they were called Doenmeh, meaning (in Turkish) either "converts" or "apostates". However, it is not clear whether this is a reference to their conversion from Judaism or to the fact of their not being true Muslims. The Jews called them *Minim* ("sectarians") and among the writings of the Salonika rabbis there are several responsa dealing with the problems of how they are to be treated and whether they are to be regarded as Jews or not. They settled in specific quarters of Salonika, and their leaders were on friendly terms with Sufic circles, and with the dervish orders among the Turks, particularly the Baktashi. At the same time they maintained secret ties not only with those Shabbateans who had not converted, but also with several rabbis in Salonika, who, when knowledge of the Torah diminished among the Doenmeh, were paid for secretly settling points of law for them. These relationships were severed only in the middle of the 19th century. This doublefaced behavior becomes clear only when their ambiguous attitude toward traditional Judaism is taken into account. On one level, they regarded the latter as void, its place being taken by a higher, more spiritual Torah, called *Torah de-Aẓilut* ("Torah of Emanation"). But on another level there remained certain areas in which they sought to conduct themselves according to the actual Torah of talmudic tradition, called *Torah di-Beri'ah* ("Torah of Creation").

The numerical strength of the Doenmeh is only approximately known.

According to the Danish traveler, Carsten Niebuhr, around 600 families lived in Salonika in 1774, and they married only among themselves. Before World War I their number was estimated to be between 10,000 and 15,000, divided more or less equally among the three sub-sects, with the *Konyosos* having a slight numerical majority. At first, knowledge of Hebrew was common among the Doenmeh and their liturgy was originally standardized in Hebrew. This can be seen in the part of their prayer book which is still extant (Scholem, in: KS, vols. 18 and 19). However, as time went on the use of Ladino increased and both their homiletic and poetic literature was written in that tongue. They continued to speak Ladino among themselves up to about 1870 and it was only later that Turkish replaced it as the language of everyday speech.

As far as social structure is concerned, there were distinct differences among the three sub-sects which developed apparently between 1750 and 1850. The aristocrats of Doenmeh society were the *Izmirlis,* who were called *Cavalleros* in Ladino or *Kapanjilar* in Turkish. These included the great merchants and the middle classes, as well as most of the Doenmeh intelligentsia. They were also the first to show, from the end of the 19th century a marked tendency toward assimilation with the Turks. The *Jakoblar* community of Jacobites included a large number of lower- or middle-class Turkish officials, while the third and most numerous group, the *Konyosos* (acording to the few available accounts) consisted as time went on mainly of the proletariat and artisan classes, e.g., porters, shoemakers, barbers, and butchers. Some say that for a long time practically all the barbers of Salonika belonged to this group. Each Doenmeh had a Turkish and a Hebrew name (for use in Turkish and Doenmeh society respectively). Furthermore, they preserved the original Sephardi family names, which alone are mentioned in poems composed in honor of the dead; many of these poems have survived in manuscript. Doenmeh cemeteries were used in common by all the sub-sects. In contrast, each sect had its particular synagogue (called *Kahal* – "congregation") at the center of its own quarter, concealed from the outsider.

Their liturgies were written in a very small format so that they could easily be hidden. All the sects concealed their internal affairs from Jews and Turks so successfully that for a long time knowledge of them was based only on rumor and upon reports of outsiders. Doenmeh manuscripts revealing details of their Shabbatean ideas were brought to light and examined only after several of the Doenmeh families decided to assimilate completely into Turkish society and transmitted their documents to friends among the Jews of Salonika and Izmir. As long as the Doenmeh were concentrated in Salonika, the sect's institutional framework remained intact, although several Doenmeh members were active in the Young Turks' movement which originated in that city. The first administration that came to power after the Young Turk revolution (1909) included three ministers of Doenmeh origin, including the minister of finance, Djavid Bey, who was a descendant of the Baruchiah Russo family and served as one of the leaders of his sect. One assertion that was commonly made by many Jews of Salonika (denied however, by the Turkish government) was that Kemal Atatürk was of Doenmeh origin. This view was eagerly embraced by many of Atatürk's religious opponents in Anatolia.

With the exchange of population that followed the Greco-Turkish war of 1924, the Doenmeh were compelled to leave Salonika. Most of them settled in Istanbul, and a few in other Turkish cities such as Izmir and Ankara. In the Turkish press at that time there was a lively debate about the Jewish character of the Doenmeh and their assimilation. When they were uprooted from the great Jewish center of Salonika, assimilation began to spread widely. Nevertheless, there is reliable evidence that the organizational framework of the *Konyosos* sect survived, and as late as 1970 many families still belonged to this organization. Among the Turkish intelligentsia, one of the professors at the University of Istanbul was widely regarded as the leader of the Doenmeh. Attempts to persuade them to return to Judaism and to emigrate to Israel have borne little fruit. Only a few isolated Doenmeh families were among the Turkish immigrants to Israel.

There is hardly any basic difference in religious opinions between the Doenmeh and the other sects who believed in Shabbetai Ẓevi. In their literature, as far as it is known, there is hardly a mention of their belonging to the Islamic fold. Their claim of being the true Jewish community is not unlike the claims of the early Christians and the Christian church. They preserved their faith in Shabbetai Ẓevi, who had abrogated the practical commandments of the material Torah and had opened up "the spiritual Torah" of the upper world as a substitute. The principle of the divinity of Shabbetai Ẓevi was firmly developed and accepted by the sect, as was the threefold nature of the upper forces of emanation, called *telat kishrei de-meheimanuta* ("the three bonds of faith"). In addition to their abrogation of the practical commandments and their mystical trinitarian belief, one factor in particular aroused great oppostion among their contemporaries. This was their obvious inclination to permit marriages which were halakhically forbidden, and to conduct religious ceremonies which involved the exchange of wives and which, therefore, bastardized their issue according to Jewish law. Accusations of sexual licentiousness were made from the beginning of the 18th century, and although many have tried to belittle their importance there is no doubt that sexual promiscuity existed for many generations. The long sermon of Judah Levi Tovah (published by I.R. Molcho and R. Schatz, in *Sefunot*, 3–4 (1960), 395–521) contains a spirited defense of the abrogation of the sexual prohibitions contained in the material "Torah of Creation". Orgiastic ceremonies in fact took place in the main on the Doenmeh festival *Ḥag ha-Keves* ("Festival of the Lamb") which fell Adar 22 and was recognized as a celebration of the beginning of spring. In addition, they celebrated other festivals, connected with the life of Shabbetai Ẓevi and particular events associated with their apostasy. They did not abstain from work on their festivals in order not to arouse outside curiosity and contented themselves with rituals on the eve of their festivals. The Doenmeh liturgy for the Ninth of Av, the birthday of Shabbetzi Ẓevi, called *Ḥag ha-Samaḥot* ("Festival of Rejoicing") is extant in Hebrew and contains a Shabbatean adaption of some of the High Holy Day prayers, with the addition of a solemn declaration of their Shabbatean creed, consisting of eight paragraphs (KS, 18 (1947), 309–10).

Bibliography: Scholem, *The Messianic Idea in Judaism* (1971), 142–66; idem, in: *Numen,* 7 (1960), 93-122 (with bibl.); idem, in: *Sefunot,* 9 (1965), 195–207; idem, in: D.J. Silver (ed.), *In the Time of Harvest* (1963), 368–86; I. Ben-Ẓvi, *The Exiled and the Redeemed* (1957), 131–53; idem, in: *Sefunot,* 3–4 (1960), 349–94; G. Attiàs and G. Scholem, *Shirot ve-Tishbaḥot shel ha-Shabbeta'im* (1948).

9

Eschatology

Introduction. Apart from basic ideas concerning reward and punishment, life after death, the Messiah, redemption, and resurrection, there is hardly a commonly held belief among the Jews regarding eschatological details. This lacuna provided an obvious opportunity for free play for the imaginative, the visionary and the superstitious, and so became the field in which the kabbalists left their mark: for they dealt extensively with just these concepts. It is understandable that with such scope they could never arrive at a decision which was acceptable to all, and thus various trends developed. From fairly simple beginnings, eschatological teaching developed in the Zohar, and in the kabbalistic works which followed it, and it had many ramifications.

Life after Death. Of great importance here are the views of Naḥmanides in *Sha'ar ha-Gemul,* of the Zohar, and of the Lurianic school as they are crystallized in the great summary of Aaron Berechiah b. Moses of Modena, *Ma'avar Yabbok* (Mantua, 1623). Generally speaking, they stress, after the time of Naḥmanides, the differing fates of the three parts of the soul, which are separated from one another after death. The *nefesh* (the lowest part) remains below by the grave, and suffers punishment for transgressions after the first judgment, which is called *ḥibbut ha-kever* ("punishment of the grave") or *din ha-kever* ("judgment of the grave"). The *ru'aḥ* is also punished for its sins, but after 12 months, it enters the earthly Garden of Eden, or "the Garden of Eden below". The *neshamah* returns to its source in "the Garden of Eden above"; for, according to the Zohar, the *neshamah* is not liable to sin, and punishment falls only upon the *nefesh* and the *ru'aḥ* (although other opinions exist in early Kabbalah). In certain cases the *nefashot* ascend to the category of *ruḥot,* and *ruḥot* to the category of *neshamot.* The *ẓeror ha-ḥayyim* ("the bond of life"), in which the *neshamot* are stored, is interpreted in various ways. It is the concealed Eden, prepared for the delight of the *neshamot;* it is the "treasury" beneath the throne of glory in which the *neshamot* are stored until the resurrection; or it is one of the *sefirot,* or even their totality, into which the *neshamah* is gathered when it is in communion and bound up with God. There are a large number of descriptions in kabbalistic literature of the details and the various degrees of punishment in the abodes of *Gehinnom,* and of pleasure in the Garden of Eden and its various standards. They dealt with the problem of how the *ruḥot* or the *neshamot* could have any experience without physical faculties; what kind of garment the *ruḥot* wore, and the method of their survival. (According to some, the garment of the *ruḥot* was woven of the commandments and good deeds, and was called *ḥaluka de-rabbanan* ("the garment of the rabbis"). Naḥmanides called the domain of pleasure after death *olam ha-neshamot* ("the world of souls"), and distinguished it absolutely from the *olam ha-ba* ("the world to come"), which would be after the resurrection. This distinction was generally accepted by the Kabbalah. In the "world of souls", the *neshamot* are not incorporated into the Divine, but preserve their individual existence. The idea of punishment in *Gehinnom* (which was envisaged as a subtle spiritual fire which burned and purified the souls) conflicted with the idea of atonement through transmigration (see p. 344, *Gilgul*). There was no settled opinion on the question of which sin was punished by *Gehinnom,* and which by transmigration. One can only say that with the development of the Kabbalah transmigration took on an ever more important role in this context. Both the Garden of Eden and *Gehinnom* were beyond this world, or on the borders of it, whereas the theory of transmigration ensured reward and punishment in large measure in this world. Kabbalists sought various compromises between these two paths, but they reached no agreed solution. Attempts were also made to remove the whole subject of *Gehinnom* from its literal sense and to interpret it either according to the view of Maimonides, or metaphorically as referring to transmigration. The eschatology of the Kabbalah, and particularly that of the Zohar, was greatly influenced by the idea of the preexistence of souls. The existence of the soul in "the world of souls" is nothing more than its return to its original existence before its descent into the body.

The Messiah and Redemption. The Messiah receives a special emanation from the *sefirah Malkhut* ("kingship"), the last of the *sefirot.* However, there is no trace of the concept of the divinity of the Messiah. The picture of the personal Messiah is pale and shadowy and does not add much to the descriptions of him in the Midrashim of redemption which were composed before the growth of the Kabbalah. In the Zohar, there are a few new elements. According to the Zohar, the Messiah dwells in the Garden of Eden in a special palace, called *kan ẓippor* ("the bird's nest"), and he will first be revealed in Upper Galilee. Some believed that the soul of the Messiah had not suffered transmigration, but was "new", while others contended that it was the soul of Adam which had previously transmigrated to King David. The letters of Adam *(alef, dalet, mem)* refer to

*A*dam, *D*avid, and the *M*essiah – a *notarikon* found from the end of the 13th century. There is possibly some Christian influence here because, according to Paul, Adam, the first man, corresponds to Jesus, "the last man" (Rom. 5:17). Descriptions of redemption in the Zohar follow in the footsteps of the Midrashim with the addition of some points and certain changes in theme. The redemption will be a miracle, and all that accompanies it miraculous (the stars sparkling and falling, the wars of the end of time, the fall of the Pope, who is called symbolically in the Zohar "the priest of On"). The idea of the pangs of redemption is greatly stressed, and the condition of Israel on the eve of redemption is pictured in terms which reflect the historical conditions of the 13th century. Descriptions of the redemption became more numerous at times of crisis, and particularly after the expulsion from Spain. However, in the later Kabbalah (Moses Cordovero and Isaac Luria), their importance declined. On the other hand, the mystical basis of redemption was emphasized – the basis that developed from the time of Naḥmanides and his school and which centered on the midrashic view that redemption would be a return to that perfection which was sullied by the sin of Adam and Eve. It would not be something entirely new, but a restoration, or a renewal. Creation at the time of redemption would assume the form that was intended from the beginning by the Divine mind. Only at the redemption would there be a revelation of the original nature of Creation which has become obscured or impaired in this world. Hence, the extreme utopian character of these ideas. In the Divine realm, the state of redemption is expressed as the end of the "exile of the *Shekhinah*", the restoration of the Divine unity throughout all areas of existence. ("In that day the Lord shall be One, and His name One" – hence the view that the true unity of God will be revealed only in the time to come, while during the years of exile it is as if sin had rendered His unity imperfect.) At the time of redemption there will be a continuous union of king and queen, or of the *sefirot Tiferet* and *Shekhinah;* that is to say that there will be an unceasing stream of Divine influx through all worlds, and this will bind them eternally together. The hidden secrets of the Torah will be revealed, and the Kabbalah will be the literal sense of the Torah. The messianic age will last approximately a thousand years, but many believed that these years would not be identical with human years, for the planets and the stars would move more slowly, so that time would be prolonged (this view was particular current in the circle of the *Sefer ha-Temunah,* and it has origins in the Apocryphal books). It is obvious, on the basis of these theories, that the kabbalists believed that the natural order would change in the messianic era (unlike the view of Maimonides). As to the problem of whether the redemption would be a miracle or the logical result of a process already immanent, kabbalastic opinion was divided. After the expulsion from Spain the view gradually prevailed that the appearance of the Messiah would be a symbolic event. Redemption depended on the deeds of Israel, and on the fulfillment of its historic destiny. The coming of the redeemer would testify to the completion of the "restoration", but would not cause it.

Resurrection at the End of the World. The Kabbalah does not cast any doubt on the physical resurrection of the dead, which will take place at the end of the days of redemption, "on the great day of judgment". The novel expositions of the kabbalists revolved round the question of the fate of those who were to be resurrected. Naḥmanides taught that after a normal physical life the resurrected body would be purified, and be clothed in *malakhut* ("the garments of the angels"), and, thereby, pass into the future spiritual world, which would come into being after the destruction of this world; and this new world would appear after the resurrection. In the world to come the souls and their "spiritualized" bodies would be gathered together in the ranks of the *sefirot,* in the true "bond of life". According to Nahmanides, the souls, even in this state, would preserve their individual identity. But afterward other views emerged. The author of the Zohar speaks of "holy bodies" after the resurrection, but does not state his specific view of their future except by allusion. One widespread view identified the world to come with the *sefirah Binah* and its manifestations. After the life of beatitude experienced by the resurrected, this world would be destroyed, and some say that it would return to chaos ("waste and void") in order to be recreated in a new form. Perhaps the world to come would be the creation of another link in the chain of "creations", or *shemitot* ("sabbaticals"; according to the view of the author of *Sefer ha-Temunah*) or even the creation of a spiritual existence through which all existing things ascend to reach the world of the *sefirot,* and return to their primeval being, or their "higher source". In the "Great Jubilee", after 50,000 years, everything will return to the bosom of the *Sefirah Binah,* which is also called the "mother of the world". Even the other *sefirot,* through which God guides creation, will be destroyed with the destruction of creation. The contradiction of having two judgments on man's fate, one after death, and the other after resurrection, one of which would appear to be superfluous, caused some kabbalists to restrict the great Day of Judgment to the nations of the world, while the souls of Israel, in their view, would be judged immediately after death.

10

Gematria

Gematria (from Gr. γεωμετρία), is one of the aggadic hermeneutical rules for interpreting the Torah (in the *Baraita of 32 Rules,* no. 29). It consists of explaining a word or group of words according to the numerical value of the letters, or of substituting other letters of the alphabet for them in accordance with a set system. Whereas the word is normally employed in this sense of manipulating according to the numerical value, it sometimes found with the meaning of "calculations" (Avot 3:18). Similarly where the reading in present editions of the Talmud is that Johanan b. Zakkai knew "the heavenly revolutions and *gematriot*", in a parallel source the reading is "the heavenly revolutions and calculations" (Suk. 28a; BB 134a; Ch. Albeck, *Shishah Sidrei Mishnah* 4(1959), 497).

The use of letters to signify numbers was known to the Babylonians and the Greeks. The first use of *gematria* occurs in an inscription of Sargon II (727–707 B.C.E.) which states that the king built the wall of Khorsabad 16,283 cubits long to correspond with the numerical value of his name. The use of *gematria* (τὸ ἰσόψηφον) was widespread in the literature of the Magi and among interpreters of dreams in the Hellenistic world. The Gnostics equated the two holy names Abrazas (Ἀβράξας) and Mithras (Μίθρας) on the basis of the equivalent numerical value of their letters (365, corresponding to the days of the solar year). Its use was apparently introduced in Israel during the time of the Second Temple, even in the Temple itself, Greek letters being used to indicate numbers (Shek. 3:2).

In rabbinic literature numerical *gematria* first appears in statements by *tannaim* of the second century. It is used as supporting evidence and as a mnemonic by R. Nathan. He states that the phrase *Elleh ha-devarim* ("These are the words") occurring in Exodus 35:1 hints at the 39 categories of work forbidden on the Sabbath, since the plural *devarim* indicates two, the additional article a third, while the numerical equivalent of *elleh* is 36, making a total of 39 (Shab. 70a). R. Judah inferred from the verse, "From the fowl of the heavens until the beasts are fled and gone" (Jer. 9:9), that for 52 years no traveler passed through Judea, since the numerical value of *behemah* ("beast") is 52. The

Baraita of 32 Rules cites as an example of *gematria* the interpretation that the 318 men referred to in Genesis 14:14 were in fact only Eliezer the servant of Abraham, the numerical value of his name being 318. This interpretation, which occurs elsewhere (Ned. 32a; Gen. R. 43:2) in the name of Bar Kappara, may also be a reply to the Christian interpretation in the Epistle of Barnabas that wishes to find in the Greek letters *τιη*, whose numerical value is 318, a reference to the cross and to the first two letters of Jesus' name, through which Abraham achieved his victory; the Jewish homilist used the same method to refute the Christian interpretation.

The form of *gematria* which consists of changing the letters of the alphabet according to *atbash,* i.e., the last letter ת is substituted for the first א, the penultimate ש for the second ב etc., already occurs in Scripture: Sheshach (Jer. 25:26; 51:41) corresponding to Bavel ("Babylon"). The *Baraita of 32 Rules* draws attention to a second example: *lev kamai* (Jer. 51:1) being identical, according to this system, with Kasdim ("Chaldeans"). Another alphabet *gematria* is formed by the *atbaḥ* system, i.e., א is substituted for ט,ב for ח etc., and is called "the alphabet of Ḥiyya" (Suk. 52b). Rav, the pupil of Ḥiyya, explained that Belshazzar and his men could not read the cryptic writing because it was written in *gematria,* i.e., according to *atbaḥ* (Sanh. 22a; cf. Shab. 104a).

Gematria has little significance in *halakhah.* Where it does occur, it is as a hint or a mnemonic. The rule that when a man takes a nazirite vow for an unspecified period, it is regarded as being for 30 days, is derived from the word *yihiyeh* ("he shall be") in Numbers 6:5, whose numerical value is 30 (Naz. 5a). Even in the *aggadah,* at least among the early *amoraim, gematria* is not used as a source of ideas and homilies but merely to express them in the most concise manner. The statements that Noah was delivered not for his own sake but for the sake of Moses (Gen. R. 26:6), that Rebekah was worthy to have given birth to 12 tribes (*ibid.* 63:6), and that Jacob's ladder symbolizes the revelation at Sinai (*ibid.* 68:12), do not depend on the *gematriot* given there. These homilies are derived from other considerations and it is certain that they preceded the *gematriot.*

Gematriot, however, do occupy an important place in those Midrashim whose chief purpose is the interpretation of letters, such as the *Midrash Ḥaserot vi-Yterot,* and also in the late aggadic Midrashim (particularly in those whose authors made use of the work of Moses b. Isaac ha-Darshan) such as *Numbers Rabbah* (in *Midrash Aggadah,* published by S. Buber, 1894), and *Genesis Rabbati* (published by Ḥ. Albeck, 1940; see introduction, 11–20). Rashi also cites *gematriot* that "were established by Moses ha-Darshan" (Num. 7:18) and some of the *gematriot* given by him came from this source even if the does not explicitly mention it (Gen. 32:5, e.g., "I have sojourned with Laban" –

the *gematria* value of "I have sojourned" is 613, i.e., "I sojourned with the wicked Laban but observed the 613 precepts", is the interpretation of Moses ha-Darshan, *Genesis Rabbati,* 145). Joseph Bekhor Shor, one of the great French exegetes of the Torah, made extensive use of *gematriot,* and nearly all the tosafists followed him in this respect in their Torah commentaries (S. Poznański, *Mavo al Hakhmei Ẓarefat Mefareshei ha-Mikra,* 73). A wealth of *gematriot* occur in *Pa'ne'aḥ Raza,* the commentary of Isaac b. Judah ha-Levi (end of 13th century), and in the *Ba'al ha-Turim,* the biblical commentary of Jacob b. Asher. The esoteric doctrines of the Ḥasidei Ashkenaz also brought about the introduction of *gematriot* into the *halakhah.* In his *Ha-Roke'aḥ,* Eleazar of Worms uses *gematriot* to find many hints and supports for existing laws and customs; with him the *gematria* at times embraces whole sentences. Thus he establishes by *gematria* from Exodus 23:15 that work which can be deferred until after the festival may not be performed during the intermediate days (*Ha-Roke'aḥ,* no. 307). *Gematriot* of the Ḥasidei Ashkenaz occupy a prominent place in their commentaries on the liturgy and on *piyyutim.* Abraham b. Azriel incorporated the teachings of Judah he-Ḥasid and Eleazar of Worms in his *Arugat ha-Bosem,* and followed their lead. These *gematriot,* which were part of the Kabbalah of the Ḥasidei Ashkenaz, established the definitive text of the prayers, which came to be regarded as sacrosanct. Some authorities forbade it to be changed even when the text did not conform with the rules of grammar.

In Kabbalah. It is possible that traditions of *gematriot* of Holy Names and angels are from an earlier date, but they were collected and considerably elaborated only in the aforesaid period. Even among the mystics *gematria* is not generally a system for the discovery of new thoughts: almost always the idea precedes the inventing of the *gematria,* which serves as "an allusive *asmakhta*". An exception is the *gematria* on the Holy Names, which are in themselves incomprehensible, or that on the names of angels whose meaning and special aspect the German Ḥasidim sought to determine via *gematria.* Often *gematria* served as a mnemonic device. The classic works of *gematria* in this circle are the writings of Eleazar of Worms, whose *gematriot* are based – at any rate partially – on the tradition of his teachers. Eleazar discovered through *gematria* the mystical meditations on prayers which can be evoked during the actual repetition of the words. His commentaries on books of the Bible are based for the most part on this system, including some which connect the midrashic legends with words of the biblical verses via *gematria,* and some which reveal the mysteries of the world of the Merkabah ("fiery chariot") and the angels, in this way. In this interpretation the *gematria* of entire biblical verses or parts of verses occupies a more outstanding place than the *gematria* based on a count of single words. For example, the numerical value of the sum of the letters of the entire verse "I have gone down into the nut garden" (Songs 6:11), in *gematria* is equivalent to the verse: "This is the depth of the chariot" *(merkavah).* Several extensive works of interpretation by means of *gematria* by the disciples of Eleazar of Worms are preserved in manuscript.

In the beginnings of Spanish Kabbalah *gematria* occupied a very limited place. The disciples of Abraham b. Isaac of Narbonne and the kabbalists of Gerona hardly used it and its impact was not considerable on the greater part of the Zohar and on the Hebrew writings of Moses b. Shem Tov de Leon. Only those currents influenced by the tradition of the Ḥasidei Ashkenaz brought the *gematria* into the kabbalistic literature of the second half of the 13th century, mainly in the work of Jacob b. Jacob ha-Kohen and Abraham Abulafia and their disciples. The works of Abulafia are based on the extensive and extreme use of *gematria.* His books require deciphering before all the associations of the *gematriot* in them can be understood. He recommended the system of developing the power of association in *gematria* in order to discover new truths, and these methods were developed by those who succeeded him. A disciple of Abulafia, Joseph Gikatilla, used *gematria* extensively as one of the foundations of the Kabbalah in *Ginnat Egoz* (Hanau, 1615; the letters *gimmel, nun, tav* of *Ginnat* are the initials of *gematria, notarikon,* and *temurah* – the interchange of letters according to certain systematic rules). This work had visible influence on the later Zohar literature, *Ra'aya Meheimna* and *Tikkunei Zohar.*

Two schools emerged as the Kabbalah developed: one of those who favored *gematria,* and another of those who used it less frequently. In general, it may be stated that new ideas always developed outside the realm of *gematria;* however, there were always scholars who found proofs and wide-ranging connections through *gematria,* and undoubtedly attributed to their findings a positive value higher than that of a mere allusion. Moses Cordovero presented his entire system without recourse to *gematria,* and explained matters of *gematria* only toward the end of his basic work on Kabbalah *(Pardes Rimmonim).* A revival of the use of *gematria* is found in the Lurianic Kabbalah, but it is more widespread in the kabbalistic works of Israel Sarug and his disciples (mainly Menahem Azariah of Fano and Naphtali Bacharach, author of *Emek ha-Melekh*) than in the works of Isaac Luria and Ḥayyim Vital. The classic work using *gematria* as a means of thought and a development of commentative ideas in the Kabbalah in the 17th century is *Megalleh Amukot* by Nathan Naṭa b. Solomon Spira, which served as the model for an entire literature, especially in Poland. At first only the part on Deut. 3:23ff. was published (Cracow, 1637) which explains these passages in 252 different ways. His commentary on the whole Torah (also called *Megalleh Amukot*) was published in Lemberg in 1795. Apparently Nathan possessed a highly developed sense for numbers which found its expression in complex structures of *gematria* (J. Ginsburg, in *Ha-Tekufah* 25 (1929), 448–97). In later kabbalistic literature (in the 18th and 19th centuries) the importance of the methods of commentary via *gematria* is well-known and many works were written whose major content is *gematria*, e.g., *Tiferet Yisrael* by Israel Ḥarif of Satanov (Lemberg, 1865), *Berit Kehunnat Olam* by Isaac Eisik ha-Kohen (Lemberg, 1796; complete edition with commentary on the *gematriot*, 1950), and all the works of Abraham b. Jehiel Michal ha-Kohen of Lask (late 18th century).

In the Shabbatean movement, *gematriot* occupied a place of considerable prominence as proofs of the messianism of Shabbetai Ẓevi. Abraham Yakhini wrote a great work of Shabbatean *gematriot* on one single verse of the Torah (*Vavei ha-Ammudim*, Ms. Oxford), and the major work of the Shabbatean prophet Heshel Ẓoref of Vilna and Cracow, *Sefer ha-Ẓoref*, is based entirely on an elaboration of *gematriot* surrounding the verse *Shema Yisrael* ("Hear O Israel"; Deut. 6:4). In ḥasidic literature *gematria* appeared at first only as a by-product, but later there were several ḥasidic rabbis, the bulk of whose works are *gematria*, e.g., *Igra de-Khallah* by Ẓevi Elimelekh Shapira of Dynow (1868), *Magen Avraham* by Abraham the Maggid of Turisk (1886), and *Sefer Imrei No'am* by Meir Horowitz of Dzikov (1877). In the literature of Oriental and North African Jewry since 1700 gematria has played a considerable role.

The systems of *gematria* became complicated in the course of time. In addition to the numerical value of a word, different methods of *gematria* were used. In Ms. Oxford 1,822, f. 141–46, a special tract lists 72 different forms of *gematriot*. Moses Cordovero (*Pardes Rimmonim*, part 30, ch. 8) lists nine different types of *gematriot*. The important ones are:

(1) The numerical value of one word (equaling the sum of the numerical value of all its letters) is equal to that of another word (e.g., גבורה (*gevurah*) = 216 = אריה (*aryeh*).

(2) A "small number" which does not take into account tens or hundreds (4 = ת; 2 = כ).

(3) The squared number in which the letters of the word are calculated according to their numerical value squared. The Tetragrammaton, יהוה = $10^2 + 5^2 + 6^2 + 5^2 = 186$ = מקום ("Place"), another name for God.

(4) The adding up of the value of all of the preceding letters in an arithmetical series (ד (*dalet*) = 1 + 2 + 3 + 4 = 10). This type of calculation is important in complicated *gematria* that reaches into the thousands.

(5) The "filling" (Heb. *millui*); the numerical value of each letter itself is not calculated but the numerical values of all the letters that make up the names of the letter are calculated (בי״ת = 412; דל״ת = 434; יו״ד = 20). The letters ה and

ו have different fillings" – הא, הה, הו and ויו, ואו, וו ; *millui de-alfin* (*alef* filling"), *millui de-he'in* "*he* filling"), or *millui de-yudin* ("*yod* filling"), respectively. These are important in Kabbalah with regard to the numerical value of the Name of God (יהוה), the Tetragrammaton, which varies according to the four different 'fillings" יוד, הא, ואו, הא (=45, in *gematria* אָדָם (Adam), symbolizing the 45-letter Name of God); יוד, הה, וו, הה (= 52, in *gematria* ב"ן, representing the Holy Name of 52 letters); יוד, הי, ואו, הי (= 63, in *gematria* ס"ג, the 63-letter Name); יוד, הי, ויו, ה' (= 72, in *gematria* ע"ב representing the Name of 72 letters, coexisting with a "Name of 72 Names" taken from the three verses Ex. 14:19–21, each of which contains 72 letters).

Other calculations in *gematria* involve a "filling" of the "filling," or a second "filling." The *gematria* of the word itself is called *ikkar* or *shoresh*, while the rest of the word (the "fillings") is called the *ne'elam* ("hidden part"). The *ne'elam* of the letter י is וד = 10; the *ne'lam* of שד"י is ין, לת and וד = 500.

(6) There is also a "great number" which counts the final letters in the alphabet as a continuation of the alphabet (500 = ם ; 600 = ן; 700 = ץ ; 800 = ף ; 900 = ך). However, there is a calculation according to the usual order of the alphabet whereby the numerical values of the final letters are as follows: ך = 500, ם = 600, ן = 700, etc.

(7) The addition of the number of letters in the word to the numerical value of the word itself, or the addition of the number "one" to the total numerical value of the word.

Criticism of the use of *gematria* as a justified means of commentary was first voiced by Abraham ibn Ezra (in his commentary on Gen. 14:14) and later by the opponents of the Kabbalah (in *Ari Nohem*, ch. 10). But even several kabbalists warned against exaggerated use of *gematria*. Naḥmanides, on the other hand, tried to limit the arbitrary use of *gematriot* and laid down a rule that "no one may calculate a *gematria* in order to deduce from it something that occurs to him. Our rabbis, the holy sages of the Talmud, had a tradition that definite *gematriot* were transmitted to Moses to serve as a mnemonic for something that had been handed down orally with the rest of the Oral Law . . . just as was the case with the *gezerah shavah* of which they said that no man may establish a *gezerah shavah* of his own accord" (*Sefer ha-Ge'ullah* ed. by J.M. Aronson (1959), *Shu'ar* 4; see his commentary to Deut. 4:25). Joseph Solomon Delmedigo speaks of false *gematriot* in order to abolish the value of that system. When the believers in Shabbetzi Ẓevi began widely to apply *gematriot* to his name and the "filling" of the name of God *Shaddai* (both equaling 814), those who denied him used mock *gematriot* (*ru'aḥ sheker* = ("false spirit") = 814). In spite of this, the use of *gematria* was widespread in many circles and among preachers not only in Poland but also among the Sephardim.

Bibliography: W. Bacher, *Exegetische Terminologie . . .* , 1 (1899), 125–8; 2 (1905), 124; F. Dornseiff, *Das Alphabet in Mystik und Magie* (1925^2), 91–118; A. Berliner, *Ketavim Nivḥarim,* 1(1945), 34–37; S. Lieberman, *Hellenism in Jewish Palestine* (1950), 69–74; H. Waton, *Key to the Bible* (1952); Z. Ch. Zalb, *Gematria ve-Notarikon* (Heb., 1955); T. Wechsler, *Ẓefunot be-Masoret Yisrael* (1968); Scholem, Mysticism, index; S.A. Horodezky, in: EJ, 7 (1931), 170–9.

11

Gilgul

Gilgul (גִּלְגּוּל) is the Hebrew term for "transmigration of souls," "reincarnation," or "metempsychosis." There is no definite proof of the existence of the doctrine of *gilgul* in Judaism during the Second Temple period. In the Talmud there is no reference to it (although, by means of allegoric interpretations, later authorities found allusions to and hints of transmigration in the statements of talmudic rabbis). A few scholars interpret the statements of Josephus in *Antiquities* 18:1, 3, and in *Jewish Wars* 2:8, 14, on the holy bodies which the righteous merit, according to the belief of the Pharisees, as indicating the doctrine of metempsychosis and not the resurrection of the dead, as most scholars believe. In the post-talmudic period Anan b. David, the founder of Karaism, upheld this doctrine, and in some of his statements there is an echo and a continuation of the ancient sectarian traditions. The doctrine of transmigration was prevalent from the second century onward among some Gnostic sects and especially among Manicheans and was maintained in several circles in the Christian Church (perhaps even by Origen). It is not impossible that this doctrine became current in some Jewish circles, who could have received it from Indian philosophies through Manicheism, or from Platonic and neoplatonic as well as from Orphic teachings.

Anan's arguments on behalf of *gilgul,* which were not accepted by the Karaites, were refuted by Kirkisānī (tenth century) in a special chapter in his "Book of Lights," first published by Poznański; one of his major points was the death of innocent infants. Some Jews, following the Islamic sect of the Mu'tazila and attracted by its philosophic principles, accepted the doctrine of transmigration. The major medieval Jewish philosophers rejected this doctrine (Saadiah Gaon, *The Book of Beliefs and Opinions,* treatise 6, ch. 7; Abraham ibn Daud, *Emunah Ramah,* treatise 1, ch. 7; Joseph Albo, *Ikkarim,* treatise 4, ch. 29). Abraham b. Ḥiyya quotes the doctrine from neoplatonic sources but rejects it *(Meditation of the Sad Soul,* 46–47; *Megillat ha-Megalleh,* 50–51). Judah Halevi and Maimonides do not mention the doctrine, and Abraham b. Moses b. Maimon, who does refer to it, rejects it completely.

In Early Kabbalah. In constrast with the conspicuous opposition of Jewish philosophy, transmigration is taken for granted in the Kabbalah from its first literary expression in the *Sefer ha-Behir* (late 12th century; see p. 312). The absence of any special apology for this doctrine, which is expounded by the *Bahir* in several parables, proves that the idea grew or developed in the circles of the early kabbalists without any affinity to the philosophic discussion of transmigration. Biblical verses (e.g., "One generation passeth away, and another generation cometh" (Eccles. 1:4), taken as meaning that the generation that passes away is the generation that comes) and talmudic *aggadot* and parables were explained in terms of transmigration. It is not clear whether there was any connection between the appearance of the metempsychosic doctrine in kabbalistic circles in southern France and its appearance among the contemporary Cathars, who also lived there. Indeed the latter, like most believers in transmigration, taught that the soul also passes into the bodies of animals, whereas in the *Bahir* it is mentioned only in relation to the bodies of men.

After the *Bahir* the doctrine of *gilgul* developed in several directions and became one of the major doctrines of the Kabbalah, although the kabbalists differed widely in regard to details. In the 13th century, transmigration was viewed as an esoteric doctrine and was only alluded to, but in the 14th century many detailed and explicit writings on it appeared. In philosophic literature the term *ha'atakah* ("transference") was generally used for *gilgul;* in kabbalistic literature the term *gilgul* appears only from the *Sefer ha-Temunah* onward; both are translations of the Arabic term *tanāsukh*. The early kabbalists, such as the disciples of Isaac the Blind and the kabbalists of Gerona, spoke of "the secret of *ibbur*" ("impregnation"). It was only in the late 13th or 14th centuries that *gilgul* and *ibbur* began to be differentiated. The terms *hitḥallefut* ("exchange") and *din benei ḥalof* (from Prov. 31:8) also occur. From the period of the Zohar on, where it is used freely, the term *gilgul* became prevalent in Hebrew literature and began to appear in philosophic works as well.

Biblical verses and commandments were interpreted in terms of *gilgul*. The early sects to whom Anan was indebted saw the laws of ritual slaughter *(sheḥitah)* as biblical proof of transmigration in accordance with their belief in transmigration among animals. For the Kabbalists the point of departure and the proof for *gilgul* was the commandment of levirate marriage: the brother of the childless deceased replaces the deceased husband so that he may merit children in his second *gilgul*. Later, other *mizvot* too were interpreted on the basis of transmigration. The belief also served as a rational excuse for the apparent absence of justice in the world and as an answer to the problem of the suffering of the righteous and the prospering of the wicked: the righteous man, for example, is punished for his sins in a previous *gilgul*. The entire Book of Job and the resolution of the mystery of his suffering, especially as stated in the words of Elihu, were interpreted in terms of transmigration (e.g., in the commentary on Job by Naḥmanides, and in all subsequent kabbalistic literature). Most of the early kabbalists (up to and including the author of the Zohar) did not regard transmigration as a universal law governing all creatures (as is the case in the Indian belief) and not even as governing all human beings, but saw it rather as connected essentially with offenses against procreation and sexual transgressions. Transmigration is seen as a very harsh punishment for the soul which must undergo it. At the same time, however, it is an expression of the mercy of the Creator, "from whom no one is cast off forever"; even for those who should be punished with "extinction of the soul" *(karet) gilgul* provides an opportunity for restitution. While some emphasized more strongly the aspect of justice in transmigration, and some that of mercy, its singular purpose was always the purification of the soul and the opportunity, in a new trial, to improve its deeds. The death of infants is one of the ways by which former transgressions are punished.

In the *Bahir* it is stated that transmigration may continue for 1,000 generations, but the common opinion in the Spanish Kabbalah is that in order to atone for its sins, the soul transmigrates three more times after entering its original body (according to Job 33:29, "Behold, God does all these things, twice, three times, with a man"). However, the righteous transmigrate endlessly for the benefit of the universe, not for their own benefit. As on all points of this doctrine, opposing views also exist in kabbalistic literature: the righteous transmigrate as many as three times, the wicked, as many as 1,000! Burial is a condition for a new *gilgul* of the soul, hence the reason for burial on the day of death. Sometimes a male soul enters a female body, resulting in barrenness. Transmigration into the bodies of women and of gentiles was held possible by several kabbalists, in opposition to the view of most of the Safed kabbalists. The *Sefer Peli'ah* viewed proselytes as Jewish souls which had passed into the bodies of gentiles, and returned to their former state.

Gilgul and Punishment. The relationship between transmigration and hell is also a matter of dispute. Baḥya b. Asher proposed that transmigration occurred only after the acceptance of punishment in hell, but the opposite view is found in the *Ra'aya Meheimna,* in the Zohar, and among most of the kabbalists. Because the concepts of metempsychosis and punishment in hell are mutually exclusive, there could be no compromise between them. Joseph of Hamadan, Persia, who lived in Spain in the 14th century, interpreted the entire matter of hell as transmigration among animals. The transmigrations of souls began after the slaying of Abel (some claim in the generation of the Flood), and will cease only with the resurrection of the dead. At that time the bodies of all those who underwent transmigrations will be revived and sparks *(nizozot)* from the original soul will spread within them. But there were also other answers to this question, expecially in the 13th century. The expansion of the notion of transmigration from a punishment limited to specific sins into a general principle contributed to the rise of the belief in transmigration into animals and even into plants and inorganic matter. This opinion, however, opposed by many kabbalists, did not become common until after 1400. Transmigration into the bodies of animals is first mentioned in the *Sefer ha-Temunah,* which originated in a circle associated with the kabbalists of Gerona. In the Zohar itself this idea is not found, but some sayings in *Tikkunei Zohar* attempt to explain this concept exegetically, indicating that this doctrine was already known to the author of that work. *Ta'amei ha-Mizvot* (c. 1290–1300), an anonymous work on the reasons for the commandments, records many details (partly quoted by Menahem Recanati) on the transmigration of human souls into the bodies of animals, the great majority of which were punishments for acts of sexual intercourse forbidden by the Torah.

In the Later and the Safed Kabbalah. A more general elaboration of the entire concept appears in the works of Joseph b. Shalom Ashkenazi and his followers (early 14th century). They maintain that transmigration occurs in all forms of existence, from the *Sefirot* ("emanations") and the angels to inorganic matter, and is called *din benei ḥalof* or *sod ha-shelaḥ.* According to this, everything in the world is constantly changing form, descending to the lowest form and ascending again to the highest. The precise concept of the transmigration of the soul in its particular form into an existence other than its original one is thus obscured and is replaced by the law of the change of form. Perhaps this version of the doctrine of *gilgul* should be seen as an answer to philosophical criticism based on the Aristotelian definition of the soul as the "form" of the body which consequently cannot become the form of another body. The mystery of true *gilgul* in this new version was sometimes introduced instead of the traditional kabbalistic teaching as found in *Masoret ha-Berit* (1936) by David b. Abraham ha-Lavan (c. 1300). The kabbalists of Safed accepted the doctrine of transmigration into all forms of nature and, through them, this teaching became a widespread popular belief.

In Safed, especially in the Lurianic Kabbalah, the older idea of *nizozot ha-neshamot* ("sparks of the souls") was highly developed. Each "main" soul is built in the spiritual structure of "mystical limbs" (parallel to the limbs of the body), from which many sparks spread, each of which can serve as a soul or as life in a human body. The *gilgulim* of all the sparks together are aimed at the restitution of the hidden spiritual structure of the "root" of the principal soul; it is possible for one man to possess several different sparks belonging to one "root." All the roots of the souls were in fact contained in Adam's soul, but they fell and were scattered with the first sin; the souls must be reassembled in the course of their *gilgulim* which they and their sparks undergo and through which they are afforded the opportunity to restitute their true and original structure. The later Kabbalah developed much further the idea of the affinity of those souls which belong to a common root. In the kabbalistic commentaries on the Bible many events were explained by such hidden history of the transmigration of various souls which return in a later *gilgul* to situations similar to those of an earlier state, in order to repair damage which they had previously caused. The early Kabbalah provides the basis of this idea: there Moses and Jethro, for example, are considered the reincarnations of Abel and Cain; David, Bathsheba, and Uriah, of Adam, Eve, and the serpent; and Job, of Terah the father of Abraham. The anonymous *Gallei Razayya* (written 1552; published partly Mohilev, 1812), and *Sefer ha-Gilgulim* (Frankfort, 1684) and *Sha'ar ha-Gilgulim* (1875, 1912) by Ḥayyim Vital present lengthy explanations of the histories of biblical characters in the light of their former *gilgulim*. Luria and Vital expanded the framework to include talmudic figures. The transmigrations of many figures are explained, according to the teaching of Israel Sarug, in *Gilgulei Neshamot* by Menahem Azariah da Fano (edition with commentary, 1907). Many kabbalists dealt in detail with the function that was fulfilled by the several *gilgulim* of Adam's soul; they also explained his name as an abbreviation of Adam, David, Messiah (first mentioned by Moses b. Shem-Tov de Leon).

Ibbur. In addition to the doctrine of *gilgul*, that of *ibbur* ("impregnation") developed from the second half of the 13th century. *Ibbur*, as distinct from *gilgul*, means the entry of another soul into a man, not during pregnancy nor at birth but during his life. In general, such an additional soul dwells in a man only for a limited period of time, for the purpose of performing certain acts or commandments. In the Zohar it is stated that the souls of Nadab and Abihu were temporarily added to that of Phinehas in his zeal over the act of Zimri, and that Judah's soul was present in Boaz when he begat Obed. This doctrine held an important place in the teachings of the kabbalists of Safed, especially in the Lurianic school: a righteous man who fulfilled almost all of the 613 *miẓvot* but did not have the opportunity to fulfill one special *miẓvah* is temporarily reincarnated in one who has the opportunity to fulfill it. Thus the souls of the righteous men are reincarnated for the benefit of the universe and their generation. The *ibbur* of a wicked man into the soul of another man is called a Dibbuk in later popular usage (see below). The prevalence of the belief in *gilgul* in the 16th and 17th centuries also caused new disputes between its supporters and detractors. A detailed debate on the doctrine of transmigration took place in about 1460 between two scholars in Candia (Ms. Vatican 254). Abraham ha-Levi ibn Migash wrote against the doctrine of *gilgul* in all its manifestations (*Kevod Elohim*, 2, 10–14, Constantinople, 1585) and Leone Modena wrote his treatise *Ben David* against transmigration (published in the collection *Ta'am Zekenim*, 1885, pp. 61–64). In defense of transmigration, Manasseh Ben Israel wrote *Nishmat Ḥayyim* (Amsterdam, 1652). Works of later kabbalists on the subjects are *Midrash Talpiyyot*, sub voce *Gilgul* (Smyrna, 1736) by Elijah ha-Kohen ha-Itamari and *Golel Or* (Smyrana, 1737) by Meir Bikayam.

Dibbuk (Dybbuk). In Jewish folklore and popular belief an evil spirit or a doomed soul which enters into a living person, cleaves to his soul, causes mental illness, talks through his mouth, and represents a separate and alien personality is called *dibbuk.* The term appears neither in talmudic literature nor in the Kabbalah, where this phenomenon is always called "evil spirit" or "evil *ibbur,*" (In talmudic literature it is sometimes called *ru'aḥ tezazit,* and in the New Testament "unclean spirit.") The term was introduced into literature only in the 17th century from the spoken language of German and Polish Jews. It is an abbreviation of *dibbuk me-ru'aḥ ra'ah* ("a cleavage of an evil spirit"), or *dibbuk min ha-ḥiẓonim* ("*dibbuk* from the demonic side"), which is found in man. The act of attachment of the spirit to the body became the name of the spirit itself. However, the verb *davok* ("cleave") is found throughout kabbalistic literature where it denotes the relations between the evil spirit and the body, *mitdabbeket bo* ("it cleaves itself to him"). It is thus the equivalent of possession (Scholem, in *Leshonenu* 6 (1934), 40–1).

Stories about *dibbukim* are common in the time of the Second Temple and the talmudic periods, particularly in the Gospels; they are not as prominent in medieval literature. At first, the *dibbuk* was considered to be a devil or a demon which entered the body of a sick person. Later, an explanation common among other peoples was added, namely that some of the *dibbukim* are the spirits of dead persons who were not laid to rest and thus became demons. This idea (also common in medieval Christianity) combined with the doctrine of *gilgul* ("transmigration of the soul") in the 16th century and became widespread and accepted by large segments of the Jewish population, together with the belief in *dibbukim.* They were generally considered to be souls which, on account of the enormity of their sins, were not even allowed to transmigrate and as "denuded spirits" they sought refuge in the bodies of living persons. The entry of a *dibbuk* into a person was a sign of his having committed a secret sin which opened a door for the *dibbuk.* A combination of beliefs current in the non-Jewish environment and popular Jewish beliefs influenced by the Kabbalah form these conceptions. The kabbalistic literature of Luria's disciples contains many stories and "protocols" about the exorcism of *dibbukim.* Numerous manuscripts present detailed instructions on how to exorcise them. The power to exorcise *dibbukim* was given to *ba'alei shem* or accomplished Ḥasidim. They exorcised the *dibbuk* from the body which was bound by it and simultaneously redeemed the soul by providing a *tikkun* ("restoration") for him, either by transmigration or by causing the *dibbuk* to enter hell.

From 1560 several detailed reports in Hebrew and Yiddish on the deeds of *dibbukim* and their testimonies about themselves were preserved and published. A wealth of material on actual stories of *dibbukim* is gathered in Samuel Vital's *Sha'ar ha-Gilgulim* (Przemyśl, 1875, f. 8–17), in Ḥayyim Vital's *Sefer ha-Ḥezyonot,* in *Nishmat Ḥayyim* by Manasseh Ben Israel (book 3, chs. 10 and 14), in *Minḥat Eliyahu* (chs. 4 and 5) by Elijah ha-Kohen of Smyrna, and in *Minḥat Yehudah* by Judah Moses Fetya of Baghdad (1933), pp. 41–59). The latter exorcised Shabbetai Ẓevi and his prophet Nathan of Gaza who appeared as *dibbukim* in the bodies of men and women in Baghdad in 1903. Special pamphlets described famous cases of exorcism, such as in Korets (in Yiddish, end of 17th century), in Nikolsburg (1696), in Detmold (1743), again in Nikolsburg (1783), and in Stolowitz (1848, publ. 1911). The last protocol of this kind, published in Jerusalem in 1904, concerns a *dibbuk* which entered the body of a woman and was exorcised by Ben-Zion Ḥazzan. The phenomena connected with the beliefs in and the stories about *dibbukim* usually have their factual background in cases of hysteria and sometimes even in manifestations of schizophrenia.

Bibliography: S. Rubin, *Gilgulei Neshamot* (1899); S. Pushinski, in: *Yavneh,* 1(1939),137–53; G. Scholem, in: *Tarbiz,* 16 (1945), 135–40; S.A. Horodezki, *Torat ha-Kabbalah shel ha-Ari ve-Ḥayyim Vital* (1947), 245–52; S. Poznański, in: *Semitic Studies in Memory of A. Kohut* (1897), 435–56; N.E. David, *Karma and Reincarnation in Israelitism* (1908); M. Weinreich, *Bilder fun der yidisher Literatur Geshikhte* (1928), 254–61; G. Scholem, *Von der mystischen Gestalt der Gottheit* (1962), 193–247; 297–306; E. Gottlieb, in: *Sefunot,* 11 (1969), 43–66.

12
Golem

The *golem* is a creature, particularly a human being, made in an artificial way by virtue of a magic act, through the use of holy names. The idea that it is possible to create living beings in this manner is widespread in the magic of many peoples. Especially well known are the idols and images to which the ancients claimed to have given the power of speech. Among the Greeks and the Arabs these activities are sometimes connected with astrological speculatations related to the possibility of "drawing the spirituality of the stars" to lower beings. The development of the idea of the *golem* in Judaism, however, is remote from astrology: it is connected, rather with the magical exegesis of the *Sefer Yeẓirah* (see p. 23) and with the ideas of the creative power of speech and of the letters.

The word "*golem*" appears only once in the Bible (Ps. 139:16), and from it originated the talmudic usage of the term – something unformed and imperfect. In medieval philosophic usage it is matter without form. Adam is called *golem,* meaning body without soul, in a talmudic legend concerning the first 12 hours of his existence (Sanh. 38b). However, even in this state, he was accorded a vision of all the generations to come (Gen. R. 24:2), as if there were in the *golem* a hidden power to grasp or see, bound up with the element of earth from which he was taken. The motif of the *golem* as it appears in medieval legends originates in the talmudic legend (Sanh. 65b): "Rava created a man and sent him to R. Zera. The latter spoke to him but he did not answer. He asked, 'Are you [made by] one of the companions? Return to your dust'." It is similarly told that two *amoraim* busied themselves on the eve of every Sabbath with the *Sefer Yeẓirah* (or in another version *Hilkhot Yeẓirah)* and made a calf for themselves and ate it. These legends are brought as evidence that "If the righteous wished, they could create a world". They are connected, apparently, with the belief in the creative power of the letters of the Name of God and the letters of the Torah in general (Ber. 551; Mid. Ps. 3). There is disagreement as to whether the *Sefer Yeẓirah* or *Hilkhot Yeẓirah,* mentioned in the Talmud, is the same book called by these two titles which we now possess. Most of this book is of a speculative nature, but its affinity to the magical ideas concerning creation by means of letters is obvious. What is said in the main part of the book about God's activity during creation is attributed at the end of the book to Abraham the Patriarch. The various transformations and combinations of the letters constitute a mysterious knowledge of the inwardness of creation. During the Middle Ages, *Sefer Yeẓirah* was interpreted in some circles in France and Germany as a guide to magical usage. Later legends in this direction were first found at the end of the commentary on the *Sefer Yeẓirah* by Judah b. Barzillai (beginning of the 12th century). There the legends of the Talmud were interpreted in a new way: at the conclusion of profound study of the mysteries of *Sefer Yeẓirah* on the construction of the cosmos, the sages (as did Abraham the Patriarch) acquired the power to create living beings, but the purpose of such creation was purely symbolic and contemplative, and when the sages wanted to eat the calf which was created by the power of their "contemplation" of the book, they forgot all they had learned. From these late legends there developed among the Ḥasidei Ashkenaz in the 12th and 13th centuries the idea of the creation of the *golem* as a mystical ritual, which was used, apparently, to symbolize the level of their achievement at the conclusion of their studies. In this circle, the term *golem* has, for the first time, the fixed meaning indicating such a creature.

In none of the early sources is there any mention of any practical benefit to be derived from a *golem* of this sort. In the opinion of the mystics, the creation of the *golem* had not a real, but only a symbolic meaning; that is to say, it was an ecstatic experience which followed a festive rite. Those who took part in the "act of creation" took earth from virgin soil and made a *golem* out of it (or, according to another source, they buried that *golem* in the soil), and walked around the *golem* "as in a dance", combining the alphabetical letters and the secret Name of God in accordance with detailed sets of instructions (several of which have been preserved). As a result of this act of combination, the *golem* arose and lived, and when they walked in the opposite direction and said the same combination of letters in reverse order, the vitality of the *golem* was nullified and he sank or fell. According to other legends, the word *emet* (אמת ; "truth"; "the seal of the Holy One," Shab. 55a; Sanh. 64b) was written on his forehead, and when the letter *alef* was erased there remained the word *met* ("dead"). There are legends concerning the creation of such a *golem* by the prophet Jeremiah and his so-called "son" Ben Sira, and also by the disciples of R. Ishmael, the central figure of the *Heikhalot* literature. The technical instructions about the manner of uttering the combinations, and everything involved in the ritual, proves that the creation of the *golem* is connected here with ecstatic spiritual experiences (end of commentary on *Sefer Yezirah* by Eleazar of Worms; the chapter *Sha'ashu'ei ha-Melekh* in N. Bacharach's *Emek ha-Melekh* (Amsterdam, 1648); and in the commentary on *Sefer Yeẓirah* (1562, fol. 87–101) attributed to Saadiah b. Joseph Gaon). In the legends about the *golem* of Ben Sira there is also a parallel to the legends on images used in idol worship which are given life by means of a name; the *golem* expresses a warning about it (idol worship) and demands his own death. It is said in several sources that the *golem* has no intellectual soul, and therefore he lacks the power of speech, but opposite opinions are also found which attribute this power to him. The opinions of the kabbalists concerning the nature of the creation of the *golem* vary. Moses Cordovero thought that man has the power to give "vitality", *ḥiyyut,* alone to the *golem* but not life *(nefesh),* spirit *(ru'aḥ),* or soul proper *(neshamah).*

In the popular legend which adorned the figures of the leaders of the Ashkenazi ḥasidic movement with a crown of wonders, the *golem* became an actual creature who served his creators and fulfilled tasks laid upon him. Legends such as these began to make their appearance among German Jews not later than the 15th century and spread widely, so that by the 17th century they were "told by all" (according to Joseph Solomon Delmedigo). In the development of the later legend of the *golem* there are three outstanding points: (1) The legend is connected with earlier tales of the resurrection of the dead by putting the name of God in their mouths or on their arm, and by removing the parchment containing the name in reverse and thus causing their death. Such legends were widespread in Italy from the tenth century (in *Megillat Aḥima'aẓ*). (2) It is related to ideas current in non-Jewish circles concerning the creation of an alchemical man (the "homunculus" of Paracelsus). (3) The *golem,* who is the servant of his creator, develops dangerous natural powers; he grows from day to day, and in order to keep him from overpowering the members of the household he must be restored to dust by removing or erasing the *alef* from his forehead. Here, the idea of the *golem* is joined by the new motif of the unrestrained power of the elements which can bring about destruction and havoc. Legends of this sort appeared first in connection with Elijah, rabbi of Chelm (d. 1583). Ẓevi Hirsch Ashkenazi and his son Jacob Emden, who were among his descendants, discussed in their responsa whether or not it is permitted to include a *golem* of this sort in a *minyan* (they prohibited it). Elijah Gaon of Vilna told his disciple Ḥayyim b. Isaac of Volozhin that as a boy he too had undertaken to make a *golem,* but he saw a vision which caused him to desist from his preparations.

The latest and best-known form of the popular legend is connected with Judah Loew b. Bezalel of Prague. This legend has no historical basis in the life of Loew or in the era close to his lifetime. It was transferred from R. Elijah of Chelm to R. Loew only at a very late date, apparently during the second half of the 18th century. As a local legend of Prague, it is connected with the Altneuschul synagogue and with an explanation of special practices in the prayers of the congregation of Prague. According to these legends, R. Loew created the *golem* so that he would serve him, but was forced to restore him to his dust when the *golem* began to run amok and endanger people's lives.

In the Arts. The legends concerning the *golem*, especially in their later forms, served as a favorite literary subject, at first in German literature – of both Jews and non-Jews – in the 19th century, and afterward in modern Hebrew and Yiddish literature. To the domain of belles lettres also belongs the book *Nifla'ot Maharal im ha-Golem* ("The Miraculous Deeds of Rabbi Loew with the Golem"; 1909), which was published by Judah Rosenberg as an early manuscript but actually was not written until after the blood libels of the 1890s, especially the Hilsner case in Polna (Czechoslovakia, 1899). The connection between the *golem* and the struggle against ritual murder accusations is entirely a modern literary invention. In this literature questions are discussed which had no place in the popular legends (e.g., the *golem*'s love for a women), or symbolic interpretations of the meaning of the *golem* were raised (the unredeemed, unformed man; the Jewish people; the working class aspiring for its liberation).

Interest in the *golem* legend among writers, artists, and musicians became evident in the early 20th century. The *golem* was almost invariably the benevolent robot of the later Prague tradition and captured the imagination of writers active in Austria, Czechoslovakia, and Germany. Two early works on the subject were the Austrian playwright Rudolf Lothar's volume of stories entitled *Der Golem. Phantasien und Historien* (1900, 1904^2) and the German novelist Arthur Holitscher's three-act drama *Der Golem* (1908). The Prague German-language poet Hugo Salus published verse on "Der hohe Rabbi Loew" and by World War I the theme had gained widespread popularity. The outstanding work about the *golem* was the novel entitled *Der Golem* (1915; Eng. 1928) by the Bohemian writer Gustav Meyrink (1868–1932), who spent his earlier years in Prague. Meyrink's book, notable for its detailed description and nightmare atmosphere, was a terrifying allegory about an artist's struggle to find himself. Other works on the subject include Johannes Hess's *Der Rabbiner von Prag (Reb Loeb)...* (1914), a four-act "kabbalistic drama," Chayim Bloch's *Der Prager Golem: von seiner "Geburt" bis zu seinem "Tod"* (1917; *The Golem. Legends of the Ghetto of Prague,* 1925); and *Ha-Golem* (1909), a story by the Hebrew writer David Frischmann which later appeared in his collection *Ba-Midbar* (1923). The Yiddish dramatist H. Leivick's *Der Golem* (1921; Eng., 1928), based on Rosenberg's book, was first staged in Moscow in Hebrew by the Habimah Theater. Artistic and musical interpretations of the theme were dependent on the major literary works. Hugo Steiner-Prag produced lithographs to accompany Meyrink's novel *(Der Golem; Prager Phantasien,* 1915), the book itself inspiring a classic German silent film directed by Paul Wegener and Henrik Galeen (1920), and a later French remake by Julien Duvivier (1936). The screenplay for a post-World War II Czech film about the *golem* was written by Arnost Lustig. Music for Leivick's drama was written by Moses Milner; and Eugen d'Albert's opera *Der Golem,* with libretto by F. Lion, had its première at Frankfort in 1926, but has not survived in the operatic repertory. A more lasting work was Joseph Achron's *Golem Suite* for orchestra (1932), composed under the influence of the Habimah production. The last piece of this suite was written as the first movement's exact musical image in reverse to symbolize the disintegration of the homunculus. *Der Golem,* a ballet by Francis Burt with choreography by Erika Hanka, was produced in Vienna in 1962.

Bibliography: Ch. Bloch, *The Golem* (1925); H.L. Held, *Das Gespenst des Golems* (1927); B. Rosenfeld, *Die Golemsage und ihre Verwertung in der deutschen Literatur* (1934); G. Scholem, *On the Kabbalah and its Symbolism* (1965), 158–204; F. Thieberger, *The Great Rabbi Loew of Prague: his Life and Work and the Legend of the Golem* (1954).

13
Lilith

Lilith is a female demon assigned a central position in Jewish demonology. The figure may be traced to Babylonian (possibly even Sumerian) demonology, which identifies similar male and female spirits – Lilu and Lilitu respectively – which are etymologically unrelated to the Hebrew word *laylah* ("night"). These *mazikim* ("harmful spirits") have various roles: one of them – the Ardat-Lilith – preys on males, while others imperil women in childbirth and their children. An example of the latter kind is Lamashtu (first deciphered as Labartu), against whom incantation formulas have been preserved in Assyrian. Winged female demons who strangle children are known from a Hebrew or Canaanite inscription found at Arslan-Tash in northern Syria and dating from about the seventh or eighth century B.C.E. Whether or not Lilith is mentioned in this incantation, which adjures the stranglers not to enter the house, is a moot point, depending on the addition of a missing consonant: "To her that flies in rooms of darkness – pass quickly quickly, Lil[ith]". In Scripture there is only one reference to Lilith (Isa. 34:14), among the beasts of prey and the spirits that will lay waste the land on the day of vengeance. In sources dating from earlier centuries, traditions concerning the female demon who endangers women in childbirth and who assumes many guises and names are distinct from the explicit tradition on Lilith recorded in the Talmud. Whereas the Babylonian Lilu is mentioned as some kind of male demon with no defined function, Lilith appears as a female demon with a woman's face, long hair, and wings (Er. 100b; Nid. 24b). A man sleeping in a house alone may be seized by Lilith (Shab. 151b); while the demon Hormiz, or Ormuzd, is mentioned as one of her sons (BB 73b). There is no foundation to the later commentaries that identify Lilith with the demon Agrath, daughter of Mahalath, who goes abroad at night with 180,000 pernicious angels (Pes. 112b). Nevertheless, a female demon who is said to be known by tens of thousands of names and moves about the world at night, visiting women in childbirth and endeavoring to strangle their newborn babes, is mentioned in the *Testament of Solomon,* a Greek work of about the third century. Although preserved in a Christian version, this work is certainly based on Judeo-Hellenistic magic. Here the female demon is called Obizoth, and it is related that one of the mystical names of the angel Raphael inscribed on an amulet prevents her from inflicting injury.

Midrashic literature expands the legend that Adam, having parted from his wife after it had been ordained that they should die, begat demons from spirits that had attached themselves to him. It is said that "he was encountered by a Lilith named Piznai who, taken by his beauty, lay with him and bore male and female demons". The firstborn son of this demonic union was Agrimas (see the Midrash published in *Ha-Goren,* 9(1914), 66–68; *Dvir,* 1 (1923), 138; and L. Ginzberg, *Legends of the Jews,* 5 (1925), 166.) The offspring of this Lilith fill the world. A transmuted version of this legend appears in the *Alphabet of Ben Sira,* a work of the geonic period, which sets out to explain the already widespread custom of writing amulets against Lilith. Here she is identified with the "first Eve," who was created from the earth at the same time as Adam, and who, unwilling to forgo her equality, disputed with him the manner of their intercourse. Pronouncing the Ineffable Name, she flew off into the air. On Adam's request, the Almighty sent after her the three angels Snwy, Snsnwy, and Smnglf; finding her in the Red Sea, the angels threatened that if she did not return, 100 of her sons would die every day. She refused, claiming that she was expressly created to harm newborn infants. However, she had to swear that whenever she saw the image of those angels in an amulet, she would lose her power over the infant. Here the legend concerning the wife of Adam who preceded the creation of Eve (Gen. 2) merges with the earlier legend of Lilith as a demon who kills infants and endangers women in childbirth. This later version of the myth has many parallels in Christian literature from Byzantine (which probably preceded it) and later periods. The female demon is known by different names, many of which reappear in the same or in slightly altered forms in the literature of practical Kabbalah (as, for example, the name Obizoth from the *Testament of Solomon*), and the place of the angels is taken by three saints – Sines, Sisinnios, and Synodoros. The legend also found its way into Arabic demonology, where Lilith is known as Karīna, Tābi'a, or "the mother of the infants." Ther personification of Lilith as a strangler of babies is already clear in Jewish incantations, written in Babylonian Aramaic, which predate the *Alphabet of Ben Sira.* A late Midrash (*Numbers R.*, end of ch. 16) also mentions her in this respect: "When Lilith finds no children born, she turns on her own" – a motif which relates her to the Babylonian Lamashtu.

From these ancient traditions, the image of Lilith was fixed in kabbalistic demonology. Here, too, she has two primary roles: the strangler of children (sometimes replaced in the Zohar by Na'amah), and the seducer of men, from whose nocturnal emissions she bears an infinite number of demonic sons. In this latter role she appears at the head of a vast host, who share in her activities. In the Zohar, as in other sources, she is known by such appelations as Lilith, the harlot, the wicked, the false, or the black. (The above-mentioned combination of motifs appears in the Zohar 1:14b, 54b; 2:96a, 111a; 3:19a, 76b.) She is generally numbered among the four mothers of the demons, the others being Agrat, Mahalath, and Na'amah. Wholly new in the kabbalistic concept of Lilith is her appearance as the permanent partner of Samael, queen of the realm of the forces of evil (the *sitra aḥra*). In that world (the world of the *kelippot*) she fulfills a function parallel to that of the *Shekhinah* ("Divine Presence") in the world of sanctity: just as the *Shekhinah* is the mother of the House of Israel, so Lilith is the mother of the unholy folk who constituted the "mixed multitude" (the *erev-rav*) and ruled over all that is impure. This conception is first found in the sources used by Isaac b. Jacob ha-Kohen, and later in *Ammud ha-Semali* by his disciple, Moses b. Solomon b. Simeon of Burgos. Both here, and later in the *Tikkunei Zohar,* there crystallizes the conception of various degrees of Lilith, internal and external. Likewise we find Lilith the older, the wife of Samael, and Lilith the younger, the wife of Asmodeus (see *Tarbiz,* 4 (1932/33), 72) in the writings of Isaac ha-Kohen and thereafter in the writings of most kabbalists, and in many incantations. Some of these identify the two harlots who appeared in judgment before Solomon with Lilith and Na'amah or Lilith and Agrat, an idea which is already hinted at in the Zohar and in contemporary writings (see *Tarbiz,* 19(1947/48), 172–5).

Widespread, too, is the identification of Lilith with the Queen of Sheba – a notion with many ramifications in Jewish folklore. It originates in the Targum to Job 1:15 based on a Jewish and Arab myth that the Queen of Sheba was actually a jinn, half human and half demon. This view was known to Moses b. Shem Tov de Leon and is also mentioned in the Zohar. In *Livnat ha-Sappir* Joseph Angelino maintains that the riddles which the Queen of Sheba posed to Solomon are a repetition of the words of seduction which the first Lilith spoke to Adam. In Ashkenazi folklore, this figure coalesced with the popular image of Helen of Troy or the Frau Venus of German mythology. Until recent generations the Queen of Sheba was popularly pictured as a snatcher of children and a demonic witch. It is probable that there is a residue of the image of Lilith as Satan's partner in popular late medieval European notions of Satan's concubine, or wife in English folklore – "the Devil's Dame" – and of Satan's grandmother in German folklore. In the German drama on the female pope Jutta (Johanna), which was printed in 1565 though according to its publisher it was written in 1480, the grandmother's name is Lilith. Here she is depicted as a seductive dancer, a motif commonly found in Ashkenazi Jewish incantations involving the Queen of Sheba. In the writings of Ḥayyim Vital (*Sefer ha-Likkutim* (1913), 6b), Lilith sometimes appears to people in the form of a cat, goose, or other creature, and she holds sway not for eight days alone in the case of a male infant and 20 for a female (as recorded in the *Alphabet of Ben Sira*), but for 40 and 60 days respectively. In the Kabbalah, influenced by astrology, Lilith is related to the planet Saturn, and all those of a melancholy disposition – of a "black humor" – are her sons (Zohar, *Ra'aya Meheimna*, 3: 227b). From the 16th century it was commonly believed that if an infant laughed in his sleep it was an indication that Lilith was playing with him, and it was therefore advisable to tap him on the nose to avert the danger (Ḥ. Vital, *Sefer ha-Likkutim* (1913), 78c; *Emek ha-Melekh*, 130b).

It was very common to protect women who were giving birth from the power of Lilith by affixing amulets over the bed or on all four walls of the room. The earliest forms of these, in Aramaic, are included in Montgomery's collection (see bibl.). The first Hebrew version appears in the *Alphabet of Ben Sira*, which states that the amulet should contain not only the names of the three angels who prevail over Lilith, but also "their form, wings, hands, and legs." This version gained wide acceptance, and amulets of this type were even printed by the 18th century. According to *Shimmush Tehillim*, a book dating from the geonic period, amulets written for women who used to lose their children customarily included Psalm 126 (later replaced by Ps. 121) and the names of these three angels. In the Orient, also amulets representing Lilith herself "bound in chains" were current. Many amulets include the story of the prophet Elijah meeting Lilith on her way to the house of a woman in childbirth "to give her the sleep of death, to take her son and drink his blood to suck the marrow of his bones and to eat his flesh" (in other versions: "to leave his flesh"). Elijah excommunicated her, whereupon she undertook not to harm women in childbirth whenever she saw or heard her names. This version is doubtless taken from a Christian Byzantine formula against the female demon Gyllo, who was exorcised by the three saints mentioned above. The transfer from the Greek to the Hebrew version is clearly seen in the formula of the 15th-century Hebrew incantation from Candia, which was published by Cassuto (RSO, 15 (1935), 260), in which it is not Elijah but the archangel Michael who, coming from Sinai, encounters Lilith. Though the Greek names were progressively corrupted as time elapsed by the 14th century new Greek names for "Lilith's entourage" appear in a manuscript of practical Kabbalah which includes material from a much earlier date (British Museum Add. Ms. 15299, fol. 84b). The story of Elijah and Lilith included in the second edition of David Lida's *Sod ha-Shem* (Berlin, 1710, p. 20a) is found in the majority of the later amulets against Lilith, one of her names being Striga – an enchantress, either woman or demon – or Astriga. In one of its mutations this name appears as the angel Astaribo, whom Elijah also encountered; in many incantations he takes the place of Lilith, a substitution found in a Yiddish

Amulet for the protection of a newborn child against Lilith, Persia, 18th century. Lilith is represented with arms out-stretched and bound in fetters. On her body is written, "Protect this newborn child from all harm." On either side of her are the names of Adam and Eve and the patriarchs and matriarchs, while above are the initial letters of a passage from Numbers 6:22-27, and below from Psalms 121.

version of the story dating from 1695. Also extant are versions of the incantation in which Lilith is replaced by the Evil Eye, the star Margalya, or the demon familiar in Jewish and Arab literature, Maimon the Black. In European belles lettres, the Lilith story in various versions has been a fruitful narrative theme.

Bibliography: G. Scholem, in: KS, 10 (1934/35), 68–73; idem, in: *Tarbiz*, 19 (1947/48), 165–75; idem, *Jewish Gnosticism* (1965^2), 72–4; R. Margaliot, *Malakhei Elyon* (1945), 235–41: Y. Shacher, *Osef Feuchtwanger – Masoret ve-Ommanut Yehudit* (1971); H. Von der Hardt, *Aenigmata Judaeorum religiosissima* (Helmstedt, 1705), 7–21; J.A. Eisenmenger, *Entdecktes Judentum*, 2 (1700), 413–21; J. Montgomery, *Aramaic Incantation Texts from Nippur* (1913); R. Dow and A. Freidus, in: *Bulletin of the Brooklyn Entomological Society*, 12 (1917), 1–12 (bibl. on Samael and Lilith); I. Lévi, in: REJ, 67 (1914), 15–21; D. Myhrmann, *Die Labartu-Texte* (1902); Ch.

McCown, *The Testament of Solomon* (1922); M. Gaster, *Studies and Texts*, 2 (1925–28), 1005–38, 1252–65; F. Perles, in: *Orientalistische Literaturzeitung*, 18 (1925), 179–80; I. Zoller, *Rivista di Antropologia*, 27 (1926); Ginzberg, *Legends of the Jews*, 5 (1955), 87f.; H. Winkler, *Salomo und die Karīna* (1931); J. Trachtenberg, *Jewish Magic and Superstition* (1939), 36f., 277f.; Th. Gaster, in: *Orientalia*, 12(1942), 41–79; H. Torczyner (Tur-Sinai), in: *Journal of Near Eastern Studies*, 6 (1947), 18–29; M. Rudwin, *The Devil in Legend and Literature* (1931), 94–107; T. Schrire, *Hebrew Amulets* (1966); E. Yamaūchi, *Mandaic Incantation Texts* (1967); A. Chastel, in: RHR, 119–20 (1939), 160–74; A.M. Killen, *Revue de littérature comparee*, 12 (1932), 277-311.

14
Magen David

The *magen David* (Heb. מָגֵן דָּוִד : "shield of David"), is a hexagram or six-pointed star formed by two equilateral triangles which have the same center and are placed in opposite directions.

From as early as the Bronze Age it was used – possibly as an ornament and possibly as a magical sign – in many civilizations and in regions as far apart as Mesopotamia and Britain. Iron Age examples are known from India and from the Iberian peninsula prior to the Roman conquest. Occasionally it appears on Jewish artefacts, such as lamps and seals, but without having any special and recognizable significance. The oldest undisputed example is on a seal from the seventh century B.C.E. found in Sidon and belonging to one Joshua b. Asayahu. In the Second Temple period, the hexagram was often used by Jews and non-Jews alike alongside the pentagram (the five-pointed star), and in the synagogue of Capernaum (second or third century C.E.) it is found side by side with the pentagram and the swastika on a frieze. There is no reason to assume that it was used for any purposes other than decorative. Theories interpreting it as a planetary sign of Saturn and connecting it with the holy stone in the pre-Davidic sanctuary in Jerusalem[1] are purely speculative. Neither in the magical papyri nor in the oldest sources of Jewish magic does the hexagram appear, but it began to figure as a magical sign from the early Middle Ages. Among Jewish emblems from Hellenistic times (discussed in E. Goodenough, *Jewish Symbols in the Greco-Roman Period*), both hexagram and pentagram are missing.

The ornamental use of the hexagram continued in the Middle Ages, especially in Muslim and Christian countries. The kings of Navarre used it on their seals (10th and 11th centuries) and (like the pentagram) it was frequently employed on notarial signs in Spain, France, Denmark, and Germany, by Christian and Jewish notaries alike. Sometimes drawn with slighly curved lines, it appears in early Byzantine and many medieval European churches, as, for example, on a stone from an early church in Tiberias (preserved in the Municipal Museum) and on the entrance to the cathedrals of Burgos, Valencia, and Lerida. Examples are also found on objects used in churches, sometimes in a slanted position, as on the marble bishop's throne (c. 1266) in the Cathedral of Anagni. Probably in

A *magen David* fashioned from Psalm 121 on an amulet for a woman in childbirth, Germany, 18th century.

imitation of church usage – and certainly not as a specifically Jewish symbol – the hexagram is found on some synagogues from the later Middle Ages, for example, in Hameln (Germany, c. 1280) and Budweis (Bohemia, probably 14th century). In Arab sources the hexagram, along with other geometrical ornaments, was widely used under the designation "seal of Solomon," a term which was also taken over by many Jewish groups. This name connects the hexagram with early Christian, possibly Judeo-Christian magic, such as the Greek magical work *The Testament of Solomon.* It is not clear in which period the hexagram was engraved on the seal or ring of Solomon, mentioned in the Talmud (Git. 68a–b) as a sign of his dominion over the demons, instead of the name of God, which originally appeared. However, this happened in Christian circles where Byzantine amulets of the sixth century already use the "seal of Solomon" as the name of the hexagram. In many medieval Hebrew manuscripts elaborate designs of the hexagram are to be found, without its being given any name. The origin of this use can be clearly traced to Bible manuscripts from Muslim countries (a specimen is shown in Gunzburg and Stassoff, *L'ornement hébraïque* (1905), pl. 8, 15). From the 13th century onward it is found in Hebrew Bible manuscripts from Germany and Spain. Sometimes parts of the masorah are written in the form of a hexagram; sometimes it is simply used, in a

The *magen David* used as the basic design for a kabbalistic drawing; Italy 17th century.

more or less elaborate form, as an ornament. Richly adorned specimens from manuscripts in Oxford and Paris have been reproduced by C. Roth, *Sefarad,* 12, 1952, p. 356, pl. II, and in the catalog of the exhibition "Synagoga," Recklinghausen, 1960, pl. B. 4.

In Arabic magic the "seal of Solomon" was widely used, but at first its use in Jewish circles was restricted to relatively rare cases. Even then, the hexagram and pentagram were easily interchangeable and the name was applied to both figures. As a talisman, it was common in many of the magical versions of the *mezuzah* which were widespread between the tenth and 14th centuries. Frequently, the

Magen David used as a printer's mark on *Seder Tefillot,* the first Hebrew book published in Central Europe, Prague, 1512. From A. Yaari, *Hebrew Printers' Marks from the Beginning of Hebrew Printing to the End of 19th Century,* Jerusalem, 1943.

magical additions to the traditional text of the *mezuzah* contained samples of the hexagram, sometimes as many as 12. In magical Hebrew manuscripts of the later Middle Ages, the hexagram was used for certain amulets, among which one for putting out fires attained great popularity.[2]

The notion of a "shield of David" with magical powers was originally unconnected with the sign. It is difficult to say whether the notion arose in Islam, where the Koran sees David as the first to make protective arms, or from inner traditions of Jewish magic. From earlier times there is only one instance connecting the hexagram with the name David, on a sixth-century tombstone from Tarento, southern Italy. There seems to have been some special reason for putting the hexagram before the name of the deceased. The oldest text mentioning a shield of David is contained in an explanation of a magical "alphabet of the angel Metatron" which stems from the geonic period and was current among the Ḥasidei Ashkenaz of the 12th century. But here it was the holy Name of 72 (taken from Ex. 14:19–21, where each verse has 72 letters) which was said to have been engraved on this protective shield, together with the name MKBY. In cognate sources this tradition was much embellished. The name of the angel Taftafiyyah, one of the names of Metatron, was added to the 72 holy names, and indeed an amulet in the form of a hexagram with this one name became one of the most widespread protective charms in many medieval and later manuscripts. (From c. 1500 onward the name *Shaddai* was often substituted for the purely magical one.) This must have provided the transition to the use of the term "*magen David*" for the sign. What caused the substitution of the figure instead of the "great name of 72 names" is not clear, but in the 16th century instructions can still be found stating that the shield of David should not be drawn in simple lines but must be composed of certain holy names and their combinations, after the pattern of those biblical manuscripts where the lines were composed of the text of the masorah. The oldest known witness to the usage of the term is the kabbalistic *Sefer ha-Gevul,* written by a grandson of Naḥmanides in the early 14th century. The hexagram occurs there twice, both times called "*magen David*" and containing the same magical name as in the aforementioned amulet, demonstrating its direct connection with the magical tradition. According to other traditions, mentioned in Isaac Arama's *Akedat Yiẓḥak* (15th century), the emblem of David's shield was not the image known by this name today, but Psalm 67 in the shape of the *menorah.* This became a widespread custom and the "*menorah* Psalm" was considered a talisman of great power. A booklet from the 16th century says: "King David used to bear this psalm inscribed, pictured, and engraved on his shield, in the shape of the *menorah,* when he went forth to battle, and he would meditate on its mystery and conquer."

Between 1300 and 1700 the two terms, shield of David and seal of Solomon, are used indiscriminately, predominantly in magical texts, but slowly the former gained ascendancy. It was also used, from 1492, as a printers' mark, especially in books printed in Prague in the first half of the 16th century and in the books printed by the Foa family in Italy and Holland, who incorporated it in their coat of arms (e.g. on the title page of Maimonides' *Guide of the Perplexed,* Sabbioneta, 1553). Several Italian Jewish families followed their example between 1660 and 1770. All these usages had as yet no general Jewish connotation. The first official use of the shield of David can be traced to Prague, from where it spread in the 17th and 18th century through Moravia and Austria and later to southern Germany and Holland. In 1354, Charles IV granted the Prague community the privilege of bearing its own flag – later called in documents "King David's flag" – on which the hexagram was depicted. It therefore became an official emblem, probably chosen because of its significance as a symbol of the days of old when King David, as it were, wore it on his shield. This explains its wide use in Prague, in synagogues, on the official seal of the community, on printed books, and on other objects. Here it was always called *magen David.* Its use on the tombstone (1613) of David Gans, the astronomer and historian, was still exceptional, obviously in reference to the title of his last work *Magen David.* Except one tombstone in Bordeau (c. 1726), no other example of its being used on tombstones is known before the end of the 18th century. A curious parallel to the development in Prague is the one case of a representation of the Synagogue as an allegorical figure, holding a flag bearing the *magen David* in a 14th century Catalan manuscript of the *Breviar d'amor* by Matfre d'Ermengaud.[3]

The symbol early moved to other communities. Its use in Budweis has been mentioned above, and the Vienna community used it on its seal in 1655. In the following year it is found together with the cross on a stone marking the boundary between the Jewish and the Christian quarters of Vienna (according to P. Diamant) or between the Jewish quarter and the Carmelite monastery (according to Max Grunwald). Apparently they were both officially recognized symbols. When the Viennese Jews were expelled in 1670 they took the symbol to many of their new habitats, especially in Moravia, but also to the Ashkenazi community of Amsterdam, where it was used from 1671, first on a medallion permitting entrance to the graveyard. Later it became part of the community's seal. Curiously enough, its migration eastward was much slower. It never occurs on official seals, but here and there during the 17th and 18th centuries it appears as an ornament on objects for use in synagogues and on wood carvings over the Torah shrine (first in Volpa, near Grodno, 1643).

The use of the hexagram as an alchemical symbol denoting the harmony between the antagonistic elements of water and fire became current in the later 17th century, but this had no influence in Jewish circles. Many alchemists, too, began calling it the shield of David (traceable since 1724). But another symbolism sprang up in kabbalistic circles, where the "shield of David" became the "shield of the son of David," the Messiah. Whether this usage was current in Orthodox circles too is not certain, though not impossible. The two kabbalists who testify to it, Isaiah the son of Joel Ba'al Shem[4] and Abraham Ḥayyim Kohen from Nikolsburg, combine the two interpretations. But there is no doubt that this messianic interpretation of the sign was current among the followers of Shabbetai Ẓevi. The famous amulets given by Jonathan Eybeschuetz in Metz and Hamburg, which have no convincing interpretation other than a Shabbatean one, have throughout a shield of David designated as "seal of MBD" (Messiah b. David), "seal of the God of Israel", etc. The shield of David was transformed into a secret symbol of the Shabbatean vision of redemption, although this interpretation remained an esoteric one, not to be publicized.

The prime motive behind the wide diffusion of the sign in the 19th century was the desire to imitate Christianity. The Jews looked for a striking and simple sign which would "symbolize" Judaism in the same way as the cross symbolizes Christianity. This led to the ascendancy of the *magen David* in official use, on ritual objects and in many other ways. From central and Western Europe it made its way to Eastern Europe and to oriental Jewry. Almost every synagogue bore it; innumerable communities, and private and charitable organizations stamped it on their seals and letterheads. Whereas during the 18th century its use on ritual objects was still very restricted – a good specimen is a plate for *mazzot* (1770), reproduced on the title page of *Monumenta Judaica,* catalog of a Jewish exhibition in Cologne, 1963 – it now became most popular. By 1799 it had already appeared as a specific Jewish sign in a satirical anti-Semitic engraving[5]; in 1822 it was used on the Rothschild family coat of arms when they were raised to the nobility by the Austrian emperor; and from 1840 Heinrich Heine signed his correspondence from Paris in the *Augsburger Allgemeine Zeitung* with a *magen David* instead of his name, a remarkable indication of his Jewish identification in spite of his conversion. From such general use it was taken over by the Zionist movement. The very first issue of *Die Welt,* Herzl's Zionist journal, bore it as its emblem. The *magen David* became the symbol of new hopes and a new future for the Jewish people, and Franz Rosenzweig also interpreted it in *Der Stern der Erloesung* (1921) as summing up his philosophical ideas about the meaning of Judaism and the relationships between God, men, and the world. When the Nazis used it as a badge of shame which was to accompany millions on their way to death it took on a new dimension of depth, uniting suffering and hope. While the State of Israel, in its search for Jewish authenticity, chose as its emblem the *menorah,* a much older Jewish symbol, the *magen David* was maintained on the national (formerly Zionist) flag, and is widely used in Jewish life.

Bibliography: G. Scholem, in: *The Messianic Idea in Judaism and Other Essays* (1971), 257–81; J. Leite de Vasconcellos, *Signum Salomonis* (Portuguese, 1918); Mayer, *Bibliography of Jewish Art,* index s.v. *Magen David;* M. Avi-Yonah, in: *Quarterly of the Department of Antiquities in Palestine,* vol. 14, pp. 64–65, pl. 23; P. Diamant, in: *Reshumot,* 5 (1953), 93–103; I. Feivelson, in: *Ha-Levanon, Me'assef Sifruti* (Warsaw, 1912), 53–56; Goodenough, *Jewish Symbols in the Greco-Roman Period,* 7 (1958), 198–200; J.L. Gordon, *Iggerot J.L. Gordon,* 2 (1894), 36–37; M. Grunwald, in: HJ, 9 (1947), 178–88; J.M. Millás Vallicrosa, in: *Sefarad,* 17 (1957), 375–8; T. Nussenblatt, in: *YIVO-Bleter,* 13 (1938), 460–76, no. 583–4; P. Perdrizet, in: *Revue des Etudes Grecques,* 16 (1903), 42–61; E. Peterson, *Heis Theos* (Goettingen, 1926), 121; J. Reifman, in: *Ha-Shaḥar,* 2 (1872), 435–7; C. Roth, in: *Scritti in Memoria di Leone Carpi* (1967), 165–84; A. Scheiber in: *Israelitisches Wochenblatt fuer die Schweiz,* 66, no. 3 (Jan. 21, 1966), 33–35; Vajda, in: *Mitteilungen zur juedischen Volkskunde* (1918), 33–42; Wolf, *Bibliotheca Hebraea,* 3 (1727), 997, 1214.

15
Meditation

The term meditation (Heb. *Hitbonenut*) first appears in kabbalistic literature from the middle of the 13th century, referring to protracted concentration of thought on supernal lights of the divine world and of the spiritual worlds in general. Many sources, however, in this connection use the terms *kavvanah,* or *devekut* ("cleaving") of thought to a particular subject, and of "contemplation of the mind" The kabbalists did not distinguish between the terms meditation and contemplation – a distinction prevalent in Christian mysticism. In the kabbalistic view, contemplation was both the concentrated delving to the depths of a particular subject in the attempt to comprehend it from all its aspects, and also the arresting of thought in order to remain on the subject. The arresting and delving in spiritual contemplation do not serve, therefore, to encourage the contemplating intellect to advance and pass on to higher levels, but first of all to gauge to the maximum its given situation; only after having tarried in it for a protracted period does the intellect move on to a higher step. This, then, is contemplation by the intellect, whose objects are neither images nor visions, but non-sensual matters such as words, names, or thoughts.

In the history of the Kabbalah a different contemplation preceded this one: the contemplative vision of the Merkabah, for which the ancient Merkabah mystics of the tannaitic and amoraitic period strove, and which was described in the *Heikhalot Rabbati* of the *heikhalot* literature. Here the reference is to an actual vision of the world of the chariot which reveals itself before the eyes of the visionary. Therefore the term *histakkelut* is used here in the exact sense of the Latin term *contemplatio* or the Greek *theoria.* The contemplation of the Merkabah mystics, in the first period of Jewish mysticism, provided the key, in their opinion, to a correct understanding of the heavenly beings in the heavenly chariot. This contemplation could also be achieved by way of preparatory stages which would train those who "descend to the Merkabah" to grasp the vision and pass on from one thing to another without being endangered by the audacity of their assault on the higher world. Even at this stage, the vision of the Merkabah is bound up with immunization of the mystic's senses against absorption of external impressions and concentration through an inward vision.

In the Kabbalah, the conception of the ten *Sefirot,* which reveal the action of the Divine and comprise the world of emanation, was superimposed upon the Merkabah world. This contemplation of divine matters does not end, according to the Kabbalah, where the vision of Merkabah mystics ended, but is capable of ascending to greater heights, which are no longer the objects of images and vision. The concentration on the world of the *Sefirot* is not bound up with visions, but is solely a matter for the intellect prepared to ascend from level to level and to meditate on the qualities unique to each level. If meditation activates at first the faculty of imagination, it continues by activating the faculty of the intellect. The *Sefirot* themselves are conceived of as intellectual lights which can only be perceived by meditation. The Spanish kabbalists in the 13th century knew of two types of meditation: one which produces visions similar in kind if not in detail to the visions of the Merkabah mystics, and the second which leads to the communion of the meditating mind with its higher sources in the world of emanation itself. Moses b. Shem Tov de Leon describes in one of his books how an intuition of the third *Sefirah (Binah)* flashes up in the mind through meditation. He compares this to the light which flashes up when the rays of the sun play on the surface of a bowl of water (MGWJ, 1927, 119).

The instructions on the methods to be employed in performing meditation form part of the hidden and secret teachings of the kabbalists which, apart from some general rules, were not made public. The kabbalists of Gerona mention it in connection with the description of the mystic *kavvanah* in prayer, which is described as a meditation concentrating upon each word of the prayer in order to open a way to the inner lights which illuminate every word. Prayer, according to this idea of meditation, is not just a recitation of words or even concentration on the contents of the words according to their simple meaning; it is the adherence of man's mind to the spiritual lights and the mind's advancement in these worlds. The worshiper uses the fixed words of the prayer as a banister during his meditation which he grasps on his road of ascension so that he should not be confused or distracted. Such meditation results in the joining of human thought to the divine thought or the divine will – an attachment which itself comes to an end, or is "negated." The hour of prayer is, more than any other time, suitable for meditation. Azriel of Gerona said: "The thought expands and ascends to its origin, so that when it reaches it, it ends and cannot ascend any further ... therefore the pious men of old raised their thought to its origin while pronouncing the precepts and words of prayer. As a result of this procedure and the state of adhesion *(devekut)* which their thought attained, their words became blessed, multiplied, full of [divine] influx from the stage called the 'nothingness of thought,' just as the waters of a pool flow on every side when a man sets them free" (*Perush ha-Aggadot,* 1943, 39–40). In such meditation, which progresses from one stage to another, there was also a certain magic element, as can clearly be deduced from the detailed description in another piece by Azriel called *Sha'ar ha-Kavvanah la-Mekubbalim ha-Rishonim.* However, this magic element was concealed or completely glossed over in silence.

A detailed elaboration of the doctrine of meditation is to be found particularly in the teachings of Abraham Abulafia. The whole of his *Ḥokhmat ha-Ẓeruf* (science of combination; see p. 54) was designed, he believed, to teach a lasting and safe approach to meditation. It consists principally of instruction concerning meditation on the Holy Names of God and, in a wider sense, meditation on the mysteries of the Hebrew alphabet. This meditation, which is not dependent on prayer, was described in his more important manuals as a separate activity of the mind to which man devotes himself in seclusion at given hours and with regular guidance by an initiate teacher. Here again the point of departure is the mortification of the activity of the senses and the effacement of the natural images which cling to the soul. Meditation on the holy letters and names engenders pure spiritual forms in the soul, as a result of which man is able to comprehend the exalted truths. At certain stages of this meditation, there appear actual visions, such as are described in the work *Ḥayyei ha-Olam ha-Ba* for instance, but these are only intermediate stages on the road to pure contemplation of the mind. Abulafia negates from its very start the magical element which was originally attributed to such meditation.

The difference between the Christian and the kabbalistic doctrines of meditation resides in the fact that in Christian mysticism a pictorial and concrete subject, such as the suffering of Christ and all that pertains to it, is given to the meditator, while in Kabbalah, the subject given is abstract and cannot be visualized, such as the Tetragrammaton and its combinations.

Instruction in the methods of meditation were widespread in the works of early kabbalists and these methods continue to be found after the expulsion from Spain among several kabbalists who were influenced by Abulafia. An anonymous disciple of Abulafia has left (in *Sha'arei Ẓedek,* written in 1295) an impressive description of his experiences in the study of this meditation. The works *Berit Menuḥah* (14th century) and *Sullam ha-Aliyyah* by Judah Albotini, one of the exiles from Spain who settled in Jerusalem, were also written in the same spirit.

The most detailed textbook on meditation into the mystery of the *Sefirot* is *Even ha-Shoham* by Joseph ibn Ṣayah of Damascus, written in Jerusalem in 1538 (Ms. National and University Library, Jerusalem: see G. Scholem, *Kitvei Yad be-Kabbalah* (1930), 90–91). The kabbalists of Safed paid much attention to meditation, as is evident from *Sefer Ḥaredim* (Venice, 1601) of Eleazar Azikri, from chapter 30 in Moses Cordovero's *Pardes Rimmonim* (Cracow, 1592) and the *Sha'arei Kedushah* of Ḥayyim Vital, part 3, chapters 5–8, propounds his doctrine on the subject. Here the magic aspect attached to meditation is once more emphasized, even though the author explains it in a restricted sense. The last steps in the ascension of the meditating mind which seeks to bring down the influx of the supernal lights to earth require meditatory activities of a magic nature, which are known as *Yiḥudim* ("Unifications"). The practical importance of these doctrines, whose influence can be recognized throughout the whole of late kabbalistic literature, should not be underrated. The doctrines of adhesion *(devekut)* and meditation in 18th-century Ḥasidism are also definitely based on the form given to them in Safed. This doctrine was not written down in its entirety in the writings of Isaac Luria's disciples and its major part was preserved orally. In Jerusalem's kabbalistic yeshivah Bet El practical guidance on meditation was handed down orally for about 200 years and the initiates of this form of Kabbalah refused to make the details of their practice public knowledge.

Bibliography: G. Scholem, *Kitvei Yad be-Kabbalah* (1930), 24–30, 225–30; idem, *Reshit ha-Kabbalah* (1948),142–6; idem, in: KS, 1 (1924), 127–39; 22 (1946), 161–71; idem, in: MGWJ, 78 (1934), 492–518; J. Weiss, in HUCA 31 (1960), 137–47; R.J.Z. Werblowsky, in: *History of Religions,* 1 (1961), 9–36.

16

Merkabah Mysticism

Merkabah mysticism, or *ma'aseh merkavah,* was the name given in Mishnah *Hagigah,* 2:1, to the first chapter of Ezekiel. The term was used by the rabbis to designate the complex of speculations, homilies, and visions connected with the Throne of Glory and the chariot *(merkavah)* which bears it and all that is embodied in this divine world. The term, which does not appear in Ezekiel, is derived from 1 Chronicles 28:18 and is first found with the meaning of Merkabah mysticism at the end of Ecclesiasticus 49:8: "Ezekiel saw a vision, and described the different orders of the chariot". The Hebrew expression *zanei merkavah* should possibly be interpreted as the different sights of the vision of the chariot in Ezekiel, chapters 1, 8, and 10[1] or as the different parts of the chariot, which later came to be called "the chambers of the chariot" *(ḥadrei merkavah).* It has been suggested[2] that the text be corrected to *razei merkavah* ("secrets of the chariot"). The divine chariot also engrossed the Qumran sect; one fragment speaks of the angels praising "the pattern of the Throne of the chariot"[3]. In Pharisaic and tannaitic circles Merkabah mysticism became an esoteric tradition of which different fragments were scattered in the Talmud and the Midrash, interpreting *Ḥagigah* 2:1. This was a study surrounded by a special holiness and a special danger. A *baraita* in *Ḥagigah* 13a, which is ascribed to the first century C.E., relates the story of "A child who was reading at his teacher's home the Book of Ezekiel and he apprehended what *Ḥashmal* was [see Ezek. 1:27, JPS "electrum"], whereupon a fire went forth from *Ḥashmal* and consumed him". Therefore the rabbis sought to conceal, i.e. withdraw from general circulation, or from the biblical canon, the Book of Ezekiel.

Many traditions relate to the involvement of Johanan b. Zakkai, and later of Akiva in this study. In the main, details about the conduct of the rabbis in the study of Merkabah are found in the Palestinian Talmud *Ḥagigah 2* and the Babylonian Talmud *Ḥagigah* f. 12–15 and *Shabbat* 80b. According to the manuscript of the latter source the prohibition on lecturing to a group was not always observed and the tradition adds that a transgressor, a Galilean who came to Babylonia, was punished for this and died. In the Babylonian Talmud, *Sukkah*

28a, Merkabah mysticism was put forward as a major subject *(davar gadol)* in contrast to the relatively minor subject of rabbinic casuistry. Traditions of this type are found, for example, in *Berakhot* 7a, *Ḥullin* 91b, *Megillah* 24b, and at the beginning of *Genesis Rabbah, Tanḥuma, Midrash Tehillim, Midrash Rabbah* to Leviticus, Song of Songs, and Ecclesiastes. Several traditions are preserved in *Seder Eliyahu Rabbah* and in small tractates, such as *Avot de-Rabbi Nathan* and *Massekhet Derekh Ereẓ*. In contrast with the scattered fragments of these traditions in exoteric sources, books, and treatises collecting and developing *Ma'aseh Merkavah* according to the trends prevailing in different mystic circles were written at the latest from the fourth century on. Many of the treatises include early material but numerous additions reflect later stages. *Re'uyyot Yeḥezkiel,* the major part of which was found in the Cairo *Genizah*[4] depicts historical personalities and the context is that of a fourth-century Midrash. Scraps of a second- or third-century Midrash on the *Ma'aseh Merkavah* were found in pages of the *Genizah* fragments (Ms. Sassoon 522, Cat. *Ohel Dawid,* p. 48). These sources do not yet show any sign of the pseudepigraphy prevailing in most surviving sources; in these the majority is formalized, and most of the statements are attributed to Akiva or to Ishmael. Several of the texts are written in Aramaic, but most are in Hebrew, in the style used by the rabbis. A great deal of material of this type has been published (mostly from manuscripts) in collections of minor Midrashim such as A. Jellinek's *Beit ha-Midrash* (1853–78), S.A. Wertheimer's *Battei Midrashot,* E. Gruenhut's *Sefer ha-Likkutim* (1898–1904), and H.M. Horowitz' *Beit Eked ha-Aggadot* (1881–84). *Merkavah Shelemah* (1921) includes important material from the manuscript collection of Solomon Musajoff. Some of the texts included in these anthologies are identical, and many are corrupt.

The most important are: (1) *Heikhalot Zutrati* ("Lesser *Heikhalot*") or *Heikhalot R. Akiva,* of which only fragments have been published, mostly without being recognized as belonging to the text. The bulk of it is in a very difficult Aramaic, and part of it is included in *Merkavah Shelemah* as "*Tefillat Keter Nora.*" (2) *Heikhalot Rabbati* ("Greater *Heikhalot*", in *Battei Midrashot.* 1 (1950^2), 135–63), i.e., the *Heikhalot* of Rabbi Ishmael, in Hebrew. In medieval sources and ancient manuscripts the two books are at times called *Hilkhot Heikhalot.* The division of *Heikhalot Rabbati* into *halakhot* ("laws") is still preserved in several manuscripts, most of which are divided into 30 chapters. Chapters 27–30 include a special tract found in several manuscripts under the title *Sar Torah,* which was composed much later than the bulk of the work. In the Middle Ages the book was widely known as *Pirkei Heikhalot.* The edition published by Wertheimer includes later additions, some of them Shabbatean.[5] Jellinek's version (in *Beit ha-Midrash,* 3, 1938^2) is free of additions but suffers from many corruptions. Relatively the best text seems to be that of Ms. Kaufmann 238 no. 6 (Budapest). (3) *Merkavah Rabbah,* part of which is found in *Merkavah Shelemah,* mostly attributed to Ishmael, and partly to Akiva. Perhaps this work contained the most ancient redaction of *Shi'ur Komah* ("the measurement of the body of God"), which later was copied in manuscripts as a separate work that developed into *Sefer ha-Komah,* popular in the Middle Ages (see G. Scholem, *Jewish Gnosticism* ... (1965), 36–42). (4) A version of *Heikhalot* which has no name and was referred to in the Middle Ages as *Ma'aseh Merkavah* (G. Scholem, ibid., 103–17). Here statements of Ishmael and Akiva alternate. (5) Another elaborate treatise on the pattern of *Heikhalot Rabbati,* but with differing and partly unknown new details: fragments have been published from the Cairo *Genizah* by I. Greenwald, *Tarbiz,* 38 (1969), 354–72 (additions, *ibid.,* 39 (1970), 216–7). (6) *Heikhalot,* published by Jellinek (in *Beit ha-Midrash* (vol. 1938[2]). and later as *III Enoch or the Hebrew Book of Enoch* (ed. and trans. by H. Odeberg, 1928). Unfortunately Odeberg chose a later and very corrupt text as a basis for his book, which he intended as a critical edition. The speaker is R. Ishmael and the work is largely made up of revelations about Enoch, who became the angel Metatron, and the host of heavenly angels. This book represents a very different trend from those in *Heikhalot Rabbati* and *Heikhalot Zutrati.* (7) The tractate of *Heikhalot* or *Ma'aseh Merkavah* in *Battei Midrashot* (1 (1950[2]), 51–62) is a relatively late elaboration, in seven chapters, of the descriptions of the throne and the chariot. In the last three works a literary adaptation was deliberately made in order to eradicate the magical elements, common in the other sources listed above. Apparently they were intended more to be read for edification rather than for practical use by those who "delved into the Merkabah." (8) The Tosefta to the Targum of the first chapter of Ezekiel *(Battei Midrashot,* 2 (1953[2]), 135–40) also belongs to this literature.

A mixture of material on the chariot and creation is found in several additonal sources, mainly in *Baraita de-Ma'aseh Bereshit* and in *Otiyyot de-Rabbi Akiva,* both of which appear in several versions. The *Seder Rabbah de-Bereshit* was published in *Battei Midrashot* (1 (1950[2]), 3–48), and in another version by N. Séd, with a French translation (in REJ, 3–4 (1964), 23–123, 259–305). Here the doctrine of the Merkabah is connected with cosmology and with the doctrine of the seven heavens and the depths. This link is also noticeable in *Otiyyot de-Rabbi Akiva,* but only the longer version contains the traditions on creation and the Merkavah mysticism. Both extant versions, with an important supplement entitled *Midrash Alfa-Betot,* were published in *Battei Midrashot* (2 (1953[2]), 333–465). Mordecai Margaliot discovered additional and lengthy sections of *Midrash Alfa-Betot* in several unpublished manuscripts.

Again, these works were arranged more for the purposes of speculation and reading than for practical use by the mystics. The doctrine of the seven heavens and their angelic hosts, as it was developed in Merkabah mysticism and in cosmology, has also definite magical contexts, which are elaborated in the complete version of *Sefer ha-Razim* (ed. by M. Margalioth, 1967), whose date is still a matter of controversy.

In the second century Jewish converts to Christianity apparently conveyed different aspects of Merkabah mysticism to Christian Gnostics. In the Gnostic literature there were many corruptions of such elements, yet the Jewish character of this material is still evident, especially among the Ophites, in the school of Valentinus, and in several of the Gnostic and Coptic texts discovered within the last 50 years. In the Middle Ages the term *Ma'aseh Merkabah* was used by both philosophers and kabbalists to designate the contents of their teachings but with completely different meanings – metaphysics for the former and mysticism for the latter.

Bibliography: Scholem, Mysticism, 40–70; idem, *Jewish Gnosticism, Merkabah Mysticism and Talmudic Tradition* (1965); P. Bloch, in: MGWJ, 37 (1893); idem, in: *Festschrift J. Guttmann* (1915), 113–24; Néher, in: RHR, 140 (1951), 59–82; J. Neusner, *Life of Rabban Yohanan ben Zakkai* (1962), 97–105; M. Smith, in: A. Altmann (ed.), *Biblical and Other Studies* (1963), 142–60; B. Bokser, in: PAAJR, 31 (1965), 1–32; J. Maier, *Vom Kultus zur Gnosis* (1964), 112–48; E.E. Urbach, in: *Studies in Mysticism and Religion presented to G.G. Scholem* (1968), 1–28 (Heb. section).

17

Metatron

The angel Metatron (or Matatron) was accorded a special position in esoteric doctrine from the tannaitic period on. The angelology of apocalyptic literature mentions a group of angels who behold the face of their king and are called "Princes of the Countenance" (Ethiopic *Book of Enoch,* ch. 40, et al.). Once Metatron's personality takes a more definitive form in the literature, he is referred to simply as "the Prince of the Countenance."

In the Babylonian Talmud Metatron is mentioned in three places only (Ḥag. 15a; Sanh. 38b; and Av. Zar. 3b). The first two references are important because of their connection with the polemics conducted against heretics. In *Ḥagigah* it is said that the *tanna* Elisha b. Avuyah saw Metatron seated and said, "perhaps there are two powers," as though indicating Metatron himself as a second deity. The Talmud explains that Metatron was given permission to be seated only because he was the heavenly scribe recording the good deeds of Israel. Apart from this, the Talmud states, it was proved to Elisha that Metatron could not be a second deity by the fact that Metatron received 60 "strokes with fiery rods" to demonstrate that Metatron was not a god, but an angel, and could be punished. This image recurs frequently in different contexts in Gnostic literature and is associated with various figures of the heavenly realm. It is however thought that the appearance of Metatron to Elisha b. Avuyah led him to a belief in dualism.

The story in *Sanhedrin* also confers on Metatron a supernatural status. He is the angel of the Lord mentioned in Exodus 23:21 of whom it is said " . . . and hearken unto his voice; be not rebellious against him . . . for My name is in him." When one of the heretics asked R. Idi why it is written in Exodus 24:1 "And unto Moses He said 'Come up unto the Lord,' " instead of "Come up unto Me," the *amora* answered that the verse refers to Metatron "whose name is like that of his Master." When the heretic argued that, if that were so, Metatron should be worshiped as a deity, R. Idi explained that the verse "be not rebellious against (תמר) him" should be understood to mean "do not exchange (תמירני) Me for him." R. Idi added that Metatron was not to be accepted in this sense even in his capacity as the heavenly messenger. Underlying these disputations is the fear that speculations about Metatron might lead to dangerous ground. The Karaite

Kirkisānī read in his text of the Talmud an even more extreme version: "This is Metatron, who is the lesser YHWH." It is quite probable that this version was purposely removed from the manuscripts.

The epithet "lesser YHWH" is undoubtedly puzzling, and it is hardly surprising that the Karaites found ample grounds for attacking the Rabbanites over its frequent appearance in the literature they had inherited. The Karaites viewed it as a sign of heresy and deviation from monotheism. The use of such an epithet was almost certainly current before the figure of Metatron crystallized. The explanations of this epithet given in the latter phases of the *Heikhalot* literature (Hebrew *Book of Enoch,* ch. 12) are far from satisfactory, and it is obvious that they are an attempt to clarify an earlier tradition, then no longer properly understood. This tradition was connected with the angel Jahoel, mentioned in the *Apocalypse of Abraham* (dating from the beginning of the second century), where it is stated (ch. 10) that the Divine Name (Tetragram) of the deity is to be found in him. All the attributes relating to Jahoel here were afterward transferred to Metatron. Of Jahoel it is indeed appropriate to say, without contrived explanations, that his name is like that of his Master: the name Jahoel contains the letters of the Divine Name, and this therefore signifies that Jahoel possesses a power exceeding that of all other similar beings. Apparently, the designation "the lesser YHWH" (יהוה הקטן) or "the lesser Lord" (אדני הקטן) was first applied to Jahoel. Even before Jahoel was identified with Metatron, designations such as "the greater Jaho" or "the lesser Jaho" passed into Gnostic use and are mentioned in various contexts in Gnostic, Coptic, and also in Mandean literature, none of which mentions Metatron. The name *Yorba* (יורבא) in Mandean in fact means "the greater Jaho" but he has there been given an inferior status as is characteristic of this literature in its treatment of Jewish traditional concepts.

Two different traditions have been combined in the figure of Metatron. One relates to a heavenly angel who was created with the creation of the world, or even before, and makes him responsible for performing the most exalted tasks in the heavenly kingdom. This tradition continued to apply after Jahoel was identified with Metatron. According to this tradition, the new figure took over many of the specific duties of the angel Michael, an idea retained in certain sections of the *Heikhalot* literature up to and including the Kabbalah in the literature of which the primordial Metatron is sometimes referred to as Metatron Rabba.

A different tradition associates Metatron with Enoch, who "walked with God" (Gen. 5:22) and who ascended to heaven and was changed from a human being into an angel – in addition he also became the great scribe who recorded men's deed. This role was already delegated to Enoch in the Book of Jubilees

(4:23). His transmutation and ascent to heaven were discussed by the circles who followed this tradition and elaborated it. The association with Enoch can be seen particularly in the *Book of Heikhalot,* sometimes also called the *Book of Enoch,* of R. Ishmael Kohen ha-Gadol, or the Hebrew *Book of Enoch* (H. Odeberg's edition (see bibl.) includes an English translation and a detailed introduction). The author links the two traditions and attempts to reconcile them. But it is clear that chapters 9–13 allude to the primordial Metatron, as Odeberg points out.

The absence of the second tradition in the Talmud or the most important Midrashim is evidently connected with the reluctance of the talmudists to regard Enoch in a favorable light in general, and in particular the story of his ascent to heaven, a reluctance still given prominence in the Midrash *Genesis Rabbah.* The Palestinian Targum (Gen. 5:24) and other Midrashim have retained allusions to Metatron in this tradition. Instead of his role of heavenly scribe, he sometimes appears as the heavenly advocate defending Israel in the celestial court. This transposition of his functions is very characteristic (Lam. R. 24; Tanḥ. *Va-Etḥannan;* Num. R. 12, 15). A number of sayings of the sages, in particular in *Sifrei,* portion *Ha'azinu,* 338, and Gen. R. 5, 2, were explained by medieval commentators as referring to Metatron on the grounds of a corrupt reading *"Metatron"* instead of *metator* ("guide").

In certain places in Merkabah literature, Metatron completely disappears and is mentioned only in the addenda that do not form part of the original exposition, such as in *Heikhalot Rabbati.* The descriptions of the heavenly hierarchy in *Massekhet Heikhalot* and *Sefer ha-Razim* also make no mention of Metatron. On the other hand, Metatron is a conspicuous figure in the *Book of the Visions of Ezekiel* (fourth century) although he is mentioned without any reference to the Enoch tradition. This source mentions a number of the other secret names of Metatron, lists of which later appear in special commentaries or were added to the Hebrew *Book of Enoch* (ch. 48). Explanations of these names in accordance with the tradition of the Ḥasidei Ashkenaz are given in the book *Beit Din* of Abraham Ḥammawi (1858), 196ff., and in another version in the *Sefer ha-Ḥeshek* (1865). According to the traditions of certain Merkabah mystics, Metatron takes the place of Michael as the high priest who serves in the heavenly Temple, as emphasized particularly in the second part of *Shi'ur Komah* (in *Merkavah Shelemah* (1921), 39ff.).

One can, thus, detect different aspects of Metatron's functions. In one place he is described as serving before the heavenly throne and ministering to its needs, while in another he appears as the servitor (*na'ar,* "youth") in his own special tabernacle or in the heavenly Temple. (The title *na'ar* in the sense of servant is based on biblical usage.) In the amoraic period the duty of the "prince of the world" formerly held by Michael was transferred to him (Yevamot 16b). This conception of Metatron's role as the prince of the world since its creation contradicts the concept of Metatron as Enoch who was taken up to heaven only after the creation of the world.

It is already observed in *Shi'ur Komah* that the name Metatron has two forms, "written with six letters and with seven letters", i.e., מטטרון and מיטטרון. The original reason for this distinction is not known. In the early manuscripts the name is almost always written with the letter *yod.* The kabbalists regarded the different forms as signifying two prototypes for Metatron. They reintroduced the distinction between the various components that had been combined in the Hebrew *Book of Enoch* in their possession. They identified the seven-lettered Metatron with the Supreme emanation from the *Shekhinah,* dwelling since then in the heavenly world, while the six-lettered Metatron was Enoch, who ascended later to heaven and possesses only some of the splendor and power of the primordial Metatron. This distinction already underlies the explanation given by R. Abraham b. David to *Berakhot* (see G. Scholem, *Reshit ha-Kabbalah* (1948), 74–77).

The origin of the name Metatron is obscure, and it is doubtful whether an etymological explanation can be given. It is possible that the name was intended to be a secret and has no real meaning, perhaps stemming from subconscious meditations, or as a result of glossolalia. To support the latter supposition are a number of similar examples of names with the suffix *on:* Sandalfon (סנדלפון). Adiriron (אדיריריון), etc. while the doubling of the letter *t* (טט) is characteristic of names found in the Merkabah literature, e.g., in an addition to *Heikhalot Rabbati,* 26:8. Among numerous etymological derivations given (see Odeberg, 125–42) three should be mentioned: from *matara* (מטרא), keeper of the watch; from *metator* (מיטטור), a guide or messenger (mentioned in *Sefer he-Arukh* and the writings of many kabbalists); from the combination of the two Greek words *meta* and *thronos,* such as *metathronios* (μεταθρόνιος), in the sense of "one who serves behind the throne". However, the duty to serve the heavenly throne was associated with Metatron only at a later stage and does not agree with the earlier traditions. It is highly doubtful whether the "angel of the Countenance" entering "to exalt and arrange the throne in a befitting manner" mentioned in *Heikhalot Rabbati* (ch. 12) can in fact be Metatron, who is not mentioned at all in this context. The Greek word *thronos* does not appear in talmudic literature. The origin of the word, therefore, remains unknown.

In contrast to the lengthy description of Metatron found in the Hebrew *Book of Enoch,* in later literature the material relating to him is scattered, while there is hardly a duty in the heavenly realm and within the dominion of one angel among the other angels that is not associated with Metatron. This applies particularly to kabbalistic literature (Odeberg, 111–25). Extensive material from the Zohar and kabbalistic literature has been collected by R. Margalioth in his angelological work *Malakhei Elyon* (1945, 73–108). In books dealing with practical Kabbalah there are almost no incantations of Metatron, although his name is frequently mentioned in other incantations. Only the Shabbatean emissary Nehemiah Ḥayon reportedly boasted of having conjured Metatron (REJ 36 (1898), 274).

Bibliography: H. Odeberg, *III Enoch or the Hebrew Book of Enoch* (1928); Scholem, Mysticism, 67–70; idem, *Jewish Gnosticism* (1965), 43–55; idem, *Les Origines de la Kabbale* (1966), 132–5, 225–31, 263.

18
Providence

The question of divine providence almost never appears in the Kabbalah as a separate problem, and therefore few detailed and specific discussions were devoted to it. The idea of providence is identified in the Kabbalah with the assumption that there exists an orderly and continuous system of government of the cosmos, carried out by the Divine Potencies – the *Sefirot* – which are revealed in this government. The Kabbalah does no more than explain the way in which this system operates, while its actual existence is never questioned. The world is not governed by chance, but by unceasing divine providence, which is the secret meaning of the hidden order of all the planes of creation, and especially in the world of man. He who understands the mode of action of the *Sefirot* also understands the principles of divine providence which are manifested through this action. The idea of divine providence is interwoven in a mysterious way with the limitation of the area of action of causality in the world. For although most events which happen to living creatures, and especially to men, appear as if they occur in a natural way which is that of cause and effect, in reality these events contain individual manifestations of divine providence, which is responsible for everything that happens to man, down to the last detail. In this sense, the rule of divine providence is, in the opinion of Naḥmanides, one of the "hidden wonders" of creation. The workings of nature ("I will give you your rains in their season," Lev. 26:4 and the like) are coordinated in hidden ways with the moral causality determined by the good and evil in men's actions.

In their discussions of divine providence, the early kabbalists stressed the activity of the tenth *Sefirah,* since the rule of the lower world is principally in its hands. This *Sefirah* is the *Shekhinah,* the presence of the divine potency in the world at all times. This presence is responsible for God's providence for His creatures; but according to some opinions the origin of divine providence is actually in the upper *Sefirot.* Symbolic expression is given to this idea, particularly in the Zohar, in the description of the eyes in the image of *Adam Kadmon* ("Primordial Man"), in his two manifestations, as the *Arikh Anpin* (lit. "The Long Face" but meaning "The Long Suffering") or *Attikah Kaddishah* ("the Holy Ancient One") and as the *Ze'eir Anpin* ("The Short Face", indicating the "Impatient"). In the description of the organs in the head of *Attikah Kaddishah,* the eye which is always open is taken as a supernal symbol for the existence of divine providence, whose origin is in the first *Sefirah.* This upper providence consists solely of mercy, with no intermixture of harsh judgment. Only in the second manifestation, which is that of God in the image of the *Ze'eir Anpin,* is the working of judgment also found in the divine providence. For " . . . the eyes of the Lord . . . range through the whole earth" (Zech. 4:10), and they convey his providence to every place, both for judgment and for mercy. The pictorial image, "the eye of providence," is here understood as a symbolic expression which suggests a certain element in the divine order itself. The author of the Zohar is refuting those who deny divine providence and substitute chance as an important cause in the events of the cosmos. He considers them to be fools who are not fit to contemplate the depths of the wisdom of divine providence and who lower themselves to the level of animals (Zohar 3:157b). The author of the Zohar does not distinguish between general providence (of all creatures) and individual providence (of individual human beings). The latter is, of course, more important to him. Through the activity of divine providence, an abundance of blessing descends on the creatures, but this awakening of the power of providence is dependent on the deeds of created beings, on "awakening from below." A detailed consideration of the question of providence is set forth by Moses Cordovero in *Shi'ur Komah* ("Measurement of the Body"). He, too, agrees with the philosophers that individual providence exists only in relation to man, while in relation to the rest of the created world, providence is only directed toward the generic essences. But he enlarges the category of individual providence and establishes that "divine providence applies to the lower creatures, even animals, for their well-being and their death, and this is not for the sake of the animals themselves, but for the sake of men," that is to say, to the extent to which the lives of animals are bound up with the lives of men, individual providence applies to them as well. "Individual providence does not apply to any ox or any lamb, but to the entire species together . . . but if divine providence applies to a man, it will encompass even his pitcher, should it break, and his dish, should it crack, and all his possessions – if he should be chastized or not" (p. 113). Cordovero distinguishes ten types of providence, from which it is possible to understand the various modes of action of individual providence among the gentiles and Israel. These modes of action are bound up with the various roles of the *Sefirot* and their channels which convey the abundance (of blessing) to all the worlds, in accordance with the special awakening of the lower creatures. He includes among them two types of providence which indicate the possibility of the limitation of divine providence in certain instances, or even its complete negation. Also, in his opinion, things may happen to a man without the guidance of providence, and it may even happen that a man's sins cause him to be left "to nature and to chance," which is the aspect of God's hiding his face from man. In fact, it is uncertain from moment to moment whether a particular event in an individual's life is of this latter type, or whether it is a result of divine providence: "And he cannot be sure – for who will tell him if he is among those of whom it is said: 'The righteous man is as sure as a lion' – perhaps God has hidden His face from him, because of some transgression, and he is left to chance" (p. 120).

Only in the Shabbatean Kabbalah is divine providence seen once again as a serious problem. Among Shabbetai Ẓevi's disciples was handed down his oral teaching that the Cause of Causes, of the *Ein-Sof* ("the Infinite") "does not influence and does not oversee the lower world, and he caused the *Sefirah Keter* to come into being to be God and *Tiferet* to be King" (see Scholem, Sabbatai Ṣevi, p. 862). This denial of the providence of *Ein-Sof* was considered a deep secret among the believers, and the Shabbatean Abraham Cardozo, who was opposed to this doctrine, wrote that the emphasis on the secret nature of this teaching arose from the Shabbateans' knowledge that this was the opinion of Epicurus the Greek. The "taking" *(netilah)* of providence from *Ein-Sof* (which is designated in these circles by other terms as well) is found in several Shabbatean schools of thought, such as the Kabbalah of Baruchiah of Salonika, in *Va-Avo ha-Yom el ha-Ayin,* which was severely attacked for the prominence it gave to this opinion, and in *Shem Olam* (Vienna, 1891) by Jonathan Eybeschuetz. The latter work devoted several pages of casuistry to this question in order to prove that providence does not actually originate in the First Cause, but in the God of Israel, who is emanated from it, and who is called, by Eybeschuetz, the "image of the ten *Sefirot.*" This "heretical" assumption, that the First Cause (or the highest element of the Godhead) does not guide the lower world at all, was among the principle innovations of Shabbatean doctrine which angered the sages of that period. The Orthodox kabbalists saw in this assumption proof that the Shabbateans had left the faith in the absolute unity of the Godhead, which does not permit, in matters pertaining to divine providence, differentiation between the emanating *Ein-Sof* and the emanated *Sefirot.* Even though the *Ein-Sof* carries out the activity of divine providence through the *Sefirot,* the *Ein-Sof* itself is the author of true providence. In the teachings of the Shabbateans, however, this quality of the First Cause of the *Ein-Sof* is blurred or put in doubt.

Bibliography: I. Tishby, *Mishnat ha-Zohar,* 1 (1957^2), 265–8; M. Cordovero, *Shi'ur Komah* (1883), 113–20; Scholem, Sabbatai Ṣevi, 861, 862; M.A. Perlmutter, *R. Yehonatan Eybeschuetz ve-Yaḥaso el ha-Shabbeta'ut* (1947), 133–41, 190–1.

19

Samael

From the amoraic period onward, Samael is the major name of Satan in Judaism. The name first appears in the account of the fall of angels in the Ethiopic Book of Enoch 6, which includes the name, although not in the most important place, in the list of the leaders of the angels who rebelled against God. The Greek versions of the lost Hebrew text contain the forms Σαμμανή (Sammane) and Σεμιέλ (Semiel). The latter form takes the place of the name Samael in the Greek work of the Church Father Irenaeus in his account of the Gnostic sect of the Ophites (see below; ed. Harvey, I, 236). According to Irenaeus the Ophites gave the snake a double name: Michael and Samael, which in the Greek work of the Church Father Theodoretus appears as Σαμμανή (Sammane). The Greek version of Enoch used by the Byzantine Syncellus retained the form Σαμιέλ (Samiel). This form still retains the original meaning derived from the word *sami* (סמי), meaning blind, an etymology which was preserved in various Jewish and non-Jewish sources until the Middle Ages. In addition to Samiel, the forms Samael and Sammuel date from antiquity. This third version is preserved in the Greek Apocalypse of Baruch 4:9 (from the tannaitic period), which states that the angel Sammuel planted the vine that caused the fall of Adam and therefore Sammuel was cursed and became Satan. The same source relates in chapter 9, in an ancient version of the legend of the shrinking of the moon, that Samael took the form of a snake in order to tempt Adam, an idea which was omitted in later talmudic versions of the legend.

In the apocalyptic work "The Ascension of Isaiah", which contains a mixture of Jewish and early Christian elements, the names Beliar (i.e., Belial) and Samael occur side by side as names or synonyms for Satan. What is recounted of Samael in one passage is stated in another about Beliar. For example, Samael dominated King Manasseh and "embraced him," thus taking on the form of Manasseh (ch. 2). In chapter 7, Samael and his forces are stated to be under the first firmament, a view that does not accord with his position as the chief of the devils. Samael is mentioned among the "angels of judgment" in the Sibylline Oracles 2:215. In the tannaitic and amoraic period, Samael is mentioned as being outside the alignment of the hosts of the Merkabah. Drawing from Jewish tradition, several Gnostic works refer to Samael as "the blind god" and as identical with Jaldabaoth, who occupied an important place in Gnostic speculations as one or the leader of the forces of evil. This tradition apparently came down through the Ophites ("the worshippers of the snake"), a Jewish syncretistic sect.[1] Partially ecclesiastical traditions of this period, such as the pseudepigraphic versions of the Acts of Andrew and Matthew 24, retain the name Samael for Satan, acknowledging his blindness. He is mentioned as head of the devils in the magical Testament of Solomon *(Testamentum Salomonis)*. which is essentially a superficial Christian adaptation of a demonological Jewish text from this period.[2] Undoubtedly Simyael, "the demon in charge of blindness" mentioned in Mandean works,[3] is simply a variant of Samael.

In rabbinic tradition the name first occurs in the statements of Yose (perhaps b. Ḥalafta or the *amora* Yose) that during the exodus from Egypt "Michael and Samael stood before the *Shekhinah"* apparently as prosecutor and defender (Ex. R. 18:5). Their task is similar to that of Samael and Gabriel in the story of Tamar (Sot. 10b), in the statement of Eleazar b. Pedat. Samael retains the role of prosecutor in the account of Ḥama b. Ḥanina (c. 260 C.E.; Ex. R. 21:7), who was apparently the first to identify Samael with Esau's guardian angel during the struggle between Jacob and the angel. His name, however, does not appear in *Genesis Rabbah* (Theodor ed. (1965), 912), but he is mentioned in the old version of the *Tanḥuma, Va-Yishlaḥ 8.* In the parallel version in *Songs of Songs Rabbah* 3:6, the *amora* has Jacob saying to Esau: "your countenance resembles that of your guardian angel," according to the version of the *Mattanot Kehunnah* (Theodor ed.). Surprisingly, in the section of the *Midrash Yelammedenu* on Exodus 14:25, Samael fulfills a positive function during the dividing of the Red Sea, pushing back the wheels of the chariots of the Egyptians. In *gematria,* Samael is the numerical equivalent of the word *ofan* ("wheel"; in Ms. British Museum, 752, 136b; and in the *Midrash Ha-Ḥefeẓ ha-Teimani,* which is cited in *Torah Shelemah,* 14 (1941) to this verse).

Mention of Samael as the angel of death first occurs in Targum Jonathan on Genesis 3:6, and this identification frequently appears in late *aggadot,* especially in the legends on the death of Moses at the end of *Deuteronomy Rabbah,* at the end of *Avot de-Rabbi Nathan* (ed. Schechter (1945), 156). In *Deuteronomy Rabbah* 11, Samael is called "Samael the wicked, the head of all the devils." The name "Samael the wicked" is repeated consistently in *Heikhalot Rabbati* (1948), chapter 5, an apocalyptic source. The Hebrew Enoch 14:2, acknowledges him as "chief of the tempters" "greater than all the heavenly kingdoms." This text differentiates between Satan and Samael, the latter being none other than the guardian angel of Rome *(ibid.* 6:26). In traditions concerning the rebellion of the angels in heaven (PdRE 13–14 (1852)) he is the leader of the rebel armies. Prior to his defeat he had 12 wings and his place was higher than the *ḥayyot* ("holy heavenly creatures") and the seraphim. Several tasks are attributed to him: Samael is in charge of all the nations but has no power over Israel except on the Day of Atonement, when the scapegoat serves as bribe for him *(ibid.* 46). It is he who rode on the snake in the course of the fall of Adam and hid in the golden calf *(ibid.* 45). In *Midrash Avkir,* one of the smaller Midrashim, Samael and Michael were active at the time of the birth of Jacob and Esau and even on the way to the *Akedah* (sacrifice) of Isaac, Samael intervened as a prosecutor (Gen. R. 56:4). The war between him and Michael, the guardian angel of Israel, will not be completed until the end of days when Samael will be handed over to Israel in iron shackles (Gen. R., Albeck ed., 166, following Mak. 12a, and similarly in the messianic chapters *(pirkei mashiaḥ)* in A. Jellinek, *Beit ha-Midrash* 3 (1938), 66f.).

Particular motifs on Samael in later *aggadah* include the following: Samael does not know the path to the tree of life, even though he flies through the air (Targ. Job 28:7); he has one long hair in his navel, and as long as this remains intact his reign will continue. In the messianic era, however, the hair will bend as a result of the great sound of the *shofar,* and then Samael will also fall *(Midrash* quoted in a commentary on *Piyyutim,* Ms. Munich 346, 91b). In Jewish astrological sources, which in time influenced those of other groups, Samael was considered the angel in charge of Mars. This idea recurs at first among the Sabans in Ḥarran, who called him Mara Samia, "the blind archon,"[4] and later in medieval Christian astrological magic literature. He appears as the angel in charge of Tuesday in *Sefer Razi'el* (Amsterdam, 1701), 34b; in *Ḥokhmat ha-Kasdim* (ed. M. Gaster, *Studies and Texts,* 1 (1925), 350); in Judah b. Barzillai's commentary on *Sefer Yeẓirah* (1885), 247, and in many other works. In demonological sources known to the brothers Isaac and Jacob b. Jacob ha-Kohen, Spanish kabbalists of the mid-13th century, an echo of the ancient etymology is still retained and Samael is called Sar Suma ("blind angel").

In later literature, Samael often appears as the angel who brought the poison of death into the world. These same demonological sources contain the earliest references to Samael and Lilith as a couple in the kingdom of impurity.[5] These sources are full of contradictory traditions concerning the roles of Samael and the war against Asmodeus, regarded in his source as guardian angel of Ishmael. Different systems were constructed of the hierarchy of the leaders of the demons and their consorts *(Tarbiz,* 4 (1932/33), 72). According to one view, Samael had two brides[6], an idea which also appears in *Tikkunei Zohar* (Mantua, 1558). The couple Samael and Lilith are mentioned many times in the Zohar, mostly without specifically mentioning the name Lilith (e.g., "Samael and his spouse"), as the leaders of the *sitra aḥra* ("the other side"; i.e., evil). In *Ammud ha-Semali* by Moses b. Solomon b. Simeon of Burgos, a contemporary of the author of the Zohar, Samael and Lilith constitute only the eighth and tenth *Sefirah* of the left (evil) emanation.[7] In the Zohar, the snake has become the symbol of Lilith and Samael rides on her and has sexual intercourse with her. Samael is cross-eyed and dark *(Zohar Ḥadash* 31, 4) and has horns *(Tikkunei Zohar* in *Zohar Ḥadash* 101, 3), perhaps influenced by the Christian idea about the horns of Satan. However, the image of Satan is linked with the goat in Targum Jonathan to Leviticus 9:3. The party, hosts, and chariots of Samael are mentioned in Zohar part 2, 111b; part 3, 29a. Different classes of demons, all called Samael, were known by the writer of *Tikkunei Zohar* (published in the main body of the Zohar 1:29a). "There is Samael and there is Samael and they are not all the same."

Conjurations of Samael often appear in magical literature and in practical Kabbalah. In 15th-century Spain a system was developed in which the heads of the demons were Samael, the representative of Edom, and his assistant Amon of No, representing Ishmael. A legend telling of their downfall at the hands of Joseph della Reina appears in several sources.[8] After Isaac Luria had introduced the practice of not pronouncing the name of Satan, the custom of calling him *Samekh Mem* became widespread *(Sha'ar ha-Miẓvot* (Salonica, 1852), Exodus; *Sha'ar ha-Kavvanot* (Salonica, 1852), *Derushei ha-Laylah* 1).

Bibliography: R. Margaliot, *Malakhei Elyon* (1945), 248–70; M. Schwab, *Vocabulaire de l'angélologie* (1897), 199; H.L. Strack and P. Billerbeck, *Kommentar zum Neuen Testament aus Talmud und Midrasch* (1922), 136–49; E. Peterson, in: *Rheinisches Museum*, 75 (1926), 413–5; J. Doresse, *The Secret Books of the Egyptian Gnostics* (1960), index; G. Scholem, *Origines de la Kabbale* (1966), 311–4; idem, *Jaldabaoth reconsidered*, in: *Mélanges H. Ch. Puech* (1973).

Part Three
PERSONALITIES

1

Azriel of Gerona

Azriel, who lived in the early 13th century, is not to be confused with his older contemporary Ezra b. Solomon, also of Gerona, Spain; this mistake has repeatedly been made from the 14th century onward. Graetz's opinion, that as far as the history of Kabbalah is concerned the two are to be regarded as one, has lost its validity since the works of both authors have been more closely studied. No details of his life are known. In a letter to Gerona that has been preserved, his teacher, Isaac the Blind, seems to have opposed his open propagation of kabbalistic doctrines in wider circles *(Sefer Bialik* (1934), 143–8). The poet Meshullam Dapiera of Gerona in various poems hailed him as a leader of kabbalists in Gerona and as his teacher. An Oxford manuscript found by S. Sachs containing his alleged discussions with philosophic opponents of the Kabbalah is the plagiarization of a genuine Azriel manuscript by an anonymous author of about a century later, who prefixed it with his own autobiography.

The clear separation of the works of Ezra from those of Azriel is largely the achievement of I. Tishby. Azriel's works have a characteristic style and a distinctive terminology. All, without exception, deal with kabbalistic subjects. They include: (1) *Sha'ar ha-Sho'el* ("The Gate of the Enquirer"), an explanation of the doctrine of the ten *Sefirot* ("Divine Emanations") in question and answer form, with the addition of a sort of commentary by the author himself. It was first printed in Berlin as an introduction to a book by Meir ibn Gabbai, *Derekh Emunah,* "The Way of Belief" (1850). (2) Commentary on the *Sefer Yeẓirah,* printed in the editions of this book but ascribed to Naḥmanides. (3) A commentary to the talmudic *aggadot,* a critical edition of which was published by Tishby in Jerusalem in 1943. This commentary represents a revision and, partly, an important expansion (in speculative matters) of the commentary of Ezra b. Solomon, particularly clarifying the differences from the version of his older colleague. (4) A commentary on the liturgy; actually a collection of instructions for mystical meditations on the most important prayers; it generally appears under the name of Ezra in the extant manuscripts. Large sections are quoted under Azriel's name in the prayer book of Naphtali Hirz Treves (Thiengen, 1560). (5) A long letter sent by Azriel from Gerona to Burgos in

Spain, dealing with basic kabbalistic problems. In some manuscripts, this letter is wrongly ascribed to Jacob b. Jacob ha-Kohen of Soria; it was published by Scholem in *Madda'ei ha-Yahadut,* 2 (1927), 233–40. (6) A number of shorter treatises, the most important of which is a large section of a partly-preserved work, *Derekh ha-Emunah ve-Derekh ha-Kefirah* ("The Way of Belief and the Way of Heresy"), as well as short pieces on the mysticism of prayer (published by Scholem in *Studies in memory of A. Gulak and S. Klein* (1942), 201–22), as well as the yet unpublished treatise on the mystical meaning of sacrifice, *Sod ha-Korban,* and the anonymous *Sha'ar ha-Kavvanah,* "a chapter on the meaning of mystical intention," ascribed in the manuscripts to "the kabbalists of olden times" (Scholem, in *MGWJ* 78 (1934), 492–518).

Azriel is one of the most profound speculative thinkers in kabbalistic mysticism. His work most clearly reflects the process whereby neoplatonic thought penetrated into the original kabbalistic tradition, as it reached Provence in the *Sefer ha-Bahir*. He was acquainted with various sources of neoplatonic literature, from which he quotes some passages directly. It is as yet impossible to say how he became acquainted with concepts belonging to the philosophy of Solomon ibn Gabirol and the Christian neoplatonic thinker John Scotus Erigena; but, somehow, Azriel must have come into contact with their way of thinking. Most significantly, the status and importance of the will of God as the highest potency of the deity, surpassing all other attributes, closely associated with God and yet not identical with Him, corresponds to the doctrine of Gabirol. Other points such as the coincidence of opposites in the divine unity, which plays a special role in Azriel's work, appears to come from the Christian neoplatonic tradition. Azriel particularly stresses the disparity of the neoplatonic idea of God, which may be formulated only in negatives, and that of the biblical God, about whom positive assertions may be made and to whom attributes may be ascribed. The former is *Ein-Sof,* the Infinite; the other is represented by the world of the *Sefirot,* which in various emanations reveals the creative movement of the divine unity. The logic, by which Azriel established the need for the assumption that the existence of the *Sefirot* is an emanation of divine power, is entirely neoplatonic. Yet, in contrast with the doctrine of Plotinus, these emanations are seen as processes taking place within the deity, and not extra-divine steps intermediate between God and the visible creation. Rather, the process takes its course in God Himself, namely between His hidden being, about which nothing positive can actually be said, and His appearance as Creator to which the Bible is testimony. In probing the mysteries of this world of the *Sefirot,* Azriel displays great daring. The same boldness is exhibited in those theosophical speculations which he reads into the talmudic *aggadah.* The Kabbalah of Azriel knows nothing of a true creation from nothingness although he uses this formula emphatically. However, he changes its meaning entirely: the "nothingness" out of which everything was created is here (as with Erigena) only a symbolic designation of the Divine Being, which surpasses all that is comprehensible to man, or of the Divine Will, which in itself has no beginning.

Bibliography: I. Tishby, in: *Zion,* 9 (1944), 178–85; idem, in: *Sinai,* 16 (1945), 159–78; idem, in: *Minḥah li-Yhudah (Zlotnick)* (1950, jubilee volume . . . J.L. Zlotnik), 170–4; G. Scholem, *Ursprung und Anfaenge der Kabbala* (1962), ch 4; G. Sed-Rajna, *Le commentaire d'Azriel de Gérone sur les priéres* (1973).

2

Naphtali Bacharach

Bacharach was born in Frankfort (the date of his birth – as of his death – is unknown) but also spent some years in Poland with the kabbalists before he returned to his home town, and in 1648 he published his comprehensive book *Emek ha-Melekh* ("The King's Valley"), one of the most important kabbalistic works. The book contains a wide and systematic presentation of theology according to the Lurianic Kabbalah. It was based on many authorities, but relied mainly on Israel Sarug's version presented in his book *Limmudei Aẓilut* (1897), which Bacharach included almost in its entirety into his own book with hardly an acknowledgement of the fact. Bacharach's claims that he brought back the sources of Luria's Kabbalah with him from Ereẓ Israel, where he supposedly lived for some time, do not deserve credit. He also accused Joseph Solomon Delmedigo, who he claimed had been his pupil, of transcribing kabbalistic manuscripts which were in Bacharach's possession, and then publishing them, with noticeable distortions, in his books *Ta'alumot Ḥokhmah* (1629) and *Novelot Ḥokhmah* (1631). However, the contrary seems much more likely; that it was Bacharach who culled from Delmedigo's work as well as from many other sources without acknowledging them. While Delmedigo's interest lay in the abstract philosophical aspect of Kabbalah, which he attempted to explain to himself, Bacharach appears as an enthusiastic and fanatical kabbalist, with a special flair for the mystical and non-philosophical traits of Kabbalah – in Isaac Luria's Kabbalah as well as in the Kabbalah of the early kabbalists. This accounts for the strong emphasis given to such elements as the doctrine of the *sitra aḥra* ("other side" – the Evil) and demonology. He wove the old kabbalistic themes together with the later ones in an elaborately detailed style. Without referring to Sarug, who is his most important source, Bacharach claims to derive his teachings from the books of Ḥayyim Vital, although important chapters of his doctrine, such as his version of the doctrine of *ẓimẓum* ("withdrawal") and all it entails, are completely foreign to Vital's writings. The merger of both these traditions characterizes this book, written with talent and clarity. Bacharach also borrowed liberally from certain parts of *Shefa Tal* by R. Shabbetai Sheftel Horowitz (1612). His style is pervaded by a messianic tension. The book *Emek ha-Melekh* had a great impact on the development of the late Kabbalah. It was widely recognized as an authoritative source on the doctrine of Isaac Luria and kabbalists from many countries, especially Ashkenazim, the great Ḥabad Ḥasidim, and the school of the Gaon Elijah b. Solomon Zalman of Vilna, quoted him extensively. His influence is also noticeable in Shabbatean literature, in Moses Ḥayyim Luzzatto's system of Kabbalah, and in the book *Kelaḥ* [=138] *Pitḥei Ḥokhmah.* On the other hand, strong criticism of the book was soon expressed. Already in 1655, Ḥayyim ha-Kohen of Aleppo, a disciple of Ḥayyim Vital, in the introduction to his *Mekor Ḥayyim* (1655), protested against Bacharach's claim that he was the true interpreter of Luria's doctrine. The protests of Benjamin ha-Levi in his approbation to *Zot Ḥukkat ha-Torah* by Abraham Ḥazkuni (1659), and of the preacher Berechiah Berach, in his introduction to *Zera Berakh* (2nd part, 1662), against misrepresentations of Luria's Kabbalah were also intended for Bacharach. Moses Ḥagiz says in *Shever Poshe'im* (1714) that *Emek ha-Melekh* is called *Emek ha-Bakha* ("Valley of Weeping"). Isaiah Bassan complains to M.Ḥ. Luzzatto about the translation of numerous chapters from *Emek ha-Melekh* into Latin, referring to the *Kabbalah Denudata* by Knorr von Rosenroth "which were among the important causes of prolonging our exile" *(Iggerot Shadal,* 29). Ḥ.J.D. Azulai also wrote: "I have heard that no genuine writings got into his (Bacharach's) hands . . . therefore the initiated refrain from reading either it or the *Novelot Ḥokhmah.*" In *Emek ha-Melekh* there is a reference to many other books by Bacharach concerning aspects of the kabbalist doctrine. Of these only a part of the *Gan ha-Melekh* on the Zohar is extant, in an Oxford manuscript.

Bibliography: Azulai, 2 (1852), 115, no. 406; G. Scholem, in: KS 30 (1954/55), 413; Scholem, Sabbatai Sevi, *passim*; M. Horovitz, *Frankfurter Rabbinen,* 2 (1883), 41–45.

3
Abraham Miguel Cardozo

Cardozo was born in Rio Seco, Spain, to a Marrano family in 1626. He studied medicine at the University of Salamanca and, according to his own testimony, two years of Christian theology as well. He lived for a time with his brother Isaac in Madrid and in 1648 left Spain with him and went to Venice. In Leghorn he returned to Judaism and later continued his studies in medicine and acquired considerable rabbinic knowledge, studying under the rabbis of Venice. Apparently, he earned his living as a physician and was trusted also by non-Jews. Even during his stay in Italy he was assailed by religious doubts and immersed himself in theological speculations on the meaning of Jewish monotheism. Most of his stay in Italy was spent in Venice and in Leghorn. About 1659 he started a life of wandering, marked by instability, persecutions, and intensive activity. According to one tradition, he first settled in Tripoli, as the bey's doctor *(Merivat Kadesh,* 9), but according to his own testimony, he first went to Egypt and lived there for five years, mainly in Cairo, where he started to study Lurianic Kabbalah. In 1663 or 1664 he arrived in Tripoli, and there he began to have revelations through visions and dreams. In Tripoli, Cardozo was respected as the religious leader by many in the community, although he had also many opponents. He stayed there presumably for almost ten years. When information about the appearance of Shabbetai Ẓevi and Nathan of Gaza was first received, Cardozo became, from 1665, one of the new "messiah's" most fervent supporters, and initiated widespread propaganda activities on behalf of "the faith." He tells of his many visions of redemption and the messiah. He persisted in his belief even after Shabbetai Ẓevi's apostasy, which he justified, although he opposed the apostasy of other Shabbateans. Some of the long letters he wrote in defense of Shabbetai Ẓevi's messianic claims between 1668 and 1707 have been preserved: among them letters addressed to his brother, to his brother-in-law, Baruch Enriques in Amsterdam, and to the rabbis of Smyrna (J. Sasportas, *Ẓiẓat Novel Ẓevi* (1954), 361–8; *Zion,* 19 (1954), 1–22. The most important of these theological pleas in defense of the messiah's apostasy is *Iggeret Magen Avraham* (published by G. Scholem in *Koveẓ al-Yad* 12 (1938), 121–55). The tract ascribed in one manuscript to Abraham Pereẓ of Salonika, a disciple of Nathan of Gaza, has now been definitely proved to be the work of Cardozo. (An analysis of the treatise is given in G. Scholem's *Sabbatai Sevi* (1973), 814–20.) During those years, Cardozo corresponded with the other leaders of the movement, particularly with Nathan of Gaza, Abraham Yakhini, and with Shabbetai Ẓevi himself. At the beginning of 1673 he sent Shabbetai Ẓevi his first theological work on his new interpretation of monotheism, *Boker Avraham.* This work was completed in Tripoli at the end of 1672, and is extant in many manuscripts. Cardozo expounds in it the new doctrine, that a distinction should be made between the First Cause, which has no connection with created beings, and the God of Israel who is the God of religion and revelation, whom one must worship by studying the Torah and by fulfilling the *miẓvot,* although He himself emanates from the first cause.

For more than 30 years Cardozo composed many books, pamphlets, and treatises in support of this paradoxical theology, which aroused stormy controversy. In 1668, when the rabbis of Smyrna accused him of misconduct relating to his observance of *miẓvot,* the *dayyanim* of Tripoli defended him in a manifesto confirming his religious integrity (Ms. Hamburg 312). Nevertheless, he was banned from Tripoli at the beginning of 1673. He stayed in Tunis until 1674, under the protection of the local ruler, whom he served as personal physician. Letters of excommunication, issued by the rabbis of Venice and Smyrna, followed him to Tunis as well. In the autumn of 1674 he arrived in Leghorn, but there too the community council demanded his isolation from the community and at the end of May 1675 he left for Smyrna. In spite of this he maintained a close relationship with the Shabbatean group in Leghorn, led by Moses Pinheiro. In Smyrna, Cardozo found many Shabbateans and had many disciples among them. The foremost among those was the famous preacher and author Elijah ha-Kohen ha-Itamari, then a young man, and the *ḥazzan* Daniel Bonafoux. His group evolved a sectarian life marked by numerous visions and revelations in which a *maggid* confirmed Cardozo's Shabbatean and general theological theories. The rabbis of Smyrna were apparently powerless in the face of Cardozo's influence and their continued persecution did not achieve his expulsion from Smyrna until the spring of 1681. During these years, Cardozo started calling himself "Messiah ben Joseph." He also made this claim in some of his books, although in his later days he retracted it, and even denied having ever made such a claim. From Smyrna he traveled to Brusa, where he stayed a fortnight and where the town's scholars became his followers. He proceeded to Constantinople. Cardozo claims that during his stay in Rodosto, by the Sea of Marmara whither he had removed from Constantinople, he received letters from Shabbatai Ẓevi's widow, proposing to marry him as "leader of the believers" and that he also met her. It was a time of profound religious ferment among the Shabbateans and Cardozo prophesied with strong conviction that redemption would come on Passover, 1682. After this prophecy came to naught, Cardozo was forced to leave Constantinople in disgrace and settled for four years in Gallipoli. During that period, mass apostasy occurred in Salonika, occasioning the birth of the Doenmeh sect. Cardozo opposed this sect and polemicized against it in some of his writings (*Zion,* 7 (1942), 14–20). Strangely enough, this fact notwithstanding, the Doenmeh literature, both in its homilies and in its poetry, is full of praises of Cardozo and refers to him as to an authority. In those years, Cardozo began to dissent also from the new kabbalistic and Shabbatean system of Nathan of Gaza, pitting against it his own system regarding the true nature of God which, according to him, was understood correctly only by Shabbetai Ẓevi and himself. He calls this secret teaching *Sod ha-Elohut* ("Secret of Divinity"). During the same period, he first visited Adrianople. In 1686 Cardozo returned to Constantinople, where he lived until 1696, under the protection of some eminent Christian diplomats despite the hostility of the town's rabbis, who persecuted him and his disciples. During Cardozo's stay in Smyrna and Constantinople, he was beset by many personal misfortunes and almost all of his children died of plague. His opponents accused him of maintaining illicit relations with various women and of fathering illegitimate children. Apparently, he was forced to leave Constantinople when his relationships with those consuls who gave him protection deteriorated. He then stayed for some time in Rodosto where he obtained the short tract *Raza de-Meheimanuta* ("The Mystery of Faith"), which was dictated by Shabbetai Ẓevi at the end of his life to one of the learned Shabbateans, who in turn passed the text to Cardozo's disciples in Constantinople. This treatise, which Cardozo viewed as strong support for his own new kabbalistic system, figured prominently in most of his later writings. From Rodosto, Cardozo tried to move to Adrianople, but failed, because of the opposition of Samuel Primo who caused his expulsion from the town after three months. During this visit some stormy discussions were held between Cardozo and Primo and his followers. There are conflicting statements about the date of this visit in Cardozo's writings. He returned to Rodosto and then he traveled to the island of Chios, and later, from 1698 or 1699 on, spent a few years in Candia, Crete. For several years, Cardozo corresponded with Polish Shabbatean leaders, such as the prophet Heshel Ẓoref, and commented also on the immigration to Ereẓ Israel in 1700 of Judah Ḥasid and Ḥayyim Malakh and their group. Cardozo was aware of the Shabbatean character of this immigration, but the opposition of Ḥayyim Malakh's disciples to his system displeased him. In Candia, Cardozo wrote some documents of specific autobiographical import, such as the homily *Ani ha-*

Mekhunneh published by C. Bernheimer, and the letters published by I.R. Molcho and S. Amarillo.

An attempt to return to Constantinople failed. Cardozo was party to the belief that Shabbetai Ẓevi would reappear 40 years after his apostasy, in 1706, and he therefore tried to settle in Ereẓ Israel. He went to Jaffa (c. 1703), but the spiritual leaders of both Jerusalem and Safed did not allow him a place in their communities. According to the testimony of Abraham Yiẓḥaki (Jacob Emden *Torat ha-Kena'ot,* 66), Cardozo met Nehemiah Ḥayon who lived at the time in Safed. Cardozo continued to Alexandria, and stayed there for about three years. He was killed by his nephew during a family quarrel in 1706.

Among the Shabbatean leaders in the last third of the 17th century, Cardozo stands out in his originality and eloquence of thought. His character was erratic, and although the main threads of his thought have coherence and consistency, his writings show many contradictions and inconsistencies regarding details. A flair for visions and all sorts of secret rituals is combined with a remarkably profound preoccupation with theological thought. His literary work alternates between these extremes. In addition to numerous letters, almost all of them concerning the messianic doctrine and claims of Shabbatai Ẓevi (two of which were in Spanish; Oxford Ms. 2481) and some about his own life, he wrote many *derushim* ("enquiries") which are not homilies but theological studies, wherein he developed his system of theology, based on a certain gnostic dualism with a reversal of evaluation. Whereas the second century Gnostics considered the Hidden God as the true God, and disparaged the worth of the Demiurge or Creator *(Yoẓer Bereshit),* i.e., the God of Israel, Cardozo disparages the value of the hidden First Cause and places supreme the positive religious significance of the God of Israel as the God of Revelation. His writings abound with anti-Christian polemic. He viewed the doctrine of the Trinity as a distortion of the true kabbalistic doctrine. His anti-Christian polemic is based on sound knowledge of Catholic dogma. He also attacked the doctrine of the Incarnation of the Messiah, which was accepted by the extreme Shabbatean groups. In practice, Cardozo adhered to the rabbinic tradition and opposed religious antinomianism. Nevertheless, his opponents interpreted his system as clearly in conflict with the fundamental tenets of traditional Jewish theology, even in its kabbalistic form. His books were prohibited from being printed and were even burnt in some places, e.g., in Smyrna and in Adrianople. An attempt, made by one of his disciples, Elijah Taragon, to publish Cardozo's main book *Boker Avraham,* in Amsterdam, shortly after Cardozo's death, failed because of the intervention of the rabbis of Smyrna. On the other hand, many copies of his writings were circulated and over 30 manuscripts containing compilations of his *derushim* are extant. He had influential disciples and admirers even in countries he never visited, such as Morocco, and England. He corresponded with many of his followers, including some in Jerusalem, between 1680 and 1703.

Among his theological works, mention should be made of the large collection of writings (Adler Ms. 1653) in New York, the major work *Sod Adonai li-Yre'av* consisting of 24 chapters (Institute Ben-Zvi, Ms. 2269), and *Raza de-Razin* (Ms. Deinard 351 in N.Y.) written against Samuel Primo. In this book, he mentioned that he wrote 60 *derushim.* Excerpts from his writings, as well as complete treatises, were published by A. Jellinek (*"Derush ha-Ketav"* in the *Bet ha-Midrash* of Is. H. Weiss, 1865); Bernheimer (JQR, 18 1927/28), 97–127); G. Scholem (*Abhandlungen zur. Erinnerung an H.P. Chajes* (Vienna, 1933), 324–50; *Zion,* 7 (1942), 12–28; and *Sefunot,* 3–4 (1960), 245–300); and I.R. Molcho and S.A. Amarillo (*ibid.,* 183–241).

Shortly after Cardozo's death, one of his opponents, Elijah Cohen of Constantinople (not to be confused with the famous rabbi of that name in Smyrna), wrote a hostile biography of Cardozo, *Merivat Kadesh* which contains many important documents (published in *Inyenei Shabbetai Ẓevi* (1912), 1–40).

Bibliography: Graetz, *Geschizhte der Juden,* 10 (1897^3), 4; G. Scholem, *Judaica* 1 (Ger., 1963), 119–46; Y.H. Yerushalmi, *Isaac Cardoso* (1971), 313–43.

4

Moses Cordovero

(Written by J. Ben-Shlomo)

Moses Cordovero was born in 1522. His birthplace is unknown, but his name testifies to the family's Spanish origins. He lived in Safed and was a disciple of Joseph Caro and of Solomon Alkabeẓ, and a teacher of Isaac Luria. His first large systematic work is *Pardes Rimmonim,* which Cordovero completed by the age of 27. Ten years later he finished his second systematic book, the *Elimah Rabbati,* and also wrote a lengthy commentary on all the parts of the Zohar which has been preserved in manuscript in Modena. He died in 1570.

The doctrine of Cordovero is a summary and a development of the different trends in Kabbalah up to his time, and his whole work is a major attempt to synthesize and to construct a speculative kabbalistic system. This is done especially in his theology, which is based on the Zohar, and in particular on *Tikkunei Zohar* and *Ra'aya Meheimna.* Since Cordovero considered this text to be by one and the same author, he felt constrained to harmonize their different and at times even opposing conceptions. Cordovero follows *Tikkunei Zohar* in his conception of God as a transcendent being. God is the First Cause, a Necessary Being, essentially different from any other being. In this concept of God, Cordovero is obviously drawing upon the sources of medieval philosophy (especially Maimonides). In accordance with the philosophers Cordovero maintains that no positive attribute can apply to the transcendent God. In his opinion, the philosophers had attained an important achievement in purifying the concept of God of its anthropomorphisms. Yet, Cordovero stresses that the essential difference between Kabbalah and philosophy lies in the solution of the problem of the bridge between God and the world. This bridging is made possible by the structure of the *Sefirot* ("Emanations") emanted from God.

In this way Cordovero tries to unify the concept of God as a transcendent Being with the personal concept. Thus, the central problem of his theology is the relation between *Ein-Sof* (the transcendent God) and the question of the nature of the *Sefirot:* are they God's substance or only *kelim* ("instruments" or "vessels")? Cordovero's answer to this question is something of a compromise between the Zohar and *Tikkunei Zohar* – the *Sefirot* are substance and *kelim* at the same time. They are beings emanated outward from God, but His substance is immanent in them. Cordovero described the *Sefirot* as instruments or tools with which God performs His various activities in the world, and as the vessels containing the Divine substance, which permeates them and gives them life, as the soul gives life to the body. By means of this attitude Cordovero wants to preserve, on the one hand, the concept of the simple and immutable God, and on the other hand to maintain God's providence in the world. Although this providence is sometimes described as a substantial immanence of God through all the worlds, Cordovero has reservations about it. In *Pardes Rimmonim,* a distinction exists between the transcendent God, who undergoes no process, and the light emanated from Him, spreading through the *Sefirot.* This emanated expansion is not of a necessary existence, but is activated by God's spontaneous will. This makes for the involvement of the will in every Divine act – the active God is the God united in His will.

It is quite understandable, therefore, why God's will has such a decisive place in Cordovero's system. Here again, the same question arises: what is the relation between God and His will? Cordovero's answer is dialectic in its character. By itself, the will is an emanation, but it originates from God in a succession of wills which approach God's substance asymptotically.

The process of emanation of the *Sefirot* is described by Cordovero as dialectical. In order to be revealed, God has to conceal Himself. This concealment is in itself the coming into being of the *Sefirot.* Only the *Sefirot* reveal God, and that is why "revealing is the cause of concealment and concealment is the cause of revealing." The process of emanation itself takes place through a constant dynamics of inner aspects inside the *Sefirot.* These aspects form a reflective process inside each *Sefirah,* which reflects itself in its different qualities; these aspects also have a function in the process of emanation, in being the inner grades which derive, each from the other, according to the principle of causation. Only this inner process, which is but a hypostasis of the reflective aspects, enables the emanation of the *Sefirot,* each from the other, as well. These inner processes are of special importance regarding the first *Sefirah* – the will. After the series of wills, which are the aspects of the *"Keter"* ("crown") in the *"Keter,"* there appear in *"Ḥokhmah"* ("Wisdom") in the *"Keter"* aspects which express the potential thought of all the not yet actualized Being. Cordovero calls these thoughts: "The kings of Edom who died before the reign of a king in Israel." This idea appears in the Zohar, but Cordovero reverses its meaning. In the Zohar this is a mythological description of the forces of stern judgment *(din)* that were conceived in the Divine Thought, and because of their extreme severity, were abolished and died, whereas according to Cordovero these thoughts were abolished because they did not contain enough judgment *(din).* Cordovero conceives of judgment *(din)* as a

פרדס רמונים . עם פרי מגדים . כפרים עם נרדים :

ספר

פרדס רמונים

פה קק קראקא

Title page of Moses Cordovero's kabbalistic work, *Pardes Rimmonim,* Cracow, 1592.

necessary condition for the survival of any existence. What is too near to the abundance of God's infinite compassion cannot exist, and therefore the highest thoughts were abolished, so that the *Sefirot* could be formed only when emanation reached the *Sefirah* of *Binah* ("Intelligence"), which already contains judgment *(din)*.

The whole world of emanation is built and consolidated by a double process, that of *or yashar* ("direct light") – the emanations downward, and *or ḥozer* ("reflected light") – the reflection of the same process upward. This reflected movement is also the origin of *din*.

The transition from the world of emanation to the lower world is continuous. Thus the problem of creation *ex nihilo* does not exist in relation to our world, but pertains only to the transition from the divine "Nothingness" *(Ayin)* to the first Being – the uppermost aspects of the first *Sefirah*. In spite of Cordovero's attempts to obliterate this transition, his stand is theistic: the first *Sefirah* is outside God's substance. This prohibits any pantheistic interpretation of Cordovero's system. The immanence of the Divine substance in the *Sefirot* and in all worlds is likewise clothed always in the first vessel, even though Cordovero hints several times at a mystical experience in which the immanence of God Himself in the world is revealed. In this esoteric meaning, Cordovero's system may, perhaps, be defined as pantheistic.

In addition to his two principal systematic books, *Pardes Rimmonim* (Cracow, 1592) and *Elimah Rabbati* (Lvov, 1881), the following parts of his commentary to the Zohar were published separately: the introduction to the commentary on the *Idrot* in the Zohar, *Shi'ur Komah* (Warsaw, 1883); and an introduction to the Zohar "Song of Songs," *Derishot be-Inyanei Malakhim* (Jerusalem, 1945). Publication of the complete commentary has begun in Jerusalem; seven volumes had appeared by 1973.

Other published works are: *Or Ne'erav* (Venice, 1587); *Sefer Gerushin* (Venice, c. 1602); *Tefillah le-Moshe* (Przemysl, 1892); *Zivḥei Shelamim* (Lublin, 1613), *Perush Seder Avodat Yom ha-Kippurim* (Venice, 1587); *Tomer Devorah* (Venice, 1589; tr. L. Jacobs, *Palmtree of Deborah*, 1960). In this work Cordovero laid the foundations for kabbalistic ethical literature, which proliferated in the 16th–18th centuries. In its short chapters he instructed every Jew in the right way to follow in order to come close and identify spiritually with each of the ten *Sefirot*. This short treatise influenced many later kabbalistic moralists in Safed and Eastern Europe. There are two existing abridgments of *Pardes Rimmonim*: *Pelaḥ ha-Rimmon* (Venice, 1600) by Menahem Azariah of Fano, and *Asis Rimmonim* (Venice, 1601) by Samuel Gallico.

Bibliography: S.A. Horodezky, *Torat ha-Kabbalah shel Rabbi Moshe . . . Cordovero* (1924); J. Ben-Shlomo, *Torah ha-Elohut shel R. Moshe Cordovero* (1965).

5

Jonathan Eybeschuetz

Eybeschuetz, a child prodigy, studied in Poland, Moravia, and Prague. In his youth, after the death of his father, he studied in Prossnitz under Meir Eisenstadt and Eliezer ha-Levi Ettinger, his uncle, and in Vienna under Samson Wertheimer. He married the daughter of Isaac Spira, the *av bet din* of Bunzlau. After traveling for some time he settled in Prague in 1715, and in time became head of the yeshivah and a famous preacher. When he was in Prague he had many contacts with priests and the intelligentsia, debating religious topics and matters of faith with them. He became friendly with Cardinal Hasselbauer and also discussed religious questions with him. Through his help, Eybeschuetz received permission to print the Talmud with the omission of all passsages contradicting the principles of Christianity. Aroused to anger by this, David Oppenheim and the rabbis of Frankfort had the license to print revoked.

The people of Prague held Eybeschuetz in high esteem and he was considered second only to David Oppenheim. In 1725 he was among the Prague rabbis who excommunicated the Shabbatean sect. After the death of David Oppenheim (1736), he was appointed *dayyan* of Prague. Elected rabbi of Metz in 1741, he subsequently became rabbi of the "Three Communities," Altona, Hamburg, and Wandsbek (1750). Both in Metz and in Altona he had many disciples and was considered a great preacher.

His position in the Three Communities, however, was undermined when the dispute broke out concerning his suspected leanings toward Shabbateanism. This controversy accompanied Eybeschuetz throughout his life, and the quarrel had repercussions in every community from Holland to Poland. His main opponent was Jacob Emden, also a famous talmudist and his rival in the candidature to the rabbinate of the Three Communities. The quarrel developed into a great public dispute which divided the rabbis of the day. While most of the German rabbis opposed Eybeschuetz, his support came from the rabbis of Poland and Moravia. A fruitless attempt at mediation was made by Ezekiel Landau, rabbi of Prague. Most of Eybeschuetz' own community was loyal to him and confidently accepted his refutation of the charges made by his opponent, but dissension reached such a pitch that both sides appealed to the authorities in Hamburg and

Jonathan Eybeschuetz, 18th century kabbalist.

the government of Denmark for a judicial ruling. The king favored Eybeschuetz and ordered new elections, which resulted in his reappointment. Yet the literary polemic continued, even prompting several Christian scholars to participate, some of whom, thinking that Eybeschuetz was a secret Christian, came to his defense. After his reelection as rabbi of the Three Communities, some rabbis of Frankfort, Amsterdam, and Metz challenged him to appear before them to reply to the suspicions raised against him. Eybeschuetz refused, and when the matter was brought before the Council of the Four Lands in 1753, the council issued a ruling in his favor. In 1760 the quarrel broke out once more when some Shabbatean elements were discovered among the students of Eybeschuetz' yeshivah. At the same time his younger son, Wolf, presented himself as a Shabbatean prophet, with the result that the yeshivah was closed. When Moses Mendelssohn was in Hamburg in 1761, Eybeschuetz treated him with great respect, even publishing a letter on him *(Kerem Ḥemed,* 3 (1838), 224–5), incontrovertible testimony to Eybeschuetz' awareness of Mendelssohn's idological approach. Eyebeschuetz died in 1764, aged around 70.

Eybeschuetz was considered not only one of the greatest preachers of his time but also one of the giants of the Talmud, acclaimed for his acumen and particularly incisive intellect. Thirty of his works in the field of *halakhah* have been published. His method of teaching aroused great enthusiasm among the pilpulists, and his works, *Urim ve-Tummim* on *Ḥoshen Mishpat* (1775–77), *Kereti u-Feleti* on *Yoreh De'ah* (1763), and *Benei Ahuvah* on Maimonides (1819), were considered masterpieces of pilpulistic literature. To the present day they are regarded as classics by students of the Talmud. They are unique in that the many *pilpulim* they include are in most cases based on clear, logical principles that give them their permanent value. His homiletic works, *Ahavat Yonatan* (1766), *Ya'arot Devash* (1799–82), *Tiferet Yonatan* (1819), also found many admirers. In succeeding generations his reputation was sustained by these works. Since (apart from *Kereti u-Feleti)* his works were not printed in his lifetime, it is clear that his great influence among his contemporaries must have derived from the power of his oral teaching and from his personality, both of which were highly praised by many writers. Of his books on the Kabbalah, only one was printed, *Shem Olam* (1891), but during his lifetime Eybeschuetz was considered a great kabbalist.

Opinions are still divided on the assessment of this striking personality, his supporters and detractors vying with one another with an extraordinary intensity. The great bitterness surrounding the controversies on the question of his secret relationship with the Shabbateans stems precisely from his being recognized as a true master of the Torah. It was hard to believe that a man who had himself signed a *ḥerem* against the Shabbateans could have secretly held their beliefs. Suspicions were aroused against him on two occasions: in 1724, with the appearance of a manuscript entitled *Va-Avo ha-Yom el ha-Ayin,* which the Shabbateans, and also several of his own students, ascribed to him. This book (preserved in Ms.) is indisputably a Shabbatean work. Even after he had signed the *ḥerem* against the Shabbateans, suspicion was not allayed and apparently it prevented his election to the rabbinate of Prague. In 1751, the dispute grew more virulent when some amulets written by Eybeschuetz in Metz and Altona were opened. Jacob Emden deciphered them and found that they contained unmistakable Shabbatean formulae *(Sefat Emet,* 1752). Eybeschuetz denied that the amulets had any continuous logical meaning, maintaining that they consisted simply of "Holy Names" *(Luḥot Edut,* 1755), and he even put forward an interpretation of them based on his system. His opponents retorted that the real interpretation of the amulets could be discovered from the work attributed to him, *Va-Avo ha-Yom el ha-Ayin,* and that they could and should be interpreted as having a meaningful content. Scholarly historical research has advanced three views concerning Eybeschuetz' relationship with the Shabbateanism: that he was never a Shabbatean and that suspicions on this score were completely unfounded (Zinz, Mortimer Cohen, Klemperer); that he was a Shabbatean in his youth but turned his back on the sect around the time of the *ḥerem* of 1725 (Bernhard Baer, Saul Pinḥas Rabinowitz); that he was crypto-Shabbatean from the time he studied in Prossnitz and Prague until the end of his life (Graetz, David Kahana, Scholem, Perlmutter). An interpretation of his kabbalistic beliefs must also depend on his relationship with Shabbateanism. Some believe that the book *Shem Olam,* which deals with the philosophical explanation of the nature of God, is a work whose kabbalistic teaching only confirms generally accepted kabbalistic teaching (Mieses); others consider that the book is undoubtedly Shabbatean in its conception of God (Perlmutter). Still others believe that the work is a forgery or was erroneously attributed to Eybeschuetz (Margulies). Recent research has demonstrated a close relationship between *Shem Olam* and *Va-Avo ha-Yom el ha-Ayin.*

Bibliography: B. Brilling, in: HUCA, 34 (1963), 217–28; 35 (1964), 255–73: D.L. Zinz, *Gedulat Yehonatan* (1930); M.J. Cohen, *Jacob Emden, a Man of Controversy* (1937); G. Scholem, in: KS, 16 (1939–40), 320–38; idem, in: *Zion,* 6 (1940–1), 96–100; idem, *Leket Margaliyyot* (1941); R. Margulies, *Sibbat Hitnahaguto shel Rabbenu Ya'akov me-Emden le-Rabbenu Yehonatan Eybeschuetz* (1941); A. Ha-Shiloni (I. Raphael), *La-Pulmus ha-Meḥuddash al Shabbata'uto shel R. Yehonatan Eybeschuetz* (1942); M.A. Perlmutter, *R. Yehonatan Eybeschuetz ve-Yaḥaso la-Shabbeta'ut* 1947); Mifal ha-Bibliografyah ha-Ivrit, *Ḥoveret le-Dugmah* (1964), 13–24.

6

Joseph Gikatilla

Joseph Gikatilla (or Chiquatilla), who was born in Medinaceli, Castile in 1248, lived for many years in Segovia. Between 1272 and 1274 he studied under Abraham Abulafia, who praises him as his most successful pupil. Gikatilla, who was at first greatly influenced by Abulafia's ecstatic, prophetic system of kabbalism, soon showed a greater affinity for philosophy.

His first extant work, *Ginnat Egoz* (1615), written in 1274, is an introduction to the mystic symbolism of the alphabet, vowel points, and the Divine Names. The title derives from the initial letters of the kabbalistic elements *gematria* ("numerology"), *notarikon* ("acrostics"), *temurah* ("permutation"). In common with his mentor, Gikatilla also links this mystic lore with the system practiced by Maimonides. This work makes no suggestion of the theosophical doctrine of *Sefirot* later adopted by Gikatilla. The *Sefirot* here are identified with the philosophical term "intelligences." On the other hand, the author shows himself familiar with the theosophical revelations of Jacob b. Jacob ha-Kohen of Segovia, although the latter is not mentioned by name. Several of Gikatilla's other writings also deal with the theory of letter combinations and alphabetical mysticism. However, in the 1280s, Gikatilla apparently made contact with Moses b. Shem Tov de Leon, and thereafter the two exerted a mutual influence on each other's kabbalistic development.

Before writing *Ginnat Egoz,* Gikatilla had written a commentary on the Song of Songs (but not the one in the Paris manuscript 790 which alleges that Gikatilla wrote it in 1300 in Segovia). This work endorses the doctrine of *Shemitot,* a theory of cosmic cycles, as expounded in the *Sefer ha-Temunah.* Gikatilla also compiled *Kelalei ha-Mizvot,* explaining *mizvot* by a literal interpretation of *halakhah* (Ms. Paris 713); a number of *piyyutim* (Habermann, in *Mizraḥ u-Ma'arav,* 5 (1932), 351; Gruenwald, in *Tarbiz,* 36 (1966/67), 73–89), some devoted to kabbalistic themes; and *Sefer ha-Meshalim,* a book of parables to which he added his own commentary, whose ethical precepts were close to kabbalistic principles. (The parables alone published by I. Davidson, in *Sefer ha-Yovel shel "Hadoar"* (1927), 116–22; the book with commentary, in Ms. Oxford 1267). While Gikatilla wrote numerous works on Kabbalah, many others have been attributed to him erroneously. A. Altmann, for instance, has shown that Gikatilla was not the author of the lengthy *Sefer Ta'amei ha-Mizvot.* Written by an unknown kabbalist about 1300 and also attributed to Isaac ibn Farḥi, it had a wide circulation. A number of treatises attributed to Gikatilla await clarification as to their authorship.

Gikatilla's most influential kabbalistic work, written before 1293, is his *Sha'arei Orah* (1559, new ed. by J. Ben-Shlomo, Jerusalem, 1970), a detailed explanation of kabbalistic symbolism and the designations of the ten *Sefirot,* starting with the last one and going up the highest. He adopted a system intermediate between that of the Geronese school of kabbalists and the Zohar. This is one of the first writings to disclose knowledge of portions of the Zohar, although it departs from its approach in several fundatmental respects.

Sha'arei Ẓedek (1559) provides another explanation of the theory of *Sefirot,* following their normal order. Other published works by Gikatilla are: *Sha'ar ha-Nikkud* (1601), a mystical treatise on the meaning of the vowels; *Perush Haggadah shel Pesaḥ,* a kabbalistic commentary on the Passover *Haggadah* (1602); a number of essays on various subjects (publ. in *Sefer Erez ba-Levanon,* ed. by Isaac Perlov, Vilna, 1899); kabbalistic works remaining in manuscript are: mystical treatises on certain *mizvot;* a commentary on the Vision of the Chariot of Ezekiel (numerous manuscripts); and considerable portions of a biblical commentary continuing the system followed in *Ginnat Egoz* (manuscript in JTS, New York, Deinard 451). A work on practical Kabbalah was extant in the 17th century (Joseph Delmedigo, *Sefer Novellot Ḥokhmah* (1631), 195a). A collection of kabbalistic responsa on points of *halakhah* from the second half of the 14th century has been erroneously ascribed to Gikatilla. Joseph Caro made use of them in his *Beit Yosef.* Problems of Kabbalah put to Joshua b. Meir ha-Levi by Gikatilla are in manuscript, Oxford, 1565. Also extant are a number of prayers, such as *Tefillat ha-Yiḥud, Me'ah Pesukim* ("100 Verses," on the *Sefirot),* and *Pesukim al-Shem ben Arba'im u-Shetayim Otiyyot* ("Verses on the 42-Lettered Divine Name"). Commentaries were written on *Sha'arei Orah* by an anonymous 14th-century kabbalist (G. Scholem, *Kitvei Yad be-Kabbalah* (1930), 80–83) and by Mattathias Delacrut (included in most editions). A summary was translated into Latin by the Apostate Paul Riccius (1516).

Gikatilla, who died about 1325, made an original attempt to provide a detailed yet lucid and systematic exposition of kabbalism. He was considered by many as the chief representative of the doctrine equating the infinite *Ein Sof,* with the first of the ten *Sefirot.* The conception was rejected by the majority of kabbalists from the 16th century onward, but his works continued to be highly esteemed and were published in many editions.

Bibliography: S. Sachs, *Ha-Yonah* (1850), 80–81; G. Scholem, *Kitvei Yad ba-Kabbalah* (1930), 218–25; idem, in: *Sefer ha-Yovel le-Ya'akov Freimann* (1937), 163–70 (Heb. section); Altmann, in: KS, 40 (1965), 256–76, 405–12; idem, in: *Sefer ha-Yovel le-Israel Brodie* (1967), 57–65; Weiler, in: HUCA, 37 (1966), 13–44 (Heb. section); Steinschneider, Cat Bod, 1461–70; A. Jellinek, *Beitraege zur Geschichte der Kabbala,* 2 (1852), 57–64; Scholem, Mysticism, 194–5, 405–6; Werblowsky, in: *Zeitschrift fuer Religion und Geistgeschichte,* 8 (1956), 164–9; E. Gottlieb, *Ha-Kabbalah be-Kitvei Rabbenu Baḥya ben Asher* (1970), 148–66; idem, in: *Tarbiz* 39 (1970), 62–89.

7
Nehemiah Ḥayon

Because of the bitter dispute which centered around Ḥayon, the information about his life is full of contradictions and must be sifted critically. His ancestors came from Sarajevo, Bosnia. From there, his father moved to Ereẓ Israel after spending several years in Egypt where, according to his own testimony, Ḥayon was born (c. 1655). As a child, he was taken to Jerusalem, grew up in Shechem (Nablus) and in Jerusalem, and studied under Ḥayyim Abulafia. At the age of 18 he returned to Sarajevo with his father and married there. His enemies claimed that from that time on he was known for his adventures. He traveled widely throughout the Balkans and spent several years in Belgrade until its occupation by Austria in 1688. He may have joined his father as an emissary to Italy for the ransoming of captives from Belgrade. According to the testimony of Judah Brieli, Ḥayon was in Leghorn in 1691. Later he served for a short time in the rabbinate of Skoplje (Üsküb), Madedonia, at the recommendation of one of the great rabbis of Salonika.

He returned to Ereẓ Israel c. 1695 and lived for several years in Shechem (Nablus). After his first wife's death, he married the daughter of one of the scholars of Safed. Ḥayon was well versed in exoteric and esoteric lore. From his youth, he was attracted to Kabbalah and he knew the Shabbatean groups intimately. His kabbalistic doctrine evades the issue of Shabbetai Ẓevi's messianic claims, but is based on principles common to Shabbeteanism. When Ḥayon received the short tract *Raza de Meheimanuta* ("The Mystery of the True Faith"), attributed to Shabbetai Ẓevi by his sectarians, he claimed that he himself wrote it and that it was revealed to him by Elijah or by the angel Metatron. Changing its name to *Meheimanuta de-Khula*, he began to write a detailed commentary. In the meanwhile, he lived briefly in Rosetta, Egypt, and from that time he became known as one who engaged in practical Kabbalah. When he returned to Jerusalem (c. 1702–05), hostility developed between him and R. Abraham Yiẓḥaki who for several years leveled many accusations against Hayon (but never directly accused him of Shabbeteanism). Later, he returned to Safed and from there he went to Smyrna, apparently intending to publish his long commentary to *Meheimanuta de-Khula* and to find supporters for a yeshivah, which he wished to establish in Jerusalem. On his return to Jerusalem, the rabbis began to harass him and he was forced to leave Ereẓ Israel. He went to Italy via Egypt (1710–11). According to the testimony of Joseph Ergas, in Leghorn (the grandson of a famous Shabbetean, Moses Pinheiro), Ḥayon disclosed to him his belief in Shabbetai Ẓevi. In 1711, in Venice, he published his small book *Raza de-Yiḥuda* on the meaning of the verse on the unity of God, *Shema Yisrael,* as an abridgment of his larger work to which he added, in the meantime, a second commentary. The rabbis of Venice gave approbations to this booklet without understanding its intent. The book did not arouse controversy. Later, Ḥayon moved to Prague where he was received with great honor in scholarly circles and gained approval for his main work, now called *Oz le-Elohim,* and *Divrei Neḥemyah,* a book of sermons. David Oppenheim approbated *Divrei Neḥemyah,* and Ḥayon altered the approbation to include the kabbalistic *Oz le-Elohim* as well. R. Naphtali Cohen, who at first befriended Ḥayon, kept him at a distance after a rumor got about that connected him with the Doenmeh (see p. 327), in Salonika. Ḥayon traveled via Moravia and Silesia to Berlin where, in 1713, supported by the wealthy members of the community, he succeeded in publishing *Oz le-Elohim.* It was daring of Ḥayon to publish a text which in many manuscripts was circulated then as a work of Shabbetai Ẓevi. With great acumen, he tried to prove in his two commentaries that this doctrine was firmly based in the classical texts of the Kabbalah. In some passages, he criticized the teachings of Nathan of Gaza and Abraham Miguel Cardozo, in spite of his doctrine being basically close to Cardozo's. Ḥayon's innovations were a new formulation of the principles governing the beginning of Emanation and the difference between the First Cause which he calls *"Nishmata de-Kol Ḥayyei"* ("Soul of All Living Beings") and the *Ein-Sof* ("The Infinite Being"). What the kabbalists call *Ein-Sof* is in his opinion only the extension of the Essence (of God) or the *Shoresh ha-Ne'lam* ("the Hidden Root", i.e., God), but paradoxically enough his Essence is finite and it possesses a definite structure, *Shi'ur Komah* ("Measure of the Body of God"). Ḥayon thought that Isaac Luria's doctrine of *ẓimẓum* ("withdrawal") must be understood literally and not allegorically. His doctrine of the three superior *parẓufim* ("aspects, or configurations, of God"), *attika kaddisha, malka kaddisha,* and *Shekhinah,* differs from the theories of other Shabbateans only in details and in terminology. His book may be defined as a strange mixture of basically Shabbatean theology and exegetical acumen by which he read the new thesis into the Zohar and the Lurianic writings. He prefaced his book with a long essay in which he argued, apparently hinting at the unorthodox sources of his thought, that it is lawful to learn Kabbalah from everyone, not only from those who conform to traditional Orthodox criteria. *Divrei Neḥemyah* contained a long ambiguous sermon in which it was possible to see an indirect defense of the apostasy of the Doenmeh sect in Salonika, but which could also be interpreted as criticism of them. In June 1713 Ḥayon left Berlin for Amsterdam. Apparently he knew of the hidden Shabbatean tendency of Solomon Ayllon, rabbi of the Sephardi congregation. Indeed, Ḥayon received the patronage of Ayllon, his *bet din,* and the *parnasim* of the community. However, a bitter and complex struggle developed between the supporters of Ḥayon and those of Zevi Ashkenazi, the rabbi of the Ashkenazi community, and of Moses Ḥagiz who knew of Ḥayon's early quarrels in Ereẓ Israel and recognized the Shabbatean "heresy" in his opinions, when they investigated his book. In this controversy, relevant factors (the true views of Ḥayon and his Shabbateanism) and personal factors (the arrogant behavior of Ẓevi Ashkenazi and personal antagonisms) are mingled. Essentially, the accusers of Ḥayon were right but from a formal and procedural point of view the Sephardi *bet din* was right. The quarrel aroused strong emotions, at first in Amsterdam, in the summer and the winter of 1713, and it swiftly spread to other countries. Naphtali Cohen apologized for his previous approval of Ḥayon and excommunicated him. So did Italian rabbis to whom both sides turned to for support. The leaders were Judah Brieli of Mantua and Samson Morpurgo of Ancona. But most of the participants in the controversy had not actually seen the books of Ḥayon and depended only on the letters from both sides. The major pamphlets against Ḥayon are: *Le-Einei Kol Yisrael* (the judicial decision of Ẓevi Ashkenazi and letters from him and from Naphtali Cohen; Amsterdam, 1713); *Edut le-Yisrael (ibid.,* 1714); works by Moses Ḥagiz including *Milḥamah la-Adonai ve-Ḥerev la-Adonai,* also including the letters of many Italian rabbis (Amsterdam, 1714); *Shever Poshe'im* (London, 1714); *Iggeret ha-Kena'ot* (Amsterdam, 1714); *Tokhaḥat Megullah ve-ha-Ẓad Naḥash* by Joseph Ergas (London, 1715); and *Esh Dat* by David Nieto (London, 1715). This book and several leaflets also appeared in Spanish. The *bet din* of the Sephardim published in Hebrew and in Spanish *Kosht Imrei Emet* (Amsterdam, 1713; in Spanish, *Manifesto).* Hayon answered his critics in several books and pamphlets in which he defended his views but denied that they contain any Shabbatean doctrine. They include *Ha-Ẓad Ẓevi Ashkenazi* (Amsterdam, 1714); *Moda'a Rabba* (1714, including his biography); *Shalhevet Yah* (against Ergas), also including the pamphlets *Pitkah min Shemaya, Ketovet Ka'aka,* and *Iggeret Shevukin* (1714). His polemic against Ergas' *Ha-Ẓad Naḥash,* called *Naḥash Neḥoshet,* is found in Ḥayon's handwriting (Oxford, Ms. 1900). Because of the controversy he had aroused, Ḥayon did not succeed in publishing his second comprehensive work on Kabbalah, *Sefer Ta'aẓumot.* A complete manuscript of the work is preserved in the library of the *bet din,* formerly that of the *bet ha-midrash,* in London (62).

Ẓevi Ashkenazi and Moses Ḥagiz were forced to leave Amsterdam. However, the intervention of the rabbis of Smyrna and Constantinople, who excommunicated Ḥayon and condemned his works in 1714, decided the struggle against Ḥayon, whose supporters advised him to return to Turkey in order to obtain the annulment of the excommunication. Ḥayon returned and attempted to achieve this but he succeeded only partially. In his old age, he went back to Europe where in the pamphlet *Ha-Kolot Yeḥdalum* (1725) he published some documents in his favor. His journey was unsuccessful because Moses Ḥagiz again came out against him in the booklet *Leḥishat Saraf* (Hanau, 1726) where he threw suspicion on several of the documents, or on the circumstances under which they were signed. Most of the communities did not allow him access and even Ayllon refused to receive him in Amsterdam. Ḥayon wandered to North Africa and apparently died there before 1730. According to Ḥagiz, his son converted to Catholicism in order to take revenge on his father's persecutors and was active in Italy, but no evidence for this has been produced.

Bibliography: Graetz, *History of the Jews* 5 (1949), 215–31; D. Kahana (Kogan), *Toledot ha-Mekubbalim, Shabbeta'im, ve-ha-Ḥasidim* (1913), 123–7; Kauffmann, in: *Ha-Ḥoker,* 2 (1894), 11–15; Scholem, in: *Zion,* 3 (1929), 172–9; Sonne, in: *Kobez al jad,* 2 (1937), 157–96; Herling, in: *Amanah,* 1 (1939), 259–74; idem, in: KS, 14 (1939), 130–5; Kahana, in: *Sinai,* 21 (1947), 328–34; A. Freimann (ed.), *Inyanei Shabbetai Ẓevi* (1912), 117–38; I.S. Emmanuel, in: *Sefunot* 9 (1965), 209–46; M. Friedmann, in: *Sefunot,* 10 (1966) 489–618; G. Levi, in: RI, 8 (1911), 169–85; 9 (1912), 5–29.

8

Christian Knorr von Rosenroth

The son of a Protestant minister in Silesia, Knorr traveled around Western Europe for several years. During his travels he came in contact with circles interested in mysticism, and was deeply influenced by the writings of Jacob Boehme. On his return, he settled in Sulzbach, in northern Bavaria, and from 1668 until his death in 1689 was a close adviser and senior official in the service of Prince Christian August, who shared his mystical leanings. Knorr became known as an inspired poet, some of his poems being regarded among the finest in German religious poetry. While in Holland, he acquired an interest in Kabbalah, becoming engrossed in the study of the source material in the original. For some time he studied with rabbis such as Meir Stern in Amsterdam, and acquired manuscript copies of the writing of Isaac Luria, coupling these inquiries with his interest in Christian mysticism. He was in close touch with the Cambridge philosopher Henry More and the Belgian mystic Franciscus (Frans) Mercurius Van Helmont, who were likewise attracted to Kabbalah as a theosophical system of great significance to philosophy and theology alike. In his lifetime Knorr was reputed to be the most profound Christian scholar of Kabbalah. His studies were summarized in the two bulky volumes of his main work, *Kabbala Denudata:* "The Kabbalah Uncovered, or, The Transcendental, Metaphysical, and Theological Teachings of the Jews" (Sulzbach, Latin, 1677–84). This work, which had a widespread influence, was superior to anything that had been published on Kabbalah in a language other than Hebrew. It gave non-Jewish readers a broad view of the first sources to be translated into Latin, and these were accompanied by explanatory notes. Here, too, appeared long disquisitions by More and Van Helmont on kabbalistic subjects (some of them anonymously), with Knorr's replies to them. In his translations Knorr aimed at precision, sometimes to the extent that the meaning is obscure to those not familiar with the original. Although the book contains many errors and mistranslations, particularly of difficult Zoharic passages, there is no justification for the contemporary Jewish claims that the author misrepresented the Kabbalah.

His book, which served as the principal source for all non-Jewish literature on Kabbalah until the end of the 19th century, opens with a "Key to the Divine

Names of the Kabbalah," an extensive glossary of kabbalistic symbolism according to the Zohar, Gikatilla's *Sha'arei Orah* and Cordevero's *Pardes Rimmonim,* and some of the writings of Isaac Luria. He also made use of an Italian work on alchemy and Kabbalah, *Esh ha-Meẓaref,* whose Hebrew original is no longer extant and is preserved only in the extracts translated by Knorr. This was followed by translations of some of Luria's writings, of the chapter on the soul in *Pardes Rimmonim,* and selections from Naphtali Bacharach's *Emek ha-Melekh,* an abridged translation of *Sha'ar ha-Shamayim* by Abraham Kohen de Herrera, and a detailed explanation of the kabbalistic "Tree" according to the teachings of Luria, after the manner of Israel Sarug. The "Tree" itself (which he possessed in manuscript form) he printed separately in 16 pages. To this were added several disquisitions by Henry More. The first part of the second volume opens with a translation of *Mareh Kohen* by Issachar Berman b. Naphtali ha-Kohen (Amersterdam, 1673), followed by a translation of the first 25 leaves of *Emek ha-Melekkh,* on the doctrine of *ẓimẓum* and the primordial world of chaos *(tohu),* an "introduction to a better understanding of the Zohar". The second part includes translations of the *Idrot* of the Zohar, *Sifra di-Ẓeni'uta* and the commentary on it by Hayyim Vital taken from a manuscript, the chapters on angelology and demonology from *Beit Elohim* of Abraham Kohen de Herrera, and a translation of *Sefer ha-Gilgulim* from a manuscript "of the writings of Isaac Luria." This manuscript includes precisely what was published in the same year, 1684, by David Grünhut in Frankfort on the Main. The volume closes with a separate work – *Adumbratio Kabbalae Christianae* – a summary of Christian Kabbalah; although it was published anonymously, the author was Van Helmont. Apart from the translation from *Beit Elohim,* all the texts in the second part of the second volume have been translated into English or French: the *Idrot* and *Sifra di-Ẓeni'uta* by S.L.M. Mathers *(The Kabbalah Unveiled,* 1887, 5th repr. 1962), *Sefer ha-Gilgulim* by E. Jégut (Paris, 1905), and the *Adumbratio* by Gilly de Givry (Paris, 1899). Knorr's major anthology to a great extent determined the image of Kabbalah in the eyes of historians of philosophy until the close of the 19th century. The philosopher Leibniz, impressed by Knorr's publication, visited him in 1687 and discussed kabbalistic subjects with him.

Late in life Knorr worked on a major book on the childhood of Jesus, based on rabbinical and kabbalistic sources. The manuscript reached his friend Van Helmont, who promised to have it published in Amsterdam; the project, however, was not realized, and this lengthy work, *Messias Puer,* was lost. During his lifetime Knorr helped to establish a Hebrew publishing house at Sulzbach, and he had a hand in the edition of the Zohar that appeared in 1684. It includes an anonymous Latin dedication to Prince Christian August, the author of which

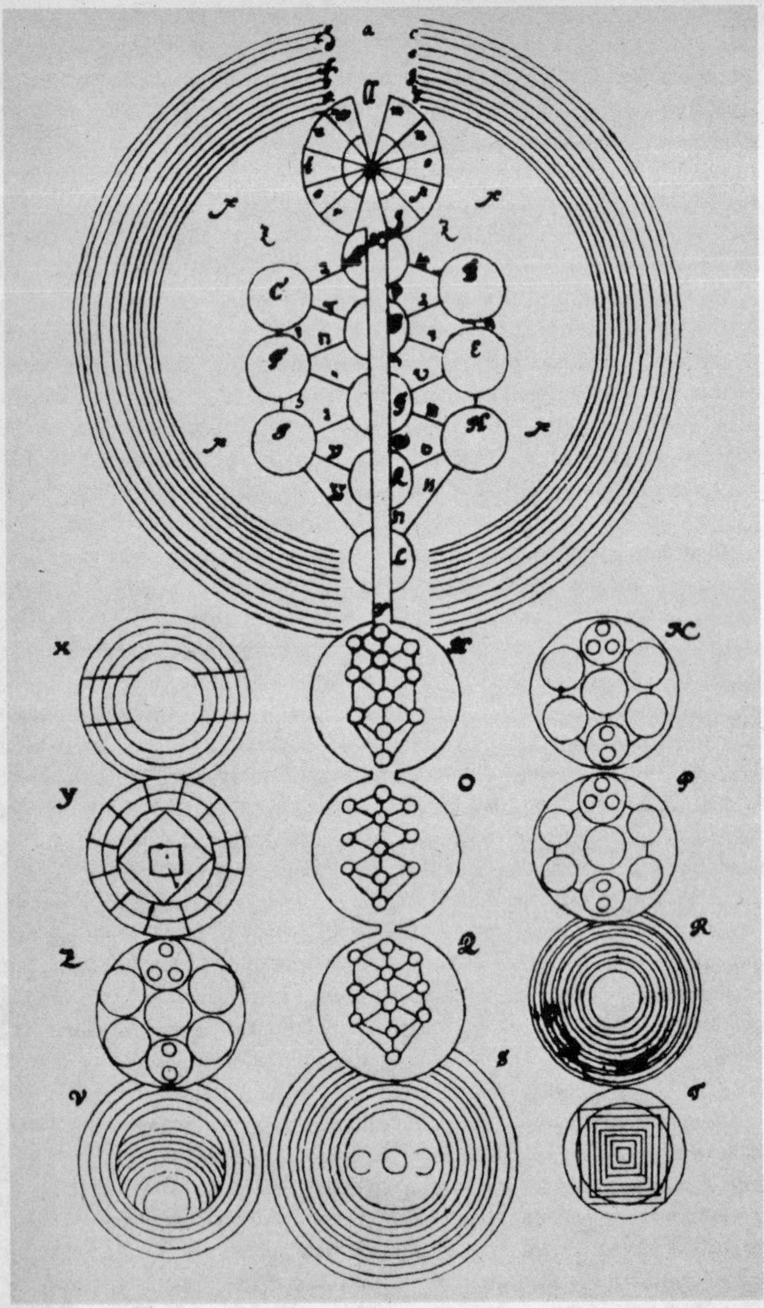

Chart showing the gradual development of the *Sefirot* in their various structures, according to Lurianic kabbalah. From Knorr von Rosenroth, *Kabbala Denudata,* Frankfort on the Main, 17th century.

was doubtless Knorr. He likewise played a role in the publication of *Ḥesed le-Avraham* by Abraham Azulai (Amsterdam, 1685), which is mainly a summary of the Kabbalah of Cordovero.

Bibliography: Wolf, *Bibliotheca Hebraea* 1 (1715), 1140–43; 2 (1721), 1232–35; 3 (1727), 677–8; K. Salecker, *Christian Knorr von Rosenroth* (Ger., 1931); Scholem, *Bibliographia Kabbalistica* (1927), 86–88; F. Kemp, in: *Neue Zuercher Zeitung* (May 9, 1971), 51–52.

9

Isaac Luria

Luria is often referred to as *Ha-Ari*(=הארי״:"the [sacred] lion" from the initials of האלוהי רבי יצחק *Ha-Elohi Rabbi Yizhak,* "the divine [in the sense of speculative or mystical theologian] Rabbi Isaac"). This cognomen was in use by the end of the 16th century, apparently at first in kabbalistic circles in Italy, but Luria's contemporaries in Safed refer to him as R. Isaac Ashkenazi (הרי״ש). R. Isaac Ashkenazi Luria (הרי״ל). also as De Luria. The Sephardim spelled the family name as Loria. His father, a member of the Ashkenazi family of Luria from Germany or Poland, emigrated to Jerusalem and apparently there married into the Sephardi Frances family. Isaac was born in 1534. His father died while Isaac was a child and his widow took the boy to Egypt where he was brought up in the home of her brother Mordecai Frances, a wealthy tax-farmer. Traditions concerning Luria's youth, his stay in Egypt, and his introduction to Kabbalah are shrouded in legend, and the true facts are difficult to establish. Contradicting the widely accepted belief that he came to Egypt at the age of seven, is his own testimony recalling a kabbalistic tradition which he learned in Jerusalem from a Polish kabbalist, Kalonymus (see *Sha'ar he-Pesukim,* portion *Be-Ha'alotekha).*

In Egypt, Luria studied under David b. Solomon ibn Abi Zimra and his successor, Bezalel Ashkenazi. Luria collaborated with the latter in writing halakhic works such as the *Shitah Mekubbeẓet* on tractate *Zevaḥim,* which according to Ḥayyim Joseph David Azulai was burned in Izmir in 1735. Their annotations of some of Isaac Alfasi's works were printed in *Tummat Yesharim* (Venice, 1622). M. Benayahu has conjectured that commentaries on passages in tractate *Ḥullin* and other talmudic tractates, extant in a manuscript written in Egypt not later than 1655 in the academy of a *ḥakham* named Mohariel, derive from notes made by pupils of Luria's yeshivah in Egypt. However, this is doubtful since the manuscript mentions *Sefer Pesakim,* a collection of halakhic decisions by the same author, and there is no evidence to indicate that Luria was the author of such a book, certainly not before he was 20 years old. It is certain, however, that Luria was familiar with rabbinical literature and was believed to be outstanding in the non-mystical study of the law. As well as religious study, he also engaged in commerce while in Egypt, as attested by documents in the Cario

Genizah. A document relating to his business in pepper dating from 1559 was published by E.J. Worman (REJ, 57 (1909), 281–2), and a second, relating to grain, by S. Assaf *(Mekorot u-Meḥkarim* (1946), 204). Assaf connects this with Luria's sojourn in Safed, but there is no doubt that it was written in Egypt. The entire document is in Luria's handwriting, the only extant specimen to date. This material supports the evidence of Jedidiah Galante (in Leon Modena's *Sefer Ari Nohem,* ed. by S. Rosenthal; Leipzig, 1840) that, like many of the Safed scholars, Luria conducted business in the town; three days before his death he made up his accounts with his customers.

While still in Egypt, Luria began his esoteric studies and retired to a life of seculsion on the island Jazīrat al-Rawḍa on the Nile near Cairo. This island was owned by his uncle, who in the meantime had become his father-in-law. It is far from clear whether this retirement, which is reported to have lasted for seven years, took place in his youth at the beginning of the 1550s or when he was older. Legend antedates it considerably. In 1558, Luria endorsed a halakhic decision jointly with Bezalel Ashkenazi and Simeon Castellazzo. In his mystic study, he concentrated on the Zohar and works of the earlier kabbalists, and of the works of his contemporaries made a particular study of Moses Cordovero. According to evidence dating from the end of the 16th century, it was during this initial period of kabbalistic study that he wrote his single work, a commentary on the *Sifra di-Ẓeni'uta* ("Book of Concealment"), a short but important section of the Zohar (published in Vital's *Sha'ar Ma'amarei Rashbi).* The book gives no hint of the original kabbalistic system that Luria expounded at the end of his life, and shows the marked influence of Cordovero. In Egypt he met Samuel ibn Fodeila, a kabbalist, to whom Luria wrote a lengthy letter on kabbalistic topics. Here he refers to his own book and asks him to examine it in his brother's house, evidently in Egypt. Luria may have made a pilgrimage to Meron before going to settle in Safed, since there are references to his presence at the Lag ba-Omer festival in Meron. In 1569, and perhaps at the beginning of 1570, he settled in Safed with his family and studied Kabbalah with Cordovero for a short time. Some of his glosses on passages of the Zohar were evidently written while Cordovero was still alive and some after his death, since Luria refers to him both as "our teacher whose light may be prolonged" and "my late teacher". On the other hand, he had already begun to impart his original kabbalistic system to a number of disciples in Safed, among them distinguished scholars. After Cordovero's death in the fall of 1570, Ḥayyim Vital drew particularly close to Luria, becoming his principal and most celebrated disciple.

Luria may have gathered around him in Safed an esoteric circle whose members engaged in exoteric and esoteric studies. The names of some 30 of his disciples are known. Vital confirms (in the manuscript on practical Kabbalah, holograph in the Musajoff collection, Jerusalem) that a week before his master died they had been studying the tractate *Yevamot.* He also gives some information about Luria's system of study in the non-mystical parts of the law. Luria occasionally delivered homilies in the Ashkenazi synagogue in Safed, but generally refrained from religious teaching in public. On the other hand, he often took long walks with his closest disciples in the neighborhood of Safed pointing out to them hitherto unknown graves of saintly personages, which he discovered through his spiritual intuition and revelations. At this period, he had already become famous as a man who possessed the "holy spirit" or was vouchsafed the "revelation of Elijah." He taught his disciples orally, instructing them both in his original system of theoretical Kabbalah, and also in the way to communion with the souls of the righteous *(ẓaddikim).* This was accomplished by "unification" of the *Sefirot* and exercises in concentration on certain of the divine names and their combinations, and especially by means of *kavvanah,* i.e., mystical reflection or meditations in the act of prayer and the fulfillment of religious precepts. He himself wrote down little of this teaching, apart from an attempt to provide a detailed commentary on the first pages of the Zohar and glosses on isolated passages. These were collected from his autography by Vital and assembled in a special book, of which a number of handwritten copies are extant.

Luria acknowledges his inability to present his teachings in written form since the overflow of his ideas did not lend itself to systematization. Nor did he select the various subjects for study in his doctrine in a logical sequence but at random. He guarded the secret of his system and did not permit its propagation during his lifetime, therefore becoming celebrated at first mainly for his conduct and saintly qualities. Some who applied to study with him were rejected, including Moses Alshekh and Joseph Caro. His relations with the scholars were friendly; a halakhic consultation addressed by him to Joseph Caro appears in the responsa entitled *Avkat Rokhel* (no. 136). Luria undoubtedly regarded himself as an innovator, preeminent among contemporary kabbalists. Certain allusions made to his disciples suggest that he believed himself to be "the Messiah, the son of Joseph," destined to die in the fulfillment of his mission. The period of his activity in Safed was brief, for he died in an epidemic on July 15, 1572. His grave in Safed was and remains a place of pilgrimage for successive generations.

Both in enthusiastic descriptions by his disciples and their pupils, written in the decade after his death, and in their careful preservation and collection of his teachings and faithful rendering of his personal traits, Luria's striking personality is attested. The relevant details are scattered in the writings of his disciples, particularly those of Vital. Some have been assembled in book form, such as the *Shulḥan Arukh shel R. Yiẓḥak Luria,* compiled from the writings of Jacob Ẓemah and published a number of times (first in Poland, 1660–70), the *Orḥot*

Zaddikim, on the precepts of Luria from the writings of Vital (vol. 2, Salonika, 1770), and in *Patora de Abba* (Jerusalem, 1905). In addition, a wealth of legend accumulated around his personality, with historical recollection and authentic fact being mingled with visionary pronouncements and anecdotes of other holy men. Such mythical elements already appear in works written 20 years after Luria's death, such as the *Sefer Ḥaredim* of Eleazer Azikri, *Reshit Ḥokhmah* by Elijah de Vidas, and the books of Abraham Galante. The legend is crystallized in two important documents, whose sequence of writing is a matter of controversy. One is the collection of three letters written in Safed between 1602 and 1609 by Solomon (Shlomel) Dresnitz, and immigrant from Moravia, to his friend in Cracow. The letters were first published in 1629 in *Ta'alumot Ḥokhmah* by Joseph Solomon Delmedigo, and circulated from the end of the 18th century under the title *Shivḥei ha-Ari* ("The Tributes of Ha-Ari"). The second document, *Toledot ha-Ari* ("Biography of Ha-Ari"), appears in numerous manuscripts from the 17th century; one version is published under the title *Ma'asei Nissim* ("Miracles") although inside it is called *Shivḥei ha-Ari;* it appeared at the beginning of *Sefer ha-Kavvanot* (Constantinople, 1720). This version of the legend was generally regarded as the later one, based on the Safed letters. However, M. Benayahu has published a complete edition of this recension (1967) and argued that it served as the source of Dresnitz' letters. Benayahu considers that the book was compiled between 1590 and 1600 by one of the scholars of Safed, and its various recensions circulated widely in the Orient and Italy. This, the first kabbalistic hagiography, compounds fact and imagination in its biographical account of the life of the saintly man.

There is no doubt that the legend of the Ari was widespread, and circulated earlier than the written sources treating his kabbalistic teaching. These compositions form an extensive literature. Although frequently described by kabbalists as *Kitvei ha-Ari*, "the writings of Luria," they are in fact the works of his disciples and their own disciples, edited and sometimes condensed. While most remained in manuscript, a few were published between 1572 and 1650. Moved by mystical inspiration, Luria expounded his ideas with many variants. His hearers seem to have noted down some of his teaching during his lifetime but mainly transmitted them from memory after his death, frequently enlarging upon them and superimposing their own interpretation. The conventicle of Luria's disciples included some important kabbalists who rated themselves highly and considered themselves faithful recorders of their master's doctrine. Personal friction and rivalry were not unknown. In the annals of the Kabbalah Ḥayyim Vital has won the laurels as Luria's chief disciple; the works of his associates and rivals have been passed over or erroneously attributed to Vital himself, in which case they acquired the reputation of authoritative sources of Luria's teachings.

In fact, different versions of these are extant which, in the main, are not interdependent but represent independent traditions recorded by his disciples, including one which must be considered spurious. There are four such principal traditions:

(1) That of Moses Jonah of Safed, crystallized in *Kanfei Yonah.* The complete authentic text is extant in numerous manuscripts, particularly (unrecognized) in Ms. Sasson 993, copied by the author himself in Constantinople in 1582. A defective edition was compiled by Menahem Azariah Fano in Mantua (first printed in Korzec, 1786). This is an important source for the study of Lurianic Kabbalah and as yet no satisfactory evaluation of it has been attempted. The author has omitted some of Luria's teachings, such as the doctrine of *ẓimẓum* ("withdrawal"; see p. 129), although, compared with Vital's rendering, his exposition of other teachings of Luria excels in clarity.

(2) That of Joseph ibn Tabul who, after Luria's death, taught Lurianic Kabbalah to several pupils, among them Samson Bacchi, an Italian kabbalist. Ibn Tabul compiled a systematic exposition of Lurianic Kabbalah divided into *derushim* ("disquisitions"), with a number of supplements. The disquisitions are extant in manuscript and for a long time were attributed to Vital under the title *Derush Ḥefẓi-Bah* and were also published in his name (1921, at the beginning of *Simḥat Kohen* by Masud ha-Kohen al-Ḥaddad). This text is most important for the version of the doctrine of *ẓimẓum* that it includes, parts of which were suppressed by Vital.

(3) That of Ḥayyim Vital. In contrast to the comparatively limited scope of the preceding disciples, Vital rendered his preceptor's teachings in detail. He augments the words which he specifically quotes as Luria's or propounded according to what he heard, with numerous additions of his own. He also wrote his first versions immediately after Luria's death, although he confirms that certain expositions were only very briefly noted after he had heard them. Luria's teachings, in a book which he calls *Eẓ Ḥayyim* ("The Tree of Life"), were mainly written down approximately between 1573 and 1576. However, he sometimes added a different version of the chapters, so that occasionally no less than four variants on the same theme are found. The existence of these differing recensions has introduced considerable confusion into Vital's writings. The original sequence in *Eẓ Ḥayyim* falls into eight parts (called "Gates"): (a) all material in Luria's hand collected by Vital; (b) *Sha'ar ha-Derushim,* a systematic presentation of Luria's theosophical doctrine; (c) *Sha'ar ha-Pesukim,* explanations of biblical passages, arranged in a sequence that follows the Bible; (d) *Sha'ar ha-Gilgulim,* the mystical doctrine of metempsychosis, *gilgul;* (e) *Sha'ar ha-Kavannot,* on the mystical intentions and meditations required for prayer *(kavvanot ha-tefillah);* (f) *Sha'ar ha-Mizvot,* the reasons for the religious

precepts; (g) the doctrine of amends for sins *(tikkunei avonot);* (h) instructions for mystical "unifications" *(yiḥudim),* which Luria transmitted to each disciple individually. This version of *Eẓ Ḥayyim* remains in manuscript. Using it, Ḥayyim Vital's son Samuel Vital compiled eight further "gates" in which Luria's own literary heritage is distributed according to its contents. These are: (a) *Sha'ar ha-Hakdamot;* (b) *Sha'ar Ma'amarei Rashbi;* (c) *Sha'ar Ma'amarei Razal;* (d) *Sha'ar ha-Pesukim;* (e) *Sha'ar ha-Miẓvot;* (f) *Sha'ar ha-Kavvanot;* (g) *Sha'ar Ru'aḥ ha-Kodesh;* (h) *Sha'ar ha-Gilgulim.* The first edition of this compilation, *Shemonah She'arim,* was published, without the title *Eẓ Ḥayyim,* in the above sequence in Jerusalem (1850–98; new ed. 1960–63). Many kabbalists, in particular among the Sephardim, recognized this version only as authoritative and rejected the rest of Luria's writings including books which were assembled from Vital's own later recensions. Since "the eight gates" remained in the home of Vital and his son and were only rarely copied by others before 1650, kabbalists wishing to study Lurianic Kabbalah used other recensions of Vital's books and eclectic anthologies of Lurianic kabbalism which circulated from 1586. Several of these, which were compiled in Safed itself, are extant (such as Schocken Ms. 97 of 1586 in Jerusalem, in the handwriting of Moses Jonah), and the manuscript of 1588 (Enelow collection 683, in the Jewish Theological Seminary, New York). Copies of Vital's writings that had remained in Jerusalem, where he stayed for several years in the 1590s, were also in circulation from the middle of the 17th century, and various collections have been compiled from them: *Sefer ha-Derushim, Sefer ha-Kavvanot,* and *Sefer ha-Likkutim* (extant in manuscripts only). It was not until the end of the 17th century that a comprehensive recension of Vital's writings relating to Luria's Kabbalah was made. This was compiled in Jerusalem by Meir Poppers of Cracow with a few additions from Luria's other associates. Poppers divided his recension into *Derekh Eẓ Ḥayyim, Peri Eẓ Ḥayyim,* and *Nof Eẓ Ḥayyim,* which in fact includes all the subjects covered in the *Shemonah She'arim.* It was in this recension that Vital's writings became widely disseminated, especially in Europe, and became familiar long before the bulk of them were first published in Korzec in 1784. The printed book thereafter entitled *Eẓ Ḥayyim* is actually the *Derekh Eẓ Ḥayyim* of Popper's recension. A number of books stemming from traditions compiled by Vital have been published in his name, such as *Mevo She'arim,* (Korzec, 1784); *Oẓerot Ḥayyim (ibid.,* 1783), both similar in content to *Derekh Eẓ Ḥayyim,* and *Arba Me'ot Shekel Kesef (ibid.,* 1804), part of which is indubitably a forgery.

(4) Superimposed on the tangled web of the three preceding traditions and their mutually interfused forms is a fourth deriving from the works of Israel Sarug (Saruk), who propagated Lurianic Kabbalah in Italy and several other

European countries after 1590. He is actualy the author of *Limmudei Azilut* ("Doctrines on Emanation"), published under Vital's name (Munkacs, 1897), which contains an entirely different interpretation of the doctrine of *ẓimẓum* and the origin of divine emanation. Since Sarug was the first to spread this teaching in Italy, his version was accepted in wider circles, although there is no doubt that he added original speculations of his own to it. Sarug was not one of Luria's disciples in Safed but based his reconstruction on those works of Luria's principal disciples that reached him. He may have known Luria personally in Egypt, since there are grounds for assuming that he was born there and his signature is appended to a kabbalistic manuscript written in Egypt in 1565 (British Museum, Almanzi 29) for Isaac Sarug (his father?). The innovations in his version in particular made a considerable impression, and for a long time it was the one accepted as authoritative, furnishing the basis for most of the earlier works on Lurianic Kabbalah; for example the *Ta'alumot Ḥokhmah* and *Novelot Ḥokhmah* of Joseph Solomon Delmedigo (Basle, 1629–31), the *Emek ha-Melekh* of Naphtali Bacharach (Amsterdam, 1648), and *Ma'ayan ha-Ḥokhmah* (*ibid.*, 1652) – which is in fact *Hatḥalot ha-Ḥokhmah,* a treatise originating in Sarug's circle. Lurianic Kabbalah, therefore, won adherents in the 17th century through the propagation of a version far removed from his original teaching. The inconsistencies in the different versions and the contradictions in Vital's own renderings gave rise to an exegetic literature which flourished particularly among the kabbalists in Italy, North Africa, and Turkey. Throughout these metamorphoses, however, the Lurianic system remained the crucial factor for the development of later Kabbalah. Apart from these variants, there are also a number of treatises and essays extant in manuscript, written by other disciples of Luria, such as Joseph Arzin, Judah Mish'an, Gedaliah ha-Levi, and Moses Najara.

Before Luria's theoretical teachings became known, he won fame as a poet. A number of his liturgical hymns, only a few with mystical content, were published in the collection *Yefeh Nof* (Venice, 1575–80). Best known of his mystical poems are three hymns for the Sabbath meals which have been included in most later prayer books. Written in the language of the Zohar they describe, in kabbalistic symbolism, the meaning of the Sabbath and the special relationship between man and the world above on this day. Also published in Venice in 1595 were his *Tikkunei Teshuvah,* "penitence rituals" (entitled *Marpe le-Nefesh*), and in 1620 his *Sefer ha-Kavvanot,* a collection of mystical meditations on prayers and rules for behavior. There is a characteristic contradiction between Luria's theoretical Kabbalah, with its numerous bold innovations in theosophical doctrine and the concept of creation which changed the face of Kabbalah, and his marked tendency to extreme conservatism when interpreting Jewish ritual customs and folkways. He upheld all the traditional usages, reading a mystical significance into them. He taught that each of the tribes of Israel could be regarded as having its own special entrance to heaven, which had resulted in differences in custom and liturgy, so that no particular usage could be considered superior to others. However, Luria did prefer the Sephardi liturgy, and the mystical meditations on prayer in which he instructed his disciples were based on Sephardi rite. This was why only the kabbalists and Ḥasidim among the Ashkenazim accepted the Sephardi liturgy in prayer, as they adopted many of his other observances.

Luria himself attempted to clarify his position in relation to the Kabbalah of Moses Cordovero, and the question has occupied a number of other kabbalists. Answering inquiries on the difference between the two kabbalists, he replied that Cordovero treated of *olam ha-tohu,* "the world of confusion," while his own teaching dealt with *olam ha-tikkun,* "the world of restitution," – i.e., each was concerned with entirely different planes and states of being in the spiritual realm of emanation, and so Cordovero's province did not impinge on that of Luria. Most kabbalists refrained from attempting to mix or combine the two kabbalistic systems. Vital too, who at first was Cordovero's disciple, wrote that he paved "the plain way *[derekh ha-peshat]* for beginners in his wisdom" while Luria traced the "inner, most important path" (stated in a dream in 1573 recorded in Vital's *Sefer ha-Ḥezyonot*). In reply to Vital's question (according to testimony in *Sha'ar Ru'aḥ ha-Kodesh*) as to why he had penetrated more deeply into the mysteries than Cordovero, Luria said that this did not come about through reliance on divine revelation or similar phenomena but because "he took greater pains than the rest of his contemporaries."

There is no justification for the theory, widely held by modern historians, that the principles Luria introduced are based on the traditions and ethical doctrine of the Ḥasidei Ashkenaz. Nor should Lurianic Kabbalah be viewed as the epitome of "practical" Kabbalah in contrast to "theoretical," or speculative, Kabbalah. The theoretical and practical aspects are blended in every kabbalistic system, particularly in those followed by the scholars of Safed. Luria's originality does not lie in his stress on the practical aspects of man's adhesion to his Creator, or on the performance of good deeds, but in his pioneer conception of the theoretical aspect of Kabbalah.

Bibliography: Azulai, 1 (1852), s.v. *Yiẓḥak Luria;* D. Kahana (Kogan), *Toledot ha-Mekubbalim ha-Shabbeta'im ve-ha-Ḥasidim,* 1 (1913), 22–42; Kaufmann, in: *Yerushalayim* (A.M. Luncz ed.), 2 (1887), 144–7; S.A. Horodezky, *Torat ha-Kabbalah shel Rabbi Yiẓḥak Ashkenazi ve-Rabbi Ḥayyim Vital* (1947); idem, in: EJ, 10 (1934), 1198–1212; I. Tishby, *Torat ha-Ra ve-ha-Kelippah be-Kabbalat ha-Ari* (1942); Scholem, Mysticism, 244–86,

407–15; Scholem, Sabbatai Ṣevi, chapter 1; idem, *Kitvei Yad ba-Kabbalah* (1930), 103–6, 115–43; idem, in: *Zion,* 5 (1940), 133–60, 214–43; idem, in: KS, 19(1953/54), 184–99; 26 (1860/61), 185–94; R. Margulies, *ibid.*, 17 (1951/52), 248, 423; M. Benayahu, *Sefer Toledot ha-Ari* (1967); idem, in: *Sefer ha-Yovel le-Ḥanokh Albeck* (1963), 71–80; idem, in: *Aresheth,* 3 (1961), 144–65; idem, in: *Sefunot,* 10 (1966), 213–98; D. Tamar, *Meḥkarim be-Toledot ha-Yehudim* (1969); J. Liebes, in: *Molad* no. 233 (Febr. 1972), 540–55 (on the three Sabbath hymns); P. Bloch, *Die Kabbala auf ihrem Hohepunkt und ihre Meister* (1905); S. Schechter, *Studies in Judaism,* 2nd series (1908), 202–306, 317–28; Rosanes, Togarmah, 2 (1938), 198–203.

10

Ḥayyim Malakh

Malakh was born in Kalish between 1650 and 1660. Nothing is known about his early career, but he became a highly respected rabbinic scholar, kabbalist, and preacher. He was soon attracted by the Shabbatean movement and became closely associated with the Shabbatean prophet Heshel Ẓoref in Vilna. In 1690 he went to Italy, probably on a mission on behalf of the movement, staying there several months with Abraham Rovigo and Benjamin Cohen, the heads of the Italian Shabbateans. They studied the writings of Isaac Luria and Nathan of Gaza, and Ḥayyim Malakh received their secret traditions concerning Shabbetai Ẓevi. From 1692 to 1694 he was back in Poland, active as a Shabbatean missionary among rabbinic circles. One of his students (about 1693) was the famous talmudist Mordecai Suskind Rotenburg, rabbi of Lublin. During this period he attracted the attention of R. Ẓevi Ashkenazi, the father of Jacob Emden, who became Malakh's bitter foe. Possibly because of a ban due to his heretic activity or possibly because of his own doubts concerning the Shabbatean theology, he went to Turkey. He stayed for two to three years with Samuel Primo in Adrianople, becoming his fervent follower and receiving the traditions and secrets of the circle of Shabbetai Ẓevi's personal pupils. He went to Bursa (Turkey) where some outstanding Shabbateans lived, and toward the end of his stay, had a vision which caused him to return to Poland and join with another Shabbatean leader, Judah Ḥasid. He arrived in Zolkiew, late in 1696, and stayed for some time, finding many influential followers. From Zolkiew he sent a letter to his Italian masters informing them that he was leaving their camp since he had found the authentic spring of Shabbatean teaching in Turkey. It is quite possible that he went back to Turkey in 1697 where he seems to have met Abraham Cardozo in Adrianople. Malakh took Primo's side in the discussions with Cardozo, whose speculative dissertations he refused to read. It is not clear whether at this time or later he came into contact with the young leader of the most radical wing of the Doenmeh sect in Salonika, Baruchiah Russo (Osman Baba), several of whose sayings were quoted by Malakh to one of his pupils (in a Shabbatean notebook, probably written in Damascus, now in Columbia University Library).

After his return he became one of the founders of the new "Society of the Ḥasidim" which advocated an immigration of ascetic scholars to Jerusalem to await the imminent coming of the Messiah. Privately this Messiah was understood to be Shabbetai Ẓevi whose return in 1706, forty years after his apostasy, had been predicted by Malakh. Apparently during these years, Malakh acquired the surname Malakh, "the angel." He became generally known by this title from the late 1690s on: whether this was because of his gifts as a preacher or because of his asceticism is unknown. Certainly he was considered the chief kabbalist of the group. In connection with the "ḥasidic" propaganda which attracted many secret Shabbateans in Poland, Germany, and the Hapsburg Empire, he spent some time in Germany and Moravia, where, at the end of 1698, he attended a council of the Shabbatean leaders of the Ḥasidim in Nikolsburg (Mikulov), an eyewitness report of which has survived. He also went to Vienna and announced that he would discuss the Shabbatean belief and teachings with any duly initiated kabbalist. Abraham Broda, the rabbi of Prague, sent his pupils, Moses Ḥasid and Jonah Landsofer, but the dispute, which lasted two weeks, ended inconclusively. Malakh then went to Ereẓ Israel where, after the sudden death of Judah he-Ḥasid in October 1700, one faction of the Ḥasidim chose him as its leader. What exactly happened in the Shabbatean circle in Jerusalem is unknown or blurred by biased and half-legendary reports. At any rate, internal dissensions between moderate and radical Shabbateans contributed to the break-up of the group, but the precise date of Malakh's expulsion from Ereẓ Israel is unknown. It is probable that he went to Constantinople and again to Salonika, meeting with Baruchiah. Since that meeting Malakh acquired the reputation of being an emissary of the antinomian wing of Shabbateanism. This led to his prolonged persecution by the rabbinical authorities. A circular letter of the Constantinople rabbis, written in 1710, denounced him vehemently. He returned to Poland where he founded the radical sect in Podolia from which the Frankist movement sprang, but he also served as an emissary for some Ashkenazi groups in Ereẓ Israel. As such he is mentioned in the records of the community of Tiktin (Tykocin) in 1708. In public he denied any Shabbatean connections, preferring to divulge his doctrine in private. Forced to leave Poland, he wandered through Germany and Holland. In 1715 he was in Amsterdam where a letter from Abraham Broda, then rabbi of Frankfort, urging Malakh's immediate expulsion arrived soon after his departure. He died shortly after his return to Poland in 1716 or 1717. He was generally considered an expert in Kabbalah and a persuasive spokesman for the Shabbatean movement after it was forced to go underground. None of his writings has survived.

Bibliography: J. Emden, *Torat ha-Kena'ot* (1871), 50, 70–71; D. Kahana, *Toledot ha-Mekubbalim, ha-Shabbeta'im ve-ha-Ḥasidim,* 2 (1913), 175–80; C. Bernheimer, in: JQR, 18 (1927/28), 125; G. Scholem, in: *Zion,* 6 (1941), 123–4; 11 (1946), 168–74; idem, in: RHR, 143 (1953), 209–20; M. Benayahu, in: *Sefer Ḥida* (1957), 73–74; idem, in: *Sefunot,* 3–4 (1960), 136–8; idem, in: *Eretz-Israel,* 10 (1971).

11

Moses ben Shem Tov de Leon

Moses was apparently born about 1240 in Leon, near Castile – he also calls himself Moses "from the town of Leon" in his *Shekel ha-Kodesh.* Nothing is known of his teachers and early studies. Apart from religious study, he was also attracted to philosophy; Maimonides' *Guide of the Perplexed* was copied for him in 1264 (Moscow, Ms. Guenzburg 771). Moses subsequently turned to Kabbalah, and when wandering among the communities of Castile, he became friendly with the kabbalists there. He immersed himself in the lore of the Geronese school of kabbalists and in the traditions of the Gnostic circle of Moses of Burgos and Todros Abulafia, and in the 1270s and 80s drew particularly close to Joseph Gikatilla. Moved by an unusual enthusiasm, combined with the urge to counteract the influence of current rationalistic trends, Moses composed various writings toward the close of the 1270s. Presented in the guise of pseudepigraphica, they were designed to propagate the doctrine of kabbalism in the pattern in which it had crystallized in his own mind. Completed before 1286, they form the *Midrash ha-Ne'elam,* or "Mystical Midrash," and are the main substance of the Zohar. The later stratum in this composite work was written by another kabbalist. The major part of these writings is in Aramaic, but Moses also composed Hebrew pseudepigraphica on ethics and the eschatology of the soul. The "Testament of R. Eliezer the Great," also called *Orḥot Ḥayyim,* is evidence of the author's hesitations in choosing between the *Tannaim* Eliezer b. Hyrcanus and Simeon b. Yohai for the hero of his pseudepigraphical construction. He also intended to compose a new Book of Enoch, parts of which he embodies in his *Mishkan ha-Edut.*

For a number of years, during the composition of the Zohar and at least until 1291, he resided in Guadalajara, circulating from his home the first parts of the Zohar, which included a partly different version of the *Midrash ha-Ne'elam* (G. Scholem, in *Sefer ha-Yovel . . . L. Ginzberg* (1946), 425–46, Heb. section). In Guadalajara he was associated with Isaac ibn Sahulah, who is the first known to quote from the *Midrash ha-Ne'elam.* He dedicated some of his books to Joseph b. Todros Abulafia in Toledo. After 1292 Moses led a wandering life until, in later years, he settled in Avila, and then probably devoted himself almost exclusively to the circulation of copies of the Zohar. Meeting Isaac b. Samuel of Acre in Valladolid in 1305, he invited him to Avila to see the ancient original manuscript of the Zohar in his home. However, on his return Moses fell ill and died in Arévalo in 1305 (*Sefer Yuḥasin*, ed. H. Filipowski, 88). His widow denied the existence of such a manuscript. The Hebrew writings which bear his name are based on the same sources as those utilized in the Zohar and they frequently make veiled allusions to it without specifying it by name. These writings and the portions of the Zohar composed by Moses frequently serve to clarify one another; the former can be regarded as the authentic exegesis of the doctrine enshrined in the Zohar (see the article Zohar).

Numerous copies of several of his works were made in succeeding generations, and it seems that Moses himself circulated the texts in different versions. According to Abraham b. Solomon of Torrutiel (Neubauer, Chronicles, 1 (1887), 105), he was the author of 24 books. Those fully or partly extant are *Shoshan Edut* (1286), which Moses mentions as his first work (Cambridge, Add. Ms. 505, includes about half the work); *Sefer ha-Rimmon* (1287), an exposition of the kabbalistic reasons for the *miẓvot*, wholly constructed on Zoharic fundaments (several Mss., e.g., Oxford, Bodleian, Ms. Opp. 344); *Or Zaru'a* (1288/89), on the act of Creation (Oxford, Bodleian, Ms. Poc. 296, other parts in Ms. Vatican 428, 80–90): this was apparently extended by another kabbalist to cover the whole section *Bereshit*, Genesis 1–6 (Ms. Vatican 212); *Ha-Nefesh ha-Ḥakhamah*, written in 1290 for his pupil Jacob, whom Isaac of Acre met after Moses' death: a corrupt text was published in 1608 which contained numerous addenda from a work by a contemporary Spanish kabbalist; a lengthy titleless commentary on the ten *Sefirot* and penances (a large part in Munich Ms. 47); *Shekel ha-Kodesh* (1292, publ. 1912; a better text in Oxford, Bodleian Ms. Opp. 563); *Mishkan ha-Edut* (1293), on the fate of the soul after death, with a commentary on the vision of Ezekiel appearing in numerous manuscripts (Berlin, Vatican, et al.) as an independent book: both here and in his introduction to *Or Zaru'a* Moses divulges the reasons for his literary activities; *Maskiyyot Kesef* (written after 1293), a commentary on the prayers, a sequel to the lost *Tappuḥei Zahav* (Ms. Adler, 1577); responsa on points of Kabbalah (ed. by Tishby, in: *Kobez al Jad*, vol. 5, 1951); a treatise on various mystical themes (Schocken Library, Ms. Kab. 14, 78–99; Ms. Vatican 428); another commentary on the ten *Sefirot, Sod Eser Sefirot Belimah . . .* (Madrid, Escorial, Ms. G III 14). Moses also wrote: *Sefer Pardes* ("Book of Paradise"); *Sha'arei Ẓedek* on Ecclesiastes; *Mashal ha-Kadmoni* (after the title of his friend Isaac ibn Sahula's work); responsa on questions concerning Elijah; a commentary on Song of Songs; and a polemic directed against the Sadducees (or Karaites), mentioned by Abner of Burgos (REJ, 18 (1889), 62). The *Sefer ha-Shem* (publ. in *Heikhal ha-Shem*, Venice, c.

1601) on the designations of the *Sefirot,* ascribed to him from the 15th century onward, was written by another kabbalist named Moses in the middle of the 14th century.

Bibliography: Scholem, Mysticism, ch. 5; idem, in: KS, 1 (1924), 45–52; idem, in: *Madda'ei ha-Yahadut,* 1 (1926), 16–29; idem, in: MGWJ, 71 (1927), 109–23; S.D. Luzzatto, *Iggerot Shadal* (1891), 259; Steinschneider, Cat Bod, 1847–56; idem, in: HB, 10 (1870), 156–61; A. Jellinek, *Moses ben Schem Tob de Leon und sein Verhaeltnis zum Sohar* (1851); I. Tishby, *Mishnat ha-Zohar,* 2 vols. (1949), general introd. and introds. to different chapters; Y. Nadav, in: *Oẓar Yehudei Sefarad,* 2 (1959), 69–76; E. Gottlieb, in: *Tarbiz,* 33 (1964), 287–313; I. Ta-Shma, *ibid.*, 39 (1969), 184–94; 40 (1970), 105–6; S.Z. Havlin, *ibid.*, 107–9.

12
Nathan of Gaza

Nathan's full name was Abraham Nathan b. Elisha Hayyim Ashkenazi, but he became famous as Nathan the Prophet of Gaza and after 1665 his admirers generally called him "the holy lamp" *(buẓina kaddisha),* the honorific given to R. Simeon b. Yoḥai in the Zohar. His father, who had come from Poland or Germany, settled in Jerusalem and for many years served as an emissary of its community, visiting Poland, Germany, Italy, and (frequently) Morocco. He was a respected rabbinical scholar with kabbalistic leanings. Nathan was born in Jerusalem, probably about 1643/44. His main teacher was the famous talmudist Jacob Ḥagiz and he seems to have been a brilliant student, quick to understand and of considerable intellectual power. Before he left Jerusalem in 1663, having married the daughter of a wealthy merchant of Gaza, Samuel Lissabonna, and settled in the latter's home town, he must have seen Shabbetai Ẓevi, then twice his age, in the Jewish quarter of Jerusalem, where Shabbetai lived for almost the whole of 1663. It is also clear that he must have heard a great deal of talk about this strange personality and his tribulations. Strongly attracted by an ascetic way of life, Nathan took up the study of Kabbalah in 1664. The combination of great intellectual and imaginative power which was his main characteristic resulted in his having visions of angels and deceased souls after a short time. He delved deeply into Lurianic Kabbalah, following the ascetic rules laid down by Isaac Luria. Shortly before or after Purim 1665 he had a significant ecstatic experience accompanied by a prolonged vision (he speaks of 24 hours) of the divine world revealing how its different stages were connected, a vision that differed in many significant details from the Lurianic scheme. Through this revelation he became convinced of the messianic mission of Shabbetai Ẓevi, whose figure he saw engraved on the divine throne. (For his further intensive activities during the following year see the major article on Shabbetai Ẓevi, above.) When the latter returned from his mission to Egypt and came to see him in Gaza, Nathan finally convinced him of his messianic destiny by producing a pseudepigraphic vision, attributed to a medieval saint, Abraham Hasid, who as it were foretold the birth and early history of Shabbetai Ẓevi and confirmed his superior rank.

Ware afbeeldinge van den genaemde prophee
Nathan Levi van Gaza:
Vraij portraict du dit prophete
Nathan Levi de Gaza.

Nathan of Gaza, kabbalist and disciple of Shabbetai Ẓevi. From Thomas Coenen, *Ydele Verwachtinge der Joden getoont in der Persoon van Sabethai Zevi,* Amsterdam, 1669.

In his ecstasy Nathan had heard a voice announcing in the name of God that Shabbetai Ẓevi was the Messiah; he therefore became the prophet of the "son of David," the mission that the biblical prophet Nathan had fulfilled for King David. As he had been vouchsafed charismatic gifts since his ecstatic awakening, many people made pilgrimages to him from Palestine, Syria, and Egypt. He divulged "the roots of their souls," revealed their secret sins, and prescribed ways to penance. Since his prophetic powers were widely acknowledged as genuine, his endorsement of Shabbetai Ẓevi's messianic claim gave the decisive impetus to the mass movement which swept the Jewish people everywhere. Remaining in Gaza after Shabbetai Ẓevi left for Jerusalem and Smyrna (Izmir), he wrote letters to the Diaspora confirming that redemption was at hand and laying down elaborate kabbalistic rules of penance *(tikkunim)* to be followed by those who wished to usher in the new age. These were widely copied and the exoteric portions of the ritual were printed in many editions during 1666. It is not known why the rabbis of Jerusalem, the majority of whom (including Jacob Ḥagiz) took a stand against the messianic claims of Shabbetai Ẓevi, did nothing to interfere with Nathan's activities. The fact that the small community of Gaza, including their rabbi, Jacob Najara, were among his followers is insufficient explanation. In the summer of 1666, during Shabbetai's confinement in Gallipoli, Nathan composed several kabbalistic tracts of which the *Derush ha-Tanninim* has survived (published in G. Scholem, *Be-Ikkevot Mashi'aḥ*, 1944), glorifying Shabbetai's mystical state since the beginning of creation. His correspondence with Shabbetai Ẓevi during this time, however, is lost.

After receiving the news of Shabbetai's apostasy, he left Gaza early in November 1666, accompanied by a large group of supporters, including his father-in-law and his family. On Nov. 20, 1666, he wrote to Shabbetai Ẓevi from Damascus announcing that he was on his way to see him, apparently on the latter's invitation. By this time he had already begun to sign himself Nathan Benjamin, the new name Shabbetai had given him in Gaza when he appointed 12 scholars to represent the 12 tribes of Israel. Nathan's faith in his messiah never wavered and from the beginning he hinted at mystical reasons which justified the apostasy. Originally he planned to travel by sea via Alexandretta (Iskenderun) but he changed his route and went with his entourage by land, avoiding the larger Jewish communities which had been warned against him by the rabbis of Constantinople. By the end of January 1667 he arrived at Bursa (Brusa) where he was threatened with a ban unless he stayed out of the town and "kept quiet." Dispersing his group he continued with only six associates, including Samuel Gandoor, a scholar from Egypt, who became his constant companion until his death. Before leaving Bursa, he wrote a letter to Shabbetai's brothers in Smyrna, opening a long series of letters, tracts, and other pronouncements defending the apostasy and Shabbetai's continued messianic mission on kabbalistic grounds. Many of these have been preserved. On March 3, 1667, he arrived at a small village near Smyrna, then stayed until April 30 in Smyrna itself; there he met with some of the believers, but kept largely to himself.

Nathan became very reserved toward all outsiders and even repelled the delegation of three northern Italian communities who were on their way to Shabbetai Ẓevi and had been waiting to hear Nathan's explanations. The Dutch clergyman Th. Coenen has left a description of his meeting with Nathan on April 25. Nathan tried to reach Adrianople, where he would see his messiah, but he was held up in the nearby small community of Ipsola and met by a delegation from Adrianople and Constantinople. After being interrogated he was forced to sign a document (dated May 31, 1667) promising not to approach Adrianople, not to correspond with "that man" in Adrianople, and not to convene public meetings, but to keep to himself; finally he admitted that all his words would be given the lie unless the messiah appeared before September 14, a date he had fixed earlier on the strength of an additional vision. Later Nathan repudiated all these obligations, claiming that he had acted under duress. He went to see Shabbetai Ẓevi secretly, then wandered with Gandoor through Thrace and Greece where sympathy with the movement was still very strong.

Early in 1668 he traveled from Janina to Corfu where he held secret conclaves with his adherents. On the initiative of Shabbetai Ẓevi himself, he then undertook a journey to Italy, with the intention of carrying out a mystic ritual at the seat of the pope in Rome. His arrival in Venice around March 20 caused considerable excitement and apprehension. Under pressure from someone in the government, he was allowed to enter the ghetto where he spent approximately two weeks, being closely questioned by the rabbis but also beleaguered by a host of admirers and followers. The events of Ipsola were repeated; the rabbis published the results of their examination in a broadsheet, including a declaration in which Nathan admitted his errors; later Nathan repudiated this in statements to the believers. From Venice he and Gandoor traveled to Bologna, Florence, and Leghorn, where he stayed for some weeks strengthening the hopes of the remaining believers. He and a wealthy Italian believer, Moses Cafsuto, then proceeded to Rome, perhaps disguised as gentiles. He stayed a few days only (end of May or beginning of June) performing some secret rituals patterned on those outlined at an earlier time by Solomon Molcho. He returned to Leghorn or, according to another source, went straight to Ancona, where he was recognized and met the rabbi, Mahalalel Halleluyah (Alleluyah), a fervent believer, who has left a detailed account of their meeting. By that time Nathan had written an account of his mission to Rome, couched in elusive Aramaic filled with kabbalistic and apocalyptic metaphors. This was widely distributed to the groups of believers. On his return to Turkey via Ragusa and Durazzo Nathan went to stay for some time with Shabbetai Ẓevi in Adrianople. After this he spent six months in Salonika where a considerable group of scholars flocked to him to receive his new version of the Kabbalah according to Shabbatean principles. For the next ten years he remained in Macedonia and Bulgaria – apart from secret pilgrimages to Shabbetai Ẓevi after the latter's banishment to Dulcigno in Albania (1673) – staying mainly in Sofia, Adrianople, and Kastoria, and paying occasional visits to Salonika. He maintained close contacts with many other leaders of the movement who continued to consider him a charismatic figure of the highest rank. Although Shabbetai Ẓevi never asked him to follow him into Islam, he staunchly defended not only the necessity of the messiah's apostasy, but also those "elect ones" who emulated him on his command. Many of the rabbis of the Macedonian communities stood by him, paying no heed to the excommunications and warnings emanating from Constantinople and Adrianople.

Nathan's letters reveal him as a strong personality, although the few that have been preserved from his intense correspondence with Shabbetai Ẓevi are couched in adoring and submissive terms. They contrast curiously with his obvious moral and intellectual superiority over his master. In spite of all this, there were periods of tension between the two. After Shabbetai's death, Nathan withdrew even more from public contact, although he continued to preach in the synagogues of Sofia on some occasions. Refusing to admit defeat, he upheld the theory that Shabbetai Ẓevi had only "disappeared" or gone into hiding in some higher sphere, whence he would return in God's own time. Israel Ḥazzan of Kastoria, who served as his secretary for about three years, took down many of his teachings and sayings after Shabbetai's death. Nathan continued to lead an ascetic life and, feeling that his end was near, left Sofia and went to Skoplje (Üsküb) where he died on Jan. 11, 1680. His grave was revered as that of a saint and over the generations many Shabbateans made pilgrimages there. His tombstone, whose inscription has been preserved, was destroyed during World War II. The many legends spread about Nathan during his lifetime increased after his death. He had two sons, of whose fate nothing is known. A sketch of Nathan drawn by a ship's mate who saw him in Gaza in the summer of 1665, which was reproduced in several contemporary broadsheets, may be authentic.

Between 1665 and 1679 Nathan embarked on a manifold literary activity. Some of his many letters are in fact theological treatises. At first, he composed kabbalistic rules and meditations for a fast of six consecutive days, *Seder Hafsakah Gedolah shel Shishah Yamim ve-Shishah Leilot,* partly printed anonymously, and omitting the passages where Shabbetai Ẓevi's name is mentioned, under the title *Sefer le-Hafsakah Gedolah* (Smyrna, 1732). These were accompanied by *Tikkunei Teshuvah,* both treatises being preserved in several manuscripts. At about the same time he began the explanation of his new vision of the process of creation, sending several tracts on this to Raphael Joseph in Cairo. Of these only the *Derush ha-Tanninim* has been preserved. After Shabbetai's apostasy he developed his ideas in a more radical way. The most elaborate presentation of his kabbalistic system, containing constant references to the function of the Messiah and his paradoxical actions, is found in the *Sefer ha-Beri'ah,* written in 1670, in two parts. It was also known under the title *Raza de-Uvda de-Bereshit,* and in some manuscripts was accompanied by a lengthy preface which may have been conceived as a separate literary entity. The work is extant, complete or in parts, in approximately 30 manuscripts and must have enjoyed a wide distribution in Shabbatean circles up to the middle of the 18th century. A short synopsis of its ideas, from Ms. Oxford, Neubauer Cat. (Bod.) no. 2394, is included in Scholem's *Be-Ikkevot Mashi'aḥ.* During the same period Nathan composed the book *Zemir Ariẓim* which, as well as other kabbalistic matters, contains long disquisitions on the state of the Torah in the messianic era and a justification of Shabbetai Ẓevi's antinomian actions (complete in British Museum Or. 4536, Cat. Margoliouth no. 856 and elsewhere). In some manuscripts it was called *Derush ha-Menorah* (partly included in the collection *Be-Ikkevot Mashi'aḥ*). These books were widely quoted by secret Shabbateans, sometimes even in printed works. Of his many pastoral letters, special mention must be made of the long apology for Shabbetai Ẓevi, published in *Koveẓ al Yad,* 6 (1966), 419–56, apparently written about 1673–74. Fragments of other writings are dispersed through several manuscripts and Shabbatean notebooks. Collections dealing with his special customs and behavior were made by his pupils in Salonika (who saw him as a reincarnation of Luria) and were distributed in Turkey and Italy. These are extant in several versions. An abridgment of Nathan's system was incorporated as the first part of the *Sha'arei Gan Eden* by Jacob Koppel b. Moses of Mezhirech and was published as an authoritative kabbalistic text (Korzec, 1803) without its heretical character being recognized.

Bibliography; G. Scholem, Sabbatai Ṣevi, *passim,* esp. chs. 3, 7–8; idem, *Be-Ikkevot Mashi'aḥ* (1944), a collection of Nathan's writings; idem, in: *Alei Ayin, Minḥat Devarim le-S. Z. Schocken* (1948–52), 157–211; idem, in: *H.A. Wolfson Jubilee Volume* (1965), 225–41 (Heb. sect.); C. Wirszubski, in: *Keneset, Divrei Soferim le-Zekher Ḥ.N. Bialik,* 8 (1943–44), 210–46; idem, in: *Koveẓ Hoẓa'at Schocken le-Divrei Sifrut* (1941), 180–92; I. Tishby, in: *Tarbiẓ,* 15 (1943/44), 161–80; idem, in KS, 21 (1945), 12–17; idem, in: *Sefunot,* I (1956), 80–117; idem, *Netivei Emunah ve-Minut* (1964), 30–80, 204–26, 280–95, 331–43.

13

Judah Leib Prossnitz

Born in Uhersky Brod (c. 1670), Prossnitz settled in Prossnitz (Prostejov) after his marriage. An uneducated man, he made his living as a peddler. About 1696 he underwent a spiritual awakening and began to study the Mishnah, and later the Zohar and kabbalistic writings. Believing that he was visited by the souls of deceased, he claimed that he studied Kabbalah with Isaac Luria and Shabbetai Ẓevi. Whether his Shabbatean awakening was connected with the movement in Moravia around Judah Ḥasid, Heshel Ẓoref, and Ḥayyim Malakh is still a matter of conjecture. Possibly he was won over by Ẓevi Hirsch b. Jerahmeel Chotsh, who spent some time in Prossnitz in 1696. Judah Leib first turned to teaching children but later his followers in Prossnitz provided for him and his family. Taking up residence in the *bet midrash* of Prossnitz, he led a strictly ascetic life; he became generally known as Leibele Prossnitz. Before long he started to divulge kabbalistic and Shabbatean mysteries and to preach in public in the manner of a revivalist preacher *(mokhi'aḥ).* He found many adherents, his most important supporter for some years being Meir Eisenstadt, a famous rabbinic authority who served as rabbi of Prossnitz from 1702. At the same time his Shabbatean propaganda, especially since it came from an uneducated lay mystic, aroused strong hostility in many circles. Between 1703 and 1705 he traveled through Moravia and Silesia, causing considerable agitation in the communities. Along with other Shabbatean leaders of this period, he prophesied the return of Shabbetai Ẓevi in 1706. His open Shabbatean propaganda led to clashes in Glogau and Breslau, where the rabbis threatened him with excommunication unless he returned to Prossnitz and stayed there. As 1706 approached his agitation reached a pitch. He assembled a group of ten followers who studied with him and practiced extravagant mortifications.

Judah Leib was widely credited with magical practices connected with his attempts to bring to an end the dominion of Samael and is reported to have sacrificed a chicken as a kind of bribe to the unclean powers. The facts concerning this and his promise to reveal the *Shekhinah* to some of his followers, including Meir Eisenstadt, are shrouded in legend, but they contain some kernel of historical truth. Since by then he was widely considered by his foes to be a sorcerer, Meir Eisenstadt left him and Prossnitz was put under a ban by the rabbinical court and sentenced to exile for three years; however, he was allowed to return after several months. He persisted at the head of a secret Shabbatean group in Prossnitz, again working as a children's teacher. Maintaining connections with other Shabbateans, in 1724 he tried to obtain the appointment of one of his closest followers, R. Sender, to the rabbinate of Mannheim (L. Loewenstein, *Geschichte der Juden in der Kurpfalz* (1895), 198–9). Jonathan Eybeschuetz, a pupil of Meir Eisenstadt in Prostejov (Prossnitz) for several years, is said to have studied secretly with Judah Leib, who was then propagating teachings close to the radical wing of Shabbateanism. Along with others in this group, he supported heretical teachings regarding divine providence. When Leib b. Ozer wrote his memoir on the state of Shabbateanism in 1717, Judah Leib was refraining from public manifestations of Shabbatean faith and was said to be working on a kabbalistic commentary on the Book of Ruth. With the resurgence of Shabbatean activities in 1724, in the wake of the emissaries from Salonika, Judah Leib again appeared publicly on the scene, claiming to be the Messiah ben Joseph, the precursor of the Messiah ben David. Once more, he found many followers in Moravia and even in Vienna and Prague. Some of his letters to Jonathan Eybeschuetz and Isaiah Mokhi'aḥ in Mannheim were found among the papers confiscated from Shabbatean emissaries. In the summer of 1725 Judah Leib was again excommunicated by the rabbis of Moravia in Nikolsburg (Mikulov) and after that led a vagrant life. When he came to Frankfort on the Main in early 1726 he was not allowed to enter the Jewish quarter, but he was given material assistance by one of his secret supporters. His last years were reportedly spent in Hungary. Whereas the friendly contact between Judah Leib and Eybeschuetz is well established, there is no conclusive proof of Jacob Emden's claim that Judah Leib saw Eybeschuetz as the future leader of the Shabbateans (J. Emden, *Beit Yonatan ha-Sofer* (Altona, 1762(?), 1b), or that he would even be the Messiah after Shabbetai Ẓevi's apotheosis *(Shevirat Luḥot ha-Aven* (Zolkiew, 1755), 18b). After Judah Leib's death in 1730 a strong group of Shabbateans survived in Prossnitz during the 18th century.

Bibliography: J. Emden, *Torat ha-Kena'ot* (Amsterdam, 1752), 34bf., 41a–42a; A. Neubauer, in: MGWJ, 36 (1887), 207–12; D. Kahana, *Toledot ha-Mekubbalim ve-ha-Shabbeta'im*, 2 (1914), 168–75, 184; M.A. Perlmutter (Anat), *R. Yehonatan Eybeschuetz, Yaḥaso el ha-Shabbeta'ut* (1947), 43–47; Chr. P. Loewe, *Speculum Religionis Judaicae* (1732), 80–82.

14
Hayyim Vital

Ḥayyim Vital was born in Ereẓ Israel, apparently in Safed, in 1542. His father, Joseph Vital Calabrese, whose name indicates his origin from Calabria, South Italy, was a well known scribe in Safed (see responsa of Menahem Azariah da Fano, no. 38). His son is also called Ḥayyim Calabrese in several kabbalistic works. Ḥayyim Vital studied in yeshivot in Safed, especially under Moses Alshekh, his teacher in exoteric subjects. In 1564 he began to study Kabbalah, at first according to the system of Moses Cordovero, although Vital did not call Cordovero his teacher. He was also attracted to other esoteric studies and spent two years (1563–65) in the practice of alchemy (probably in Damascus), which he later regretted. After Isaac Luria's arrival in Safed, Vital became his principal disciple, studying under him for nearly two years until Luria's death in the summer of 1572. Later he began to arrange Luria's teachings in written form and to elaborate on them according to his own understanding. Vital tried to prevent Luria's other disciples from presenting their versions of his doctrine in writing, and he gathered around him several who accepted his spiritual authority. But he did not entirely succeed in his ambition to be the only heir to Luria's spiritual legacy and to be accepted as the sole interpreter of Lurianic Kabbalah. In 1575, twelve of Luria's disciples signed a pledge to study Luria's theory only from Vital, promising not to induce him to reveal more than he wished and to keep the mysteries secret from others (*Zion,* 5 (1940), 125, and see another copy of the agreement in *Birkat ha-Areẓ* by Baruch David ha-Kohen (1904), 61). This study group ceased to function when Vital moved to Jerusalem, where he served as rabbi and head of a yeshivah from late 1577 to late 1585. In Jerusalem he wrote the last version of his presentation of the Lurianic system. He returned to Safed early in 1586, staying there until 1592. According to tradition, he fell seriously ill in Safed around 1587; during his long period of unconsciousness the scholars of Safed are said to have bribed his younger brother Moses, who allowed them to copy 600 leaves of Ḥayyim Vital's writings which were then circulated among a select group (according to a letter written by Shlomel Dresnitz in 1606, in *Shivḥei ha-Ari).*

In 1590 Vital was "ordained" as rabbi by his teacher Moses Alshekh. (The text of the ordination is published in *Sefer Yovel le-Y. Baer* (1961), 266.) He was in Jerusalem once more in 1593 and perhaps stayed there several years, returning to Safed from time to time. According to the tradition of the rabbis of Jerusalem, he moved from Jerusalem to Damascus; in any case, he was in Damascus in 1598 *(Sefer ha-Ḥezyonot* (1954), 87) and remained there until his death. For a time he served as rabbi of the Sicilian community there *(ibid.*, 92, 116). After a severe illness in 1604, his sight was impaired and at times he was even blind. During his final years a kabbalistic group gathered around him. He died in 1620. Vital was married at least three times and his youngest son, Samuel (1598–c. 1678), inherited his writings. While he was in Damascus, mainly between 1609 and 1612, Ḥayyim Vital assembled autobiographical notes which he called *Sefer ha-Ḥezyonot,* mainly stories and testimonies to his greatness, but also including his dreams and those of others; these form an important source for the study of the course of his life and the complexities of his soul. The work is preserved in his own handwriting and was published by A.Z. Aescoly (1954), from the autograph in the possession of Rabbi A. Toaff of Leghorn. (This publication aroused considerable embarrassment in some rabbinic circles.) From this work it is apparent that strained relations existed between Vital and Jacob Abulafia, one of the rabbis in Damascus, who doubted Vital's claims to be the sole interpreter of Lurianic Kabbalah. The early editions of *Sefer ha-Ḥezyonot* were published from fragmentary and corrupt copies, in Ostrog (1826) as *Shivḥei R. Ḥayyim Vital,* and in Jerusalem (1866) as *Sefer ha-Ḥezyonot.* Vital's epitaph was published in David Zion Laniado's *La-Kedoshim Asher ba-Areẓ* (1935), 43. Besides his son, his other disciples in Damascus included Japheth ha-Miẓri, Ḥayyim b. Abraham ha-Kohen of Aleppo, and Ephraim Penzieri. Many legends about Vital circulated even during his lifetime, and are preserved in *Toledot ha-Ari* and in the letters of Shlomel Dresnitz, first published in 1629 in *Ta'alumot Ḥokhmah* by Joseph Solomon Delmedigo. In subsequent generations many other legends were added.

Vital was a prolific writer. His proficiency in exoteric subjects is attested by his ordination and by his rabbinical function in Jerusalem. However, few of his talmudic teachings have been preserved: one responsum from Damascus was published in the responsa of Joseph di Trani (Constantinople, 1641 ed., 88c.) and ten halakhic responsa are included in Samuel Vital's *Be'er Mayim Ḥayyim* (Ms. Oxford Neubauer Cat Bod no. 832). His commentaries on the Talmud are extant, together with those of his son (in Ms. Guenzburg 283) and have been published at the end of every tractate of the El ha-Mekorot Talmud, appearing in Jerusalem since 1959. A complete volume of his sermons on esoteric subjects and popular Kabbalah is preserved in *Torat Ḥayyim* (unpublished Ms. in the written list of the collection of R. Aryeh L. Alter of Gur, no. 286) and several of his sermons can also be found in Badhab Mss. collection 205, now in the Hebrew University, and in Columbia University (Ms. H533, foll. 150ff., New York). His *Sefer ha-Tekhunah* on astronomy was published in Jerusalem in 1866. His autograph manuscript of his work on practical Kabbalah and alchemy was extant in the Musayoff collection in Jerusalem in 1940.

According to his son, Vital assembled his major writings into two vast works *Eẓ ha-Ḥayyim* and *Eẓ ha-Da'at.* The former is the inclusive name for all those writings in which he elaborated on the teaching of Isaac Luria. These works went through several versions and adaptations, for Vital began to arrange what he had heard from Luria immediately after his death and, according to Meir Poppers, remained absorbed in this task for more than 20 years. The first version *(mahadurah kamma)* remained in Damascus with Vital's son, who did not permit it to be copied for many years. He himself reedited and rearranged the *Shemonah She'arim* and this version was widely circulated from around 1660. The Middle Eastern kabbalists, especially those in Palestine, considered this the most authoritative version of Lurianic Kabbalah, and some confined their studies to this version only. A magnificent manuscript written in large letters, which served as the paradigm for other copies, is preserved in the National Library in Jerusalem (4°674, three folio vols.). So that it might have greater authority, this manuscript, which was actually written in the late 17th century, has false dates added to it to make it appear that it was copied in Aleppo and Damascus in 1605.

The copies of Ḥayyim Vital's works which circulated during his lifetime among the kabbalists in Palestine were not arranged in good order. Around 1620 Benjamin ha-Levi and Elisha Vestali (or Guastali) assembled them into a three-volume edition. This, too, was not printed but was very popular in subsequent generations. It included *Sefer ha-Derushim,* mainly composed of material belonging to *Sha'ar ha-Hakdamot* and *Sha'ar ha-Gilgulim; Sefer ha-Kavvanot;* and *Sefer ha-Likkutim.* Vital's writings first reached other countries in this edition, which is extant in several libraries. The torn and tattered pages of the "last version" *(mahadurah batra)* which Vital arranged in Jerusalem were discovered by Abraham Azulai and his colleagues, apparently shortly after 1620, in a *genizah* in Jerusalem. From these writings Jacob Ẓemah arranged several books, such as *Oẓerot Ḥayyim* (Korets, 1783), *Adam Yashar* (1885), and *Olat Tamid* on meditations in prayers (1850). Another version of Vital's system which corresponds to the *Sha'ar ha-Hakdamot* was discovered and published as *Mevo She'arim* or *Toledot Adam.* His grandson, Moses b. Samuel Vital, reports that he found the author's own manuscript in Hebron (Ms. British Museum, Margoliouth CMBM no. 821). Copies reached Italy in the middle of the 17th century, but it was first published in Korzec in 1783. Parts of the beginning of the work are missing in both the printed and manuscript editions, but a complete version was still extant in Jerusalem in 1890, and was also preserved in the collection of Aryeh Alter of Gur. From all the previous editions that reached the Jerusalem kabbalists, Meir Poppers, the disciple of Ẓemah, arranged the final edition of Vital's writings, which was completed (according to testimony in some of the copies) in 1653. All matters pertaining to the *Sha'ar ha-Hakdamot* were arranged in *Sefer Derekh Eẓ Ḥayyim,* in five major sections and 50 sub-sections including the "first version" and the "last version" and even at times other versions (third and fourth), side by side. This book alone was given the name of *Eẓ Ḥayyim* when it was published in Korzec in 1782 by Isaac Satanov (of Moses Mendelssohn's circle). The best editions are those published in Warsaw (1890) by Menahem Heilperin, and Tel Aviv (1960), by Y.Z. Brandwein. Everything pertaining to matters of prayer and mystical meditations *(kavvanot)* was arranged in *Sefer Peri Eẓ Ḥayyim* in four sections: *Kavvanot;* the reasons for the *mitzvot (Ta'amei ha-Miẓvot); Tikkunei Avonot;* and *Yiḥudim.* The section on mystical meditations alone was published under the name *Peri Eẓ Ḥayyim* (Dubrovno, 1803). The book, which was published earlier under this name in Korzec 1782, is not based on Poppers' edition but was a separate adaptation by his colleague Nathan Shapira called, *Me'orot Natan.* The third and fourth sections were published together under the name *Sha'ar ha-Yiḥudim* and *Tikkun Avonot* in Korzec in 1783. All material pertaining to other matters was arranged in *Sefer Nof Eẓ Ḥayyim* in four sections: *Perushei ha-Zohar; Perushei Tanakh; Perushei Aggadot;* and *Gilgulim.* A complete manuscript of this work is found in Oxford (Neubauer, Cat Bod no. 1700). The first section was never published in this form; the second section (which also included the *ta'amei ha-miẓvot)* was published as *Likkutei Torah Nevi'im u-Khetuvim* (Zolkiew, 1773); an incomplete version of the third section was published as *Likkutei Shas* (Korzec, 1785); and the fourth section was published earlier than all Vital's other works as *Sefer ha-Gilgulim* (Frankfort on the Main, 1684). A version in 70 chapters revised according to Nathan Shapira's version was published in Przemyśl in 1875. Hence it is clear that Vital's writings exercised their main influence on kabbalists through manuscript copies, despite the fact that all his works were later published several times. In a few places in Palestine, Turkey, Poland, and Germany, Vital's writings were copied wholesale. *Sefer ha-Kavvanot* (Venice, 1620) was merely an abridgment and adaptation of one of the copies which circulated in Palestine during Vital's lifetime. The major part of the first section on *Perushei ha-Zohar* was published as *Zohar ha-Raki'a* (Korzec, 1785).

In all these works Vital's presentation is dry and matter of fact, quite unlike the flowery language common in his day. In one place in *Eẓ Ḥayyim* (39:16) he inserted an adaptation from Moses Cordovero's *Pardes Rimmonim* without mentioning that it was not Luria's teaching. In most parts of the *Shemonah She'arim* Vital added statements from Luria's other disciples, mainly on matters which he himself did not hear directly, but he rarely mentions them by their full names. Vital was most exact in transmitting Luria's teachings, pointing out on many occasions that he could not remember exactly, or that he had heard different statements on different occasions, or that he had forgotten. It would seem that on first hearing them he recorded many statements in copybooks and notebooks which were occasionally cited. He also presents some statements of which he admits that he cannot recall the meaning. Indeed, his works include more than a few contradictions, some of which have their source in his teacher and others in the development of Vital's views while he was editing. These contradictions gave rise to a kind of *"pilpul"* literature on Vital's statements comprising many volumes.

Before his association with Luria, Vital wrote a commentary on the Zohar according to the system of Cordovero, to which he later added occasional remarks alluding to Luria's views. Discovering this commentary in Jerusalem, Abraham Azulai inserted it in his compilation, *Or ha-Ḥammah* (1896–98). Vital's affinity to Cordovero's teaching can also be recognized in his second major work, *Eẓ ha-Da'at,* only parts of which are extant. It apparently included commentaries on most of the books of the Bible, but what he calls *peshat* ("the literal meaning") and *remez* ("the allegorical meaning") are in many cases Kabbalah, although closer to the literal meaning of the Zohar. According to one testimony, he began this work as early as 1563 at the age of 20, but according to another he wrote it in 1575. Chapters 2 and 6 of this work were preserved in his own handwriting in the collection of R. Alter of Gur (no. 185; dated 1575). His commentary on Psalms was published from this manuscript, *Sefer Tehillim* (1926). The part on the Torah was published as *Eẓ ha-Da'at Tov* (1864). The second part, including various eulogies, sermons for weddings, circumcisions, on repentance, and commentaries on Proverbs and Job, was published in Jerusalem in 1906. Vital himself arranged various editions of this work. In addition to these works, he also wrote moralizing tracts; the most important, *Sha'arei Kedushah,* was first published in Constantinople in 1734 and many times afterward. His tract *Lev David* was published from his own manuscript by Ḥ.J.D. Azulai (Leghorn, 1789) and several other times. It is assumed that in addition to these works Vital wrote many disquisitions on Kabbalah not included in the printed editions, such as *Hakdamah Kodem Derush Mayim Nukvin* quoted by his son and partly published in the introduction to Meir Bikayam's *Me'ir la-Areẓ* (Salonika, 1747). Of doubtful authenticity is *Goral Kodesh,* on geomancy according to the Zodiac (Czernovitz, 1899). *Arba Me'ot Shekel Kesef* (Korzec, 1804) is apparently an extract from Vital's known works with additional autobiographical remarks and allusions to other works, but it is highly doubtful that Vital could have written them. The book purports to have been written in 1615 but it cites names of later versions arranged by Benjamin ha-Levi and Ḥayyim Ẓemah. It would seem that in fact it was written in the second half of the 17th century, and was known in Morocco in the early 18th century. A scroll containing graphic descriptions of the celestial worlds of the Kabbalah, written by Vital and brought from Damascus, was found in Yemen, and in 1858 was sold to the traveler Jacob Saphir *(Sefunot,* 2 (1958), 270). Writings of Israel Sarug, such as *Limmudei Aẓilut* and a commentary on *Sifra di-Ẓeni'uta* (1897), were erroneously attributed to Vital. Vital was also interested in early kabbalistic literature, although he hardly used it in his works. His anthology of early works was found in his own handwriting as late as 1930 in Tunis (Ms. Tanuji). His son Samuel's copy is preserved in manuscript in the Jewish Theological Seminary in New York.

Although he possessed no truly creative powers, Vital was one of the most important influences on the development of later Kabbalah, attaining this position as the chief formulator of the Kabbalah of Luria. No thorough study of his personality and activities has yet been attempted.

Bibliography: N. Shapira, *Tuv ha-Areẓ,* ed. by J. Hirschensohn (1891), appendix 23–25 (based on a complete manuscript of *Mevo She'arim);* G. Scholem in: *Zion,* 5 (1940), 113–60; M. Benayahu, in: *Sinai,* 30 (1952), 65–75; idem, *Sefer Toledot ha-Ari* (1967), index; D. Tamar, in: *Tarbiz,* 25 (1956), 99f.

15
Moses Zacuto

Moses Zacuto, who was born into a Portuguese Marrano family in Amsterdam about 1620, studied Jewish subjects under Saul Levi Morteira (an elegy on the latter's death by Zacuto was published by D. Kaufmann in REJ 37 (1898), 115). He also studied secular subjects. According to tradition he later fasted 40 days "in order to forget the Latin language." He was a student in the *bet midrash* of Amsterdam and in his youth traveled to Poland to study in the yeshivot there. Zacuto was attracted by Kabbalah and refers in his letters to his teacher Elhanan, perhaps "Elhanan the kabbalist" who died in Vienna in 1651. He moved to Italy, remaining for some time in Verona. From 1645 he lived in Venice and served for a time as a preacher under Azariah Figo. Afterward he became one of the rabbis of the city and a member of the Venetian yeshivah. Between 1649 and 1670 he was proofreader of many books printed in Venice, especially works on Kabbalah. He edited the *Zohar Ḥadash* in 1658, and also wrote many poems for celebrations and special occasions. Zacuto tried to acquire the manuscripts of the Safed kabbalists, especially those of Moses Cordovero and the different versions of the works of Ḥayyim Vital. He befriended the kabbalist Nathan Shapiro of Jerusalem and the old kabbalist Benjamin ha-Levi, who served as an emissary from Safed in Venice for two years (1658–59).

At the outset of the Shabbatean movement, Zacuto tended to give credence to the messianic tidings, but he was opposed to innovations such as abolition of *tikkun ḥaẓot* ("midnight prayers") and other customs. In the spring of 1666, in a letter to Samson Bachi, he took a positive but cautious stand in favor of the movement, mainly supporting its advocacy of repentance. After the apostasy of Shabbetai Ẓevi he turned his back on the movement and joined the other Venetian rabbis in their action against Nathan of Gaza when he came to Venice in the spring of 1668. At the same time he openly opposed the Shabbateans in a letter to Meir Isserles in Vienna, and in subsequent years rejected Shabbatean propaganda, despite the fact that his favorite students Benjamin b. Eliezer ha-Kohen of Reggio and Abraham Rovigo were among the "believers" *(ma'aminim).* Relations between Zacuto and these two disciples became strained because of their differences, when, for example, the Shabbatean scholar Baer Perlhefter came to Modena and Rovigo supported him. On the other hand, he tried to procure from his pupils copies of Nathan of Gaza's writings on Shabbatean Kabbalah. The Shabbateans on several occasions criticized Zacuto, whose conservative temperament displeased them. In 1671 he was invited to serve as rabbi in Mantua, but he did not go until 1673, remaining there until his death in 1697. He enjoyed great authority as the head of the contemporary Italian kabbalists and corresponded with kabbalists in many places. He never realized his desire to settle in Ereẓ Israel.

Zacuto's published exoteric works include his commentary on the Mishnah, *Kol ha-ReMeZ;* he was known throughout his life as ReMeZ, from his initials (Rabbi Moses Zacuto). Part of the work was published in Amsterdam in 1719. Ḥ.J.D. Azulai, in his *Shem ha-Gedolim,* noted that the manuscript was twice as long as the printed edition. A collection of halakhic responsa was published in Venice in 1760. A commentary on the Palestinian Talmud is lost. His major activity, however, was in Kabbalah. Zacuto opposed the mingling of the kabbalistic system of Cordovero with that of Isaac Luria which was then current in some circles (Tishby, in *Zion,* 22 (1957), 30) and for this reason he criticized Solomon Rocca's *Sefer Kavvanat Shelomo* (Venice, 1670) even though he composed a poem honoring the author (see Zacuto's *Iggerot,* letters nos. 7, 8). He went over the entire corpus of Luria's and Vital's writings and added many annotations under the name *Kol ha-ReMeZ* or the abbreviation *MaZaLaN (Moshe Zakkut Li Nireh* – "It seems to me, Moses Zacuto"). Many of them are collected in the books *Mekom Binah* and *Sha'arei Binah* of Isaac Sabba (Salonika, 1812–13) and they have partly also appeared in different editions of the works of Vital and Jacob Ẓemah. Zacuto wrote at least two commentaries on the Zohar. In the first, he continued *Yode'ei Binah* begun by his contemporary Joseph Ḥamiẓ (up to Zohar I, 39). Here, Zacuto used many commentaries from the school of Cordovero, the commentary *Ketem Paz* by Simeon Labi and the first commentary of Ḥayyim Vital. The printed part contains the commentary up to Zohar I, 147b (Venice, 1663). For unknown reasons it was never circulated. One copy is extant in the library of the *bet din* in London, but there exist complete manuscripts (e.g., British Museum, Ms. Add. 27.054–27.057). *Mikdash ha-Shem,* his second commentary on the Zohar, was written for the most part according to the Lurianic Kabbalah, and was published in abridged form in the *Mikdash Melekh* of Shalom Buzaglo. The complete commentary is found in the Oxford manuscripts Opp. 511, 512, 513, 515, 516, 517. *Mezakkeh ha-Rabbim* (Oxford, Bodleian Library, Ms. Opp. 120) though ascribed to him was not written by him. A long kabbalistic responsum to the rabbis of Cracow on the copying of Torah scrolls, *tefillin,* and *mezuzot* was published several times, in *Mekom Binah,* in *Kiryat Sefer* by Menahem Meiri (pt. 2, 1881, 100–8; separately, Berdichev, 1890). Zacuto arranged *tikkunim* ("special prayers") for several religious ceremonies according to Kabbalah. These were often reprinted and had great influence, especially on the religious life in Italy. They include *Shefer ha-Tikkunim* (a *tikkun* for the eve of Shavuot and Hoshana Rabba; Venice, 1659), *Mishmeret ha-Ḥodesh(ibid.,* 1660), *Tikkun Shovavim* (the initials of the first six sections of Exodus), i.e., a *tikkun* for fasts undertaken in expiation for nocturnal ejaculations *(ibid.,* 1673), and *Tikkun Ḥaẓot (ibid.,* 1704). All these were arranged under the influence of Benjamin ha-Levi and Nathan Shapiro.

A major part of Zacuto's poetry is devoted to kabbalistic subjects, such as his poems in the book *Ḥen Kol Ḥadash* (Amsterdam, 1712), in *Tofteh Arukh* (a description of hell; Venice, 1715). Besides this he arranged voluminous *collectanea* on kabbalistic subjects. The first was *Shibbolet shel Leket,* on all the books of the Bible (Scholem, *Kitvei Yad be-Kabbalah,* 1930, p. 153, para. 107). This was followed by *Remez ha-Romez* on numbers, *gematria,* and explanations of Holy Names according to numerology (Ms. British Museum, Margoliouth 853); *Erkhei Kinnuyim,* selections from the Lurianic Kabbalah in alphabetical order (complete in Ms. Jerusalem 110). Parts of this work were published at the end of *Golel Or* by Meir Bikayam (1737) and at the end of Bikayam's *Me'ir Bat Ayin* (1755). Another anthology, in alphabetical order, was published as *Em la-Binah,* part of his *Sha'arei Binah* (1813). *Shorshei ha-Shemot,* also called *Mekor ha-Shemot,* is a collection of practical Kabbalah according to the order of the magical "names." This work was widely circulated in manuscript and went through several versions by North African kabbalists. A complete manuscript is in Jerusalem (8° 2454). Essays on kabbalistic subjects have remained in several manuscripts; also a number of important collections of Zacuto's letters are perserved, e.g., Budapest 459 (in his own handwriting); Jerusalem 8° 1466; British Museum Ms. Or. 9165 (in his handwriting); Jewish Theological Seminary, N.Y. Mss. 9906 and 11478; and in the Eẓ Ḥayyim Library in Amsterdam, C15. Only a few were published in *Iggerot ha-ReMeZ* (Leghorn, 1780).

Bibliography: A. Apfelbaum, *Moshe Zacut* (Heb., 1926); Ghirondi-Nepi, 225; Landshuth, *Amudei ha-Avodah* 2 (1862), 214–21; J. Leveen, in: *Semitic Studies . . . Immanuel Löv* (1947), 324–33; G. Scholem, *Kitvei Yad be-Kabbalah* (1930), 150–5; idem, in: *Zion,* 13–14 (1949), 49–59; idem, in: *Beḥinot,* 8 (1955), 89; 9 (1956), 83; Scholem, Shabbetai Ẓevi, 653–4; A. Yaari, *Ta'alumat Sefer* (1954), 54–56, 67–75, idem, in: *Beḥinot,* 9 (1956), 77 M. Benayahu, in: *Sinai,* 34 (1954), 156; idem, in: *Yerushalayim,* 5 (1955), 136–86; idem in: *Sefunot,* 5 (1961), 323–6, 335 I. Tishby, *Netivei Emunah u-Minut* (1964), index; Steinschneider, Cat Bod, 1989–92.

16

Joshua Heshel Ẓoref

Ẓoref, who was to become the most important figure of the Shabbatean movement in Lithuania, was born in Vilna in 1633. He was a silversmith with a modest Jewish education who early inclined to an ascetic way of life. During the persecutions in the wake of the Polish-Swedish War he took refuge around 1656 in Amsterdam, but returned later to Vilna where he started the study of moral and mystical writings, but remained without talmudic learning. During the messianic upheaval of 1666 he had visions which many compared with those of Ezekiel. He became the outstanding spokesman of the believers in Shabbetai Ẓevi and persisted in his belief throughout his life. He continued his strictly ascetic behavior, and during several years was said to have never left his home except for the synagogue or the ritual bath. Shortly after 1666 he started to put down the revelations he received in five books, intended to correspond to the books of the Pentateuch. He assembled around him a circle of fervent followers who considered him an oracle, and played in this group a role very similar to that of the later ḥasidic *ẓaddik*. Stories told about him already have a noticeable "ḥasidic" flavor. He used to make pronouncements not only about the messianic developments and the related mysteries but also concerning political events of his time, such as are recorded by Ẓevi Hirsch Koidanover in *Kav ha-Yashar* (ch. 12; 1705). People flocked to Ẓoref from all over Poland to ask his advice or to strengthen their Shabbatean faith. He considered himself the Messiah ben Joseph, and Shabbetai Ẓevi the true Messiah and saw his own role as revealer of the secrets of redemption between the first and the second coming of the Messiah. His written revelations center around the esoteric meanings of the *Shema Yisrael* and by the time of his death were said to have covered about 5,000 pages. Those parts which have survived show clearly that the book was completely built upon elaborate numerological speculations following the *Megalleh Amukkot* of Nathan Nata b. Reuben Spiro (Spira). These speculations are essentially founded on the *gematriot* of Shabbetai Ẓevi and his own name Joshua (Yehoshua) Heshel (814 and 906), frequently alluding to the year 1666 (in *gematria* 426) as the beginning of redemption. Although the Shabbatean character of Ẓoref's revelations is clear, he did not divulge his faith except to the members of his intimate circle who had to take a formal vow to show discretion and dissimulation before unbelievers.

He maintained, directly or through his confidants, a lively correspondence with Shabbateans in Italy and Turkey. A letter written by the Shabbatean leader Ḥayyim Malakh in 1696, after some visits to Heshel Ẓoref, acknowledges his extreme ingenuity with numbers but expresses great reservations as to his kabbalistic initiation and his psychic powers. During the last years of his life, Ẓoref transferred to Cracow where he married (in second marriage?) the daughter of Jacob Eleazar Fischhof, one of the protectors of the ḥasidic group of Judah Ḥasid and Ḥayyim Malakh. When this group prepared to journey to Jerusalem, Ẓoref participated in a meeting of its Shabbatean leaders in Nikolsburg toward the end of 1698 or beginning of 1699. Ẓoref died in Cracow. His manuscripts were scattered. Some parts of the collection of his revelations, *Sefer ha-Ẓoref,* came into the hands of the kabbalist Nathan b. Levi, a member of the *klaus* of Brody who hid them; however, another part, including his writings from his last years, found its way to Israel b. Eliezer Ba'al Shem Tov, the founder of Ḥasidism, who held these writings in high veneration without seemingly having been aware of their Shabbatean character. He frequently spoke in their praise, and the tradition of his pupils identified them with those of the mythical rabbi Adam Ba'al Shem which his son was said to have given to the Ba'al Shem. Adam Ba'al Shem, a legendary figure of the 16th century, and Heshel Ẓoref in the generation preceding that of the Ba'al Shem, coalesced into one figure. Toward the end of his life the Ba'al Shem ordered a copy of the *Sefer ha-Ẓoref* to be made, but this order was executed only more than 20 years after his death in 1700. Copies of these copies have been preserved among the descendants of the ḥasidic rabbis Nahum of Chernobyl and Levi Isaac of Berdichev. An attempt by the latter to have the book printed in Zholkva (Zölkiew) was foiled by Ephraim Zalman Margulies of Brody who recognized its Shabbatean character.

Bibliography: G. Scholem, in: RHR, 143 (1953), 67–80; idem, *Kitvei Yad be-Kabbalah* (1930), 157f., 161f., 239f.; idem, in: *Zion,* 6 (1941), 89–93; 11 (1946), 170–2; W.Z. Rabinowitsch, *ibid.,* 5 (1940), 126–32; 6 (1941), 80–84; Ch. Shmeruk, *ibid.,* 28 (1963), 86–105; A. Freimann, *Inyenei Shabbetai Ẓevi* (1912), 99–103; M. Benayahu, in: *Michael* 1 (1972), 13–17, 72–76.

NOTES

THE HISTORICAL DEVELOPMENT OF KABBALAH

1. *Zion,* 23–24 (1958/59), 33–34, 141–65.
2. See S. Poznański, in REJ, 50 (1905), 10–31.
3. See G. Scholem in *Sefer Assaf* (1953), 459–95; the text itself is translated into German in *Lieber Amicorum,* in honor of Professor C.J. Bleeker, 1969, 175–93.
4. *Tarbiz* 40, 1971, 301–19.
5. Ed. Vaillant, 1952, p. 39.
6. J. Levy, in *Tarbiz,* 12 (1941), 163–7.
7. For example, in the *Ma'aseh Merkabah,* para 9, ed. by Scholem in *Jewish Gnosticism* . . . (1965), 107.
8. See JE III, s.v. Bibliomancy.
9. Ph. Bloch, in MGWJ, 37, 1893.
10. For the important differences between the two versions, see A. Epstein, in MGWJ, 37 (1893), 266.
11. For example, S. Karppe, *Etude sur la nature et les origines du Zohar* (1901), 16ff.
12. Cf. S. Morag, in *Sefer Tur-Sinai* (Torczyner; 1960), 207–42.
13. GV 175
14. *Das Alphabet in Mystic und Magie,* 1925.
15. E. Urbach, in: *Kovez al Yad,* 6 (1966), 20.
16. Ed. by Bialik and Rawnitzki pt. 2, no. 58.
17. Davidson, in HUCA, 3 (1926) 225–55 and additions by E. Baneth, in MGWJ, 71 (1927), 426–43.
18. In KS 6 (1930), 385–410.
19. G. Scholem, in KS, 4 (1928), 286ff.
20. See G. Scholem, in *Tarbiz,* 16 (1954), 205–9.
21. For an example of this see Scholem, *Jewish Gnosticism* (1965), 84–93.
22. G. Scholem, *Les Origines de la Kabbale* (1966), 175–94.
23. See *Tarbiz,* 32 (1963), 153–9 and 252–65, the dispute between I. Weinstock and G. Scholem, and Weinstock's reply in Sinai, 54 (1964), 226–59.
24. The greater part were assembled by E.M. Levin in *Ozar ha-Geonim* to *Hagigah* (1931), 10–30, and in the section on commentaries 54–61.
25. See J. Dan, *Torat ha-Sod shel Hasidut Ashkenaz,* 1968, 124–28.
26. Jellinek, *Beit ha-Midrash,* pt. 2 (1938), 23–39, and, with a commentary, in *Nit'ei Ne'emanim,* 1836.
27. Cf. the view of Abraham Parnes, *Mi-Bein la-Ma'arakhot* (1951), 138–61.
28. Ed. S. Rosenblatt, 2 vols. (1927–38), with the title *The High Ways to Perfection.*
29. G. Vajda, in JJS, 6 (1955), 213–25.
30. HUCA, 25 (1940), 433–84.
31. Scholem, *Origines de la Kabbale,* 254–5.
32. See J. Dan in: *Zion,* 29 (1964), 168–81.

33. Ed. E. Urbach, 1939–63; see the introduction (vol. 4) in the section on mysticism.
34. Scholem, *On the Kabbalah and its Symbolism,* 173–93.
35. Ed. J. Dan, in *Temirin* I, 1972, 141–56.
36. Scholem, *Reshit ha-Kabbalah,* 206–9.
37. In *Ha-Ḥoker,* 2 (1894), 41–47.
38. J. Dan, in *Tarbiz,* 35 (1966), 349–72.
39. British Museum Ms. 752; Adler Ms. 1161 in New York, and the commentary of Moses b. Eliezer ha-Darshan to the *Shi'ur Komah;* see Scholem, *Reshit ha-Kabbalah, 204ff.*
40. Scholem in MGWJ, 75 (1931), 72–90.
41. *Archives d'histoire doctrinale du moyen-âge,* 28 (1961), 15–34.
42. See Werblowsky, in *Sefunot* 6 (1962) 135–82.
43. Scholem, *Origines de la Kabbale,* 59–210.
44. Scholem *Origines de la Kabbale,* 213–63.
45. Scholem, *Origines de la Kabbale,* 252.
46. *Tarbiz* 40 (1971), 483–507.
47. *Sefer Bialik* (1934) 143ff.
48. Published as an appendix to G. Scholem, *Ha-Kabbalah be-Provence,* 1963.
49. For an analysis of his thought, see Scholem, *Origines* .... 263–327.
50. Ibid. 414.
51. Ibid. 241.
52. See the list in *Reshit ha-Kabbalah,* pp. 255–62; *Origines* ... 283–91.
53. Scholem, *Origines* ... 413.
54. JQR, 4 (1892), 245–56.
55. His poems were collected in *Yedi'ot ha-Makhon le-Ḥeker ha-Shirah,* 4, 1938
56. Collected by M. Hasidah in *Ha-Segullah* (fascicles 17–30, Jerusalem, 1933–34).
57. *Madda'ei ha-Yahadut,* 2 (1927) 233–40.
58. Altmann, in JJS, 7 (1956), 31–57.
59. See *Sefer Bialik* (1934), 141–62.
60. Scholem, *Origines* ... 416–54.
61. E. Gottlieb, *Tarbiz,* 37 (1968), 294–317.
62. KS, 6 (1930), 385–410.
63. *He-Halutz,* 12 (1887), 111–4.
64. A list of such tracts in KS, 10 (1934), 498–515.
65. *Kelal mi-Darkhei ha-Kabbalah ha–Nevu'it;* see G. Scholem, *Kitvei Yad be-Kabbalah* (1930), 57.
66. Ed. Jellinek,, *Jubelschrift* ... H. Graetz, 1887, 65–85.
67. Scholem, *Mysticism,* 146–55.
68. *Madda'ei ha-Yahadut,* 2 (1927), 168.
69. Ibid. 276–9.
70. G. Scholem, in *Tarbiz,* 3 (1932) 181–3; KS, 6 (1929), 109–18.
71. See Scholem in KS, 4 (1928), 307–10.
72. Ibid., 302–27.
73. G. Scholem, in *Sefer Yovel le-Aron Freiman* (1935), 51–62.
74. KS, 40 (1965), 405–12.
75. Casablanca 1930; see E. Gottlieb in KS, 48 (1973), 173–78.
76. *Kovez al Yad,* 1951.
77. Scholem, in KS 21 (1945), 284–95, and E. Gottlieb in *Benjamin de Vries Memorial Volume,* 1969, 295–304.
78. KS 10 (1934), 504, no. 52.
79. See Sinai, 5 (1939), 122–48.
80. Vajda, *Recherches sur la philosophie et la kabbale* (1962), 115–297.

81. A.M. Habermann, *Shirei ha-Yiḥud ve-ha-Kavod* (1948), 99–122.
82. A. Altmann (ed.), *Jewish Medieval and Renaissance Studies,* 4 (1967), 225–88.
83. Vajda, in REJ, n.s. 15 (1956), 25–71.
84. 1574; Vajda, in *Mélanges E. Gilson* (1959), 651–90 (partly due to forgery) and E. Gottlieb in *Tarbiz* 39 (1969–70), 68–78.
85. *Kovez al-Yad,* 5 (1950), 105–37.
86. Scholem, in *Tarbiz* 6 (1935), 90–98.
87. Z. Edelmann's collection *Ḥemdah Genuzah* (1855), 45–52.
88. S.A. Horodezky, *Ha-Mistorin be-Yisrael* vol. 2: *Ginzei Seter* (1952), 341–88; Baer, *Spain,* 1 (1961), 369–73.
89. G. Scholem, in KS 21 (1945), 179–86.
90. *Tarbiz,* 24 (1955), 167–206.
91. JQR, 21 (1931), 365–75; Yael Nadav, in *Tarbiz* 26 (1956), 440–58.
92. G. Scholem in *Sefunot* 11 (1973), 67–112.
93. Paris Ms. 849; KS, 5 (1929), 273–7.
94. S. Assaf, in *Jubilee Volume for D. Yellin* (1935), 227.
95. E. Gottlieb, in *Studies Religion and Mysticism . . . in honor of G. Scholem* (1968), Hebr. part, 63–86; idem, in *Michael,* Tel Aviv University, I (1972), 144–213.
96. KS 6 (1930), 259ff.; 7 (1931), 457ff.
97. Schechter, in REJ, 62 (1892), 118ff.; KS, 9 (1933), 258.
98. *Sullam ha-Aliyyah,* see Scholem, *Kitvei Yad be-Kabbalah,* 225–30; KS, 22 (1946), 161–71.
99. M. Benayahu, in *Kovez ha-Rambam* (1955), 240–74.
100. G. Scholem, *Kitvei Yad be-Kabbalah,* 89–91.
101. Hirsch Ms. 109, Schwager and Fraenkel 39, 5–10, now in New York; A. Marx, in ZHB, 10 (1906), 175–8.
102. I. Tishby, in *Perakim,* 131–82; S. Assaf, in *Sinai,* 5 (1940), 360–8; M. Benayahu, *Ha-Defus ha-Ivri be-Cremona* (1971), 119–37; E. Kupfer, in *Michael* 1 (Tel Aviv, 1972), 302–18.
103. Y. Baer, in *Me'assef Shenati Zion,* 5 (1933), 61–77.
104. G. Scholem, ibid., 4 (1933), 124–30; J. Dan, in *Sefunot,* 6 (1962), 313–26.
105. M. Benayahu, in *Areshet,* 5 (1972), 170–88.
106. R.J.Z. Werblowsky, *Joseph Karo, Lawyer and Mystic,* 1962.
107. G. Scholem, *Shabbetai Zevi,* (1967) 47–49.
108. M. Benayahu, *Toledot ha-Ari,* 1967.
109. D. Tamar, in *Sefunot,* 7 (1963), 169–72.
110. G. Scholem, in *Zion,* 5 (1940), 133–60.
111. Scholem, in KS, 19 (1943), 184–99.
112. *Zion,* 5 (1940), 214–43; 9 (1954), 173.
113. D. Tamar, in *Sefunot,* 2 (1958), 61–88.
114. G. Scholem, *Lyrik der Kabbalah?* in *Der Jude,* 9 (1921), 55–69; A. Ben-Yisrael, *Shirat ha-Ḥen,* 1918.
115. See the mass of material in Dembitzer, *Kelilat Yofi,* 2 (1888), 5–10, 117–26.
116 *Revue de l'histoire des Religions,* 143 (1953), 37–39.
117. For a detailed list of the Bet El kabbalists see Frumkin, *Toledot Ḥakhmei Yerushalayim,* 3 (1930), 47–54, 107–21.
118. A. Geiger, JZWL, 4 (1866), 192–6.

THE BASIC IDEAS OF KABBALAH

1. *Kovez al-Yad,* new series, i (1936), 31.
2. Scholem, *Origines . . .* 367–75.

3. Ibid, 295.
4. Scholem, *Kitvei Yad be-Kabbalah,* 89–91.
5. *Tarbiz,* 39 (1970), 382.
6. See G. Scholem, *Tarbiz,* 2–3 (1931–32).
7. See *Tarbiz,* 39 (1970), 382–3.
8. See Altmann, JJS, 9 (1958), 73–81.
9. See *Midrash Talpiot* (1860), 113c.
10. See E. Gottlieb, *Papers of the Fourth World Congress of Jewish Studies* (1969), Vol. 2, 327–34.
11. See I. Tishby, *Mishnat ha-Zohar,* 2, 237–68; G. Scholem, *Messianic Idea in Judaism* ((1971).
12. See Enelow, *Jewish Studies in Honor of Kaufmann Kohler* (Berlin, 1913), 82–107; G. Scholem, MGWJ, 78 (1934), 492–518.
13. See Marmorstein, in: MGWJ, 71 (1927), 39 ff.
14. KS 4, 319.
15. Scholem, *Mysticism,* 142.
16. Scholem, *Mysticism,* 147–55.
17. Joseph Tirshhom's *Shushan Yesod Olam,* see M. Benayahu, in *Temirin,* 1 (1972), 187–269.
18. *Festschrift fuer Aron Freimann* (1935), 51–54.
19. *Sefunot,* 11 (1971), 86–87.
20. Y. Perles, *Festschrift fuer H. Graetz* (1887), 32–34; see also Eliahu Kohen ha-Itamari, *Midrash Talpiot,* under *devarim nifla'im.*
21. See P. Bloch, MGWJ, 47 (1903), 153ff., 263ff.

ZOHAR

1. He-Ḥalutz, 4 (1859), 85.
2. G. Scholem, in: *Jubilee Volume . . . L. Ginzberg* (1946), 425–46.
3. On these documents, see I. Tishby, *Mishnat ha-Zohar,* 1 (1957²), 110–2.

DEMONOLOGY IN KABBALAH

1 See the exposition *Zur altjüdischen Dämonologie,* in Strack-Billerbeck, *Kommentar zum Neuen Testament aus Talmud und Midrasch* IV (1928), 501–35.
2. *Tarbiz,* 4 (1933), 208–25.
3. *Tarbiz,* 19 (1948), 160–3.
4. Cf. *A. Friedmann Jubilee Volume* (1935), 51–53.
5. G. Scholem, *Kitvei Yad Be-Kabbalah* (1930), 182–5.
6. *Tarbiz,* 19 (1948), 165–72.

MAGEN DAVID

1. Hildegard Lewy, in *Archiv Orientālnī*, vol. 18 (1950), 330–65.
2. See Heinrich Loewe, *Juedischer Feuersegen,* 1930.
3. Ms. of Yates Thompson 31 in the British Museum.
4. Jacob Emden, *Torah Ha-Kena'ot,* p. 128.
5. A. Rubens, *Jewish Iconography,* no. 1611.

MERKABAH MYSTICISM or MA'ASEH MERKAVAH

1. According to S. Spiegel, in: HTR, 24 (1931), 289.
2. Israel Lévi in his commentary on Ben Sira, *L'Ecclesiastique,* 1 (1898), and 2 (1901).
3. Strugnell, in: VT, 7 supplement (1960), 336.
4. Best edit. I. Gruenwald, in *Temirin* 1 (1972), 101–39.
5. See G. Scholem, in *Zion,* 7 (1942), 184f.

SAMAEL

1. Theodore Bar Konai, ed. Pognon, 213.
2. Ed. McCown (1922), 96.
3. Ginza, trans. M. Lidzbarski (1925), 200, and *The Canonical Prayer Book of the Mandaeans* ed. E.S. Drower (1959), 246.
4. D. Chwolson, *Die Ssabier und der Ssabismus,* 2 (1856); *Picatrix,* 3d. H. Ritter (1933), 226.
5. Isaac ha-Kohen's treatise on *aẓilut, Maada'ei ha-Yahadut* 2 (1927), 251, 260, 262.
6. Resp., *Sidrei de-Shimmusha Rabbah, Tarbiz,* 16 (1945) 198–9.
7. *Tarbiz,* 4 (1932/33), 217f.
8. G. Scholem, in: *Zion,* 5 (1933), 124f.

ABBREVIATIONS

A. Bibliographical abbreviations

ARN *Avot de-Rabbi Nathan.*
Avot *Avot* (talmudic tractate).
Av. Zar.
Avodah Zarah (talmudic tractate).

Baer, Spain
Yitzhak (Fritz) Baer, *History of the Jews in Christian Spain,* 2 vols (1961–66).
BB *Bava Batra* (talmudic tractate).
Bek. *Bekhorot* (talmudic tractate).
Ber. *Berakhot* (talmudic tractate).
Beẓah *Beẓah* (talmudic tractate).
Bik. *Bikkurim* (talmudic tractate).
BK *Bava Kamma* (talmudic tractate).
BM (1) *Bava Meẓia* (talmudic tractate).
(2) British Museum.

Charles, Apocrypha
R.H. Charles, *Apocrypha and Pseudepigrapha ...*, 2 vols. (1913; repr. 1963–66).
Deut. Deuteronomy (Bible).
Deut. R.
Deuteronomy Rabbah.

Eccles.
Ecclesiastes (Bible).
Eccles.R.
Ecclesiastes Rabbah.
EJ *Encyclopaedia Judaica* (German, A–L only)
10 vols. (1928–34).
Er. *Eruvin* (talmudic tractate).
Ex. Exodus (Bible).
Ex.R. *Exodus Rabbah.*
Ezek. Ezekiel (Bible).

Gen. Genesis (Bible).
Gen.R.
Genesis Rabbah.

Ḥag. *Ḥagigah* (talmudic tractate).

HTR *Harvard Theological Review* (1908ff.).
HUCA
Hebrew Union College Annual (1904; 1924ff.).

Isa. Isaiah (Bible).

JBL *Journal of Biblical Literature* (1881 ff.).
JE *Jewish Encyclopedia*, 12 vols (1901–05).
JHSET
Jewish Historical Society of England, *Transactions* (1893ff.).
JJS *Journal of Jewish Studies* (1948 ff.).
J.N.U.L.
Jewish National and University Library.
JQR *Jewish Quarterly Review* (1889 ff.).
JSOS *Jewish Social Studies* (1939 ff.).
JTSA Jewish Theological Seminary of America (also abbreviated as JTS).
JZW *Juedische Zeitschrift fuer Wissenschaft und Leben* (1862–75).

KS *Kirjath Sepher* (1923/4 ff.).

Lam. Lamentations (Bible).
Lam.R.
Lamentations Rabbah
Lev. Leviticus (Bible).
Lev.R.
Leviticus Rabbah.

Mak. *Makkot* (talmudic tractate).
MGWJ
Monatsschrift fuer Geschichte und Wissenschaft des Judentums (1851–1939).
Mid.Ps.
Midrash Tehillim.
Mid.Sam.
Midrash Samuel.

Nid. *Niddah* (talmudic tractate).
Num. Numbers (Bible).
Num.R.
Numbers Rabbah.

PAAJR
Proceedings of the American Academy for Jewish Research (1930 ff.).
PdRE *Pirkei de-R. Eliezer.*
PdRK *Pesikta de-Rav Kahana.*
Pes. *Pesaḥim* (talmudic tractate).
Ps. Psalms (Bible).

REJ *Revue des études juives* (1880 ff.).
RhR *Revue d'histoire des religions* (1880 ff.).
RSO *Rivista degli studi orientali* (1907 ff.).

Sanh. *Sanhedrin* (talmudic tractate).

Scholem, Mysticism.
G. Scholem, *Major Trends in Jewish Mysticism* (rev. ed. 1946; paperback ed. with additional bibliography 1961).

Scholem, Shabbetai
G. Scholem, *Shabbetai Ẓevi ve-ha-Tenu'ah ha-Shabbeta'it bi-Ymei Ḥayyav,* 2 vols. (1967). English edition: *Sabbatai Sevi: the Mystical Messiah* (1973).

Shab. *Shabbat* (talmudic tractate).

Song Song of Songs (Bible).

Sot. *Sotah* (talmudic tractate).

Steinschneider, Cat. Bod. Steinschneider M., *Catalogus Librorum Hebraeorum in Bibliotheca Bodleiana,* 3 vols. (1952–60).

Tanh. *Tanḥuma.*

VT *Vetus Testamentum* (1951 ff.).

ZAW *Zeitschrift fuer die alttestamentliche Wissenschaft und die Kunde des nachbiblischen Judentums* (1881 ff.).

ZH *Zohar Ḥadash*

ZHB *Zeitschrift fuer hebraeische Bibliographie* (1896–1920).

B. General abbreviations

anon. anonymous.

Aram. Aramaic .

b. born; *ben, bar.*

B.C.E. Before Common Era (= B.C.).

c., ca. circa.

C.E. Common Era (= A.D.).

ch., ch.
chapter, chapters.

d. died.

ed. editor, edited, edition.

Eng. English.

Heb. Hebrew.

Ms., Mss.
manuscript(s).

n.d. no date (of publication).

Pol. Polish.

R. Rabbi or Rav (before names); in Midrash (after an abbreviation) – *Rabbah.*

tr., trans(i)
translator, translated, translation.

GLOSSARY

This glossary presents only general terms used in the text. For explanations of technical Kabbalistic terms, the reader is referred to the note to the index.

Aggadah, name given to those sections of Talmud and Midrash containing homiletic expositions of the Bible, stories, legends, folklore, or maxims.

Amora (pl. *Amoraim)*, title of Jewish scholars in Ereẓ Israel and Babylon in 3rd to 6th centuries who were responsible for the *Gemara.*

Av Bet Din, head of communal religious court.

Bar, Ben, "son of", frequently appearing in personal names.

Baraita, statement of *tanna* not found in Mishnah.

Bet Din, rabbinic court of law.

Dayyan, member of rabbinic court.

Etrog, citron, one of four species used on *Sukkot.*

Galut, exile; condition of Jewish people in exile.

Gaon, head of academy in post-talmudic period, especially in Babylon; title of respect for great scholar.

Gemara, traditions, discussions and rulings of *amoraim* commenting on and supplementing the Mishnah, forming bulk of Talmud.

Genizah, depository for sacred books, best known being that discovered in Cairo.

Ḥaliẓah, biblically prescribed ceremony (Deut. 25:9–10) performed when man refuses to marry his brother's childless widow.

Ḥasidei Ashkenaz, medieval pietist movement among Jews of Germany.

Hoshana Rabba, seventh day of *Sukkot.*

Haskalah, "Enlightenment"; movement for spreading modern European culture among Jews, c. 1750–1880.

Levirate marriage (Heb. *Yibbum*), marriage of childless widow by brother of deceased husband (Deut. 25:5); release from obligation is called *ḥaliẓah.*

Lulav, palm branch, one of four species used on *Sukkot.*

Maggid, 1) popular preacher; 2) angel or supermundane spirit who conveys teachings to scholars considered worthy.

Maḥzor, festival prayer book.

Marranos, descendants of Jews in Spain and Portugal whose ancestors had converted to Christianity under pressure but who continued to observe Jewish rituals in secret.

Midrash, 1) method of interpreting scripture to bring out lessons by stories or homiletics; 2) name for collections of such rabbinic interpretations.

Minhag, ritual customs

Mishnah, earliest codification of Jewish Oral Law.

Ofan, 1) hymn inserted into a passage of the morning prayer; 2) the wheel of the vision of Ezekiel (Ezek.1:15 ff.).

Parnas, chief synagogue functionary.

Pilpul, sharp academic argument, casuistry.
Piyyut, Hebrew liturgical poem, written by *paytan*.
Shemittah, Sabbatical year.
Siddur, among Ashkenazim, the volume containing the daily prayers.
Sukkot, festival of Tabernacles
Tanna (pl. *Tannaim*), title of rabbinic teacher of mishnaic period.
Targum, Aramaic translation of Bible.
Tefillin, phylacteries.
Ẓiẓit, fringed four-cornered garment prescribed in Numbers 15:37–41 and Deuteronomy 22:12.

ILLUSTRATION CREDITS

Jerusalem, J.N.U.L., frontispiece, pp. 97, 146, 256, 403, 418, 436.
Jerusalem, Sir Isaac and Lady Wolfson Museum in Hechal Shlomo, p. 321.
Photo David Harris, Jerusalem, p. 321.
Jerusalem, Israel Museum (Feuchtwanger Collection), pp. 360, 363.
Photo R. Milon, Jerusalem, p. 363.
Formerly Detroit, Feinberg Collection, p. 364.
Photo Manning Brothers, Highland Park, Mich., p. 364.
Jerusalem, J.N.U.L., Schwadron Collection, p. 406.

PUBLISHER'S NOTE

This book is based on the major entries written by Gershom Scholem for the "Encyclopaedia Judaica," which have been revised and re-edited by Professor Scholem for this volume. "Kabbalah" therefore represents the most recent synthesis of Professor Scholem's researches covering all major manifestations of Jewish mysticism and esoteric doctrine (except Ḥasidism).

The entry on Moses Cordovero was written by J. Ben-Shlomo for the "Encyclopaedia Judaica."

INDEX

GENERAL INDEX

Numbers in bold typeface refer the reader to pages in which kabbalistic terms in Hebrew – not explained in the Glossary – receive fullest explanation.

INDEX OF BOOK TITLES

About the Author

Gershom Scholem is one of the towering figures in modern Jewish scholarship. He left Germany in 1923 and joined the Hebrew University, Jerusalem, first as librarian and eventually as Professor of Mysticism and Kabbalah. His combination of painstaking analysis, penetrating philosophical insight and profound historical understanding has added new perspectives to Jewish Studies. Since 1968 Professor Scholem has been president of the Israel Academy of Sciences and Humanities.